Launching the War on Poverty

THE OXFORD ORAL HISTORY SERIES

J. TODD MOYE (University of North Texas), KATHRYN NASSTROM (University of San Francisco), and ROBERT PERKS (The British Library Sound Archive), *Series Editors*
DONALD A. RITCHIE, *Senior Advisor*

Launching the War on Poverty

An Oral History   SECOND EDITION

MICHAEL L. GILLETTE

OXFORD
UNIVERSITY PRESS

2010

OXFORD
UNIVERSITY PRESS

Oxford University Press, Inc., publishes works that further
Oxford University's objective of excellence
in research, scholarship, and education.

Oxford   New York
Auckland   Cape Town   Dar es Salaam   Hong Kong   Karachi
Kuala Lumpur   Madrid   Melbourne   Mexico City   Nairobi
New Delhi   Shanghai   Taipei   Toronto

With offices in
Argentina   Austria   Brazil   Chile   Czech Republic   France   Greece
Guatemala   Hungary   Italy   Japan   Poland   Portugal   Singapore
South Korea   Switzerland   Thailand   Turkey   Ukraine   Vietnam

Copyright © 2010 by Oxford University Press, Inc.

Published by Oxford University Press, Inc.
198 Madison Avenue, New York, NY 10016

www.oup.com

Oxford is a registered trademark of Oxford University Press

Library of Congress Cataloging-in-Publication Data
Gillette, Michael L.
Launching the war on poverty : an oral history / Michael L. Gillette.—2nd ed.
p.   cm.
Includes bibliographical references and index.
ISBN 978-0-19-538727-8 (pbk.)
1. Poverty—United States.   2. Economic assistance, Domestic—United States.
3. United States—Social policy.   4. United States—Politics and government—1963–1969.
5. Politicians—United States—Interviews.   I. Title.
HC110.P63G54 2010
362.5'80973—dc22   2009038655

9 8 7 6 5 4 3 2 1
Printed in the United States of America
on acid-free paper

For LeAnn, who shares my life and my projects

Contents

Acknowledgments

The creation of this book has been largely a collective enterprise. I am pleased, therefore, to acknowledge my numerous obligations to those who made it possible. My largest debt is to the interviewees themselves, who generously explored their memories and allowed their recollections to be published; the book is actually their story of the War on Poverty.

I am also indebted to the former staff of the University of Texas Oral History Project under the direction of the late Joe B. Frantz. His fellow interviewers were Stephen Goodell, T. Harrison Baker, David McComb, Dorothy Pierce McSweeney, and Paige Mulhollan. The project relied on Colleen Kain and Ruth Matthews for transcribing and editing.

To my former oral history staff at the LBJ Library belongs the lion's share of credit for the research, transcribing, and editing involved in building an oral history collection of 1,700 interviews. Over a span of almost two decades, the staff included Christie Bourgeois, Gary Gallager, Gianzero, Sibyl Jackson, Donna Cook Jones, Mariella Krause, Jenna McEachern, Lois Martin, LouAnne Missildine, and Laura White. I owe special gratitude to Regina Greenwell, Lesley Williams Brunet, Jennifer Velez, Joan Kennedy, and Ted Gittinger, the long-term veterans whose professionalism sustained the program throughout its duration.

The Lyndon Baines Johnson Foundation, under the leadership of W. Thomas Johnson, funded the LBJ Library Oral History Program for many years. Although the foundation has assisted the library's researchers in many ways, I am especially grateful to the foundation board for facilitating our effort to complement the written records. Former LBJ Library Director Harry J. Middleton played a vital role in the program's longevity while providing guidance and inspiration throughout my career there.

The archival staffs of the LBJ Library and the National Archives graciously facilitated my research in the relevant textual records. I am especially grateful to archivists Tina Houston, Laura Eggert, Linda Seelke, and Rita MacAyeal. E. Philip Scott, Suzanne Barchus, Margaret Harman, Allen Fisher, and Nick Natanson were invaluable in tracking down the photographs that appear in this book.

Launching the War on Poverty was conceived at the suggestion of my colleague Donald Ritchie, formerly editor of the original Twayne Oral History Series and presently senior advisor to the Oxford University Press Oral History Series. His encouragement and advice have advanced this project through both editions. For their work on the Twayne edition, I am indebted to editors Anne Jones and Mark Zadrozny, copy editor Cindy Buck, and production editor Susan Gamer. Two colleagues, Donald C. Bacon and John Constance, provided helpful feedback on the manuscript.

For this new edition of *Launching the War on Poverty*, I extend my deep appreciation to Nancy Toff, vice president and executive editor of Oxford University Press, for her thoughtful insight and encouragement, and to series editors J. Todd Moye, Kathryn Nasstrom, and Robert Perks for their valuable guidance. Sonia Tycko, editorial assistant at Oxford, kept track of myriads of details, while my extraordinary assistant, Julia Aguilar, rescued me from several technological impasses. Liz Bohman Barger assisted me with the index. I am also grateful to senior production editor Joellyn Ausanka, copy editor Patterson Lamb, and designer Adrianna Sutton for helping to transform the manuscript into this book.

Finally, there are the personal debts that are the most difficult to measure. My three sons, Rob, Kenneth, and David, and my daughter-in-law, Anna, have always aided my work with their support, insight, and encouragement. My wife, LeAnn Lakin Gillette, has had an even more direct role, assisting with the editing, proofreading, and solving the mysteries of the computer. I could not have begun the project, much less finished it, without her loving help.

Introduction

On April 24, 1964, President Lyndon B. Johnson took a trip that he declared should have been unnecessary. He flew on Air Force One to Huntington, West Virginia, and then by helicopter to the eastern Kentucky community of Inez. From there, he traveled by motorcade up an Appalachian mountainside. He stopped at the three-room, tarpaper-covered shack of Tom Fletcher. As the president of the United States sat and listened, Fletcher described the daily hardships that he, his wife, and their eight children endured. He had been a coal miner before losing his job, and later a saw-mill worker, but he was now unemployed. He had earned only $400 in the past year. His family subsisted on monthly distributions of surplus food. Two of his children had already dropped out of school—a fate he feared would also befall the others. Fletcher had been up all the night before with a sick neighbor who could not afford to go to the hospital.[1]

The fact that the Fletchers' tired, gaunt faces projected an image of tragic despair was significant. They had been "chosen" by the White House to personalize poverty—to symbolize the 35 million Americans who in 1964 earned less than $3,000 a year. A president can do more than propose legislation; he can create public awareness. Johnson hoped that this poignant scene from the Appalachian hollows would focus the nation's attention on the plight of the poor in America and dramatize the need for his War on Poverty. As he explained to a reporter early in 1964, "I don't know if I'll pass a single law or get a single dollar appropriated, but before I'm through, no community in America will be able to ignore the poverty in its midst."[2]

As president, Lyndon Johnson marshaled the resources of the federal government to extend prosperity and democracy to society's least fortunate. Through sweeping civil rights legislation, massive federal aid to education, and landmark health care provisions, Johnson's "Great Society" transcended the New Deal agenda by assisting those who had been left behind in an era of prosperity. But even in this decade of unprecedented government activism, the War on Poverty stood out as a bold experiment. It targeted one of humanity's ancient enemies in its strongest redoubts—urban ghettos and pockets of rural poverty—where it had spanned

President and Lady Bird Johnson visit the Tom Fletcher family in Inez, Kentucky, April 24, 1964. C293-4-WH64, 4/24/64. *Photo by Cecil Stoughton, Presidential Collection, LBJ Library*

generations. By providing opportunities to those who were unable to help themselves, the War on Poverty sought to break the cycle of the culture of poverty.[3]

When Johnson, in his 1964 State of the Union Address, declared "unconditional war on poverty," he defined the term "poverty" in its broadest sense. He enumerated all of the weapons that he hoped to have in his arsenal, including medical insurance; an expanded food stamp program; an extension of minimum wage laws; federal aid to education; the construction of libraries, hospitals, and nursing homes; mass transit; and urban renewal projects. He even included his tax cut measure, accurately predicting that it would create new jobs. The War on Poverty seemed to embrace the entire Great Society agenda.[4]

Yet Johnson's War on Poverty was also a specific legislative initiative: the Economic Opportunity Act of 1964. As the foundation of the antipoverty offensive, this measure created a new agency, the Office of Economic Opportunity (OEO), dedicated solely to the eradication of poverty. OEO was expected to chart a new course by striking at the causes of poverty as well as its consequences. In addition to launching an array of antipoverty initiatives, OEO was mandated to coordinate a government-wide attack on poverty. The War on Poverty became synonymous with OEO.[5]

If the War on Poverty failed to achieve total victory, its accomplishments were, nonetheless, significant. The offensive prodded government, the media, and the population generally to focus attention on what had been largely an invisible problem. Changes occurred at all levels of government. Fresh ideas and approaches came forth. While personal testimonies recounted the transformation of individual lives, statistics documented the numbers of Americans touched by OEO's programs. The poverty rate dropped precipitously from 22.4 percent in 1959 to 12.6 percent in 1970. While other Great Society measures were instrumental in achieving this decline, the test of longevity is another measure of the War on Poverty's success. Although OEO lasted only a decade, virtually all of its components have survived for more almost half a century under nine presidents. If such familiar programs as Head Start, Work-Study, the Legal Services Corporation, Foster Grandparents, and Community Health Centers have gained broad acceptance, their War on Poverty lineage has been all but forgotten.[6]

From the moment the War on Poverty was unveiled, it became a target of conservative criticism. Opponents charged that the antipoverty experiment was politically motivated, that it exceeded the proper role of the federal government, and that it would stifle private efforts and individual incentive. Once the program became operational, new charges were added: that it was wasteful, mismanaged, counterproductive, and a cause of social and racial turmoil. Even those who supported OEO complained about its shortcomings and conceded that it was the most controversial program of the federal government.[7] Negative perceptions increased in subsequent decades as the failure of the welfare system became more apparent. Critics blamed the War on Poverty for expanding the cycle of welfare dependency and propagating a huge urban underclass.[8]

These negative assessments represent a striking contrast to the intent of those officials who created the War on Poverty. For, while the planners' objective was clearly visionary, their strategy—to enable the poor to help themselves—reflected orthodoxy deeply rooted in the American work ethic. "A hand up, not a hand-out," was Lyndon Johnson's description of the poverty program. After signing the Economic Opportunity Act in 1964, he instructed an aide as follows: "Now, you tell Shriver no doles.

We don't want any doles." Sargent Shriver himself was equally adamant that the program was designed to stimulate self-help rather than welfare dependence. "The War on Poverty was never a handout program," he insisted, "and we never handed anybody anything for nothing. Never. Not a nickel."[9]

What then was the strategy of the poverty warriors as they mounted their controversial offensive? This book depicts the War on Poverty of the 1960s through the voices of the creators of the Office of Economic Opportunity. In oral history interviews, the participants recount the program's genesis in the councils of government, its formulation in the task force organized by Sargent Shriver, and its implementation by OEO. What were the planners' experiences, assumptions, and biases? How did these shape their endeavor? Did all the antipoverty warriors share the same original intent and expectations? What other approaches did they consider and reject? What were their successes and their regrets?

The interviews excerpted here are from the large oral history collection in the Lyndon Baines Johnson Library. Approximately 1,700 interviews have been recorded to fill the gaps in the written record. These narratives reflect on the life and presidential administration of Lyndon Johnson, with many of the participants focusing on federal policies during the 1960s. Begun under the auspices of the University of Texas at Austin, the initial interviews were conducted during the last year of the Johnson presidency. Dr. Joe B. Frantz directed the project from its inception until 1973, when it was transferred to the Johnson Library. I then succeeded him, and the program continued through 1991. Most of the initial War on Poverty interviews were conducted by Stephen Goodell from 1969 to 1970; I recorded a second series a decade later.

Reliance on interviews entails certain limitations. Memories are often vague, biased, and erroneous. Significant gaps occur in terms of both subject matter and sources. Inevitably, some relevant topics and some people were overlooked by interviewers. A few poverty warriors declined to be interviewed; some others declined to make their transcripts available. The interviews, of course, vary widely in expansiveness, precision, and frankness. To encourage candor, each narrator was given an opportunity to review and edit the transcript and seal the interview for a period of time. The narrators' embellishments have been primarily stylistic rather than substantive; and despite the potential for conflicting memories and varying perspectives, the degree of consensus among interviewees is remarkable. The interviews have been excerpted and arranged topically in order to tell the story of the creation of the poverty program while highlighting corroborative and divergent recollections.

The 2010 edition adds Lyndon Johnson's voice to the War on Poverty story. Excerpts of his recorded telephone conversations document a president's extraordinary efforts to prevail in one of his most difficult legislative struggles. The reader can now eavesdrop on LBJ as he utilized his formidable powers of persuasion and the abundant resources of his office. The conversations also reveal how the president and his advisors reached many of the administrative and policy decisions in developing the antipoverty initiative. A surprising number of the issues that the Office of Economic Opportunity would later confront were considered in these conversations. Where should the new agency be located within the Executive branch? How could it coordinate the work of the cabinet departments while operating its own programs? Should nonprofit organizations be eligible to receive Community Action funding, and should these grantees be under the control of local government? Why were the costs of Job Corps training so high?

Both the interviews and the conversations constitute oral sources, but they are very different kinds of records. The interviews, conducted years after the fact, employ a format of questions and responses to construct a reflective narrative from the perspective of hindsight. The telephone recordings, on the other hand, are the actual conversations that not only describe events in the narrative as it is unfolding but are themselves significant elements of that narrative.

For example, Sargent Shriver's interview recounts how the president persuaded him to head the War on Poverty. His description, while remarkably detailed and accurate, as the conversations now confirm, is limited by the quality and selectivity of his memory. On the other hand, the three recorded telephone conversations capture the negotiation itself, providing a verbatim record that conveys even the nuances in each man's voice. The audio recordings of Lyndon Johnson's telephone conversations are available online on the website of the University of Virginia's Miller Center for Public Policy.

The telephone conversations document the president's actions, advocacy, and inclinations at particular moments, but not necessarily his long-term views. As the legislative process unfolded, LBJ pragmatically adjusted his stated preferences to advance the measure. If the circumstances of the moment influenced his statements, so, too, did the person to whom he was speaking. Labor leader Walter Reuther heard one set of appeals, while a conservative southern senator heard another. Since the conversations were spontaneous, unlike the more reflective oral histories, LBJ's mood at the time of each recording was another factor that influenced his words. Momentary vexations, even those unrelated to the poverty program, affected what he said. President Johnson's White House aides understood when to take his declarations literally and when to discount them as letting off steam. Readers of the telephone transcripts should exercise this same judgment.

As a case study, this book traces the evolution of a new government program. First, influential writings publicized a pressing social problem, calling it to the attention of policy makers. The White House responded by analyzing the problem and proposing solutions through the mechanism of a task force. After the group's findings and recommendations became part of the president's public policy agenda, specific measures were incorporated into draft legislation. The president's advocacy provided the moral suasion necessary to generate public support and congressional action. The legislation established a new government agency, which had to formulate its administrative structure and procedures. Its operations influenced existing government departments, which in turn affected the course of the new agency.

A portrait of the 1960s also emerges from these oral records of the War on Poverty. The voices reflect the manifest idealism of the period, its sharp distinctions between right and wrong, and its belief that government could solve even the most intractable of society's ailments. As the interviewees reminisce about that decade, its dynamic historical movements seem like freeze-frame images. From our historical perspective thirty years later, the dramatic transformation in race relations, the impact of the women's movement, and the broad advance of empowerment come sharply into focus. Not only do the accounts vividly show how sweeping these changes have been since the mid-1960s, but the entire scenario of a circle of white males concocting a government program demonstrates how narrow participation in policy councils was in that era. Although some women and minorities were involved in creating the poverty program, they were far fewer in number than we would expect today.

Still, the poverty warriors were an assorted lot. They included borrowed government officials, corporate lawyers and other professionals, university-based economists, reigning experts on poverty, and freelance kibitzers. As products of the nation's finest law schools and graduate programs, the planners took an intellectual approach to the problem of poverty and an activist approach to its solution. The participation of intellectuals was noted by one observer who recalled that "there were suddenly a lot of guys in funny shoes running around the corridors." Yet there were fewer social dreamers and fugitives from ivory towers than there were lawyers and other private-sector professionals and experienced government officials. The academicians, too, had had tours of public service. A significant number of the participants had apprenticed in the Bureau of the Budget. The few who were old enough to have had minor roles in the New Deal drew from that experience. Most of these planners had come of age during the Great Depression and were veterans, in one way or another, of the World War II era. Having conquered two of the twentieth century's greatest challenges, this generation possessed extraordinary self-confidence, determination, and idealism. No task was too formidable. Through vigorous, enlightened government action, society could be improved. Even poverty—a timeless human condition—could be eradicated. The poverty warriors believed that it was their responsibility to help those in need.

Although the War on Poverty would be unveiled as Lyndon Johnson's first major legislative initiative, its origins lay in John F. Kennedy's White House. In response to popular writings that revealed grinding poverty amid plenty, Kennedy's advisors began to focus on the problem. An interagency task force reviewed hundreds of antipoverty proposals submitted by the cabinet departments. By the time of Kennedy's assassination in November 1963, it had become clear that identifying the problem of poverty was easier than prescribing a cure. What ultimately emerged as the most acceptable solution was a "community action" approach that had been used in a series of small pilot projects run by the Justice Department's Committee on Juvenile Delinquency and Youth Crime. This strategy emphasized mobilizing the residents of a target neighborhood to determine the community's needs and energize its resources. Controversy would ultimately engulf the community action approach as empowerment of the poor ignited scores of local power struggles.[10]

Kennedy's successor did not have to be persuaded to put his imprimatur on the antipoverty initiative. By both temperament and experience, Lyndon Johnson, a modern populist, was attracted to the plight of the poor. As a young teacher in rural south Texas, he had witnessed firsthand the ravages of poverty among his Hispanic students. During the New Deal, he had served as the state director of the National Youth Administration, providing jobs and training to unemployed young people. Johnson learned of the proposed antipoverty initiative the day after Kennedy's assassination. He immediately embraced it as "my kind of program" and instructed aides to push ahead "full tilt." He quickly expanded the program's scope from a limited demonstration project to a nationwide offensive. The solution, he believed, must match the magnitude of the problem. Moreover, Congress was unlikely to fund a program that would benefit only a few areas of the country. After declaring "unconditional war on poverty," Johnson announced that his objective was total victory.[11] This inflated rhetoric has been criticized as raising expectations that the program could never fulfill, but his hyperbole was deliberate—it was designed to create awareness and rally the nation.

On February 1, 1964, Johnson appointed Sargent Shriver as the commanding general to lead the government-wide offensive. Shriver, a man of extraordinary energy and imagination, was an ideal choice to launch the experiment. As Kennedy's brother-in-law, he brought to the assignment the prestige and mystique of the Kennedy family. As the founding director of the Peace Corps, he had already transformed one novel experiment into a widely acclaimed success. As a salesman nonpareil who knew how to lobby Congress effectively, he would be a convincing advocate in winning support for a controversial new program.

Shriver threw himself into the task with characteristic energy. Almost overnight, he organized the President's Task Force in the War against Poverty as a planning mechanism. Recruiting members from his wide network of business and political contacts as well as from the Peace Corps and other government offices, Shriver attracted a band of volunteers who reflected his own tireless enthusiasm. The group met at all hours of the day and night, routinely moving from one temporary location to another. Their equipment and supplies had to be "borrowed" from government agencies; their funding had to be improvised.

There was no shortage of proposals for the task force to consider. Some projects had been submitted to Congress in previous years but rejected. Others had evolved from the New Deal experience, from university sociology departments, and from current notions about poverty. In ten weeks of frenetic deliberations, the Shriver task force drafted legislation encompassing an array of different antipoverty measures, with community action as the centerpiece.

Despite the wording of Johnson's declaration of war, the War on Poverty was not "unconditional." The president had assured Senator Harry Flood Byrd that the budget would not exceed $100 billion. This compromise—which had been necessary to liberate the administration's tax cut measure from the Senate Finance Committee—left the War on Poverty with modest resources. The new offensive was funded at the $1 billion level, including $500 million for antipoverty programs in existing federal agencies. (In contrast, in 1934 the New Deal's work relief appropriation bill was more than $4 billion, plus nearly $880 million of previously authorized funds.) Lack of funding sharply limited the War on Poverty's choices of weapons. One option, a large-scale employment program, was discarded for budgetary reasons. Although the poverty program's appropriations would increase modestly in subsequent years, the escalation of the war in Vietnam would prevent the domestic offensive from receiving its full potential funding. Promises were made and expectations were raised, but the budget for OEO remained modest.[12]

One sentiment that was almost universal among the poverty warriors influenced the design of the program. Their belief that the federal bureaucracy was not focusing on the poor led the task force to propose a new agency instead of assigning the mission to the existing federal departments. The Office of Economic Opportunity was created to administer the programs, to devise new antipoverty weapons through experimentation, and to coordinate the efforts of other federal agencies. To give the new agency clout and prestige, it was placed in the Executive Office of the

President. Yet OEO would never attain the leverage necessary to direct the cabinet offices' activities. Moreover, the combination of coordinating and operating responsibilities would intensify bureaucratic competition.[13]

The Economic Opportunity Act, which Congress passed in August 1964, was a multifaceted attack on poverty. The Job Corps and Neighborhood Youth Corps offered impoverished teenagers vocational and educational training, a primer on the work ethic, and a modest stipend. Through the Work-Study program, low-income college-age students were able to earn money on campus to stay in school. The Adult Basic Education Program provided financial assistance to states for adult literacy initiatives. The Work Experience Program was designed to raise the basic educational level of the unemployed poor sufficiently for them to secure and retain a job. Rural components included loans to low-income rural families for local enterprises, a loan program to encourage farmers to establish marketing and processing cooperatives, and aid for migrant laborers. Another loan program targeted small businesses and offered them incentives to hire the long-term unemployed. The Volunteers in Service to America (VISTA) program was, in concept, a domestic Peace Corps: VISTA recruited and supported volunteers to live and work in low-income communities.[14]

The heart of the antipoverty program was the Community Action Program, which funded a wide assortment of initiatives. This component typically funded local community action agencies to mobilize an area's resources in planning and implementing a coordinated attack on the causes of poverty. Cities and rural communities could assess their own needs and design a program accordingly. To advance this process, the legislation called for "maximum feasible participation" of the residents of the target neighborhood. This ambiguous term became the subject of intense debate and was cited in countless local power struggles. Did "participation" mean control? Did "residents" mean only the poor? The architects of the War on Poverty clearly considered involvement of the poor central to the concept of community action. Not only was participation a form of empowerment—providing a forum in which the poor could articulate their own needs—but involvement in itself was seen as a way to energize impoverished neighborhoods to combat the poverty in their midst.[15]

Community action became the Great Society's lightning rod. Forces that had been unleashed by the civil rights revolution and embittered by the hopelessness of the urban ghettos defiantly challenged local establishments for control of community action boards. Even allies of the War on Poverty felt threatened by federally sponsored radicalism, while Republicans anticipated the inevitable conservative backlash. Community action gave a voice to the poor, but that voice was often angry and shrill.

Several antipoverty initiatives that had broad appeal became known as "national emphasis" programs. The most popular was Project Head Start, the development program for preschoolers that dramatically transformed conventional attitudes about early childhood education. Legal Services gave the poor greater access to the courts and the local administrative process by providing attorneys to assist low-income residents in civil matters. Under the Foster Grandparents Program, unemployed elderly poor people were trained to work with neglected and mentally retarded children. Comprehensive Health Services brought basic medical care to low-income neighborhoods. Upward Bound enabled disadvantaged students to prepare for college.[16]

Launching the War on Poverty is not a definitive history of the Office of Economic Opportunity, although the subject deserves a comprehensive study. Nor does the book encompass the reflections of people whom the poverty program was intended to help or of those who participated at the local level, such as community action agency directors, VISTA volunteers, and Job Corps alumni. Eventually, these other perspectives will add important insights to our understanding of the poverty program and its impact.

Launching the War on Poverty covers three phases of the program. Chapters 1 through 6 trace its genesis and evolution through the passage of the Economic Opportunity Act. Chapters 7 through 12 deal with the initial implementation of the program during 1964 and 1965. The succeeding years—when the War on Poverty was itself under siege—are covered in Chapters 13 through 16. Finally, in Chapter 17, "Epilogue and Assessments," participants combine the benefits of hindsight and experience to offer their evaluations of the program's successes and failures.

Launching the War on Poverty

1

CAMELOT CONFRONTS THE CULTURE OF POVERTY

IT WAS A SEQUENCE *of diverse factors that put the problem of poverty in America on the public policy agenda. The pivotal West Virginia primary in the 1960 presidential campaign brought the candidate John F. Kennedy face to face with the impoverished hollows of Appalachia. If that experience sparked his initial interest in the problem, other influences soon followed. A series of books and magazine articles dramatically detailed the conditions of poverty. Michael Harrington's* The Other America *cogently unveiled the invisible poor in the nation's midst, and Dwight Macdonald's essay-review in the* New Yorker *gave Harrington's exposé a more elite audience. Homer Bigart's 1963 articles in the* New York Times *recounted the plight of coal miners in eastern Kentucky. When these sources found their way into the president's stack of night reading, the idea of alleviating poverty began to gather momentum.[1]*

The burgeoning civil rights movement and Martin Luther King Jr.'s March on Washington gave the issue a sense of urgency. African Americans, pressing for jobs as well as justice, drew the nation's attention to its urban ghettos. Increased awareness of America's troubled youth also added to the focus on poverty in the inner city. Searching for the roots of juvenile delinquency was no longer merely a preoccupation of sociologists but a topic of broad public concern.[2]

Within the White House, the most persistent messenger was Walter Heller, Kennedy's chief economist. Heller used his position as chairman of the Council of Economic Advisers (CEA) to advance the antipoverty cause with two presidents. He also set in motion within the government a series of deliberations on the causes of poverty and solutions for it. The discussions, led by Heller's economists, first took place during informal Saturday "brown bag" lunches. As the participants pondered the implications of census data for the nation's poor, it became apparent that poverty was not one problem but a constellation of interrelated problems. Moreover, for millions of Americans, poverty was neither a temporary state nor a condition of unemployment caused by disability or old age. The deeply rooted affliction that spanned generations became known as the "culture of poverty."[3]

*The 1960 presidential campaign had provided insights into the problem of poverty;
the 1964 race concentrated deliberations on the development of a program. In the fall of
1963, the informal Saturday discussions gave way to a CEA-led interagency task force.
After sifting through hundreds of antipoverty proposals, the task force seized on the
concept of "community action": local residents organizing to address common problems.
The models for community action programs were several urban Gray Areas projects
funded by the Ford Foundation and a series of community-based antipoverty initiatives
sponsored by the President's Committee on Juvenile Delinquency and Youth Crime.[4] As
the participants in the task force's deliberations traced the emergence of the idea of community action, it is clear that they viewed it primarily as a flexible approach to developing tailor-made programs for local circumstances. Yet the planners also addressed
the need to involve the poor in decisions affecting them, and the fact that established
institutions had often actually added to the problem of poverty rather than contributing
anything to its solution.*

*The day after Kennedy's assassination, Heller broached the notion of an antipoverty
offensive with the new president. Lyndon Johnson instantly embraced the proposal and
within weeks declared "unconditional war on poverty." By expanding the initiative
from a few demonstration projects to a national effort, he raised the stakes—and the
potential for controversy. Neither his extravagant vision of a Great Society nor his
visceral impatience with the nation's ills completely explain his abrupt action. Johnson
understood the imperatives of selling a new program to Congress and the nation. He
recognized, too, that his opportunity to effect change was unique and fleeting.[5]*

"NEW WORLDS TO CONQUER"

*Charles L. Schultze served as assistant director of the Bureau of the Budget (BOB) from
September 1962 to February 1965; in June 1965 he succeeded Kermit Gordon as director.
Schultze was a veteran of World War II and had received his M.A. degree from Georgetown University and his Ph.D. in economics from the University of Maryland. He
worked as a staff economist for the Council of Economic Advisers throughout the 1950s
and as a professor of economics at the University of Maryland in the early 1960s.*

SCHULTZE: The basic germ of this came probably from two places, maybe others.
One, in 1963, with the tax bill submitted and with some hope of its passage, Walter Heller then was looking for new worlds to conquer and quite clearly saw the
point that, hopefully, we had got the economy on the road to full employment
for the economy as a whole. Now where is the next big area of economic need?
He started it that way. Clearly, it's the pockets of poverty in the midst of what is
hopefully affluence. And he got to the president, saying, "Look, the next logical
step in this, since we have gone after the aggregate economy, is to find ways of
going after the pockets of poverty, not in the depressed-area sense of rural areas
which you can bypass—or not *solely* them—but rather just poor people who full
employment will help in part but won't fully cure." That's one. I suspect Michael

Harrington's book on poverty [*The Other America*] got a lot of stir. Kennedy had read it, and it impressed him. Finally, Kennedy's own trips through West Virginia and some of the other poverty areas [had influenced him]. I also think there was just the beginning, at least, of the recognition on the part of the civil rights people that legal remedies were not going to be enough—just the beginning glimmerings of that. All of these came together, but I think it was Walter Heller who probably first put the idea in Kennedy's head.

Kermit Gordon, an economist, was director of the Bureau of the Budget during the last two years of Kennedy's presidency; he left BOB in 1965 to join the Brookings Institution. Gordon was a native of Philadelphia who was educated at Swarthmore and was a Rhodes scholar at Oxford in 1938–1939. After returning to the United States, he worked for the Office of Price Administration (OPA) during the early 1940s and then joined the faculty of Williams College, where he taught until 1962. His appointment to the Council of Economic Advisers in 1961 led to his move to Washington.

GORDON: There have been a number of versions of the origins of the war on poverty—all of them partly accurate, partly inaccurate, in my recollection. My impression is that [it] really began in the summer of 1963 in an approach that Walter Heller made to President Kennedy.

Kennedy had developed a deep concern about the poverty he himself had observed in the hills of West Virginia during the presidential primary of 1960. There was a series of articles on the suffering of the poor people in the hills of eastern Kentucky which ran in the *New York Times*, I think sometime in the winter of 1962–1963. These articles were written by Homer Bigart, a *New York Times* reporter. These captured Kennedy's attention and imagination and aroused his concern. He ordered a crash program—it must have been in the late fall of 1962—without new legislation, but simply focusing existing programs and funds on the situation in eastern Kentucky. And on Kennedy's own initiative, with Ted Sorensen taking the lead, a number of federal agencies were mobilized to concentrate, in effect, relief programs in the hills of eastern Kentucky among the unemployed miners in that area. This was a clear response to Kennedy's concern over these articles he read in the *New York Times* by Homer Bigart. This just foreshadowed the growing concern in the administration with the problem of the people who had been left behind—the people who in a generally prosperous and affluent society were subsisting on the level of severe deprivation and hardship.

Perhaps it was a result of that experience that Walter Heller approached Kennedy, first in the spring of 1963, and asked for a license to conduct a quiet investigation of the dimensions of the poverty problem in America—the dimensions meaning racial, geographic, by age, etc.—and with the thought that as a result of this type of quiet investigation, it might be possible to come up with some preliminary ideas about an effective program to deal with these problems.

Heller got such a go-ahead from Kennedy, and on the basis of that license, he brought a man named Bob Lampman, an economist in the University of Wisconsin, to the Council of Economic Advisers in the summer of 1963.

He's a very able economist who had worked for some years prior to that summer on the problem of poverty in America. Lampman did some very good work at the council that summer; and on the basis of his studies, Heller went to Kennedy in the fall and got from Kennedy, if I remember correctly, a green light to assemble a little task force to try to begin the job of putting together a program.

Robert J. Lampman was working on the staff of the Council of Economic Advisers during the period from 1962 to 1963 when he and his colleagues in the Kennedy administration began to study the problem of poverty. A native of Wisconsin, Lampman had received his Ph.D. in economics from the University of Wisconsin, where he had held a professorship from 1955 to 1962. His book Low-Income Population and Economic Growth *(1959) had established him as an early expert in the field of poverty.*

LAMPMAN: My involvement was through the Council of Economic Advisers, for which I was a staff member, beginning first as a consultant in 1961 and then coming on board in Washington in June of 1962, where I stayed until the fall of 1963. Prior to 1961, I had gotten involved in the poverty question in doing a paper for Senator Paul Douglas's Joint Economic Committee of the Congress on the question of low-income population in the United States. It was a kind of response to John Kenneth Galbraith's book *The Affluent Society*, published in 1958.[6] In undertaking that, I had gotten acquainted with what information there was on the very low-income end of the spectrum: who the people were and where they were located, what kind of occupations and ages and so on they had. And that particular paper was used by a certain number of people, including Hubert Humphrey, in some of the campaign preparations at least leading up to the 1960 election. It got a certain amount of press, and it was part of the discussion at least that went on among reviewers and journalists and speechwriters. People began to think about the agenda for the 1960s.

One of the people who read it was Walter Heller, whom I had known before and who was teaching at that time up in the neighboring state of Minnesota. When we talked about my coming to join him as a staff member at the council, he talked about that paper, and he talked about the interest I had had in the distribution of wealth, as opposed to income, and my interest in social security and tax questions. So when I got to the council in 1961, I worked first on some consumer packages, consumer legislation, consumer council work.

But by the spring of 1963, Heller's interest turned to the question of income distribution. Partly this was due to sort of the national media attention to the problem of poverty. One thing I dug out of my file here was something that came to the council from the president's office about letters that had come in response to Howard K. Smith's TV program on poverty. The memorandum I have is dated March 22, 1963.[7] And we were asked to suggest ways that the White House might respond to this rather extraordinary expression of concern. There were other things like that that enabled Heller to open up again his interest in this particular aspect of the American economy.

Heller was very quick to note those at least flickers of interest that came along. But, of course, his big interest and big push in those first years was the innovative tax cut of what he had hoped would be early 1963 and which ended up being 1964 as the date of its beginning. He was certainly well geared up in his own thinking to the things to do after the tax cut, including, among other things, attention to the special problems of the people passed over, left out, somehow remaining in Depression-like conditions even though we'd had this great period of prosperity after World War II.

So that's how I got interested, and that's how it came on the agenda, as I remember it. The council then carried forward with not only responding to questions from the White House but putting new thoughts forward. On April 25, 1963, I wrote a memorandum to Heller on changes in the distribution of wealth and income through 1961–1962. Two days later, Heller wrote back, with scrawling on the margins: "This is very illuminating. The president should see a simplified version of it." Then two days later, I sent him back a simplified version, and he sent it over on May 1, 1963, to President Kennedy.[8]

It was about the point that there was some disappointing performance of the economy with respect to the numbers of people moving out of what could be called poverty—a total money income under $3,000. As economists, we generally tended to link this up in considerable part to the general slowdown in the economy in the late fifties. This became sort of additional ammunition for the general tax cut, but it also was part of this way to bridge over to the next step you're going to take after that.

So that memorandum did go to the president. I don't have any written notices here of what happened at that point, but my general memory is that Heller got favorable response again from President Kennedy sometime after that, and that as they began to gear up for thinking of at least beginning to explore possibilities for the 1964 campaign for reelection, one of those possibilities might be something about poverty, something about depressed areas, something about the disadvantaged.

THE SATURDAY GROUP

LAMPMAN: In that period, May to June [1963], somewhere along in there, Heller asked me to take part in writing up the possible meaning of an attack on poverty— lots of different phrases were used—and to meet with a group of people around Washington at the assistant secretary level and pick brains and get suggestions and criticisms of the idea. We dealt with people from the Bureau of the Budget;

from HEW [Health, Education, and Welfare Department] (Wilbur Cohen was an assistant secretary, as I recall, at that time); from Labor (Pat Moynihan [Daniel Patrick Moynihan] was the assistant secretary [of Labor]); from Agriculture; from Department of Justice.

There were just a few meetings, as I recall. We'd meet for an afternoon once every couple of weeks or something like that. It was all very tentative and very low-key, at least to start with. People were just speaking their minds. It was almost an academic sort of seminar. Indeed, it was interesting how many people there were Ph.D.s or were backed up by a scholar who was associated with the work. And we had represented people from different disciplines. There were people like Moynihan, who was a political scientist; and Cohen, who was an old hand in the income maintenance field but who was especially interested in this as an issue. There were statisticians, and then there were lawyers. People had very different approaches to the whole question.

We would get into discussions about the definition of poverty. What kind of a concept and what kind of a numbers frame would you have in mind? Some people would say poverty obviously means lack of money income. That had the great merit of being something we had some numbers on. We could say how many people there were above and below some line and where they were and so on. But other people said that's really not what poverty means; poverty is more or sometimes even less than money. It's a spiritual concept; or it's a participation-in-government concept; or it's a lack of some kind of self-esteem, sort of a psychological or image problem that people had. Or people would say, well, it really has to do with race; it has to do with sort of a near caste system in the United States. Still others would say it really has to do with lack of opportunity. It has to do with lack of public facilities like schools and so on. That's what makes people really poor.

So we had pretty long philosophical discussions, at least some of the time. I think that difference in concept was also later on reflected in the kinds of remedies that people would come up with. For example, the political concept of poverty—of this lack of power and so on—clearly got its expression in the community action approach as a remedy. In general, there were the economists against the rest of the disciplines. The economists tended to have a more optimistic view that you could do something about it. Sociologists, my impression, generally were very pessimistic about that. These are very deep-rooted social, psychological, attitudinal, value-laden concepts. As people bring their own purposes to the poverty question, you can't change those very rapidly and so on.

So there was a kind of sociological theory of poverty with its lack of remedies, and the economic theory with easy optimism that you could do something about it all. All you have to do is get money to people somehow, get them a job, get them education, training, something like that. So there was a kind of naive optimism, maybe; but at least it was strikingly different from some of the other attitudes expressed. That was one of the preoccupations at one or more meetings of this group. But there was, in general, receptiveness to the idea that was coming from Heller, and perhaps via him from the president himself, that this might be a good emphasis for a campaign to reelect.

Now this heated up sometime in the summer of 1963, and Heller got apparently a signal that the number of possible things to be emphasized in a campaign was down to just a few. It wasn't one of twenty different things, it was one of two or three. I don't remember exactly what the others were. But I think one of the ideas had been what we now call the environmental emphasis, but I think it went under the heading of conservation of resources and conservation of the environment. So there was a conscious exploration then of who would listen, who would be attracted to this as a political emphasis. In connection with that, some of these same people I mentioned were drawn in, but more a new group, for me at least, [including] some of the Irish Mafia from the White House who were Kennedy's very close political advisers, Myer Feldman, Ken O'Donnell, and Ted Sorensen. We had quite a lot of conversation with Ted Sorensen. They had to test for themselves the water of poverty as an issue. They pointed out, and other people were quick to see it too, that the poor don't vote. If you're going to attract them, you aren't going to attract much. And probably any of those who do vote already voted Democratic anyway, or many of them did. So the political interests turned around the question of which parts of the nonpoor would be attracted. And from the Howard K. Smith letters and some of these other responses that the president had had, it was concluded this was a good suburban issue politically, because there were a lot of churchwomen and League of Women Voters people, or I guess you might call them opinion leaders in the country, who were quite outspoken in [their] interest in this question.

Bill Cannon in the Bureau of the Budget was a very important figure in this story. There were other people in the Bureau of the Budget; there's sort of a rotating cast of characters. But Bill Capron, who had been with the council and had moved over to be with Kermit Gordon at the Bureau of the Budget, was in and wearing different hats at different times. So there were a group of people—and I guess I was one of them for a brief period of time—who were spending a good deal of time meeting with and listening to and communicating back and forth about this as a possible theme, as I said, for future legislation, for future campaign slogan use, for future action, perhaps at the departmental level if not at the White House level.

We didn't cover a lot of bases that you might have thought we would. I don't remember that we were encouraged to reach off into some of these things very far. For example, this original group didn't really touch the community action issue much. That was a big surprise to me after—that that came into prominence very late. It was the end of 1963 when that kind of got into the priority list of remedies. There was a little attention through the attorney general's office. They had been working, of course, on juvenile delinquency questions and had had a lot to do with the Ford Foundation's efforts in a few cities to get community action against a recognized problem with some federal government help. So that was a different approach than we had talked about in those meetings and in formal probings that we had done.

The impetus through the Council of Economic Advisers was much more in the direction of taking going programs that we had in the country and expanding those or extending them in some way to reach people who had been kind of left out. So there would be new efforts on the unemployment side to reach the very poor among the unemployed with new training programs or new job-seeking programs or something. Then there would be new efforts to get out into the schools where kids from the poorest and most disadvantaged families were to be found—and to use the Agricultural Extension Service in a new way to deal with the noncommercial farmers. So those were some ideas. Also, one of Pat Moynihan's ideas was to use the Department of Defense to some extent, more than it had been, as a kind of recovery device for kids who were really ineligible for the draft. That was a thought that attracted a lot of people in this initial group. Moynihan, among other people, had had [something] to do with a research project that came out about that time, as I remember, [about] the percentage of rejectees who were in some sense from very disadvantaged backgrounds.[9]

William M. Capron, a native New Yorker, was a staff member with the Council of Economic Advisers when he began working with the interagency task force on poverty in 1963. He had been a fiscal analyst for the Bureau of the Budget in the mid-1940s, a professor of economics at the University of Illinois and Stanford during the 1950s and early 1960s, and an economist with the Rand Corporation from 1951 to 1956. Capron became assistant director of the Bureau of the Budget in 1964.

CAPRON: I was a senior staff member with the Council of Economic Advisers beginning in 1962. In June of 1963, I became actively involved in [the question of poverty]. But even earlier than that, I was aware that another senior staff member, Robert Lampman, who was on leave from the University of Wisconsin, was working on updating and pulling together information drawn from the 1960 census on the distribution of income and particularly the distribution of income at the lower end of the spectrum. And indeed, [that was] the material that later—in January of 1964—was made public in chapter 2 of the 1964 "Economic Report of the President," which laid the groundwork for what came to be known as the War on Poverty.[10] That work was begun in the spring of 1963 by Bob Lampman, who was and remains one of the distinguished experts in the field of income distribution.

Walter Heller, the chairman of the council, was already talking about the need to think ahead to the legislative program that President Kennedy might introduce in 1964. The centerpiece of the 1963 program had been the tax cut. As Heller pointed out in conversations with the president and with Ted Sorensen over the summer, the tax cut was fine, and yet it didn't do anything directly for those at the very bottom of the income distribution.

There were some other events that I recall, not in necessarily exact chronological order. There was a very important magazine article in the *New Yorker* by Dwight Macdonald. The president got a marked-up copy of the Macdonald article. We do know that Homer Bigart's concern about the possibility in the winter of 1963–1964 of real hardship and starvation in the coal-mining areas exercised President Kennedy sufficiently so that a very targeted crash program was organized, which involved some of the same people early that fall who were also working on the poverty effort. As a result of that, some funds, particularly [Department of] Agriculture food funds, were channeled into that area, and some other emergency relief measures were undertaken. In any case, I'm mentioning that because it was quite clear during the summer that there was real interest in developing some kind of program—programmatic responses from the federal level to the problem of low-income people or poverty problems.

Heller, as was the custom in the Kennedy administration, right around Labor Day met with Ted Sorensen, who was President Kennedy's domestic policy chief of staff, and out of that came an instruction to the Council of Economic Advisers to take the lead in pulling together ideas for a program or group of programs in this area. Those of us who were involved in this at this point were really grasping for ideas.

Another thing that occurred over the summer of 1963 was that Lampman and I convened a Saturday-morning informal "brown bag" lunch group which included ourselves and two or three others from the CEA staff, and some of the people from the Labor Department, HEW, HHFA [Housing and Home Finance Agency], and the Bureau of the Budget. We met in a small conference room in the Executive Office Building in the council quarters. We used to usually get together about twelve and go until two-thirty or three on a Saturday afternoon. We did this several times over the summer. Some people were off on vacation part of the time; the group varied. Some people brought along with them others who they thought might have something to say. The focus of that exercise was to increase our own understanding of poverty. Several of the key people, in addition to Lampman, were those who knew a lot about the database. I remember some of the most important people in that group, in terms of the impact they had on educating people like myself who came to this with no background in the field at all, [were] Ida Merriam, who was a longtime Social Security Administration policy analyst—I do not remember her exact title, but that was her role—quite senior and a very effective person; Phil Arnow, then in the Labor Department as some kind of special adviser, I believe, or maybe an economist in the Manpower Administration; Wilbur Cohen joined us from HEW a couple of times, because Wilbur, in addition to his very effective political role as undersecretary, goes way back as a student of the whole income distribution area and certainly had an effect. From the Budget Bureau, Bill Cannon may have joined us toward the end of the summer, but Mike March, who was at that point in the division that managed the HEW and Labor budgets, participated.

Did the Saturday group focus on any particular aspects of poverty, such as employment or income distribution or income maintenance, or was it simply an open-ended discussion group?

CAPRON: Well, I have to qualify my ability to remember clearly, because I was learning from lots of conversations from those meetings and from trying to read a lot of stuff all at the same time, so it's very difficult for me to stand back and say, "That I first heard there," and so forth. My impression, though, is that one of the things that developed out of those discussions certainly was a sharpened view of the need, when one was thinking of going from analysis of what is the problem, to recognize that it wasn't *a* problem. It was a whole constellation of problems with very different sources. And some of the themes that were picked up in the council's "Economic Report of the President" that winter and have been part of the dialogue about poverty ever since were first identified then—the fact that a large number of people in any year will statistically be measured as poor because of transitory reasons. They're out of work for a large part of the year. They suffer some kind of injury or temporary disability. They are transitory poor. There may need to be some kind of programs to help them over that dip in the road, but they are very different than the people who are "trapped in poverty" or seem to be. The elderly poor were recognized as a special kind of problem. Manpower and education programs are not designed to help the elderly.

So the distinction [was made] between alleviating poverty for the elderly and the disabled and trying to eliminate poverty for those who still had a chance, through retraining, relocation, or whatever, to earn their way out of poverty through the world of work. We got fascinated with some of the data. Lampman had picked up a little of it. I remember it was at a couple of those Saturday-morning meetings that some data that was developed someplace in HEW [was presented] which identified what we came to call for a while the "culture of poverty." These are intergenerational families that for at least two or three generations have clearly been in poverty. Mothers or parents who are or were under the Aid [to] Families [with] Dependent Children would, in response to questionnaires, be asked [whether]—and indeed it was discovered that—their parents had also been in poverty. Trying to break the cycle of poverty became one of the themes that some of us tried to build into some of the specific program suggestions.

Of course, a lot of the programs were explicitly not designed to focus on the poor. But there was something that's become more commonplace. One of the things that I remember—some of the more sometimes heated discussions in that Saturday-morning group (I had forgotten about that)—was that some of us were beginning to read enough of things like Dwight Macdonald, for example, to be very skeptical of the whole social work establishment, managing people's lives in detail and almost putting people in second-class citizenship dependent status and keeping them there, because that's the way the programs ran, by keeping them there. Rather than encouraging people to move out of poverty, you'd put them in a dependent position and lock them into it. So it was to get out of the traditional mold. Oh, Mike Harrington, too, had written stuff that influenced us.

There was not, at least consciously, a notion in those Saturday-morning meetings that we were there designing a major part of the Kennedy program for 1964. We were not at that point. The real initiation of those meetings was Lampman trying to get some of the experts in Washington to react to some of the data that he was putting together and the way he was organizing it as a result of his very detailed and careful study of the 1950 and 1960 census information on income distribution. We knew that we were going to say something in the council report, but not necessarily in the president's program, about what was happening to income distribution and make general suggestions about government policy in the area. But this was before anyone had a notion of—and Lampman at that point didn't have in his head—a "war on poverty."

THE INTERAGENCY TASK FORCE

So then, after the summer, you took over as Heller's principal assistant on poverty?

CAPRON: That's right. Lampman had to return to the University of Wisconsin at the end of the summer. His leave was up. So Heller turned to me and one of the younger members of the CEA staff, Burt Weisbrod, and he and I together became Heller's point men on this whole subject. As part of that operation, a group of cabinet officers was put together as kind of an informal task force. It was decided by Sorensen and Heller, as I was told, that they would not use the technique which was used in the Kennedy years and later in the Johnson years very often to establish a task force which included outsiders. In this case, it was just the cabinet officers; the secretaries of HEW, Agriculture, [and] Labor; the administrator of Housing and Home Finance; the director of the Bureau of the Budget, of course; and the secretary of Commerce, although my memory is that Commerce played almost no role in this. There were a couple of meetings held, at least one meeting of that group that I remember, and then with Heller in the chair, and then a couple of meetings later on during the winter organized or called by Sorensen. I'll come to those a little later because they're important in explaining how we got to the Shriver task force.

The primary purpose of this kind of informal task force was to get the departments and agencies to come up with suggestions for items that might be included in a program should Kennedy decide to go ahead and make this part of his 1964 program. The results were perhaps predictably disastrous. That is, Heller got a lot of junk. These were warmed-over revisions of proposals that had been around for a long time, coming up out of the bureaucracy, programs that had been already rejected by the Congress. Very little imagination.

Were they weak primarily because they didn't have much prospect of passing?

CAPRON: No. Part of the problem was that they were terribly categorical; and from my point of view, they didn't fit what was emerging as our diagnosis of the problem, because they were completely unintegrated. They were little bits and pieces that didn't really hang together. What we'd struggled for through November of 1963 was an organizing theme. To the extent we got one, I would say it was the Community Action Program, which we viewed as a device to focus many different federal and local programs to match the needs in particular localities. We were particularly concerned about federal programs. It was this lack of focus and the fact that we knew there were lots of different patterns out there and that no one piece of legislation was going to affect more than a relatively small part of the problem in a relatively few places.

James Sundquist joined the War Against Poverty Task Force with two decades of experience in government and politics. Born in Utah, he worked as a reporter for the Salt Lake City Tribune in the late 1930s before he received a master of science degree in public administration from Syracuse University. In Washington, he worked as an administrative analyst with the Bureau of the Budget in the late 1940s, and as chief of the reports and statistics branch in the Office of Defense Mobilization in the early 1950s. From 1957 to 1962, he served as legislative and administrative assistant to Senator Joseph Clark of Pennsylvania. Sundquist's political activities were also extensive. After a brief detail as a speechwriter for President Truman, Sundquist was assistant to the chairman of the Democratic National Committee (1953–1954), and a speechwriter for Kennedy and secretary of the platform committee during the 1960 presidential campaign. In 1963 he became deputy undersecretary of Agriculture.

SUNDQUIST: The word went out to the departments during the late spring and early summer [of 1963], on a fairly informal basis, as I remember. But in the fall, there was a formal instruction to each department to come up with ideas for what might go into a poverty program. At that point, it was entitled "Widening Participation in Prosperity." There's a memorandum signed by Heller and Kermit Gordon which outlined the concepts of the program and divided it into three elements—preventing entry into poverty, facilitating exit from poverty, and ameliorating the condition of those who remained in poverty. Those were the three headings. We [in the Department of Agriculture], as other departments did, sent the memorandum to our bureaus and asked them for their ideas. They came up with innumerable suggestions, which then, in our department, Turley

Mace and I winnowed down and processed, so to speak. But generally speaking, unless they were obviously outlandish, we sent them on to the Council of Economic Advisers for their consideration.

William Cannon was born in Iowa in 1910. He received an M.A. from the University of Chicago, where he served as assistant vice president for development from 1954 to 1959. He joined the Bureau of the Budget in 1959 and in 1962 became assistant chief of the bureau's Office of Legislative Reference. In this capacity, he was responsible for health, education, and welfare issues.

CANNON: I was in the Office of Legislative Reference; this was my area—health, education, and welfare, and things like that. We saw a laundry list that the task force had generated as a first effort. There must have been 150 separate proposals. They may not have all been different, but they were all separate, and they represented the kinds of things that line agencies had been thinking about for years. It was a fairly unimaginative list.

As I recall, there was a big White House meeting with Sorensen somewhere in mid-October, early October maybe, to begin fashioning a program. You had to decide what the program was going to be because you had to get specs and you had to begin drafting legislation and things like that. But the meeting was a bomb. I wasn't there, but I was told. And Sorensen really in effect said to this task force, "Go back and do some more homework."

About that time we were getting anxious. It was October, and January comes up a lot faster; and running the legislative side of things, we had to make sure we had something. There was kind of an implicit responsibility in the office to be a ramrod for the White House, which is to keep the process moving fast enough to the end. So it was from that angle that we began to get concerned if the president really wanted a program like this. That wasn't clear. That was not at all clear. In part, the agencies weren't paying a lot of attention because they weren't sure that the president really wanted it. But if he really wanted it, we had to act on the assumption that he did and had to make a judgment as to whether he was going to get a program the way the process was working. And we were very dubious about it. This is Sam Hughes and me.

I'd had some dealings with David Hackett, who was Bob Kennedy's roommate in school and a very close friend, in connection with what eventually became VISTA but was set up as the domestic [National] Service Corps. I'd known Dave through those contacts, and I had kept in touch with Dave. Now I began talking to him about [the fact that] I was worried about the interagency process. They tend to be ineffectual, and this one was proving to be as ineffectual as most. So I began prodding Dave to prod the attorney general, Robert, to tell the White House this thing didn't seem to be going anywhere and somebody ought to be taking charge of it. Now, whether he ever did that or not, I don't know. There's some evidence from things later that he did. I began the argument, which was later fulfilled in a different way, that what you really needed was not an inter-agency task force but someone who was really going to run the program and who had a stake in it and therefore ought to be in on the shaping of it and the selling of it to Congress, which is exactly what happened with Shriver, which I thought was a marvelous development when it came.

I'd argued this with both Gordon and Heller, because by now it's mid-November. It's the tenth of November, somewhere around there, the eighth, and there was another White House meeting. This time [it was] on the same laundry list shortened—maybe there were only 75 [items]—and Sorensen couldn't do anything with that either. They were sent back again, because all you can do with it is to tell them to try it again. But after all, this was November 10, and everybody was beginning to get worried. There would have to be a decision whether to go ahead, and on the basis of what they had at that point, they couldn't go ahead. So Hackett began, I'm sure, to talk to Bob Kennedy.

On the other hand, Willard Wirtz [Secretary of Labor] was pushing for a utopia, a $5 billion-a-year job program. That wasn't in the works at all, but that's what he was pushing for. And he thought he was going to get it; that was the other side.

Walter Heller, as chairman of the Council of Economic Advisers under Kennedy, emerged as perhaps the most influential of the New Frontier economists. After earning an undergraduate degree from Oberlin and graduate degrees from the University of Wisconsin, Heller launched a career that included government service as well as academia. During World War II, he helped devise the withholding tax system while working at the Treasury Department; after the war, he provided fiscal advice to General Lucius Clay, the military governor of Germany. While an economics professor at the University of Minnesota, Heller became the principal tax adviser to Governor Orville Freeman. Hubert Humphrey introduced Heller to Kennedy during the 1960 presidential campaign.

HELLER: Ted Sorensen had told me, "Keep at it, it's the kind of an issue we should sign on to, and it's a terribly important thing." I'd had sessions on it with Kennedy in October, and again three days before the assassination. The reason I had seen Kennedy before leaving for Japan was that I had made a big staff commitment to it. I had Bill Capron rounding up opinions all over the government on the poverty program, and I then heard from Ted Sorensen some rather disquieting comment about, "We may have to put more emphasis on the suburbs," or something like that. So I thought the only thing to do was to go directly to Kennedy and find out how he felt about it. And he said, "Yes, Walter, I am definitely going to have something in the line of an attack on poverty in my program. I don't know what yet. But yes, keep your boys at work, and come back to me in a couple of weeks." This is what Kennedy told me on November 19.

CAPRON: Gordon and Heller and I had chatted the middle of that week before the assassination, on that Tuesday or Wednesday, because I know Walter was leaving. He was on the plane with the cabinet group going to Japan. They left, I guess, the day of [the assassination]. He was leaving in a couple of days, and I was with Heller at the White House mess [dining hall], and Kermit joined us for a few minutes. Maybe we stuck our heads in Sorensen's office, or he came in, but I remember at that time both Heller and Gordon saying, "Ted, we're not going to have anything if you don't start knocking heads." This was the idea.

Meaning heads of cabinet officers?

CAPRON: Yes, and Sorensen's sardonic response was that he didn't mind knocking heads, but he didn't see what he was knocking for, because he didn't have anything from us that anyone could put their teeth in. One of the doubting Thomases—the "man from Missouri"—at this point was Kermit Gordon, then the director of the Bureau of the Budget. He didn't think that we had a real set of programmatic ideas. He'd seen this list of things that he as budget director recognized were kind of typical add-ons to various agencies' programs, and he didn't see the glimmer of an idea. He had been quite intrigued with Lampman's summary of the character of poverty, which was attached to one of these early memos, almost an outline of chapter 2, although it wasn't put forward that way. It's one of the early [memos].

The day after Kennedy's assassination, Walter Heller was able to meet with Lyndon Johnson.

HELLER: We had something like 40 minutes together. And it was a very satisfactory discussion of issues and of approaches and of the problems of the tax cut, and particularly I got the green light from him on the poverty program.... I told him very early in our conversation that the very last substantive conversation that I had had with Kennedy was about a poverty program.... I related this conversation to Johnson, and his reaction immediately was, "That's my kind of program. I'll find money for it one way or another. If I have to, I'll take away money from things to get money for people." His response was favorable and immediate.

Judging from subsequent events, was this reaction one of sincere interest in poverty, or was it a means of gaining your support in the council and in the government?

HELLER: His response was so spontaneous and so immediate—and without knowing that we were sort of battling within the administration to get this kind of a program adopted—that I thought that it was an instinctive and intuitive and uncalculated response, [not] calculated in the sense that your question suggests. The play for support came in the comments as he led me to the door, telling me that he was really a Roosevelt type of liberal and I should be sure to tell my friends that. I mean, there he was: Lyndon Johnson, the politician working on the human relationship and a matter of gaining your support and loyalty and so forth by saying, "Yes, I am committed to the same general ideals you are." That was very clear in that context. But I did not have [that] feeling in the more formal part of our discussion, as we sat there going over issue by issue. I had written up a little agenda of things that I wanted to go over, and he held still for all of them. I got through the whole thing from A to Z.

THE PRESIDENT'S COMMITTEE ON JUVENILE DELINQUENCY AND YOUTH CRIME

CAPRON: Bill Cannon put me together during October or early November with Dave Hackett and Dick Boone from Bobby Kennedy's juvenile delinquency (JD) operation.[11] I knew absolutely nothing about it. I knew the name, but that was all I knew. And that was my introduction to the notion of what came to be known as community action. Bill Cannon gets a lot of credit for holding my feet to the fire and making me think about it, because he was coming at this from the vantage point of the division of legislative analysis in the Budget Bureau. They're the people who have to worry about what will sell on the Hill and how to package a program. Like Kermit and Sorensen, for that matter, he was very well aware that we didn't yet have handles that you could put a program on, and he latched on to this.

Dave Hackett was a very hard-driving, effective, caring person. He really cared about what he was doing in the Juvenile Delinquency Program. He very quickly excited me by the possibility. I do get credit for one piece of the business here, because I put Boone and Hackett together with Heller for what was supposed to be a half-hour and [the meeting] ran for nearly two hours. Walter got sold on the idea of community action as being the organizing principle.

How was the program presented to you by Boone and Hackett? Do you recall how they described it?

CAPRON: I think one of the main themes was the tremendous energy and potential there were in lots of communities that looked from the outside like they were desolate, dead, and disorganized. With a little federal seed money, there was the possibility of local groups to really come together and do something to help themselves. The fact [was] that [if] people thought they were going to have some control over what happened to them—or in this case their young people—that a lot could happen. There was tremendous variety—this was the other thing—from one part of the country to another, from ghettos to smaller cities and all the rest of it.

Jule Sugarman was recruited by Richard Boone in the summer of 1964 to assist with the administrative organizational work of setting up the Community Action Program. Before coming to OEO, Sugarman served as budget officer for the Bureau

of Prisons, and from 1962 to 1964 as chief of budget and management planning at
the Department of State's Bureau of Inter-American Affairs. As deputy associate
director of the Community Action Program, Sugarman was instrumental in the
creation of Project Head Start, and in 1965 he became associate director of Head
Start.

SUGERMAN: One of the peculiar twists of history here is that I wrote the executive order that set up the President's Committee on Juvenile Delinquency [and
Youth Crime, PCJD] years ago when I was in the Bureau of Prisons and was
working with Dave Hackett, who set that up. Then I really was not involved in its
activities at all during most of its life but came back into contact with all these
people later on.

After Robert Kennedy was appointed as attorney general, he appointed
Dave Hackett, who had been his college roommate, to look into problems
of juvenile delinquency. As first parts of that effort, Dave came to the Bureau
of Prisons, talked to the director of the bureau, and eventually wound up
talking to me and a couple of other people from the bureau at some length.
At that time, I think it would be fair to say, he knew nothing about juvenile
delinquency, and he was quite candid in admitting it. But he had the kind of
mind and the kind of interest that caused him to probe people rather deeply
and to sort of draw out their ideas. He apparently talked to quite a few people
around town and then eventually came back and said to me, "It seems to me
we've got three major agencies here that ought to be working together on
the juvenile delinquency effort: one Justice, one HEW, and the other Labor.
Would you do something to put together an organization which could do
this?"

So we did draw up a draft of what such an organization might be. We figured
out how it could be financed without actually having to go to the Congress
for the initial appropriation and wrote a draft of the executive order which the
president eventually issued. At that time, I don't think that there was very much
detailed involvement with university people. I think it was mostly with governmental people. But shortly after the program came into being, university people
began to appear on the scene. And I think it's fair to say that they're the ones
who actually gave it shape and character in terms of a program. All we had was
an organizational framework when we began.

Many of the basic concepts did grow out of the president's committee. And
certainly many of the first community action agencies had had their origin in a
prior JD project.

What were the kinds of programs the committee sponsored?

SUGARMAN: They had a wide range, but their favorite, I think, was the comprehensive neighborhood approach to working on juvenile delinquency, which was

almost indistinguishable from the comprehensive neighborhood approach to working on poverty—the feeling being that the origins of juvenile delinquency and the origins of poverty are awfully close together. The JD program ran into a pretty heavy barrage of criticism in the Congress eventually, because it couldn't clearly be identified as being a juvenile delinquency program. Particularly among those who were not too happy with the community action concept, it became quite a target.[12]

The original concern for the problem of juvenile delinquency, with the subsequent studies and evaluations and investigations into this particular problem, broadened into a larger concern because of the findings—the relationship between juvenile delinquency and the much broader problem of poverty.

CAPRON: There's no question that the community action idea—and this stayed with it and plagued it to some extent all the way through—was very urban. The juvenile delinquency people were mostly working, not surprisingly, in an urban setting. We didn't talk much about the rural problem. That came up first in the community action context when I got Paul Ylvisaker, who was then with the Ford Foundation and head of a private community action experimental or demonstration program, to bring Mike [Mitchell] Sviridoff and another guy whose name I never can remember.[13]

This began as a breakfast meeting [and] went on for part of the morning. I remember I was so frustrated; I had wanted to get Ylvisaker in to talk to Kermit Gordon—but I couldn't work it out, Gordon's schedule was just too jammed-up or something, I can't remember—because Ylvisaker took us then a major step, for me at least, beyond the Hackett-Boone discussion. Partly he was able to organize his thinking in a not so directly, [not so strictly] nuts-and-bolts operational way, which is the way Hackett naturally approached things. He's a can-do sort of person. There was more of a structure in Ylvisaker's mind, because he had been designing programs.

You mean "structure" in terms of how you set up a program?

CAPRON: That's right, and a lot of the ideas that ended up actually in the legislation, the ground rules for how you would go about organizing CAPS [community action programs], really were developed out of the Ford experience. We were not drafting legislation at that first meeting, but I got some of this in me, and some of the things that were said then started appearing in the memoranda going out over Heller's name and ended up being reflected in the Council of Economic Advisers chapter and then flowed into the Shriver task force when it was organized.

Do you recall any particular projects that either Ylvisaker or Hackett and Boone referred to, something like the HARYOU program?

CAPRON: HARYOU was discussed, and of course we heard a lot from Mike Sviri-doff about New Haven and Dick Lee's efforts. And also Terry Sanford's efforts in North Carolina.[14]

THE EMERGENCE OF COMMUNITY ACTION

CANNON: Then came the assassination, and the great decision was what to do: (a) we didn't know what Johnson would want to do, and that was critical; and (b) we didn't have a program. Even if he wanted to do something, what the hell is it that he would do? And those are two major [points]. Really, the lines of communication were just beginning to form. I mean, we hadn't worked with Johnson. You know how vice presidents are, or at least used to be: they're fairly isolated from things, at least like this.

But we decided just to move ahead, and I took various key ideas we were kicking around—education, jobs, and so on—and I wrote a memorandum, which Sam Hughes sent to Wilbur Cohen and also to Capron and Heller. And they bought it. It had the germ of the Community Action Program, but it had more than that. Around this germ and some other ideas, you could get a coherent program. Really what the memorandum did was, while it specified going ahead in certain areas on education and so on, it also said what you need is a very flexible program, because poverty is a flexible problem. And you need authority organized around some concept, comprehensive community action. Then you don't have to worry about 158 programs or 75; you've got some coherence to it.

After we surfaced this idea, then Kermit bought it after Capron and Heller bought it. Incidentally, there's a document from the council to Sorensen, December 14, which has the label "Comprehensive Community Action Program," recommending a comprehensive community action program as a centerpiece. Capron had lifted those words from my memorandum, in which they were not side headings or anything; they were just in there in a sentence. I hadn't recognized the value of it.

But they were also popping in another direction in that Gordon himself began to get in on the act. We had a meeting with him, and he said, "This sounds an awful lot like some of the stuff the Ford Foundation is doing." He'd been with Ford, and I had no notion of it myself, none whatsoever. I didn't know what they were doing. But we then had a series of meetings with Ylvisaker and Mike Sviridoff, who was then at New Haven, Yale. And yes, as far as I could tell, they were talking about something else. The resemblances were really very super-ficial. Now, I checked this out, because I thought maybe I'd gotten it through Hackett, who, after all, I did know and I just kind of picked it up without attri-bution. He was vehement about it in the sense that, by God, he wasn't going to have anything to do with their silly little concept, you see. So he was, if anything, giving me the negatives of it rather than the positives of it.

No, it really came out of the framework in which I was operating plus my own personal background, which was an attempt to put a legislative package together and try to figure out a way to unify, politically and intellectually, things that were very different—and organizing it around a political appeal that I thought would be very effective and would sell on the Hill, which was localism.

SUNDQUIST: I had taken over to the Council of Economic Advisers the list of proposals after Turley Mace and I had shaken it down, and there may have been twenty that we felt [were] worthy of forwarding. Bill Capron had received, I suppose, a couple hundred suggestions altogether. It was during this period—when they were swimming around, wondering how to make a selection from among all these proposals, all of which had some merit but none of which had outstanding merit—that the community action idea began to come to the fore, not only as a program in itself but as the means for mediating among all these other programs. I reported at a staff meeting in the Agriculture Department. I recall that I said that every proposal we sent over had been approved. The people around the table beamed, and then I went on to explain that this was subject, of course, to the communities' deciding that these were the programs they wanted and initiating proposals for them. The reaction around the table was, "Well, that's fair enough. We won't have any trouble working with the community action agencies, and we'll be prepared to carry out the programs that they recommend." But this got everybody off the hook. I was very conscious of it myself, and I assume that the people in the Budget Bureau and the council felt the same way, that community action was the solution to their problem of selection.

ESTABLISHING A NEW AGENCY

CAPRON: The other thing that was very evident and became much more overtly clear when we met in Sorensen's office in December with the relevant cabinet officers, [was] a fierce desire on their part to keep programs in their own departments and not let loose of anything.

The meeting I remember best was December 20, just before Christmas. There is a December [20] memorandum from Heller to Sorensen, and a couple of days before that he sent a covering note with a draft of that memorandum to the cabinet officers concerned.[15] That was a very unpleasant meeting. It has to be understood that a number of us—and I guess most particularly it was obvious to me that Ted Sorensen, Kermit Gordon, and Walter Heller—were still most deeply affected by Kennedy's assassination. Especially Ted, not surprisingly. He was morose. He did not, as I had seen him in the past, control the meeting.

We were already way down the road in terms of putting the budget together in the program. Because of the inability [to agree on an antipoverty program] in November at an earlier meeting, which I don't remember as well—I'm quite sure I was there, but this was before the assassination—and there was just no agreement at all and a good deal of confusion as to what the next steps were. We took it that the next steps were to identify what came to be known as the Community Action Program, which was then just a kind of glimmering possibility dimly seen and I think looking different to everyone who used the phrase.

So the meeting on December 20, if that's the right date, was at Johnson's insistence that he needed something, and we didn't have anything for him in terms of a real program. He was about to leave—he probably left that weekend for the ranch—and the annual go-round on the budget and the legislative program.

My memory is that [Willard] Wirtz was the most aggressive. I believe he stalked out of the meeting, to coin a phrase. He argued that we didn't need any more damn new agencies, that he and [Anthony] Celebrezze, secretary of HEW, between them could work out a coordinated attack on poverty, that there wasn't enough money going to be in the budget. We knew at that point that we were operating with a terribly tight budget, and the numbers seem unreal in today's world. But the magic figure for that period was $100 billion. There was a marvelous minuet publicly danced between the budget director, Kermit Gordon, and Lyndon Johnson. Johnson and Gordon knew quite well that they could, by pushing things around a bit, come in under $100 billion, and a lot of people have forgotten why that was an important number: that was the number that seemed to be necessary to get one of the great barons of the Senate, Harry Byrd, to agree to the tax cut. So that magic number was very real. Anyway, as the budget was finally printed, it showed only a half-billion dollars of new money. This, of course, gave a lot of people a great deal of trouble.

It's very hard for me not to let hindsight influence what I say now. We started out with the notion that we were not talking about big new budget resources, and that was a constraint from the outset. That's why in the initial design of what came to be known as community action we talked about a targeted demonstration program. We used the argument that we were all terribly ignorant about poverty and programmatic ways to do something about it, that we had to learn a lot more. We were not talking about a massive War on Poverty that fall at all. That was very much the Johnsonian impact. And by saying that, I'm not saying that President Kennedy would not have also insisted on going much bigger if he was going to go at all. By the time of that meeting in late December with Sorensen and the cabinet members concerned, it was already clear that there wasn't going to be a big new program of any kind. And it was partly on that argument that Wirtz argued that it didn't make any sense [to create a new agency].

The big debate that went on through that fall was whether or not you did some restructuring of programs and agencies, within particularly Labor and HEW, or whether you needed something bureaucratically separate from those. Charlie Schultze, who was then assistant director of the Bureau of the Budget, Bill Cannon, and I were the three people who were most insistent that nothing was going to happen if you put particularly the small number of dollars we were talking about into the existing agencies. [The money] would just get gobbled up in the usual bureaucratic crap. It would get tied into the categorical programs with these very strong bureaucratic links between the feds, the state, and the local governments. You wouldn't be able to see anything happen. There would just be a little more business as usual.

SUNDQUIST: We had a couple of meetings at the White House on how the program should be organized. The meetings were chaired by Ted Sorensen or Mike Feldman, or both, and the departmental representatives came. One of the meetings was preceded by the distribution of a paper, setting up alternative organization plans. This was at the point where community action was the program, and the question was, "How do you organize community action?" There were several alternatives, the two basic ones being HEW or an independent agency. Then there may have been a third or fourth alternative involving an interdepartmental committee, with perhaps HEW as the operating agency. But the question at the White House meeting was, "Does HEW get this program, or doesn't it?"

Our department had taken a stand strongly against HEW running it. As I recall it, nobody supported HEW in the meeting except Secretary Wirtz, which surprised me at the time. Secretary Celebrezze made his opening remarks on behalf of HEW, and then Wilbur Cohen, who was sitting behind him, took over, and they made their case. This was the period after the assassination, and Ted Sorensen was visibly in a state of shock. He didn't have his heart in mediating this nasty jurisdictional dispute. He lost control of the meeting at times and left for a while and came back, so that there was no decisive hand at the helm at that point.

WHERE DOES THE POVERTY PROGRAM BELONG?

The poverty program's location within the government involved both administrative and political considerations. The following conversations illustrate the organizational dilemmas the president and his advisors faced in establishing a new authority outside of the existing bureaucracy.

LBJ's conversation with John Kenneth Galbraith, January 29, 1964[16]

JOHNSON: ...I saw your speech on this poverty thing.[17] We're going to have quite a problem because it's scattered all over the government. We're going to have difficulty setting up a new agency and getting much done because you can't get good people to come and run it. You can't set up all the checks and balances and all the payrolls and auditing and all that kind of stuff—the administrative angles. I talked a good deal to Walter Heller and Gordon about it. I don't know when you're going to be down this way, but if you could sometime in the next week, I sure would like for you to sit down and talk to me and talk to Walter Heller and talk to Kermit Gordon, the director of the Budget, and get any ideas you might have as to just the best approach we could make to this thing because it means so much to the whole country. And it's got them all stimulated and inspired. We just can't afford to have it be a WPA flop.

GALBRAITH: Absolutely not. Well, I'm absolutely at your command, Mr. President.

JOHNSON: Walter Heller will be back tomorrow. He has been talking to various cabinet agencies. Now, what we think, we are asking for new obligational authority of $500 million. We thought that's as much as we could get by with to start it off. We don't know whether we can get by with that or nor. We've got a pretty rough Congress. We can't get youth employment and some other good bills through that ought to be through because of fellows like Clarence Cannon. He just abolished the supplemental appropriations [sub]committee on me yesterday. Just kind of a dictator type. But we asked for $500 million. We think we'll have another $500 million in the existing programs if we get it through. But the question is: how do we coordinate, and how do we develop and how do we pick out some real pilot projects—New York, Chicago, or Los Angeles, some of these places? The Justice Department, I guess, will have something to do with it because of juvenile delinquents. Labor will have a good deal to do with it. HEW will have a good deal to do with it, but you can't run a program like that by committee, as you well know. You've got to have some good strong administrator.

GALBRAITH: I've got two thoughts on it, Mr. President. One, let me urge one thing: don't use the word "pilot project." That's got to be a cliché, as an excuse for not doing anything. But my main point is one of the reasons, I think, that the Roosevelt programs are, on the whole, identified with liberalism and one of the reasons that the Peace Corps was [identified] was it got somewhat out of the bureaucratic rut. I was down a few weeks ago and had a talk with Frank Roosevelt. The one concern I came back with was I hope this doesn't get buried so deep in the government that nobody gives you credit or the Democrats credit for doing it. It should have the visibility and also the inspiration that goes with a new group of people attacking it. I don't know how you feel about that, but I have a feeling that if this gets too deep in the government, it will just be lost sight of.

JOHNSON: Yeah, I think that's right. On the other hand, how are you going to tell Celebreeze what to do with his money that's appropriated to him?

GALBRAITH: Of course, someone's going to have to do that; no question about that.

JOHNSON: I would think what you ought to have is a top-flight, imaginative young Sargent Shriver-type as executive director and maybe an advisory committee of the cabinet most concerned with it, say, five men on it like Secretary of Labor, Health Education and Welfare, and so on and so forth.

GALBRAITH: I think that's right. And right in the White House.

JOHNSON: Probably so.

GALBRAITH: But is there a possibility of giving that sort of man education— even at the cost of hurting Tony's feelings—of lifting something out, so that he also has something to run?

JOHNSON: It's pretty difficult. You see, these cabinet officers are really going to hold on with their teeth to everything that's theirs because they take the position that Congress has appropriated [it] to them for their administration.

GALBRAITH: Yes, but the presidency is a powerful office.

JOHNSON: When Walter Heller gets back here, why don't I get him to call you and get Kermit Gordon and the three of you get together with me and let's see what we might work out of it?

GALBRAITH: All right. This is very close to my heart, and I'll come down anytime on any notice. You think Walter's getting back tomorrow?

JOHNSON: I believe so.

GALBRAITH: Suppose I have a talk with him tomorrow in any case.

JOHNSON: I wish you would and get his thinking. Then you chew on it a little bit and maybe talk to Kermit Gordon—he's been working on it some. Then see what date would be good for them. Any date will suit me; I'm going to be here every day. I want to put it ahead of anything else. You just give them a call and get back in touch, and you come down within the next week.

GALBRAITH: How are you feeling otherwise, my good friend?

JOHNSON: I couldn't be doing better. Is Kitty doing all right?

GALBRAITH: She's doing fine. This all agrees with you?

JOHNSON: Yes, sir.

GALBRAITH: You always did like work, though, better than any man alive.

JOHNSON: I'm feeling wonderful, and I'm looking forward to seeing you. Tell Kitty I want another dance with her pretty soon.

GALBRAITH: Okay, she hasn't forgotten the last one. I can tell you that.

LBJ's conversation with Kermit Gordon, January 29, 1964[18]

JOHNSON: I talked to Ken Galbraith this morning. Did you all give any more thought as to how we're going to administer this poverty program?

GORDON: There are some papers coming to you, Mr. President. My own judgment is that the central authority ought to be in a small independent agency, either in the Executive Office [of the President] or outside the Executive Office, with an administrator and advisory council composed of representatives of the cabinet departments that are involved.

JOHNSON: When Walter Heller gets through touring, will you get a hold of him and tell him, by God, never let anybody else leave this capital. These folks are taking trips to Tokyo and everything. They really do throw us out of joint. You get a hold of him, and see what we're doing on that message, and see what we're going to do on the administration end, and tell him to call or you call Ken Galbraith, and arrange a date to get him down here this week or the early part of next week, and let's try to get that in shape.

GORDON: We're working on the message, Mr. President. As a matter of fact, Ted Sorenson, I think, is working on the administrative arrangements. There was some disagreement between Celebrezze and Wirtz, on the one hand, and the rest of us on the other. My own very strong view is that it would be a mistake to lodge this coordinating authority in HEW. I don't think that anybody in HEW could bring the other cabinet departments into line and really coordinate the thing effectively. I think it has to be done outside the cabinet departments. And since I know you didn't want it too close to the White House, our best judgment was a small, quite small, independent agency with an administrator and an advisory council composed of cabinet members.

JOHNSON: That sounds pretty good. You get with Walter and try to work it out and get Ken Galbraith down here. Let's spend a lot of time working on the organization and the message, too.

LBJ's conversation with Walter W. Heller, February 15, 1964[19]

JOHNSON: Sorenson just tore Shriver to pieces yesterday. He just went back to where I was at the ranch with you. He said that they're just not going to give any special assistant to the president this money in a political year. You've got to handle it through existing agencies. I listened to it for an hour. Then I just felt so depressed—I had to go to St. Louis—I got up and left. But that poverty thing is going to cause us a lot of headaches, because we're not going to get it passed if you don't get it in the right channels.

HELLER: I had a couple of hours with Shriver today and later on with Bill Wirtz. In that connection, of course, Shriver has the idea that if we put these camps under the McNamara umbrella, we'll take a lot of the heat off of you and off the whole charge that it'll be sort of a slush fund and so forth for the president. At the same time, we're going to have to be damned careful the make sure we don't lose the conservationists, who are, you know—they're strong on the CCC camp idea. To balance all these different things is obviously very tough. I myself think Shriver is making good progress. I think he's got a pretty realistic grasp of a great deal of this. While there are still a lot of holes in it and it's a damned tough program, I can't think of a better man to have charge of it.

JOHNSON: I think that's right from the standpoint of selling it up on the Hill. But I think we've got to agree here—and you and Kermit are going to have to sit down with him and see that we get some agreement and see that Wirtz and Celebrezze and the rest of them go along. Now, are they ready to go along and give their money to him to administer?

HELLER: Their attitude has improved 1,000 percent on this score since Shriver was appointed. As I think I mentioned earlier, I thought that was a brilliant move, because he is, of course, the kind of guy that commands respect, and they are all cooperating with him.

JOHNSON: What I think we'll have to do is let the money stay with them and let him write drafts on it some way or other.

HELLER: . . . In substance he's got to have control of that money if he's going to make a go of this.

JOHNSON: Well, he can write the draft, and they can have it subject to a veto some way or the other. We can't start it out with a new political agency—a guy running for vice president and a president—in an election year. Now, Walter, I just know that much about politics.

HELLER: Right. They're not going to—

JOHNSON: They won't object to the bureau of education and the bureau of labor employment or whatever you've got over there.

HELLER: How about the Pentagon? I suppose that—

JOHNSON: If they don't go military. I just don't want a Hitler outfit started over there. McNamara is the smartest guy in the cabinet. He's just got it. If he'll buy it—I doubt that he'd buy it. If Shriver can get him to buy it and he'll go up and swing for it, that is the best chance we've got out of it.

LBJ's conversation with Lawrence F. O'Brien, March 11, 1964[20]

O'BRIEN: Mr. President, I talked to several of the people that would be key on the Hill as we fight this out, and the consensus certainly is that the bill should point out the route is through the director, that the director is the key in it, and that this thing operates through him and out. . . . The view on the Hill obviously…[is that segmenting it into various departments] will make it much more difficult to enact this legislation.

JOHNSON: They want to ask him, "Well, all right, Mr. Director, they're giving you the power here. Who's going to administer this program under your direction?" Doesn't he have to say Labor Department?

O'BRIEN: Well, he's going to certainly spell it out in hearings along those lines, but…there has to be a centralization of this in the view of those on the Hill. And the centralization obviously has to be through the director. And the director is the key in the minds of many of these people up there, [and] that if they get into departmentalized initial authority at the early stages of this operation that it's just going to make it more difficult to sell this.

JOHNSON: In other words, HEW has got its group; Agriculture has got its group, its congressmen; Labor's got its group. We wind up—we're going be kind of like we are with the Food Stamp, Wheat—Cotton bills. We haven't got enough for any of them unless we combine them.

O'BRIEN: That's right. That's right.

SELLING THE PROGRAM

SUNDQUIST: About the same time, the Council of Economic Advisers had reached the conclusion independently that we needed someone with stature and political appeal to handle the salesmanship of this program to the Congress. And Bill Capron's name is on a memorandum to the president pointing out that the program was going to need both specific development and most of all salesmanship, and that someone ought to be designated by the president in whom he had confidence. Two names were on that piece of paper: Abe Fortas and Sargent Shriver. This memorandum, I assume, went forward, so that you had two factors, then, bearing on the decision. One was the squabbling that was going on as to how the thing would be organized; the other was the feeling on the part of the president's staff advisers that somebody had to be charged with the congressional presentation.

This was not something that the council or the Budget Bureau—either one—felt equipped to do, and they were quite right. It was an enormous lobbying job that had to be organized, and those agencies aren't set up for that purpose and don't have any skill at it. So I don't know how these two lines of influence converged on the president, or whether they did converge. At any rate, at the point where he decided he wanted a man to sell the program to Congress, he decided at the same time that he would have an independent agency rather than giving the community action job to HEW.

HELLER: In the poverty program, [Johnson] was extremely demanding. Kermit Gordon and I went down to the ranch. And the president just threw that back at us time and time and time again. He said, "Look, I've earmarked half a billion dollars to get this program started, but I'll withdraw that unless you fellows come through with something that's workable." He made very clear that it had to have some hard, bedrock content, and he kept referring time and again to his National Youth Administration experience in the thirties. He liked the idea of learning while doing, learning through doing. I recall quite vividly a night in that living room with the big fireplace down there at the ranch.

GORDON: I remember a meeting in the cabinet room to which the president called all of his most trusted advisers. There were a number of cabinet members around the table. Clark Clifford was there. Abe Fortas was there, and I'm sure Larry O'Brien was there, and a number of other such people, to talk specifically about the poverty program. The one thing every person in the room agreed with was that under no circumstance must this be called a poverty program, because it was felt poor people would be offended to be told they were living in poverty, and secondly, it would be bad for the American image abroad for the government to acknowledge this bluntly and flatly that it had a serious problem of poverty. An interminable amount of time was spent in thinking up euphemisms for the poverty program with all this high-powered talent around the table. I think the reason it was called the War on Poverty, the poverty program, was that nobody around the table, despite a lengthy effort to identify such a title, could think of any euphemism which didn't sound silly. The meeting broke up kind of inconclusively. In the absence of something better, it was called the poverty program, the War on Poverty. I remember that later with a good deal of amusement.

CAPRON: So finally, the president did [appoint Sargent Shriver] at the end of January.[21] I'll never forget that announcement, because Walter had gotten some tickets to A Funny Thing Happened on the Way to the Forum. It was a big hit that winter of 1963–1964 on Broadway. I worked my tail off on the report, and Walter and his wife couldn't go up that Saturday because they had something they had to do or whatever, so he very kindly gave me the tickets, and we went up. We came out of the theater—it was Saturday night—in Times Square, picked up the Sunday morning New York Times, and there was the announcement that Shriver had been named. I went back to the hotel, and I said to Peg, "I'll make a bet that I have a message," and I did. Walter had called. I had to go back.

2

THE WAR ON POVERTY
TASK FORCE

BY ENLISTING SARGENT SHRIVER to head the President's Task Force in the War Against Poverty, President Johnson instantly escalated the offensive. First and foremost, Shriver was a Kennedy, the slain president's brother-in-law—a fact that had enormous significance in 1964. Yet the charismatic Shriver brought more to the task than the Kennedy mystique. The Peace Corps, which Shriver had launched in 1961 and which he still directed, was celebrated as a symbol of national idealism. Even more important was his well-deserved reputation as an effective salesman who understood how to mobilize public opinion and lobby Congress.[1] He was just the leader who could convert a government program into a crusade.

Shriver tackled the assignment with characteristic gusto. Telephones immediately began to ring, summoning former associates in the business world, the Kennedy presidential campaign, and the Peace Corps. Shriver's reach extended beyond his own circle to acquaintances of friends and to experts on poverty. A number of those who had been part of the CEA interagency task force gravitated to Shriver's group. Although most of the regulars were on government payrolls, they did not necessarily represent the views of their departments.

Establishing the task force required imagination in logistics as well as in planning. As poverty planners camped in one temporary office after another, they borrowed equipment and supplies from other departments and enlisted people on government, corporate, and university payrolls. Since many of the task force members, including Shriver, had responsibilities at other agencies, planning the poverty program was a nocturnal activity. One participant has recalled that the task force's familiar routine was to meet at midnight.[2]

The hectic, after-hours operation of the task force undoubtedly contributed to its chaotic atmosphere, described by one veteran as a political campaign train and as comparable to being in a hotel lobby during a convention. Moreover, Shriver's ad hoc organizational style encouraged the intellectual free-for-all that ensued, as did the fact that the problem of poverty itself defied rigid institutional boundaries.

The pressure of time also quickened the pace of activity. The task force had to design a comprehensive antipoverty program and draft a presidential message and legislation to implement it. All of this work had to be completed early enough to allow the measure to go through both houses of Congress before adjournment.[3]

Sargent Shriver's appointment as director of the War on Poverty task force and subsequently as head of the Office of Economic Opportunity (OEO) capped an extraordinary career of civic and humanitarian service. A graduate of Yale University and Yale Law School, he served in the navy for five years before he became manager of the Chicago Merchandise Mart. His work with the Joseph P. Kennedy Jr. Foundation led to his involvement with a variety of educational and mental health programs advanced by the foundation. He served as president of the Chicago Board of Education from 1955 to 1960. After working in the 1960 presidential campaign of his brother-in-law John F. Kennedy, Shriver became the organizer and first director of the Peace Corps in 1961.

The president met with you on January 31, right after your return from the trip around the world.

SHRIVER: Yes. I recall that I went to the White House to meet him, because customarily when I went overseas for the Peace Corps I always came back at the end of the trip and talked to the president, just to give him a personal report. I did that with Kennedy, and now in 1964, when Johnson was president, I did the same thing.

[Johnson] received me over there either in the cabinet room or in his office—I don't remember which—and then he got up right away and walked out of the office into the Rose Garden. We walked from the Rose Garden around the White House driveway. Then we walked back the same way into the Rose Garden and into his office. During that stroll, I suppose I talked to him maybe three or four minutes about the trip I had just finished, which was and is a story by itself. It was a remarkable trip, and he had given me a lot of letters to present to various heads of state, and so I did have something to tell him. But when it was all over he said, "Well, that's very nice, Sarge. Thank you very much," and immediately changed the subject. He never responded in any manner to my report about the Peace Corps. Now he said, "You know we're getting this war against poverty started. I'd like you to think about that, because I'd like you to run that program for us."

Then he started to tell me about his ideas about the War on Poverty, most of which had been worked out and announced in the State of the Union Message while I was overseas. I was totally unfamiliar with the whole project, having been in Asia when he announced the proposal. All I knew was a little item I read in a Bangkok newspaper, that Johnson had in his State of the Union Message indicated that he was going to mount a war against poverty. Then my friend Bill Moyers, who was, of course, working in the White House then, told me that Johnson had some ideas about that war against poverty which involved me.

Moyers didn't elaborate on what they were, though?

SHRIVER: Oh, no, no. No. Moyers is too smart to do that; that wasn't his job. He was more or less alerting me to the fact that Johnson might say something to me about it, but he never even made a statement that would have committed Johnson to saying something to me about it. So that's all I knew, when President Johnson spoke to me at the White House and said he'd like me to think about the program and think about running it.

I tell you the truth of the matter: I didn't think about it very much. It's not a very laudatory thing for me to say that about myself, but it's a fact. I had been overseas; Jack Kennedy had just been killed; I was in a very unusual psychological and emotional situation. I was home for the first time in months. I was, so to speak, remeeting my family. My wife was still under the influence, the aftermath, of the president's assassination. And my meeting with the president was within three or four days of when I came home. I was also working my head off at the Peace Corps, trying to catch up. When I'd go home at night, my business was to get myself reorganized or reestablished and get things going again at home. Not that something was wrong—I don't mean that, even by implication. Nothing was wrong. But to get back into a pattern of living with my family, and with the new reality that Jack Kennedy was dead. He'd only been killed sixty days before, and there was huge tension about that in the United States and especially, obviously, within the members of the Kennedy family and at the Peace Corps. Consequently, I don't believe I really thought about the war against poverty, which President Johnson had told me to think about. It was really a dereliction on my part; but I didn't really think about the new program.

So I think it was a Saturday; I was at home. The president called up, and if my memory serves me right, I was out playing with my children. He was on the other end of the phone, and he said, "Sarge, what do you think about that war against poverty? What have you thought about that?" I said, "Mr. President, I'm very embarrassed to tell you, I haven't really thought about it at all. I'm sorry, I guess I should have, but I didn't realize that you were that concerned about it in terms of time." Then I told him what I just got through telling you, more briefly than I told it to you, but nevertheless, explaining to him my need to get on top of things at the Peace Corps, my need to concentrate on things at home, etc.

He said, "Well, Sarge, I'd like to have a press conference today at noon, and I'd like to announce you as the head of my new program." Then I really got concerned. I said, "Well, Mr. President, if you don't mind, I think it would be better to postpone that announcement. I don't know anything about poverty. If you make an announcement like that, the press is sure going to ask me something about it, for my opinions, etc. I don't know what to say, anything about it. There's nobody in the Peace Corps that knows anything about it. I've just come from a trip around the world. The Peace Corps people will wonder, why haven't they been alerted to it? I think it's much too precipitous. Why don't we wait? I'll be happy to talk to you about it and think about it and discuss it with your people this coming week. And we've got plenty of time." He said, "Well, no. I really want to do it at twelve o'clock. You think about it, and we'll talk again."

It was about ten o'clock in the morning, and I went out and talked to my wife, and I said, "I don't really want to run this thing." Frankly, I was somewhat tired, and I was very happy with the Peace Corps. It took a long time to get the Peace Corps and a lot of work to get the Peace Corps where it was in 1963, early 1964. It was really running well. And it was "a success." Everybody rather liked it. It had taken a lot of effort to get it to that point, and I was just as happy to stay with that.

What did your wife say when you talked to her about the poverty program?

SHRIVER: She said, "It's a terrific compliment that Johnson would ask you to do that," that it was a question for me to decide myself, that she thought that he was right, that I would be good at it. On the other hand, she thought I ought to just tell him what I thought. So either I called him back or he called me, I don't really know which it was. I said, "Look, Mr. President, I have talked to Eunice about it, and I have thought about it, and I honestly think that it would be better to postpone this decision or this announcement, and let's us think about it this coming week. There's got to be people in the United States that can do this better than I can. Moreover, you've got a new administration; you're the new president. It would be useful to bring in some celebrated person—this is a big job—and give that new person this important new job. You want to build up your own situation by bringing in really good people into your administration. I'm very happy where I am. You don't have to give me any job. I'm not concerned about anything. Why don't we just take it easy? We've got all this next week. If next Saturday you want to do it, we can still do it next Saturday." He said, "No, Sarge. I really want to do it now." Well, then it was about eleven o'clock. I said, "Please, Mr. President, really, I would much prefer it if you don't do it." He said, "I really think that it's important to do it," and so on. I said, "Well, I understand that you do," and then I repeated my litany of things. He said, "Well, you think about it."

Then about a half-hour later, there he was on the phone again. And he said to me in a very subdued voice, low tone of voice, as if he was very confidential, "Sarge." I said, "Yes." "This is your president speaking. I've interrupted a meeting going on right now in the cabinet room. I shouldn't be interrupting it. But I thought about what we discussed. You'll just have to take my word for it. There's nobody that can see the whole picture like the president can. I need you to do this job, the country needs you to do this job, and I'm going to announce you as the director of the war against poverty at the news conference at twelve o'clock." Bang! Down went the phone.

So then I called up the Peace Corps headquarters. There was a fellow there who was my right-hand man, a wonderful person named Warren Wiggins. I said, "Warren, you won't believe this, but here's what happened." He sort of listened and said, "Sshu...," something like that. I said, "We've got to get ready. It sounds to me as if he's really going to do it. I don't seem to be able to stop him. We ought to compose a cable that we will send to all of the directors of Peace Corps operations in the fifty countries, telling them what's going to happen and telling them I'm not going to leave the Peace Corps, telling them that it's merely a study group, working group, telling them that I'm not quitting the Peace Corps." To many of those guys, I really symbolized the Peace Corps at that time. I had hired them all. Most of them had a rather close feeling of a personal relationship with me. I surely had with them. I didn't want them to suddenly pick up the USIA [U.S. Information Agency] wire service or something and get this story all mixed up. He and I agreed on a text. I said, "Let's just listen to the radio and see what happens. If he announces it, send the telegram. If he doesn't announce it, tear it up." Johnson went on the radio and made the announcement.

In your discussions with him up to this point, was it assumed that you would stay on as Peace Corps director, and how was this decision reached?

SHRIVER: Well, no, it wasn't assumed by me. In fact, I was screaming my bloody head off that I shouldn't run the War on Poverty but should stay with the Peace Corps.

Did he want you to give up the Peace Corps?

SHRIVER: No! He said to me, "Listen, Sarge, you're not half the man I think you are if you can't run both those jobs very easily." I remember it just as if it happened twenty minutes ago. He didn't want me to give up the Peace Corps. He wanted me to run both of them. I said, "You can't do that. It's illegal!" He said, "Well, we'll get around that; we'll take care of that." Somewhere around here I have a funny letter—I don't know whether it's in this office now or where it is—from him to me, saying that in accordance with title such-and-such, statute such-and-such, etc., "your compensation will be zero." [Laughs.] Not many people have that. Because it is illegal to pay a federal officeholder for two jobs at the same time. In fact, I wasn't getting paid for either, because I was a dollar-a-year man for the Peace Corps. That's all I needed; a dollar-a-year man for two jobs at the same time.

A real bargain.

SHRIVER: Yes, that's right. That was probably the reason why I got that job. [Laughs.] Oh, God.

Why do you think he chose you to head the War on Poverty?

SHRIVER: I think I know why. Johnson believed, rightly or wrongly, that it was going to be very hard to get that program through Congress. That's number one.

Number two, I had developed an extremely good rapport with Congress. That came about for a lot of reasons I won't bore you with right now, but it's a fact that I got along very well with the Congress, both the House and the Senate, but particularly the House. One of the reasons is I happen to like the Congress. I like congressmen; they are the kind of people I like. Most of them are extroverts and happy personalities, and I enjoy the atmosphere over there. I also respect them—which I find, to my disappointment, not everybody does. But I do literally respect them. I got along very well with them, and Johnson knew that. He knew that better than anybody, because Congress was a subject that he was the master of.

I think he gave me the job, or forced the job on me, because he thought it was going to be difficult to get it through Congress and he thought I could help get it through. He as much as told me that when I suggested men like Sol Linowitz or LeRoy Collins.[4] He said to me, "Sarge, look, those men are excellent. But let me tell you something. It will take them a year to get their feet on the ground in Washington. It isn't a question of them being incompetent, but it's a question of just getting accustomed to what's going on down here and how to operate in Washington. We don't have a year. This thing has to work. And it has to (a) get through Congress, and then (b) it has to work right away. It's going to get a lot of opposition; people are going to attack it. And we cannot afford to have it run by somebody who's inexperienced in Washington. You can get it through, and you can succeed in this very initial stage with it." Truthfully, there is little question in my mind that that was the crucial reason.

LBJ RECRUITS SHRIVER

Sargent Shriver's elaborate account of his February 1, 1964, telephone conversations with the president is remarkably detailed for an interview recorded sixteen years after the fact. The actual conversations, while generally confirming his recollections, add several significant dimensions. Shriver's desire to retain his Peace Corps position emerges as a much larger factor in the conversations than the oral history narrative suggests. His description of the conversation with the president while the latter was meeting with other officials[5] omits the primary reason for LBJ's inability to speak freely—the fact that at least some people in the room opposed Shriver's selection to head the poverty program. The president's daily diary indicates that those present in the cabinet room when Shriver called were Walter Heller, Theodore Sorenson, Jack Valenti, and Bill Moyers.

LBJ's conversation with Sargent Shriver, February 1, 1964, 1:20 PM[6]

JOHNSON: Sarge?

SHRIVER: Good Morning, Mr. President. How are you?

JOHNSON: I'm going to announce your appointment at that press conference.

SHRIVER: What press conference?

JOHNSON: This afternoon.

SHRIVER: Oh God, I think it would be advisable, if you don't mind, if I could have this weekend. I wanted to sit down with a couple of people and see what we could get in the way of some sort of a plan, because my thought is that what happens is [if] you announce somebody—me or somebody else—and they don't know what the hell they are doing or what the program is going to be specifically and who's going to carry it, then you're in a hell of a hole because they all are going to call you up and say, "Well now, what are you going to do? You haven't thought this out. You don't know what you're talking about."

JOHNSON: Just don't talk to them. Just go away and go to Camp David and figure it out. We need something to say to the press. We've got to say to them and I've got to tell them what I talked to you about yesterday. And you can just take off and work out your Peace Corps any way you want to. You can be head of the committee and have some acting operator. If you want Bill [Moyers] to help you, I'll let him do that. I'll do anything. But I want to announce this and get it behind me, so I'll quit getting all these other pressures. You've got to do it. You just can't let me down. So the quicker we get it behind us, the better. You can talk to them as Special Assistant to the President a hell of a lot easier than you can talk to them just as Peace [Corps] administrator. If they want to talk to you, tell them to speak to me. Don't make me wait till next week, because I want to satisfy this press with something. I told them we were going to have a press meeting.

SHRIVER: Can I make just one point?

JOHNSON: They're going to have all these damn questions, and I don't want to seem indecisive about them.

SHRIVER: I understand, but I think that there is a point that's worthy of your consideration. It's this: number one, I'm not going to let anybody down, last of all you. You've been terrific to me. Second, this appointment, if it's announced without the proper preparation with our people abroad around the world, as I tried to indicate to you yesterday—and I think Bill will confirm this to you, Mr. President—will cause an awful lot of internal apprehension. I would like to have a chance to prepare the Corps, not only my top people here in Washington, which I can do, but I got four or five guys coming back here from abroad right now.

JOHNSON: But that'll leak out over forty places. Why don't I tell them that you are not severing your connection with the Corps, that you're still going to be identified in the Corps, and the details of what you'll do there can be worked out later, and you'll announce them? But generally speaking that I'm—

SHRIVER: Could you say this: that you've asked me to study how this thing should be carried out and that's the way I did for President Kennedy when he asked me to look at the Peace Corps and to study how it should be organized and carried out, and that I will do that for you. And based on what I propose, then you will make your move. Now what I will propose, of course, is what you want to have done, but at least it doesn't look ask if I have left the Peace Corps.

JOHNSON: Let me make it clear. Let me say that I have asked you to study this, and I'm going to ask you to direct it. That that does not mean that you're losing your identification with the Peace Corps and what responsibilities you'll have with the Peace Corps you'll announce at a later date.

SHRIVER: Could you just say that you've asked me to study this?

JOHNSON: No. Hell, no! They've studied and studied and studied. They want to know who in the hell is going to do this, and it's leaked all over the newspapers for two weeks that you're going to do it, and they'll be shooting me with questions. They're already doing it.

SHRIVER: Yes, yes, I'm all set on that, that Shriver is going to be the person that is going to organize this thing. He's going to study it, come in with a report to me on what he wants to do with it, within the two or three weeks, whatever it was. We spent a month at the Peace Corps.

JOHNSON: I want to say that you're going to be Special Assistant to the President and the executive in charge of the poverty program, and how that affects your Peace Corps relationship—you'll still maintain it, but you'll be glad to go into that with them at a later date. At present, you're working up the organization for this. What's wrong with that?

SHRIVER: The problem with it is that it'll knock the crap out of the Peace Corps.

JOHNSON: Not if I tell them you're not severing your identification with the Peace Corps.

SHRIVER: Do you say that I'm going to continue as Director of the Peace Corps?

JOHNSON: Well, I'll just say you're going to continue your identification with the Peace Corps. Whatever identification you want, whatever you want to do with it.

SHRIVER: I think it would be better if you would say that I'm going to continue as the Director of the Peace Corps.

JOHNSON: They're going to say then: "Are you going to have him directing two jobs?" And I'm going to say "I don't know." That's the next question, see. I'd say, "he's going to continue his identification with the Peace Corps, and in what capacity he'll explain to you in great detail. But he's going to see that it functions, and he's also going to take on the poverty assignment."

SHRIVER: Of course, you've got the sense of the situation. I must say that I would prefer it, Mr. President, if I had forty-eight hours even to work with our staff around the world so that they won't hear this over the worldwide Voice of America or something like that...

JOHNSON: It's not going to be anything but a compliment to you. They're going to be proud of you. They're going to be applauding you. Everybody is.

SHRIVER: The point I'm trying to make—namely, that within the Peace Corps right now there is a sort of a personal problem about me with a whole lot of people who are in it.

JOHNSON: I'm not taking you away from there. I'm just giving you a billion dollars more to work with. And you figure out how you want to work.

SHRIVER: I was thinking about this last night, and I talked to a couple of fellows this morning. The returning Peace Corps volunteers could be of tremendous assistance.

JOHNSON: Of course they could. You could build your organization out of a good many of them.

SHRIVER: That's right, but what I'd like to do is get back—the way this is going to be integrated, so that when we announce something, we're really ready to talk about it intelligently.

JOHNSON: I don't think you can do that until you come up with this whole study and you come up with a message, and all that will go in the message. But I'm talking about the man that is evolving the organization and in charge of perfecting it right now. And his name is Sargent Shriver. He still has his identification with the Peace Corps, and he will keep it to such extent as he deems desirable. If you can't run a hundred million program in your left hand and a billion one with your right hand, you're not as smart as I think you are.

SHRIVER: Deciding the money, that's no problem at all; it's the people that I'm . . . I want to keep all these people for the government that are in the Peace Corps and bring them into any other programs so that they can—

JOHNSON: That's good. I'm not going to sever you from the Peace Corps at all. I'm going to say that you're going to maintain your identification with the Peace Corps. And how much of the details you do, whether you hire them or sweep out the room is going to be a matter for you to determine. I'm going to make that clear. But I'm going to make it clear that you're Mr. Poverty, at home and abroad, if you want to be. And I don't care who you have running the Peace Corps. You can run it, wonderful. If you can't, get Oshgosh from Chicago and I'll name him.

SHRIVER: I can't get anybody—the only guy who could possibly do it, Mr. President, is Bill [Moyers].

JOHNSON: You can write your ticket on anything you want to do there. I want to get rid of poverty, though. You can organize the poverty [program] right from the beginning. You'll have to get on the message Monday. The Sunday papers are going to say that you're Mr. Poverty, unless you've got real compelling reasons, which I haven't heard. And I'm going to say that you're going to maintain your identification with the Peace Corps and operate it to such extent as you may think desirable.

SHRIVER: As I looked over the papers, it seems to me this is a thing which really ought to operate out of HEW. I don't mean at this moment...

JOHNSON: It can't work out of HEW. You wait till we get by an election before we go to operating out of HEW. We've got to get by this election. I've thought of all those things and got some good ideas on them which you would approve of, but I've got an election ahead of me now.

SHRIVER:...these Peace Corps people.

JOHNSON: Well, go talk to them. Talk to them.

SHRIVER:...up here in Washington. This will be a bombshell.

JOHNSON: Not if you—hell, it'll be a promotion! You've got your identification with the Peace Corps. You've got everything you ever had there plus this. I don't know why they would object to that. Unless you've got some women that you think you won't have enough time to spend with them.

SHRIVER: [laughs]

JOHNSON: You've got the responsibility. You've got the authority. You've got the power. You've got the money. Now you may not have the glands.

SHRIVER: The glands?

JOHNSON: Yes.

SHRIVER: I got plenty of glands.

JOHNSON: Well, all right. I haven't. I haven't. I'd like to have your glands, then.... I need Dr. [John R.] Brinkley, myself, and some of those goat glands.

SHRIVER: You feel that you've got to do it this afternoon?

JOHNSON: I think I ought to. I think I ought to. I think that I'm going to keep you identified with the Peace Corps, and I'm not—

SHRIVER: Why not Monday?

JOHNSON: Because I've got a press conference at three o'clock, and it's announced. And this is going to be the thing I tell them. I'm just going to say this: that we have a government that's going to be strong, and a government that's going to be secure, and a government that's going to be solvent, and a government that's going to be compassionate. Now, I've looked over this thing very carefully. There are going to be several departments involved, but I think that one man is going to have to be Special Assistant to the President that leads the way and directs it, and I'm going to appoint Sargent Shriver as a Special Assistant to the President to be the executive head of the poverty program. And I've asked him to work on the details of the message and on perfecting the organization, and this does not mean that he is severing his identification with the Peace Corps. But what capacities he carries on there will be a matter for him to determine, which he will announce at a later date. Now that gives you both jobs. It couldn't do anything but please everybody in Tanganyika or Panama, where you're bragging about keeping those people.

SHRIVER: Why don't you just say, "This does not mean he's severing his connection with the Peace Corps, period?" In other words, at least he's still the Director of the Peace Corps.

JOHNSON: All right. All right. And then they say: "Is he going to handle both jobs?" Then what do I say?

SHRIVER: I think, if you will, say that if there's anybody that can do it, he can.

JOHNSON: All right. I'll do that. Yeah, I'll do that. That's a matter for you to determine.

SHRIVER: The problem—I don't want to overemphasize this; it gets repetitious, but the thing is that Bill Moyers and Sarge Shriver really to 99 percent of the people abroad with the Peace Corps are the personal leaders of this operation...

JOHNSON: Well, don't you think that they're not damn glad that both of them have taken over the White House?

SHRIVER: [laughs] They know that nobody ever did that with you there.

JOHNSON: I remember one day when I came in here when they had you completely out of the White House and over in the State Department.

SHRIVER: I remember; you took care of it.

JOHNSON: The people are not ever going to get worried when you're going up, my friend. Not your friends. And this is not a demotion for you.

SHRIVER: I appreciate that, and I think it's terrific that you have the confidence in me to do it. It's just that I wanted a little time to work on some—

JOHNSON: Well, you've got all the time you're going to from here on out. Just go to work with them. But you're Mr. Poverty, so take it and run with it.

SHRIVER: It's an awful lot of stuff. Wow.

JOHNSON: Figure out where you get your best people and where you are going to get them. And figure out who ought to be on that committee of seven. I would think it ought to be HEW, Labor, Interior, Agriculture; that's four. You're five. Attorney General's six. And maybe Commerce, I don't know. I wouldn't think State or Treasury would need anybody on it.

SHRIVER: Do you think that there's got to be this committee?

JOHNSON: Well, I think that you've got to have them as an advisory board, that you can say the President wants you to do this, and then the head of the agency can make them give you that money that you use.

SHRIVER: Because I think one of the great things that's made the Peace Corps possible is the fact that we've had the authority to run something ourselves—

JOHNSON: I'm not going to have any government by committee. I'm going to have a cabinet committee with the power lodged in the executive director, whatever you call him in your bill. That's where the power's going to be.

I don't expect to run the poverty program anymore than the advisory committee ran the Peace Corps. But I think you do have to tell the Attorney General that the President has said to you that he wants this done in the field of juvenile delinquency. And I think it has a little more effect than if you just say "I'm the executive director, and I'd like to see this done."

SHRIVER: Well, take the title executive director; that's not very good…

JOHNSON: Well, get it whatever you want to. Director? What are you going to call it?

SHRIVER: Well, I don't know. I haven't…

JOHNSON: Well, you're the Director of the Peace Corps, and you're the director of the poverty. Do you want to call it director of the poverty program?

SHRIVER: Well, I was thinking, if we had a paper…

JOHNSON: You've done pretty damn well with this Director of the Peace Corps title.

SHRIVER: That's right. I tell you, we had an idea, Mr. President—I shared this with Jack when he was alive—of a whole new approach toward getting people interested in doing things for their country. Not just the Peace Corps abroad or a domestic Peace Corps at home, but it fits in a lot with what you've got with this poverty program. That's what I really wanted to go back and propose to you, that you come out with a program which improves this but which involves people in a very big way. It gives a place to the returning Peace Corps volunteer to come in and work on these local programs as well as helping the—

JOHNSON: Well, what do you want to call it? What do you want me to say?

SHRIVER: To tell you the truth, I don't know because I haven't had but two hours to think about it.

JOHNSON: I'm going to say director until you put in the bill otherwise. When the bill's drafted, you can put whatever you want to. You can put executive vice-president or anything you want to.

SHRIVER: … the magnitude of what we were hoping to accomplish—

JOHNSON: I'm going to say that I'm going to ask you as the Special Assistant to the President to take over the direction of the poverty program, period. And then you can work out whatever title you want. Is that all right?

SHRIVER: [laughs] Well, I'll tell you, I would have much preferred to have had forty-eight hours...

JOHNSON: Oh, I know. You've had forty-eight weeks. You've known this the whole time. It's been in every paper in the United States.

SHRIVER: The problem is I've been away. I haven't read anything about it. Until you gave me these things last night I didn't know beans about it, because I've been overseas....

JOHNSON: Well, you don't need to know much; you just go ahead and do it. You've got your Peace Corps now. They can't be mad at you. They're all going to be with you. And besides, you'll have a place for every damn one of them when they come back. You'll have an international Peace Corps— one abroad and one at home.

SHRIVER: If somebody says to you: "Is he going to run the Peace Corps?" you can say: "It seems to me that returning Peace Corps volunteers are exactly the kind of people who can help in an attack on poverty in this country," or something, so that there is some link between these things.

JOHNSON: All right. All right. I'll do that. I'll do that. I'll do that.

SHRIVER: Now, about Bill [Moyers]—Bill can come back [to the Peace Corps from the White House staff] if I need him?

JOHNSON: For just as little as you can spare him. I need him more than anybody in the world right here. And you need him here too. He's good for Shriver here.

SHRIVER: I know he's very valuable to you, but you don't want this whole damn thing to go down. You know, I don't want to give you a whole lot of sap about it.

JOHNSON: No, you can find some others. I can't. He'll help you and work with you, and he's on your team. He reports to you.

SHRIVER: ... He couldn't come and take on the acting direction of this thing while I'm on the other thing?

JOHNSON: Not and run the White House too. And that's what he's doing now. He's in there writing up what we're going to say on Cyprus, and he's trying to say what we're going to do about this plane they shot down. And he's trying to explain what we had in—

SHRIVER: How about [Myer] Feldman?

JOHNSON: No, now don't go to raiding the White House! Go on and get your own damn talent.

SHRIVER: The trouble is that Bill's got three of my people in the White House now.

JOHNSON: Well, they're not people that you have to rely on. Peace Corps—hell, you've got a baby-sitter for every ten! For Christ's sake, if your wife—if the Kennedys had—they wouldn't have this fortune if they had as many baby-sitters as you've got in the Peace Corps. You've got ten thousand people and you've got 1,100 administrators—

SHRIVER: I'll tell you one thing. I'm glad you're not still over in Congress asking me questions.

JOHNSON: Well, that's right. There's not a Kennedy compound that's got a baby-sitter for ten. And you've got it in the Peace Corps around the world. All right, I'll see you later, and good luck to you. And happy landing!

SHRIVER: Okay, thank you.

JOHNSON: Bye.

LBJ's conversation with Sargent Shriver, February 1, 1964, circa 3:30 PM[7]

JOHNSON: I couldn't talk to you freely.... I had the Secretary of State and everybody, fifteen in the room, peppering me with questions. Now, I don't want to make you feel bad because you're too successful and I'm too proud of you to ever pour cold water on it, but to one minute before I appeared [for the press conference], I was meeting violent protests to naming you. Now, I couldn't let that grow and continue. I've had other folks recommended and other people pressed. And when I came in, after I talked to you this morning, I got another recommendation immediately that it had to go to a fellow in HEW. And they come from about as powerful people as we have in this government.

SHRIVER: Yes.

JOHNSON: Now they all think it's terrible to have the Peace Corps and this together. They all think that you're a wonderful man, but when you get down to, say, an election, one of them said this morning, "he's never had anything to do with anything like this." I said, "Well he had all the businessmen in the campaign that I know about and had the small business committee for Kennedy. I participated in it, and I thought that he brought the best men into the government. I know he brought the best in the Peace Corps. He stole some of them from me. And that's what we've got to have in this thing. We've got to have somebody that people respect and can attract people and good people will follow and all of those things." They said, "Well, as a public relations expert, he's the best." But I think as an administrator and as a candidate that you have great potentialities and that you have demonstrated them. And what I am trying to do is not put myself in the position of waiting until Monday when I couldn't do it. I could get some requests that I just couldn't do it. And I just couldn't for those requests because waiting two hours got me some hell of a pressure that makes people mad and will probably give me some resignations because I just had to ride roughshod over them. But I couldn't tell you that when some of them were sitting there....And I was trying to be as gentle as I could with you and "let's go along on what we did this morning" without emphasizing all that. Now don't go trying to figure out who it is because it's nothing to worry about. It's done. The decision's made. The water's behind us. Now you do whatever you need to do with your Peace Corps and whatever you need to do with poverty, and let's get this advisory group together and then let's figure out how we're going to get this money through and get you the brains of this government. And I'll support you all the way to the hilt....This is the best thing this administration's done. I've got more comments, more popularity on the poverty thing than anything else, but they'll defeat it and kill it if we let them do it....You're just beginning to move, my friend. Now, come on and let's do it and let's quit worrying about headaches we're going to have. We're going to have a lot of them. We're going to have a lot of hell and a lot of problems, but you're going to do this all right. If it can be done, you'll do it. If it can't, why we'll find something else for you to do. We'll make a hero out of you for failing. That's the kind of team we play on.

SHRIVER: Okay. Thank you for taking the trouble to—

JOHNSON: Don't quote me. I just had to tell you the reason I was so obstinate. I would gladly give you two weeks if you wanted it, but I couldn't do it with the people that sit at my elbow.

SHRIVER: Okay, so thank you very much.

JOHNSON: And I would have had more [alternative recommendations] that they would have generated because this is a popular enough thing that they had some candidates.

SHRIVER: I see.

JOHNSON: And I disagreed with them a time or two before.

SHRIVER: Who were they proposing?

JOHNSON: Well, Boisfeuillet Jones was the last one. The Attorney General was the first one. They've had all different groups. The Secretary of Labor's one. The Secretary of Health, Education and Welfare's another one.

SHRIVER: To do this thing?

JOHNSON: Yes, yes. And very confidentially if you were Secretary of Health, Education and Welfare, we might do it that way. A lot depends on where you are. Do you follow me?

SHRIVER: Yes.

JOHNSON: So all I could do was act with what I had, and I did it. I did it with the best intentions, and, I think, the best judgment. I think you would have done the identical thing if you'd have been here and I'd have been in your place and you'd have been in mine, because you want to get the job done.

SHRIVER: Well, fine.

JOHNSON: I had to be as adamant—

SHRIVER: I'd love to have a chance sometime to talk. [I know you've been] preoccupied—

JOHNSON: You'll have a chance anytime you want to. Anytime you want to. You can come tomorrow, if you want to. Whenever you get where you're full enough of it to let it flow out, you just come on. There's a fellow named Moyers here who handles some of my business. He has a talking acquaintance with you, so you just tell him you're on your way, and he'll work it out for us to meet in a dark alley somewhere.

LBJ's conversation with Sargent Shriver, February 1, 1964, 6:28 PM[8]

JOHNSON: Now, what you do is you've got to get together and see how in the hell you're going to administer this thing. Then you're going to have to get that bill and that message together. Then you're going to have to get up to that Congress and walk it through. You've got to get on that television and start explaining it. And you have to get this advisory committee in and see that every damn thing that can be done for poverty is done. If McNamara can take any Defense funds and put it around to these poor sergeants that are getting less than $3,000 a year, let's find out [what] you can do there. Let's find out…how we can use [any dollars appropriated] for poverty. You can have advisory committees in every place. You can have county commissioners' courts. You can have mayors, and each one of them have to be sponsors. You'll have more influence in this administration than any man in it, because this will have to come if they want to get things. And you'll have a billion dollars to pass out. That's damn near as much as McNamara and Jim Webb got in contracts. And theirs have got to be for materials, and yours are for people. So you just call up the Pope and tell him you may not be at church every morning on time, but you're going to be working for the good of humanity.

ONLY COMMUNITY ACTION?

CANNON: All of a sudden, I remember getting a call on Saturday morning from Kermit [Gordon] saying we're starting over. Shriver's going to plan to head a task force. By Sunday night, the next day, Kermit and I and Heller and Mike Feldman—I think maybe Charlie [Schultze] was there, and maybe Capron—met with Sarge. He had Warren Wiggins and Frank Mankiewicz and Adam Yarmolinsky and maybe one or two others there.

The whole aim of the meeting was to sell Sarge on what we'd been doing and particularly [on] community action. By this time, community action had begun to get that peculiar kind of attaching feature; people would learn about it and like it. And Sarge hardly heard us, to be very frank with you. He told me many months or a year later or so that he never thought much about community action. Sarge's focus that night was, and continued to be for a long time, to repeat the political success of the Peace Corps. He wanted something glamorous, easily understood, apparent in its workings, and which you could succeed at. The concept of community action was much too complex and diffuse. It would take a lot of time, and Sarge wanted it fast. It would take a lot of time to work out community action, there's no question about it. But he underestimated some of the enormous political interests that community action could generate. He was just not listening to us, as hard as we kept trying to sell him. He was much more interested in what eventually became the Job Corps because that fitted [his goals]. He could take these tough ghetto kids off the street and make citizens out of them.

But Sarge was obviously listening to something else, [as were] Yarmolinsky and Mankiewicz. You never knew what the hell Mankiewicz was doing. But Wiggins was operating, trying to protect Sarge on this new untried rapids crossing. Nothing was decided. All it basically did, for me at any rate, was to say I knew where there was a core of support for community action. For the next ten days or so, I was out of the game completely, for reasons I'm not at all clear about. I wasn't invited back.

As special assistant to the secretary of Defense, Adam Yarmolinsky was loaned to the War on Poverty Task Force to serve as its chief of staff. He had been one of a group of Kennedy aides who had recruited talent for the New Frontier. At Defense, Yarmolinsky had been responsible for civil defense preparations during the Berlin crisis of 1962 and for desegregation at military bases. A former law clerk for Supreme Court Justice Stanley F. Reed, Yarmolinsky had an undergraduate degree from Harvard and a law degree from Yale.

YARMOLINSKY: It was to be *all* community action, half a million dollars of community action. It was presented to Shriver and me and others at the first session we had after Shriver was appointed that Sunday night. Shriver's immediate reaction, and I guess mine, was that this just wouldn't fly, that you couldn't make a whole program out of community action because you wouldn't get results soon enough, clearly enough, to be able to carry it forward in the successive years and get appropriations the second year. You needed to put in other elements in the picture. It was then that we began to reach out for these other elements. So there was no question in our minds that community action was a good idea.

Frank Mankiewicz was both a journalist and an attorney before joining the Kennedy administration. He earned a master's degree in journalism from Columbia and a law degree from the University of California at Berkeley. After working at the Western Reporters Washington news bureau, he became city editor of the Los Angeles Independent. *Mankiewicz practiced law in Beverly Hills in the late 1950s before enlisting in Kennedy's presidential campaign. He was director of the Peace Corps in Peru when the War on Poverty Task Force was organized.*

MANKIEWICZ: I think it was the first of February 1964. I came to Washington for two days to testify before the House Foreign Affairs Committee as director of the Peace Corps in Peru. The Peace Corps appropriation was being considered, and what the Peace Corps did was to pick the directors of two or three fairly typical programs to come back and testify. That's what the committee wanted. I think that's why I was here. It was to testify, anyway, for a couple of days. I called Sarge Shriver that day, as I always did when I came to town, and read that he had been appointed the head of the War on Poverty. The result was that I stayed for six weeks working on the task force that would later become the OEO. But at that time, I was still the Peace Corps director in Peru; I was on loan, in effect, from the Peace Corps to that task force, just as other people were on loan from the Labor Department or whatever it might have been.

I was reading the Sunday paper in my hotel room, and I saw this [article on Shriver's appointment] and talked to Sarge about it. He was his usual ebullient self. I had done a lot of reading on the question, and I knew some of the players. I knew Mike Harrington, and I had a close friend named Paul Jacobs who was very active in some of the research on the question. Sitting in Peru, I had done a lot of reading; I hadn't done much talking to people. Sarge asked me, as a matter of fact, if I knew anything about the general question of poverty, and I said, yes, I did. So he started asking me about it, and I talked to him about Harrington, about that book of his, about Paul.

Had Shriver read the Harrington book?

MANKIEWICZ: I don't believe so. I think he'd read the long review in the *New Yorker* by Dwight Macdonald, but I don't think he'd read the book. We talked about Harrington; I told him what kind of a person he was, and he said, "Well, let's get him here. See if he'll have lunch with me tomorrow." And I said, okay, I'd call him. I told him I'd call Paul Jacobs—he wanted to talk to him too. The upshot of it was I sensed that I was going to be doing some things, but I knew I had to leave the following night, and I knew that Sarge knew that. And at about three or four o'clock that afternoon—it was a Sunday—I was over in the Peace Corps office writing up my testimony for the next day to the House committee. I got a call from Sarge's secretary, Mary Ann Orlando, who said to me, would I come to a meeting at Shriver's office in the

Peace Corps at six o'clock? I said, "Sure, what's it about?" And she said, "Well, it's about the poverty war."

So I went. At that meeting were present, in addition to Shriver and myself—I think Adam Yarmolinsky was there by that time, and the rest of the people were all from other branches of the government. Secretary Wirtz was there; Kermit Gordon, who at that time was the director of the Bureau of the Budget, was there; Charlie Schultze, who was his assistant, was there; I think Jim Reynolds from the Department of Labor and some others—I can't recall too well. And at that meeting, the Labor Department guys and the Bureau of the Budget presented what was apparently a first draft of a poverty message or bill—I think maybe both. But the point of it was all community action. I forget how much money they were going to spend; it was not very much, because a lot of that money had already been allocated.

Was it about $500 million?

MANKIEWICZ: That's right, that's the figure. But it was an illusive figure, because some of it was going to come from other programs for which money had already been appropriated. And it was the first I had seen of it; there was a draft submitted to everybody.

At the beginning of the meeting, Shriver introduced me to the people I didn't know and said that I was his executive assistant, or functioning as his assistant on this project, or whatever it was, which was news to me. But I functioned that way at the meeting and gave my opinion of this approach. And the upshot of the meeting was that we didn't want to do that, but we were going to start from scratch and write up a program that might include some of that community action approach.

Who felt that it should be a wider approach?

MANKIEWICZ: Shriver, Yarmolinsky, and myself. Everybody else who was there regarded it as practically a foregone conclusion that [community action] was what it was going to be. It wouldn't be that version. That was a first draft, but clearly that was going to be the substance. We weren't even sure what should go in it, but we thought it shouldn't be just that. There was talk about youth employment, talk about other things. So we left it at that. Shriver would, in effect I supposed, convene a task force in which these other fellows would, if not participate, at least play a role in the counseling of it.

SHRIVER: When Johnson asked me to run the War on Poverty, he told me that he had $500 million in the budget for this effort, and that I was to organize a program spending the $500 million to eradicate poverty. First of all, $500 million in 1964 was a lot more than $500 million today. So far as I was concerned, it was a colossal sum of money. I didn't know how to spend $500 million intelligently to eradicate poverty. Therefore, when it was proposed to me by Walter Heller and Kermit Gordon that the entire War on Poverty should be that one effort [community action], and Ken Galbraith supported that idea, and Ken Galbraith had written a draft presidential statement, I just wasn't of the opinion that the United States government could spend $500 million intelligently in one year in that way or according to that formula. But I wasn't sure.

So I called up Dick Lee, who was the mayor of New Haven. I called him because New Haven had been one of the cities selected by the Ford Foundation and by the juvenile delinquency operation for a community action program. I said, "Hey, Dick, you've been running this [Ford Foundation–sponsored] Gray Areas Program up there in New Haven for a couple of years now. Is that right?" He said yes. I said, "Well, how much are you spending on it?" I think he told me it was something like $3.5 million. So I said to him, "Dick, you've got a city of 150,000 people. Tell me, how much money could you spend in New Haven, if there were no restriction whatsoever, to combat poverty and you could do whatever you think is necessary?" My memory is that he said, "Well, we could probably spend $9 or $10 million."

I talked to him about other matters and hung up the phone. [I] went back, and I put down the cities of the United States where there [were] more than 150,000 people. Then I extrapolated from that list of cities—most of which would have to start a community action program from scratch, not like New Haven, which had been in business doing this for a number of years—how much money it was physically possible to project, with any degree of intelligence, as being capable of being expended in that year. If you just took the rubber band off the bankroll, spread the money around like snowflakes, you couldn't efficiently spend maybe more than $300 million at a maximum on community action. Now, the exact figure I can't remember, but that's somewhere in the record. So I said to myself, this one program cannot be the whole $500 million War on Poverty.

So in all the meetings I had, I kept probing businessmen, economists, labor leaders, etc., to get their ideas of what could be done that would be effective. In the back of my mind, I always was saying to myself, "I've got maybe $200 million that I can spend here on things that have nothing to do with community action."

Almost from the day it was handed to me, I knew damn well that community action could not be the sole thing in the War on Poverty. That had nothing to do, however, with the conceptualization of community action, which I favored from the beginning. In fact, community action—which the people in community action thought was so revolutionary—was something that we had been running in the Peace Corps for four years before it ever got into the War on Poverty. So I thought community action was absolutely sort of normal. To me it was routine; to them it was a giant revolution. Many of them had been struggling to get community action accepted more widely in the United States. So they had what you might almost call an idée fixe, or fixation, about how important it was, and how it was necessary to have a lot of money spent on it, and from that it was easy for them to say that it was the only thing. But having run the Peace Corps and having been on the Board of Education in Chicago, I knew well that it wasn't the only approach to poverty.

There's been some suggestion that you were initially skeptical of community action, and that it was Robert Kennedy who met with you and convinced you to retain that in the War on Poverty.

SHRIVER: I've heard that said before, but that's just false. The reason why it's false is that, with all due respect to the people who were interested in community action, I think I knew more about community action than they did. For example, since Saul Alinsky had been a friend of mine in Chicago, I knew all about the Back of the Yards movement.[9] Moreover, we'd been running community development in the Peace Corps for three years before it ever started here in the War on Poverty. My wife and I had started the program on juvenile delinquency in the Department of Justice. So there wasn't anything new that anyone had to sell me. I think the misapprehension may have come because I did not think we ought to try to spend our entire $500 million on community action. I did play down the idea that community action could be the totality of the War on Poverty. Of course, I still think that decision was correct, to make community action an essential part but not the whole of the War on Poverty.

THE TASK FORCE GEARS UP

MANKIEWICZ: Then we got together that [first] night and talked about what kinds of things we might look into. By the next night, Mike Harrington was in town, and Paul Jacobs. I think Pat Moynihan had already come over from the Department of Labor. And we began writing that night a series of memoranda to Shriver on some ideas that we all had sort of come up with about what kinds of things ought to be included in a poverty program.

Then we began moving. We had some offices at the Peace Corps. Pat Moynihan brought some office help over. At that time, we were talking about all kinds of [things]. It was sort of a grab bag of proposals. I think for the first time we began to talk about the cigarette tax for employment.

Then we started bringing people in. We decided we needed lawyers, so I thought of Hal Horowitz, who was at that time deputy general counsel at HEW but was leaving anyway July 1, and so we thought that wouldn't disturb things too much if we got him. Eric Tolmach was an old friend of mine, and he was at that time a press guy. He had quit his job at Newhouse about six weeks before on a matter of principle, the nature of which I can't recall. He was a good guy. He was at that time married to a very close friend of all of my family's, which was how I knew him. We decided we needed a press fellow, and he was at that time assigned as special assistant to Wirtz; there was thought that he would do press work. Pat Moynihan had met him and liked him, so we brought him over. Some people started participating regularly by the third or fourth day. For quite a while, it was still a very small group. There was a guy named Jim Adler [who] was employed at the [Commerce] Labor Department. Jim Sundquist came over early from Agriculture.

President Johnson's economic report—the one that was done in late 1963 and, I think, delivered to Congress in early 1964—that plus Harrington's book and other related books and articles and so forth: were these the sources that you used?

MANKIEWICZ: Well, most of the people who were talking at that time—Moynihan, Jacobs, Harrington, me, to some extent Horowitz, Tolmach, Sundquist—were all sort of familiar with most of the literature. In fact, another thing we did: we got up a list that first night of books and magazines and all kinds of things that we suggested Shriver start reading immediately. Oh, there might have been fifteen or twenty books on that list, not just Harrington—Harry Caudill's book; and Ben Bagdikian had a book; and Herman Miller, *Rich Man, Poor Man,* something like that; [and] statistical material that Pat Moynihan had run across in the course of that report on the draftees. We even put James Agee's book in

Sargent Shriver chairs an early meeting of the Poverty Task Force. *RG-490-GC-19-F8076-9, National Archives Still Picture Unit*

there, *Let Us Now Praise Famous Men,* and we had a secretary who didn't know what we were talking about.[10] I remember that in the memo that book was listed as *Let Us Now Praise Farmers, Men,* which we thought was not a bad title for a different book.

Edgar May had just published a book about poverty, The Wasted Americans, *when he was invited to join the War on Poverty Task Force in 1964. May was born in Zurich in 1929; his family fled Europe in 1940 to escape the Nazis. He attended Columbia University night school and in 1957 earned a degree in journalism from Northwestern. Working as a reporter throughout the 1950s, May won a Pulitzer Prize in 1961 for a series of articles on poverty and welfare. During his tenure at OEO (1964–1968), he served as special assistant to the director, deputy director of VISTA, and inspector general. He later joined Sargent Shriver's staff at the American embassy in Paris; still later, he was elected to the Vermont state senate.*

MAY: I remember it was a Friday night, and I was in an office in New York City where I was doing some work in the public welfare area, which was in part a quid pro quo for getting some Field Foundation support for a book I was doing. It was after five o'clock, and my secretary said, "There's a call for you from Sargent Shriver in Washington." I picked up the telephone, and this voice said, "My name is Sargent Shriver, and I'm down here in Washington with the Peace Corps, and we're trying to put together a task force to do something about poverty. I read your book last night, and I just want to know, how long are you going to criticize this stuff, and when are you going to *do* something about it?" And that is almost verbatim, as I recall the conversation.

My response was, "Well, Mr. Shriver, what do you want me to do about it?" He said, "Well, for openers, can you come down here?" I said, "Sure, I'd be glad to do that. When would you like me to come?" He said, "What are you doing tomorrow?" There was a moment's pause, and he said, "No, no, no, wait a minute, tomorrow's out. I've got one too many things to do. But how about Sunday?" So I said, "Sunday I'm leaving for Texas, as a matter of fact—for Austin, to give a speech to the Texas Welfare Association." "What time is your plane?" I said it was at, I think, three or four in the afternoon. And he said, "Well, that's plenty of time for you to come down here. We'll get you back to Kennedy Airport to get your plane." So I said, all right, I would try. That was vintage Shriver.

Then, of course, in those days he had all the accoutrements of the White House at his disposal. So I wound up at National Airport—here's a nice country boy from Vermont, and there's a White House uniformed chauffeur and a limousine taking me out to Shriver's house. All designed to do exactly what it did: it was to get me to drop everything and come to Washington. And that was really my first exposure.

Did he give you an indication of how he intended to use your expertise?

MAY: Well, he wanted several things. He wanted some input on the problem of poverty. I had spent more than a year doing this book, *The Wasted Americans*. The book really started with a newspaper series that preceded it when I was working as a reporter for the *Buffalo Evening News*. That had gotten some national attention, and as a result, the book followed. When I say vintage Shriver, Shriver collected a diverse and sometimes exotic group of people, most of whom had done something that had made a headline, whether they were Davis Cup tennis players or downhill skiers or left-handed pool shooters or Pulitzer Prize winners. Then he could say, "Well, I've got these people on my staff...." That was a touch of his, and I suppose that was part of the chemistry of it all.

He wanted some input on these various problems. Also, since I had given some indication that I could write a clear English sentence, he wanted me to do some of that. I said that I would for about a week. He had a few things to do that were on a crash basis at the time. So I went down for a week or two, as I recall, then went back to New York to finish up whatever I was doing. He said, "Would you come down a few weeks later again?" And I agreed to come for thirty or sixty days. That lasted ten years before I finally got out.

Did Shriver discuss the writings that were influencing him at the time, or did he ask your assessment of these various writings on poverty?

MAY: I think Mike Harrington's *Other America*. I'm sure he was influenced by what Mike had written. I like to think he was influenced somewhat by what I had written. There were people brought in who had experiences with poverty and with working with the poor for many years, all of whom contributed to that thinking.

The difficult part of the task force days was sheer organization and logistics, together with trying to get so many different things going at the same time. All of this, of course, took place in a framework of Shriver having a full-time job and running the Peace Corps. So we were scattered in three or four nooks and crannies around Washington, most of them within walking distance of the Peace Corps. He would call us at a moment's notice to come over and have a meeting in the Peace Corps building, which is really where we met until we wound up at an old abandoned hotel, which in its previous incarnation was, I'm told, a second-class whorehouse, not a first-class whorehouse. But before our whorehouse days, we were really scattered from hell to breakfast throughout Washington. I remember during the summer of 1964 making these crazy dashes through ninety-eight-degree temperatures in order to get to Shriver's office. That kind of heat always impresses a boy from Vermont.

MANKIEWICZ: We talked a lot about "lighted schoolhouses." We talked about reforming some of the uses of educational materials in institutions. We talked about "nonschool" schools, that is, neighborhood schools to be run in people's houses, garages, where people could learn trades and where other people—in other words, instead of bringing the machine shop to the school, so that in an academic atmosphere people would study machine shop, we talked about bringing the academic atmosphere to the machine shop or the garage.

Through all of this period, Shriver was perfectly willing to let us do anything in a sense, come up with all kinds of suggestions, and these would all go into a pot and people would talk about them; we'd discuss it. It was rather informal. We spent a lot of time at Shriver's house. We would stay up late because it was the best time to get work done, because there were no phones ringing. The press was now starting to come around, and that was posing a problem.

How much of what you did and what you talked about was done with an eye cocked to Congress as to what could get through?

MANKIEWICZ: Practically none. Our job, as we saw it, at least for the first four weeks, was to come up with a maximum program, and then we'd start paring a little bit later down the road. But that process, of course, began earlier, and things would be jettisoned and toned down and so forth as a result of various meetings that Shriver would have. Then, all during this time, Shriver and I were talking to an awful lot of people, at first to get their ideas, and secondly, with an eye that they might join the program.

I remember we got an awful lot of industrialists to come in, presidents of large companies and so forth. I remember particularly going to lunch with the president of the Chrysler Corporation, whose major contribution to the War on Poverty, and the only one he really suggested, was that he thought that the whole problem could be solved if only the cost of domestic servants could be made tax-deductible. He felt that this would open up wide avenues of employment for otherwise unemployable Negro women and provide a great boost to the middle class. He talked at length about how his wife was unable to get servants. It was rather a disappointing luncheon.

We talked to a lot of people at that time—Jack Conway too. We gave him a very hard sell at a luncheon. I'm trying to think of any of the other industrialists who were a little disappointing. But generally they were good people that we tried recruiting. Ted Patrick, I remember, came in and we talked to him, Ben Heineman...a lot of good people...Howard Samuels.[11] And some of it got a little politically crossed. Occasionally we'd hear, "Don't have so-and-so. He's...," you know, but it never bothered us an awful lot.

Hyman Bookbinder, a native of Brooklyn, received a B.S. degree from City College in 1937. After service in the navy during World War II, he worked for the New York Laundry Workers Union in New York before joining the national headquarters of the Amalgamated Clothing Workers of America as a research assistant. In 1953, Bookbinder became Chief of Congressional Research for the president of the CIO, Walter Reuther.

After seven years as a labor lobbyist for CIO and then AFL-CIO in Washington, Book-
binder, who had aided Kennedy in the 1960 campaign, was appointed assistant to the
Secretary of Commerce. In February 1964, he joined the Shriver task force while still on
the payroll of the Commerce Department. After OEO was created, Bookbinder became
its Assistant Director for Private Groups.

BOOKBINDER: In those early weeks that I was around, Shriver [would] have that
series of consultations with a wide range of men and women from around the
country. It may sound naive now and simplistic, and I guess it was in a way, but
Shriver would bring down people. He'd sit them on one side of a conference
table and he and two or three of us—sometimes only one—would be on the
other side of the conference table, and Shriver would say, "The president has
given me an assignment to eliminate poverty in this country. What would you
do if you had to eliminate poverty in this country? Where would you start? Give
me some ideas." We'd make some notes. So this was going on constantly; every
hour or two another group would come in. It was a way of involving people,
getting them interested, but to some extent you also got substantive advice from
people.

One of those sessions I shall never forget. The man brought in was James
Patton, the head of the National Farmers Union, who evidently was an old
friend of Shriver's, and I had known him over the years from the labor movement. After he went through a half hour of specific content about what needs to
be done, Patton said something to this effect, "I don't really care what you do,
how you do it. The important thing is that you're doing something and you're
different and you're new. I know this goddamned bureaucracy; I know this government. They get stale. So you have to have somebody new come in and just
kick them in the ass and make them aware of the new problem and have them
do something, compete with them, create a new entity." He said, "Shriver, I want
to tell you now: about ten years from now, we're going to have to come back and
kick you in the ass too."

SUNDQUIST: Nothing ever seemed very systematic, but there may have been more
system in it than appeared on the surface. Shriver called people that he thought
would have something to contribute, asked them to come in, and then whoever
was around would sit with them and pick their brains. He did at one point ask
two or three people to put together a list of people who ought to be brought in,
and that was a little more systematic. We then looked at different segments of
the population—industry, labor, education, and so on—and tried to get a representation from these various groups. Then we showed him the list, and he said,
"Fine, go ahead and set up a series of meetings, and I'll attend as many as I can."
So we invited most of the people who had experience in community action in
the various Ford Foundation and juvenile delinquency projects that were the
forerunners of community action. Governor Sanford came in, and Mayor Lee,

and people like that, Mayor [John] Houlihan of Oakland; we had [Raymond] Hilliard [director of the Department of Public Aid of Cook County, Illinois] in from Chicago and so on. Jim Patton appeared one day.

How about Ford Foundation people?

SUNDQUIST: I had Marion Crank [Speaker of the Arkansas house of representatives] come in from Little River County, Arkansas. Ylvisaker was in the original February 4 meeting, and he maintained contact with us throughout. He was always available if somebody needed to consult with him or wanted him to critique a piece of writing. Howard Hallman also joined the task force, full time for a while, from New Haven, where he was Mike Sviridoff's deputy. And Mike himself, of course, was down.

HEW was asked to designate somebody, and Wilbur Cohen came over for the meeting on February 4. I assumed that Wilbur was going to stay, just as Pat Moynihan and I stayed. He didn't, and in his place turned up, after a few days' gap, Harold Horowitz. Horowitz confided to me at one point that he was unsure whether he was there as a legal draftsman or whether he was there in Wilbur's stead to represent the whole range of interests of the department. I don't believe that was ever cleared up.

He became a legal draftsman, didn't he?

SUNDQUIST: Yes, but he didn't represent Health and Education and Welfare in a substantive way—as completely as Moynihan and I represented our departments and maintained liaison with them. I've used that word "representation" again. There was an element of representation in it, in the sense that we were to look out for their interests and keep in touch with them and bring them in where they were concerned. We didn't necessarily represent them substantively in the discussions within the task force, and there were occasions when I took a view opposite to the view of the department. When I told Freeman this, a time or two when it became uncomfortable, he told me that was exactly what I was supposed to do and not to give it a second thought. I don't think that Pat Moynihan had that same kind of understanding with Secretary Wirtz, for instance. In the field of education, [Commissioner of Education Francis] Keppel himself came over and got into the act very intensively, so there was no problem about the representation of the education side of the government. There were no representatives of educational institutions in the early phase, but then, there weren't representatives of other outside interests either.

Harold Horowitz was associate general counsel at HEW when he was detailed to the War on Poverty Task Force. A native of Los Angeles, he received his B.A. from UCLA and his L.L.B. from Harvard. He was a professor of law at the University of Southern

California from 1950 to 1960. When he left the government in 1964, he returned to California to join the faculty of UCLA's law school.

HOROWITZ: I was associate general counsel of HEW, working only in part on matters related to what eventually came about in the Economic Opportunity Act. I think I got into the task force through Frank Mankiewicz. Frank and I had known each other for years from Los Angeles days. Where did we go? I guess it must have been to the Peace Corps [building], and an ever-expanding group of people began to turn up. One of the glorious things about it [was that] it was just a bringing together of a lot of highly charged people with a marvelous mission.

My typical day was to do my day's work at HEW. I don't know if all people were doing that, but my work on the task force was at night. It threw our car-pooling arrangements just utterly out of whack completely. We lived out in Maryland. I really had a logistical problem, because I could no longer come and go with the people I regularly rode with in HEW. So I don't remember what I was doing. I guess I was riding buses or something. No, I'd leave HEW at the end of the day with everybody else and hop on a bus and go over to the Peace Corps and start the second shift.

Had you thought much about poverty before the task force?

HOROWITZ: No. Certainly not as a student. Just to the extent that I became aware of it in my career at HEW. I was an academician. I was teaching at the University of Southern California, and really, aside from a generalized liberal interest in the programs of the New Deal and the New Frontier, I had not thought about the question. I got steeped in it when I went to HEW in 1961, because the lawyers were working with the innards of the various substantive programs; and I fell, among other things at that time, under Wilbur Cohen's spell, and I began to see the world the way Wilbur does.

Throughout this whole affair, I was not a theorist. There were a lot of us like that. Jim Adler was not a theorist. I mean, people who could try to ask questions, try to synthesize.

Would you divide the task force into people like you and the theorists?

HOROWITZ: Yes, I think I would. I don't know, I'm not sure now who I would put in which category. I think Pat Moynihan was a theorist, whatever I mean by that term. [Sanford] Kravitz would be a supreme example of that. I'd put Jim [Adler], people like that, on the other side: hard workers, good minds, and just opening, continuing to peel the layers off the onion, or whatever the simile ought to be, to just see to it there was a lot of information, a lot of ideas floating around.

I remember one night when Paul [Jacobs] had to fill out—what was it called—the government form 57, the standard employment application form, the thing you fill out when you become an employee. I was standing right next to him, and he got to the question, "Have you ever been a member of the Communist Party?" and he wrote yes. He said, "I love to do this for government agencies, because so many people in government agencies have told me it makes their time worthwhile. They sit, and they never get interesting answers to questions. Now somebody's going to have to look into this because I answered yes." Then he got to the section where they asked for references. [He wrote], "Honorable Robert Kennedy," and two others of similar stature. And he smiled, and he said, "They're going to have fun with this one."

But Paul and Mike [Harrington] were the yeast of that group. When you have a brainstorming session, from them would come the really wild, wild notions, things other people just wouldn't think of.

Eric Tolmach was a journalist serving in the federal government when he joined the poverty task force in 1964. After graduating from Columbia and attending law school for a year, Tolmach worked first as a reporter for a Long Island newspaper and then for Newhouse newspapers. Since his focus had been labor issues, he was recruited to work at the Labor Department drafting speeches and serving as a public information officer. During the fall of 1963, Tolmach was asked to prepare some written materials on the subject of poverty and unemployment. He learned about the Shriver task force soon after it was formed and, through Patrick Moynihan and Frank Mankiewicz, was invited to join. During the summer of 1964, Tolmach worked with Jack Conway's group planning the Community Action Program and ultimately became chief of evaluation for the program's Training and Technical Assistance Division.

TOLMACH: On the evening of February 6, I simply walked over to the Peace Corps, where all of this was taking place and [I] was expected, and the secretary introduced me. I asked Shriver when we were starting, and he said, "Now." So I began work Friday night, when most people go home.

What had Moynihan told you about what was going on?

TOLMACH: Actually, he had told me nothing. I simply knew that he was at the Peace Corps, that he had been detailed by the Labor Department to represent it in the activities of the task force. Since Pat had been a friend and associate, I asked him if I could get with the action, but I hadn't had any time to be briefed by him. I just knew that it sounded like the kind of thing that interested me. I had been working on related things, and it appeared to be an exciting group that was shaping up.

What were you asked to do?

TOLMACH: Specifically I was asked to keep the press off Shriver's back. I had been a newspaperman, and Pat knew this, and I'm told that that's the way Moynihan introduced the idea of my coming over to Shriver. There was someone else also on the task force at the time, Frank Mankiewicz, who was a personal friend, who seconded apparently the idea of my usefulness. I came over to more or less be the spokesman to the press, because the deliberations of the task force were in such an early stage, no one knew what was going to be recommended. So many ideas were being batted around that there was considerable speculation about what was going on in the discussion rooms, and the press was clamoring for information. In those rather frenetic days over at the Peace Corps, there were literally half a dozen reporters roaming around in the halls at any time collaring people, and there was clearly a need to get them off people's backs. So that's what I was assigned to for the first couple of months.

Incidentally, there were additional press spokesmen brought on board after about a month of operation. But I did attend every single meeting that I knew of. I'm not sure I knew of every single meeting, and I know of some, as a matter of fact, that I didn't get to. Those would involve Shriver and Wirtz more or less privately, if such a meeting took place. There were some more precious groups, rooms that I just didn't get into. But I would say ninety-nine percent of the meetings which took place at the Peace Corps, with the exception of certain more or less administratively confidential huddles or personal huddles in Adam Yarmolinsky's office, I did attend. So I had a pretty fair knowledge of how things were shaping up.

Were any records kept at these meetings?

TOLMACH: Not formally, no. Most of the meetings were designed as working meetings to produce papers leading up to recommendations either for the president's message on poverty or for the bill itself. So the papers that were generated became actually the records of these meetings in a way, but there were no recorders, or there were no secretaries, to my knowledge, at the meetings. No minutes were kept. There are memos based on people's interpretations of what took place at the meeting. There are no word-for-word accounts.

CANNON: I was invited back to attend a meeting. I was invited as a kind of technician, carrying out a Budget Bureau function, to price out what the task force had come up with. I joined the meeting that Yarmolinsky was chairing and had the core group of the task force on it. Mankiewicz was there again, Tolmach, Moynihan, Ylvisaker, Jacobs, Hal Horowitz; Wilbur Cohen was there occasionally, but Wilbur never stays put. Jim Adler from Commerce. Andy Brimmer [Deputy Assistant Secretary of Commerce], I think, was in on it also. They had been sitting about the table obviously for days and nights.

So I was there to price out a program. For the first time, apparently, they had reality involved, because they had to tell someone what the program was so he could price it up. I listened to them all, and it was just incoherent. So I went back and wrote out a pricing table. I developed a two- or three-page pricing table from everything they'd say, Job Corps, etc. But I put community action back in the list, because they hadn't said to take it out, and I put a price on it.

Community action was out at that point. The group had rejected it, and I kind of encouraged Ylvisaker to bring it back up again in these meetings. But then I put it down in the list, which really became the legislation, and put the price on it. That made it look very real when you put $500 million here and $200 million for the Job Corps and how many enrollees you're going to have. This little paper crystallized the discussions. These discussions then went on for several days.

They were mad as hell at the second meeting when I came back with this piece of paper which was very concrete and very brief. Yarmolinsky threw it on the table and said, "Another goddamn Budget Bureau trick. They always make things look real with numbers." I'm quoting him almost exactly. But there wasn't anything he could do. They were running out of time. They had really been retracing steps that we had been retracing for months—which is all right, that's fine, but they're finding the same set of problems, and they're coming up with the same laundry list. So community action becomes, again, an organizing principle for the thing.

During this period, Yarmolinsky and Moynihan were the two chief honchos, and they were saying Sarge really wasn't going to buy community action. So I went to Hackett, and I said, "You've got to do something about this. You've got to get the attorney general [Robert Kennedy] to talk to his brother-in-law." In a couple of days, there was no bar against having community action. I don't know whether the talking was ever done, but all of a sudden community action was in.

HOW THE TASK FORCE OPERATED

LAMPMAN: I hadn't been back here very long when the president announced he was appointing Shriver to work on this, February 1, 1964. Shortly after that, Kermit Gordon called me, I remember, and asked me to give some time to Shriver or to people in Shriver's group, and that began a very fitful kind of relationship, from my point of view. I did do some work, but I could never figure out what I was doing.

It was sort of like a campaign train or something. First of all, Shriver was exploring very widely the nature of this charge he was undertaking. He met with all kinds of people, and I knew that I was just one of many [with whom Shriver consulted] all the time I was there. I never was fitted into a particular kind of reporting pattern. I felt a little bit like every time I would get there, there would be a different car on the train, sort of a different company. I was sort of on the idea side of the train. By "idea people" mainly they meant people who were good communicators and who could sell this idea of poverty as a problem and the government as a remedy, and the great merit the War on Poverty's achievement would have.

So that meant that one time I'd arrive and I'd be talking to Frank Mankiewicz, whom I had never met before and I didn't get to know really. But he was certainly a political expert, a public relations sort of expert, I guess [a] campaign manager sort. And this was to him just like any other sort of promotion problem. He had a way of digesting material and moving it into TV shorts or into movies. You could almost see him kind of moving it into some kind of a visual presentation. Well, I wasn't any good at that; I didn't understand or appreciate some of this sort of imagery. Then the next time I'd go, I'd be there with Paul Jacobs, who was a journalist, novelist, writer. I don't know how to characterize him—poet, almost. Somewhere I have a list of the various people I met in this sort of task force phase. They were most extraordinary.

I wasn't ever in many meetings. I would just kind of wander around the halls, or somebody would come wandering into my office or a part of [an office]. I'd have a desk in some office, a different one every time I went to Washington. It was extraordinarily chaotic. I never knew what to expect.

There was some organization, I guess, but it seemed more like the organization in a lobby of a big hotel or something to me, where you just wander around from one corner of the big room to another. Various things would be going on, and you could sit down if you wanted to or you could listen in or raise your hand and say something. Various pieces of paper would float by, and then you could comment on those if you wanted to. I never knew quite to whom I was reporting, but I would get requests for things like, "Tell us about some of the special problems of poverty in West Virginia," or something like that. Some questions I couldn't answer, and some I thought I could say a little bit about.

YARMOLINSKY: Shriver picked many of [the task force members] himself, and some I suggested. A number of people I brought in from the Pentagon on loan to work mostly on some of the technical, logistic aspects of it. My own special assistant, Colonel John Carley, did a lot of the logistics work for the Job Corps. And then we recruited people. Some were volunteers from outside government. We managed to run that whole task force operation for a budgeted figure of something like $10,000 or $20,000, which was absolutely incredible, because it was all borrowed people and volunteered people and borrowed space and borrowed telephones and all the rest of it.

We had to be particularly careful because there was a congressional rider—because of congressional resentment of the task force that President Kennedy had set up on the domestic volunteer corps, the thing that later became VISTA—that no money could be spent to develop such a proposal within the executive branch. No money could be spent out of executive departmental appropriations, so we had to be very careful that any work that was done on that part of the program was either done by volunteers or with White House funds.

We brought in a lot of people as consultants and advisers, whose names have been more prominently displayed in the histories of the task force [but] who, in fact, played considerably lesser roles, primarily because they didn't think programmatically. People like Michael Harrington and Paul Jacobs. They were very good at giving us a start and saying, "Here are the dimensions of the problem," but they weren't the kind of people who had experience putting together a government program. Therefore it was others, less famous perhaps, who did play the essential roles.

Christopher Weeks, senior examiner in the Bureau of the Budget's Foreign Aid and International Economic Policy Division, was a member of the Peace Corps task force and the group that drafted the Peace Corps Act. When the War on Poverty Task Force was announced in February 1964, he was one of the first members recruited by Shriver. Weeks served as program troubleshooter and special assistant to Shriver until July 1966 and also worked as deputy director of the Job Corps for nine months in 1965. Weeks was born in 1930; he received degrees from Yale and the University of Michigan and an M.P.A. in public finance from Harvard.

WEEKS: During the early days, particularly during the six-weeks process, Shriver was very much concerned about what I would call the political problems of trying to sell a program on Capitol Hill. He was spending quite a bit of time talking with congressmen and senators, trying to figure out what a package would have to contain in order to be able to get through up there. As various proposals from the poverty program leaked out from time to time, congressmen, senators, and one person or another would call up and yell and scream about some aspect of it. Shriver would immediately react to that. He was not at all involved in any of the substance of putting the program together. Under Shriver you had Adam Yarmolinsky, who was the primary person who was involved in trying to put this kind of [program together] and trying to pay attention to what I would call interior substance as opposed to political salability.

MANKIEWICZ: Adam was very close to Sarge. He had two roles. One is that he could crack heads pretty good. Adam in effect became the chief of staff, which was a role that Sarge was willing to let him have because he was quite good at it. He'd say, "Do this," or, "What's happened to the such-and-such proposal?" and somebody would say where it was. And Adam would say, "Well, that's not an adequate answer. Do it faster." Or somebody would say something, and he would say, "That's silly. We can't do that because...." And he was smart enough and sharp enough and direct enough to get away with it. That's why a lot of people didn't like him. So he was a coordinator, and he was also an indefatigable worker and, I suspect, did a lot of things for Sarge along the way. You know, "Talk to so-and-so, and tell him this or that. Size up this and that thing." I don't know—he worked very much with Sarge, and it was clear early on that he was going to be the deputy.

YARMOLINSKY: How did the task force function? It did not function as a democratic body. We had staff meetings, but the staff meetings were just to keep everybody abreast of what people were doing. We were formulating legislation. We agreed that people would take on assignments, and the person who took on the assignment really got to put together the proposal. The proposal would come back and presumably be discussed in a meeting of whoever happened to be around, because the final decision was going to be Shriver's anyway. If it wasn't Shriver's, it was mine in Shriver's absence, or I would make a decision and bring it to him to make sure he agreed with it.

The members didn't take a vote, then?

YARMOLINSKY: Oh, no. No. None of that sort of foolishness.

Let's say, Wilbur Cohen would present a background paper on education.

YARMOLINSKY: But it wouldn't be a background paper in an academic sense; it would be a set of proposals. It would be programmatic: "Let's propose this to do this, and this much money." And then we—and whoever "we" was is hard to remember, but it was whoever happened to be around and wanted to participate and offer suggestions, with the understanding that this was not a democratic organization.

What was the atmosphere like in these discussions? Was it like a college seminar room, where different people would argue?

YARMOLINSKY: It was very open. It wasn't like a college seminar room. It was more like a college seminar room today, I suspect, because there wasn't very much theoretical argument. It was more, "How are we going to do this?" and it kept coming back to, "We've got to make up our mind; we've got to stay within budgetary guidelines; we've got to have it done by a certain date. We're under a great time pressure." There was no question of, "You're on the task force, and you're not." It was whoever happened to be around, and nobody was excluded. People generally excluded themselves when they did not take an interest in a programmatic process, in a practical process. But I think, when we were putting together the legislation, that either Shriver or I was in the chair, and that didn't mean terribly much. I probably chaired more meetings than Shriver because very early on he was spending hours and hours and hours on the Hill.

I know that I did not go through a process which I might have gone through with somebody who was more formal and systematic. I would always say to people who were involved in a meeting, "You don't like my decision, you should always feel free to go to Shriver." But I don't remember cases in which they did, although there must have been some. I don't remember being reversed, but then that may be selective memory.

The task force was organized to the extent it was around the major divisions of the legislation, which would also be the major administrative divisions of the agency. Early on it came out that there was one person in charge of Community Action, one person in charge of Job Corps, one person in charge of Neighborhood Youth Corps, the interagency coordination, and they corresponded to the titles of the act and the eventual assistant directors of the agency.

HOROWITZ: I can remember, for example, presentations. Experts would come in. Somebody came in to give a presentation on unemployment or whatever it might have been, and people would ask questions. There were some true wild brainstorming sessions, just what kinds of programs could be dreamed up.

Did Yarmolinsky generally head these sessions?

HOROWITZ: Yes. He would give assignments, to get papers written or what have you, and that was done to some extent on the basis of agency expertise. I got an assignment to outline HEW programs that could somehow be built into an expanded manpower training program. I got in touch with one of the lawyers in the HEW legislative division, where Sid Saperstein and Ted Ellenbogen were, one of the young lawyers, and asked him to develop that catalog and got that material from him and turned it into a memo. And just people from all over the place were doing that sort of thing and just building files.

The one other thing I remember about that time would be, we'd be in a meeting with Adam, and he'd say, "Okay, I want that paper, and we'll discuss that one at midnight." That was the way the thing was running, yes.

Ronald L. Goldfarb served as special assistant to the attorney general in the organized crime section from 1961 to 1964, when he was recruited to work with the War on Poverty Task Force. He entered private law practice in Washington, D.C., the following year. Goldfarb, a native of New Jersey, received his law degree from Yale in 1960.

GOLDFARB: [Decision making] was done in a very disorganized way. To a great degree, it seemed to me that it was by virtue of people's own energy and imagination, they would evolve as activists who were in on meetings where things were done, and it had an awful lot to do with individuals' energies as well as their expertise. So different people emerged as influential simply because they were activists and became influential. I would, for example, describe Sundquist as a person who came there with a particular expertise in a particular field and was doing his job; and a guy like Weeks as somebody who was a generalist who came in there, but by virtue of the fact that he was energetic and assertive and involved, he came to have a relatively major role in that task force. It was due more to his own personality and initiative than to his expertise.

John Baker, as assistant secretary of Agriculture for rural development and conservation, had extensive experience with rural poverty by the time he joined the War on Poverty Task Force in 1964. Baker, who was a native of Arkansas, earned a graduate degree from the University of Wisconsin and served in the navy during World War II. Baker worked in the Farmers Home Administration (FHA) for fifteen years. During the 1950s, he was director of legislative services for the National Farmers Union.

J. BAKER: One thing that I presented, and said that I could talk the Extension Service into doing it if nobody else is willing, was "family planning." Every other member of that task force literally goddamned near threw me out the window on that one. I said, "Well, I don't mean what you think." They said, "Well, you said it!" Boy, they just ripped me, everybody from Lisle Carter to the guy from Avis. I don't know whether they were all Catholics or not. But god damn it, I took a ripping that day. They didn't think that the government ought to be putting money into birth control. They translated that [incorrectly]. Davis and I kind of introduced the word innocently. We were thinking in terms of teaching [the poor] to budget and keep records.

James N. Adler was working in the Department of Commerce on an economic development program for Appalachia, an initiative that would ultimately become the Appalachian Regional Commission. Before the commission was created, however, Adler was sent to the poverty task force as a Commerce representative. Adler was born in Kansas City, Missouri, in 1936. He received his undergraduate degree from Princeton and his law degree from the University of Michigan and was a law clerk for Justice Charles E. Whittaker and Chief Justice Earl Warren in 1961–1962, before joining the Department of Labor as special assistant to the solicitor. From 1964 to 1965, he served as acting director of the men's urban Job Corps centers.

ADLER: Title VI, which was one I was particularly interested in and which was virtually a lost title in the program, was designed to induce states on a one-at-a-time basis to adopt AFDC [Aid to Families with Dependent Children], what was then called AFDCUP [Aid to Families with Dependent Children–Unemployed Parent]. At that time the law permitted states to have an option—still does permit that option, as a matter of fact—with regard to whether to include a family headed by an unemployed parent in the welfare program, in the Aid to Families with Dependent Children program. Most of the industrial states had adopted the AFDCUP, but most of the nonindustrial states had not. And that title was designed to say to a state, "If you will adopt an AFDCUP program, and with a work and training component, we'll essentially fund it the first year." The thinking was that the program would prove sufficiently popular that the state would have difficulty pulling out of it once it had committed itself to it. Therefore, it would pick up the cost and that money [could] then the next year be rolled over to induce other states.

Ann Oppenheimer Hamilton, a Wellesley graduate in economics in 1958, earned an M.S. in international economics from the London School of Economics in 1961. That year she also became international relations officer in the Peace Corps' Office of Program Development and Coordination. As Hamilton was leaving the Peace Corps in early 1964 to accept a position in the Bureau of the Budget, she learned about the poverty task force. She arranged to be detailed to the task force from her new assignment.

HAMILTON: It was very open, very free-flowing, very unstructured in the early days, the kind of place where ideas were freely and hotly exchanged. Those are characteristics that I associate with Shriver. He came in, as he had done to the Peace Corps, without preconceptions; didn't mind, indeed encouraged, debate; brought in all kinds of people with all kinds of ideas.

Another interesting Shriverism in the early days—I recall he turned an awful lot to his friends, colleagues, and contacts in the business community for ideas on this kind of administrative thing, on the theory that they knew how to solve problems. They were essentially problem solvers. You set yourself an objective in the business world and went out and achieved it, and there was no reason why that shouldn't apply to an administrative challenge like eradicating poverty. So there were all kinds of millionaires popping in and out for a day at a time.

THE TASK FORCE VERSUS THE BUREAUCRACY

ADLER: Shriver came into the meeting—I think it was a Monday or Tuesday—and he had spent the weekend, he said, considering what the outlines of the program should be. He then laid out his conception of the program, and at that meeting he described some of his rationale in what he was doing. But what he had done was pull a number of programs that were already in the budget into the poverty program. I think that he wanted to have a billion-dollar price tag on it, in terms of this was a billion-dollar effort, and yet he didn't have $1 billion of new budgetary money to spend. I think he had been given $500 million of additional budget, but he had to pull the other $500 million from existing programs that were already in the budget. So part of his strategy was to utilize existing programs that had already been submitted but would have been assigned to other departments, and to pull them into a coordinated effort and to utilize their money that way.

One of the things which I think he expressed at that time was a desire to put together a program that could go to one [congressional] committee. The concern was that we were dealing with, in what became the various titles of the department, subject matter which traditionally would have gone to probably five or six committees. And to go through five or six substantive committees on both sides, and then the appropriation committees they've got on both sides, would have taken a long time and been undesirable. So the desire was to pull it together into a comprehensive program.

GOLDFARB: I did a lot of day-to-day, ad hoc things which I don't remember now: wrote an article for the *ABA Journal*, gave a speech to this group or that group. There was a lot of that kind of thing. In terms of projects, I remember one of them was to go through all of the government programs that existed in all of the agencies and see which ones of them touched on poverty-related projects. I made a book on all of those programs and where they were and what they did and what their budgets were, etc. I talked to the people who were running them so that we could find out what existed at that time, however diffused and spread out around government it was.

Was the object of this to achieve a measure of coordination?

GOLDFARB: Yes, that was exactly what it was.

And maybe take over some programs too?

GOLDFARB: Oh, exactly, sure. The idea was that, if there was a new agency, might it be a logical thing to pull all those things out, and then how much budget were we talking about, and how dear were they to different agencies, how well were they being administered, and did they add up to a program in and of themselves?

What did you conclude about the status of poverty programs in the existing government framework?

GOLDFARB: Essentially, it was that we had the best of worlds and the worst of worlds in terms of social programs at that time affecting poverty. There were all kinds of programs around. It evidenced an interest on the part of Congress and the executive to do something about specific programs, and that was the best of worlds.

The worst of worlds was in the typical fashion that critics would criticize the federal government: they were all over the lot, they were duplicative, it was a many-headed monster, and the people in one department didn't know what the people in another department were doing. An obvious conclusion to one who went through an exercise like this would be that there was a clear need for coordination of these programs, getting rid of some, consolidating others, accenting others, but bringing it all under one umbrella. An example was, as I recall, that there were lots of programs about dealing with rats, and you found them in the Interior Department under one rationale, and in the Agriculture Department under another rationale, and at HEW someplace else. It was smart and wise and sensible that we would do something about the problem of rats, but no one had heard of the other one's program, it seemed, and so it was operating kind of catch-as-catch-can and in not such an effective way. And that, in a small way I thought, was duplicated in a lot of other situations.

Was there a good deal of squabbling among the departments with regard to how the program would be formulated and which departments would handle it and whether there would be a new agency?

J. BAKER: The struggle was mainly between HEW and the Department of Labor, against each other and against the White House in terms of the location. All the rest of us knew we couldn't get it, so we were in favor of having it go to the White House. No, we thought if you really wanted to put it upstairs instead of being buried down in the hierarchy somewhere, the thing you had to do was to put it in the White House.

Was there a general feeling among the task force members that the existing cabinet departments were not really focusing on the poor?

J. BAKER: I think that all of them thought that they were, but that it was like outdoor recreation, and water resources, and water resources research, and later beautification: it needed a White House focus if you were going to get it up above the threshold of national conscience. They all thought they were doing an awful lot. That's human. They all were, in their own ways, coming out of the New Deal, but it lacked a central focus. Then there were others who were not representing departments, like Ylvisaker and Yarmolinsky and some of those young Yale lawyers that Sarge brought in, that felt like nothing that had ever been done was any good. Nobody ever really found out what they thought needed to be done except rehabilitate criminal offenders. Each one had different kinds of things. We never did know for sure what they were focusing on. Maybe that was just us deep-in-the-mud bureaucrats and country boys, and we didn't understand the greater things that [Kingman] Brewster [president of Yale University] had taught his young lawyers at Yale.

Was your main interest developing local leadership for rural programs?

J. BAKER: To use the words I've been using a long, long, long time, my purpose and the purpose of the department—in the sense that you can say that anything as big and complex as the department has got a purpose—was to eliminate the complex, interrelated causes of rural poverty. There was still an awful lot of rural poverty. We had made an awful run at it with the Resettlement Administration and Farm Security. Since about 1937, when Roosevelt put the Resettlement Administration into the Department of Agriculture, the elimination of the causes of rural poverty and amelioration of its symptoms had been one of the major things the Department of Agriculture was supposed to be in business for, primarily through what was then called the Farm Security Administration.

Did the task force have an antirural bias?

J. BAKER: Yes, but really, I think not the consensus, but kind of the majority drift of the task force was focusing on low-income, black, inner-city, and a little bit resent[ing] it having anybody else be poor too, or being admitted that they were poor. There was lip service given to the fact that there are a whole lot more poor white people than there were poor black people in the United States. But when they started talking plans and policies, their stereotype that they were trying to get operating programs to operate on was the inner-city black poor. This, of course, heightened after [riots in] Watts and Detroit and 14th Street [in Washington, D.C.].

DRAFTING THE ECONOMIC OPPORTUNITY ACT

CANNON: I began talking to John Steadman, who's a lawyer, and Hal Horowitz; and I began, from my Office of Legislative Reference point of view, saying, "We've got to get some legislation." I don't remember the dates exactly, but that got set up, and I don't know quite who did it. So we went over to Justice—it must have been mid-February—on a Friday, and there was [Norbert] Schlei. It was a typical Yarmolinsky operation. The way I reason it is, I told Adam, and others undoubt-edly told him, "You need a bill." So in typical fashion, Yarmolinsky, being a law-yer himself, said, "Well, if I need a bill, I need a lawyer who drafts bills. Who's the government lawyer who drafts bills?" It was Schlei. So, "Norb, draft a bill."

So I sat there with Schlei and Steadman, and there were people trooping in and out. We had a separate caucus of people. We sat there, and we drafted from Friday to Sunday night or something, and we had a bill for a meeting on either Monday or Tuesday of the chief participants, all agency heads, the Wirtzes and the Celebrezzes and the Cohens and the so on. Yarmolinsky chaired the meeting to clear the legislation.

HOROWITZ: I guess at some point there must have been a basic document just plotting out what was going to be in the bill. That was what these bull sessions were about all the time—should this program be in or not, and somebody else would dream up a new program and argue it ought to be included, etc. And that began to take shape. Then [there was] discussion about which one should come first in the bill, etc. At some point that got organized enough that the time came to start to attempt a draft.

When we went to work, it was with a basic framework of the statute before us, and each of us in the drafting group was assigned a chunk of the bill to come up with the first draft. I had been sitting in on all of these discussions of community action and what have you, and [I] came from HEW, which of all government agencies was most closely involved with the sorts of things that community action programs would include. I can't remember, but I must just naturally have inherited Title II then as the chunk I would do. I don't remem-ber who did the other pieces of it. But then there was a meeting finally of the drafting group when the pieces were there, and then Norbert just set us to work, and we started on page 1 and said, "Okay, here's the preamble." We'd just talk it through word by word and make changes in whatever the first draft of the preamble was. So that was the way that the drafting group worked.

John Steadman joined the Department of Justice in 1963 after having practiced law in San Francisco since 1956. He was recruited by the Shriver task force in 1964 to help draft the Economic Opportunity Act. Later in 1964, Steadman became deputy undersecretary of the army for international affairs. The following year, he was appointed special assistant to the secretary of Defense, and he later served as general counsel to the air force. Born in Hawaii in 1930, Steadman had an undergraduate degree from Yale and a law degree from Harvard.

STEADMAN: Norb called me in one day, and he said, "Look, there's this thing about to happen involving some presidential decision to do something in the area of improving the lot of poor folks," or something. And he told me that there was this whole bunch of people over in Shriver's area in the Peace Corps building, which I'd never been to. [He said] to go on over there and see what's going on and give them a hand in whatever kind of drafting or whatever might have to be done.

I went over to this place in the Peace Corps, which was just absolutely chaotic. People were just running all over. To me, being a guy from the sticks, to see all these people around like Pat Moynihan and Willard Wirtz and Charlie Schultze and these people you had heard of but didn't know, like Paul Jacobs and Michael Harrington, it was a very heady experience for me, because it sort of threw me. I felt, all of a sudden, here I was involved in a process in which the whole domestic part of the government cared. So I saw all these people, and I just remember it was an extraordinarily exciting time for me.

I remember Shriver getting together with—maybe Norb was there, and I know I was there, and maybe like Horowitz and others of us that were cutting and pasting. And the exhortation was, "Make the language as general as possible, because we want to be able to do anything that we think of that will lead to an improvement in the economic condition of people." And so I know at least our early drafts were written in extraordinarily general language; that is to say, I remember we wrote the preamble to say we're going to do all kinds of good things. Even when we were sort of describing the program, we always put in, "...and do anything else that might kind of cope with this general sort of situation." I'm trying to remember if we went from the general to the specific. It seems to me as the bill went along it kept getting more specific.

LOGISTICAL PROBLEMS

WEEKS: Simply logistically, the problems of operating were enormous. When I reported for work in early February, I went to work in an office on the fifth floor of the Maiatico Building. Within two or three weeks, I moved to the twelfth floor in a completely new set of offices. Within about sixty days after that, we moved to the Court of Claims building. That would have been in roughly June, I would guess. By the end of July, they were building a building next door to it, and one of the pile drivers hit one of the foundation stones of the Court of Claims building and knocked a big crack in the wall. It's a 130-year-old building, I guess. It was structurally unsound. We had parts of the ceiling falling down—and the ceilings in that building are a good thirty feet high—and we had 200-pound chunks falling on the floor. So at one point in time, we were told to evacuate the building because it was dangerous. And it was.

And we moved from the Court of Claims building to an old hospital building about two blocks away. So in a period of three or four months, on top of the tremendous substantive problems we had to deal with, we were moving continuously. Every time we moved, we had a completely new set of telephone numbers, so you couldn't even call anybody. You didn't know what anybody's telephone number was. That meant, for example, that you couldn't get stationery; you couldn't get paper clips; you couldn't get any of the other kinds of things either, because they weren't available. We had to raid other agencies in order to get operating supplies. You couldn't even figure out what the telephone number was of the guy to call and get stationery and things like that. So just the simple problems of day-to-day functioning were pretty enormous, aside from the pretty awesome problems of trying to put the overall program package together.

How did the task force operate during the time you worked with it?

MAY: By fits and starts. Shriver was so damn cheap that he wouldn't let us spend any money. He had this thing in his id about being frugal if you're going to be involved in poverty, and also he got so much mileage out of giving money back to the Treasury of the United States from the Peace Corps budget every year when there were some dollars left over. That really impressed Congress. Other agencies usually spent their last dime.

As a result, you really had to cajole people into coming to help you. For example, I never was paid a dime while I was a member of the task force, and I think I might have gotten paid two or three trips from New York to Washington, but that was all. [Bill] Moyers gave [Shriver] a specific amount of money the president gave him. It was a small amount, whether it was $50,000, $100,000—I believe it was $50,000—but he insisted on not even spending that. So we were on the cheap. In fact, all of our telephone bills are still unpaid. I don't know if you've talked to Bill Kelly; he knows some of those things. We were hitchhiking on the Defense Department, which like always is the fattest cat in town. As a matter of fact, the Bible that we used to swear in Shriver on August 20, 1964—that was the date the Economic Opportunity Act was passed—Emedio Tini stole out of a warehouse belonging to the Department of Commerce. We always felt that was appropriate, because where else would the Department of Commerce keep a Bible but in a warehouse? So that's where we copped the Bible from.

Chris Weeks described a crisis in communication between the leadership of the task force and the working groups within the task force when Shriver was on the Hill and Yarmolinsky was recuperating from an automobile accident. Yarmolinsky insisted, however, that he was not out of commission for very long.

YARMOLINSKY: As soon as I was taken from Arlington County Hospital to Walter Reed, and possibly before, I was having people come to the hospital suite and running things from the hospital bed as much as possible. The director was on the Hill all the time, and the deputy director wasn't there, but I think the interval was shorter [than a month], and I suspect that the effects were not as serious.

After working with Sargent Shriver for two years at the Peace Corps as director of contracts, William P. Kelly Jr. was associate assistant administrator for procurement policy at the Agency for International Development (AID) when Shriver recruited him for the poverty task force. Kelly brought with him more than a decade of administrative experience with the army, the air force, and the National Aeronautics and Space Administration (NASA), where he was chief of the procurement branch. When OEO was created, Kelly became the assistant director for management. He also filled in as acting director of the Community Action Program before his appointment as the third director of the Job Corps in December 1966.

KELLY: I happened to be in Pittsfield, Massachusetts, on leave in early May of 1964 when I got a telephone call from Mr. Shriver. It started out on kind of a facetious note. He asked me, "What are you doing in Massachusetts?" I said, "I'm taking a little vacation." He allowed as how he didn't think I needed a vacation, and then he asked me if I would come and join the task force and work in the administrative areas. As a matter of fact, he said, "I would like you to run the administrative area. We need to put together the first budget. Nobody has done anything about that. We need to put together a personnel shop, and I would like you, if you could do that, to do it." I pointed out to him that that would be well and good, but that it would probably be necessary for him to talk to David Bell, who was then the administrator of the AID program. He said that he would. He asked me when I was going to return to Washington. I told him in a few days. Then he asked me to contact Adam Yarmolinsky, who was functioning as his deputy, as soon as I returned to town. And that I did.

There was a subsequent meeting between Bell and Shriver and Bill Moyers of the White House, at which time Dave Bell agreed to my being freed up to work half time on the task force. I might add for history that I worked half time one day and, although I stayed on the AID payroll until January of 1965—because

OEO had no payroll until November of 1964—that I did work full time on the task force.

The first thing that I tried to do was to bring some semblance of logistic logic out of what we had. It wasn't quite clear as to how many people we had on the task force, because they were scattered all over town. The task force had a very debilitating problem in that it didn't have any money, and we couldn't pay for such simple things as printing. We didn't have any office space per se; we were squatting on other people's office space. The authorizing legislation was proceeding through the Congress, but aside from the gross kinds of figures that you use in that process, there was no budget for appropriations hearings. We had no personnel functions even though we had people working all over the place on other people's payrolls. We had no housekeeping. So that the first thing that I tried to do was to create the semblance of some logic in the logistics area and then start to work very hard on putting together the aspects of budget presentation for the Congress. This encompassed the period May, June, July; and by mid-August we did have a budget put together in detail. As a matter of fact, Congressman John Fogarty [of Rhode Island], who headed our appropriation subcommittee, said it was the most complete presentation he had ever seen on the part of a new agency.

You said that task force members were in a sense being paid by other agencies. Was this general for that task force?

KELLY: Yes. As a matter of fact, what we tried to do—when we'd identify people that we wanted to come and help us that couldn't do it for free (and we had a lot of people who did it for free, did it out of their own pockets, or stayed on the payrolls of universities if they happened to be academic types, or if they were industrial people stayed on the payroll of their industrial corporation), we had to scurry around town and try to find a place to get them on a payroll. So that we had people on payrolls from the Federal Trade Commission (FTC); we had them on CAB [Civil Aeronautics Board]. One of my assistants was on the Civil Aeronautics Board payroll. We had them on Agriculture, Interior, the Department of Defense.

SCHULTZE: How do you get money to put the task force together and get some kind of planning done? So Elmer Staats and my deputy apparently suggested to Shriver that they ask the president for the use of a couple of hundred thousand dollars out of his special projects fund. The president blew up. He didn't want anybody to know about that special projects fund. And his comment to Elmer was, "Look," he says, "I don't fool around in your budget, and that runs into hundreds of billions. You leave *my* budget alone."

KELLY: We did ultimately get some money out of the president's contingency fund. But there were so many demands on that fund, and that fund is limited in terms of its size. Finally, in June of 1964, we did get a small amount of money, and we finally got, in November of 1964, some additional money to pay bills. What we tried to do was to run on the largesse of other people, but there were certain things that you could not ask other people to absorb. So as a result, we had some transportation costs of people that were in the academic community whose universities would pay their salaries but not their transportation. We had costs of such things as some commercial printing jobs that we had to have done. We did buy some supplies that were not available through GSA [General Services Administration], and we did have some bills. As I recall, we ended up with about $45,000 or $48,000 coming out of the president's contingency fund. But that was a small amount of money. In my experience, this was the first time we ever undertook anything of this magnitude without any money. We had to do some really extraordinary things, like steal franked envelopes at one point in time to get a mailing out.

Was it the feeling among task force members throughout the congressional review that the act would be passed?

KELLY: I think we were always very optimistic. There was an excellent esprit de corps in the task force. We had some remarkably able people, people who were very deeply committed to this whole notion of waging a war on poverty. We knew that this was President Johnson's first major piece of legislation after taking office, one that clearly had his stamp on it. People on the White House staff were very supportive of what we were doing. The leadership in the Congress was very supportive. It was something that everybody believed in. Everybody was optimistic during the late spring and summer of 1964.

I think the task force went through really a couple [of], or maybe even three, stages. There were the people who were here early on in February and March and April, May, even into June and July, who were kind of the theoreticians about poverty. They were people like Harrington, the author; Vern Alden, who is president of Ohio University—those two come to mind—and Pat Moynihan. They were kind of the theoreticians; they kind of described the parameters. And they worked with people in the Budget Bureau and on the Council of Economic Advisers, people like Bill Cannon in the bureau.

Then next you got in kind of the planners. People like John Carley, who was a colonel in the army [and] had been an aide to Adam Yarmolinsky; [he] was a logistician. He worked on the logistics of where would you locate Job Corps centers, what did you have to have in terms of building them, creating them? You had people like Glenn Ferguson, who came in from the Peace Corps for the VISTA operation, who was, again, kind of a logistician—not a theoretician, but a more firm planner—who had been Peace Corps representative in Thailand [and] before that had been a management engineer with McKinsey and Company.

And then the later stages of the game, along about late summer or early fall of 1964, you had the people who were operationally oriented, people who could run things. By that time, Otis Singletary, who was later to become director of Job Corps, had been identified. He was a university president or chancellor, and we had those kinds of people who are operationally orientated. But those were, as I recall it, the three stages it went through.

THE TASK FORCE AND THE WHITE HOUSE

SUNDQUIST: I don't recall that the White House had any impact whatever on the content of the bill. Now, they must have acquiesced at some point in putting into the bill the various pieces of legislation which were pending on the Hill already, and in the case of one bill, this was fairly delicate. This was a bill that was being handled by Bobby Kennedy, the juvenile delinquency bill.[12] At one point it was considered putting that in too, but Kennedy objected that he was getting it through all right on his own and not to muddy the waters, and Shriver yielded. But no, to my knowledge, no positive ideas came from the White House. They all were generated within the task force context.

KELLY: There was a good deal of liaison [between the task force and the White House], and it occurred at a number of levels. Mr. Shriver was talking regularly to the president as the bill moved through the congressional cycle. You also saw [him] talking to Larry O'Brien, who, of course, was very interested on behalf of the president. Adam Yarmolinsky was talking to Bill Moyers, as was I, so that there was a liaison constantly. There was hardly a day didn't go by in the summer of 1964, as I remember it, that, in conversations with Yarmolinsky and conversations I had with Shriver, there wasn't at least a reference to the fact that somebody had been talking to somebody in the White House.

There was a deep and abiding interest, as I recall, [on] the president['s part] in what were some of the costs of this program, in greater detail. I can remember putting together, or helping to put together with some of the members of the Job Corps task force, what were the unit costs that made up a job corps. These were gross slices. But what was it going to cost for food, what was it going to cost for clothing, what was it going to cost to rehabilitate x or y military establishment?

So one of my preoccupations, of course, was really trying to get Bill Moyers to cough up some dough. I had any number of memoranda that I prepared, that either I signed or Adam Yarmolinsky signed, in which we pointed out our plight: "We are being hounded by our creditors and trying to get Bill to free some of the contingency money"—which he ultimately did, as I mentioned before, in June.

YARMOLINSKY: Sarge and I reported to [President Johnson] primarily through Moyers, who was the staff man and who was responsible. Occasionally, we would get word that on this or that aspect of it, he had some view subsequently. But no. Of course, there were a lot of legislative problems, and we counseled every day with Larry O'Brien and his staff, worked very closely with the White House staff on getting the bill through. But the president himself—there were occasions when we asked the president to telephone leading members of Congress.

When we had the proposal for legislation in form to present as a proposal, Shriver presented it at a cabinet meeting, which I attended as an observer. The president naturally expressed his view and supported certain parts and did not favor other parts that were proposed, particularly the proposal for a public employment program to be supported by an increased tobacco tax. He felt that they couldn't ask for a new tax at the same time he was asking for a reduction in taxes. That was dropped out.

THE PRESIDENT'S POVERTY MESSAGE

MANKIEWICZ: I left Washington the day the bill went to the Congress and the message was approved. Now, Pat Moynihan and I worked on the message a lot. Pat had a draft of the message, which I worked on with him, and then Ken Galbraith came in, and we worked on a Galbraith draft for a while. I guess Bill Moyers finally drafted it. The only final draft I saw was full of short sentences.

HAMILTON: Galbraith was certainly not actively involved. I remember him well as the man who saved the message. It had been through any number of drafts, each one not significantly better and sometimes worse than the one before. Nobody was quite satisfied with the drafting process, which was the principal reason that it got delayed. The whole thing was tied up together. First of all, the substantive issues were being sorted out at the same time that the message was being drafted. And secondly, the drafts weren't any good. Galbraith came in, and in two days at the outside of what must have been marathon sessions on his part, all-night sessions, he redrafted it essentially into the message that was finally delivered.[13] And it was qualitatively better. I mean, you could feel the difference. And then I don't remember ever seeing him again.

ASSESSMENTS OF THE TASK FORCE

KELLY: We did suffer some problems in terms of not having the kind of money we needed. But I think that no program ever got off the ground faster in this city than the War on Poverty. I watched the development of the Peace Corps, from its very beginning in 1961, and it didn't move as rapidly as the War on Poverty. And it had all the money it needed. Like the War on Poverty, the Peace Corps had excellent support at the presidential level, but it didn't move any more rapidly or any more efficiently. I think that it could have been easier if we would have had that one ingredient that the Peace Corps had—money. I'm not sure that anybody could ever measure whether it was more efficient or not if we would have had that kind of support from a fiscal point of view.

HAMILTON: The task force by its very nature consisted of a fair number of zealots who probably were not excessively realistic in assessing the real negative consequences of their ideas. They realized, of course, they would make some problems. This was a gauntlet. I think they thought probably that the intensity of its political support would help carry it through more easily than it in fact did. And anyway, problems were inevitable.

LAMPMAN: I do have curious little memories, and I don't know how important they are. I remember in that period things like this. One day I was seated there, writing on some memorandum, and Isador Lubin came in. A real old man at that point, a former commissioner of the Bureau of Labor Statistics, a much respected and close confidant, I think, of Averell Harriman—he came in to talk about the New York program. It had been called Harriman's "attack on poverty" when he had been governor. Those were just precious moments for me. I always had a lot of respect for Isador Lubin. I had never met him.

The thing that was remarkable and memorable about it was not only this great enthusiasm and infectious spirit of Sargent Shriver, but all the people who came out of the woodwork to give a cheer for this sort of thing. There were ministers of the gospel and radicals like Paul Jacobs, people from all persuasions, it seemed, who would volunteer. They'd go out of their way to come and say what a good idea this was and what an important thing it was for a rich country to do. That is the leading memory I have of that task force period. It was a period of kind of unusual harmony, even though there were people who wouldn't speak to me and so on, or I felt they wouldn't anyway. And where there were fundamental disagreements about ways to go about it, there was still a belief some of it was important to say.

3

CREATING THE COMMUNITY ACTION PROGRAM

HOW DID THE SHRIVER *task force envision community action? To what extent would community action organizations bypass city hall or even threaten local establishments? As the concept advanced from the discussions within the CEA interagency group to enactment as Title II of the Economic Opportunity Act, there were clearly various interpretations of its intent. In his book* Maximum Feasible Misunderstanding, *Daniel Patrick Moynihan argues that the activists who planned the implementation of the Community Action Program (CAP) discarded its original purpose in favor of a more radical agenda of arousing the poor.[1]*

While hindsight has not produced unanimity, the participants clearly agreed that the residents in the target areas should be involved in determining the programs that affected them. Involvement, however, did not mean control, any more than bypassing local government or encouraging reform of local institutions would inevitably degenerate into class warfare. Although there is some support for Moynihan's analysis, on balance the task force participants describe more continuity throughout the evolution of the program than he has suggested. The participants' views may have varied in degree, but empowerment, not conflict, was their common objective.

FOCUS ON JUVENILE DELINQUENCY

Was your Peace Corps experience applicable or critical in formulating the concept of community action?

SHRIVER: That's a huge question. There were many, many things in the Peace Corps which were applicable to the War on Poverty, and you put your finger right away on one of them right away. That was the approach which we in the Peace Corps called "community development." In fact, doing community development in Ecuador is, philosophically and substantially, no different than doing the same thing in some West Virginia hollow. Now, I'm not trying to say West Virginia hollows are like Ecuador, but the concept of going into Ecuador to try to help people decide their own problems, and to energize them, motivate them, assist them to be able to handle their own problems themselves, is no different than the psychology you take into West Virginia or to the South Bronx. In the Peace Corps, one called this process "community development"; in the war against poverty, we called it "community action."

Norbert A. Schlei, assistant attorney general in charge of the Office of Legal Counsel, was detailed to the Shriver task force in 1964 to draft the Economic Opportunity Act. A Yale graduate and former law clerk to Supreme Court Justice John Harlan, Schlei had been a practicing attorney in Los Angeles from 1959 to 1962, when he joined the Kennedy administration.

SCHLEI: [Community action] was a concept that had various ideas associated with it. But any two people you talked to about what a community action program was and what was important about it would grab hold of a different part of the elephant.

The Community Action Program was in many respects an outgrowth of the experience that the Juvenile Delinquency Committee, of which David Hackett was the executive director, had had over the past years. They had concluded that if you wanted to do anything effective, you had to involve various people, including the target population, the local officials. If you tried to come in from on high and do something effective about a problem like juvenile delinquency, you were going to fail. And in order to make a lasting impact, you had to get everybody singing from the same sheet music, so to speak, and being mutually supportive. That was a key input in the development of what became the Community Action Program in the statute.

Frederick O'R. Hayes was born in Utica, New York, in 1923. He graduated from Hamilton College and later earned graduate degrees from Harvard in public administration and in political economy and government. After a year in Albany with the New York state comptroller, he joined the staff of the U.S. Bureau of the Budget, initially as a fiscal economist and later as a principal budget examiner. In 1961, he was appointed an assistant commissioner in the Urban Renewal Administration; while in that position, he participated in the work of the task force on the War on Poverty in 1964. After the Economic Opportunity Act was passed, Jack Conway recruited Hayes as assistant director of the Community Action Program with responsibility for program operations. Later, Hayes was appointed deputy director, serving until late 1966, when he became the New York City budget director.

HAYES: I really didn't know very much about the program [President's Committee on Juvenile Delinquency and Youth Crime (PCJD)]. I had a very general understanding of its dimensions and purposes and a limited exposure to a few of its projects. It was a planning, research, and demonstration program, with only a handful of projects. At the end of 1963, it was still a relatively new program, and I doubt that there was enough evidence to support any solid judgment on the worth of the program. My impression, perhaps based largely on the massive HARYOU-ACT and Mobilization for Youth [MFY] study reports, was that much of the effort up to that time had gone into planning and that other grantee program operations were still quite limited.[2] I knew that PCJD was involved in some, probably only a few, of the Ford Foundation Gray Areas Programs; and that—like Ford NIMH [National Institute of Mental Health] and OMAT [Office of Manpower, Automation, and Training] in the Department of Labor—[PCJD was] interested in experimental or pilot community antipoverty projects.

The project that drew the most attention was, of course, Mobilization for Youth, because of its comprehensive scope. But Mobilization was probably too ambitious, too focused on one target group, and in a sense, too academic to be a model for community action. I never heard anyone suggest that it should be. If there was a model for community action, it came from the Ford Foundation Gray Areas Program, not from PCJD.

WEEKS: The specific theses that came from the juvenile delinquency program were first that the local organizations—concerned in the initial instance, of course, with juvenile delinquency—had to get together. The juvenile delinquency program found that the employment agencies and the probation agencies and the police agencies and so on in cities quite frequently were completely separate and not only didn't work together but were sometimes warring with each other to see who could get responsibility. Before a juvenile delinquency grant could be made, the groups had to get together and form an umbrella organization to demonstrate that they would in some way work cooperatively together to eliminate juvenile delinquency, supposedly. That thesis—the umbrella thesis, a collective action thesis—carried specifically over into community action.

The "maximum feasible participation" thesis was a little less present in the juvenile delinquency program and came more out of the specific feelings of Dick Boone and others in the government at the time—Sanford Kravitz being another major thinker—who felt that one of the major problems with government programs oriented toward the poor, urban redevelopment, and so on, was that most of the planning had been done by agencies in Washington or by city bureaucrats sitting in city offices: that in a lot of cases things had been done that simply didn't make sense in light of what was going on in a particular neighborhood. Everything was characteristic of planning from the top down, and they felt that there should also be a process for planning from the bottom up, which obviously calls for something called "maximum feasible participation."

THE TASK FORCE EXPANDS COMMUNITY ACTION

SUNDQUIST: Dave Hackett first put into the Council of Economic Advisers planning system a proposal for community action. He proposed ten areas and proposed that a comprehensive survey be made in each area, which would take about a year, prior to the enactment of legislation to authorize community action programs.[3] That was how cautious he and his advisers were. One thing that influenced him was the proposition, of which that group was so conscious, that nobody quite knew what needs to be done to eradicate poverty. It's not a simple thing. They had a research approach, research and demonstration. So along with the planning is a notion that there has got to be some very hard thought and perhaps some experimentation as to what you want to do.

In the February 4 meeting, there was a sharp focus on this point. The community action people, in their presentation, had suggested that the planning approach be taken along the lines of the way that the President's Committee on Juvenile Delinquency had run its projects. But I think in their original presentation they acknowledged that they would use what was called the "building-block" approach.

I remember my own contribution to the meeting, just before noon, was a plea in that direction—that when the president had declared unconditional war on poverty, you couldn't first limit the number of areas. That had been in the original proposal. In fact, it had been in the thinking from the very beginning. At the time Shriver took over, the Budget Bureau and the council had been thinking in terms of not more than fifty areas. This was one point I made my pitch against. You can't have unconditional war on poverty and, after you've designated your fifty areas, tell all the other mayors and county commissioners and civil leaders to go back and wait—they could fight their war on poverty later. It just didn't respond to the president's leadership, which he was asserting then, and it was not in accord with the country's response to that leadership. The country was ready to move on a truly unconditional war on poverty.

At that point or shortly afterward, there seemed to be no question that the consensus of the meeting was clear on both those points: that we would go universal at once, and we would use the building-block approach. My complaint about Moynihan's book is that he treats the suggestion that this be a universal program as though it were a kind of conspiracy of the social scientists to thrust their untried theories on the country. It was the social scientists who were the most cautious. It was they who said, "Let's hold this to ten areas," in Hackett's original proposal, or fifty at the time the Budget Bureau got hold of it. It was the politicians who said, "Let's take this idea and make it universal, whether or not we know what we're doing."

When the War on Poverty Task Force was formed, Samuel V. Merrick was assistant to the secretary of Labor for legislation, a post he held from 1962 to 1968. His earlier career in government included five years as special assistant general counsel at the National Labor Relations Board (NLRB) in the early 1950s and work as a professional staff member of the Senate Labor Committee from 1959 to 1962. Born in Pennsylvania in 1914, Merrick received his undergraduate and law degrees from the University of Pennsylvania.

MERRICK: The President's Committee on Juvenile Delinquency was a tripod organization basically under the direction of the Justice Department, with Bobby Kennedy being the nominal head of it. And he was. He was not only nominal, but he would come in at times of serious decision making. But Dave Hackett was his deputy and really the person who ran the program, and I was the Labor Department's representative on that tripod organization. There's sort of a sequence about this. There's the Ford [Foundation] Gray Areas thing, and then came along the juvenile delinquency program. Then came along community action. Then the fourth step in this was the Model Cities Program. Each one sort of built on the other.

In the case of the juvenile delinquency program, $2 million or $3 million a year was all they were working with, on a very experimental basis. In the eyes of somebody like Hackett, [he was] aghast at the sudden increase in the size of this thing, with all of its troubles, as it evolved in the poverty program. I was astonished that the task force should multiply the program a hundred times. It was just buying trouble. Even at [the] $2 million level, it was trouble in the cities where it was going on because the mayors were faced with power centers taking antagonistic positions.

My primary memory of cities coming into Washington asking for some piece of this two-and-a-half million was a group of people around a room asking questions. They would describe what they were doing, and these people on board [would ask], "Well, why isn't so-and-so part of it?" And, "Unless we have more community involvement, or more charitable organization involvement, or unless we have more of the city administration part…," or, "Unless we have less city administration control over it…," etc. [They'd say,] "Well, no, you'd better go back and redo your thinking and come in and smooth that out, and then we'll give you a couple of hundred thousand," or whatever. My overwhelming impression was that the effort to make an ideal kind of "everybody aboard" thing was just agonizing in the process of approving these plans.

The key feature of the juvenile delinquency program was that there's no point in giving money for schools alone unless you do something about housing and jobs and health and family structure, [which] are important deficiencies and all interrelated. But there's no point in throwing money at one without dealing with the spectrum of social ills. The other key thing was being sure that you just didn't have the established political heads but that you had community groups putting in their vision, their perception as to what is wrong at the local level.

HAYES: We started with a draft of Title II, perhaps written by Norbert Schlei or someone else in Justice. I believe that the draft included the "maximum feasible participation" requirement, which would suggest that Dick Boone had had a hand in its preparation. I do not recall any discussion of participation, but the requirement would not, at that point, be seen as potentially controversial. I remember the discussion of only two significant issues.

One was whether private nonprofit organizations as well as public agencies should be eligible for grants. This issue had arisen in the meetings of the community action planning group because of the concern expressed by some that some local governments in the south might decide not to participate in the program. In that event, authority to make grants to nonprofits would provide an alternative means of initiating the program in those jurisdictions. The provision was included. The concern about program participation in the South proved groundless, but the nonprofit option was widely used in all parts of the country. The nonprofit structure offered freedom from civil service requirements and the onerous red tape of government. It provided a neutral site and a highly flexible, easily created organization that could be tailored to reflect sponsorship by several governmental units [city, counties, school boards] and participation by the poor.

The second issue was the proportion of the funding that would be available for research, pilot, and demonstration projects. The group accepted my proposal to allow up to fifteen percent of the money to be used for such projects. This was a relatively large share, and I proposed it on the basis of a general conviction that we had tended throughout government to underfund knowledge building and knowledge dissemination.

You may know that Dick Boone and I had initially proposed that we start, not with an operating program, but with a very large research and demonstration program. The proposal was rejected by Ted Sorensen, who said to forget about the notion of a $100 million demonstration program and to start instead with a full-scale program.

Was your desire for planning and experimentation based on the experimental nature of the President's Committee on Juvenile Delinquency?

HAYES: No, it was not. There were two reasons. First, the program would demand an extraordinary combination of imagination, responsiveness, political skill, and managerial ability from its local sponsors. We knew from experience with urban renewal and other programs that we could expect, at most, only a handful of communities to create antipoverty agencies with these capabilities. A program open to eligible organizations in every American community was likely to result in many uninnovative and uninspiring or incompetently managed programs and few stellar performances. This approach would make sense only if its likely results were clearly recognized in advance, and if it were seen as a developmental and educational effort that might over, say, a half-dozen years create a more widespread and perceptive understanding of poverty and what might be done about it.

The second reason was our very limited knowledge of the effectiveness of various antipoverty programs. One can produce some fairly solid conclusions on the factors contributing to the reduction of poverty—the absorption of millions of poor immigrants, and the growth of national wealth over the past 100 or 150 or 200 years. But we knew next to nothing about the most effective means of getting people out of poverty in the short run. Paul Ylvisaker described our problem as the need to discover that act of social jujitsu that would make it possible to do in one generation what had taken two or three generations before. There was no certainty that we would learn much from a large pilot and demonstration program, but the chances were better than for a full-scale program.

WEEKS: At the end of March, I went over to meet with Dave Hackett and Dick Boone to try to come up with examples of community action programs that could be mounted. Along with myself were Annie Oppenheimer and Barry Passett, a guy I had working with me that I had borrowed from the State Department.

It was one of those meetings in which there is a surface agenda and then there is a subsurface agenda. I remember very clearly that as we walked out of the room we all looked at each other, and we said, "We lost both the surface agenda and the subsurface agenda." The juvenile delinquency program at that time was trying to create a role for itself as the community action agency in each of the cities in which these organizations had been set up. They were doing that by trying to give as illustrations of community action programs that might be done what ABCD [Action for Boston Community Development] was doing in Boston, what HARYOU-ACT was doing in New York, and what [the Chicago Commission on Urban Opportunity] was doing in Chicago, and so on.[4]

So the bureaucratic rivalry was very, very evident right from the beginning. The other side of the juvenile delinquency [program] claim was, if the Community Action Program really got under way, there would hardly be any use for a juvenile delinquency program. It would be kind of subsumed in the whole thing.

[The conflict] was essentially resolved because, as Jack Conway came in and took over, he was powerful enough and influential enough to be able to bring Dick Boone over. Dick Boone came over as one of the principal thinkers and planners, director of policy and programming for Community Action. What essentially happened was that the juvenile delinquency program thinking was subsumed into Community Action thinking by subsuming the main thinkers of the juvenile delinquency program. So what could have started out as a rivalry in fact turned out not to be so much of a rivalry. Jack Conway and Dick Boone thought along similar lines.[5]

THE TASK FORCE VIEWS OF COMMUNITY ACTION

TOLMACH: As the task force saw it, and as the people who staffed the Community Action Program—certainly in the early days—[saw it], the whole idea was that it was a new approach. And that in its very newness, especially newness in some of its principles of involving people and the way it was to be structured and what it was to be concerned with and so forth, it was a virtuous way to proceed. Now, it hadn't worked before; we were trying some kind of new way of doing it. It doesn't necessarily make it the answer. It seemed to join together some of those elements which appeared to be lacking in previous approaches, and of course nobody knew exactly what all the consequences of it would be. They didn't know everything that was meant by "maximum feasible participation." I don't know that one needed to know everything.

SCHLEI: As I understood the Community Action Program, the key idea was that you tried to coordinate within the community everything that was being done to deal with the problem of poverty. You would involve both all of the levels of government that were involved and elements of the community as well, particularly including the target population, the poor people themselves.

Involving them in the policy level as well as the implementation?

SCHLEI: I personally disagreed with the idea that you really had to put the whole thing under the control of poor people in the community, because I didn't think they would be up to the job.

But that's not stipulated in the act, is it?

SCHLEI: No—rather to my surprise, I may say—but that is what came to be thought to be the concept of this "maximum feasible participation" language that appears in Title II.

Did you notice any change in the prevailing thinking of the task force with regard to community action?

SCHLEI: Yes. I heard a lot of talk about community action programs that made me wonder if it was the same concept that we had been talking about when I was in touch on a daily basis with the thinking. I think the whole concept began to evolve, and it got to be much more this matter of putting the target population in charge, putting the local people in charge of the federal money. That sort of thing began to move along. I really hadn't understood that that was part of it.

Was this while the program was still under consideration on the Hill?

SCHLEI: I think so. I think that even while it was not yet passed, there appeared some drift in the whole thinking about community action.

Who was articulating this new concept?

SCHLEI: Well, some of it came out of Shriver. I would hear Shriver say things that made me feel that there had been some evolution in thinking since I was directly involved. All I can recall is that the idea of putting the target population in a power position and the idea of putting the local government people in a power position seemed to me to be talked about like they were much more integral to the whole idea than I had understood originally.

COMMUNITY ACTION AND LOCAL GOVERNMENT

YARMOLINSKY: I didn't realize until after the bill was passed that [Lyndon Johnson's] perception was not as close to reality as one might have thought. Because I think it was after the bill was passed, or shortly before the bill was passed, he was saying to [Bill] Moyers things which led Moyers to conclude that Johnson assumed that community action would be handled entirely by local government or agencies of the federal government, like the NYA [National Youth Administration], which Johnson had been involved in as a young man. Moyers had to explain to him, no, it wasn't going to be that way. So I really don't think he got involved in the detail of the program.

LBJ'S VIEW

On the eve of the Economic Opportunity Act's passage in the House, Johnson describes his original understanding of the antipoverty initiative.

LBJ's conversation with Bill Moyers, August 7, 1964[1]

JOHNSON: I'm going to rewrite your poverty program. You boys got together and wrote this stuff. I thought we were just going to have NYA, as I understood it. You know what I think of the poverty program? What I thought we were going to do? I thought we were going to have CCC camps.

MOYERS: We got that.

JOHNSON: I thought we were going to have community action, where a city or a county or a school district or some governmental agency could sponsor a project. The state highway department could sponsor it, and we'd pay the labor and a very limited amount of materials on it, but make them put up most of the materials and a good deal of supervision, and so forth, just like—

MOYERS: We got that.

JOHNSON: I thought that we'd say to a high school boy that's about to drop out: "We'll let you work in the library, sweep the floors, or work in the shrubs, or pick the rocks, and we'll pay you enough so you can stay in school."

MOYERS: We got that.

JOHNSON: I thought you'd let a college boy do the same thing, and a college girl.

MOYERS: We got that.

JOHNSON: Now I never heard of any liberal outfits where you could sub-sidize anybody. I think I'm against that. If you all want to do it in the Peace Corps, then that's your private thing. That's Kennedy. But [in] my Johnson program I'm against subsidizing any private organization. Now if we had a hundred billion, we might need to. But with all the govern-mental agencies in this country, I'd a whole lot rather [Chicago Mayor] Dick Daley do it than the Urban League. He's got heads of departments, and he's got experienced people at handling hundreds of millions of dol-lars. And every one of these places, I'd make them come in and sponsor these projects. I just think it makes us wide open, and I don't want any-body to get any grants. Now you got the grants [taken] out for farmers, didn't you?

MOYERS: Altogether and got that thing out on handicapped that I men-tioned to you last night. Everybody has to work.

SHRIVER: I think President Johnson may have thought that the way community action was going to work was through local government. But frankly, that never was my idea. My idea always was, by analogy, that a local community action board would be like a local board of education. Now a local school board in Tuscaloosa, Alabama, or any other place in America is an independent agency. The board is responsible for the schools. I thought a community action agency ought to enjoy that same type of independent status on the local political scene that a board of education had. Just as a board of education speaks out on behalf of education, on behalf of teachers, on behalf of schoolchildren, the local community action agency should speak out on behalf of poor people and the needs of poor people, whether they were needs for jobs or housing or health care—whatever those needs happened to be. Therefore I wanted the local community action agency to be composed of distinguished people at the local level: private businessmen, private philanthropy people, poor people, and government people. I wanted it to be what I used to call the "community." Ours was not the poor community versus the rich community, or the business community versus the labor community.

In these discussions of community action, did the group assume that the poor did not have sufficient control over their own affairs and social programs that were being offered them?

HAYES: The answer is yes, but I believe there were significant differences among us in our perceptions of the extent and importance of the problem. Most of us saw the primary problem as the way in which the professionals in the school systems and social service agencies tended to deal with the poor. David Seeley, an assistant to [Commissioner of Education] Frank Keppel, thought most of us naive about big-city public schools and [that we] were in for a rude surprise if we thought they could be easily influenced just with money. The schools constituted a closed system, defensive about outside criticisms and ideas, and imbued with a self-conscious professionalism.

We were not talking about any radical shift of authority to the poor. Both the schools and social services needed to improve what business would call "customer relations" by doing a better job of listening to, responding to, and communicating with their clients—pupils and parents. In addition, there was a strong case for a more participative pedagogy, the core of the changes advocated for years by progressive educators, and its equivalent in social services for poor children and adults where traditional modalities had been least successful.

Was community action viewed as a vehicle for bypassing these local governmental institutions?

HAYES: No. There was no way in which the school system could be bypassed and, at best, limited prospects for doing so with respect to most social services. We were skeptical about the effectiveness of direct funding for the school systems. If, however, we provided funding to community action umbrella agencies for public school programs for poor children, the umbrella agencies, as rational and prudent purchasers of services from the schools, might be able to obtain better results and greater accountability.

We did want local umbrella agencies set up independently rather than as an arm of a department of welfare or social services. But otherwise, we did not propose or assume that community action would bypass local government or the mayors. In fact, I know of no CAA [community action agency] that was organized without the sponsorship and participation of local elected officials, although there may possibly be a few exceptions in rural areas.

Did you see it working under the aegis of local government?

HAYES: Conway, Boone, and I all assumed that would be the case. Before the program was funded, I met with over a dozen mayors and Conway probably saw as many more in an effort to induce them to begin work on program planning and organization. In addition, Conway and I met with the governors of Georgia, North Carolina, and Vermont to discuss plans for programs in rural areas.

Did the language of the original draft legislation require community action agencies to come through the local political power structure?

MANKIEWICZ: Yes, I think [it] did, because one of the things we were very conscious of when we were writing and working was to keep it *out* of city hall. And indeed, our feeling was that in almost every one of these areas, the institution responsible for solving the problem was in large part responsible for the problem; that is to say, that people were being badly educated because of the public school system. The people were not finding jobs because of manpower training programs. And indeed, the welfare program was a mess because of social welfare agencies, officials, city hall, county government. Now, we may have been too strong on that; maybe it was more of a gut feeling than a researched analysis, but it was a strong feeling that a lot of us held.

The way the legislation was drafted, funding did not have to be funneled through local government. Was this done for fear that local governmental institutions in the south would discriminate against blacks?

SCHLEI: Well, that may have been an element in some people's thinking. I think the dominant element was the idea that if you left it up to local government, it would never get done. There had to be an element of pressure on the local government stemming from the fact that if they didn't go along at all, you could just do it without them. With that pressure, you would be able to involve them in the job and wind up probably with their support. But if you were totally subject to their veto, in many places nothing would happen.

Was this discussed among the members of the drafting committee or among the task force members as a whole?

SCHLEI: My recollection is that on the drafting committee we were for a maximum federal freedom to act, and in various other quarters we struck the feeling that the local people had to be in control—they had to be given an option or veto. I guess I ultimately, personally, came to accept the view that you really were never going to do anything effective and lasting unless you involved and brought along with you the local governments; that maybe you could defy them and go and do your thing, but they would keep undoing it or uprooting it unless they were brought in. So I believe that is the concept that is in there, to the extent that any concept is in there, that the local government authorities must be brought in and participate in the program.

Did you envision that some of the local community action programs would turn on city hall and cause problems?

SCHLEI: Well, yes. But somehow I didn't envision the extent to which these programs would wind up being under the control of the target population. That was just not my concept. I haven't looked at the bill for a long time. My impression is that the bill isn't very precise about exactly how this is going to work, and the reason for that is that nobody could be very precise at that stage. But as it turned out, the people who set up the program and made it happen were very much more committed to the idea of putting the target population in charge of the whole thing than we were in the formative stages. Certainly, as far as I personally am concerned, I thought they went clear over the edge.

Do you think that the bill was not specific enough about what sort of local control or local input there would be?

SCHLEI: I think that if we had it to do over again—with the hindsight, with the benefit of all these years of experience—I could draft a statute that I would be a lot happier with. But in those days, and even now, you might have to make do with a vague statute because you couldn't get agreement to a more precise statute. If it leaves the matter open, everybody can vote for it. There isn't anything in there that is objectionable. But when you start becoming more specific, then you start making enemies.

Was that the reason the legislation was vague? Because being more specific would have caused more opposition on the Hill?

SCHLEI: I think there were three reasons why the proposal we sent up was, to some extent, vague. One was that there was not enough agreement in the administration to formulate a more precise bill in some respects. Secondly, none of us were able to know what problems would be encountered and how they should be resolved, so that we didn't have the knowledge, the foresight, to make it more precise. We had to leave it vague because we didn't know what the future would hold. And then, finally, I think there were some areas in which it was made vague because it was thought that a more precise formulation of what we were trying to achieve would unnecessarily make enemies up on the Hill. But the problems existed in the task force itself, that people could not arrive at a precise solution to the issues that they could all go along with.

Was community action designed to work under the aegis of local government?

YARMOLINSKY: It was, and it never occurred to us that local government would get into a big fight with the community. It was a real blind area. We thought the fight would be between the traditional charitable organizations on the one hand, and the local government and the poor on the other hand. It was recognized that CAP could be used to bypass some local power structures, but that was primarily in the context of black and white, that you would have to have ways to protect the rights of poor minorities.

I remember that the first big meeting was the one that Shriver chaired, and the second one I chaired. I think it was the one that Shriver chaired with a lot of outside advisers, the Tuesday or so after the Saturday that he was appointed. Dick Boone kept bringing up the idea of "maximum feasible participation." Whether he used those words then, I don't recall. I said to Dick, "You've brought that idea up several times," and he said, "Yes, I have. How many more times do I have to bring it up before it gets into the program?" and I said, "Oh, two or three." He did, and it did.

My conception of what [maximum feasible participation] meant was that you involved poor people in the process, not that you put them in charge. It was partly a means of ensuring black participation in the south. That was one of its [elements].

We were aware of Saul Alinsky's views of community organization. I think we thought they were [about] using conflict. I think we were a little too much a bunch of do-gooders to be really attracted to those ideas. Our discussion of the implications of participation of the poor did not assume the kind of confrontations that later developed. We didn't really talk about [the] question of what the proportions would be.

GORDON: At that stage, up to the time of Shriver's appointment as the first director of OEO, I don't remember ever having heard any discussion of the issue of "maximum feasible participation" by the poor, which later became a central issue of the community action concept. I mean that literally. I can't remember in numerous meetings and discussions and planning sessions that the issue was ever raised as an important issue. I'm sure all of us at that time thought of community action as organized, controlled, and managed in a sense by elite groups—by the city government, by business groups, by churches, by labor unions, by nonprofit social organizations, welfare bodies, etc.

This conception of the poverty program as consisting mainly of community action had a number of ramifications to it which I think are pretty important. I remember arguing very, very strongly that there ought to be no money for program activity for the first year, that the first year ought to be spent in organizing community action groups and financing studies, diagnoses, and analyses of local poverty problems and the design of local programs. The first year as a planning year, with the federal government picking up the tab for the planning effort, but no substantial program money. This was apparently politically impossible. Once the sales pressure to get Congress to accept the program was mounted, the pressure was so strong that the administration felt it simply had to go ahead and try to make tracks and achieve results quickly. This was Shriver's instinct. I'm sure politically he was right. Having sold the program as a matter of the highest urgency, it would have then been very difficult to say we needed a year for planning.

SCHLEI: I just have a general recollection that the consensus was to try to get real local autonomy in the administration of programs affecting the poor. My own view was that that would not work.

I thought that the administration of many of these programs required great intelligence and the ability to harmonize a lot of very complex things to administer the efforts of a lot of people and resources. I felt that, whereas maybe a bunch of poor people would have a better insight into where they hurt, they would never ever be able to successfully administer a large, complex program. They just would not be able to. I continue to believe that that is the fact. For one thing, you cannot have anything administered by a committee. You can have a committee that has legislative-type functions, or a committee that has a policy input function, or some kind of an advisory discussion group function. But if you actually put control of something in a Hydra-headed monster like a committee or some group, you are going to have a mess. That's my own personal conviction. When I hear somebody talk about administering something through a democratic mechanism, I feel that I'm dealing with somebody who has not got hold of reality with a good grip.

THE MEANING OF "MAXIMUM FEASIBLE PARTICIPATION"

CANNON: Now, in drafting the bill, there were a lot of things that I had had in my memo that I put in which became transformed. The preference clause in the Economic Opportunity Act, for example, was a watered-down version of what I'd proposed in my December memo [about] a waiver giving the president the right to waive certain requirements in existing programs. That came from that. "Maximum feasible participation," according to my understanding, came out of the separate drafting session we had, in those same offices in Justice, of Hackett and me and [Hugh] Calkins. I don't know whether Boone was there, but Fred Hayes was there, and Hal Horowitz. Hal was doing the drafting for us, and it was Hal to whom we told the concept of participation, and he came back with a draft labeled "maximum feasible participation of the poor."

So you felt the language was his?

CANNON: Yes. Well, unless he got it from somebody else; but that's the way it came back, because we immediately noticed it. As a matter of fact, I had goofed on it. When I took the language back to clear it within the bureau, I went to the chief of the Labor Welfare Division; he said, "Well, this isn't your concept, 'maximum feasible participation of the poor.'" I said, "By God, you're right." So we crossed it out and wrote in "maximum feasible participation of the residents of the area," because we weren't looking at just a program to organize the poor. We were looking at a program to organize the community. So that part I know— "residents of the area." But Hal did the drafting on Title II, or at least somebody for him in his office or something.

Was there, within this drafting group, a difference of opinion with regard to what local participation should be?

CANNON: I don't think so, though Dave Hackett kept raising that question, and it came up in another context. In his typical way, he would simply say, "Now, is this what you mean? Is this what you mean?" And we couldn't answer that. And we talked about it. But it came up in another context. I went over to the small group within the task force that Yarmolinsky was chairing. Ylvisaker was there, and Moynihan was there; I was sitting right next to Moynihan. When Moynihan says in *Maximum Feasible Misunderstanding* that he did not understand community action, it wasn't because he wasn't exposed at least three times. I was sitting right next to Pat, and Ylvisaker was across the table, and someone raised the question: "What if," they said to Paul, "you're up testifying, and they suggest to you that one of the effects of community action will be to undermine the mayor's control of the city?" And Paul said, "If they ask me that question, I'll ask them another question." That was his direct answer. And there was Pat sitting there. Well, beyond that, I patiently explained to Yarmolinsky and Moynihan two or three times the concept of community action.

What did you say?

CANNON: I obviously put it in the terms I believed it, which is: It was a method of organizing local political action, community action. It was just that. It was not a delivery system. We were always clear: it was not supposed to be just a delivery system. It wasn't a mechanism for dispensing services, though it would dispense services and money. But the major point was maximum feasible participation in the local community problems. Now, this does have implications for mayors.

Did you see community action as working within the structure of local government, or did you see it as a way to bypass local government?

CANNON: No, I saw it both ways. That was the key to it. This is exactly the question Pat raised to us after the act was passed. He called a meeting with Gordon, protesting that we were subsidizing the opposing parties and so on and so forth. He raised that exact same question, and my response was that the concept of community action is its flexibility. That is, it could be something different in New York. It would certainly be something different in Chicago, where Dick Daley was in charge, and it would certainly be something different in Saginaw. And that was the point. It was supposed to fit local political, social, and economic circumstances. And in Chicago it did. There was no problem with community action in Chicago. I worked that beat. Daley had that firmly under control. Pat was worried about what was going on in Harlem with HARYOU and things like that.

But the point of community action was its adaptability and flexibility. You see, this is a big country. I spent a lot of time going around it after this was all passed, visiting various cities, and in Saginaw the government doesn't want to have anything to do with community action. They've got enough to do doing urban renewal. So that in there they want a separate community action, and if they're told they're going to have one out of the government structure, there won't be any.

In the South, where blacks were traditionally excluded from the local government process, did you see community action as a way to give blacks more power?

CANNON: No, that was not our orientation. I know Frances Fox Piven and [Richard] Cloward raised the thesis that the War on Poverty represents the rise of the civil rights movement.[7] I think that overstresses what was going on at that time. Community action and the War on Poverty were not black-designed, minority-designed programs. They weren't designed to deal with that problem specifically. As a matter of fact, the larger percentage of poor in this country at this time were white. Substantially. So it wasn't, no. I don't want to be misunderstood, because we were very concerned about how community action would operate in the south, not as a minority program but as a community program. That's why "maximum feasible participation" was such important language—and other parts of Title II—because they were designed to make it work on a community level with "maximum feasible participation." And I don't care; in our minds it could be rednecks who were being excluded and ought to be in.

Am I right in saying that you saw it as a program that would challenge local government where it needed to be challenged, but would otherwise work within local government?

CANNON: Exactly. Exactly. It was designed not to destroy. It was supposed to be positive, constructive. Obviously, there was going to be at some times friction, but that's the nature of politics and change. But it was designed from a national point of view—which is a funny thing to say, but what I mean is that it was designed to fit situations all over this very diverse country—rural, city. One of the big successes of CAP was in the rural areas, which was not a surprise to me. It was a surprise to a lot of people, but it wasn't to me.

HOROWITZ: It's a marvelous question: where did those words ["maximum feasible participation"] finally come from? My records can demonstrate chronologically when those words appeared. We can narrow it down to sometime in a period of a few days. Who was the actual author of them? I don't know. I think I was, but there's no way I can demonstrate that. What was meant by it? Precisely what those words say. The notion was, to the maximum feasible extent, that you would have whatever is meant by participation of the people involved in whatever a community action program was.

Did you see it in terms of a percentage—say, thirty percent or sixty percent?

HOROWITZ: No. That's the glorious thing about statutory drafting or writing contracts or things like that. You can fall back on words like "maximum" and "reasonable" and "feasible" and what have you and fend off questions about what that means specifically. What it would mean if you were trying to administer it would be that there's got to be some demonstration that you made all good-faith efforts to have participation of the people involved in the programs, and that going farther than that just wouldn't make much sense.

SCHLEI: I think ["maximum feasible participation"] was just a way of expressing an idea that somebody in the group hit upon, and once it got used, it began to be used in other places. But the particular place that we started out talking about, the "maximum feasible participation" by people in the community, the target population—I forget exactly the words—I think that came from the pen of Harold Horowitz.

What did it mean to you?

SCHLEI: As best I can recall, it had two ideas. One was that the poor people would be consulted about what needed to be done. There would be perhaps advisory committees of people from the target population who would alert the administrators when they were hitting the wrong target. One of the great things about democracy, in my judgment, is that it enables the people who are hurt to do something about it by throwing out whoever is hurting them. One of the things about our welfare-type programs is that they are typically administered from on high, and maybe the relatively well-paid people who administer those programs are shooting at the wrong target; they are doing the wrong things. It made sense to me that there should be some regularized input from the target population, so that there would be an opportunity to learn what they thought about whether you were hitting the target or whether you ought to shift your aim.

Secondly, there was the idea that poor people should actually be utilized to do some of the work connected with these programs, because they could use the work. They could use the money. It would be constructive to involve them in the solution of their own problems. It would be good for them economically and socially, if you will, in the sense of giving them a sense of responsibility, being in control of their own destiny, and the like.

J. BAKER: ["Maximum feasible participation"] meant starting with the most downtrodden. It meant that women ought to have an equal say-so with men. It meant that poor black folks ought to have equal say-so with upwardly mobile, upper-middle-class [people] like Lisle Carter, that Lisle Carter ought to have an equal voice to John Baker. At the community level, everybody that perceived themselves to have a unique concern or contribution should be geared into the decision-making mechanism.

Did you see a set formula of certain percentages of neighborhood residents or poor people being involved, or a certain percentage of people from agencies and city governments?

J. BAKER: No. I was kind of on the other side on that, recognizing the importance of having some rules of thumb, but every community is different. Pick a percentage, and it's wrong the next place you stop. The other is, if you seem to be trying to force everybody into a quota system—so many of this kind and so many of that kind and so many of that kind—you overcome or set aside the benefits you get from maximum feasible participation.

Maximum feasible participation in a typical pre–World War II southern county is really an upheaval at just the thought, when you let black sharecroppers come in and have a say and take it seriously, give them a vote. But even in the Appalachians, where it's all white and all English, it's still a revolution to talk about it sometimes.

"A RIVET ON THE COUNTRY'S CONSCIENCE"

KELLY: I can remember the night that Mr. Shriver decided to appoint Jack Conway deputy. He talked to me about his decision. Conway had been functioning as director of the community action part of the thing during the task force days. I said I thought it was a good decision, and then he paid Jack Conway one of the most extraordinary compliments I've ever heard Shriver pay anyone. He said, "Jack Conway is the only man I know of who had the guts and vision to put together the Community Action Program." That was pretty high praise.

SHRIVER: There were a number of reasons for bringing in Jack Conway. First of all, he knew a great deal about the task of organizing programs locally. He had been in the United Automobile Workers for a long time; he knew how to organize unions, which is normally from the grassroots up. He believed in "participatory democracy." So that was one big factor.

Secondly, he was known as a person here on the Washington scene who knew how to get things done in Washington. He had lots of contacts in the Congress; he had lots of contacts in the labor union movement; he had lots of contacts within the executive branch. That was another very strong factor in his favor.

Third, he was well respected, highly regarded by the people who had been working on the anti-juvenile delinquency effort. He had credentials, credibility, with Bobby Kennedy, the attorney general; with Dick Boone; with Dave Hackett; and [with] others who were devoted to the effort which they had been making through the Committee on Juvenile Delinquency, or through the office concerned with juvenile delinquency. They trusted him and believed that he would be a good leader of the community action effort.

A veteran of the labor movement, Jack Conway served from 1946 to 1961 as administrative assistant to Walter Reuther, president of the United Automobile Workers. After working in Kennedy's 1960 campaign, Conway joined the administration as deputy administrator of the Housing and Home Finance Agency. He served as director of the Community Action Program from October 1964 to February 1965, and as deputy director of OEO from February to October 1965. Conway, a native of Detroit, graduated from the University of Chicago in 1940.

If you were to characterize the thinking of the people that you drew together, how would you?

CONWAY: They were young activists, smart as hell. They took the essential objective of the program and put it into action.

Some of these people—Hackett and perhaps Boone and Tolmach and Horowitz—were around from the very start of the task force. Did they sense that there had been a transformation, or was the formulation of the program proceeding as it had from the beginning?

CONWAY: There was a break. All the planning and stuff that led up to the drafting of the legislation that was submitted by the president was one period. What happened after the president submitted the legislation and the law was passed and put on the boards is another period. I was not associated with the first one. I was associated with the second one.

David Hackett had almost nothing to do with the Community Action Program. He was part of the earlier thing because he was on the Juvenile Delinquency program. Eric Tolmach was a stray dog in the sense he had been a reporter with the Newhouse newspapers. He was over in the Labor Department. I don't know whether they knew what to do with him or something. Maybe he rubbed Moynihan the wrong way, I don't know. But I was asked could I absorb him in[to] the staff. I forget who asked me. I put him in the labor training staff, and he fit nicely, no problems at all. He was with some mature people. As far as I was concerned, he was just a nice guy that did what he was expected to do, carried out his job well, no problems with him, didn't have any serious influence in the scheme of things. Boone, yes, very important man. Fred Hayes, yes, very important man.

There is some continuity there.

CONWAY: Not Hayes, he was a new guy. I brought him in new. One of the reasons I made the switch is that I felt that it was important that there be a break and that people not carry out things that they had considered their own.

Dick [Boone] had been the captain in the police force. [He] was a pragmatic street guy, he thought, an operator. But he was a good idea man. Instead of having him head up the field operations, which would have been more of the same, I brought him over into the idea side. And I took Fred Hayes, who had been handling the program development in the planning period, and put him in charge of operations. It was an actual switch in the sense of they were doing something they had never done before, and it worked beautifully. Temperamentally, they took to the assignments, and in many ways Boone, as an operator, had a chance to look over the shoulder of Hayes, the planner, who was operating, and vice versa. They kept each other honest. They both reported to me, and we were a team of three. When I added Brendan Sexton as the fourth person in charge of the training side of it, we had a top team.

HAYES: Jack made it clear almost from the beginning that he wanted Dick and me to work with him. Conway said he had a long debate with himself, but only on which function Dick should serve and which I should serve. He decided that Dick should be responsible for research and demonstrations and that I should manage operations. I was a little surprised. Neither of the two positions I had held in URA had anything to do with urban renewal program operations. I was then running the open space and planning grant programs, and earlier I had been responsible for policy planning, research, and demonstration projects. But after both reflection and experience, it seems quite clear to me that Conway was right. I had gone to URA because of my interest in urban problems, but my experience there, as Conway knew, had increasingly turned me toward problems of management and organization. On the other hand, Dick had decided advantages for the research and demonstration job because of his long involvement in poverty-related problems and his wide acquaintanceship among the most insightful people in the field.

Moynihan asserted in Maximum Feasible Misunderstanding *that after the legislation was submitted, the original task force members returned to their various departments and the most forceful community action advocates presided over a radicalizing of the community action structure.*

HOROWITZ: What would and what would not be a radical view of community action? But assuming you came to terms with that, I don't know that I would agree with that description exactly. People returned to their agencies, but I don't know that if they had not returned to their agencies, anything would have been different. I mean, there was a concept, and that concept took hold. It was written as faithfully as possible into the bill as we could do it. So I don't know that it took later concerted effort [by] a narrow little band of people then somehow to turn it into something that it wasn't designed to be in the future.

You drafted the community action provisions; therefore you saw the way it was when it was submitted to Congress. You are also one of the people Moynihan alludes to as having presided over the radicalization.

HOROWITZ: Yes. I don't know what to make of that, because we left before anybody turned it into an agency. I have to be very careful here. I cannot testify to what actually went on in OEO when the group that started to run Title II [took over]. What happened when that occurred, I have no information. But my comment would be that I don't know that anything that happened thereafter was contrary to the original conception. Maybe the point is that people really tried to do what the legislation said, and that that came as a surprise to a lot of people. That's possible.

MANKIEWICZ: We thought about the poor in the United States at least in many ways as an underdeveloped society. Now, that was rather primitive and maybe inaccurate, but I think Pat Moynihan is wrong. I don't think much of what he says is wrong, but I think he is wrong when he says that this concept of community action as an essentially revolutionary activity was not understood by the people who drafted it or by the OEO. It was pretty clearly understood by us.

CONWAY: I didn't even enter the picture until after the other task force was dissolved and until after the legislation had been sent up. I was in charge of the "Chevrolet division of the General Motors Corporation."[8] And whatever happened, I'm responsible for. The fellows that worked with me—Boone, Kravitz, Hayes, etc.—were working under my direction to design and implement a community action program. Nobody told me "you can't do this" or "you can't do that," or "this isn't what we planned." I took the law as it was passed, I took the objectives as they were very clearly set out, and we designed a program and put it on the boards and hit it with as strong a mule kick as we could. Now if that's radicalizing it, that's what we did.

Did you foresee the degree of conflict between the Community Action Program and local government and local establishments?

CONWAY: I'd have to say yes to that. But the conflict was isolated. It was in a few places, not many places. In most places, the program got off the ground smoothly and with enormous good results right away. It was a very exciting, very—and it was only in Syracuse, New York, and Chicago and Mississippi and a few places like that where the cutting edge of the conflict was.

HAYES: Moynihan has been among the most insightful observers of the social and urban problems of our time, but in this case the misunderstanding is his. As I remember, he built his case on a critique of the views of Lloyd Ohlin and the authors of Mobilization for Youth. There is no point in commenting on the merits of that critique, since—contrary to Moynihan's assumption—the Ohlin-MFY position had, for all practical purposes, no influence on the administration of CAP. [Also,] there was very little change in the basic cadre working on CAP between the submission of the legislation and the beginning of operations.

The statutory requirement for "maximum feasible participation," the only radical aspect of community action, was not intended to be so. Those of us involved in the drafting of the legislation can be criticized for our blindness to its potential for controversy and trouble, but neither the White House nor the Congress [was] any more prescient. We were inclined to regard the appointment of poor people or their representatives to program governing bodies or advisory committees as a more symbolic than substantive form of participation and were taken by surprise when representation emerged as a furiously contested issue. We were much too slow in recognizing the need for OEO guidelines setting the proportion of governing body seats to be allocated to the poor.

The implementation of the participation requirement raised a storm of protests from the mayors, but OEO administrative policies and practices, contrary to general belief, were consistently conservative. OEO, throughout its history, assumed that the CAAs [community action agencies] would and should be organized under the aegis of local government. There was not a single case in which OEO rejected a government-sponsored applicant in favor of a competing private group. Moreover, there was not a single instance in which OEO supported demands by representatives of the poverty areas for a controlling voice in the CAAs.

OEO funds for over 1,500 local community action umbrella agencies covered perhaps 10,000 to 15,000 individual projects and programs. I would doubt that any projects or programs of a clearly revolutionary or politically radical character survived OEO review. The only even arguably radical projects approved by CAP arose from a handful of controversial research and demonstration grants to organizations other than CAAs.

Do you think that Conway had different or more radical ideas about community action?

HAYES: No, definitely not. Jack Conway was a liberal, even something of an idealist, but he was very practical and politically realistic. He saw the Community Action Program as depending upon the cooperation of all of the different entities involved. He repeatedly used the analogy of the three-legged stool, although the rest of us tended to become confused in identifying the specific legs.

Local government being one?

HAYES: Yes, local government was definitely one of the legs of the Conway stool. Jack's basic notion of consensus and participation was realized in the many CAAs organized on the basis of an agreement negotiated by the city government, the school system, representatives of poverty neighborhoods, sometimes one or more county governments, and, often, private social service agencies. I called them "treaty organizations," for obvious reasons.

Jack saw the Community Action Program as a means of bringing the attention of the public in communities all over the country to the problems of poverty, problems that most people, in Jack's opinion, were only barely aware even existed. He said: "If they give us three years with this program, we'll put a rivet on the conscience of this country they'll never take off."

4

EMPLOYMENT VERSUS POVERTY

REDUCING POVERTY THROUGH *employment programs was the "road not taken" by the War on Poverty. The emphasis on community action and the creation of the Shriver task force were clear indications that the program was not going the way that Secretary of Labor Willard Wirtz had hoped. Budgetary constraints alone were sufficient to defeat Wirtz's proposal for a massive job-training and job-creation program. The issue arose at a cabinet meeting in March 1964. When Shriver and Wirtz unveiled Wirtz's proposal for a $1.25 billion employment program funded by a five-cent tax on cigarettes, the president merely ignored the suggestion.[1] If the president's rejection of the employment initiative in favor of a new antipoverty agency was a slight to the turf-conscious Wirtz, allowing the new agency to run its own youth training program, the Job Corps, was an affront. The only concession to the Labor secretary was that his department would administer the Neighborhood Youth Corps, a more limited program which would provide local training and funds to keep low-income students in school.*

The best-known antecedents of the Jobs Corps were the Depression-era Civilian Conservation Corps (CCC) and the National Youth Administration. In 1958 and 1959, Senator Hubert Humphrey sponsored legislation to revive CCC as a Youth Conservation Corps, which would employ 150,000 boys, ages 16 to 21, on state and federal conservation projects. Although Humphrey's proposal passed the Senate (by a narrow margin), the House took no action. The Kennedy Administration added Humphrey's initiative to its legislative agenda and broadened his measure to include job training as well as conservation work. Again, however, the legislation stalled in the House.[2]

The creation of the Job Corps reflected the expansiveness of the task force's planning. Corporate executives were asked to lend their expertise in training programs; and the military was drafted to provide logistical support, although a larger role for the military, actually operating the program, was rejected in favor of civilian control. Shriver hoped to enhance the program's prestige and emphasize its educational mission by naming a university president as the program's director. He persuaded the president of Ohio University, Vernon Alden, to head the Job Corps planning effort. Alden was involved only part time, however, and ultimately the demands of launching the new program became more than he could manage.[3]

The people most obviously excluded from participation in the Job Corps were women: as proposed, the program provided only for young men. This omission would be remedied as soon as the measure reached Congress and Representative Edith Green of Oregon, a powerful member of the House Education and Labor Committee.

Task force planners had serious doubts that the Labor Department's U.S. Employment Service could function as an effective recruiting mechanism for the Job Corps. The poor were simply not the focus of the network of state employment offices. Fearing even greater concessions if Wirtz appealed to the president, however, the poverty warriors accepted a compromise which allowed them to supplement the employment service's recruitment with their own initiatives.[4]

"OUR CHARM SCHOOL"

MANKIEWICZ: By the second or third night [of task force meetings], we were talking about employment programs, our "charm school." It was a thought that we had had for some time. It went to the whole question of the fact that the establishment, in a sense, was responsible for a lot of the problems of poverty, and one of them was that people who didn't fit the established culture didn't tend to get jobs. We thought that one thing could be done: there should be some money for an educational program to, in effect, teach people how to apply for a job. If you can't beat them, join them. We called it a "charm school," which was unfortunate. It made the Labor guys very mad. I think it made them mad because it suggested, in the first place, a kind of class bias which they felt was directed against them, but I think really it made them mad because it was a way in which members of minority groups would be able to get jobs and probably that way get into the union. Nothing was more likely to get the building trades mad than the suggestion that they might have to put up with some black members.

Jack Howard worked as a labor reporter for the San Francisco Chronicle *before going to Washington as a congressional fellow in the late 1950s. He joined the staff of the House Government Information Subcommittee in 1960, worked in Kennedy's presidential campaign, and in 1963 became executive assistant to the undersecretary of Labor. As the official in charge of all poverty planning in the Labor Department in 1964, Howard was assigned responsibility for administering the Neighborhood Youth Corps.*

HOWARD: Philosophically, Wirtz felt that training and jobs and minimum wage were much more fundamental to increasing employment and defeating recession than investment and tax credits. His fundamental position was the full-employment philosophy: that is, that certainly the earnings from jobs and resultant tax revenues, etc., etc., the resulting shift of people off unemployment and off welfare—that all of that made much more sense than practically anything else, including community action. Hence, the whole manpower program that had just come in a couple of years before and the intense attempt within the Labor Department—in which we were doomed to fail—to convert the [U.S.] Employment Service [USES] into a useful bureaucracy.

YARMOLINSKY: One of the choices we said we had to make was whether to concentrate on preparing jobs for people or preparing people for jobs. We decided for the latter, partly because we thought that the president's tax cuts would in effect be job-creating, partly because we thought it takes more time to prepare people for jobs than jobs for people, and I guess partly because we didn't see where we'd get the money for the job part.

But the minority view, as represented by Bill Wirtz in the Labor Department, was always there. At the last minute, we put in this notion of the job program, which was hedged about with some protective devices to keep it from being an employment security program for the Union of Operating Engineers, who said they had to be low-paying, unskilled jobs. There had to be a certain percentage of people from the area where the work was going on and so forth. But we really had not thought it through. It appeared as an afterthought.

Then Shriver presented it, and the president said no. Then Bill Wirtz spoke up at the cabinet meeting—this was the one that Shriver took me along to, so I was there—and said, "Mr. President, we really need something like this." The president just ignored him. It was a shocking demonstration of the way Johnson sometimes handled things. He didn't even bother to respond; he just went on to the next item on the agenda.

Wirtz, because he was in the labor business, wanted the program to provide jobs. That was point one. And we had made the decision that that was not going to be our order of priorities. Second, Wirtz, I have to say, even more than being concerned about substance, was concerned about turf. He was a very jealous bureaucrat in this as in many things. The stories about Wirtz's temperament are legion. He would much have preferred to run the whole poverty program, and if he wasn't going to run the whole thing, he certainly wasn't going to let Shriver run any piece of it that might go in the Labor Department.

There were two fights: one was over the Neighborhood Youth Corps, and the other was over whether the United States Employment Service would be used for the Job Corps, or whether the Job Corps would run its own recruiting program. I insisted—I think successfully, as I recall, and maybe I'm dreaming—that we couldn't accept the statements of the Labor Department that they would beef up and rejuvenate the USES, but that the best way to do that would be for us to have a competing activity, in Rooseveltian fashion. So I believe we won on that one.

MERRICK: [Wirtz] certainly thought the Labor Department should run what became the Neighborhood Youth Corps—and unfettered by somebody else telling him [what to do]. He certainly felt that the Labor Department should be the central figure in the Youth Conservation Corps. That's the thing that I had been working on. Certainly that much.

Did he see the Job Corps as something that would detract from the Youth Conservation Corps?

MERRICK: Yes, I'm sure that he thought that the Job Corps was just another name for Youth Conservation Corps. The idea of having the Job Corps operate in places like Camp Kilmer, rather than out in the woods somewhere, were alterations in program content which could have been accomplished, calling it Youth Conservation Corps. I think "Job Corps" is just a name that probably was invented with the idea of getting away from the notion that it was just another CCC [Civilian Conservation Corps]. I'm sure that Wirtz felt strongly that the Labor Department should not be divested of that piece.

I did go to one meeting of the task force, and I think this was done because at some point where Wirtz thought that Moynihan was giving the safe away to the enemy, he insisted that perhaps I should be there to talk about the Youth Conservation Corps and have my input as to why it should be in the Labor Department. And I went. This was eight or ten people in the room, and what I did when I got there was to explain the product of our planning activity, which had really gotten quite advanced. I had had regular meetings with people in Agriculture and Interior as to how the interrelationships—complicated, obviously—would work. I discussed what kinds of planning activities I had conducted. I might just as well have saved my breath, because I think most of the decisions had been made.

The philosophy that OEO should run it may have been based on its notion that existing departments were not focusing on the poor. Was the Labor Department focusing on the poor at this point?

MERRICK: I think the Labor Department, with my preparations for handling the Youth Conservation Corps and preparations for handling the Neighborhood Youth Corps, was prepared to focus on the poor. We didn't have programs that especially did—although there was probably a mistaken perception that if we really wanted to focus on the poor, we'd get the Employment Service to do it more. But the Employment Service is a strange beast of state control. The Labor Department has very limited political capacity to make everything happen in the Employment Service. As a matter of fact, the operating incentives in the employment problem really push the Employment Service to give the "poor" a lower priority. The Employment Service's role is to get people into jobs. Inevitably, it's much easier to get jobs for employable people than those who are less employable. So if you're going to have any success story at all, any reason for existence, you'd better get people jobs. How to get "very difficult to employ" people employable and employed is going to take more than the Employment Service, try as it might. The point is that it was fashionable to talk down the Labor Department on the basis of the reputation of the Employment Service.

SCHLEI: The initial draft of the bill, as it came out, struck Willard Wirtz as very drastically skewed toward the point of view of HEW and away from his, and he was quite angry. I think he was personally angry at me. I had difficulty at first even understanding what was bothering him because, of course, I had no bias of any kind whatsoever. I was simply trying to reflect what I had heard and my own thoughts as to how it should be refined and brought along. But he felt that the terminology was the kind of terminology HEW would use, and it would not really appeal to his labor constituency. At some point, we did go through the bill and attempt to change the terminology. In some respects, I'm sure the changes were substantive, but in a great many respects the changes were simply to use terminology that would be more understandable and would touch the concerns of the people that Willard Wirtz was trying to represent.

For example, I think in the initial draft of the bill we called this thing the Human Resources Development Agency, or something like that, which was a name that I had coined. Willard Wirtz thought that was terrible. So it ultimately became known as the Economic Opportunity Act. What became the Job Corps was initially named something else, but it came to be called the Job Corps because that was a term that was more reflective of the problems that the Labor Department's constituents wanted to see addressed by the bill.[5]

Do you recall Wirtz's efforts to get the program in the Labor Department, and why he lost that struggle?

SCHLEI: I remember that he was fit to be tied in that first meeting that was held after our first full-fledged draft of the proposed statute was circulated. He had gone to some early meetings, and he thought it was on track. And he didn't come around for a month. Then he saw this proposal, and it had taken obviously many turns that he was not sympathetic with. He was very angry; he was very upset. There were various substantive things he objected to, and there were all these coloring items that he thought were bad also. We came very close to having him so alienated that he just was going to start publicly throwing bricks at the whole thing.

I did speak to him privately and tried to reassure him that nobody was trying to run around him or do anything behind his back or anything like that.

Did the president side with Shriver or Wirtz in delegating the Neighborhood Youth Corps to the Labor Department?

WEEKS: There was not so much an argument on that, because when you came right down to it, there really wasn't an option for the poverty program to run the Neighborhood Youth Corps. It would have created such a fracas at a time when we had plenty of other fracases going that we didn't need one. And it would have created a situation that clearly wouldn't have worked. It wouldn't have worked politically; it wouldn't have worked bureaucratically inside the government. So I regarded it as one of those things in which there's a fair amount of argument going along, but in which everybody knows what the answer is going to be if you really sit down and look at it and say, "Hey, are you really going to have a situation in which you have a poverty program in which the Labor Department has no role whatsoever? That's silly."

Do you recall any particular meetings in which Shriver and Wirtz went to the president?

WEEKS: There were meetings in about the first week of March. I was aware of what was going on, but I was not deeply involved. Wirtz had basically gone to the president and said, "Hey, this whole poverty thing is getting out of hand. What you really ought to do is maybe establish a coordinating committee or an overall cabinet committee for the poverty program or something like this. But this idea of setting up a separate agency and having them running programs is really off the wall." Shriver and Wirtz basically were called over to see the president to resolve that question. And I guess I would say, if it was resolved in anybody's favor, it was resolved in Shriver's favor. Shriver said, "Hey, look, Mr. President, you asked me to pull together a poverty program. A poverty program can't be just a cabinet committee or something like that if you want to be serious about it." And he's right.

HOWARD: I know we certainly agreed to the whole Job Corps thing with great skepticism. It was a source of irritation as long as I was in the operation.

Why was it so regarded?

HOWARD: Well, there are real reasons, and then phony reasons. First of all, we were annoyed as hell from the bureaucratic point of view that the person running Job Corps was, I think, a presidential appointee class 5, or something of that sort, for a much smaller program than we were doing. Secondly, they had an enormously higher per capita expenditure rate. They could just do anything they wanted. Thirdly, they hid all their figures, so that for the first couple of months the dropout rate was camouflaged. Fourthly, we felt that fundamentally it was bad policy to pick up kids from Harlem and put them out in Oregon. We felt that that magnified the separation from home, what little support they might have gotten from home, but at least from peers and so forth. It invited all the racial problems, and it was a disaster, and it was fantastically expensive.

I mean, the transportation costs and all that kind of crap. We thought it made much more sense, if you're going to put them into a camp situation, to do it much more closely to home, where there are weekend possibilities, where there are family possibilities, where there is a greater similarity in culture and all that kind of stuff. So that all of this, plus the heavy PR that was devoted to the Job Corps and the parallel hold-down on our own [Neighborhood Youth Corps] operations—we saw this as the favored program that was laying a big egg. And so we had a great deal of bitterness on it.

REVIVING THE CIVILIAN CONSERVATION CORPS

Vernon R. Alden was president of Ohio University when he was asked by Shriver to direct the planning effort for the Job Corps. He agreed to a part-time commitment in order to continue in his university office, which he held until 1969. He was one of the organizers of the Young Presidents Organization. Alden, who was born in Chicago in 1923, served in the navy during World War II. He received his M.B.A. from Harvard Business School.

ALDEN: [The conservation projects] were part of our very early discussions. We read a lot of material on the CCC and their useful projects, such as cleaning up the country and improving the national parks, etc. Not knowing much about the CCC, I was impressed with what the program had accomplished. I felt that taking kids out of Harlem, Watts, or the Hough District of Cleveland and into a national park or the wide open spaces of the United States would be a very good element of the program. The conservation corps aspect was included from the very beginning of our discussions.

J. Baker: Certainly the Forest Service experience in the CCC camp was dug right out of the files, used by our part of Job Corps....The Forest Service and I had recommended, and President Kennedy had sent up, and the Congress approved, something called Youth Conservation. In the way of psychology instead of logic, this got into the picture too: there was a deep belief on our part, which many of the urban types didn't agree with, that there was something about just living out in the woods and doing hard work on nature things that helped to rehabilitate the human soul. We had a real belief that that was true of CCC. We kept telling ourselves but never did really believe that the [Job] Corpsmen were a different clientele than the CCC was, so that the lessons of CCC couldn't be bridged perfectly across to Job Corps. Every effort was made [to get Job Corpsmen who were] people off the bottom rungs. CCC was anybody that was unemployed. This was everybody up to and including the banker's son in most of your small towns around the country.

The Job Corps planners would argue that there was a need to get these young people out of their environment because the environment was part of what was impairing their advances to begin with.

HOWARD: We dismissed that as just being part of the rationale for using the camps. One of the problems is, they had to use camps where they existed. They had to use agriculture and forestry camps and places; they couldn't start from scratch. To a degree, one of the rationales was, that's why they're all in the west, because they had all these ex-CCC camps. What's a good rationale for that? Well, we have to get them out of their environment. I could invent any kind of thing you want. There were good folks over there. I'm not just saying that they're totally misguided. I just think that that wasn't the real reason. They're getting out of the environment, that's true. But then, when you end up with race riots in Oregon and other northern cities and problems down in Texas, you just begin to wonder, what kind of environment are we putting them into? So I don't think that was satisfactory. I would think it would take much more sophisticated screening and selection than the Job Corps people had to identify those who could benefit from a transcontinental environmental change, and they didn't operate on that basis. They had quotas, and they had everything else to fill. So that I just don't accept that. And I've got some bad things to say about my own program too. Don't get me wrong.

REACHING THE POOREST OF THE POOR

HAMILTON: One of the better lines, which I have quoted repeatedly since, was in one of the early discussions of the Job Corps. The issue was how to tackle the really hard-core unemployed, almost untrainable young people, and get them back on the ladder of economic development, as the expression was. How to get them on the bottom rung, and did we try for that? Did we try to tackle the problem of real hard-core poverty, or did we take the easier cases who just happened to be suffering from a much more superficial combination of adverse circumstances and give them the little boost that was necessary: the ones that were already motivated, willing, and *only* poor. Somebody—I believe it was Vern Alden in a meeting on one occasion, in support of the same theory I'm expounding—said that he really felt we ought to start with the "cream of the crap."

That was a philosophy which tended to prevail, for very obvious reasons. You don't go for the most difficult cases first, because your chances of failure— and therefore the failure of the whole program—are greater. You go for areas where your chances of success are greater and hope that once you've gotten the program established, you will learn enough and develop enough of a basis of support to go for the harder cases later. I don't recall funding being an issue.

YARMOLINSKY: It's a characteristic of any social program in which you take the people you can do the most with, but who need it the least. You take the cream off the top. One of our objections to using USES to recruit for the Job Corps was, we figured they would "cream." I don't know whether we used that word at the time. But they had over the years and decades become adept at finding jobs for middle-class people, who were the ones who needed them least; and not good at all at finding jobs for poor people, who needed them most. If they did the recruiting for the Job Corps, they would give us nice middle-class kids who really weren't the ones who needed it. But whether we were reaching down below the run-of-the-mill poverty person to the real poorest of the poor, I can't tell you whether we thought that's what we were going to do.

THE ROLE OF THE MILITARY IN THE JOBS PROGRAM

YARMOLINSKY: I determined early on that the thing that the Department of Defense was best at was housing, clothing, feeding, training, moving people; and in the Job Corps we tried to use them that way as much as we could despite the anguished cries of knee-jerk liberals. And the department was perfectly willing to be used that way, provided they got reimbursed. We said, "Yes, you'll get reimbursed, so don't worry about it."

The people that came crying that this was a bad thing couldn't persuade me, and they couldn't persuade Shriver, and they couldn't persuade Moyers, and they didn't have a focus in the Congress. So I was able to say, "I hear what you're saying, but I think you're wrong, and we're not going to do it that way."

But wasn't the role of the military greatly reduced in the Job Corps?

YARMOLINSKY: Not in the planning stage. I saw the military as the logistics people, and only the logistics people. Now, it may be that in the rural Job Corps camps, once they got started, that the Interior and Agriculture bureaucracies did battle with the military. I don't know. I was out of it by that time. But in the planning stage, no. I don't think there was any reduction in the original intention.

Initially, when the Job Corps proposal was first going through the task force, wasn't there a plan to have the military play a larger role?

J. BAKER: There was a discussion of two things in regard to the Pentagon. One was that these centers ought to be operated by trained military officers—same argument as had come up thirty years earlier with CCC.

The other had to do with the draftees who couldn't cut it—this program of [Defense Secretary Robert] McNamara's where he was trying to rehabilitate draftees that they got that either psychologically or mentally or [by their] educational background or so forth couldn't cut it in the military. Somehow these could be filtered into the Job Corps centers, or the two programs could operate parallel. I never was in on the top-level fighting over that, except that, along with Orville Freeman and I guess a lot of the rest of the more liberal civilians, we didn't want the military to get their dirty paws on it, in [two senses]. One is that they were losing an awful lot of liberal support for the Job Corps if they looked on it as a training for World War III. Then [there was] a great deal of liberal feeling that the background of an infantry officer doesn't necessarily teach him how to rehabilitate people from the lowest rungs of society.

But hadn't the military also worked with CCC?

J. BAKER: Oh, yes. As I recall, the actual commanders of the camps were military officers. Some of the boys who graduated with me from high school instead of going up to the University of Arkansas went halfway through CCC camp. One of my closest friends, a guy by the name of Leonard Zimmer—[he] was the head of a big office machine repair outfit in Kansas City and has been for years now—won the "golden football" in high school, and he went up to CCC camp, and that's where he got his college education, CCC camp. If I recall, his commander was an army captain. Some of them were lieutenants, first lieutenants. According to where the CCC camp was located, the number two man would be either a Forest Service person or what is now called a Soil Conservation Service person.

But [in] the Job Corps, there wasn't any military around. That might have overcome some of those early logistical problems. But I haven't given much thought to how it would have turned out differently if they'd used the military instead of civilians.

VERNON ALDEN'S ROLE IN PLANNING THE JOB CORPS

ALDEN: I was invited in the winter of 1964 to Hawaii to speak at a convention. It seemed like a marvelous quasi-vacation, because I had been going at my job eighteen hours a day, seven days a week. I looked forward to giving my speech and relaxing on Waikiki Beach for four or five days. I had given my speech and had been on the beach no more than half an hour when I was paged for a call from the White House. I picked up the phone, and after a long wait President Johnson came on with an invitation to fly immediately to Washington. Then he said, "I'd like to have Mr. Shriver explain what this is all about." Sargent Shriver said, "We want to talk to you about being part of an exciting new program we're developing." I replied, "Well, yes, I can be in Washington next week sometime." Shriver said, "What do you mean, next week? We expect you tomorrow." I said, "I had planned to stay here a little bit longer." He said, "No, you've got to come right away. After all, it's the president of the United States inviting you."

So I got on a plane and flew all the way back to Washington and then sat around a day and a half waiting to be seen by Lyndon Johnson and Sargent Shriver. They said they wanted me to drop everything at the university immediately and come to Washington to chair the task force planning the Job Corps portion of the War on Poverty. I responded, "Look, I've been at this university only two years, and we have a number of very substantial programs just beginning. I just can't run out on people." Shriver said, "Well, maybe you can be part of the task force for a period of time, and then you'll be able to leave and join us full time." I replied, "That's not possible. I really doubt whether I can take any time at all, even spending a day or two a week in Washington."

Sargent Shriver then flew down to Florida and talked to the chairman of the Ohio [University] board, who was John Wilmer Galbreath, not the John Kenneth Galbraith from Harvard. Shriver told him that it would be important to the university that I chair the task force. John Galbreath called me and said, "You know, I think this will be difficult for the board of trustees and for the people of Ohio to accept, being as conservative as they are. But if you feel that you really want to do it and should do it, I think the board would okay your going there for maybe a couple of days a week for the next three months or so." He went on to say, "I gather from what you said to Shriver that there's no way that you'd leave the university to take on the full-time responsibility as head of the Job Corps." I said, "That's true. I will make whatever inputs I can to the task force, and I will do those things that Mr. Shriver described to me, but obviously, I am not going to be a candidate for the directorship of the Job Corps."

So I flew to Washington a couple of days a week for a period of about three months. I would get up about five in the morning, fly to Washington, work all day long, talk with Shriver until well in the evening, and then work all the next day before flying back to Ohio late at night.

I would guess that the reason Sargent Shriver asked me to become involved was that I had gone to the Harvard Business School and worked there on the faculty and in the administration for twelve years. I also served on some corporate boards and knew the business community very well while being a member of the academic community. He apparently wanted somebody who was comfortable in both worlds, because the Jobs Corps looked to him to be a combination of the practicality of business with the research and teaching inputs that the academic world could give.

Do you recall what President Johnson said to you at that first meeting and the circumstances of the meeting?

ALDEN: It was not a long meeting. It was in the so-called Fish Room. With the president were Mr. Shriver and a black man. I've forgotten his name, but I don't think he ever became a member of the task force. He probably was a visitor whom the president was trying to impress with his plans for the War on Poverty. President Johnson reminisced about his youth, his teaching experiences, and his very early concern for poor people. He said that he had been dirt-poor himself, that he had always wanted to do something for poor folks. He went on to say that he had talked with Sargent Shriver about a program that would eradicate poverty in our lifetime. He described various elements of it—community action,

Sargent Shriver and Vernon Alden at a Job Corps meeting, April 1964.
RG-490-GC-8119-36, *National Archives Still Picture Unit*

the VISTA volunteers, and a job-oriented program that would be modeled after the CCC camps, only they would be better. He spoke in generalities. It was a brief meeting, and then I went off with Sargent Shriver to the first building we occupied.

I did not get too deeply into the detailed planning of the Job Corps camps or the logistical work that had to be done with the Departments of Defense or Labor. Bob McNamara and Pat Moynihan were both friends of mine from Harvard days, so in the initial meetings I took our small team over to talk with them. But then John Carley or Wade Robinson or other members would carry on the day-to-day detail work with their staffs. I perceived my role—and I assumed that Sargent Shriver agreed—as an outreach to the business and academic communities. I also knew several leading sports figures who could help us make the Job Corps camps attractive to young people. I spent some time running around the country talking to business leaders, to academics, to the press, inviting them to share their ideas with the task force.

Many Republican-oriented businessmen were skeptical of the War on Poverty. I visited several business leaders, trying to explain that the Job Corps was practical, businesslike, and focused on the problem of poverty. I shall never forget my interview with Neil McElroy, the chairman of Procter & Gamble. Because he was a graduate of Harvard and the Harvard Business School, I thought that he would be one of the more understanding and liberal businessmen. I was wrong. I argued, "Do you have any idea how much money we're spending on kids who have dropped out of school, have gotten into lives of crime, and are now locked up in prisons or detention homes? We are spending millions, even billions of dollars on these lost kids. What if we had a program that would take unemployable youngsters out of predominantly black neighborhoods, or hollows of Appalachia, and first of all bring them up to a decent condition of health, then give them some basic skills, so that they could at least read and write and learn how to use a telephone or cash a check—just those elementary skills that we take for granted? Now, what if we were able to take these kids out of their dead-end environments and, as Lyndon Johnson said, no longer give them a 'handout' but give them a 'hand-up'? What if a million of them could be made employable, find jobs, and have spending money? How much more Crest toothpaste could you sell? It's a very practical problem. We plan to take these lost youngsters off welfare, out of detention homes, out of dead-end situations, and make them employable."

McElroy's response was, "Well, I've heard from President Eisenhower and others that this is a boondoggle, so that's good enough for me."

But happily enough, there were several businessmen who took an interest, and we set up an advisory board of business leaders. I helped Mr. Shriver put together that list, and we invited them to meet with us from time to time in Washington. They served as an advisory group, but more importantly, they were emissaries to the rest of the business community.

When we began to talk about where the Job Corps camps should be located and who should run them, we discovered early on that academic people wanted to use them as research laboratories. They were looking for grants from us so they could study these kids, like specimens. We were disappointed that few academics had practical ideas for meeting our goal: making unemployable young people healthy, skilled, and useful to society. So we decided that several Job Corps camps would be run by business corporations. There was a business recession in 1964, and in many companies there were sophisticated Ph.D.'s who really didn't have an awful lot to do or were about to be laid off. It occurred to me that running a Job Corps program could be attractive to Xerox, Litton, CBS, or other companies. Looking at the record, some of the best Job Corps camps were run by goal-oriented, well-organized business corporations.

The only times I saw the president were, once, when he initially talked to me briefly about serving. Secondly, one time Representative Gerald Ford [of Michigan] attacked the Job Corps on the floor of the House, calling it a boondoggle and a waste of money. Sargent Shriver was told about it by Wilson McCarthy. I happened to be in Sarge's office at the time, so he grabbed me and said he was going over to the White House right away to talk to the president. We were ushered into the president's office, and Sarge was hopping mad about Gerald Ford's attack. That's when the famous statement was made: "Don't worry about Gerald Ford, because he can't fart and chew gum at the same time." It was polished up and reported as: "Gerald Ford can't walk and chew gum at the same time." Maybe the president said it again in a different context, but I was in the office when he said that, trying to calm down Shriver.

We were concerned that the public would think that this was a program only for black kids, for ghetto kids. So we emphasized in all our speeches that there were hundreds of thousands of young people trapped in the hollows of Appalachia or in other rural areas, and that this was not just a black program; it was a white and black problem. We were afraid also that the public would believe that the Job Corps was designed primarily for youngsters with prison records, [for] juvenile delinquents or drug pushers. We planned to take kids with poor records, but they were not going to be the only ones in the program.

We also talked about the poor health of kids. We discovered that many were going to need an awful lot of remedial work on their teeth, for example. We talked about the number of young people in high schools who could not read at grade-school level. We invited representatives of publishing firms to discuss the teaching tools that would be needed.

Do you know how Otis Singletary was chosen to head the Job Corps?

ALDEN: Otis at the time was [chancellor of the University of North Carolina at Greensboro]. He was not on the original list of people I gave to Sarge. I knew Otis, but I thought it would be impossible to wrest him away from the University of [North Carolina]. I think that Sarge must have gotten his name from one of the representatives or senators from [North Carolina]. Sarge asked me about Otis, and my response was that I thought Otis was a fine fellow but he probably couldn't be persuaded to take the job. But Shriver talked him into it.

Did Shriver feel that the Job Corps director should be a college president?

ALDEN: Yes. Shriver felt all along that the program had to have prestige in the eyes of the public. The Job Corps was not going to be just another outfit where we would get a government veteran from the bureaucracy to run it. He wanted to have the Job Corps identified as an educational opportunity for people. He could have had a school superintendent or a school board member, but I think that Sarge really wanted to give the program a little bit of distinction by saying a university president would run it.

In those days, people were much more in awe of university presidents than they are today.

5

RURAL PROGRAMS

ALTHOUGH JOHN KENNEDY *had been awakened to poverty in the United States when he traveled to the hollows of West Virginia, the President's Task Force on the War against Poverty focused largely on urban areas. Yet the inclusion of rural programs was at least recognized as a legislative necessity, if not a priority.*[1]

The tension between the task force's urban and rural advocates stemmed from a cultural gulf as well as a difference in regional emphasis. The agrarians' recycled New Deal remedies seeemed quaint beside the experimental social engineering proposed by the urbanists. Agriculture's southern orientation alone was sufficient to make some of the eastern liberals suspicious of their counterparts' commitment to racial justice. Yet the task force's rural representatives reflected a long tradition of government action to relieve the plight of poor farmers. It was no accident that a strong dose of populism laced the rural antipoverty proposals which flowed into the legislation.

The bill's provisions for community action, job training, adult education, and small businesses pertained to rural areas as well as cities, but it was Title III that specifically addressed the needs of rural communities. One component, to be administered by the Department of Agriculture, provided for loans to low-income farm families for business initiatives, and for loans to farm cooperatives. This program will be discussed in Chapter 12. Another provision brought aid to migrant farm families in the form of housing, sanitation, education, and child care programs. A controversial "land reform" section, which proposed the creation of farm development corporations to buy land and sell it cheaply to poor farmers, was deleted by Congress. Other significant antipoverty initiatives, including food stamps, water and sewer loans, and the Appalachian Regional Development Act of 1965—which was designed to stimulate economic development in that depressed region of the country—were enacted in separate pieces of legislation.[2]

THE RURAL POOR AS AN AFTERTHOUGHT

SUNDQUIST: When it comes to the solution to the poverty problem, a good many of the urban poverty thinkers have written off the rural areas and have concluded that the only way to deal with rural poverty is to let the people move and then handle them in the cities. Some of this is conscious and some is unconscious, but insofar as it's expressed consciously, the argument is made that only if people come together in cities can you hope to provide them with the public services necessary to make them employable and then provide them with the employment opportunities. Now formally, of course, the Kennedy and Johnson administrations both supported rural development in the Area Redevelopment Act and the Public Works and Economic Development Act and the Appalachia Regional Development Act and in a number of the Agriculture Department measures. But these tended to be looked on by the group that might be called "urban fundamentalists" as gestures, not as serious efforts to stabilize the location of population and deal with poverty where it existed.

It's just the whole nature of our culture. The rural areas are looked on as backwaters. The people who live there are looked on as unenterprising and hardly worth saving, because if they had any gumption, they'd get up and leave. Our culture is thoroughly urban-centered. Our newspapers, our magazines are published, and our radio and television programs originate, in urban centers. If there is any attention to rural areas, it tends to be the kind of treatment that is given the Indians in cowboy-and-Indian shows, as a sort of a relic from the past.

So throughout this period, it was always my fight and my frustration to get some attention paid to the rural areas. In discussions, the topic would always tend to come up as an afterthought. After they had discussed the urban poverty problem and the crisis of the ghettos, then they would say, "Oh, yes, of course, there's also the rural areas." I believe that the weight of economic and intellectual opinion was against programs like Appalachia and Area Redevelopment. Certainly we encountered great resistance to these programs in the Budget Bureau and in the other elements of the Executive Office, other than the political elements. There was a sensitivity in the White House, but not in the career agencies.

The movement of population has been away from rural areas for half a century, quite dramatically. So the assumption underlying so many people's thinking is that this is inevitable and will continue, and therefore why worry about the rural areas, because in a little while they won't be here at all, except for those rich farmers who are being subsidized too much already. This was part of the difficulty we had in putting through the community facilities measures, the water and sewer system development. The attitude in the Budget Bureau at the point where these were buried was that, "Well, this is just throwing money down the drain, because these communities are withering away. It's apparent in the statistics." We tried to say that this was a confusion of cause and effect, that they were withering away because they didn't have the basic public services. There were plenty of illustrations of how the population trend itself could be reversed by the provision of basic water and sewer systems that would make these places fit to live in, but we got nowhere until the Congress took the matter in hand itself some years later.

It may not be in the preamble of the act, but it certainly is the underlying rationale for the Appalachian Regional Commission—that is, to improve the areas in order to keep the people there.

SUNDQUIST: That's right. That's what the area itself wants, of course, and that's why the politicians tend to take that view and have some empathy toward rural areas, because rural areas are filled with voters. But the objective analysts, the cost-benefit economic types, fall back upon a higher wisdom.

I gather that your function when you were detached and became a member of the task force was to press for solutions to rural problems. Is that correct, or did you have a much broader scope?

SUNDQUIST: Well, it was both. My first responsibility was to develop the rural side of the program, and in one of my first conversations with Shriver, I said that what he ought to have was a rural title, because the bill as a whole was bound to be urban-oriented. I told him of the success we'd had in getting housing bills through, omnibus housing bills, by virtue of always having a Title V dealing with rural housing. That was good for quite a number of votes, and when it came on the floor of the Senate or the House, people could look at it and say, "Well, it's a balanced bill. It's predominantly urban, but there is some rural language and an acknowledgment that there's a rural problem." Shriver caught this immediately and, without any significant discussion, said, "Fine, go ahead, we'll do it that way. Draft something." So then I took the best of the material that had bubbled up out of the department in the fall, and we refined that and worked it up and put it in.

Who else besides yourself represented the Agriculture Department on the task force?

SUNDQUIST: Let's pause a minute on that word "representation." It was understood that I was not representing Agriculture. I was part of Shriver's staff and was detached from the department, so that when it came to the question of representation, then John Baker headed that up. He came to meetings representing the department. Working with him were Turley Mace, the head of the Office of Rural Areas Development, and on the Farmers Home Administration items Joseph C. Doherty was the man who came over and sat with me. Doherty developed most of the supporting documentation. All the items that wound up in the bill were Farmers Home Administration proposals.

Everybody there, to the extent he wanted to, kibitzed on everything, so that I had a chance to get my licks in on community action or the Job Corps or whatever it might be. A task force, I guess, is always a fluid kind of organization without any fixed lines of responsibility. Shriver was in no position to discipline anybody, or fire them, because they belonged to somebody else in the first place, and he needed them anyway. So if there was a meeting going on and you walked into the room and began to take part, nobody told you to leave. There were several of us that made it a point to get in on most everything.

The best [rural proposals] were the ones that finally got into the economic opportunity bill, the proposed loans and grants to poor farmers and rural non-farmers to permit them to set up small businesses. We had a community facilities program, sewer and water works for rural areas. Each bureau tended to say, "If we only had more money to do what we're now doing, we could do it much better and reach more poor people." The Extension Service in particular made a strong pitch for inclusion in the program, contending that extension work was essential to helping people help themselves. I remember the Agricultural Conservation and Stabilization Service came up with a proposal for more "ACP"—Aid to Conservation Practices.

A bureau would have to be singularly lacking in self-respect if it couldn't figure out some way that it could participate in this enterprise which the president was leading. We realized that many of the proposals weren't worth much, and we finally put our emphasis on the three that seemed to represent substantial innovations.

The Agriculture Department made a strong pitch for getting the Extension Service programs back in there. The Extension Service is the organization that embraces the county agricultural agents and the county home demonstration agents, which in many communities have lost the adjective "agriculture" and are engaged in a general adult education activity. They have been active in some cities. In Providence, Rhode Island, and Milwaukee, Wisconsin, for example, the state extension service is doing a lot of work with poor people. This involves going into their homes, and in the case of the home demonstration agents, working with them in housekeeping, child-rearing, consumer education, how to buy and how to cook and prepare food, and so on. They've been working in conjunction with the welfare departments in some places. The Extension Service felt that as part of the War on Poverty they could vastly expand their efforts in this kind of work. While they do it on a professional level, it's not unlike what later developed in the poverty program using sub-professional aides.

THE FOOD STAMP PROGRAM

J. BAKER: What turned out later to be one of the largest antipoverty programs in the government at that time was in the process of moving from an experimental demonstration program that Freeman and Kennedy had started by executive order, now called the food stamp plan. I remember right in the middle of one of the task force meetings, when Sarge was by that time chairman—must have been sometime in the late winter or early spring of 1964—one of Sarge's legislative liaison lieutenants came huffing and puffing in and handed Sarge a handwritten note. Sarge read it and looked up at me, and he said, "Well, Congress beat your goddamned food stamp plan." Like he thought, well, the food stamp plan wasn't worth a damn in the first place, and the goddamned rural congressmen had done it in the second place. It took me three or four days after that to climb back up to ground level again, he was so mad.[3]

Was that vote considered a bad omen for the War on Poverty program?

J. BAKER: They were of two minds. It wasn't part of the War on Poverty because it had started the first week Freeman and I were in office. In fact, I think that's the first thing Jack [Kennedy] sent up. Therefore, it was very much a farmers' [program]; really, farmers were wanting to sell more food, even if they had to sell it to poor people. The Ylvisakers and the Yarmolinskys and the Dick Goodwins and the deep-breathers really and Lisle Carter and the rest of them just kind of snarled when they'd think about rural or white southerners, like the president turned into. Anything that came out of the agriculture committees, just like anybody that talks with a southern or southwestern accent, was suspect to those fellows. That was their attitude toward the food stamp plan. It did turn out though to be—gosh, it's a multibillion-dollar thing now.[4] Willard and I knew it was going to be.

THE COMMUNITY FACILITIES PROGRAM

SUNDQUIST: The water and sewer proposals were rather favorably received by Shriver, who tended to look favorably upon any new idea—a very open-minded person. The Budget Bureau took a stand against this. Shriver was reluctant to take it out, and he went along with taking it out only when the Budget Bureau gave him a firm promise to consider it on its merits when it was presented separately. Maybe they considered it on its merits, but it came out in the same place it had before. It was rejected until Senator [George] Aiken [of Vermont] initiated it on the Hill, and then it went through Congress easily.

J. BAKER: What's now called [the] Community Facilities Program was started in the 1930s, again, under the president's emergency [powers], and then was emblazoned in marble by Congress as a water facilities program, still in the 1930s, as primarily a way of loaning money to low-income farmers in the so-called semidesert areas to get irrigation. Then this turned into water for home use as well as irrigation. And the expansion of the Community Facilities Program from its then existing stature was in Kennedy's very first message.[5]

I talked to the guys on the Hill—which I had been working with daily for ten years previous to that—found out what they thought they could pass (that's what I'd urge the White House to put in the message), and get that little bit passed. Then, over a long period of time, that little water facilities program is now a multibillion-dollar community facilities program, with a little add-on every year, as it were.

Actually, we got some simultaneous legislation expanding the Community Facilities Program at that time. Senator Aiken, who was from Vermont, was very strong for getting water out to those dairy farms. Aiken originally wrote up a proposal that this be an added third function to [the] Rural Electrification Administration [REA]. For whatever reason at that time, Norm Clapp and Clyde Ellis felt like they had enough fights on generation and transmission loans to not look like they were trying to expand their [REA] empire. Howard Bertsch [administrator of the Farmers Home Administration] was just drooling to get it. So Bertsch and I went up and talked the old man into saying it would be administered by Farmers Home instead of REA. It went through the Senate as a vastly expanded water distribution loan program of the kind they got now. It got over to the House, and Bob Poage wasn't going to let it rest at that. He added sewer to it. And of course, Howard and I thought that was good too. It passed as a water and sewer loan and grant program.[6] In other words, it's kind of on a separate track. We didn't really fight for it as being part of the OEO, partly because by that time Sundquist had convinced me there wasn't any point in fighting the Ford Foundation crowd and all these human resource deep-breathers.

LAND REFORM

SUNDQUIST: [The land reform scheme] was a proposal to resettle some poor people with farm experience on land of their own. It wouldn't take care of very many people. But particularly in the south, there is a lot of absentee ownership of rather large estates, and as these come on the market, rather than selling them as one piece, the theory was that some kind of governmental corporation would buy them and then divide them into family farms and permit the reestablishment of displaced farmers.[7]

J. BAKER: In the late Truman years and the Eisenhower time, the Congress, mainly as a result of the hearings of the so-called [Rep. Stephen] Pace Committee, had completely removed all of the authority that the Farm Security Administration [FSA] had to buy land and sell it to tenants. When the president's emergency [powers] ran out, we didn't have that authority in the department.

Sometime in the early 1960s, I got the idea that if we would use Title III of the old Bankhead-Jones Farm Tenant Act, which is the submarginal land purchase title—instead of Title I, which was the "helping poor folks" title—that maybe we'd get it back. In 1961, Dr. Orville Scoville, who is now my son's father-in-law, and I went up about seven o'clock in the morning to Senator [Allen] Ellender's office—he was chairman of the Senate Agriculture Committee at the time—to present all of the amendments we wanted to the Bankhead-Jones Farm Tenant Act. He said, "Uh-huh, uh-huh, uh-huh, uh-huh...," and then he sees this thing—I caved in as fast as Sargent did five years later. There wasn't any way to talk that old man into letting the government buy any land that morning.

We decided—Freeman agreed—we'd just put it in the OEO package. Those urban do-gooders, revolutionaries, kind of thought, "Well, good God, the Department of Agriculture didn't recommend something like this." They just bought it without much discussion. LBJ wasn't opposed to it. Hell, coming out of Texas, he thought it was a good thing. The Kennedyites, who were still his staff people at that time, didn't object in the White House. It went sailing up there, and the Republicans and some of the deep-dyed southern reactionaries on the committees—just exactly like the obstacles they tried to throw in our way in Japan and Korea—said, "That's a communist thing." They took out after Sarge, and he folded. That was the end of that.

MIGRANT LABOR

J. Baker: I read a memorandum the other day in which I said that over the years this has been one of the most talked-about and least done-about problems in America: migratory rural workers. There was always a dichotomy. A lot of do-gooders thought what we really ought to do is spend a whole lot of federal money and make living conditions and schools and housing and everything real good for migrant workers. Another point of view was: that's subsidizing a bad system. What the hell would a landowner spend any money to build a good house if the federal government builds a fine dormitory on his vegetable patch? Throughout the fifties, there was a considerable argument among well-meaning people over this one subject.

My position was that what we ought to do is pass regulatory legislation and do other things Willard Wirtz was talking about to make migratory labor unnecessary. In other words, labor-saving machinery, rationalization of agricultural production, and providing other opportunities for these people to drop off the migrant stream seemed like the constructive thing to do.

You've got extremely poor people in Mexico, and now the Caribbean Islands, who even at a substandard minimum wage in the United States make more in a day than they can make at home in a month. From the standpoint of humanity as a whole, why not let them come up here and get some of this? But the other point of view is organized labor saying it undercuts our bargaining power, which it does. It was in the OEO time, and in the pre-OEO time, always this struggle of organized labor not wanting any of them to come in—which, as I understand it, even led to the first immigration acts way back in the twenties— and the conservatives and other kinds of liberals that thought that from a worldwide standpoint one way of helping poor people in Mexico is let them come up here and work at substandard wages.

The worst kind of exploitive capitalist industrial owner in the United States loves to have barefooted men in entries, they used to say in my hometown, a coal-mining town. If you've got enough barefooted men in the entry, you can go tell a guy to go dig that chalk over there whether he likes the looks of the roof of the mine or not. If you haven't got any barefooted men in the entry, you've got to put up with those fellows. That was constantly discussed in the early OEO discussions, these various things.

It's the seasonal nature of agricultural production, of course, that made this so necessary. The reason they're so opposed to strikes and so on, if tomorrow is the day to pick your cucumber crop, the day after tomorrow ain't the time. I mainly served as Freeman's liaison man [to the] secretary of Labor throughout this time on migratory farm workers, largely based, if we possibly could, [on] just giving Wirtz our full support for whatever he came up with was the right thing to do.

I know we didn't give [reform of migrant farmwork] very much visibility, partly because market people and manufacturers like Campbell Soup and the consumer representatives—and I used to argue this with Bill Batt [Jr., administrator, Area Redevelopment Administration] on his Pennsylvania program—they really didn't want to help migratory workers by raising their wages, because that increased the price of Campbell soup and watermelons and everything else. They didn't feel badly enough about the poor migratory worker to be willing to pay higher prices in the grocery store. Maybe out of all that experience, and because the Department of Agriculture was kind of out of the migratory farm labor business by then anyway, we didn't put it in, and I haven't got the faintest idea why Willard Wirtz didn't put it in.

I think maybe we decided the best way to improve the so-called migratory farm worker problem was, instead of attacking it direct as a mandatory income requirement on your so-called users or employers, to do it by eliminating their need for migratory workers in the first place by improved machinery and so forth. And in the second, of making alternative opportunities available to people who were in the migrant stream; [then] the users wouldn't have anybody unless they did pay them a decent wage.

6

THE ENACTMENT
OF POVERTY
LEGISLATION

THE EFFORT TO LEGISLATE *a crusade against poverty could hardly have come at a more opportune moment. The assassination of President Kennedy had imbued the national conscience with a spirit of altruism. President Johnson, whose own popularity was near its peak, had both the instinct and the inclination to make the most of his unique opportunity.*[1]

But timing was not the War on Poverty's only advantage. When the bill was introduced in April 1964, it was assigned to the House Education and Labor Committee, chaired by Rep. Adam Clayton Powell, Jr. This panel, which would handle much of the Great Society legislation, was perhaps the most liberal in the House of Representatives. Although the legislation could be expected to receive sympathetic scrutiny from progressives, Rep. Phil Landrum's sponsorship of the bill in the House made it politically acceptable for conservatives to support it. Landrum, a Democrat from Georgia, had established his own conservative credentials and earned the enmity of organized labor as one of the authors of the Landrum-Griffin Act of 1959.[2]

Did Congress really understand the Economic Opportunity Act of 1964? As with most legislation, only a few members who carried the measure in committee were likely to possess comprehensive knowledge of the details. Moreover, legislators were surely even less familiar with a bill as unconventional as the poverty program than they would have been with more traditional measures. Yet it should be noted that Congress was sufficiently cognizant of specific elements to strike out the most radical section, the "land reform" proposal. Moreover, the Senate subcommittee focused closely enough on the community action program to amend section 202 (a) in an attempt to ensure that local government would not be bypassed and state agencies would be encouraged to participate.[3]

Whether the new agency would have the authority to make grants to private organizations was a primary concern. Representatives with large Catholic constituencies favored giving the agency such authority, while members from predominantly Protestant regions invoked the principle of separation of church and state. The formula for resolving the issue was to allow grants to religious organizations only for secular activities. To ensure that the poverty program's funds would be equitably distributed, Congress added an apportionment formula requiring that OEO grants be allocated in proportion to a state's low-income population (as determined by a combination of statistics). Congress also granted governors the authority to veto Job Corps and Community Action projects within thirty days.[4]

Several provisions in the poverty legislation were designed to ensure that the program did not neglect the rural areas in favor of cities. Title I required that at least forty percent of Job Corps enrollees be assigned to rural camps working on conservation and recreation projects. Within a state, an equitable distribution of community action program funds between urban and rural areas was stipulated. Title III, the principal rural section of the act, provided for loans to local processing or marketing cooperatives and aid for migrant workers; it also contained an irrelevant rider about indemnity payments to dairy farmers as compensation for unsold milk containing pesticides.[5]

A loyalty oath for Job Corps enrollees and VISTA Volunteers was added as an amendment proposed by Rep. John Bell Williams of Mississippi. This provision compelled recruits to swear an oath of allegiance to the United States and required other program recipients to sign an affidavit affirming that they did not advocate overthrowing the government.[6]

Enactment of the poverty program was by no means assured. Although the Johnson Administration pressed Democrats to vote for this election-year measure, Republican opponents were vocal, denouncing it as a "boondoggle," a "hodgepodge of programs," and a "throwback to the 1930s." Concern that a coalition of southern Democrats and Republicans would defeat the bill led Shriver and Johnson to capitulate on Adam Yarmolinsky's involvement in the program. After Landrum's announcement that Yarmolinsky would have no role in the antipoverty initiative, the legislation passed the House on August 8 by a wider margin than expected: 226 to 185.[7]

WORKING THE HILL

C. Robert Perrin joined OEO in March 1966 as assistant director for governmental relations. In this capacity, he served as liaison between OEO and other federal agencies as well as local and state public officials. Perrin—a native of Michigan and a veteran of World War II—graduated from the University of Minnesota and then worked as a reporter for United Press International and the Detroit Free Press, where he became labor editor. In 1955 he moved to Washington to join the staff of Senator Patrick V. McNamara of Michigan. Perrin served as McNamara's administrative assistant until he joined the poverty program. He became acting deputy director of OEO in March 1968.

PERRIN: There's no question that the timing is important. I think that the poverty program is an example of that. It really came into being in those rather awful moments following the Kennedy assassination and the new Johnson administration. One can't really predict what would have happened if Kennedy himself had lived and had proposed this program. I don't think it would have

Lyndon Johnson presents a pen to Sargent Shriver at the White House bill-signing ceremony for the Economic Opportunity Act, August 20, 1964. Robert Weaver, Kermit Gordon, Gale McGee, and Bill Mullins are standing next to Shriver. 341-27-WH64, 8/20/64. *Photo by Cecil Stoughton, Presidential Collection, LBJ Library*

happened, certainly not as fast as it did, because he wasn't really having a great deal of luck with his domestic programs, and something as controversial as this, being added to the others that he was trying to get through Congress—I just don't believe it would have happened. But the timing and circumstances were such that it could happen with Johnson.

YARMOLINSKY: Why did they want it in such a hurry? If you're legislatively oriented, you want to get it up there as soon as possible because one of the easiest ways you can lose legislation is just [to] run out of time, and we were worried about running out of time. Whenever you got a new bill, one of the major worries is, not that it will be defeated, but that it just won't get all the way before the session is over, and then you have to start over again, or half over again. I don't doubt that Johnson wanted it, in part, for the 1964 election. He was so determined to have a landslide that he wanted everything. Johnson always wanted everything.

If anything, we were working harder [after the legislation was drafted], because then we had the job of getting the bill through—which was the thing in which Shriver really showed such extraordinary achievement, skill, imagination, and energy—and the job of putting together the organization so that it would be ready to go once the bill was passed. Identifying the people and settling all these troublesome questions of: How many supergrade authorizations would the agency have? How would they be divided among the various proposed bureaus within the office? Those were all questions that I had to cope with. So I would say we were working harder at the end than we were perhaps even at the beginning.

How important was White House lobbying, which was credited at that time with being so effective in Congress?

YARMOLINSKY: Well, what was terribly effective was to have the master strategist Larry O'Brien and his staff working in daily, hourly cooperation with us. But I think the most important thing of all was Shriver.

LAMPMAN: I accompanied Shriver to the opening hearing at the House Education and Labor Committee. I had, I guess, something to do with drafting some of the things he was going to say or had been saying about that period. I can't remember now who all went, but there weren't too many people from the office who went. But I didn't know Shriver really. I was impressed by how he easily went to the Republican side of the table and apparently knew all these people and had been at Yale Law School with half of them, I guess. [I was impressed] also with how well he seemed to get along with Adam Clayton Powell and the other side of things. What a strange world it is where you get people as diverse as Adam Clayton Powell and Carl Perkins!

Perkins, early on, wanted to know what it was going to do for the water systems in Kentucky. He thought the way to combat poverty was to build and perfect the water systems and sewage systems and so on in rural eastern Kentucky. Not a bad idea, really. And, of course, Adam Clayton Powell had his Harlem youth organization, HARYOU. I think it was a period of a lot of harmony really, and the Republican opposition was not total at least. It was in a compromising kind of mood, it seemed to me.

AN UNLIKELY SPONSOR IN THE HOUSE

Lawrence F. O'Brien, Jr., John F. Kennedy's chief campaign strategist since the early 1950s, became his special assistant for congressional relations in the White House. O'Brien continued in the legislative role for Lyndon Johnson, who appointed him postmaster general in 1965. After serving in the Johnson administration, O'Brien held the positions of chairman of the Democratic National Committee and commissioner of the National Basketball Association. He was born in Springfield, Massachusetts, in 1917.

O'BRIEN: It wasn't a matter of suggesting Phil Landrum; it was a matter of exploring with appropriate members of Congress this concept in its initial stage, getting a feel of attitudes, and finding that Phil Landrum was very receptive. From the outset, he evidenced an interest in the concept.

Were you yourself talking to Landrum?

O'BRIEN: I talked to him; others talked to him; and we agreed, to our utter surprise, that Phil Landrum seemed to be a fellow who not only had an open mind but seemed to be leaning strongly in the direction of a program. We realized that if by any chance Phil Landrum would take the lead in this, it could be just a tremendous plus for us.

Because he was not known for advancing progressive social legislation?

O'BRIEN: That's right. At what moment Landrum agreed, I don't remember. But I recall that labor was disbelieving. I went to the labor headquarters and met with George Meany. I believe Sarge may have been with me. In any event, I talked to George, told him about this coup, and he was disbelieving. Finally, by the time I left his office, he had to conclude one of two things: that I had just lost my head totally, or this was true. Landrum coming aboard in the leadership role was a real blockbuster. If you were to look over the House membership, you'd find he would be among the very last that anybody would ever suggest in this area. But that's what happened, and he stayed consistent throughout.

To what do you attribute his espousal of this legislation?

O'BRIEN: I honestly don't know. All I can say about Landrum [is that] I didn't find him to be the ogre that he was portrayed to be by labor. But I'm talking in human terms, because Landrum was a very pleasant fellow who I enjoyed. That wasn't the case with every member of Congress. I enjoyed my contacts with Landrum. I was leery of him because of his background, Landrum-Griffin. But I must say, I found him a very easy fellow to be associated with.

Whatever his motivation, I know this: there's no way that Phil Landrum would have taken on that task through any effort from the president or anyone else. This would be purely a personal decision on his part. He didn't envision that he would be in that role, but once we realized that he had a basic personal interest in pursuing it, asking him to take on the role was not that difficult. I'm not at all sure George Meany wound up being pleased he was doing it, but I guess he accepted that it would be a significant plus in getting enactment. But I'll never forget that meeting with Meany, because he just was thunderstruck.

Do you think that Landrum's support had to do with the poverty in his own Georgia district?

O'Brien: Probably. Who knows? But I think it's like anything else. We were talking about Lyndon Johnson in that regard. I guess if you've been exposed to this directly in the context of representing people, you probably have a soft spot in your heart, and the day is going to come when the spark will be there and you feel comfortable. It's hard to figure that out in terms of his opposition to labor, but maybe not that hard. Talking about poverty is different than talking about organized labor and its power. It probably wasn't even on the same wavelength, in Landrum's mind.

LBJ'S CONVERSATIONS WITH LAWRENCE F. O'BRIEN

February 10, 1964

O'Brien: I just want to check one item with you on the poverty bill.[8] I've been exploring just how we would hit it committee-wise in the House. Of course, the bill would undoubtedly go to the Education and Labor Committee....Phil Landrum has never taken a position on a subcommittee since [Adam Clayton] Powell's been chairman of that committee. Phil would be awfully pleased to chair a subcommittee given this assignment, and, I think, would do one whale of a job. I have reason to believe at this point that Powell would acquiesce to that. I just wanted to mention it to you, if there's any other thought in your mind. If you think this procedure is okay, I'll follow through on it.

Johnson: Do you think Phil would report it?

O'Brien: Yes, Phil, I think, would enthusiastically work on it. I think it would make a hell of an impact frankly on the floor to have Phil handling it.

Johnson: I think it would on the floor, if he'll handle it. I'm afraid he'd kill it.

O'Brien: Oh no, no. No, I talked to Phil. Phil, I am very confident, would do one whale of a job with it, but we haven't made any decisions on it. I thought at this point that at least you ought to know that we're kind of playing around the fringes of this, because otherwise, I honestly don't know how we would bypass the Education and Labor Committee....I know Phil is enthusiastic, is anxious to do everything he can, if we should travel this route and that off our experience with Phil over the last couple of years, he's been terrific.

JOHNSON: I'd go that way then. I'd talk to Shriver about it.

O'BRIEN: All right.

JOHNSON: That sounds all right to me, if you're sure of Phil.

O'BRIEN: Yes, I would pin that down completely, but at this point, off my conversation with Phil, I firmly believe he would enthusiastically lead the fight on it. He has been, as I say, damn good with us over the last couple of year on a variety of items.

March 11, 1964

O'BRIEN: The general view of labor toward Landrum has changed considerably.[9] There is a recognition of the fact that he, in turn, on the record has changed considerably. Secondly, from the point of view of passage of this bill, obviously, the key people—and Landrum is certainly damn key—have to be considered. This is going to be a damn difficult bill. We're going to have plenty of roadblocks. It's not going to be an easy road. I've been asked for a candid opinion. I have to give it. That is that we just have to do it pretty much the way these people on the Hill feel it should be done in order to accomplish it. It's going to be tough as hell at best.

JOHNSON: Well then, what do you think? Why don't you and Wirtz and Shriver try to see labor before we do this thing, and have somebody sponsor it in the Senate who is clearly pro-labor and have them understand that this is labor's bill and Shriver's bill and the [Bureau of the] Budget's bill. Landrum hasn't put a damn thing in the bill. He's not going to get anything out of it, except we're just going to use him to get it passed.

O'BRIEN: I feel confident we can do it....

JOHNSON: We could go up there and have Jimmy Roosevelt introduce this bill and get it killed, or we could get Landrum to introduce it and get it passed.

O'BRIEN: That's just it.

JOHNSON: We can administer it anyway we want to once we get it passed.

O'BRIEN: That's exactly right. Furthermore, on the Senate side, we'll certainly, from the point of view of labor, be able to have people playing key roles that would be pleasing to them and take any onus that they might feel is on this.

THE HOUSE EDUCATION AND LABOR COMMITTEE

Since the poverty bill cut across various jurisdictions of congressional committees, how was the decision made to refer it to Powell's Education and Labor Committee?

O'BRIEN: The makeup of the committee. I don't recall all the names, but as difficult as Adam was to deal with as the chairman, there were any number of members of that committee whom we could look to quickly.

You look at the Democratic side of that committee, and you see that it's a liberal group. The Republican side would be the normal Republican situation you would run into on any committee. But you had Carl Perkins from Kentucky, for example. There's got to be a spark there too. And Landrum was the big surprise factor. Then Jimmy Roosevelt and Frank Thompson—"Thompy" Thompson was as liberal as he could be—[John] Dent, [Roman] Pucinski, Dom[inick] Daniels, [John] Brademas, and Jim O'Hara, one of the solid, hardworking members of that committee whom we looked to for assistance consistently over the years. You have Hugh Carey, who was emerging as a very bright and able guy on the committee. Gus Hawkins. On the Democratic side, that was a very strong committee in terms of a proposal of this nature.

Was Edith Green a factor on the committee?

WEEKS: Oh, yes. Edith Green was a very, very powerful factor on the committee. I would say, after Phil Landrum and the committee chairman, Adam Clayton Powell, she was probably the next most powerful person on the committee, for several reasons. She comes out of an educational background. She was previously a schoolteacher herself, and therefore there were parts of the program that she felt very sincerely about. Secondly, she was a very, very capable congresswoman. She did her homework. She studied, thought, and it was very clear that when she said something, it wasn't something that had just occurred to her off the top of the head. It was something that she'd done a considerable amount of homework and analysis on. She was well prepared. And third, she was perfectly prepared to be personally nasty if necessary in order to gain her point of view. I remember one point in time when she brought down the roof of the committee room when some Republican congressman—I can't remember who it was—had asked a relatively stupid question. It was a question that just didn't reflect very much intelligence or kind of study, and she proceeded to tear him apart. Just so much so that he just went back and was discouraged from asking any further questions. Adam Clayton Powell was soaking all this in with a big grin, and after she finished, he said, "Edith," he said, "you're the only woman I know who's been going through menopause for forty years."

WOMEN'S JOB CORPS CAMPS

Were there any aspects of the bill that were put in to accommodate Representative Green?

WEEKS: The obvious one was the Job Corps for women. Her immediate reaction when the legislation went up was: "Are there going to be girls in these Job Corps camps, in addition to men?" We'd all thought about that possibility before. None of us were very anxious to establish a whole separate Job Corps for women, and some people were really completely opposed to it, because they felt that the problem was the male high school dropout and getting him a job. A female high school dropout was a completely and totally different situation. [They felt] that we should draw a line and say, "Hey, that's somebody else's problem," and, "We can't pull them out of the communities in the same way that we're planning to send males to Job Corps centers," and so on. So there was a lot of opposition at the staff level to the idea of a women's Job Corps; but politically, once Edith Green said, "There are going to be women in these Job Corps centers," it was obvious that the answer was going to be yes, there would be. In addition to that, I would say that her influence stretched rather broadly across the entire program.

Why was the Job Corps restricted to men to begin with?

SCHLEI: I think we saw this as a sort of outdoor, "hard physical work" type of program that really, in the vast majority of cases at any rate, would not be suitable for women. It would be a man's program, primarily at least. If women were included, there would only be a few women, and then you'd have to duplicate facilities of various kinds. You would run into social problems. These would be people from the lowest stratum of society, and maybe there would be unwanted pregnancies. We just thought that, for those reasons, it would be simpler to have that program for men and something else for young women.

THE APPORTIONMENT FORMULA

WEEKS: Now, one thing that happened in the process of getting the legislation through the House was that the staff of the House Education and Labor Committee, as compared to the Senate committee, took a very, very different position with respect to cooperating with OEO. By and large, the staffs of the House committees generally are given much, much less authority than the staffs of Senate committees. Congressmen, because there are 435 of them, [each] maybe on two committees. If it's a junior congressman, he has a relatively minor role even then. And the congressman himself will do a lot of the homework, a lot of the research, a lot of the analysis, and so on, and will make up his own positions. On the other hand, a senator—there only being 100 senators—may be on four or five different committees and may do a great deal of outside public speaking and so on over and above his legislative duties and therefore delegates much more authority to the staff to prepare positions on legislation.

The House Education and Labor Committee staff director was a woman named Deborah Wolfe, a black woman who I recall as a college professor from a college in New York. It became pretty obvious after several weeks after we sent up the congressional presentation that she simply wasn't going to deal with the OEO staff on any basis. They simply took off in the wrong direction, and we simply couldn't get any kind of feedback from her as to what direction—what any congressman was thinking, or where the staff was going, or anything else like that. And we had to rely on the traditional channel of communication—which was back through the congressional office of the Office of Education and the congressional office of the Department of Labor—in order to get any information about where the congressional staff was going.

So we kept getting telephone calls from Sam Hildebrand, who was the legislative liaison for the Office of Education. He'd been developing his contacts on the Hill for six or eight years. And he took those folks out to lunch all the time and really did his job in developing a close working relationship. We couldn't match that, because we were newcomers. And I think we were regarded on the House side as being intruders.

[It was] very different on the Senate side; on the Senate side, we had no problem dealing with the folks. Don Baker, of course, was one of the main people that we were dealing with. I think he regarded us as not being particularly well qualified in many ways, but after all, Don Baker and the folks on the Senate side, many of them had been working on reviewing legislation and budget appropriations for labor and public welfare programs for 10 or 15 years. And they did, in fact, know a heck of a lot more about that than we did.

Basically, what the House Education and Labor Committee did was insert in the poverty program the same kind of formula which was typical of most Office of Education or health or welfare programs, which divided the money, or a portion of the money, among states according to certain criteria. And all the argument in HEW programs usually revolves around the criteria—what criteria are going to be used—rather than the substance of the program in many ways. Jack Conway in particular felt very strongly that to insert an apportionment formula among the states in community action removed from his control and from Shriver's control the basic decision-making authority, which was the authority as to whether a certain area was going to get money or whether it wasn't going to get money.

The thought was that if a state is apportioned according to the formula—let's say, $5 million—that Jack Conway's decision-making responsibility was only: How was the $5 million going to be spent within the state? Maybe he could decide that so much was going to go to Birmingham, Alabama, versus Montgomery, Alabama, but that wasn't the kind of decision which he wanted. He wanted to decide between Birmingham, Alabama, and Chicago, Illinois. Of course, there were provisions for reapportionments of unused funds, but that was a very, very major change that was inserted by the House Committee over Jack Conway's dead body.

The opponents at the time argued that there would be nothing to prevent Conway from spending all $200 million in Cleveland or New York or something like that.

WEEKS: That's right. And I remember we were preparing legislative positions about how Congress always had control, and that if any program director did anything like that, that the implications for what would happen to him next year, we were arguing, would be as controlling as any formula that Congress might establish.

That was not persuasive, I gather.

WEEKS: Absolutely not. Absolutely not. I remember when I first came back, after I saw the first House committee markup of the bill, that was the biggest change that they had made of a great many changes in the [bill]. I told Jack Conway that he was in the House bill, though it was a state apportionment formula, and that was the number one issue in the whole markup.

Do you think, in retrospect, that the issue was important?

WEEKS: I think, in retrospect, it really was not a major issue at all, that the position that we took—that any reasonable and responsible program administrator who had a sense of political astuteness would tend to divide the community action funds up in some reasonable way among the states so that no state would be shortchanged—is very forceful. If anything, it might possibly have helped a little bit, because without a formula, it would have been possible for any state to have come up with its own way of determining what it should have gotten versus what it did get in effect, and if [it] claimed that it was being shortchanged, then it provided a benchmark or a ruler against which one could say what was equitable and what was not. And, too, the idea that such a benchmark was available may have been a help in the final analysis.

Did this apportionment formula contribute to the tendency to spread the program too thinly over many areas rather than focusing on the experimentation projects?

WEEKS: The effect of any apportionment formula is to spread funds evenly across a large number of districts, and this is built into the legislative process for almost all governmental programs. I think most legislation that goes to Congress that involves giving out grants or loans or looking at the distribution of funds—there's a natural tendency in Congress to, I guess what I would call, "detarget" funds. In the last five or six years, one of the major issues in congressional appropriations has been so-called targeting: the extent to which antipoverty funds or antirecession funds or urban redevelopment funds would be specifically targeted to the cities that were worst off—hence the inevitable tendency of Congress to spread the funds broadly across the cities rather than to work on a more strictly targeted basis. It's a natural tendency because of the necessity to generate a specific number of votes, and congressmen tend not to vote for programs that are not going to shunt money into their districts.

CONGRESS AND COMMUNITY ACTION

WEEKS: There were definitely, particularly on the congressional side, congressmen who expressed very, very severe reservations about certain aspects of the program, which represented positions that they would not take publicly. I remember at one point in time—this would have been in roughly July of 1964, when it was well understood that Wilbur Mills [of Arkansas] was quite opposed to the poverty program as a whole. We prepared a kind of a position statement to deal with a number of the questions that it was understood that he had about the program. I was sent personally by Shriver up to Wilbur Mills's office to sit down with the congressman and go through this.

The appointment was made. I went up and was ushered into the congressman's presence, just myself and the congressman. And I said, "We've prepared this document which we think deals with some of the questions that you have about the program and tells why we think perhaps we may have taken care of your concerns or recognized your concerns in some way." He took that piece of paper and threw it across the room and said a few words about how he was not going to be involved in any program to help a bunch of niggers and threw me out of the office. That was about a three- or four-minute meeting, and I scurried back downtown with my tail between my legs.

Congress changed the Community Action Program by allowing assistance to local public groups or private groups for noncomprehensive, noncoordinated programs. Did you see this as a watering-down of community action?

WEEKS: I think this was made largely because there were a number of groups that went back to Congress, that had very specific and limited charters—for example, adult education—[and] that saw themselves as being, if not excluded, as certainly having a very, very tough time getting what they would like to see as [their] share of the community action funds, and they didn't always want to be wrapped up in the comprehensive program idea. They wanted to make sure that they could get a separate piece.

Donald M. Baker was counsel to the Senate Select Subcommittee on Poverty when the Economic Opportunity Act was passed; he joined OEO as general counsel in November 1964. A veteran of World War II who had earned three degrees from the University of Michigan, he had served as administrative assistant and secretary to Representative James G. O'Hara of Michigan, from 1959 to 1963, before moving to the Senate side. There his position was counsel to the Labor Subcommittee of the Senate Committee on Labor and Public Welfare.

D. BAKER: I anticipated many of the problems that the bill in fact precipitated for the agency. I perhaps only a little blindly anticipated one of the basic problems. I started out viewing community action from the "programmatic" perspective, not the "community organization" perspective. And even focusing on that, I perceived that it was going to cause a great deal of difficulty trying to get institutions to change their way of doing business, and I knew that any agency that tried to do it was going to get into trouble. We were going to be a challenge and a threat to all ongoing institutions, public and private, and that was going to cause us a fairly substantial amount of heat. As a matter of fact, I told Pat McNamara once—I think after the first reading of the bill—"If the members read community action and understand what it means, it'll never get through." But they didn't, of course.

Carl Perkins of Hindman, Kentucky, was elected to Congress in 1948 and represented his Appalachian district until his death in 1984. He became chairman of the House Education and Labor Committee in 1967. Perkins, a veteran of World War II, practiced law in Kentucky and served as Knott County attorney, as a member of the General Assembly, and as counsel for the state highway department.

PERKINS: I thought we should let local governments get involved more. But the legislation was so important, we kind of bypassed that aspect of it at the time. There were those on the committee who thought we should bypass, and others who thought we should include, and others who thought the local governments should just more or less act in an advisory capacity. That may have been the original idea, but it didn't work out that way. I know they'd hold some meetings and run meetings all night to get rid of the local elected officials in some areas of the country behind the local elected officials' backs and so forth. We knew there had to be greater coordination, and that's the reason we [later] tied it together.

Do you think the legislation was too broad?

PERKINS: No, it wasn't too broad. I mean, we gave the community action agencies themselves broad authority in bypassing city governments. We let them establish employment and training programs and everything of that nature.

It has been said that if Congress had understood what community action really was, the legislation would never have gotten through the Congress. Do you think that Congress understood the implications?

PERKINS: I do. I think we understood it. The thing was to get the local communities involved for putting people to work and educating and training people, and that was the purpose of it. They were to elect their leaders. They started off; we had some leaders that got far afield, I think, from the local communities and from the local governments, and that was what brought about the subsequent legislation to tie it to local governments.

Were there conflicts between community action agencies and local governments in your district?

PERKINS: Some, yes. Some, but they were not insurmountable. The fellow that was the director of community action felt that they were in a position that they ought to be on their own, that the city hadn't done these things, or the county hadn't done these things, and we are going to do them. Sometimes they would duplicate, and that was one of the things that wasted money that we wanted to make sure did not reoccur.

THE CHURCH-STATE ISSUE

CHURCHES AND NAVY YARDS

Sectional differences regarding the separation of church and state threatened to stall the legislation in the House of Representatives. Several northeastern Democrats with large Catholic constituencies vowed to oppose the measure if it excluded parochial schools from receiving community action funding. Southern Democrats and the National Education Association opposed an amendment that would stipulate the inclusion of private educational

institutions. Further complicating the issue was the fact that the three north-
eastern Democrats, Hugh Carey, James Delaney, and Tip O'Neill, used their
strategic committee positions not only to press their case for including private
schools but also to forestall the administration's plans for reductions at the
Brooklyn and Boston navy yards. Carey was a member of the House Educa-
tion and Labor Committee, while Delaney and O'Neill sat on the Rules Com-
mittee. In the following telephone conversations, President Johnson discusses
this stalemate with Lawrence F. O'Brien, Sargent Shriver, Rep. Phil Lan-
drum, and Bill Moyers. While venting his irritation with Carey and O'Neill
to O'Brien, the president makes his case for the Catholic legislators' support.
After rejecting Shriver's suggestion of seeking southern support of an amend-
ment, Johnson and Landrum agree that the entire community action section
should be jettisoned if northerners insist on amending the legislation. When
the president presents this option to Moyers, the latter explains community
action's rationale and its importance to the poverty program.

LBJ's conversation with Lawrence F. O'Brien, May 11, 1964[10]

JOHNSON: Larry, Charlie Halleck's going to try to keep us from peeing a
drop from now till the session is over with. Like that little resolution of
his. I just think maybe we ought to start trying to get some of these Democratic members that are friendly to us from the committees in to see us on
some of these things. It looks like to me a damned outrage that O'Neill
and Delaney are opposing administration things in that committee. I'm
not going to take any more threats from O'Neill. I stopped [the closing of]
the Boston Navy Yard like I did Philadelphia. You know it.

O'BRIEN: He ought to know that too. He does know it.

JOHNSON: Now he wants to bring the church into this poverty fight.

O'BRIEN: In fact when you called me, I was on the phone with Carey. I've
been on the phone with him for an hour.

JOHNSON: Carey just can't do that. I've got a Catholic in charge of it. I
can't put the Pope in charge of it. I've got the nearest thing to the Pope
I can get. I've got a Catholic running it. Get me by the election, and I'll
help them every damn way in the world I can. Nobody ever charged me
with not being pro-Catholic. So Carey can't have us kill a bill by saying
you got to appropriate to private schools. You know they're not going
to do that.

LBJ's conversation with Sargent Shriver, May 13, 1964[11]

SHRIVER: Mr. President, we were talking to Henry Wilson and Wilson McCarthy. The thought came up that if we could get the leading southern people like Mills and Harris and Landrum and Sikes, Mahon, Vinson, and so on, to hold the southern vote in line if we accepted this new language, which is acceptable to the northerners—to Carey and Delaney and the rest of them that...

JOHNSON: In the bill or in the report?

SHRIVER: In the bill. That it would be a tremendous coup for you personally.

JOHNSON: I don't think you can do that, though. I just talked to a bunch of them, and I think that you're just going to have a war if you try to rewrite the bill we sent up there. They're going to say that [Cardinal] Spellman rewrote it. It's that simple. They'll say we had a bill for all the country, all the people, treated them all well, but Spellman rewrote it. He sent down the word from the Pope and that's it. I've just been to the Hill and had lunch with twenty-three of them, and they just tore right in. That's the first thing they wanted to talk about. I told them, "Now here's what we're going to try to do. Under NYA we had every kid regardless of what church he belonged to, regardless of what race he belonged to, regardless of what section of town he was in, we treated them all alike. We're going to pass this bill as we sent it up there, but we're going to put a provision in the report, and the administrator is going to treat all kids alike. It's nothing for you all to get hot and bothered about now, because Bill Moyers is in on this program, and he's not going to turn it over to the Pope." But you have no idea how that feeling—and Halleck's got it going. He's outsmarted you. He's just got them going just 100 percent. He tried the Negro thing, and that didn't get off the ground, and now he's got the religious thing, and he's got it working for him 100 percent. You've got no more chance to hold that Bible Belt with changing a comma that involved the church thing than you have of just flying to the moon, in my judgment, as of now. I talked to Landrum about it this morning, and he says, "Well, you can get a bill through the Rules Committee, but you'll get it killed on the floor."

SHRIVER: Now that's a question that came up, and it seemed to me that this was a possibility, namely, let's say that it goes onto the floor. You go through the Rules Committee, which would accept it easily. You get on the floor, and there's an eruption against this particular part. If you have to take an amendment there, so then you take the amendment, and nothing is lost. If, on the other hand, they lose on the amendment, and it is beaten off—

JOHNSON: No, the Republicans will vote with the Catholics to kill the bill, and then they'll vote to kill the bill.

SHRIVER: Well, that's the question, of course. If those fellows could be held in line not to kill the bill, then two things would happen—this was Wilson's theory and I thought it was pretty good—number one, you would get not only the credit for putting through a fantastic education bill, which Wilbur Cohen, for example, describes as the best thing on aid to education that's happened for years. But second...

JOHNSON: I can't put it through though. I've already sent a bill up, you see. [If] I go to amending my own bill, I get in deep trouble.

SHRIVER: The bill has been amended—

JOHNSON: I know that. That's right. That's right, but not by my leadership. Not by my leadership. Now, I'm not close enough to it, Sarge, to know exactly what to do, but I know this feeling is deep. You'd almost have a fistfight if you put Bob Poage and Wright Patman in a room with Jim Delaney and Tip O'Neill.

SHRIVER: Of course, what they're saying, according to Wilson, is that Bob Poage, for example, he gets everything he wants, but the northern guys, who have to run against opposition, don't get anything, that when the cotton-wheat thing comes up, they vote to help out in the way that the South needs it. Like on the IDA [International Development Association] vote today, as Wilson says, who's voting with it is the northerners; who's voting against it is the southerners. For once, if they would stand on this one, they would show that the South is staying with you, and that the South is going to help the North. And you've got a united Democratic Party, united in a way it's never been united before. In fact, without losing a thing in the South, or damn little, you gain fantastic support in the North. You get all these guys in the North behind you as the guy who, like when you brought the first civil rights bill through the Senate in this history since the Civil War, you bring through the first aid-to-education bill—

JOHNSON: I can't do it if it involves changing the bill you sent up, because they just won't take it. And no human being can do it. God couldn't get them to do it.

SHRIVER: I see.

JOHNSON: I think what you better try to work out is to say: "Please, give me the discretion, give me power. Put it in the report, where the report doesn't attract much attention. The bill's the same as [we] sent up there. If you can't trust me and Johnson, you can't trust anybody." I think you better just tell your folks that, and if they can't do it, they kill themselves a bill. We were for this bill, and we all thought it was treating everybody all right. Now the Catholics raised this question. Walter's scared to death that they're raising the question. They're going to get the thing made an issue. I think that's a terrible thing for them to make it the issue.

SHRIVER: You mean Walter Jenkins?

JOHNSON: Yes.

SHRIVER: I think the truth of the matter is that they're not so much worried about that as they are, let me say, irritated about these other things that bear on the same issue. Namely, as Carey put it to me over there in Phil Landrum's office: "They're closing up my navy yard; now they're going to close up my schools. What the hell have I got to run with? And I've got a Republican against me."

JOHNSON: Well, we can save his navy yards. I've saved his navy yards, but I am prepared to close them. They were on the list to close, both Brooklyn and Boston. If he and O'Neill want them closed, I can act forthwith, right quick. He doesn't have to get a religious argument started to do that. I asked McNamara to make a study of every one and take twelve months to do it. That study hasn't come in. But they oughtn't to blackmail me on that. I told John McCormack I didn't blackmail on that yesterday. I'm the one that kept the navy yard from closing. Nobody else, but little Lyndon. They ought to be closed. They're WPA navy yards. They're operated for the basis of giving jobs to people that we do not need the work done. It's a poverty program. That's what it is. But I've kept them open in Boston and Brooklyn and Philadelphia. And I did it because Ken O'Donnell came in here and said, "We can't afford to close them." But I'm not closing Carey's navy yard, and if that's what he's doing on this, why we can close it if that helps his pain any.

But we don't want to. We're trying to do our damnedest. I'm not wedded. I don't have to have a poverty program. If they want to kill it, they can kill it. I think the wise thing for them to do though would not [for] just the church to lower its boom here on a bill that's up there, because I think it'll be unfortunate for them. Maybe unfortunate for the Democrats, too. I think that if they can't trust one of their own to administer this bill when they got language in the report that says that all kids will be treated alike. I don't know what kind of language it is, but Larry O'Brien said they had five different types of it. They could put it in the report, and then you've got discretion. You've got power, and this doesn't involve parochial schools. Just leave the power with you. And you operate it like—

SHRIVER: Actually, I think that what they claim, at any rate, what O'Brien claims and Wilson tells me—the truth of the matter is—that they're not raising the religious issue and that that's sort of a superficial thing, that it's these other considerations that are—

JOHNSON: Well, what can I do about the others? I've kept them from being closed. Now how much farther can I go? Can I build a new one there? Is that the point they're raising?

SHRIVER: No, of course not.

JOHNSON: Well what is the point then?

SHRIVER: I don't know the whole thing. The way Wilson put it to me, Mr. President, was that if the South will go along with the North—

JOHNSON: The South ain't going to go along with anything except that bill. And Wilson knows that. If he's got sense enough to pour piss out of a boot, he knows it. If he hadn't, he oughtn't try. What he says is that you go and turn the South because I can't turn the North. That's the nut of what he says. What we've got to do is find an agreement that both of us can get on. And that's in the report.

SHRIVER: Okay. Fine. We'll go back. I thought this was worth trying out.

JOHNSON: Well, we've tried that. I tried that last night. I tried that this morning. I called Landrum this morning. Landrum said, "You [will] get through the Rules Committee, but you [will] get a bill killed." That's what he told me on the phone.

SHRIVER: Henry Wilson said to me that he thought maybe—his opinion was that Landrum might be reflecting what used to be the situation, but which is not the situation, in fact, right now.

JOHNSON: If I were you and had to guess on the House's sentiment instead of listening to Henry Wilson or Wilson McGowen or Wilson whatever his name is—

SHRIVER: McCarthy.

JOHNSON: McCarthy. I'd listen to Phil Landrum. He's the man that's going to have to get you the southern votes. Neither one of those boys is going to be able to pee one drop. [Henry] Wilson can't get [the] North Carolina vote, where he comes from. Wilson McCarthy can't deliver one. Before they go to evaluating for you—you picked out Landrum, which was a smart move. Now you get down with Landrum and do what Landrum says you got to do and find some way that you can do what these other fellows want you to do administratively.

SHRIVER: Okay, Fine. Thank you.

LBJ's conversation with Phil Landrum, May 14, 1964[12]

JOHNSON: Phil.

LANDRUM: Good morning, Mr. President.

JOHNSON: They tell me that you've got to change your bill or he [Carey] won't have it. I told them just not to change it, just go on and vote it up or down. If we lose, why we'll just lose, and we'll let the Catholics take over the country. But I ain't going to be browbeat or blackmailed. If I can get it out [of committee] without it, all right; if not, I'd take the whole goddamn section out. We don't have to have that part of it.

LANDRUM: Well now, I think that's a wise decision. I think we can get it out of committee without Carey. I believe if we get this thing out of committee, then we can blame the responsibility for any roadblocks after that on the Republicans and the Catholics.

JOHNSON: Yes, that's what I'd do. Has Carey got any votes in the committee?

LANDRUM: No, sir. As a matter of fact, the two leading Catholics on the committee besides him are going to go with us either voting the bill out as it is—I mean with this language in this section as it is—or as a last resort just take this paragraph out entirely. I had felt that we might weaken it a little bit by taking it out entirely with some of the school people. I had a conference last night with the National Education Association fellows, and they're studying it. They think maybe, as a last resort, it might be all right to take it out. I still think we have to stay with the language as it is, Mr. President.

JOHNSON: Well, my judgment would be if you could. We don't have to get everything in one year. If we don't get anything but a work camp, we're all right. If I had to and the Catholics made an issue, I'd just lay it right in their lap with the Republicans and say "All right, you vote it out." And let them vote it out.

LANDRUM: Here's what we can do. We can justify this $900,000,000 with the first title of this bill.

JOHNSON: Yes, that's right. Is that your work camp?

LANDRUM: Yes, sir. Work camp and the work-study program for the poor college boys and girls.

JOHNSON: What do you do there on a Catholic college?

LANDRUM: We don't do anything.

JOHNSON: You pay it directly to the kid?

LANDRUM: That's right. Through the college after the child makes the choice. There's no direct line from the director to the school.

JOHNSON: ...I don't want to be quoted, but if I were you, I'd just seriously— that's what we're going to have. What you need is three camps in Gainesville, Georgia, that will take these kids and prepare them where they won't stay on relief all their life.

LANDRUM: Community action could be junked entirely.

JOHNSON: To hell with community action.

LANDRUM: Damn, I don't know how I can think any more of you, but every time I talk to you, damn, I realize more the complete knowledge you have of government in this country.

JOHNSON: Well, Phil, I feel the same way about you, and I'm awful glad I got you. I would just do it. I'd just tell the Speaker and them that the Catholics upset it, and you can't do it.

LBJ's conversation with Bill Moyers, May 14, 1964[13]

JOHNSON: Bill, I see our poverty's in a hell of a shape. They're quitting and adjourned over till Monday.

MOYERS: I knew they did that. Basically, they did it [because] Adam Clayton Powell wanted to go to Puerto Rico. Although it's just as well from the standpoint of reaching a compromise [on the church-state issue] because we couldn't do it today. [Rep. Hugh] Carey just is adamant. But we met with the NEA. Larry met with them a good while this afternoon, and I talked to them this evening. They're bending a great deal. In fact, they have been grossly misinterpreted in early conversations this week. I'm right here now with the bill in front of me, and I just got off the phone with [Adam] Yarmolinsky, reworking a section in a way that ought to satisfy everybody. This comes from NEA. It took their guidance in it. We're going to meet—Larry [O'Brien] and Shriver and Yarmolinsky and—in the morning.

JOHNSON: Why does NEA hate to see a Catholic get any aid?

MOYERS: They believe that it will eventually lead to a deterioration of support for public schools, that it [will] start draining off funds that they badly need now. There are two men—this fellow Fuller and then the executive secretary of NEA, Bill Carr—who is just violently opposed to any aid to parochial schools.

JOHNSON: How are you going to get them to go along then if they're violently opposed to it?

MOYERS: What they don't want to establish, Mr. President, is the principle of legislation which says that aid can be given to parochial schools. They are realists and know that peripheral aid is going to have to be given sooner or later, like textbooks or like buses, but they don't want to establish a legal legislative precedent which admits aid to parochial institutions. So if we can fuzz it in such a way that the administrator can use Catholic or parochial schools after hours without saying such, they'll take reality that way. That's the only hope we have now, I think.

JOHNSON: What do we care if we take it out and just let all that money go for camps?

MOYERS: This is a vital part of the poverty program, getting communities and facilities in what's decided. Shriver thinks it's as important as the camps because if you ever prove that a community can get together to solve its problems, you're halfway on home.

JOHNSON: Yeah, but I'd get the camps and let the Catholics go to hell if they messed with it.

MOYERS: I certainly think that is the fallback position, that if we do not reach a compromise tomorrow that by the time they come back here Monday, we just have to give up Title II. But the compromise we're thinking about right [now] is just to knock out any reference to educational institutions at all in the language and not fool around with the schools. This is your idea, really, of taking out the whole section, but instead of the whole section, just that part that deals with education, and for the first year, get by without it. NEA will buy that, and we think that Carey will. We're going to meet tomorrow with this specific language, and Larry's going to talk to him.

JOHNSON: Okay.

WEEKS: Another question that arose very early on—an intriguing one that got a lot more attention than "maximum feasible participation of the poor"—was the church-state question. The question specifically was: Would we make grants to religious organizations? Obviously, there are Jewish organizations, Catholic organizations, Protestant organizations, and all sorts of organizations who would be delighted to be able to get poverty program funds to run day-care centers, to do all sorts of things. This sprang off all sorts of side issues: Would we rent space in churches or synagogues? Could overall community action organizations use religious organizations as delegate agencies?

I remember very clearly that the legislation simply fuzzed this issue specifically, and this was one of the major questions that came up in the first day of hearings when Mayor [Anthony] Celebrezze, who has a very short fuse, started to get questioned during his testimony about how they would operate Title V, the work-study program, but got into broader questions of the church-state issue. Obviously, he's an Italian-Catholic mayor. I've forgotten which congressman it was—[Charles] Goodell [of New York], I think. A match of wits between Goodell and Celebrezze leaves Goodell on the winning side by a large margin. Charlie Goodell was a very bright congressman.

Willard Wirtz seems to have fared much better in those hearings on the same questions.

WEEKS: Yes, Willard Wirtz has a brilliant mind. His testimony before the House Education and Labor Committee on all sorts of questions was just a terrific testimony. I remember at one point in time, one of the Republicans asked Wirtz a question about the Job Corps, and whether there wasn't something that was basically wrong about taking young men out of their homes and putting them in camps. Wirtz's question—well, he said, "Don't you realize that that is specifically what Plato proposed in *The Republic* as the ideal way to organize young men into the kind of strength that's needed in order to defend the country?" The poor questioner just sat back in his chair and kept his mouth shut after that. [Wirtz] was a very intimidating testifier in the sense that his answers are so good that it discourages probing.

On the church-state question: Was there a formula in some of the government education programs that you could apply?

WEEKS: No. No, as a matter of fact, at the time we really didn't have a good answer for the whole church-state question. The answer evolved out of approving specific applications for the Community Action Program over time. I can remember one of the first things that Shriver wanted publicized— that one of the very first community action grants was to a Jewish group to run a program for Spanish American kids in a Protestant church in a white Catholic neighborhood, or something like that. He said, "If you want to talk about church-state issues, this is what it's all about." Well, it was one of Shriver's wonderful ways of answering an issue with a specific case, which tended to block further questioning; but the answer that he gave really was not an answer to the issue in a broad sense. And in a broad sense there really is not [an answer]. The church-state question is so involved and complex that it's not a question which in any sense you can answer definitively. It's one which you deal with over time in all its variations.

It was very clear that we would not make a grant directly to a religious organization. The whole question was, "Well, then, what is the role of religious organizations under community action programs?" When the Head Start program started, this became even more poignant, because most or a great many day-care centers are run either in churches or by religious organizations or in some way under religious affiliations. It comes down to all the questions of: If you're going to run a day-care center in a Catholic church, do you have to get them to take down all the Christs that are hanging on all the walls of the building? It gets really convoluted very quickly when you get to the particulars.

SCHLEI: It was my position—which was expressed as the administration's position—that there was no constitutional infirmity involved where you assisted people, even through sectarian institutions, if there was no sectarian content to what you were doing. If you're going to make milk available to children, the fact that you find some of them in a parochial school is not an establishment of religion. It becomes more difficult if you are providing some sort of facility to the institution itself. Suppose you are going to build hot-lunch facilities so that all schools can feed their kids a hot lunch, because that's in the interests of the national health; then you begin to have a problem, because some people feel if you aid the sectarian institution, you cannot help but aid their sectarian purposes. I know that at one point we took the position that so long as the facilities and assistance provided were totally unrelated to any sectarian activity or purpose, it was all right.

This must have been a thorny political problem, because on the one hand, you have people like Hugh Carey [of New York], who had large parochial constituencies, and on the other hand, you had other members that were dead set against any sort of aid. Do you recall trying to thread this particular needle between the two factions?

SCHLEI: I recall testifying a time or two. Basically, it was a Catholic versus Protestant split—well, a lot of Protestants in the middle. The Jewish point of view is very much against any kind of government assistance to religious institutions. The Protestant view varies [but] basically is against. The Catholic view tends to favor it because the Catholics are, it seems, the ones who have their own schools the most, their own colleges, and are struggling to keep them alive. So when you hear from a politician who is a Catholic or who has a lot of Catholic constituents, you can expect to hear a tolerant attitude toward assisting religious institutions. When you hear from a rural legislator whose constituents are mostly Protestant, when you hear from a legislator whose constituents are primarily Jewish or very much interested in civil liberties, you'll get a very strongly "anti" point of view in relation to assisting religious institutions.

"MONEY, MARBLES, AND CHALK": THE FIGHT IN THE HOUSE

Although the Economic Opportunity Act passed the Senate by a wide margin, the legislation seemed destined for defeat in the House. Many southern Democratic members opposed the measure as too liberal, too urban, and too minority-centered. With the election only three months away, southerners felt increasing pressure from a white backlash after the passage of the 1964 Civil Rights Act and an outbreak of black riots in Harlem, Rochester, Philadelphia, and New Jersey. George Wallace's withdrawal as a third-party presidential candidate strengthened the candidacy and the party of Barry Goldwater in the region.

The House Republican caucus was virtually united in opposition to the anti-poverty bill. Minority leader Charles Halleck employed an effective strategy of delay, taking advantage of absenteeism caused by primary races in Tennessee, California, and North Carolina and delays in the Education and Labor Committee and the Rules Committee. He calculated that the breaks for two national conventions might also be helpful in stalling the legislation until adjournment. As Halleck stalled for time, formidable business groups as the Chamber of Commerce, the National Association of Manufacturers, and the Farm Bureau lobbied against the bill.

Securing House passage required Lyndon Johnson's full arsenal of presidential powers, legislative tactics, and persuasion. He worked day and night, concentrating on southern Democrats in Texas, Florida, North Carolina, Georgia, and Tennessee, while labor allies Walter Reuther and George Meany courted moderate Republicans and Democrats in urban states. LBJ's bargaining chips were judicial appointments, ambassadorships, and a large inventory of public works projects. He threatened to close military bases and intervened to keep them open. To provide cover for vulnerable Democrats, he enlisted the support of friendly southern governors, senators, and senior House members like Carl Vinson, Mendel Rivers, and George Mahon. By working through such intermediaries, Johnson also avoided charges of excessive White House pressure and bribery. Even wavering members were dispatched to influence their more uncooperative colleagues. If a congressman feared the wrath of public opinion in his district, LBJ sought to alter that factor through the influence of publishers, bankers, religious leaders, and campaign contributors.

Johnson's appeals were as varied as his inducements. In addition to touting the program's merits, he defined the vote in terms of his personal pride, loyalty to the Democratic Party, and—in the aftermath of the Gulf of Tonkin incidents— patriotism. He invoked the analogy of Franklin D. Roosevelt's ill-fated Court- packing bill, arguing that a defeat would weaken LBJ's presidency as it had FDR's. When congressmen still refused to support the legislation, Johnson per- suaded several to do so only if their votes were critical to secure passage. Others agreed to be absent or vote in pair. In the end only Johnson's Herculean effort saved the poverty program.

LBJ's conversation with Sargent Shriver, July 28, 1964[14]

JOHNSON: Now you've got a problem trying to get the Tennessee delegation back. I just got off—I talked to seven of them this afternoon. I've been here thirty-two years, and I've never had as much hell on any bill in my life. I had McCormack who agreed to give them an extra week when they didn't even ask for it. Then North Carolina decides they would go home this week. And then Tennessee can't be here next week. The only way they can get them is Friday afternoon. We're just doing everything that plays into...[the Republicans'] hands. If some guy doesn't screw it up, another one does. If not an admiral, it's a general. I didn't look at the rule. I don't know [what] kind of rule they had, but somebody ought to be watching that before it came out of there....

What is it that Carey wants? Carey's got a shipyard in this district?

SHRIVER: Carey's got the Brooklyn Navy Yard, that's right. But a letter arrived today over there to all the guys in the New York delegation saying that five hundred to eight hundred jobs were going to be taken off the Brooklyn Navy Yard payroll on the second of October. It seems to me whether they take them off on the second of October or the third of November, there's not a matter of cataclysmic importance to the Defense Department or to their savings or to their budget. After all, it's eight hundred guys' jobs for one month. What's more, they don't have to, it seems to me, send the letter up there the day before the Rules Committee is going to meet, and Dela- ney's sitting on the Rules Committee. You know these guys are edgy any- how. I'm not trying to defend them, but we got to have the eight votes.

LBJ's conversation with Lawrence F. O'Brien, July 28, 1964[15]

JOHNSON: I got your note; I talked to Sargent. I saw this story in the paper three weeks ago in New York about the Brooklyn Navy Yard being cut.

But I talked to McNamara about it, and he says that he'll try to work out something, put it off till the first of the month.

O'BRIEN: ...I told Sarge I felt that we could handle this problem, and if we can touch up Hugh a little bit in the next few days, all right, we'll do it. That's all. You know, and get him calmed down. But I must say, this guy [Carey] is getting it pretty regularly, and, God, he won by 180 votes, and the guy running against him is heading the drive to hold the yard there. So it really placed him in a miserable situation....

JOHNSON: Now, Larry, I want you to use me twenty-four hours a day until we get 218 votes.

O'BRIEN: Right.

JOHNSON: And I want you to use Bill Moyers and Walter Jenkins and everybody. And I want you to meet Carl Albert every day. I want you to put all your time on this one until we get fixed. It's next Friday now. We're going to take it up Wednesday, Thursday, and Friday.... Let's report. Check in with me every night and tell me who to talk to and who they can talk to.... I'd rather lose every bill we got than this one. I want to get this one bill passed, and get these kids at work. And then, by God, they can be through with it.

LBJ's conversation with Senator George Smathers of Florida, August 1, 1964[16]

JOHNSON: Now you get over there and you call me back on that damn [Rep. Charles] Bennett and [Rep. Paul] Rogers, and I'll go to work on your ambassador and your judgeship. But you hang those on the wall. If they've got to have a canal or whatever they've got to have, we'll do it. This one vote I cannot lose. Charlie Halleck has told every Republican that "if you vote against me, you're out of the Republican Party. I'll eliminate you." So he's going to get a solid vote. And I've got about twenty-nine of these damn whorey southerners like Bennett and Rogers and [Rep. Walter] Rogers from my own state. Some of them are taking walks for me, and some of them are going off, and some of them are going to say, "Well, hell, I had to get him to give me this canal." You'll just see what they've got to have, and then let's get it. But let's get those two votes.

SMATHERS: Okay.

JOHNSON: Call me back now, George.

LBJ's conversation with Governor Carl Sanders of Georgia, August 1, 1964[17]

JOHNSON: I've got two votes I sure do need to put my poverty program through and I can't get them. [Rep. Russell] Tuten, what do you call him: T-u-t-e-n...

SANDERS: Russell Tuten. Tuten's not going to vote for it?

JOHNSON: No, and damn it; it's the finest thing in the world for the South. I could make you an allotment down there, and you could fill it up with these boys in every community and work on it. And Landrum is the author of it. And I don't understand Tuten and Hagan.

SANDERS: Elliott Hagan won't vote for it?

JOHNSON: No, he hasn't agreed to yet.

SANDERS: Let me see if I can't talk to him.

JOHNSON: Now I went to bat for all the boys in Georgia and South Carolina and North Carolina on their cotton bill and on their textile bill. I moved heaven and earth, and I made every New Yorker and every Philadelphian and every one of them vote for it, 100 percent. Now the Republicans—they told them if they don't vote against me because they don't want me to have this billion dollars to employ these people—they want them to be unemployed and be rioting around the country—they tell every Republican that "If you don't vote against Johnson's bill—this is the biggest bill Johnson's got; the one he's most interested in—then we'll make you get out of the Republican Party. We won't give you a penny."

　　Old man [Carl] Vinson was down here today, and he went right back and got Mendel Rivers to endorse me from Charleston, South Carolina. So he's supporting it. But [Vinson] left me two names.

SANDERS:...if somebody could put a bug in Tuten's ear—because this [Cross-Georgia Canal proposal] cuts all across his counties—that the Corps of Engineers might at least look favorably upon at least making a study of the damn thing, I think you could get Tuten to do just most anything you want him to....

JOHNSON: You get me the number of the bill and tell him you called me up and talked to me about it and said you wanted me to do it, and I said, well, by God, I want a little help out of him and I don't know whether it's feasible or not, but I'll get the chief of the Corps of Engineers and get him [Tuten] both in my office next week and sit down with them and tell them to go to bat and help them if it's at all possible. But, by God, I don't want him voting against me. If he can't vote for me, just don't vote.

SANDERS: Right. That's what I was going to tell him.

JOHNSON: But be careful what you say to him. Don't let him say we pressured him or anything unless you....

SANDERS: Elliott Hagan I can talk to. Let me talk to Elliott Hagan and see—

JOHNSON: Call him and tell him he's got Camp Stewart, and I'm his friend and I want to help him. And I like him, and I like his wife. And this is my blood. This is it. I'm going to lose twenty-five Democratic votes, and the Republicans are going to vote together to the man. I've got to have his help. If I don't, I want him to go to Georgia.... I've got 196 votes today. I need 210 to pass it....

SANDERS: All right, all right.... Let me ask you this: now when I get through talking to Tuten, if Tuten tells me he wants to come over there....

JOHNSON: You just call me back or call Walter Jenkins, if I'm not here, and say "Get Tuten and the Chief of the Corps of Engineers in the President's office any day this week." And we'll get them there.... He'll sure get the chief. The chief will be right at my desk with him any day you say so, whether he votes for the bill or not if you want it. But you figure out some way to get him to vote for us without bribing him or without exposing yourself. Lead him around and say, "Now listen, I called up there and I'm trying to help you. Two or three things. Now isn't there some way in the world if I can get you all to sit down there and talk it over that you don't have to fight the president?"

SANDERS: All right, I'll call him this afternoon.

JOHNSON: Tell him Carl Vinson's going along with us. Landrum's going along with us. Herman Talmadge voted for the bill. Ain't a damn thing wrong with the bill. Dick [Russell] voted against it, but Herman Talmadge voted for it. Dick ought to have voted for it. Dick put the amendment in that allows the governor to veto it. If a governor don't like a damn thing we do, all he's got to do is veto it. And what will happen is, it will be a hell of a thing for the states and help them. And our section needs it more than any section.

SANDERS: You're right. You're absolutely right. I'll call Russell Tuten and Elliott Hagan both this afternoon...

JOHNSON: Then you call me back.

LBJ's conversation with Rep. George Mahon of Texas, August 1, 1964[18]

JOHNSON: I've got to get you to help me on my poverty. This damned [Rep.] Albert Thomas now said he's going to follow Mahon. I got 195 votes. Charlie Halleck has told them all that, "you leave the Republican Party if you vote for this. We won't give you a dime. We won't do anything." I've taken it up from ten agencies. I've put it all in one bill. I've got the best administrator up there, Sargent Shriver. I got 195 votes. I got Mendel Rivers this afternoon, which is 196. I have counted you, and I have counted Thomas. Now somebody saw Thomas today, and Thomas said, [LBJ mimics Thomas's voice.]: "Well, I've been thinking about this thing, and I just believe I'll follow my chairman. I'll get you the money, but I'll just have to follow my chairman, and he hadn't made up his mind."

MAHON: Well, I've been very quiet. I haven't talked to all—

JOHNSON: You get something else. You vote against me on a dozen things, but, for God's sakes, we've only got five in the Texas delegation against us at this moment. [Rep. John] Dowdy, [Rep. O. C.] Fisher and [Rep. Omar] Burleson—by God, he never can vote with us. I don't know why.

MAHON: Well, I've been very quiet. I've made no statement.

JOHNSON: I know it, but I've got to have you unquiet. I've got to have you help me with some. I've got old Sikes on there. You ought to help me with him some. I talked with Carl Vinson down here. He says he thinks he can help me with—he got me Rivers today and maybe Hagan. I got Rivers, and [Rep. John L.] McMillan [is] against me in South Carolina, and [Rep. Porter] Hardy and [Rep. Thomas] Downing in Virginia. You see, they pick off four or five. They pick off five or six Democrats in Texas and three or four from these other states. That winds up, and that gives them thirty Democrats, and they hold a solid Republican line. And they rub my nose in it. I passed it two to one in the Senate, two to one. I got ten Republican votes for it in the Senate.

Every one of these boys that will work on this job will become taxpayers when they get out of here, instead of tax-eaters. I got a good program, if they'll just let me do it. They're rioting in every damn district. I want to get these boys out of these damn cities and put them to work and having them doing something instead of having them loitering around, breaking in store windows, and everything else. I passed it through the Rules Committee, eight to seven. I passed it through the Senate. I passed it through both committees. All the Republicans voted against me on the Labor Committee. I had nineteen to thirteen, strictly party vote. I've got to have a strictly party vote on the floor, and I've got to have my chairman of my Appropriations Committee to get out there and make some of these wayward fellows get in line, like old Bob Sikes. He's got every damn thing in the world down there in his district.

MAHON: That's right.

JOHNSON: This is a party measure. This is party responsibility. If I lose this, it's telegraphed around the world that, by gosh, the Republicans roll me and roll me good on the key measure, the only single Johnson measure that was sent up. Everything else was Kennedy.

MAHON: Well, let me have a prayer session with Thomas.

JOHNSON: You just get Thomas. Don't have any prayer session. And you get one with Sikes. And you bail me out of this one, and I'll try not to have you bail me out of any more. I'll be bailing you all out. And anything you got to be bailed out on—I'll move the navy to Lubbock, or I'll do anything you need done, whatever it is; I don't care. But this is one—you've got to get Thomas. I didn't know you had that kind of influence on him.

MAHON: I didn't either....

LBJ's conversation with Speaker John McCormack, August 4, 1964[19]

JOHNSON: ...I'm going to tell them to go to hell in about another week—all of them—because I've got a belly full. If I can't pass one bill, I can't lead the country. They can get somebody else to lead it. I have enough hell in my own outfit. I spend all day answering Bobby Kennedy's leaks, and he's got all the people hired around here giving us hell. You've got no loyalty in the government. You can't get your own people. They'd rather go with Halleck. I can't understand what's in a man's mind that he would go to Halleck against us, but they do.

McCormack: Who?

Johnson: George Mahon. A good fellow like him. He just said well the United States Chamber of Commerce came up and got him to make a broadcast denouncing poverty. I said, "Now, George, don't tell another person this, but go on and vote against my Appalachian bill—poverty. And maybe we can get some Republican votes from Ohio and Pennsylvania. If we can't, well we can't pass it. But don't vote against this bill, because this means more to me than all the bills put together all year.

McCormack: What did he say?

Johnson: Well, he just said that he kind of half way committed, and the [news]paper was after him, and he's afraid of the paper. So he left. I don't know what he's going to do. I talked to this fellow, Tuten, and he swore me to absolute secrecy, not to tell a human being, but he said that they had a barber shop poll in his district, about five hundred to fifty, something like that. Six hundred to eighty. And that the civil rights thing was just something terrible, and that he had gone down and told them that he loved Johnson, but they hated all the civil righters and all the Kennedys, and all the administration, and it was just suicide for him. But he said, "Now if you won't tell anybody and won't quote me"—and I'm not going to quote him to anybody but you. I'm not even going to tell Walter Jenkins. He said, "I'm going to sit in the well [of the House chamber], and when they get to the 'T's, if my vote will make the difference, you've got it. I'll get kicked out of Congress if I have to, but I'll vote with you. If you've got it won anyway, don't make me do it." And I said all right. So don't even let them know it. Don't count him at all, but remember that he's a courageous fellow, that he's willing to stand up.[20]

LBJ's conversation with Lawrence F. O'Brien, August 4, 1964[21]

Johnson: We picked up two or three different ones today and lost two or three, and one of them is [Rep. Robert A.] Fats Everett. Do you know anything about that?

O'Brien: No.

Johnson: His administrative assistant told some of them up on the Hill that he wasn't coming back. He told Bill [Moyers] that he wasn't going to be able to make it or was afraid he wasn't.

O'Brien: Yes. I hadn't heard that, but Henry Wilson, just as I was leaving a while ago, reported that the National Association of Manufacturers and the Farm Bureau and others have cranked up tremendous forces up there. They're all over the Hill. Henry is to call me a little bit later on some of these things that we wanted to check out. I didn't get any details from him. He certainly didn't mention Fats Everett to me.... We've had some opposition harden. Otis Pike, for one, that I had hoped would finally come, has said flatly under no condition. He's afraid that, as he put it, we're trying to move Harlem Negroes into his district. We haven't had any changes. We went over that thing up there with Landrum and Carl Vinson and the leadership...

Johnson: What agreement did you reach?

O'Brien: Well the judgment was they would go with the [governor's veto] amendment. We went over the names and decided that ten or eleven of these people were more reasonable targets conceivably with the amendment than without it. Finally, it was just an overwhelming opinion, as you'll undoubtedly detect in your office, so that's where we are. I'm not really concerned that we'll lose any of these guys. I'm just going to make damn sure that they don't start getting a little nervous. None of them—I talked to Hugh Carey today, and he wasn't at all nervous about it.

Johnson: Now, what's your last count?

O'Brien: I have 198 Democrats and Republicans.... Sarge is claiming one in Ohio.... [Rep. William H.] Harsha.

Johnson: Harsha, Ohio. Bill [Moyers] says no; it's a question mark.... What effect is our asking Congress for a resolution to support us in Southeast Asia and bombing hell out of the Vietnamese tonight? What effect will that have on this bill? Will it kill it or help us?

O'Brien: It won't hurt us. I just don't know that it will help or not.

Johnson: I think it would be a little more reluctant to vote against the president.

O'Brien: I would think so. But certainly as McNamara has said—

JOHNSON: They oughtn't to be personally attacking us to much.

O'BRIEN: No, I wouldn't think so.

LBJ's conversation with Edwin L. Weisl, July 30, 1964[22]

WEISL: I talked to Sam Newhouse. He's calling his editor in New Orleans to put the pressure on [Rep. F. Edward] Hebert on the antipoverty bill. Bill Moyers called me up and asked—

JOHNSON: Yes, that's very important. We're going to lose that bill with five or ten votes. It's just a few people. We can't get any Republican votes. The liberal Republicans ought to be with us [and] fellows like Hebert that are southerners—they're under heat since Wallace got out of the race. They're just not for us. We've just got to win it. We can't lose it.

WEISL: I know we must. What else can I do, Lyndon?

JOHNSON: I don't know. I don't know where he's got [news]papers.

LBJ's conversation with Rep. Robert Jones of Alabama, August 5, 1964[23]

JOHNSON: Does it beat you to vote for poverty?

JONES: It's going to be awfully close, Mr. President.

JOHNSON: Does this Birmingham paper of Newhouse's help you any?

JONES: Hell no.

JOHNSON: Would it?

JONES: Hell, they're going to vote for Goldwater.

JOHNSON: I talked to [Sam Newhouse] today, and I told him I had a good friend that was for the country, but he really had a problem. I wondered if he'd mind asking his editor to help him if he could help me with my poverty. He said, no, he'd be glad to, and he helped me with one or two others, one or two of the Republicans. I don't want to mess with anything that doesn't [help you], but I heard somebody say yesterday that you said that it just murdered you unless others went along, and the others weren't going along, but if your vote would kill the bill, that you might try to help us. I thought if I could I might get him to try to compensate for it some by...

JONES: Sarge called me three weeks ago, and I gave him an unqualified "yes."

JOHNSON: I know that. We want you here now. We've got two or three Alabama boys that are good but not going [along]. I'm for you money, marbles and chalk, quietly. I'll hide, and I won't embarrass you. But I think if we ever get the bill passed—you see, we're going to put in the governor's [veto] amendment, where he can veto anything. Any governor can veto any project. We're going to turn over jobs in every one of these colleges, which will really be helpful, I think, so far as the young people are concerned, because they'll need them the most.

JONES: I know the virtue of the bill. I want to be for it....

JOHNSON: ...Well, I'll tell you this, Bob. If it costs you, I don't know what it will be that I can do, but I'll guarantee that I'll more than make up with it. I'll make up with it with interest.

LBJ's conversation with Rep. Olin E. Teague of Texas, August 5, 1964[24]

JOHNSON: I know how much trouble that you've got on this poverty for me, but Walter indicated that if it meant the difference that you'd go there. I appreciate it, and I'll make it up with interest. I don't know how, but I'll start tomorrow. Any way in the world that I can get even with you, I'll sure do it, because I appreciate the guts it takes. But I want you to talk to some of these folks like you that look to you. If they roll me on this one, it would be just like when they beat Roosevelt. I'll lose my leadership to Charlie Halleck, but I'll never get that all back. It's the only bill I got to have this year. They can take the rest of them. I don't care about—I want them—I'd like to have Appalachia—but they can vote against it if they have to. I'd like to have ARA, but they can vote against it if they have to. This one, if I don't get it, I'm in deep trouble as far as being leader of this country is concerned. They oughtn't vote against me now. It doesn't do any good for some of these liberals to go around and say that. They can't get any votes. But if you can say it to two or three folks, you can make the difference. We're within five votes of winning this thing.

TEAGUE: Well, Mr. President, I don't want to vote for the bill, but if my vote means passing [it], I'm going to vote for it.

JOHNSON: Walter told me that.

TEAGUE: I'll talk to some of these others. In fact, I already have.

JOHNSON: I'll run these kids out of their ears at [Texas] A&M though with this bill. It will be a real thing for old [A&M President] Earl Rudder. I'd put enough stuff down there that, by God, they'll be calling it Olin Teague College.

TEAGUE: Well, I've talked to them and I've told them that I'm on the team and that I owe some obligations to the Democratic Party. As bad as I'd hate to, if it means me for me to stand up and change a vote and say I'm voting for it to pass it, I'll damn sure do it.

JOHNSON: Cliff [Carter] and Walter told me that, and I'll never forget you. But you can help me with—Joe [Kilgore] wants to help. He's a good boy, but he's going to leave, and he's afraid some of his clients will be mad. He doesn't want to vote for the bill to begin with.

TEAGUE: I'm not so sure. I've talked to Joe, and I think Joe may vote for it.

LBJ's conversation with Lawrence F. O'Brien, August 5, 1964[25]

JOHNSON: Walter Reuther said he'd gotten [Rep. John] Lesinski, [Jr.] and [Rep. Harold] Ryan. Do you count either one of them?

O'BRIEN: I count Ryan "yes." Lesinski we've been counting "right—question mark," and that's a damn good one to firm up.

JOHNSON: [Reuther] said he went through the church, and he's got him. I told him that I wanted him to be positive [and] for him to call you tonight and tell you. He said he's working on [Rep. William S.] Broomfield, too.

O'BRIEN: Well that's damn good too.

JOHNSON: Also, he's going to call [Rep. Ogden R.] Reid and [Rep. John V.] Lindsay and [Rep. Otis G.] Pike with some New York liberals and bankers and people that he works with. He thinks that because this ought to be a good bill for New York that maybe some of them will help. I think he might have a chance to help a little with Lindsay.

O'BRIEN: Yes, I would think so. Now Lindsay—Halleck has given him the word that if he's off the reservation that he can forget any future New York Republican activity and all that sort of thing. They're working him over hard. He'd normally be firm on something like this, and he just isn't firm. So that's a damn good one.... Pike—every damn check, and there's been about ten of them on him in the last few days—he still comes back "wrong."

LBJ's conversation with Senator Everett Jordan of North Carolina, August 5, 1964[26]

JOHNSON: I passed it through the Senate, two to one. But now if these boys from the South—forty of them—leave me and go over and join Halleck. I know damn well, I can do more for North Carolina than Halleck can. Now, how in the hell do I get that over to them?

JORDAN: Do you say that Phil [Landrum] is all right if you agree to take that amendment?

JOHNSON: Phil Landrum's going to be the author of the bill. He's putting it through, and he got me to agree to take the amendment this morning. He said it would help with some of the other southern boys. It has helped with fellows like Mendel Rivers, but the ones that I'm really troubled about [are] your damn boy [Rep. L.H.] Fountain and your boys [Rep. Horace R.] Kornegay and [Rep. David N.] Henderson. The whole North Carolina delegation's in trouble. I thought Luther Hodges could talk to them and you could talk to them. Hell, when you all talk to me, I just get out there and get the job done, if it's possible. I thought they'd go along, but they tell me they haven't made up their mind yet.

JORDAN: I have Fountain and Kornegay and...

JOHNSON: [Rep. Ralph J.] Scott?

JORDAN: No, Scott was out sick yesterday. He hasn't got back. They say he's drunk, to tell you the truth.

JOHNSON: Well let him stay drunk. Just keep him away. That'll be just as good if you'll just keep Scott away....

JORDAN: Now Kornegay told me yesterday—and I told Walter about it last night—that [Rep. Harold D.] Cooley was wobbling. He said, "Now if Cooley votes against this thing," he said, "I just can't possibly. We've got the same type of people down there." That is, that's what Henderson said. They do have adjoining counties and districts. Now Cooley can do a whole lot for that whole situation if he will.

JOHNSON: Now who can I get to talk to Cooley? Do I have to talk to him myself?

JORDAN: I believe it would be better for you than anybody in the world.

JOHNSON: All right, I'll do that.

LBJ's conversation with Sargent Shriver, August 9, 1964[27]

JOHNSON: ... I want to congratulate you. You did a mighty wonderful job. I'm mighty proud of you.

SHRIVER: Thank you very much. They were really pleased with themselves over there, the leadership was. Hale Boggs and the rest of them. They knocked their blocks off. They worked hard, but they nearly got caught with their pants down, too.

JOHNSON: Yeah, they sure had lots of problems, but I hope that we got the worst of them behind us now. You ought to be thinking of who you're going to get in for that [bill] signing and let's get the leaders all over the country....

I know that we all got worked to death and upset every night, but the proof of the pudding's in the eating. When you get a forty-vote margin, why that's said. You'd have been ruined and I would have, too, if it had been forty the other way.

SHRIVER: Although we did a hell of a job with the Peace Corps without tremendous assistance from the White House, this thing could not have got through without you being on top [of it.] You know that, I'm sure. A lot of those calls from you over there were the ones that turned the tide. I think John McCormack really worked hard for us.

JOHNSON: He sure did. He did a wonderful job. You ought to thank him.

SHRIVER: Yes, I've already talked to all those men over there....

JOHNSON: We've got the damnedest record of any Congress since the republic started. That IDA thing, [the Republicans] beat it, but we made them come back and put it going again: $750 million. They beat our Mass Transit by thirty votes, and we came back and made them pass that. They had our farm bill beat, and we made them pass that. Civil Rights, we had cloture; we passed that. The tax bill, Harry Byrd had it locked up, wouldn't even have a hearing on it. We passed that. Now poverty was where they were really going to make their record. We passed that. So it looks like to me Halleck ought to resign.

SHRIVER: If I was a Republican, I'd sure be calling for his resignation. They were talking about that over there, as a matter of fact, over the weekend.

JOHNSON: You ought to let some of them know it up there. Some of these folks that are giving me hell in these columns all the time, you ought to whisper to them that Halleck—that you heard it all over the place that they're going to ask him to resign. That'd be good for him right now.

SHRIVER: Yes, okay....

LBJ's conversation with Rep. Phil Landrum, August 9, 1964[28]

JOHNSON: I thought that you not only did a very able job, but you did one that I think was mighty patriotic. I want you to give a little thought to the pitfalls in it. When I get back up there and we get settled, right after we sign it, I want to kind of get you to be an unofficial advisor as to how we can keep this thing clean, just anticipate the problems that are going to come from our region and our section. Let's pick out one or two that could be real models and try to make our dreams come true.

LANDRUM: We do have wonderful potential in this thing, Mr. President, and I've complimented you—I don't know whether I can be any value or not, but I'll certainly help you and way in the world I can.... I'm delighted that you're pleased with our effort. We couldn't have ever done it without the assistance we've had from the executive branch of the government. But we did outvote Judge Smith. Didn't we?

JOHNSON: I don't even tell myself some of the things we did, Phil.

LANDRUM: It was a bloody, bruising battle on the floor. I've got a mean, nasty fight going on down here in the primary. If I can get by without a conference on that, it would give me a few days to campaign—

JOHNSON: Well, I'll sure do it. We don't mix in primaries, but anything that you want us to do, you let me know.

LANDRUM: I don't think—

JOHNSON: I know I could hurt you more than I could help you, but any way in the world—if you've got anything pending around there that's got any problems in them, let us quietly clear them up.

LANDRUM: If you could tell that fellow up there in Detroit whose name starts with an R, you know—

JOHNSON: Yes, sir. Yes, sir, I'll do that. I'll do that today.

LANDRUM: Tell him to call off this General Motors crowd in Doraville, Georgia.

JOHNSON: Give me that name.

LANDRUM: That's UAW.

JOHNSON: Yeah, I know it, but I mean the town in Georgia.

LANDRUM: Doraville.

JOHNSON: D-O—

LANDRUM: R-A-V-I-L-L-E. That's the Buick, Oldsmobile, Pontiac plant just outside of Atlanta. They're riding this boy around, and that's where he's getting his breakfast from.

JOHNSON: Thank you, my friend. I'll let you hear from me.

LBJ's conversation with Walter Reuther, August, 9, 1964[29]

JOHNSON: Now, I've got to ask you to do something else that you may not like to do, but this is something that's just got to be done. There's a fellow down in Doraville, Georgia, with the UAW, Pontiac Division, or something, that's giving Phil Landrum hell. We just can't do that. We've just got to save him.

REUTHER: You don't know who this is?

JOHNSON: No, he just says that he's got a fight in the primary [against Zell Miller]. He's going to win it two or three to one, but [he] says, "I've been here murdering on your poverty bill day and night, and they called me a turncoat and a counterfeit Confederate and everything else. I brought along the boys from North Carolina and Georgia and everything." And he did. If we hadn't have made that selection of strategy [in getting Landrum to sponsor the legislation], they would have murdered us. I think that this is the biggest bill this year. It has to be authorized again through this committee. We're going to use this fellow to get a billion dollars worth of appropriations, and it will probably be twice that much next year. He has had some bad labor votes back there. No question about it. But they're not going to beat him. They're not going to touch him. They're not even going to come close to it. He's the best man we've got. If I could have Landrum or Johnson or Reuther, I'd rather have Landrum, because he appeals to a good many people that you and I can't ever touch.

REUTHER: That's right. All right, I'll go to work on that right away. I'll get on the phone right away on that.

JOHNSON: You let me know something that I can report to him, because he holds this thing in the palm of his hand. What I'm going to do, without sacrificing anything, where people are going to be there anyway, I'm going to try to make them Johnson leaders instead of Johnson haters.

REUTHER: Sure. All right. I'll go to work on that right away this morning.

THE SENATE LABOR AND PUBLIC WELFARE COMMITTEE

PERRIN: In 1964 the antipoverty bill was drafted primarily by the Johnson administration. We [Senator McNamara's staff] were not involved at that stage in the actual drafting of the bill. Our first connection with it, really, was when Senator McNamara was asked by the White House to be the Senate sponsor of the bill.

Do you know the reason for that request?

PERRIN: I knew that they weren't about to get Senator Lister Hill of Alabama, who was the chairman of the Senate Labor and Public Welfare Committee, to be the sponsor of it. And I don't know that they asked anyone else before they came to Senator McNamara, but he seemed like a logical person to do it. There may have been more to it that I've either forgotten about or don't know about, but in any event, we were asked to sponsor the bill. I think my first real knowledge of it came when Adam Yarmolinsky and a couple of other people came by my office to give us a draft of the bill and discuss it. Senator McNamara then introduced the legislation, along with the House sponsor, who I believe was Congressman Landrum, of all people.

Why Landrum in the House and McNamara in the Senate, when they seemed to be at different poles?

PERRIN: That was part of the strategy, to have people of this nature being the sponsors of the bill. Then they could point to the southern conservative and the northern liberal as the sponsors; ergo, the bill must be a great one. It's rather a juvenile strategy, I guess, but nevertheless somebody dreamed this up.

I don't have a timetable in front of me of the legislative process that then took place, but we conducted rather short hearings on it in the Senate. The bill was generally pretty straightforward as to what was to be expected—except for community action, which I don't believe anyone really fully understood then, except for some ideas that were floating around. I've always thought with some interest of the impact that the phrase "maximum feasible participation of the poor" has had over the years, and I've thought back as to what it meant to us at that time. It never really became the subject of much discussion during the legislative process. In my own recollection, the word "feasible" was the key word. Every time you use the word "feasible," you have the option of going as far as you want to or stopping as short as you want to. And I always considered it in that context, that the idea was good. "Participation" obviously was good, but "feasible" would control how far you had to go. So I think this was one of the reasons that we never really considered it an all-powerful tail that was going to start to wag a dog one of these years.

D. BAKER: There were no radical changes in the Senate. As the easiest way of handling the thing from a tactical point of view, we basically took the House bill and tried to operate with it. We had relatively brief hearings. Senator McNamara was always unenthusiastic about hearings. He didn't think they accomplished a great deal except to give the enemies of a piece of legislation a forum. So we more or less adopted the hearings of the House committee in bloc as part of our own hearings and went forward with the House legislation.

Probably the major thing that occurred in the Senate side during the committee deliberations was the adoption of the migrant worker provisions—the housing, education, sanitation, day-care operations—which, of course, were based on legislation that had passed the Senate from [New Jersey] Senator Harrison Williams's subcommittee on migratory labor. There had been housing, day-care, sanitation, and education programs for migrants which had passed the Senate separately and got stalled over in the House. When the poverty bill was before the committee, these were sort of pressed together into one lump package and attached to it.

THE GOVERNORS' VETO

SHRIVER: [The battle over governors' veto of community action programs] came up principally when we were trying to get the OEO legislation through the Senate. I was having a very difficult time, especially with Senator Richard Russell of Georgia. Richard Russell was one of the behemoths, one of the giants of the Senate, and normally wouldn't even have concerned himself with a peripheral thing like the War on Poverty. He was a big man dealing with big defense issues and geopolitical issues and huge national political issues. He had been a candidate for president of the United States and all that kind of thing. So this really wasn't a matter of great concern to him. But it was to his constituents, because Richard Russell and many others from the South were traditional believers in the doctrine of states' rights. Well, I was not unsympathetic to that doctrine, truthfully, because I came from the state of Maryland, and in the state of Maryland when I grew up, one of the absolute cardinal principles of the Democratic Party was our belief in states' rights. So I think I understood the philosophical and political milieu out of which Richard Russell came.

Similarly, I was rather close at that time to Herman Talmadge, the senator from Georgia. Talmadge was and still is an extremely astute southern politician. One day I was talking to him, and I said, "Look, this is the problem, Senator. We can't allow all this money to become bogged down in the state and local government apparatus, and we cannot allow a system to be established whereby the purposes of the legislation can be frustrated totally by the clique that might be hanging around a particular governor. How in the name of God can we get around that problem? Moreover, I think that's the problem that is preventing Senator Russell from supporting us. He is being badgered by some of his constituents from Georgia"—which is where Talmadge is from.

Talmadge looked at me—I remember it very well. He had a big cigar he used to smoke, and he flipped the ashes in a spittoon in his office. And he said, "Well, Sargent, have you ever considered a veto by the governor?" He used to be a governor, Talmadge. I said, "Well, no, I never have. What do you mean?" He said, "Why don't you consider the possibility that you will allow the governor to veto any program that is going to take place in his state if he disapproves of it? Now, first of all, they're not going to disapprove of many of them, because the governors all want to have the money come into their states. Secondly, the governor politically doesn't want to be in the position of being the person who is preventing a certain program from taking place in his state. My guess, Sargent," he said to me, "is that you will get very, very few vetoes from governors. But if you put it in the legislation that the governor has the veto, then Senator Russell will be able to say that the doctrine, the principle of states' rights, state authority, has been maintained." I said, "Thank you, Senator. That's all I want to know." I got up and walked out of the office. That's where the governors' veto came from.

O'BRIEN: Then there was the question of the governors' veto of Job Corps camps. That became a major problem, and we compromised on that. There was some element of veto put right into the bill. That "right" became something we had to agree to or cave on, because it could have been extremely disruptive if we didn't work out some kind of an accommodation. Of course, that had the civil rights aspects to it too.

But that was something we just had to accept. That was a splendid opportunity for those in opposition or those worried about civil rights. It was a way of getting around the corner. Supposedly now we're in states' rights, which suddenly some people have great concern about who normally wouldn't be concerned. But you had to accept it for what it was: it was a maneuver. By the same token, that did provide an opportunity for people to either leave the reservation or not join the reservation. So it had to be accommodated, reluctantly, but the practical aspects dictated it, and it happened. I'd prefer not to, but it did. I don't recall the exercising of any of these prerogatives particularly, as time went on, but there should not have been any authority in the bill for governors to make determinations. It was a political accommodation.

YARMOLINSKY: Well, I remember, very close to the end, when it was almost through, Moyers calling me, saying, "How important is this governors' veto?" and I gave him the pros and cons. He said, "Okay." And that happened several times on things. "What would happen if you couldn't have X or Y or Z?" and I would tell him, "It's not the end of the world." This is a familiar sort of question one is often asked by the White House and people in the White House: "You've got this in your legislative program. What's it worth?"

THE LOYALTY OATH

Congress also added a section requiring a disclaimer or an affidavit by individuals employed under the act. Do you recall this loyalty oath?

WEEKS: It was a loyalty oath, particularly applied to Job Corps enrollees, but not to civil servants, as I recall. I think it was for VISTA volunteers and Job Corps enrollees. There was universal opposition on the part of everybody who was involved in the task force at the time to the concept of a loyalty oath, and this went right up to the top of the organization, including people like Jack Conway, who this didn't affect directly because he wasn't concerned with Job Corps or VISTA in a supervisory position. I think it raised concerns about McCarthyism and the idea that you would require a loyalty oath of a sixteen- or seventeen-year-old high school dropout who never got past the fifth or sixth or seventh grade; [it] struck many people as being something that was just plain wrong.

Furthermore, most of us saw this, and I think correctly, as a tactic by a group of very conservative southern congressmen to create a nuisance area, something which would create difficulty and which might be controversial and which would be more like a roadblock. Because I don't think it does make sense to give sixteen- and seventeen-year-old kids a loyalty oath. This was sponsored by one of the congressmen from Mississippi, as I recall.

INDEMNITY PAYMENTS TO FARMERS AND AID FOR MIGRANT WORKERS

Do you recall how indemnity payments for dairy farmers were added to the bill?

WEEKS: Oh, yes, I remember. That was very controversial. That was something that appeared literally out of the blue. Nobody could figure out why or where. This was strictly a special interest thing that was tacked onto the bill. I forget whether this came from [Representative Robert] Poage [of Texas], or whether it came from some other area. There was horror in OEO that this thing was getting tacked onto the bill, not over the substantive question of indemnity payments to farmers, but simply because it obviously had no relationship to anything that we were dealing with, and that adding this on suddenly added a controversial new aspect to the bill that certainly didn't simplify the task and could make it a lot more complicated.

Congress also added aid for migrant farmworkers at the legislative stage. Do you recall that addition?

WEEKS: Yes, I do, and I think the initial reaction was that perhaps this could be covered under [the] Community Action [Program], but that when we sat back and said, "Migrant farmworkers are migrant, and therefore perhaps this [amendment] makes some sense." I recall that trying to figure out how to administer it—that it created a complication from the management point of view. It was kind of a rat's nest. Everyone realized that there was a problem with migrant farmworkers, but nobody was quite sure how to deal with it or what to do about it. We were faced with a problem of having to develop what everyone saw as a new and difficult area of activity.

GOLDFARB: We didn't do anything about migrant farmworkers. Not because some-one sat down and said they're not important enough or they don't fall into this jurisdiction, but simply because nobody knew about it or said anything about it. Fortuitously, when Sundquist took our package up to the Hill, two people on the Hill—one, [James] Roosevelt in the House; and the other, [Harrison] Pete Williams in the Senate—said, "I'll buy your agricultural program, such as it is; but I have for years been pushing some pet programs, and they must be added." Sundquist said, "It made sense to me. It was no great concession, because I thought it was a good idea." So we said, "Sure. If that's the price, we'll pay it." And that's how we got into the OEO package eventually what treatment there was for an obvious constituency in this program which had never been planned into the program.

YARMOLINSKY IS SACRIFICED

RE: ADAM YARMOLINSKY

As vice president, Johnson had worked with Adam Yarmolinsky on the Equal Employment Opportunity Commission. Although he was aware of Yarmolinsky's background, LBJ respected his abilities and coyly resisted pressure to exclude him from the program. Not only did the president believe that the attacks on Yarmolinsky were unfair, but he was also determined to protect his prerogative to appoint whom he wished.

LBJ's conversation with Sargent Shriver, March 26, 1964[30]

SHRIVER: I was just chatting with Bill Moyers because Adam Yarmolinsky has had a talk with Bob McNamara, and it's okay with McNamara for Adam to come over here and become, so to speak, the deputy special assistant here, to be the key fellow with me in the development of this program. I was just talking to Bill about it. He said he thought that you would be interested. Naturally, if you are, I wanted to talk to you about it because you know how bright Adam is and how much interested he is in this particular area of work that we're involved here with this urban thing.

JOHNSON: I think he's very able, very fine, wonderful fellow. I like him. He's a good friend of mine. You want to watch that background on the Hill, though. I'd be worried a little bit about that on poverty.

SHRIVER: Yes. Of course, it is in a sense, less of a situation than over in the Defense Department, so that's really terrific, I think. I'm all set on that. I'm not worried. He's got terrific, particularly good contacts with the liberal groups over on the Hill where maybe I'm not the strongest guy in the world. What I was wanting to do was—since, if he leaves the Defense Department and comes over here, he would have to become, let's say a deputy special assistant, and I was hoping that you would give me permission to talk to Jenkins or somebody about the paperwork involved with that.

JOHNSON: All right. Yeah. Yeah. Talk to him. I don't know what's involved, but...

SHRIVER: I thought maybe I might assign my salary to him.

JOHNSON: Yeah. [laughs]

SHRIVER: Is that all right?

JOHNSON: Yeah, it's all right. I don't know anything about the details; talk to Walter. Thank you, Sarge.

LBJ's conversation with Rep. George Mahon of Texas, August 6, 1964[31]

JOHNSON: ...I haven't appointed a single human, and you can tell every one of them. They say I'm going to appoint this radical fellow or that guy. Nobody's talked to me. I haven't committed myself to anyone....

MAHON: This Adam Yarmolinsky, or whatever his name is, he is not an asset.

JOHNSON: He is McNamara's lawyer.

MAHON: I know and—

JOHNSON: They borrowed him from McNamara. His father had a bad two or three organizations he belonged to. The kid defended his father. McNamara has plans to send him up as Assistant Secretary of Defense. He didn't want to do it before the election because he thought it would be a red herring and there would be an issue.

MAHON: There would be.

JOHNSON: He thought he would wait until after the election, and sit down, and we could reason it out even with the Republicans. He says there is nothing against the boy himself. He hasn't done anything wrong. He's been one of the best men he's had for three years.

MAHON: Yes, he is—

JOHNSON: But we just borrowed him for this drafting. And he did. He's the best drafter. He's kind of like they used to raise hell about Ben Cohen. He was a great wild man. Well he's the most conservative man in town now. But he is a skilled artist. I guess a dozen talked to me yesterday about it. I said I've never talked to him. I've never offered him any job. I've never recommended him for anything. I don't want to just go out and say the man is no good and [that] I've disqualified him. But I'll assure you [that] before I appoint him to anything, I will be very damn careful, and I will sit down and look at it, and I'll consider all of your views. I'm not in the habit of bringing in people that irritate everybody on the Hill.

LBJ's conversation with Speaker John McCormack, August 6, 1964[32]

McCORMACK: That fellow Sampleton [Yarmolinsky]...let's see, what the hell's his name. I don't know what his name is. You know that poison's floating around.

JOHNSON: Yes, it's been floating around by the NAM. It's all a lie, but you can't denounce a man because somebody's starts to lie on him.

McCORMACK: Can I tell them that he won't be even appointed?

JOHNSON: No, I wouldn't say that about Capone. You can tell them that I've never had him mentioned to me; that he's never been recommended; that I've never considered it; and that I couldn't and wouldn't think of what I was going to do unless I had the authority to do it; and that this is pure propaganda lie.

McCORMACK: Yes. All right, Mr. President.

JOHNSON: My judgment is that he will be nominated for Assistant Secretary of Defense next January. He's been with McNamara for three years. This is a McCarthy-type action, which you are going to see a lot more during Goldwater's administration.

McCORMACK: Yes, I know.

JOHNSON: How they would know when I don't know—that answers the question itself.

McCORMACK: I understand. I entirely agree with you, but you understand my calling up.

JOHNSON: Sure. I'd just say that "I talked to the President. He told me: number one, he had never considered him or thought of him in connection with any place, number one; number two, that no one had ever talked to him about it, recommended him or otherwise; that, number three, he had made no commitments to anyone on any appointment and would not do so, either for or against, until the bill is passed." But I don't think you need to worry about me doing anything that's very bad.

McCORMACK: All right, fine. This is enough for me to talk around....

JOHNSON: How's it look to you today?

McCORMACK: Close. It will be won or lost by five votes, in my opinion.... We're going to do a little repair job in the North Carolina delegation on this Yarmolinsky.

JOHNSON: Well go do it and just tell them that you've talked to me and I've given you assurance I have not considered him. Nobody's recommended him. I'm not entertaining any thought of appointing him. I wouldn't say that I wouldn't appoint anybody, but that I'm not going to appoint anybody unless I talk to you.

LBJ's conversation with Bill Moyers, August 7, 1964[33]

JOHNSON:...Did you all have any good speakers on poverty? I guess Landrum was the best, wasn't he?

MOYERS: Good speeches and good speakers.

JOHNSON: Who wrote the speeches?

MOYERS: Ira Walsh, Hal Pachios, Adam Yarmolinsky...

JOHNSON: How did you get by with Yarmolinsky today with—

MOYERS: It did not come up on the floor. Jimmy Roosevelt inserted the letter that Yarmolinsky wrote to McNamara two years ago clarifying his record and denying these charges. He put that in the record. Roosevelt and some of these liberal congressmen are very upset. They feel that Yarmolinsky's got the shaft. It's been tough holding some of them down today from saying anything on the floor, but it would have been unwise for Yarmolinsky for them to say anything.

JOHNSON: Yes, unwise for Roosevelt too; he's a plain damn fool. Yarmolinsky [had] better stay in the Defense Department. McNamara is the best defender he's got and the safest one he's got. He ought to tell him that's where he wants to stay until we can get him confirmed as Assistant Secretary of Defense.

MOYERS: That's great. I'm glad to hear you say that. I won't tell him that, but I'm glad to hear it.

JOHNSON: I'd tell him that I think that he ought to stay there. McNamara's told me he wants to try to get him Assistant Secretary of Defense. I wouldn't mind going to bat if his record's clean. Has he belonged to any liberal organizations?

MOYERS: Liberals, yes, but no Communist organizations. And in those liberal organizations he has opposed the Communists and has driven them out.

JOHNSON: Now what liberal organizations that are questionable does he belong to.

MOYERS: The American Veterans Committee. Are you familiar with that?

JOHNSON: No.

MOYERS: That's a small group of veterans who organized to fight for liberal causes twenty, twenty-five years ago. Wirtz is a member, et cetera. In the beginning, there was a big fight over whether the Communists would dominate it or not. Yarmolinsky helped expose and drive them out, and that's a matter of record in the *Daily Worker*.

JOHNSON: Has it been cited?

MOYERS: No, sir. It has not been cited by the Attorney General's list. His mother and father at one time joined to an organization that was cited, but they got out of it before it was cited when they learned that it was Communist-oriented.

JOHNSON: Well, we'll just put up a fight if we win this election. McNamara told me he wanted to make him Assistant Secretary of Defense, and I told him that's fine if he can do it. And that was three months ago, four months ago. Now that's good.

LBJ's conversation with Sargent Shriver, August 9, 1964[34]

SHRIVER: The only sad thing here was this business about Adam Yarmolinsky of course. I wonder—have you had a chance to speak to him?

JOHNSON: No. No, I haven't.

SHRIVER: I think it would be terrific, Mr. President, if you could call him. He has a terrific respect for you. The only thing he's ever said to me in the course of the whole business—his attitude has been just perfect—was that he was concerned about what you thought and that he was a little unhappy, you might say, that he hadn't heard anything from you.

JOHNSON: Well I was unhappy as hell for him giving out that interview, and I was unhappy with him being up in the radio gallery yesterday. I think that we've got to teach—

SHRIVER: Giving out what interview?

JOHNSON: He had an interview [as] long as a whore's dream in the Scripps-Howard papers, of all places, about what's going to happen in the Peace Corps; that I guess I had to talk to thirty congressmen about.

SHRIVER: That was out there today?

JOHNSON: No, no. This was three or four days ago. That's what all our fight's been about. We'd have had this bill passed by fifty votes if he hadn't been giving out his interviews and they hadn't been circulating these letters on him.

SHRIVER: Well, the letter he wrote, of course, was something he wrote some time ago, and I think he should have written that, Mr. President.

JOHNSON: I'm not talking about what he should have done. I'm just talking about what he did do and the hell that it caused us. I told Bill Moyers that you can't have everybody in your shop giving out interviews. If they're going to do some talking over there, you do the talking for them. But don't have Yarmolinsky any more than we have some in my shop. Roosevelt told me one time that "some of the very best men in government completely destroyed themselves and are no longer useful to me because they can't stay out of the paper." ... I don't think [Yarmolinsky] ought to ever be in any front job for a good many reasons, but I won't enumerate them. I like him. I think he's smart. I'm for him. I'm for him in his place, just like I'm for my wife in her place. I don't want to put her out driving any tractor. And he's got no business giving out interviews or being out in front.[35]

WEEKS: Yarmolinsky came into the Kennedy administration through the Defense Department, and in the Defense Department he was instrumental in a number of ways. But one of the main things that he was instrumental in was declaring segregated facilities off-limits to military personnel in the south, which meant that bars, restaurants, taverns, and so on near military bases had to be integrated or else military personnel were not allowed to patronize them. This created a furor in congressional districts all across the south, because there are a lot of military bases in the south, and there are a lot of commercial establishments right around them that have grown up patronizing military personnel.

In addition, it was well known that Adam Yarmolinsky's mother, I guess, is Babette Deutsch, who was a known and professed "communist," [and] that Adam himself, of course, is Jewish. He came out of an egghead intellectual university, and he was the guy who had integrated all those places in the south. So he had at least four reasons, any one of which would have made a southern congressman oppose him. By the time you added those four reasons together, you got a pretty powerful group of southern congressmen who said that this is the kind of person that as far as we're concerned is persona non grata—anywhere. Certainly not to run the poverty program and do the kind [of things] that he's been doing with commercial establishments, making commercial establishments off-limits to servicemen.

O'BRIEN: That was the last effort on the part of the opponents: attack Adam. I remember that for its gross unfairness to Adam, which, in my judgment, was a cheap shot. If they could deflect attention to Adam, take a little detour, maybe they could muddy up the waters. And they went at it.

Adam was subjected to a great deal at that time. The attacks on him were an example of people reaching desperately for one other handle that might derail [the bill]. I don't know what the record shows or [what] the history of this reflects, but the opponents at that stage would find it awfully difficult to attack Sarge. He had a broad base of support, and in fact, he was well thought of by people in opposition to the program. Adam would go along with Sarge to these meetings on the Hill. Some wise guy one day probably decided a shot could be taken that might bear fruit.

Apparently, there was a fear that the North Carolina delegation would not deliver the needed votes.

O'BRIEN: As I recall—and some of these things I probably get entwined with other activities—there was actually a caucus of the North Carolina delegation, which we requested [Representative Harold] Cooley [of North Carolina] to have to try and shore up that situation. There was a fear, and I think we did ask the delegation to caucus as an entity, which is fairly extreme. And that did occur. But that's my best recollection. We had no other state caucuses or delegation caucuses; that was the one I remember.

The Yarmolinsky situation became the most significant controversy in that fight. After everything was tried by the opposition—whether you're talking about community action, family planning—it did zero in on Adam. I can't testify to Sarge committing to Adam that if he, Sarge, ran the program, Adam would be his deputy, but let's assume that happened. It became clear to us at the White House that there had to be a definitive position taken on Adam's future role in order to avoid ultimately losing this fight. Whether Adam was sacrificed, or whether it was a totally exaggerated situation, it was easy to say, "Well, no, there's no contemplation that Adam will be involved." I rather think—and Sarge would have to testify to this—that it was widely assumed on the Hill Adam would probably be deputy. He had played a key role throughout, and it would be very logical to assume he would have a key role in implementation once enactment took place. The opposition was able to create concern, but the concern seemed to focus on the North Carolina delegation and Harold Cooley. And Landrum was leader of this fight, and finding that he might stumble in the last mile, there had to be an assurance on noninvolvement. Maybe Landrum also demanded it, and he'd be in a position to make a demand of that nature, because we were depending on him to carry the ball.

I was not directly involved in any of the intrigue. All I know is, if Sarge had publicly announced that Adam would be the deputy when the program was enacted, I think we still would have made it, but it would have been much more difficult. In fact, I'd never known whether Adam had any interest in being part of the program.

[Yarmolinsky was] an extremely able fellow who you were happy to have aboard. Adam would step forward and take the personal sacrifice without even blinking an eye, but I thought the whole thing was a smear that was repugnant to all of us. I wasn't at a meeting where a demand was made. I know that.

SHRIVER: We were meeting in John McCormack's office. Cooley, the chairman of the North Carolina delegation and chairman of the [House] Agriculture Committee, was there, and some other congressmen, and all the whips. The Speaker had all the whips in. These people, led by Cooley, said that if Adam Yarmolinsky was in the program, they would not vote for it to pass the Congress. The Democratic whips said that if they did not have the votes of these congressmen, this particular group—I can't remember whether it was fifteen or twenty-five votes that Cooley and his supporters had gotten together—that they couldn't get the legislation through the Congress without those votes. There was a terrific harangue and argument.

They wanted me to say that I could guarantee them that Adam Yarmolinsky was not going to be in the program. My position was very complicated, but it was also straightforward. I told them that I did not intend to be in the program myself, which was true. I didn't want to be the director of it. I had told Johnson that I would organize it and try to get it through the Congress, but I wanted to go back and run the Peace Corps. So I said, "I'm not going to be the director of it. I have no desire to be, and I'm going to propose people to the president who can run it. Therefore, I'm not going to say a thing about this. Adam Yarmolinsky is an extremely competent person. I think he would be great in the program. But I do not have the right to put him in or put him out. That position will be a presidential appointment, just like the director's is, and that's for the president to say."

So they said, "Well, then, get the president on the phone." I said, "Well, that's not my business." The Speaker of the House told me to go get the president on the phone. When the Speaker instructed me to do so, I stepped into a little room adjoining the Speaker's office, and I called the White House. I got the president on the phone, and I told him what the problem was. I said, "From what our friends over here tell us, you can have the War on Poverty bill through the Congress. But the price of it is that you would agree not to appoint Adam Yarmolinsky."

The president wasn't going to sit still for that, because he wasn't going to have people in the Congress tell him in the executive branch whom he could appoint and whom he could not appoint. So in his typical imaginative and artful way, Johnson said to me, "Well, you tell them that you won't recommend that I appoint him." I said, "Well, that won't make any difference, Mr. President, because I've already told them that as far as I'm concerned I won't even be in there to make a recommendation one way or the other." He said, "Well, all the easier then. If you're not even going to be there, then you don't have to worry about making the recommendation." I said, "Yes, but I don't want to do that, because Adam Yarmolinsky is my friend, and I don't want to say that to these particular congressmen because"—they were anti-Jewish and they were antiliberals and they were anti-anybody named Yarmolinsky. It was just real, lowdown racial bigotry and political venom and all kinds of odious hatred. I said, "I don't want to kowtow to these guys." He said, "That's okay. Don't you worry about them. You just tell them that the president will act on these matters in his own judgment, and that in that process that he will consider recommendations from everybody, and that nobody's recommendations are going to be controlling, and so on." I went back, and that wasn't satisfactory. They said, "No, we have to have an assurance that Adam Yarmolinsky will not be named as a deputy director," or, as a matter of fact, that his name will not be sent to the Congress.

So did you call the president back?

SHRIVER: I called the president back, yes. Here's where, in fact, the actual wording of what I was then authorized to say by Johnson skips my memory.

That was the most unpleasant experience I ever had in the government of the United States. In fact, despite the fact that I didn't think I had any choice, I felt then as if I ought to just go out and vomit, it was such a despicable proceeding. And in fact, I didn't admire myself for the role I had to play in it.

D. BAKER: There was a great deal more nervousness about its passing in the House than, from the benefit of hindsight, needed to have existed. If we'd known what the votes were going to be, the White House and Mr. Shriver might have told the South Carolina delegation to go jump in the lake on the Yarmolinsky affair. I read all the stories, but I was told the story by a member of the Congress who happens to be a personal friend of mine, who was present in the Speaker's office when this matter came up and was resolved. It was considerably different than has appeared in print. The way I understood [it], [Representative] Mendel Rivers [of South Carolina]—either through his antipathy to Yarmolinsky because of his association with McNamara, or because of some alleged personal affront, or because [Yarmolinsky] was a Jew, or because he was a liberal, or for whatever reason—he had mobilized the South Carolina delegation and some of the North Carolina delegation to threaten that they would not support this legislation and, in fact, would oppose it unless they were assured that Yarmolinsky was not going to be the deputy director. This ultimatum was presented to Mr. Shriver in Speaker McCormack's office. As I understand it, he said he could not make this kind of commitment. He went to the phone and called the White House; my informant told me that it was his impression that he had spoken to the president. He came back and said, not that he was committed, not that Yarmolinsky would not be the deputy, but that his commitment was that he, Shriver, was permitted to say that he would not recommend Yarmolinsky to the president to be deputy. It was that fairly limited commitment that was made.

Subsequently, in the course of the debate on the floor of the House in response to a question raised by someone—I believe it was some Republican—Phil Landrum alleged that it was his understanding from, as I recall he said, the "highest possible source," that Yarmolinsky was going to have no part of this operation, which was a distinct enlargement upon the original commitment as I understood it.

Are you suggesting that there was some sort of a communication breakdown between the president, Shriver, and Phil Landrum? Or is there something more to it?

D. BAKER: I really don't have any way of knowing how that occurred, except that I am confident that the person that confided this—in the view that I gave on the matter—to [me] is an objective and honest reporter of the facts as he perceived them. Whether there was a later communication with Phil Landrum, I don't know. But the fact of the matter is, once he had made that statement, even though he was in McCormack's office when the other events took place.... Now, if [Landrum], in fact, misunderstood, it really didn't make a lot of difference at that point, because he was the sponsor of the legislation in the House, and the agency was in no position—nor was the White House, in fact—to make a liar out of him. So it really didn't matter whether he misunderstood or whether he was informed. The fact of the matter is, once that statement had been made on the floor of the House, the matter was accomplished.

Once the statement was made, it had the effect of putting Shriver on the spot.

D. BAKER: That's right. Sarge was very severely criticized for the whole affair, and I think unfairly, as I view it. I think within this agency, in matters of that kind, I came to be as close to Sarge as anybody on the real tough issues. And one of the things that was always remarkable to me is that in this sort of thing in which the White House was involved, he never complained. Whatever the press was saying, he never said, "The White House told me to do this," or, "Somebody told me to do that." He always took the responsibility, and like a good loyal soldier, he kept his mouth shut, even to those of us who were very close to him.

YARMOLINSKY: I was dimly aware that there was some problem with some of the southern congressmen. I had been the object of attack by the famous General Edwin Walker a couple of years before. I knew that some of the southern congressmen felt I was the architect of a more intensive integration policy in the Defense Department, although I think I would be exaggerating my role to say that I was the architect. I was the fellow that was given a job to do by the secretary, and in fact it wasn't really done effectively until a year or more after I left.

The person who really should get the credit for it, more than anybody else, other than the secretary and Cy Vance, is probably Alfred Fitt.[36] But they had picked on me, and they had gotten all kinds of stuff. Of course, I was persona non grata in various circles because I had done *Case Studies on Personnel Security* back in 1955, although it was quite all right with the people that I worked with in the FBI and the government. But this thing kind of blew up, apparently. I was not told about it, I'm sure, out of consideration. Sargent Shriver and Wilson McCarthy, who was the legislative liaison fellow, indicated to me what was going on. I suppose it was going on for about a week, and then it blew up.

I remember Shriver coming back at the end of the day that day, coming into the office and saying to me, "Well, we've just thrown you to the wolves," and, "This is the worst day in my life."

D. BAKER: It might be observed that [sacrificing Yarmolinsky] probably was the most unfortunate thing that ever happened to the poverty program; that single occurrence probably did us more harm than anything else that ever happened. I have tremendous respect for Yarmolinsky and his abilities, and his innate good judgment, and his brains, and his capacity to administer. He and Sarge Shriver obviously had a very good working relationship. Sarge was the outside, and Yarmolinsky was the inside guy. Yarmolinsky ran a very taut ship, and he made most of the inside decisions, and he stopped most of them at his level. Sarge was free to go ahead and deal with the legislature and the outside groups and whatnot, and Adam did the housekeeping for him.

As it happens, after [the] bill was passed, he left. Sarge was without a deputy and, for reasons I've never quite understood, continued to try to run the Peace Corps and this place too. There was no number two man. Finally, after months went by, he elevated Jack Conway to the position of number two. This was after there had been an awful lot of shots taken at the program and Sarge. I think he personally had gotten himself very much overfatigued and overworked. He appeared to lack the confidence in Conway that he had in Yarmolinsky, but in any event, they did not work as well together as I think Yarmolinsky and Sarge would have. And for practical purposes, even after Jack got in here and after he left, Sarge never had a deputy. He never quite got to the position again where he could identify with his deputy as his alter ego. He just never did it in the history of the agency after Yarmolinsky left. A lot of the problems that subsequently came up would have been resolved much more quickly and much more certainly than in point of fact occurred. For instance, the conflict between the concept of what community action was all about—whether it was a coordinative, innovative, program-related effort as against an effort designed to organize the poor, and to whatever degree you want to charge it with responsibility for bringing on conflict in change or confrontation, those two polar positions—I think the agency would have arrived at some compromise or some decision as to where it was going in that area, and we would have operated on that thesis.

As it was, I think we sort of vacillated on a case-by-case basis. I don't blame Sarge for this. He was immensely put-upon. The critics from the outside and the inside, and the disloyalty in some respects—I considered it such, the leaks from the inside that were making life difficult for him—the attacks from the Hill, from areas in the administration, and from newspapers and whatnot, just kept him so busy, he really couldn't possibly keep up with what was going on. And I really think if Yarmolinsky had been here, it would have been a much better program.

SCHLEI: I think that Adam was a key figure in the development of the legislation and the program and the building up of the staff. He was a key figure in what made it good, because he supplied some elements that [Shriver lacked]. Sarge has tremendous enthusiasm and charm, and he can persuade people. He's tremendously creative, has lots of ideas. But he has more ideas, by far, than he has good ideas, and he needs somebody who is close to him who can shoot down the bad ideas and preserve the ones that are brilliant and good. Sarge is not able, like many people, to do that himself.

Secondly, Sarge is not a good methodical administrator. He works in bursts of tremendous creativity and energy, and then he has to regroup and do his thinking and so on. When he had Adam, the whole operation kept right on going, because Adam administered it and made it all happen and went around picking up the pieces. When he left, I felt that the whole operation began slowly to unravel. I think that he was a very, very significant loss to the whole operation.

THE APPROPRIATION PROCESS

What happened between the time that the bill was actually passed and the appropriation hearings and the election, and when OEO finally got started?

KELLY: Of course, there are certain benchmarks in this period. The twentieth of August was the day on which the president signed the authorization bill.[37] We then turned our attention completely to appropriations hearings and preparations for those. Those were held in late September, first before the Fogarty subcommittee [Representative John Fogarty of Rhode Island], and then before the subcommittee in the Senate which John Pastore chaired. We spent a great deal of time polishing up the budget presentation during late August and early September. I spent a good deal of time working with Bob Moyer, who was the clerk of the Fogarty subcommittee, in terms of trying to fathom what the members of that subcommittee would be interested in, what Fogarty himself was interested in. Fogarty asked a number of questions in writing to Mr. Shriver, and we prepared answers, which became kind of the bedrock of the testimony. We appeared before those two subcommittees, and then we worked very closely with the various clerks, John Witeck in the Senate side, and again Bob Moyer in the House side, until markup took place. Then ultimately, on the eighth of October, there was a bill signed which gave us an appropriation.

During the same period, I finally succeeded—again, looking at my functions in this matter—in getting ninety-five percent of the task force drawn together in one place, thanks to some assistance from the GSA. We had everybody, or at least most everybody, finally housed in the old Colonial Hotel—it was called the New Colonial Hotel, but it was about fifty years old—at the corner of M Street and Fifteenth, and that made logistics a little bit easier. Everybody had a bathroom in their office.

After the bill was passed in October, the next thing was to try and get people off of other people's payrolls and create our own, and to do the necessary personnel things that you have to do in the federal government in order to comply with civil service regulations. So that took a good deal of our time, really, in October, November, and January. We had been instructed by the president that we were only to proceed with planning, with putting people on the payroll, and we were not to proceed to let contracts or make grants on any of the programs until after the election. That was explained to me by Mr. Shriver in terms of the fact that the president did not want to create any impression that the War on Poverty was being used as a vote-getting device in the 1964 election.

7

THE OFFICE
OF ECONOMIC
OPPORTUNITY

"The Most Action In Town"

WITH SHRIVER AT THE HELM, *the new Office of Economic Opportunity had a leader of great vision and tireless energy, who seldom became mired in the day-to-day routine. His dislike for administrative minutiae would not have been a significant handicap if he had had a strong deputy. After Adam Yarmolinsky's departure in August 1964, however, Shriver did not have an assistant director to whom he could comfortably delegate. Instead, he attempted to fill both of the agency's top positions himself. An added complication was the fact that Shriver did not resign as head of the Peace Corps. He spent two days a week presiding over that agency as well until 1966.*[1]

In its administrative style and structure, the Office of Economic Opportunity resembled the Peace Corps. Three assistant directors presided over the major program components—Job Corps, VISTA, and the Community Action Program. The principal staff offices, which also had assistant director status, were: Management; Inspection; General Counsel; Congressional Relations; Interagency Programs; Public Affairs; Private Groups; and Research, Plans, Programs and Evaluations. To maintain close contact with local OEO projects, the agency established seven regional offices to whom state directors reported.[2]

The task of launching a new agency with an uncharted mission would have been difficult even under ideal circumstances. Inevitably, start-up logistics, interagency coordination, and control of thousands of grantees were going to be challenging for any director. Although Shriver's portfolio included government-wide coordination of antipoverty efforts, he never had the standing or the presidential leverage to assert this role over the cabinet officers. These essentially contradictory roles—coordinating and monitoring the initiatives of other government departments while at the same time administering a set of competing programs—forced OEO to concentrate on its own efforts.[3]

No sooner did the War on Poverty become operational, after the 1964 elections, than the agency had to prepare its budget for the next fiscal year—with little program *experience to aid the planning process. By the summer of 1965, Shriver tried to sell the president on a dramatic escalation in the attack on poverty. The proposed ten-year plan, which called for a large-scale jobs program, increased social services, and a negative income tax, would require up to $10 billion annually. Although the funding requirement was modest when compared with the magnitude of poverty in America, Johnson balked. He knew that Congress was unlikely to support more than a small incremental increase. Also, by mid-1965, domestic expenditures had to compete with the increasing cost of the war in Vietnam.[4]*

SHRIVER AS DIRECTOR

WEEKS: As the legislation was being passed, it was well known that there was a serious question as to whether or not Shriver was going to be the director of OEO. Shriver made it clear a number of times in the hearings that he didn't know whether he was going to be director, and he personally hoped that he would not be the director. And I know personally that Shriver did not want to be director of OEO. From the beginning, Shriver made it clear to me that his job—and he had been asked by the president—[was] to put together the legislation and to get the legislation passed. As soon as the legislation was passed, he expected that somebody would be selected to head the program, and that would be it. Furthermore, he was still very much wrapped up in the operations of the Peace Corps. He still loved the Peace Corps. He was starting to carry out a few specific assignments that were not strictly Peace Corps–related, but they were kind of diplomatically related. I think at one point in time Lyndon Johnson sent him to meet the pope in Jerusalem, or something like that, for example, as a presidential representative. And he enjoyed the role that he was playing there very much. He really did not see himself as being the head of the poverty program and didn't seek it, and I don't think he wanted it.

Everything that was involved in all his actions after the basic legislation was passed in August of 1964 were actions which saw him basically staying away from the main issues of the program at that point in time and clearly waiting for a signal from the president as to whether he was going to run the Peace Corps or whether he was going to run the poverty program. And it was a signal which did not come for a long period of time; he was head of both programs for quite a long period of time. This was to some extent a problem for OEO, because it was difficult enough to run one agency like OEO, much less run OEO and Peace Corps besides.

Otis A. Singletary Jr., the first director of the Job Corps, headed the program for a year beginning in the fall of 1964. Initially a professor of history at the University of Texas at Austin, he rose through various administrative posts to become chancellor of the University of North Carolina at Greensboro. His board of trustees granted him a one-year leave of absence to accept the Job Corps assignment.

SINGLETARY: I had the feeling that Shriver had a considerable degree of respect for the president. Of all of the Kennedys—if I may call him a Kennedy—I think that he had a better sense of the obligation he had to serve faithfully for the government, whether that man had been of his choosing or not—although from what I saw, I would be willing to say that Shriver had some appreciation for the real strengths, raw though they frequently were, of the president.

On the other hand, I think that the president rightly viewed Shriver as an extremely intelligent, hardworking, active, able man. I heard him say [as much] out there at the ranch at the time that Shriver was filling both jobs—both OEO and the Peace Corps. Shriver asked him the question, "Mr. Johnson, I'm getting queried about this all the time, and I'm just simply saying that that's your decision, that I will give up either or both jobs any time you ask me to."

He said, "That's just the right answer, and I will just tell you this. I have you doing those jobs because I think you're the best man in the United States to do those jobs." And he said it not in some fawning way. It was a direct statement. There was nobody standing there. I happened to be in the golf cart going back from the plane to the house and heard that statement. I was impressed, knowing what little I've known of the president. He didn't just throw that around to people. You didn't wallow in praise when you were around him.

Herbert J. Kramer was appointed OEO's director of public affairs in September 1965. He remained in the position until June 1968. A native of New York City, he received a doctorate in English literature from Harvard and a law degree from the University of Connecticut. Throughout the 1950s, he worked for Travelers Insurance Company, where he became vice president of public information and advertising. During a one-year appointment as the insurance industry's coordinator for the National Advertising Council's campaign on mental retardation, Kramer had become acquainted with Sargent Shriver, who brought him into the War on Poverty.

KRAMER: I concur with the thesis expressed by many that, from the very beginning, with Mr. Shriver dividing his time for two years with the Peace Corps—spending three days a week here, two days a week at the Peace Corps, trying to run both operations, and without a strong deputy of his own choosing—the program suffered greatly. Internecine warfare was permitted to be carried out—assassinations in the night, cloak-and-dagger activities—and [there was] a general failure, I think, really to subject programs and procedures to hard evaluative judgments.

Edgar Cahn and his wife, Jean Camper Cahn, wrote an influential article in the Yale Law Journal on legal aid as an antipoverty measure, "The War on Poverty: A Civilian Perspective." It was based on Jean Cahn's pioneering work with a community program in New Haven, Connecticut, and it brought the Cahns to the attention of the War on Poverty Task Force. Edgar Cahn, who was then employed by the Department of Justice, was detailed as a special assistant to Sargent Shriver. At OEO, the Cahns were instrumental in the establishment of the Legal Services Program. Jean Cahn, although employed by the Ford Foundation, was on loan to OEO from November 1964 to March 1965.

Edgar Cahn—the son of Edmund Cahn, a distinguished legal philosopher—was educated at Swarthmore and at Yale, where he received a doctorate in English and a law degree. Jean Camper Cahn, the daughter of a prominent Baltimore physician who had been a civil rights leader and founder of the Baltimore branch of NAACP, was educated at Northwestern, Swarthmore, and Yale Law School. After leaving OEO in 1965, the Cahns founded the Urban Law Institute in Washington, D.C., which later became Antioch Law School and, ultimately, the District of Columbia School of Law.

E. CAHN: I have a recollection, too, that Shriver was trying to be extremely careful not to be viewed as disloyal or being part of a Kennedy plan, but really being part of a team and working very closely with Bill Moyers, whom he'd known in the Peace Corps. I have a feeling that Shriver was always way out on a limb, using both personal [and political] capital, doing his damnedest, but that his relationships with the White House were some [what] shaky. If anything, he was the token Kennedy member that was being included; he came to have a genuine commitment, and a personally almost tortured commitment, because he understood that he was going to be using up all of his personal and political capital. There were times when he talked about: Should he quit? Could he do any more good? This particularly became clear as the Vietnam War and the priority issue became clearer. And he would say, "Somebody has got to hang in there, and I can't figure out anybody who's got more sort of credibility with Congress and more political capital who would be willing to go to bat to keep this program alive in Congress, because it's so controversial."

So starting off from a very amorphous kind of understanding—and he'd really let Yarmolinsky run the thing for him—he walked in, and there he was on a half-time basis trying to get hold of a bucking bronco which internally had everybody at each other's throats.

SUGARMAN: Let me say, when I first came to OEO, I was not an admirer of Mr. Shriver. I found it rather difficult to communicate with him, and in fact, we didn't communicate very well for a long time. But as I worked with him over a period of time and watched him in operation, I became convinced that he was one of the real geniuses of America. I've never to this day seen anyone with the capacity to continually innovate, to continually push for development, that he has. And I've never seen anyone who was any better at analyzing the potentials and the problems and situations, not always knowing what the answers were, but at picking out the weak points in arguments. Gradually, we learned how to work with one another, and while I never considered myself one of the Shriver crowd, we found that we respected one another pretty well and found that we were both interested in accomplishing the same kinds of things and could work pretty comfortably together.

TOLMACH: I suppose in a way he's a guy that you admired and couldn't stand at the same time. He was, as everyone attests, handsome and forceful and had a great sense of humor and so forth, and in that way was a national leader. Some of his administrative practices made a lot of hair stand on end on a lot of scalps. While he developed a feeling for poor people and the problems of poverty—much in the way that he did for similar people in other countries through his Peace Corps experience—and believed in this whole thing overall, I don't think he really understood beans about the deeper problems of social change, what really had to go into bringing about change or dealing with some of the problems in welfare systems and in education systems. I think this showed itself in his frequent inability to understand some of the projects that were proposed to him and consequently in his drawing back from support of them.

Perhaps it's unfair to ask that a man of his background have the same understanding as, say, a man like Mitchell Ginsberg, who comes out of years of the social work profession.[5] But then, you can't have everything. He also was a salesman of such ability that we got quite a bit more than we might have if it hadn't been for him. I don't mean money, but support from many quarters.

D. BAKER: It was utterly impossible for Sarge to conceive of himself as part of a bureaucracy. He was very intolerant of bureaucratic types. He saw himself as being part of a monumental effort at innovation, of helping to find new ways of charting new routes, and with a lesser emphasis placed on resources as such. He always recognized that you had to have the resources, but he was interested mainly in the innovation to the degree that he was able to give attention to it. He was never so happy as when he was talking with a bunch of people, trying to develop a new idea—talking to a bunch of child psychologists, educators, psychiatrists, medical people, and whatnot in the development of the Head Start program. It was an area of great excitement for him. There was nothing he liked better than that. He threw himself into that, and into a number of the new problems, with a great alacrity, and to the degree that he didn't have to spend all his time keeping the agency alive, he spent most of the rest of the time trying to help develop new programs. To give you an example, we were among the first of the federal agencies to overtly, blatantly, and clearly make grants for family planning purposes.

"Family planning" being a euphemism for birth control?

D. BAKER: Yes. Well, that was one thing we insisted on, that it always be called "family planning." But the fact of the matter is, he was deeply involved in getting us started in that. Among other things, I attended a number of dinners out at his house in which this subject was discussed. There were doctors, theologians, and general practitioners, and gynecologists, and psychologists, and people that had been over advising Rome, and all manner of people attending these things. We'd discuss at great length the pros and cons of this approach and that approach and this rule and that rule and the other one. The thing that he really delighted in was the development of new ideas. He just delighted having around him people who were able to work on new ideas and find imaginative ways. The last thing he would ever have wanted to do was administer an agency that was handing out money in a routine way, putting it in an envelope and sending it off year after year after year.

William G. Phillips joined OEO in 1966 as assistant director for congressional relations. Phelps—a native of Pennsylvania and a veteran of World War II—earned two degrees from American University. He became a congressional staff member in 1955 and served as administrative assistant to Representative George M. Rhodes of Pennsylvania. Phillips was the first staff director of the liberal Democratic Study Group (DSG) in the House, from 1959 to 1965.

PHILLIPS: As far as organization, the structural management area, Shriver had made some reputation of being an efficient manager, in dealing with agency people and in coordinating and controlling what they did. One of the favorite ploys Shriver used to use—he was noted for it—took place at his senior staff meetings, attended by about fifteen people: his special assistants, the assistant directors, the program directors [for] Community Action, Job Corps, VISTA, the director of the Office of Inspection, and his general counsel. These were senior staff. He would play one person off against the other. He'd set up a premise and call on one of his senior staff to expound upon his views in that area and then encourage others to take him apart in the dialogue. I've never been in such stimulating staff meetings. No one ever went to sleep, because you were always guarding your flank against somebody else.

But there was a purpose to all this in the decision-making process. Shriver would say, "Well, how do you think we ought to handle this grant?" He would call on the person who was most familiar in the program area administering the grant. He would make the pitch why it ought to be re-funded, say, at the level of $2 million. Then he would call on his public affairs director and say, "How is the press going to handle this? Are we going to get any bad press if we re-fund? What's the local paper going to [report]? What's their reaction going to be? Have they supported any parts of our program?"—the *Elmira News* or whatever town it was in. And he'd ask me, "What would be the political repercussions? What would the senators from that state [say]? How would they feel toward OEO? What about the congressman? Have you talked to him about it?"

Everyone would have an input, and quite often there would be a strong difference of opinion. In fact, most of the time there was some difference of opinion. Shriver would let us argue it out, however long it took, and he would make a decision based largely on that discussion plus whatever input he might have had from other sources either before or after the final decision. But once a decision was made, that was it. We were all expected to do our best to implement it fully.

Would the meetings degenerate into personal attacks?

PHILLIPS: Sometimes they did. Of course, if you had thin skin, that was not the place to work. I guess maybe Shriver pushed people harder than anyone I've ever known. I know I worked longer hours under more intense pressure there than even I could possibly have imagined. At the Democratic Study Group, I was used to long hours: a twelve-hour day for me was nothing. At OEO it was not unusual to work sixteen, seventeen hours a day.

Did you feel that this process of free fire in the meetings was productive?

PHILLIPS: I enjoyed it. Some people don't. But after the initial shock, I found myself being embarrassed for someone else at the meeting. Maybe I didn't even know him, or maybe I had just met him the day before, or didn't have any real dealings with him, but I found myself being embarrassed because he was being subjected to this kind of pressure. But after a while I began to see some purpose to this technique.

THE DIFFICULTIES OF COORDINATING THE WAR ON POVERTY

A habitual complaint among the administrators of the poverty program was that Shriver never really had a coordinator's status.

SUNDQUIST: The reason that the War on Poverty never did get coordinated was that the president and his advisers either didn't see the administrative requisites of coordination or didn't pay any attention to them. The president was concerned about the substance of the program and the politics, and he was going to have Shriver there as a coordinator, and that would be that. Administration would take care of itself. Had he thought about the coordinating role in administrative terms, he would have recognized that Shriver was not the man for that kind of a job. Shriver had certainly no interest. Nobody knows what his talent would be if he had the interest, but since he didn't have the interest, the question is moot. An intragovernmental coordinating job: that's a job—not for a public figure who has vice presidential aspirations—it's a job for a Bertrand Harding, an anonymous Budget Bureau type. Shriver was not the man for that.

But didn't you also need somebody who could wield authority in the cabinet? The program certainly was going to involve conflict and friction between the prerogatives of the new agency and those of the old departments.

SUNDQUIST: You don't have conflict with cabinet members except when you are competing with them. The Budget Bureau doesn't compete with them. The Council of Economic Advisers doesn't compete with them. If OEO had been a staff coordinating body, there wouldn't have been any conflict. The conflict came as to who was going to run particular programs, and OEO was one of the organizations that wanted to run the programs.

Certainly they didn't want any additional competition in the Executive Office. The president decided that, "Well, we'll put it in the Executive Office for the first year." This was his concession to Kermit [Gordon, of the Budget Bureau]. And then, of course, after that inertia kept it there, but it never did function as an Executive Office agency. So the intent was there to coordinate, but it was simply that the mechanism wasn't set up adequately and, added to that, the personality of the person.

LAMPMAN: We started an argument that nobody could settle. The first big collision was about that budget. Putting together a billion dollars didn't do much for anybody, because there was some money in there for a couple of things, and there was also money in there for this community action thing. Nobody knew how much that was going to cost. And there was money in there for a coordinating role by Shriver.

He had two kind of conflicting roles. He was supposed to do two things. One, he was supposed to try out some new programs on a very small scale, like Project Head Start, that would just be a trial sort of thing; and the Job Corps would be another one. He would run some of these directly, and then he would spin them off to Labor or HEW or wherever, and then he would take up another group and try some more experiments. That was one idea, of sort of a pilot running the ship for trial runs, you might say. The other one was to be the president's coordinator, the president's manager of an antipoverty budget and of sitting in on a budget process with the director of the Bureau of the Budget and asking all along of each department, "What are you doing for the poor? What are you doing for this goal?" Those are somewhat in conflict. On the one hand, he's sort of challenging departments; and on the other hand, he's supposed to get a message out to the departments.

So he was spending the money that was appropriated directly for this and kind of elbowing the departments aside. And then, out in this community action stuff, he was making life miserable for them—that is, organizing protests against the welfare administration in Chicago and the schools in Denver and so on. So you had a bitter kind of a feeling from some people that Shriver and his team of activists that were there were just embarrassing the government at either the federal or the state level. It was a difficult role or set of roles for Shriver to carry off. I guess I had tended to see, before this community action thing came in, this other role of coordinating and of pushing the established agencies as a kind of backroom operation, just as the director of the Bureau of the Budget is kind of a quiet role.

THE CHALLENGES OF A NEW PROGRAM

PERRIN: The flexibility of the OEO charter was such that you could do practically anything and justify it under the law. Now, whether you could justify it politically or through common sense was something else again.

Are you talking about the Community Action Program now?

PERRIN: Primarily Community Action, yes. Although it was reflected to an extent in the Neighborhood Youth Corps at that time or the Work Experience Program and things that we delegated to other departments to run; we didn't administer those, but we had something to do with the policy of them. "Maladministration" may be too harsh a phrase. I think Shriver just wasn't interested in administration. He wanted to be out there swinging with these tools that had been given to him in this legislation and try different things.

The whole approach, of course, the fantastic speed with which they moved to get this program started and the political implications of that—to have this huge package of announcements ready by November 1964 and so forth; the chartering of these community action agencies all over the country before anyone really knew what the Community Action [Program] was or all of the pitfalls that they were heading into—all of these things we've lived with ever since. But because of all of this, I think OEO would have been about the last place I would have chosen. But as I got to thinking about it, my interest in getting into the executive branch—and really an abhorrence of going down to one of the old-line federal agencies with those endless halls and doors, I just couldn't see that either. I realized that, for all its flakiness, OEO was still probably the most action there was in town, and maybe the most fun to work for. And certainly Shriver was interesting to work for, and that entered into my consideration at the time. So I said okay, and I came aboard.

James Gaither had responsibility for the War on Poverty as a staff assistant to President Johnson from 1966 to 1969. Born in California in 1937, Gaither held an economics degree from Princeton and a law degree from Stanford. Before joining the White House staff, he was a law clerk to Chief Justice Earl Warren and a special assistant to Assistant Attorney General John W. Douglas. After leaving government service, Gaither became an attorney in San Francisco.

GAITHER: They launched that incredible mass of programs in a very short period of time, with almost no constraints on the money. If you read the original OEO act, it is an unbelievable piece of federal legislation, because it basically said, "Here is a big pot of money, and you can spend it to alleviate the problems of the poor." They just launched these programs without worrying too much about being able to account for every last penny, feeling it was more important to start addressing the program, start training people; to start getting kids in school, start giving them their first dental checkup, their first health exam; getting parents involved in early childhood education. All of those things they first got started, and the controls came later.

KELLY: The War on Poverty moved out very rapidly. One of the things that I think is interesting to note is that the resources for conducting the War on Poverty in this nation in many places did not exist. This was the first time in a long time that a program had been devised where its operation was back at the grass roots. I suppose if there was anything that ran counter to what had been the New Deal and Fair Deal philosophy, where you centralize things in Washington, it was the War on Poverty. The War on Poverty in New York was not Sargent Shriver's war; it was [Mayor] Robert Wagner's war. The War on Poverty in Atlanta was not Sargent Shriver's war; it was [Mayor] Ivan Allen's war. And what we did was to give great autonomy—in the community action area particularly and in VISTA—to local auspices and local sponsorship.

One of the really unfair things that would happen—and it constantly happened—is that somebody in Great Falls, Montana, would do something that the citizens or maybe some of the politicians in Great Falls didn't perceive to be in their self-interest, and all of sudden it was Sargent Shriver's screwup.

I think that the Job Corps, and the rest of OEO for that matter, during the first couple of years was never adequately reported. Somehow or other, the press just wanted to preserve the notion that centralization continued, that the War on Poverty was not a decentralized operation, that somehow or other, if somebody in the hinterlands said something that people didn't like, it was Sargent Shriver speaking. I think that the operation of the War on Poverty during the period of 1965 and 1966 was just one of the most enormously successful undertakings, at least—I have been in the federal government for about eighteen years—that I'd ever seen.

The whole thrust of OEO was to give as much autonomy for the operation of this program out at the grass roots [as possible]. Instead of the federal government sitting around trying to decide what was best for New Haven, the people in New Haven ought to decide what was best for New Haven. That was the philosophy that pervaded, and to this day pervades, the whole operation of the

War on Poverty, at least in the community action area and to a great extent in the VISTA area. The same is true of the Neighborhood Youth Corps. There are local sponsors that run the Neighborhood Youth Corps. In the case of New York, it's the Human Resources Administration. What we were trying to do here was not set up an enormous bureaucracy here in Washington. There never have been any more than 3,000 people on the whole OEO payroll, including Washington and seven regional offices.

D. Baker: To be perfectly candid, we've made some mistakes. We've failed in some areas. Parenthetically, I can say a very substantial part of our failure was at least influenced or encouraged by the very rhetoric that got us passed in the first place, that caused us to speed the damned thing up so fast and to do it and get it out, get the money out. But that first year—first seven, eight months—was just absolutely the most hectic of my life; that last month of June when we were just literally pushing the money out the window, it was just mad. It was sort of insane—that you have to say. But the fact of the matter is, every member of the House and Senate—at least it appeared to me then—every one, friend and foe, were all beating us across the head and shoulders because they wanted *their* money for *their* program, and they wanted this Job Corps camp here, and they didn't want one there, and it was just—but mainly they wanted them. And they wanted the CAP money, and they wanted everything, and they wanted it out there, like, yesterday.

The fact of the matter is, we really never had enough people. I never had enough people in my office, have never been up to staff in my office in this agency, until we got that tax bill free. For the first two years of this agency, I just didn't have time to hire people. It was just such a madcap operation. But even if I'd had the people, I wouldn't have had enough, and a lot of the program people never had enough people to do the job that they set about doing. I remember once—when was it, '66—Stu Udall [secretary of the Interior] and the Bureau of Indian Affairs [BIA] were catching such hell from the Congress for what was happening on the Indian reservations, what BIA was not doing. I happened to be in Sarge's office. He called Sarge and said, "You guys are doing such a great job with the Indians; I want some help. I've obviously got to reorganize the BIA. Can I borrow a team?" Sarge said, "Who do you want?" "I want a whole team of people." Well, you know, we've got two professionals and a secretary! And they were running our Indian program. We just never have had enough people to be able to provide technical assistance in monitoring and keep[ing] an eye on even the controversial sort of thing that any sane man would watch very closely.

Now, having said that, and excused it, there were some bad program judgments. I think we have always had a rash of people—we attracted a certain element of people, probably at the extreme edges, who can be considered almost sick, who would go out for confrontation for its own sake as a perfectly justifiable

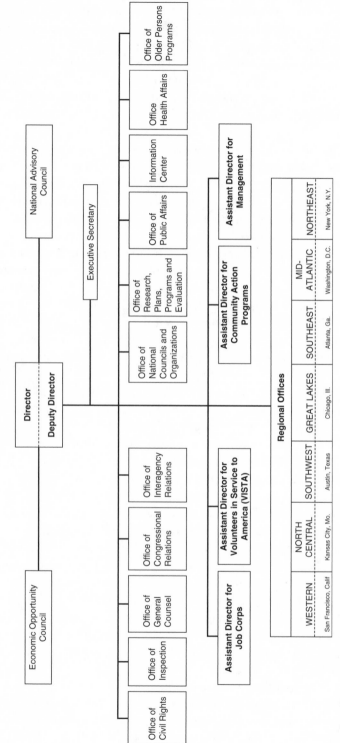

OFFICE OF ECONOMIC OPPORTUNITY
Executive Office of the President

National Advisory Council

Director
Deputy Director

Economic Opportunity Council

Executive Secretary

Office of Civil Rights

Office of Inspection

Office of General Counsel

Office of Congressional Relations

Office of Interagency Relations

Office of National Councils and Organizations

Office of Research, Plans, Programs and Evaluation

Office of Public Affairs

Information Center

Office Health Affairs

Office of Older Persons Programs

Assistant Director for Job Corps

Assistant Director for Volunteers in Service to America (VISTA)

Assistant Director for Community Action Programs

Assistant Director for Management

Regional Offices

WESTERN	NORTH CENTRAL	SOUTHWEST	GREAT LAKES	SOUTHEAST	MID-ATLANTIC	NORTHEAST
San Francisco, Calif.	Kansas City, Mo.	Austin, Texas	Chicago, Ill.	Atlanta, Ga.	Washington, D.C.	New York, N.Y.

OEO organization chart, May 1967.
National Archives RG-381, "Management Summary of Anti-Poverty Programs," May 1967

thing. There's a few of them in-house here, and more of them got hired out to various places around the country. They did us—and did the program, I think—immeasurable damage with some of their wild antics.

ADMINISTRATIVE CONTROLS

PERRIN: Our management procedures are quite good, really. We've established a lot of procedures that I don't think many federal agencies even today have. Ours haven't always worked precisely right, but on the other hand, no one has ever had to deal with these kinds of programs before and these kinds of grantees. Our audit procedures, our inspection, the management training are all quite unique in the federal establishment. I think we've taught other agencies quite a bit about it. But as far as problems that I have to face, they're [the] usual ones; quite deep in the budget process each year, as we develop the needs, [we] conduct in-depth interviews with each of the regions as to their capabilities and their requirements. The personnel matters generally fall into my jurisdiction. Not only the staffing problems of the various offices but the specific problem cases, grievances, quite often find their way up to me. I'm the chairman of the Executive Selection Board, [which] interviews candidates for all supergrade positions.

Bertrand Harding, a career civil servant, became a specialist in planning and management. Harding, a native of Texas, worked for the Bureau of the Budget, the Veterans Administration, the Atomic Energy Commission, and the Internal Revenue Service (IRS). He was deputy IRS commissioner in 1966 when he was asked to direct a management survey of the poverty program. Harding became deputy director of OEO in May 1966, and acting director in March 1968.

HARDING: [OEO] was a very controversial concept. It was also viewed as a potential source of great fraud. Many examples of fraud, of course, occurred in WPA [Works Progress Administration] and in the other early New Deal agencies, and I think the Congress—and particularly the Republicans—perhaps with justification, felt that this was an opportunity for a great deal of maladministration and perhaps dishonesty. And therefore, there were frequent forays from various staffs on the Hill, GAO [General Accounting Office], FBI [Federal Bureau of Investigation], etc., to look into our activities. Fortunately, perhaps even because of this exposure, the agency has been very careful, particularly in elements of misuse of funds. We have made extensive use of audit of the grantees, and there has been relatively little fraud compared to what I would have anticipated.

MAY: The administrative structure—internal service components for the agency—was set up largely by Bill Kelly. If there was a model, I didn't know what the model was, because I was new to government as well. I think the administration of OEO improved markedly when we got a deputy director who was a career administrator—that was Bert Harding. But as far as the lines of authority and who reported to whom, I don't know what that was patterned after.

There were program heads who were very bothered by the function of the Office of Inspection, which reported directly to the director. In part, that was structure; and in part, that was personality. For Shriver, it began in the Peace Corps as an information-gathering system, and it was transferred over to OEO to serve the same purpose, and I think it served that purpose.

It got difficult sometimes, because the Community Action people were convinced that the Office of Inspection was in fact operating as a line operation and telling people what to do. During my tenure, we never did that, or at least I hope we wouldn't do that. I also provided the department head—the director of a program such as the Job Corps or Community Action or VISTA—with a copy of an inspection report at least twenty-four hours before I would give it to Shriver, so that the program director would not be placed in a position of having to respond to something from Shriver that he didn't see. I think that helped take the sting out of things.

Typically, how would you investigate a community action program?

MAY: We would take a program like Community Action, or when we did the Job Corps series, we would go to twenty or thirty Job Corps centers, and people would be told to find out what's going on: What are they doing, what are their goals, what are their programs, what's their retention rate, how are they teaching? And my inspectors would go in a class and listen and sit there, talk to corpsmen in Job Corps centers, look at the grant application—which says what they were going to do—and find out if they're doing it.

Were local project directors told who you were?

MAY: Oh, yes, sure. Always identified.

Did you usually initiate investigations or monitoring simply on a routine basis? Or would you get reports that perhaps something was wrong with a particular program or a local operation and it needed an investigation?

MAY: Both. For example, we initiated a whole series of reviews of both urban and rural Job Corps centers. Similarly, a random sample of VISTA projects. Then there was a separate component, which really is a traditional inspection component, which is responding to complaints or somebody stealing something. I had a deputy who was an ex-FBI agent, and he ran that. But the major thrust was really a program information and evaluation system that was quick and hopefully based in fact, as well as a kind of journalistic report: "This is what's going on." Some of it was done by lawyers, some of it was done by social workers, and some by newspaper people.

Then there were the crisis issues, programs that—because of bad newspaper publicity—we needed, or Shriver needed, to respond [to], or the program director needed to respond [to], and we needed quick, fast facts. During crises, we had the capacity to move very fast. The major crisis was right after the riots, when there was a determined effort by certain congressional forces to pin the riots on the Office of Economic Opportunity. We went into twelve to fifteen cities in twelve days and developed a report on each one of them to permit Shriver to testify accurately that that was not, in fact, the case—that poverty workers were not involved but actually made efforts to calm the situation. There frequently was controversy in community action.

KELLY: I would be constantly asked by Mr. Shriver, "Are those financial controls of such a nature that we should want to...fund the program or...refund it or...cut off funding?" And it would be our judgment in management that he would rely upon in those areas.

What kinds of criteria do you use?

KELLY: Usually what we did was: One, I put auditors into the field to determine whether or not there was an accounting system extant before we made a grant or a contract award. Was the accounting system based on good professional practice? Was it auditable? Secondly, were there people in place that could operate an accounting system? You can have all the systems in the world [but not] have people who know how to operate them. And, three, had arrangements been made so that we could expect that external audits would be made not by us but by respected, registered professional accounting and auditing firms? Those were the three criteria. If I could say yes to those things, then we would go ahead.

Now, sometimes we said yes, and what would happen would be that personnel would change, and we would not be aware of it. We would find that the accounting system was not being operated; even though the system was good, it was being circumvented. In those cases, then, we would say, "Cut it off." We would suspend funding until such time as we could get in there [and] help with the identification of people that could move in and operate the system. In some instances, we operated the system until personnel could be located.

INADEQUATE FUNDING

SUNDQUIST: A lot of us felt that $500 million was not going to turn out to be enough, but this was the first year, after all, and we set something in motion. What we were concerned with then was getting a national commitment to an objective. At that point, you don't quibble very much about the specific content of the program. In fact, the more conservative and cautious you are, the more likely you are to get the commitment. But we felt that once the act was passed and the OEO was in being—and the president's leadership at that time on these matters was superb—that these other problems would work themselves out.

It's like a declaration of war. I think the military analogy, while it's been decried by the liberals, is a very useful one. I thought of it in those terms. When we declared war on the Axis powers in 1941, we didn't define with much care at all how we were going to win that war, but, by God, we knew we were going to do it. This was the bridge I wanted to cross.

PERRIN: I think that the White House realized that it was going to be a very expensive proposition, but I don't know that there was a cause and effect there, as far as OEO was concerned. The president was bragging about the fact that over $25 billion in federal funds were going to programs for the poor, so the total amounts didn't seem to bother him.

Yet each year OEO, within the framework of the way budgets are worked out, always asks for more than it actually receives.

PERRIN: Yes, that's right. I'm sure that if we'd had a more sympathetic ear in the president in terms of deeper understanding of what we were doing, we probably would have come out with a higher budget each year, if he had been totally approving of our activities.

Have programs suffered because you haven't gotten the money that you wanted?

PERRIN: Yes and no. I think that there's one attitude around here that we could have used double the money that we've gotten—triple. Certainly the need is there, but I don't think OEO could have handled funds like that. Where we have been handicapped, however, is in our inability to significantly follow up after the first-year funding to increase the allocations to the community action agencies and other programs which we were funding, particularly the CAA[s]; after that first year, very few of them actually got much of an increase in their level of operation. This not only handicapped them [but] disillusioned them, because this was supposed to be just the beginning of a program that was going to grow. Instead of growing, it stayed static. It not only disillusioned them, but it also prevented us from funding more community action agencies, particularly in rural areas.

WEEKS: My main experience with the president and the poverty program came when we were putting together the budget for the second year of the poverty program. The appropriation which we received in October of 1964 was for the fiscal year ending June 30, 1965; and in October and November of 1964, we had to put together the budget for fiscal year 1966 as well. As I remember, the budget for the first year was something like $947 million, and we didn't get all of that appropriated, but we got a good bit of it appropriated. We put together a budget for the second year of something like $1.8 billion. It was a big number, and it was partly justifiable. The first year we were only operating for seven or eight months anyway, so it's bound to cost more in the second year.

The Budget Bureau came back with a number of something like $1.2 billion as an allowance. We rifled through the meaning of that and told Shriver that what it meant was that the second year for most efforts would be lower, and we'd have to start closing Job Corps centers as soon as we opened them up. [That was] a little bit of an overstatement, but it was definitely a tough number to deal with. So Shriver called the president and said that we'd have a hard time living with that number. And the president talked with Bill Moyers, I know, and then I got a call from Shriver. He said, "I'll meet you downstairs in the lobby as soon as you can get there. We're going over to see the president to make our case for a higher number." This [time frame] would have been about mid-December.

So I met him, and it was just Shriver and myself and the president. We went into the Oval Office and sat down, and before Shriver had a chance to say a word—and it's a rare occasion when Shriver doesn't have the first word—the president said, "Well, Sarge, I want you to know that there is nothing dearer to me than the War on Poverty program, and there's nobody who wants to see it succeed more than me, because this is the first program that really has my name on it, and this is Lyndon Johnson's program. It is not Sargent Shriver's program"—something else like that. He said that in a kindly way. He wasn't trying to say that Shriver was taking it away from him, but what he was trying to say was that he felt that it was his, Lyndon Johnson's, program.

At this point in time—this is a side note—we're already starting to get a considerable amount of flak from cities that their applications hadn't been approved [and] from Job Corps centers that there were fights going on over where there was to be a Job Corps center somewhere. All the initial eruptions were starting to take place, and they were all floating back to the president. So the president said, "I just want you to know that nobody wants this program to succeed more than I do. But we just don't have the coonskins yet to hang up on the wall." That's the specific phrase that he used. I understand he used it fairly frequently. He said, "I want this program to grow and to be the kind of thing that we all want it to be, but I think that we need to move carefully, and I think we need to take our time here. Therefore, I've gone over with"—I'm pretty sure it was Kermit Gordon at that point in time—"the Budget Bureau. We're going to stick [with] it,"—whatever the number was, $1.2 [billion] or $1.3—"and that's my decision. That's where I am."

Of course, what he succeeded in doing was taking the offense away from Shriver right away, because he had already killed most of the arguments that Shriver had. So we stayed there for ten minutes or so and talked. Then we left, and when we were riding back in the car, we both said, "Well, we lost that one,

I guess. We never even got a chance to get the ball in the court; [he won] before we even got the ball."

Well, about a half an hour later the president called Shriver, and he said, "I want you to know, I've sat down and talked this over with Bill Moyers and with Kermit. It's against my better judgment. I really do not think that this is the way we should do, but I'll raise the budget allowance," I think it was to $1.6 [billion]. That's an approximate framework. I think we asked for $1.8 [billion] or $1.9, and the mark came in at $1.3 [billion], and he finally came in at $1.6 [billion].

It was my very strong impression that the president was concerned that things might not be happening as [they should]. We had better do things right as well as fast. We were perhaps under more pressure from Sarge himself to achieve quick results than from the president himself. Sarge is a very results-oriented person. It was quite clear the president wanted to get the legislation passed quickly and wanted to get something under way, but after that, I think the president was very aware of the fact that administrative complications and failure to do your homework with the local townships and the local cities and the local counties and the local people can create problems which can subvert even the best of programs.

Has President Johnson pushed hard for OEO? When OEO goes to the Hill, what kind of support do you get from the White House?

HARDING: I feel the president has been very supportive, in spite of his irritation at times. I know he has had irritation with the program. For example, when he called me over when Sarge left, really the only question he asked me was whether or not I was prepared to go up and fight for that full budgetary request. And no matter what anybody said to me about what his views were, he wanted every dollar that he had requested for this program. He wanted me to go over there and fight for every dollar, which is exactly what I did. I remember at one point during the appropriation hearings before Congressman [Daniel] Flood [of Pennsylvania], who was chairman of our subcommittee, the question of that sort came up. "Well, what does the president really want?" I related to the congressman that the president had told me that he wanted every dollar that he had requested. Mr. Flood, who is quite a theatrical gentleman, sort of screwed up his face: "Well, that's not in accordance with what I understand to be the president's views." I said, "Well, if you have any information to the contrary, Mr. Flood, I'd be happy to know about it. That's my instruction from the president, to tell you and to tell the Senate that he wants appropriated every dollar that he has requested." And to the best of my knowledge, he stood with us throughout that whole process. I'm not sure that he [did] personally, but I know that members of his staff interceded with Congressman [George] Mahon [of Texas] in the final juggling that went on between the House and the Senate in order to get the best deal that could be gotten between those two figures.

PHILLIPS: By this time, it was clear that there was going to be a cutback in the amount of money requested under the authorization. As I recall, the administration's original OEO budget called for $1.75 billion for that fiscal year. As it became clear that our military commitment in Vietnam was going to be greater than originally estimated, there was a scaling down of the appropriation requested under the authorization bill that was finally passed. The eighty percent would spread it out and permit more community action programs that were in operation to be refunded, even if it were at a lower level. We were always concerned about getting hopes aroused for a magic formula to solve poverty problems in every community when there just was not enough money available—even if money alone would have solved the problems. There never would be enough money to be able to do the job. If you get people's hopes up to a point where they cannot even be partially fulfilled, all you're doing is fueling the fires of racial unrest, unrest over the Vietnam War, and causing more and more community unrest, sometimes of a violent nature. We were all very much concerned about the level of funding possible in 1966. Nobody thought it was adequate, but there were other competing demands. This is what every agency had to go through.

The New York Times *reported that in the summer of 1965 Sargent Shriver met with Johnson at the LBJ ranch in Texas and told him that the War on Poverty was working but reaching only half of the people who needed to be reached.*

SHRIVER: I certainly didn't say it was reaching half the people. It was probably reaching something like a third or a quarter of the people, and we therefore had developed a whole budget for what we believed was necessary to eliminate poverty over a ten-year period. At that time our budget was, let's say, a billion and a half, or a billion seven, something like that. The budget I laid in front of the president was, let's say, six billion per annum—maybe six, seven, eight billion dollars per annum—to eliminate poverty within ten years. And I laid it out to him; I said, "Look, Mr. President, this is what is needed financially to eliminate poverty in our country. With this amount of money, I think we really hold out the hope of eliminating poverty over a ten-year period."

Well, that was at the time that the war in Vietnam was heating up and taking a lot of money, and the president said, "Sarge, we can't go from a program of one billion or one billion and a half to a program of six billion. You can't do that. In Congress, you have to go by increments. Maybe we can go up another $150 [million] or $250 million, but we can't go from one billion to five billion overnight." In addition to his decision that [such an increase] was politically impossible, there was also the fact that the demands on the treasury for the war in Vietnam made it economically impractical at that time.

The fundamental thing is that we never had enough money to defeat poverty. Of course, one of the objections to the statement I just made is made by people like George Will, or other conservatives, saying, "All Shriver or the people in the War on Poverty were interested in was throwing money at the problem." That was a cliché of those days. That is a calumny for which there is no foundation whatsoever. One of the things I was always frankly quite proud of was that in the War on Poverty, every program required a poor person to do something to get any benefit from the program. They, in a sense, had to volunteer. For example, in the Job Corps, nobody was drafted into the Job Corps. Young men and women had to look at the opportunity offered by the Job Corps and volunteer; leave their home and go someplace; subject themselves to a year or two of tough discipline for those people, a lot of training; and they had to have the guts and determination to see that through to a successful end. That's what I was trying to get from them, that internal commitment to do something to help themselves. And everything in the War on Poverty was on that basis. That's where we got that slogan, "A hand up, not a handout." The Republicans liked to always say it was a handout because that's an easy thing to accuse Democrats of—handout programs. The War on Poverty was never a handout program, and we never handed anybody anything for nothing. Never. Not a nickel. And that's a fundamental, philosophical fact about the War on Poverty which never gets talked about.

Was Shriver simply being loyal to the Johnson administration, or did he really believe that we could have the "guns" as well as "butter"?

KELLY: No, I think that he believed that this nation was wealthy enough to wage both a War on Poverty—on a much bigger scale than the war we were waging on poverty in terms of dollars and cents—and also the war in Vietnam [with] the amount of resources it was taking at that period of time. He used to say it was the same war. That the War on Poverty here at home was to secure people's freedom, to secure their rights, to secure their safety in the streets, to secure their decent education and the good life. And that the war in Vietnam was the same thing, to try and do those things for the people of South Vietnam.

I think he believed that you could do both, but he was intensely loyal to the administration. He was intensely loyal. He was always being faulted for not being loyal; thoughts were always being attributed to him. I don't know how you look into a person's mind and divine what they are thinking when they don't say it. Because I worked for him longer than anybody else in Washington, and I saw him angry with the administration, but I never saw him disloyal.

COMPETING FOR FUNDING

The following conversations illustrate the conflicting pressures on OEO's appro-
priation. While Shriver and the Community Action Program's constituents lob-
bied for increased funding, the advocates of delegated programs competed for a
larger share of the poverty budget. Shriver threatened to resign over the inad-
equacy of funding, but Vietnam's escalating costs forced the president to limit his
domestic programs to modest increases.

LBJ's conversation with Sargent Shriver, January 22, 1966[6]

SHRIVER: [I wanted to tell you] that I was having a press conference here at 2:30 to explain to the press the effects on the local community action pro-grams—like the one in Dallas—of the congressional action. I am doing that because we are getting a large number of letters and telegrams, et cetera, from people in these community action programs, mayors, gov-ernors, et cetera, who are worried about what's going to happen to these programs locally. And, rather than wait and have this come out one by one in a way which would harm you and this program, I was going to have a press conference this afternoon on that. They are coming over here at 2:30....

JOHNSON: The only thing I want to be careful about—I want you to operate the most efficient setup you think you can, the best way you think you can. I want to be careful this period that we avoid some of the lobbying we got last year through the papers and the columnists and the leaks and the [Joseph] Loftuses and the rest of it. I would caution your people on that until we have a chance to make our decisions.

SHRIVER: Yes, well—

JOHNSON: Because we don't want poverty to become an instrument of harassment for the president and a pressure group and so forth. It's a crea-ture of the administration and not a pressure group. I know the cities can do that without our aiding and abetting them, without my trusted lieu-tenants becoming parties of it. Some of the underlings may do that unless you stay pretty close to it.

SHRIVER: Well, what I am saying here is that if your bill had been passed as you sent it up there, then we would have been able to make modest progress on the entire front, you might say. But, that what happened was that some things were increased out of proportion, which means that the salient, you might say, stick out, but other parts of the program necessarily go back or remain constant, despite the fact that some people want them. I just wanted them to understand this was not your doing, that your bill would not have caused this, but that the congressional changes are causing the dissatisfaction, which is already beginning to appear substantially across the country.

LBJ's conversation with Willard Wirtz, October 1, 1966[7]

WIRTZ: Could I have you for one minute on the appropriation for the poverty thing?

JOHNSON: Yes, all you want to.

WIRTZ: Just to inquire as to whether you have been in that point—budget—

JOHNSON: No, my point is this—all I've been in it is this—I told them that the budget we sent up was what I stood behind, what I recommended, what I believe in. The people on the Hill, off the record, know what I feel very kindly toward the Neighborhood Youth Corps and that I don't get upset when they recognize what it's done. I've submitted my budget. I don't want to go beyond that budget on this or anything else. I can't consistently when I'm cutting three billion out of it.

WIRTZ: I don't want to go beyond it either. The question is to whether within it we are free to reshuffle.

JOHNSON: I let them reshuffle up on the Hill without fussing about it. Is there some contemplated? What's happened? Has the Senate reshuffled you out of business?

WIRTZ: No. Oh, no. I've got nothing to lose, and the fact of having something to gain isn't the principal thing. I think if we really want to stay within $1.7 billion, the way to do it is to do some reshuffling, and that if we don't do that reshuffling, then whether one or the other of them is going to carry us above it. The Senate will carry us above it. Do you see what I mean?

JOHNSON: Yes.

WIRTZ: I think by doing a little reshuffling, I could get pretty complete concurrence with the—

JOHNSON: I won't fuss at what you do. As a matter of fact, if you want to know my whole feeling, in a very short time, I would rather you and some of these folks handle things than some of the other things that are taking place around here. I've got commitments out of the House people; they'll stay by the House figure.[8] I don't know what the Senate will do. I would guess that they might run way over it, because they just want me to impound it. And that makes it embarrassing for a socially conscious president to hold up any poverty funds.

WIRTZ: This is exactly—frankly, it's between $300,000,000 and $496,000,000 in Neighborhood Youth Corps. That's a secondary matter. My point is, Mr. President, is I think one way to get them all to stay within the $1.7 billion is to do enough shuffling around within it that we can satisfy the demands of those who want to go on up.

JOHNSON: Try to do whatever you think is wise without saying the president ordered this, so I can stay consistent. But you just do what you think is best in the general interest without getting me involved and without forcing me into it, because I'll have to deny it. But I'm for my budget as it went up, and I'm going to stand on it. I'm not going to go above a billion seven fifty. I gave them $250,000,000, and I'll give them twice that much if I can get out of Vietnam. But I can't deny a soldier. It's hell for me to carry on both of them.

WIRTZ: If I can try to get some reshuffling within it—

JOHNSON: Meany, I think, might give you a little support. He told me last night that he didn't think we ought to go wild on education and poverty right now because we'd ruin it all. We're going to have a backlash on that that's going to be worse than the backlash on the Negro if we're not awfully careful, because they're telling me that.

LBJ's conversation with Mayor Richard Daley, December 14, 1966[9]

JOHNSON: In the poverty program we gave them last year—I recommended $1,750,000,000. I had $800,000,000 the year before; I doubled it last year. Shriver came in, and he put every pressure on me that he could. He wrote mayors. He called governors. He sent in people working for him. He went before television. He had a big press conference a week ago. He couldn't have been better if he had been a Republican, pressuring me; knowing all the time that I authored the program; that I brought it to existence; that I'd done everything I could to fund it. I recommended a billion seven, fifty. It got to the Senate. Kennedy got up and offered an amendment in committee to bring it to two and a half. He got it adopted. That made everybody that had been supporting it mad. It came out on the floor of the Senate. Dirksen offered an amendment to reduce it to the billion, seven fifty, where it was. Kennedy fought him, and Kennedy got twenty-six [votes], and Dirksen got seventy, putting it back where it was. So now they started the hearings to pressure you to add a good deal more money. I want to add some if there's any possible way I can, but they might near foreclose it by their television and by their pressure and things of that kind. Now both leaders told me yesterday that, first, they didn't believe they'd have any program in poverty. Second, if they did, they'd believe they'd cut it in half. Now that is what I am working with them against. I can't go as fast as they want to. I think a president that takes twelve billion for the poor and doubles it—

DALEY: You've done a great job.

JOHNSON: And that's better than they've done in all—I have added more to the poor budget in three years than all the presidents preceding me. And President Kennedy added three billion. I've added twelve. If Bobby and Shriver knew so damn much about the poor, why didn't they do something about them in three years when they ran the government? All they do now is divide me and to cause my polls there and to criticize me, and to piss in a well in the water I've got to drink. And they do it every day.

LBJ's conversation with Bill Moyers, December 26, 1966[10]

JOHNSON: [Shriver's] decision to quit will be the signal that the Congress will not pass it, because I don't believe he will quit if he thinks they will pass it....If he quits, then I don't think they will. Now, I'm not anxious for him to stay more than I am [McGeorge] Bundy. I would like for him to and I think he's the best one for it. He has my support and my confidence and so forth. Whatever figure I give the budget I will fight for it as I did last year, but I cannot keep him from being the victim of Bobby and Ribicoff and Joe Clark and [Wayne] Morse. I cannot keep him from being victim of the communists who were out here yesterday. [They] said "give the money to poverty, not Vietnam." I think that's hurting poverty more than anything in the world, is that these commies are parading—these kids with long hairs, saying, you know, that they want poverty instead of Vietnam and the Negroes. I think that's what the people regard as the Great Society....In my judgment, the bigger request I make for poverty, the more danger it is [in of] being killed. I don't think they're just going to cut it. I think the same thing about AID. I think if I ask for two billion or three billion for poverty when I've got three billion jobs and I'm spending $24 billion in other fields, I think they'd say, "Good God, it goes up every time he gets somebody a job; it costs you more." I think if we increase it a reasonable amount, then we have a much better chance of fighting and holding it.

8

THE JOB CORPS

THE JOB CORPS, *the most logistically complex component of the War on Poverty, was expected to achieve the most rapid progress. Even before the legislation was signed, the president announced the locations of twenty-two proposed conservation sites. In the haste of opening and staffing centers around the country and recruiting 10,000 corpsmen by June 30, 1965, the Job Corps' overly optimistic projections and the negative publicity it received overshadowed its accomplishments. A high dropout rate, tensions with local communities, a high cost per enrollee, disciplinary problems, and even violence in the centers tarnished the new program's image during its first year. Thereafter, however, significant improvements were made.¹*

There were two types of Job Corps centers. Urban training centers, frequently established on abandoned military bases, offered intensive and specialized vocational training. Corporations proved more successful than universities in operating these centers. Smaller conservation camps, managed by the departments of Agriculture and the Interior, emphasized human renewal while providing physical labor in forests and recreational areas, along with a modest educational curriculum.² To underscore the program's educational nature, Shriver recruited a university chancellor, Dr. Otis Singletary, as the first director of the Job Corps.

Lyndon Johnson, who had been a state director of the National Youth Administration, viewed the Job Corps as a modern version of his own effort to combat poverty during the Depression. Not only did he understand the program, but he became personally involved in ensuring that Camp Gary, the Job Corps center in his old congressional district in Texas, was among the first, the largest, and the best.³

Unlike its New Deal predecessors, the Job Corps targeted society's "least likely to succeed": sixteen- to twenty-one-year-old high school dropouts, most of whom came from troubled homes or impoverished environments. Many of the corpsmen had suffered such severe cultural deprivations that they could not move into more sophisticated trades. Thus, the Job Corps faced the problem of providing meaningful training, preparing corpsmen for jobs they could actually fill, demonstrating a pattern of success, and yet targeting the poorest of the poor.⁴

LBJ EXPLAINS THE JOB CORPS

In the following conversation with Dick West, editorial director of the conservative Dallas Morning News, *the president gives a "tough love" analysis of the Job Corps's mission.*

LBJ's conversation with Dick West, August 31, 1964[5]

JOHNSON: If my poverty thing works out, I'm going to be pleased with it. I'm going to take a bunch of these strapping boys out of these damn rioting squads that they're engaged in, put them out and put them to work. Feed them and clothe them and try to get them where they can get in the army, particularly a lot of your Negro youth. They've got nothing to do and they can't get a job. You know, it's hard to believe what you see in a good many of these places. If you had the same population density in New York that you've got in Harlem, you could put the whole United States in three boroughs.... People living that way—the bottom's going to blow off the tea kettle. It's just got to. We've got to get them out and put them to work some way. Sixteen percent of our young people are unemployed. That's where all our crime rate's coming from. It's these damn youngsters. So we've got to put them to work. We're going to do it and make them—scrub them up, get some tapeworms out of their bellies, and get them where they get up at 6 o'clock in the morning and work all day. And then we can get them where they can serve. One out of every two that come into us now in the draft are being turned back They're not fit physically or mentally. We think we can clean them up this way and shoo them on in there and maybe teach them to be a truck driver or something.

GETTING STARTED

SINGLETARY: I was in Greensboro, North Carolina, in the fall of 1964. I just got a call one morning that said, "Dr. Singletary, this is Sargent Shriver. I wonder if you'd mind coming up here and talking to me." I said, "What about?" He said, "I don't want to tell you, because you won't come if I do." So I said, "Okay, in that case, I'll come." So I went up. Shriver was a very shrewd recruiter. He talked to you about all the big jobs and all around, but he never did get right down to any specifics. He wanted to see whether he was interested in you and whether you had any interest in what they were doing.

I went back a second time. This must have been in late September or early October of 1964. We got down to talking specifically about the Job Corps, and specifically about the directorship. It is my feeling, in retrospect, that Sarge had decided that he wanted an educator to head that program—for better or for worse. Secondly, I think that once he'd decided that he had some interest— this delay was going on while he cleared me politically, as they do these things and otherwise. I had no reason to believe that if he approached Johnson, that Johnson would have had anything for or against me, one way or another.

When Shriver offered you the job, did he have a clearly formed notion of what the Job Corps would be? My impression is that he made it up as it went along.

SINGLETARY: There was some planning. Some of it was pretty good, and some of it was hopelessly unrealistic. Sarge knew some things he wanted. He had a concept of two kinds of centers. He had a basic concept that I still am kind of in love with. He knew that out there were in fact millions of kids in that sixteen- to twenty-one-year age group who were out of school and out of work and for whom the normal system wasn't working. He saw two ways— one through the conservation center, and the other through the urban job training center—[to make] these people, in a sense, as he liked to put it in that good old way of his, "taxpayers rather than tax eaters." You'd hear that all the time!

I took the job with him under the clear stipulation that I would take it only if my board of trustees would give me a leave of absence for a specified time; that I had no interest in staying up there very long; that I would help him get it started and do what I could do to help him find a successor. And then I wanted [to come] back, because my commitment clearly was to university and not to government work.

Right after the election, I flew out to the ranch with Shriver to brief Johnson about what we were doing—in the prepping of the poverty program, which, as you know, he placed great stock in early in the game. It was a pretty long day for me because Johnson really zeroed in, in the way he can do. He's a very intense man. He asked me a whole flock of questions about the Job Corps and then took me in at lunch and sat me next to him and continued all through lunch.

On the way back to Washington that night, Sarge and I were flying in that Jet Star. Shriver said to me—and I assume you want it the way he said it—being the devout Catholic he is, he said: "Jesus Christ, when did you decide all that!" I said, "Just sitting there answering those questions!"

Were the Job Corps offices set up, or did all that have to be worked out too?

SINGLETARY: That was the intriguing thing. When you get right down to it, what he was saying was, "Look, here's an idea that's only partially formed, and an empty office practically, and a desk, and $150 million! Come on up here and create a program!" That is, in a sense, the chance and opportunity of a lifetime, and that is clearly what attracted me, along with—I'll admit this—Shriver himself is a very attractive and persuasive guy, and he helped con me into that.

Did you have to do most of your own recruiting of administrative personnel, or did you have a good bit of help in that?

SINGLETARY: We had some already onboard from the task force and earlier planning groups when I got there, but we grew tremendously and were recruiting all the time we were there. We were just continually adding.

You didn't have time for a lot of meditation and reflecting; you had to make some decisions pretty quickly. How did you arrive at the decision to have rural Civilian Conservation Corps–type centers as well as urban centers?

SINGLETARY: There were clearly two needs to be met. One was for the kind of youngster who had no reading skills and who could fit the pattern that had already been advocated for some years by a fairly powerful group on the Hill— the conservation line. And the conservation center concept came out of that. What these kids were going to do is presumably work half time on the public lands and the public parks and on projects and improve [them], as they did in the thirties.

As time went by, the CCC became kind of popular in retrospect.

SINGLETARY: Absolutely. And as you look back in the forties and fifties at the park facilities in this country, anybody who knew anything about it understood how valuable the CCC had been, in a way nobody ever saw very much. But there was literally millions of dollars' worth of labor being done by these youngsters in the way of improving and expanding park and recreational facilities in this country, clearing out new trails, and all this kind of stuff. And indeed there was, and is today, a very real need for more of that.

At the same time there was an educational program built into [the Job Corps], which was aimed at improving basic literacy skills, with the idea that later, when those skills were improved enough, they might well go to one of these urban centers, which were in a sense more sophisticated. That was to deal with the kid who was just a dropout, not necessarily illiterate, but who needed to be turned into some kind of productive guy, such as a welder or an automobile mechanic or any one of a number of things you can think of.

Where did you recruit training personnel?

SINGLETARY: We begged, borrowed, and stole. Part of the problem we had was that you couldn't get anybody on the payroll, even though you had the money.

The Washington problem of dealing with the Civil Service Commission and the Bureau of the Budget almost was as great, in my opinion, as the problem of trying to create and operate the program. I left there, in my short time, feeling that they made it doubly difficult for you to get the job done, even after the Congress appropriated the money for you to do it.

You even have an academic problem: you're coming in in the fall, and everybody's already contracted.

SINGLETARY: Yes. Coming in in the fall like that, though, we began running training programs right away. Our big problem in the beginning wasn't just [the need] for teachers. We needed people who could help us plan curriculum, do these things. We went to the universities and borrowed professors. We went to other government agencies and got people transferred on loan. We went to the Pentagon and got used equipment and clothing and everything for these kids. We begged and we borrowed and we stole from every place we could find.

CHOOSING JOB CORPS SITES

WEEKS: There were quite a few policy issues. I remember, for example, we had one proposal [to] put a Job Corps center at a place called Big Bend National Park in Texas. We discovered that it's something like 120 miles to the nearest town. We said, "Hey, look. These are kids—sixteen-, seventeen-, eighteen-, nineteen-year-old kids. You can't put them in a situation where the nearest town is 120 miles away. They've got to have some kind of off-site recreational opportunities." The Park Service really thought that Big Bend was a wonderful area. We had a fair fight over that one.

We had a list of the first conservation centers that Interior and Agriculture had sent over as their preliminary proposal. All it was was a list of names; it wasn't anything else. We were trying to look at it and trying to figure out how on earth to make a decision about it. We sent the list up to Shriver, and Shriver sent it over to the president, because, he said, "Hey, there are some political implications here." Obviously, one of the things about the Job Corps that had been controversial from the beginning was what control will local officials and state officials like governors have over whether there is a Job Corps center in their town or state? Can the federal government simply come and put one in regardless of whether the local folks want it or not?

Anyway, this list was sent over to the White House simply from the point of view of, "Say, hey, you got any reactions to this list, good or bad?" We hadn't even started to figure out how much it would cost to put anything there or whether these were good sites or bad sites. The next thing we know, the president is up there reading the list at a press conference. That's absolutely and literally the way that it happened. I was sitting in Shriver's office. Larry O'Brien called up, and he said, "Hey, what's this list of Job Corps centers?" Shriver said, "Hell, that's something very tentative." This was Saturday morning about ten o'clock, or something like that. Larry O'Brien called back about five minutes later; he said, "Well, the president just announced your list of Job Corps centers as being the first centers that will open. They're all going to open in the next three months." Well, we hadn't contacted a single governor, a single mayor, a single congressman or senator, or anything else like that. I'll never forget that day.

Was there any conscious attempt on the part of the Job Corps, either before or after you came, to put Job Corps centers in areas of most need?

KELLY: I don't think that that was an objective back in 1964 and 1965, when most of the centers were picked. I think the objective, particularly in those areas where the conservation centers [were sited]—and, of course, they were the most numerous—they picked them on the basis of facility, that is, what was it going to cost to construct something; and, two, where was there conservation work that wouldn't be all completed in the first six months or the first year but something that had a long-term conservation benefit. Now, they didn't succeed in doing that in every case, because right now, some four years later, after the Job Corps has been in operation, we find that there are some conservation centers that may have only a year's work left in that locale.

However, what happened here was that probably three-fourths of the conservation centers ended up in poor counties, in depressed areas, either depressed in terms of median family income [or] depressed in terms of having an unemployment statistic which was multiples ahead of the national average. We had conservation centers before this close down here last week [April 1969] in areas where the unemployment rate was fifteen percent, as compared to 3.4 percent in the nation. So that it did occur. And what happened was that we ended up with conservation centers being the most important economic activity in a given locale, in terms of its payroll, in terms of the kind of money it spent in the town, in terms of the kind of money the youngsters spent in the town. They spent their $30 a month, which was what they received, in that town. You multiply that by 150 to 200 youngsters in a conservation center in a town of 2,000 people: that's a whale of a lot of dough.

Are there any Job Corps centers in the deep south?

KELLY: No. There was one in St. Petersburg, Florida. It was a women's center, which was closed in early 1966, as I recall, before I became director of the Job Corps.[6] It was located in St. Petersburg, Florida, in a hotel in a residential area which was populated fundamentally by senior citizens who didn't like the jukebox. It was run by the board of education of the county down there. They didn't do a very good job of running it, but boards of education are not famous for running anything very well, at least from all I can tell working in American education. That was the only one.

The problem has been, at least in the early days when the Job Corps was being logistically created, the problem of the veto. Job Corps represents a non-segregated training establishment. I think there were some feelers in terms of putting something other places down there, but with the exception of Florida, it never came to any fruition.

Have there been subsequent feelers?

KELLY: Yes, as a matter of fact, we were in the process before this cut of putting one of the Job Corps skill centers in Louisiana, with the entire backing of the Louisiana delegation. Every member, including Speedy Long [and] Otto Passman, all signed a letter to me petitioning me to put one in there. They understand clearly that it will be an integrated training program. So that's a change.

Was that change partly motivated by a desire to reap the economic benefits?

KELLY: I think that the South is moving. They're going to have it whether they like it or not. There have been some benefits that have been denied them in certain locales because they have not been willing to obey the law. So I think they're coming around.

THE LOGISTICAL PROBLEMS

WEEKS: The Job Corps was an administrative mess. More than anything else, the Job Corps suffered from the contradiction of being administratively by far the most complex program and yet the one that had to bear the brunt of getting under way the fastest. The administrative complexity was simply the complexity of establishing 100 Job Corps centers—staffed, managed, organized, with all the equipment, materials, and supplies, training programs, and everything else like that. There's no problem in selecting the kids to go there and getting them there. The problem was in getting the Job Corps centers organized, with a staff that knew what to do with them when they were there.

I understand that sometimes the kids would arrive almost before the staff got set up.

WEEKS: Yes, that was one problem. We didn't receive appropriations until late October of 1964. Sarge set a goal of having 10,000 kids in the Job Corps by June 30—the end of the fiscal year at that time—of 1965, which is about eight months. We hit 10,000, but those kids were sleeping on high school gymnasium floors because the centers weren't finished. We were paying for them to eat in restaurants and sleep in motels and so on, because we met the goal. We met the goal in numbers, but we didn't meet it in having the places ready for them.

Most of the staff had only been there three or four days. They didn't know what on earth they were supposed to do. They didn't have the books. They didn't have the materials. They didn't have the equipment. They didn't have the beds, the blankets, the sheets, the towels, the washing machines, any of the other kinds of things that are needed to get things off the ground. All the conservation centers, of course, were in rural areas where things don't arrive overnight, and there's not a Sears, Roebuck store in the shopping center five miles away [where] you could go and buy stuff on an emergency basis.

RECRUITING CORPSMEN

SINGLETARY: We blanketed the country with what we called "opportunity cards," which [was] the Job Corps announcement. You filled it in and sent it in if you thought you were interested, or wanted more information, or wanted to be considered as an applicant. We had them in every post office, in every selective service office, in every employment office. We sent them to all the schools for people they might know to refer them to. In the case of the rural kids, we even got them into the trunks of the cars of every county agent that we could discover in the country and had them taking them out. I will say, that was a clearly successful throwing of the net, because while there was some argument about whether or not there was a demand or need for this program, what we got were hundreds of thousands of those cards sent back to us immediately.

How did a boy get turned down?

SINGLETARY: Availability of space at the moment. He was interviewed, first of all, somewhere near where he was, by some member of a team, whether it was a local employment office or something, and certain criteria came through. It was a computer operation to a considerable extent—as was, in the earlier days, where you assigned him. While there was a lot of talk about how you assigned him, the original concept was that you started at the center and you moved out in a concentric circle until you found the nearest Job Corps center to him where a vacancy for his particular interest and concern existed, and you put him there.

What did you do about those boys who were too ignorant to know what their concerns were?

SINGLETARY: We had a lot of that. Many of those who went to the conservation centers were like that. They didn't really know what they were interested in. They went out there to try it out. And a lot of the first kids we got were really dumped on us by properly motivated, but very, very unreliable welfare workers in the city. They were just getting rid of their problems.

Did you ever feel that you were running a reform school in some cases?

SINGLETARY: They dumped all over us from these cities. We found other cases later where they said to the kid, "Instead of sending you up, if you'll take this Job Corps assignment, we'll let you go there." And that hurt us a lot. The quality of input was one of the real weaknesses of the program. And could we have moved slower, could we have had fewer centers and fewer kids and more careful screening, I think we could have had a more durable and more defensible program in the long run.

OEO would argue that the Employment Service did a miserable job of recruiting for Job Corps. Is this the case?

HOWARD: It's quite possible, quite possible, yes. You have to look at the history. The Employment Service was set up to appeal to employers and to place persons who needed work. Obviously, they liked the best possible candidates for the jobs. They liked to tell employers they've got great people for them and so forth and so on. Suddenly, we're going to make them a social agency. To me, it's akin to deciding that suddenly the school system is going to be our mechanism for integrating the neighborhoods of the United States of America after a couple of hundred years of discrimination. Schools can't hack it. The Employment Service couldn't hack it. The Employment Service didn't want to hack it. Part of that is history, and part of that is the state structure. They're fat, dumb, and happy out in the states, and they see a federal program dumped on them, and they don't want it. They just didn't want it. Who would care about it? Who cares about picking up twenty kids out of this town and moving them out to Oregon for a Job Corps camp? They could care less. They just didn't care.

Sure, I sympathize with the Job Corps on that. So they turned to private recruiting, or agency recruiting, things of that sort.

WEEKS: The one thing where the Job Corps did not step back from a tough problem was that it tackled almost the toughest kids in the sixteen- to twenty-one-year-old age group to deal with. When I say "almost the toughest," there was a considerable amount of debate over criteria for getting into the Job Corps and what it should do. It also related somewhat to the other programs in the poverty program package. Where we had a work-study program for college kids, that clearly is not much of a poverty program. It's in there because it was something that HEW wanted to pass, and they'd been trying to get passed for a couple of years on its own and hadn't been able to. So we decided to stick it in, and maybe we could get it passed as part of this. The Neighborhood Youth Corps program was basically kind of a temporary public works program for kids in their own setting, and the kids were going to be selected by the Employment Service. We well knew that a lot of the worst kids never come into contact with the Employment Service and won't go near them. So a very basic decision was made early on that the only kids that we would select out of the Job Corps, at the bottom, would be those with serious criminal records and those with some kind of serious mental or physical handicap, which meant that they really needed some kind of very, very special treatment. The Job Corps is obviously not able to offer advanced kind of sessions for [the] mentally retarded. Nor did we feel we were very able to handle kids with repeated convictions for assault and things like that, although I think it was pretty clear that many of the U.S. Employment Service offices, which were the primary screening agents for Job Corps kids, purposefully overlooked criminal records in referring kids and recommending kids to be enrolled in the Job Corps. We had a lot of kids with pretty heavy criminal records in there. But the point I'm making is that, in setting policy, we decided to go for the hardest group to deal with, with those few exceptions—that is, criminal records and mental or physical disabilities.

Did you have to decide which kids to aim for: those who had a reasonably good chance of benefiting from the program, or those who were strictly at the bottom of the barrel?

SHRIVER: That, of course, was a continuing fight all the time. Not only was there [that] conflict, but there was also the conflict between the rural people and the urban types. I believe that with the Job Corps, like with the Peace Corps, the idea had to work right away. Not because it was wrongly conceived or a bad idea, but because Congress wasn't going to give us any running room . . . or a second chance. I used to say to the people at the Peace Corps: We're like a guy going up for his first parachute jump. When we jump, the chute has to open. So pragmatically, to go back to your question, I felt we had to get some proportion of the kids who would be "success stories." That meant that we just couldn't focus exclusively on the bottom of the barrel, to use an old cliché.

But then the big complaint comes from all the hot-rock experts who accuse you of what they call "creaming." That means you're skimming the cream off of the container of milk. You're doing the easy part of the problem. Therefore, you're a bum, because you're not handling the really tough cases. You're not out there in the muck; you're creaming—that's the allegation. Well, we had to cream some. Otherwise, we would have had a disaster record on our hands. But we didn't consciously—at least, I never consciously said, "Look, we're going to take seventy percent cream and thirty percent milk," or like a barrel, ten percent on the bottom of the barrel and ten percent off the top, like a bell curve. I never went into that kind of an analysis, but pragmatically and simplistically, we had to succeed to some degree.

Was the fact that many of the kids you were dealing with had police records a problem?

SHRIVER: That was another thing everybody was yelling about. "My God, you're taking crooks! You're taking thieves, felons, into this Job Corps!" We're funny, aren't we? People are. We're so damn funny. Because you'd think that if we took some felons in and could turn them around, we ought to get the Croix de Guerre with five palms, because that not only saves a life but saves society. But people aren't like that. They don't want to give a break to a fellow who's down; they don't want you to give a break to a guy who's a crook, a felon.

SINGLETARY: First of all, we really had to create a program that would not just take a kid who was in poverty, but take a kid who was in poverty and who had a domestic situation of a kind that made it important to put him into the residential situation. We had to have a program that would really do something for that kid in terms of moving him from one plateau to the next in terms of his earning capability and his ability, in a sense, to cope with this century in that way. We ultimately had to find a way to do this at a cost that could be made acceptable to the taxpayer in the country—and to do it in a milieu in which there was a considerable degree of hostility to the program and which tended, particularly in the news media, to inflate the incidents that occurred.

KELLY: This whole notion of skill centers in which there were nonresidential components: all of our experience in the Job Corps going back to 1965 had indicated that the nonresidential component doesn't work. Yet [the Bureau of the Budget officials] want to try it over again. They keep trying to reinvent the wheel, hoping against hope that their mythology will somehow be borne out in the real world.

The minute you put a nonresidential component in with the residential components, within two or three weeks it fails. Because the kids don't come. They're like day-hops in college. If you've ever known anybody that went to college and lived at home, he has an entirely different life than kids who are residents on that campus. He's kind of an outsider, and that's exactly what has happened in the Job Corps. The kid who's a nonresident is a day-hop. He's an outsider, and he doesn't get integrated into the program. Pretty soon he just never makes it to the bus stop.

THE JOB CORPS AS NATIONAL PROGRAM

Would it have been preferable to have the programs more localized, closer to the large urban cores where a lot of the unemployed youth were coming from?

SHRIVER: I don't think so. I realize there's a vast body of opinion that does think so, so I may as well just say why I don't think so. First of all, the Job Corps was a national program; and the problem of poor, unemployed, badly educated young men and women was a national problem; and I didn't think that it was fair to just concentrate the effort where those people lived. I thought it was a national effort, and to take everybody on a national basis and treat them as citizens of the United States was an exemplification of that. If you join the Marine Corps or you join the army, you just don't stay where you are—in Arkansas, let's say. You become a part of the army, and you go into the army, and you go wherever the army wants you to go. I had the same attitude about the Job Corps: it was not a little local effort; it was a national effort to deal with a national problem.

The second thing is: The mere traveling—perhaps quite a long ways away from your previous existence—is an educational activity, and it has an emotional and cultural impact on the people who experience that kind of travel.

Third, it was my belief—still is my belief—that a large number of the poor, unemployed teenagers in America are to some extent victims of their surroundings. They grow up in a certain social environment which is almost conducive to keeping them the way they are. I felt it was important to extract them out of that environment and to put them in a different environment, twenty-four hours a day, 365 days a year, two years, a totally new environment, a new culture. Expose them to a new culture: a culture of work, a culture of discipline, a culture of responsibility, personal responsibility. I thought that to take them away from where they were and to put them into this new culture, the culture of the Job Corps, would be profoundly transforming to them and beneficial to them.

JOHNSON AND CAMP GARY

SINGLETARY: I remember one day—a particularly harried day—at noon I was over at that desk, and I was having a glass of milk and one of those miserable sandwiches. The phone rang, and it was Bill Moyers. Bill said, "Otis, I just left the president's office, and as I was going out the door, he asked me if you had that heavy equipment in at Camp Gary yet." And I said, "I do not know." He said, "Well, go get on the phone and find out and tell him, by God, to get it in there, and I don't want any excuses. I want it in there." You know, that stuff.

Well, Bill hit me at the wrong moment. I was already uptight about lots of things. I said to Bill, "Well, Bill, you go back in there and tell the president of the United States that you've relayed his message to me, and that I have heard it, and that I have this reply. And that is, that this is his program, and he can have it run any way he wants to. He has that right. But he doesn't have the right to have me run it any way he wants to. I am getting that equipment as fast and as best as I know how." Bill said, "Cool down. Be glad of one thing—at least you're in a different building!"

The president, whatever else he kept his interest alive in, he kept his interest alive in his old congressional district for a long time. I remember very clearly being there for the [Camp Gary] opening. He and Mrs. Johnson were at the ranch and came down and later took a group of us back with him to the ranch to spend the day. When he arrived that morning for the dedication ceremony, he was so pleasantly surprised at seeing a refurbished Camp Gary. We had at that time, I think, 1,000 or 1,500 Job Corps enrollees scheduled to come into this facility. We took him on a tour and showed him these printing plants and places for mechanical drawing, language laboratories, the recreational facilities.

I think it moved him, because on the helicopter going up to the ranch after that was over, he got Governor [John] Connally and me in there and said, "Can you double it?" I looked at Connally, and Connally at me. It was a problem for both of us, because it was clear we were having to raid a lot of the public schools to get the kind of staff you needed in there. The president then told one of those stories of the type that you've probably heard from many other people. He said, "You know, when I was in the NYA, we had a fellow out here, and we asked him if he could do something. If he didn't sound like he could do it, we always sent him to El Paso.[7] By the time he got out there and got back, we had it done. So I'm now going to ask you again, can you double it?"

I said, "Mr. President, I have been to El Paso. We can double it." So the decision was made on that helicopter ride to expand that from its then size to double its size.

Other than your recruitment of faculty, the state had no real part in it, did it? You had no tenderness of federal-state relationships here?

Shriver, Johnson and Governor John Connally attend the opening of Camp Gary Job Corps Center in San Marcos, Texas, April 10, 1965. A264-27, 4/10/65. *Photo by Yoichi R. Okamoto, Presidential Collection, LBJ Library*

LBJ and Lady Bird Johnson visit with Job Corps recruits at the opening of Camp Gary Job Corps Center. *A259-6, 4/10/65. Photo by Yoichi R. Okamoto, Presidential Collection, LBJ Library*

SINGLETARY: There was a little tenderness that involved the president and the governor....John Connally has some pride and temper of his own. He and the president are both typical Texans in lots of ways. The first fight I got caught in was that the president had apparently not read his legislation carefully enough to know that the governor could veto that project. The president went to San Marcos and made a speech, and in the speech he said the first one was going to be there at Camp Gary, and indeed [we] had not cleared it yet with the governor. So I inherited the situation where the governor really didn't want a Job Corps center, or at the moment didn't think he did.

Do you think he was showing pique, or he just didn't want it?

SINGLETARY: In the beginning, Governor Connally had real reservations about the program. I think there was a little pique too, although I would leave that for him and the president. I later saw them in situations that led me to believe that they didn't stay mad very long when they got mad.

I want to say this about Governor Connally. This is an important part of this story. Once he decided to go, they did a lot more than recruit staff. John Connally himself took the lead in pulling together in there some of the major corporations and corporate talent in Texas—Texas Instruments and some of the large oil companies—and helped them design and set up the training programs.

And it is my belief even today that Gary was the best of the urban-type Job Corps centers.

George D. McCarthy was a staff director in the Office of Civil Defense when he joined the War on Poverty Task Force in 1964. He served as special assistant to the director of the Job Corps in 1965, and in 1966 he was appointed deputy assistant director for congressional relations. The following year, he succeeded William G. Phillips as assistant director for congressional relations. A native of Butte, Montana, McCarthy received his bachelor of science degree from the Montana School of Mines. After serving in the army during World War II, he operated an engineering firm and a war surplus business in Butte until 1961.

McCarthy: The Gary Job Corps center was run by the state of Texas. So that wasn't run by any university or private enterprise; that was Lyndon Johnson's and John Connally's. [Connally] said, "Damn it, if there's going to be a Job Corps center in Texas, I'm going to run it." I remember at the time Otis was director, and Otis thought that he should run it. Connally disabused Otis of that pretty quickly. Otis was down in his office, and he called Lyndon on the phone, and he said, "Who the hell is going to run this Job Corps center?" And Connally was going to run it. But from the facts of the case, and those are the records—like old Al Smith used to say, "Go back and look at the record"—Camp Gary had the lowest cost per enrollee. They had the highest percentage of completions. They had the greatest number of placements. All around, it was the best-run Job Corps center in the United States.

Do you think that, in addition to Connally's influence, Camp Gary's success may have been due in part to Johnson's being from Texas?

McCarthy: Yes, but it was a whole combination again, and I think it was what I spoke of earlier: they were enthused. The president was enthused. Connally, even in his mean, ornery way, was enthused and wanted to be a part of LBJ's program. But where he succeeded and the others didn't—I think the secret of his success is that Connally brought all of the leading businesspeople of Texas in and told them that he wanted this program to succeed. He said, "I want these boys to have jobs, and you tell me how many each of you are going to hire." He put together a group that represented the private interests and the potential employers of these enrollees. And that's why he had such a successful program.

RURAL AND URBAN JOB CORPS CAMPS

Weeks: Certainly the Job Corps didn't work, in my opinion, and in fact I was deputy director of it for the first year and a half of its operations—reluctant deputy director. Whether the Job Corps helped [is debatable]. It hurt a lot of kids, and it helped some kids. I'm not even sure that it helped more kids than it hurt. There were a lot of kids who came into the Job Corps with the hope that they were really going to get into something, not always completely realistic. A lot of kids came in feeling that they were going to have their own personal bulldozer as soon as they got in, and that within a couple of days they would be driving it all over wherever it was they were going. They had their own illusions. But we gave them the promise that they were going to get a leg up on a new life, and what they got frequently was a Job Corps center in which the big black urban kids with an awful lot of street sense ran the center, no matter what the staff did. That included protection—all the kinds of things that go on in a big high school.

I don't want anybody to take that as a racist statement. What I should say is, the big urban kids. What you had in many Job Corps centers was a mixture of big, black, urban, street-smart kids with physically small, underfed white kids from rural poverty, many of whom had hardly really seen a black before. It was a pretty explosive mixture. Until you could see the kids come off the buses—and you could count the rural kids as they got off the buses, because they would be four or five, six inches shorter than the rest, and their weight would be thirty, forty, fifty pounds lighter. Half their teeth would be gone. They would be obviously victims of malnutrition. Their faces would be covered with poor skin conditions, the whole works. You put a bunch of kids like that together with a bunch of street-smart urban kids, and you've got a tough problem. And part of the naiveté of the Job Corps was that until the Job Corps centers opened, nobody ever figured that one out.

Would the corrective have been more localized camps?

WEEKS: Yes. Certainly one of the problems was taking kids and putting them 2,000 miles away. When you did that, that distance from home is too far to send them back every couple of months; and these kids came from homes with chaotic conditions in many cases, where sisters were getting beaten up, or mothers were getting beaten up, or other things like that were happening. It was tough if you're a kid and you get a letter or a telephone call that says there's a disaster condition at home: "Ma's left again, and your pa is here, and he's beating up on me, and I can't take it anymore," and the kid is sitting there in a Job Corps center. What's he going to do? He's going to take off and hitchhike back home.

There were a lot of things that were not true in the Job Corps that reflected the fact that it was hastily patched together, without leadership—without any consistent leadership. I think it gradually improved over time. Certainly the second and third and fourth years it was more effective than it was the first year.

There were basically two kinds of Job Corps centers: large centers run by corporations for the most part, and small centers run by the Interior Department and the Agriculture Department. Small centers had maybe seventy-five to 100 kids at them, and the large centers had anywhere from 1,500 to 2,500 kids at them, some of them 3,000 or 4,000. I think the general impression was that the larger centers had far better educational programs but couldn't control the kids, that the kids ran the centers, in fact, and the staff could never really enforce any kind of discipline or organization on the kids.

[In] the small centers, the kids had a wonderful time in the country, and they got good food. I've been out to several Job Corps conservation centers there in beautiful areas, and the kids basically were pretty well-behaved. They stayed in line. They didn't learn a heck of a lot out there either. They were out there chopping brush and clearing paths and doing fairly menial work. They got a good chance to get a year, fifteen months, or two years in the countryside. Whether they came back with really usable skills is very questionable.

J. BAKER: Our impression from the results of the evaluation studies is that the conservation centers came out with cost-effective results. Now, that doesn't mean that you couldn't find somebody that left two days after he got there because he was homesick and those kinds of things. But as distinct from the urban centers, the Forest Service centers had tried-and-true leadership of very high caliber—the Forest Service officers—in terms of knowing human nature and all those kinds of things. I visited at one time or another at least twenty-five or thirty of the conservation centers. I've got everything from cups to all kinds of things they'd give me when I'd be out there.

How did those on the bottom rung of society respond when they got out in the country and worked on these conservation projects?

J. BAKER: This is based purely on my own personal observation now rather than reading evaluation reports. I was greatly impressed with the educational component of Job Corps. Instead of working all day chopping trees, Job Corps would spend, say, the morning learning basic arithmetic and reading and so on. The teaching materials that were developed by Job Corps were—again, my observation—the most attractive and effective kinds of materials that I have ever seen in and out of colleges or grammar schools or whatnot. I was greatly impressed with that. Those kids—never 100 percent—but those kids were in there really looking at those picture books and learning English, learning basic mathematics and so forth.

Again, I was a big shot from Washington, and everybody, including the camp commander, wanted to look good because I was there. So what I saw and what they told me was undoubtedly biased in the direction of being favorable to the experience. We had very little trouble with drugs, for example.

I really still believe that there is a big difference between having up to 100 kids way out in the woods working [at] something and having 500 or 600 in a high-rise. I was later confirmed in this as a consultant to the University of Massachusetts. One of their big problems—they had built three high-rise dormitories right in the middle of the campus, and then they immediately started hiring psychiatrists to find out what all the problems were. I just think there's something about people having a little bit more room to live that....

Weren't these kids going to be moving back to the cities? Weren't they basically city kids who wouldn't be content to live out there in the country?

J. Baker: Well, I've often thought about that. These thumb-suckers of the *Washington Post* have started me thinking again on it. I'm inclined to think that Job Corps, in one sense, was more like vocational education and Boy Scout training than it was like a manpower development course. In other words, it wasn't the final; it shouldn't have been thought of as the final. I think a lot of people thought of it as being that somehow you get out of Job Corps and then get placed. I think maybe the Job Corps experience for the enrollees was more of a generalized benefit than it was a specific benefit. A lot of them became expert machinists, for example, and went immediately [to work].

Then of course the Forest Service anyway developed memorandums of agreement and cooperation, actual operating cooperation, with labor unions. That worked a whole lot better, of course. Part of being a carpenter is getting that union card that you're a carpenter. Unless the carpenters' union will accept Job Corps experience, you don't ever get to be a carpenter unless you start over again at the bottom of that four-year apprenticeship. Whereas if the time in Job Corps worked out toward apprenticeship, he got a hand-up on it. But it took them from 1964 to 1968 to get that developed with major labor unions. The first breakthrough was in Tennessee.

There was a great to-do about how much it cost per corpsman, and it cost about the same—as much per corpsman per year—as it does a student at Harvard for a year. We used to argue which product was better. But that was after Kennedy was gone and after LBJ [was there].

Was there a problem with discipline in the rural camps and conservation camps?

J. Baker: The answer is, not very much, partly because they were so thin, if you know what I mean. There were 100 in one place, and there weren't 10,000 more around close. Partly because many of these Forest Service officers who were their supervisors had had from one to three or four years' experience with CCC. And partly because Forest Service officers, riding herd over forests and grazing, had to learn as a public service how to keep people from fighting with six-guns. I'm going back now seventy-five years. Partly I think also—and you'll find a memorandum in this extra material I gave you—there was early on something that came up in Montana that [Lee] Metcalf wanted to be damn sure didn't break out. Chief [Edward P.] Cliff of the Forest Service and I and [Clare] Hendee and other Forest Service–Job Corps guys and I think [Senator Mike] Mansfield got in on it, developed an agreement. Mansfield got it out of Sarge some way, or one of Sarge's successors that selected input. We weren't going to take the worst ones at his word. We kind of insisted on creaming the crop from the cities. Some of our early experiences led us to believe that you couldn't just take absolutely unbriefed people that they sent you from the sidewalks of the large city. I realize that's kind of contrary to some of the higher-level thinking, most soft-hearted of the group, but that kept down [trouble].

But there were something less than 1 percent of the camps had any trouble at all, and them only minor. There never was this business of them threatening to blow a building down or drug rings. There weren't enough corpsmen in one place to have a drug ring. I think I had the communications system set up well enough that I would have heard about it, and fully eighty to ninety percent of the camps never had any trouble at all. Now, I'm talking about the Forest Service ones. I was never closely familiar with the details of the Bureau of Land Management and Park Service conservation centers. But I never did hear any of my colleagues talking about any particular trouble. The trouble came up in places like Omaha—as I remember, it was one of the bad ones—in these big urban centers where they'd have people stacked up. And they had as many troubles later in one of the women's centers as they did the men's centers.

Was there much criticism about the expense of flying these Job Corpsmen such long distances to these remote camps and back?

J. BAKER: There was a great deal of external criticism of the sheer expense involved. Internally, the signals I got from the people that worked with me was that the closer the Job Corps centers could be to the corpsmen's home bailiwick, the better things worked out. In spite of the fact that a lot of us, on an intellectual basis, really thought that a good thing to do was to get somebody as far from a damn Baltimore ghetto as they could get him before they started trying to rebuild him.

I think we had kind of a mystical, religious attitude about this [conservation center concept] too: that if you are going to take kids out of the slums and try to give them a new slant on life, that there was something to being out there with God's trees and fresh air and everything that was over and above what you taught them in those wonderful math and reading books and the discipline that was inherent in not cutting each other's head off with a knife.

Some memos point to confusion within OEO on directives and policies, and a lack of coordination within the poverty agency itself. Was this a problem with respect to the Job Corps?

J. Baker: More of an irritant than a problem. An irritant in two ways: One, because the other people that were administering non–Forest Service Job Corps centers were not doing as good a job as we were, and we were taking some of the heat out there locally because of what somebody else was doing wrong. The other was—and I realized it at the time, but I didn't let it bother me very much—you had a completely new outfit of people that hadn't worked together six months, much less seventy years, up against one of the most highly efficiently organized and operated outfits in the world, the Forest Service. So that no matter what OEO did, it looked clumsy compared to what Forest Service could have done if it was doing it itself.

DISCIPLINE IN JOB CORPS CAMPS

Singletary: Given the youth revolt and the youth movement and all the rest of it as we know it today, the Job Corps was really the first place this hit. If you bear in mind that we were bringing together the most difficult age group in the country: that age group—out of school, out of work—they're tough kids, mostly. We were bringing them into the residential situation. We really had our hands full. It was such a hot publicity item that a fistfight appeared to be a riot. And if it involved a black boy, it was a race riot, as the papers got hold of it! But anybody who would not have anticipated that we were going to have a hell of a lot of disciplinary problems with that age group in the residential situation, particularly as isolated as many of these were, simply missed the point. We did have those problems from the very beginning.

There was a special set of problems with the women's center, the kind of people it attracted around it—males in particular hovering around. Anytime you pull together in a residential situation that number of girls, it's going to be sort of like a dormitory. There's going to be a lot of traffic in and out. And the public pretty generally put a bad light on that. But the need was certainly no less for the women.

One interesting feature, though, about the women was the number of volunteer recruiters we had working for us across the country, including Junior Leaguers, giving time to interview and identify. In many ways, I had the feeling that there was a more selective job done in choosing the women than the men for Job Corps.

THE DROPOUT RATE

Singletary: Hell's bells, if the dropout rate was thirty-five percent or so—which is pretty high if you compare it to some things—you've got to remember that it's not high compared to the freshman class that enters college this year, if you consider their graduating year. That's going to be about fifty percent, as I recall: about half of them are going to get degrees.

But far more important than that is the simple fact that you started with 100 percent dropout, and that for two-thirds of those kids, the program was to some degree working! As you saw the youngsters, and as you were made aware, as I was—having lived so many of my recent years on the campus, where in spite of all the talk these days about repression and all the rest of it, they're the freest and most privileged kids in the world. That first bunch of Job Corpsmen very nearly broke my heart, the first kids that came into the program. And I'll never forget watching them come off that bus down there [in Catoctin, Maryland].[8]

But the dropout rate, I think, is easily defensible. They talked about the cost of the program a great deal. You know the old cliché about, "You could send a boy to Harvard for what you could send him to the Job Corps." Except you couldn't send this boy to Harvard! I once said to a committee up there: "Fine. You can fill that stadium up there with Job Corps boys, and I will take out of this program the full payment for as many of them to go to Harvard as you can get Harvard to accept." That pointed up the ridiculous fact of trying to argue Harvard.

But if you look at it another way, if you looked at the number of American dollars that had been spent on that boy who enrolled as a freshman in Harvard that year, in the first eighteen years of his life, as compared to what had happened to the kids we were dealing with, that's where you saw the real difference.

The critics of Job Corps would charge that it costs more to educate a student at Harvard.

McCARTHY: Which was a crockful. They didn't take the capitalization; they just took the tuition costs of sending the kid to Harvard. They didn't amortize the costs, like you had to in the early days. The Job Corps has been in existence now since 1965. It's been fifteen, sixteen years now. You take those costs and amortize them today and put it back in. But what they were doing then was taking all the capital costs. They were taking the costs of all of the upgrading of the buildings, all of the initial [costs], and they were trying to put all of that into the cost. When you took it and annualized it and amortized costs out, there was no comparison, and I remember doing many of them. The only real comparison— and they were very comparable, and in many cases less—Job Corps was costing about the same as it was for keeping someone in a penal institution.

The Gottlieb report observed that, as a result of substantially higher dropout rates among white recruits, the Job Corps was becoming less of an integrated institution.[9]

KELLY: That's been the case [with] Job Corps from its beginning. It has held pretty steady in the last two years. It's about sixty percent black. It has held there—fifty-eight to sixty-two percent—over the last two years. I think what Gottlieb's analysis shows is that Negroes perceive that the Job Corps is their last opportunity. They tend to have greater staying power than whites, who tend to be younger, who tend to be rural. As a result, young white rurals have much less staying power.

Poverty is not as grinding in an Appalachian hollow when you can sit down on the side of a hill and look at a graveyard down at the bottom of the hill in which six generations of your family are buried. There is a culture in Appalachia, even though poverty may be grinding. It's very hard to find a culture in Woodlawn or in Anacostia. So that kids that come out of the West Virginia and Kentucky hollows miss them, and there's a hold on them; whereas the black kid who comes out of the garbage-strewn middle of Harlem wants out of that place so bad that the Job Corps represents an exit. They have much better staying power, and they're tougher.

UNIVERSITY-OPERATED CENTERS

SINGLETARY: We contracted with some universities. We contracted with the Texas Education Agency.[10] We contracted with some private corporations. And strangely enough—it is kind of hard to judge out of this, except to say that, on the whole, the universities were the least effective operators of Job Corps centers. The corporations did pretty well, [and] the Texas Education Agency did very well. But I have always in my own mind thought that resulted more from John Connally's help with the high-powered industrial folk there who helped set the training program up.

KELLY: [University officials] thought they were running an educational undertaking, and Job Corps is not an educational undertaking. It's a whole host of other things. So their only expertise was in higher education, and they tried to fit the higher education ideas into a Job Corps center at Breckenridge, Kentucky, off the campus, with a number of people who were castoffs from their university. And it just didn't work out. Then they got disenchanted, and they didn't like it. They were looking for a way out, and so it became a kind of mutual agreement to get them out and get somebody else in.

SINGLETARY DEPARTS

SINGLETARY: I really didn't quit. I stayed the time that I agreed to stay. I took a leave of absence till the beginning of the second semester, and I really left on January first. I think I was back at my desk January second in Greensboro. I stayed exactly as long as I agreed to stay.

Your successor, Dr. [Franklyn] A. Johnson, stayed only through the next November, or at least he announced his resignation then. Was the job a bit of a killer that used you up pretty fast?

SINGLETARY: Yes, it was a killer. There was no question, it was a killer. Although I was very much engaged in the business of helping to locate him, Frank was, in my judgment, as it worked out—although let me make it clear, I supported him for the job. Of the people who were then available, I thought he was the best candidate. I will tell you now, in retrospect, I don't think that was a good judgment. Frank became more a ribbon-cutter and a program-appearer at the time when the program still had to prove itself. It still had to have that internal gut decision. And Dave Squire, who was his second man, did a very good job with the inside.

Otis Singletary discussed President Johnson's relationship with the Job Corps.

SINGLETARY: I believe that Lyndon Johnson's own career as an NYA administrator and so forth did in fact give him a special feeling for this youth program. There was never a time when I was there that I did not think that he was properly interested.

The other thing is that I am satisfied that, until this day, his vision was a correct vision of the need to do something about that aspect of this population for whom little is being done and yet who [are] potentially in mind a very explosive element in the population.

[Johnson] also saw [the Job Corps] as an investment, not just in camp sites and more jobs, but also an investment in what he liked to call the human potential; that along with those things, some benefits come into the nation at large and some benefits come into the man through increased earning power, and to the government. [There was] also that thing he used to talk about, the quality of life. A lot of people think that a politician is always a phony when he starts in on that. In plain fact, he can have those feelings as well as the next man. And having seen him—we were at Gary together, and I've forgotten where else; I saw him a number of times, both in and out of the White House when I was there—[I] never had any reason to doubt his interest in or sincerity in that program. I was always impressed by that, although I found him to be a very difficult man to work for.

Did you ever consider another position under him?

SINGLETARY: No.

You had your taste of public service?

SINGLETARY: The university never looked better.

9

THE COMMUNITY
ACTION PROGRAM

LIKE THE JOB CORPS, *the Community Action Program had to organize an administrative structure and develop guidelines. Since its mandate was significantly broader than that of the job training program, defining the scope of that mandate was a primary task. The program was designed to assist local communities in mobilizing their own resources to combat poverty. Through local community action agencies (CAAs)—either private organizations or creatures of government—social service professionals, civic leaders, and residents of target areas would develop antipoverty plans tailored to their particular needs. The CAAs were intended to mobilize the poor in developing and implementing these plans, and to coordinate local antipoverty resources at all levels. OEO would fund up to ninety percent of the cost of these initiatives.*[1]

Although diverse local circumstances spawned scores of different kinds of community action initiatives, OEO also developed projects that had broad application and appeal. Such "national emphasis" programs as Head Start, Legal Services, Upward Bound, Foster Grandparents, and Comprehensive Health Services were services commonly provided by local CAAs. Some Community Action officials regarded these programs warily because they competed for funding and short-circuited the agency's effort to stimulate local planning and coordination.[2]

With more than 1,000 new CAAs in operation, problems were inevitable. The notoriety of a few controversial programs tarnished the image of the entire effort. Power struggles frequently erupted over control of the local agencies. Would the poor merely be involved in the decision-making process, or would they actually dominate it? Some projects became forums for bashing the local establishment; some others were criticized as captives of city hall. As programs organized opposition to local political leadership, members of Congress voiced their complaints with OEO and the White House.[3]

Most participants agree that the Green Amendment saved the controversial program and OEO's 1967 authorization. This measure, proposed by Representative Edith Green, placed the community action agencies under the control of local government by requiring that an agency be either an entity of state or local government or a private nonprofit agency designated by local or state government. By making community action more palatable to southerners and representatives from northern cities, the Green Amendment thwarted a Republican effort to spin off OEO's programs to established departments.

Although only forty-eight CAAs were taken over by local governments, OEO's guide-lines for implementing the Green Amendment became so controversial that they too were amended.[4]

"A VERY POWERFUL PROGRAM"

CONWAY: We put together under Dick Boone a planning program development team—Sandy Kravitz, a number of others. It was out of that team that Head Start came, Legal Services, Foster Grandparents, Upward Bound, most of the substantive programs that lasted. Under Fred Hayes, the field services operation was really a top-notch thing. Then we had a team of people that I pulled from the labor movement: Brendan Sexton and Fred Hoehler and Judah Drob and Tom Cosgrove. These were all labor educators; and just as we had trained illiterate working people to become effective union people, we trained illiterate, inexperienced blacks and Chicanos and Indians to become effective leaders in their own right and to take on responsibilities. That's the permanent contribution, in my judgment, of the Community Action Program: the enfranchisement, the empowerment, of literally hundreds and thousands of people who had been out of it before. That was never reversed. As a matter of fact, Marion Barry, the mayor of Washington, and all of the people who are in various places in the Carter administration come out of the OEO programs. It's all there. It's had its successes, excesses, and in many ways it's run its course, but nevertheless, it was a very powerful program, in my judgment.

The juvenile delinquency program had worked under the local government. Community action agencies could be creatures of the local government, counties, cities, whatever. They could be private groups, and many of them were. They could be a combination. In the case of Los Angeles, they were a consolidation of several governmental agencies creating the EYOA [Economic and Youth Opportunities Agencies], or whatever it was, which was the county and the city and the school boards. The Joint Powers Act was used to do this. But my theory was supportive of the proposition that local governments should look at this as an additional tool. But if local governments refused to, we were not precluded from going in and working out [with] private agencies, nonprofit corporations, programs that were focused on the same things.

MAY: The program development grant, the initial funding that created the CAP, created a structure and gave those people a microphone, whether it was on an Indian reservation or in a South Side neighborhood of Chicago, where a group of people would get together who never either (a) got together or (b) had a microphone. So it wasn't a question of setting up, in my view, an alternative system to deal with the problems of poverty, but [of] develop[ing] an entity that could speak on behalf of the poor and reorient local programs so that in fact they were helping the poor. Now, that was the idealistic goal. What happened in a number of places—you got into feifdoms, and you got into power struggles, and you got into who had the action, who didn't, and then, when the dollars started to come in, who got the dollars and who didn't.

JOHNSON'S VIEW OF COMMUNITY ACTION

Johnson, in The Vantage Point, said that he perceived community action as a means of shaking up existing institutions, and he asserted that local governments had to be challenged to be awakened. Was this the view that he seemed to put forth at the time?

CONWAY: I am hesitant to describe what Lyndon Johnson's view was. I always assumed that he knew what was in the legislation and what the law, once it passed, permitted. The only time that I ever sat [with him] and talked about what we were doing was at the ranch when we flew down on one of the air force planes and made a direct report to Lyndon on the progress. This was in November, I guess, just about the time we were rolling. I was the last of the people to report; the Job Corps, others, reported first; Sarge did. Then I laid out what we were doing in the cities and counties and in various states and so on. And Lyndon listened very attentively and cautioned me. He didn't admonish me; he cautioned me. He in effect said that, "There are a lot of these places where civilization is pretty thin, and you have to be sure you don't ride roughshod over people and create your own problems"—something to that effect. I didn't interpret that to mean that he was opposed to what we were doing. He just was fearful that if we hit too hard, too fast, and too many places, [if we] tried [to] create our own counterrevolution, so to speak, [we would] give him too many problems to deal with, as well as ourselves. But I assumed that he knew what he was doing.

I think he would have preferred for a lot of the programs to go through state agencies, like the traditional state agencies that he was familiar with from earlier experiences in Texas. But I think he accepted, as something he agreed with, the objectives of the program, to shake it all up. It wasn't going to change unless you did, particularly in the South. And we did shake it up.

KRAMER: I think at the very beginning, when the president realized what "community action" and "maximum feasible participation" were going to mean, and that federal money for the first time would be going to private, nonprofit corporations, he, being a good politician, knew that it would be very difficult to make it work; that it would set up rival organizations to the mayors; that the governors would rebel against having their turf invaded. And, of course, the president was right. I think his defense against that was to kind of back-step and say, "Well, I really don't have anything to do with it."

Did he have an understanding of what community action was in 1964, when the bill was passed under his aegis?

KRAMER: No, I don't really think he did. I don't think anybody fully had an understanding of what community action was. I think that the president was wary of community action. It may or may not be apocryphal, but the president is said to have said to Mr. Shriver or others, "I just want you to make sure that no crooks, communists, or cocksuckers get into this program." We were plagued by all three at various times in our career.

GAITHER: The fact is that the poverty program and Title I of [the] Elementary and Secondary Education [Act], which were the main programs for the poor, were kept year after year only because of the very strong support that the president gave to them. Both of them got into trouble almost immediately after Johnson left office. It's understandable. There's just no constituency there.

[The] Community Action [Program] was probably the most troublesome, because it was a broad umbrella under which communities could try almost anything they wanted to try as long as it was directed at problems of the poor. Almost by definition they had problems of accounting and charges of rip-offs. Some of them were bad, and some of them were very good. But they created enormous political problems in the cities. The mayors were always complaining about them because they didn't have control over them. Originally, all community action grants went directly to community groups, and the local political types didn't like that at all. Over time, because of political problems and political pressures in Washington, the local governments got control over community action programs, at least veto power.

But it was understandable. They were doing tough and difficult things. One organization would have a program for ex-convicts; another would have a program for juvenile delinquents. An ex-con commits another robbery—that's not much of a story; but if he's at that point working for a community action agency, it's very interesting political news. Those things were happening all over the country.

Community action was everything. It was everything to everybody. While you knew what voting rights meant, and you knew what fair housing meant—and [President Johnson] fought very hard for those—I don't think that anybody knew exactly what community action was. Because all it was saying is that each community ought to have some funds to try to develop programs to meet their own needs. In one community, it was a water purification effort. In another, it was dealing with ex-cons. They really ran the full gamut. I never had a sense that the president was out in front the way he was with some of the other programs, [that he was] saying there's something about community action that really is going to, through the political process, change the lives of these people.

By the time you started working with OEO from the White House, did you have a well-defined view of what community action ought to be?

GAITHER: No, I guess not. The longer I was there, the more important I thought it was that local communities have funds to try new things. And the longer I tried to find answers to all of society's problems, the more convinced I became that it was far better than for Washington to tell people what to do, to let [local communities] try, and recognize at the outset that a lot of mistakes would be made. In that sense, I was very supportive of community action. I also became very troubled about some aspects of community action, particularly as more and more requirements were built on for representation. [Community Action boards] basically became places where people screamed at each other rather than doing something.

LBJ'S NEGATIVE VIEW

During his last gloomy months in office, Johnson privately railed against Community Action. In this instance, his anger was ignited by a grantee's potentially embarrassing employment of Mrs. Johnson's niece.

LBJ's conversation with Bertrand Harding, December 6, 1968[5]

JOHNSON: [Community Action grants to nonprofit organizations are]...just tearing us all to pieces, and they just have all kinds of fights. There are just bitter, vicious threats. This is not what I set up poverty—I set up poverty for people to just work like hell and get paid so they'd have something to eat. All this theoretical stuff with a bunch of goddamn social workers going out and shoveling money to a bunch of half-baked organizations [is] the biggest, crappiest thing that I ever saw. I don't think it's worth a damn. I put it in an interview the other day [for] my history that it was the most disgraceful thing I had was poverty, and the boys made me take it out. I said I think it's a waste. I think it is graft. I think it is mismanagement. I think it's political. I really do. I just feel terrible about it. Then when you get into things like this—paper organizations being made overnight, and the taxpayers' money going out—you have no idea how Nixon's going to make us look. You just don't have any [idea].

GRANTS AND GUIDELINES

D. BAKER: It was a wild sort of operation in those early days, making the first grants. We didn't have any guidelines and didn't have the time really to draft them to start out. Many of the communities, in anticipation of the passage of the act, had been putting together applications; obviously, the applications came in in a variety of forms. And what, in effect, happened was that we used those original applications as a means of learning, little laboratory experiments in which we would study and decide what our policies were going to be.

For instance, one of our most acute and difficult problems early on was the church-state issue. The original poverty act that had gone up provided for education programs to be administered only through the public school systems. Some of the members that traditionally had been insisting upon services going to children in parochial and private schools also objected to that. And the way the compromise worked out, instead of the authority for the agency to grant, in effect, general aid to education to be run through the public school systems in the ghettos—an authority which probably was so broad that it meant that the federal government could virtually have hired the teachers and run the schools and dictated the curriculum—the compromise prohibited general aid to education but permitted what the act called "special, remedial, and noncurricular educational assistance." Thus, it was conceived that directing the assistance to special children with special needs—who were the legitimate concern of the federal government—and providing only a limited kind of assistance for them, the federal government could aid the child wherever he was, and that we could and would be expected to make grants to parochial institutions where they were running programs for kids in need.

What we did in that first batch of grants was to get some of the people that the mayors had appointed: some of the public school people, some of the parochial school people, some of the welfare agencies, and other groups from Detroit, New Haven, Chicago, and Pittsburgh. We had them in here, and we sat down for a couple days at least with each one. We probed the geography of the city and the cultural breakdown of the city and what they proposed to do and how they proposed to do it. Out of their fact[ual] situations, and [taking into consideration] why they thought they wanted to go one way rather than another, we eventually came up with some ideas as to how we could structure this thing so that it would be least subject to attack in the courts and most in keeping with what the Congress intended, and we came up with our church-state guidelines.

That's what we did on many things. There would be program people who would sit down with one or more of my lawyers and some others, and they would go over the grants and the applications and discuss with the people what they wanted to do. We gradually evolved what came to be a sort of a common law of decision that the agency was going one way rather than another in this particular area. We had some guidelines that would apply to education programs; then we began to have some ideas about preschool programs which we tried out a little bit and [which] we gradually expanded upon into the Head Start thing and a wide variety of things. We began getting experience, and our program people got experience.

As more people came in, we began to write some of this stuff down, and then we developed the guidelines. What happened, as a practical matter, was, we divided up into regions, even though we were physically in the same building. One batch of people were going to handle the New York-New England region, and they were up on one section of a floor, and somebody else was someplace else. And then eventually that became the cadre.

There might be a team of people from Detroit—as there were—who came into town, and we'd all sit around a table and discuss what some of their problems were and how we could mutually resolve them. The general counsel's office never considered itself standing off from the program people. I decided early on that we were not going to issue a bunch of legal interpretations as separate memorandum, particularly since we wanted our program and the guidelines to be understood, or capable of being understood, by most people. We would see that the legal input was put as much as possible into layman's terms [in] the guidelines, the requirements that were issued by the program people. So we've always been very close—much closer, generally, than most general counsels' offices were.

This caused some problems. As a practical matter, Sarge and Conway and many others in the Congress were pressing the program people to get the money out and to go, go, go, and make the grants and make the contracts. It became obvious after a while that the only safety valve in the place was our office. What was happening otherwise down below in the program element was that people were looking at increasingly discrete and small elements of an application package. And it just happened that our office came to be the only place, in fact, where one mature, rational, individual took a look at the total package. This caused some fury on our part, and eventually we had to discipline the program people. But it was even left for us, for instance, to find arithmetic errors and budgeting errors and whatnot. In any event, we came to view ourselves as sort of the last protection, the ditch, for the director; and again, this caused some flap among some of the program people.

We made them defend their decisions. In the early days, Sarge also took these packages after we had signed off on them or refused to sign off on them or something. They were simply taken en masse to Sarge, who sat around with program people, and he explored and tested the decisions that were made. We would feel perfectly free in challenging and making an educator justify a program that he was making, or a grant that he was proposing to make, even though there wasn't strictly a legal decision. People would say, "That's none of your business; it's not a legal issue." Our position was, more or less, "If it's a waste of taxpayers' money, that's a legal issue." Or, "If it's bad judgment, we are not authorized by Congress to be using bad judgment with the taxpayers' money." And, in effect, we did stick our nose into a great number of areas.

As mayor of Cincinnati in 1964, Theodore M. Berry developed a community action plan for that city after the passage of the Economic Opportunity Act. His discussions with Sargent Shriver and other OEO officials led to his appointment in March 1965 as assistant director for Community Action Programs, a position he held until 1969. Berry received his undergraduate and law degrees from the University of Cincinnati. In the 1940s he worked as the assistant prosecutor of Hamilton County before his election as a Cincinnati city councillor and vice mayor in the 1950s. Through Berry's national prominence in civil rights organizations, he had strong ties to leaders of the African American community. He served as president of the Cincinnati branch of the NAACP and became a member of NAACP's national board of directors. He was also a delegate-at-large to the National Urban League.

BERRY: When I came aboard in March [1965], I think the second or possibly the third round of grants had been made. There were applications from all over the country. It was a centralized operation, very hectic. We had not reached any point of decentralized or regional offices. We had very hurriedly outstationed community action personnel in certain areas where we thought regional offices would be ultimately approved, but they were outstationed personnel of headquarters, to be more closely related to communities. We had a number of applications from various and sundry groups that did not conform to the language of the statute of what community action was intended to be. So we were concerned with qualifying those agencies, quantifying their proposals—[to ensure that] they seemed to be making sense—and making grants, so that we would have shown at least a record of having reasonably, prudently, consistent with the legislation, used money that Congress had made available. So half the fiscal year was gone when I came aboard in March. We had practically one quarter remaining to obligate something like more than fifty percent of our appropriation. It was a very hectic operation.

One of the two critical issues that were on the table was qualifying the community action agency for Cleveland. The other was a very hectic operation with reference to the city of Chicago. The city of Chicago had brought down—figuratively, I would say—a bushel basket of proposals, wanting them all funded. This was a case of the big hog getting to the trough first and wanting it all, and we had to make some judgments. We had to sort of hold back. First of all, was there a properly constituted community action agency? And secondly, to quantify at least these proposals that we couldn't just go overboard merely because they asked for it, that they were all going to be funded. And believe me, the city of Chicago was trying to use all the pressure it had politically and otherwise to get as much as they could. There were problems that arose with other big cities of wanting to get large grants, and we had to keep also always reminding the director that our legislation called for an equitable allocation of these funds between rural and urban [areas].

We made a number of planning grants. Many communities were not prepared; many, many communities did not have the sophistication or the resources [of] a city like New York, Chicago, [or] Philadelphia, that could turn the wheels of their council of social agencies to generate a lot of proposals that would command dollars.

Part of my task [was] reviewing and at least recommending to the director the final content of the guidelines that would help communities to qualify for OEO Title II grants. We drew the guidelines in a manner that administratively interpreted what we felt the language of the statute meant. The format of our guidelines addressed themselves to the kind of grants we could make, and who was eligible and how these organizations might be brought into being. They could be a public agency or they could be a private, nonprofit agency. We brought attention to the matter of the participation of residents, both in representation on the boards, the policy-making bodies at the community level. We tried to spell it out in understandable ways. Then we dealt with the types of eligible programs that we could fund. They covered a rather broad spectrum, because the language was very general. We included, of course, remedial education, employment training, job training and counseling, health, vocational rehabilitation, housing and home management, consumer information education, legal aid. We were identifying areas of service which later developed into national emphasis programs. But it covered a rather broad spectrum because the language was broad.

KELLY: We have never gotten an appropriation until late fall or early winter during the entire history of this institution, going back to its first year, 1964, when we got the first appropriation on October 8. It has always made it very, very difficult to plan. I think that this is probably more deeply felt in the community action area than it is in the Job Corps, because the Job Corps, after 1966, really became a fixed program in terms of its size. It had pretty finite boundaries.

The problem of planning the Community Action Program becomes really enormous because of the fact that you have cities out there, community action programs that are in cities and towns out in the rural areas—not too many of them, but there are some out there who are funded on what amounts to a hand-to-mouth basis. They present the OEO with a plan, and they say, "We need $10 million." And the OEO says, "Well, look, this is August. We don't know whether or not your fair share of the allocation is going to be $10 million or not." "When are you going to know?" "Well, we hope we're going to know next month, in September." Then you find out in December, and then you find out that what happens is that it's $9 million rather than $10 million.

And then you have the complications that intelligent community action agencies have done the same thing we've done: they've held back so that they're running sixty to ninety days behind their plan. Then people say, "Well, it's not very efficient." It isn't, but it doesn't lie with the OEO or with the community action agency. It lies with the fact that the Congress has been traditionally so late in passing legislation. As a matter of fact, we never testified until last year before our appropriate appropriations committee in the Senate. We always ended up with the supplemental subcommittee rather than the subcommittee that would ordinarily hear our appropriation, because we were so late in the game.

NATIONAL EMPHASIS PROGRAMS

BERRY: As we proceeded with the day-to-day work of reviewing proposals coming from communities in our own program planning section—which at that time was headed by Dick Boone—we did conceive of programs that were initiated through our research and demonstration funds that—as we conceived it, if they were successful—might be replicated, packaged, replicated by getting them accepted by communities to extend it.

Was this the building-block approach?

BERRY: Yes, that's right. While many communities came in with tutorial education—there was a heavy orientation toward education in the beginning—there was a modicum of at least the beginnings of the idea of the multiservice center or system, community neighborhood service system. It came in various forms in various communities. But I have frequently referred to it as probably the most "indigenous" national emphasis program, in the sense that it was not one that we conceived in Washington, but by the very spontaneous manner in which it came in various forms from all over the country, that this was an instrument which local communities felt would meet some of their needs or enable them to attack the problems in the target areas. Out of that has developed this whole matrix of what we call the "neighborhood service center." I refer to it as a neighborhood service system because it takes various forms in various localities. It needs a good deal of improvement in many areas, particularly in our rural areas.

Foster Grandparents was a program which was conceived in our shop. I remember [Dick Boone] coming into my office—his office was right next-door here—and we discussed it. It was first funded out of our demonstration funds. It had a very novel approach to the whole question of child care, particularly foundlings in institutions. It was going to serve two purposes: provide forms of employment for older persons and [transfer] their natural love and affection for children. It caught on in many institutions.

Upward Bound was an experiment with our demonstration money. We tried it, I think, with thirteen institutions the first summer. Most of these institutions were Negro, or black, institutions. There were some colleges up in the northeast. But that first year's experience validated our theory, so much so that in the next year we were able to go out and try to enlist under Dick Frost—he really did a tremendous job of opening the eyes and the minds and the interest of the staid college institutions—to begin to marry the gown with the problems of the town, in terms of motivating, helping poor youth who had low academic achievement to begin to get a sense of their own capability, [and developing] the interest of these institutions in them.

We felt it could be a national emphasis program because it was so closely related to the established college institutions. It had to be linked with them, against the wishes of most of the college institutions; they did not want to be tied to the tail of community action. And yet we sold them on the idea that if they were going to do a job, they ought to relate to an organization or an institution in the community that had access that could reach those kids that needed to be reached. So in most cases the college institution that receives the grant is

committed to a program of working with community action agencies in identifying the kids that needed the service of the Upward Bound program.

PARTICIPATION OF THE POOR

KELLY: The fall of 1965, of course, was the great conflict that finally made the
newspapers—the participation of the poor. The memo that had been written
internally in OEO, in [the] Community Action [Program]—in which [it] was
made known to a select group of people, ultimately the whole United States,
that there was a great deal of trepidation on the part of the Budget Bureau—[was
made public]. The implication was that [the trepidation] was located even at a
higher level about further involvement of the poor. And that, of course, created
a terrible hugger-mugger, because the press wrote it, and the National Council
of Churches got involved. God, everybody got involved. That was the time in
which they said the sellout was at work, and they blamed the president.

I can remember Archbishop [Robert E.] Lucey [of San Antonio], who was a very
strong advocate of participation of the poor [and] who served on our National
Advisory Council. In December of 1965, when we had a meeting of that council
and I was acting director of CAP, he delivered himself of a peroration for about five
minutes up in the conference room, room 823 of the Brown Building. He was talking about [how] we hadn't really gotten the poor involved. And Mr. Shriver turned
to me—I guess maybe he didn't want to quarrel with the archbishop, although
that wasn't like Mr. Shriver—and he said, "Well, what do you think about that,
Bill?" I said, "You know, a year ago there were exactly zero poor people involved in
anything in this nation. Now we've got about 800 to 900 community action agencies, and poor people represent twenty-seven percent of all the boards that we've
got. I think we've come a hell of a distance, Bishop Lucey, from zero in a year to
twenty-seven percent. I don't know what you want, maybe you want fifty percent
or 100 percent, but I think twenty-seven percent is better than we were a year ago.
And God knows, it is a lot better than we were twenty years ago."

One of the things that I can't emphasize strongly enough is the fact that
there were a lot of people arguing about a lot of things for ideological purposes
only. They couldn't have arranged to run a War on Poverty. They couldn't get
your garbage collected. But as theoreticians, they were brilliant and articulate
and noisy.

E. CAHN: There was a tug-of-war between Fred Hayes, Jack Conway, and Dick
Boone, with Jack Conway being the decision maker, really. The issue was how
tough you were on the citizen-participation dimension of the organizational
structure of the program—whether it was the board, the staffing, whatever—
before you gave them the money. With Fred Hayes saying, "Look, we've got
to move fast to shovel out the money, because a few precious, perfect projects
won't do anybody any good in a dynamical move." With Boone saying, "Yes,

that's true; we've got to shovel out the money. But we've got a maximum bargaining leverage at the front end, and that's when we ought to hold the line as tough as we can." So [then] you begin to make projections about the first wave of communities that would get funded—where you had to have a splash, and you had to have some geographic spread, and you had to worry about which congressmen's districts they were in, and so forth.

SUGARMAN: There was a very deep and enduring struggle between the Community Action Program and the inspector general's corps which had a substantial impact on the eventual evolution of the community action policy. In a way, it was a little hard to tell who was more community action–oriented at that time. The community action people were deeply concerned by the problem of spending money. Yet it was proving almost impossible to get programs organized and to get communities organized in time to do that. That's one of the things that undoubtedly contributed to the success of Head Start—the inability to spend money on the other programs in the early stages. They simply weren't ready. Head Start wasn't afflicted by that same problem.

What was the nature of that division of interest between the Office of Inspection and the Community Action Program?

SUGARMAN: The nature of it was, the [William] Haddad [Office of Inspection] group had very strong convictions about the importance of involving the poor in decisions and very strong convictions about the problems of racial balance and racial representation. Since the Community Action staff had not really defined the precise conditions which would meet the test of representation, you were left with an open field for battle as to whether you need thirty-one percent or thirty-seven percent. In fact, of course, it's pretty hard to develop a single set of definitions that would cover all communities.

The Community Action representatives would agree to one set of conditions only to have Inspection overturn them. Then there would be a battle back and forth. It was quite a numbers game that was played between the two staffs, and many times with the community in the middle, or at least sitting on the sidelines, waiting for it to be fought out within OEO.

During this period, the "three-legged stool" concept enunciated by Jack Conway...

SUGARMAN: Right. That was it, but even there, the proportional balance wasn't firmly established and certainly wasn't commonly accepted by all the members of the staff. OEO has attracted more bright and more individualistically thinking people than almost any federal program I've ever seen. But the result of that was, nobody was willing to accept the authority of anybody else to make a decision. Every issue had to be fought out time and time again.

TENSIONS WITH LOCAL ESTABLISHMENTS

MANKIEWICZ: I know very well that Shriver knew what community action was. I remember sitting at a Peace Corps meeting sometime in late '64 or '65, after things were going. Shriver used to have meetings twice a week of his senior staff of the Peace Corps. And at one of these, he was joking with us, and he was saying, "I had a phone call from [Senator] Clinton Anderson, saying, 'Shriver, what are you doing? A bunch of your people are picketing the Albuquerque City Hall, and they want to go to the city council meeting, and the demonstration is being led by an ex-Peace Corps volunteer who's working in the Community Action Program now.'" Well, he happened to be one of my ex-volunteers who had been in Peru and who had done that very successfully in the city of Arequipa. And Sarge said, "You know what I told Clinton Anderson? I said to him, 'That's the best evidence I have that both of the agencies I'm running are successful. A guy who agitated the poor in Peru for two years took that training and used it and is now working for OEO to get the poor to demand that they be allowed to participate in city council meetings. That's what it's all about.'" So he knew.

SHRIVER: To me the interesting thing was always that some of the places which were most enthusiastically for community action were rock-ribbed Republican places, like Dallas. The mayor of Dallas [J. Eric Jonsson] was a big booster, and Dallas ran the program perfectly. Cincinnati, the home of the Taft family, perfect. They had a communal kind of a pride or background in those places that just made it work. Now, you could go to another place where the culture and political atmosphere was poisoned; and when you brought community action in there, the whole town exploded. The hostilities between classes, the hostilities between rich and poor—which were there; we didn't create them—they would just explode. I used to say that community action was like a doctor coming in and putting a thermometer in your mouth to find out what your temperature is, and the temperature comes out 110 degrees, and then you curse the doctor. That's what happened in a lot of communities: the community leaders cursed us for revealing how lousy the community situation was; it was terrible. It wasn't our fault. Our activity brought it into the open.

It has been suggested that by 1965, OEO had to back down under political pressure.

MANKIEWICZ: Well, they backed down in some specific instances. They backed down in Syracuse; they backed down in Mississippi. But only where the pressures became intolerable, and as a tactical matter. You can argue with those decisions; you can say Shriver should have been tough and hung in there and fought for those people, and I think it's probably right. But somebody made a political judgment, and that may have also turned out to be right. It may have saved the program for another three years by not making it explicit what was implicit, which is that the purpose of this program was to have what you had in Syracuse. I don't think you'd want to go running to Congress and rubbing their nose in Saul Alinsky, but the fact of the matter is that philosophically our program was an Alinsky-type program.[6]

Was community action thought of as a way to help blacks participate in local government in the South?

CONWAY: That was a major part of it. That's why we worried about the governors' veto. Conceivably, the program could have been blocked. We worked out a compromise on the governors' veto that allowed the director to proceed after thirty days. In other words, the governor could veto, and if the director felt that it was an improper thing, he could go forward. Consciously and deliberately in November, after the election and when the law was operative and the department was operating, I put a planning grant on the desk of every southern governor, with $35,000, $50,000, whatever it was. And I gave them a chance to veto it, and none of them did. So I figured that I was home free, and so I just kept going. [Governor] Ross Barnett went out of his mind when we put that big Head Start grant into Mary Holmes Junior College in Mississippi and made it the administrator of the program. But we did that because he would have vetoed that.

BERRY: Our position was not to foster polarization, and most of our functions and efforts during those hectic days of assisting communities to get an understanding of what we regarded as community action was trying to encourage the traditional decision makers to be open, to arrive at an accommodation of this desire, this acceptance of the word as it was spelled out in the act. By those groups in the community, particularly in the big cities, there was already the seeds that had been germinating in the whole civil rights movement. We were trying to interpret to slow-reacting communities that the day was at hand when they should be willing to sit down and to share some of the seats in the decision-making process. At the same time, we were also trying to interpret to this new emerging power that wanted to confront that confrontation in and of itself was not necessarily community action.

D. BAKER: Community action gets to be a problem for a congressman when it's doing a good job or when it's doing a bad job, or sometimes when it's not doing a job at all. It may be that the community action agency was pressing a school system to do something, or there might have been militants threatening or leading a demonstration on city hall.

Were there ever instances of a direct challenge, not perhaps to a congressman, but to a congressman's political friend, such as a mayor?

D. Baker: Oh, yes. Typically, congressmen—though not invariably—most frequently are not good friends with their mayor. The fact of the matter is, normally a congressman and a mayor or the superintendent of schools or whatnot will have arrived at an accommodation with each other. Any threat to the status quo frequently is perceived on both sides as a threat. And yes, there are not infrequently those troubles. In the early days, they had CAP people running around making speeches all over the place and jumping into a race for the school board, or running against the mayor, or for county supervisor or such whatnot. This caused a great deal of hysteria and hurt feelings. There would be criticism that some agencies got grants and others didn't, and we did it through the local CAP, or the regional office did it, and there would be threats to cut off some program or not to go forward.

Newark, probably as much as any city in the country, influenced the changes in legislation in the sense that a great deal of what is thrown together in the so-called Green Amendment was really a result of Newark, either through the testimony of the police and mayor or through their investigations as to what was going on.[7] It was clear that the members of the committee who might not have been disposed otherwise decided that, one, Newark has too large a proportion of poor, that there was too much poor domination, not enough establishment, not enough [of] the rest of the community [on the CAA board]. It was clear that they were impressed that the Newark board was so big that it couldn't possibly function; that, again, the mayor and the city councilmen and the local doctor and the various and sundry other people who were on the board who might have provided some guidance couldn't stay up until two or three o'clock in the morning, because they had to go to work the next day.

A lot of people had recognized that San Francisco, which was another "poor-dominated" board, and Newark, and various other case examples had demonstrated that this good thing gets carried too far, and that a majority of the poor on the board means very damned little or no program out there, [and difficulty] getting services to people that need them. It just means a mishmash of nothing at all except organizing people for the sake of organizing them, and frequently enough to cause the program harm—organizing them for attacks, rational and irrational, on what they perceived as the evil establishment.

Essentially, the mayor wants to be able to control everything that goes into that town. In most cities where the public officials are reasonably competent, they have found a way of getting a very substantial voice in the community action program. They did so before the Green Amendment, and they're doing so after the Green Amendment. And the fact of the matter is, the situation hasn't changed that much. The mayor somehow now pretty much runs that damned operation, and he isn't a formal party in any sense in any way. Yet mayors and city council and local politicians, where they're bright and not a lazy bunch of idiots, have managed to run it. Let's face it, Dick Lee in the city of New Haven has run the community action program up there and has run it through Mike Sviridoff and that outfit up there since the beginning. Before we came into existence, he was running that program.

PERRIN: I think the mayors [in 1966–1967] by and large had gotten over their antagonism; and while many of them weren't completely happy with what they had, they had come around to accept this as a price really for new federal money, new federal emphasis on the city problems. They'd agreed generally that the community action agencies were a going thing and a necessary thing. That doesn't mean that they were uniformly happy with the ones they had in their cities. In fact, I feel that that's the lesson we have from the outcome of the Green Amendment exercise: very few mayors actually exercised the rights that they had to alter the sponsorship of the CAAs and make them public agencies.

Some of our people like to hold this up as proof that CAAs have demonstrated their acceptability and the mayors and CAAs are getting along just fine. I don't think that's necessarily true. But I think what it does prove is that most mayors, despite their troubles with CAAs, have learned to get along with them and recognize that there's a need for them and will exercise their influence in a more quiet way rather than taking them over or destroying them. And then they also recognized the challenge from the states that was beginning to mount. The governors were beginning to try to press their point that all of these programs should be run through the state house. There's nothing that scares a mayor more than that. So there were those kinds of forces going for us too in this battle: the antagonism among the public officials.

PHILLIPS: The only community action programs that we really remember are the ones involved in controversy. We don't think much about all the hundreds and hundreds of programs [about which] there was never a peep of a financial scandal, or never a peep of controversy or conflict between the people who participated in the programs and the local community. Many, many of them had 100 percent support from the local governments. We only think of the relatively small percentage where there were problems, and some of those problems were, I think, deliberately caused by people on both sides of the ideological fence who wanted to use it as a springboard for their own political ambition or to advance their own philosophic goals.

In Republican districts where you had Republican mayors and states with Republican governors, and even in many Democratic states where you had Democratic officeholders at that level, you had a lot of antipathy against the program politically because of its aggressive nature and its tendency sometimes to pit one group against another, one establishment against another. There were significant political considerations involved. I think a lot of people genuinely thought that it was a waste of money.

TOLMACH: There were those of us who think that the Green Amendment didn't ameliorate but crippled. Nevertheless, it should also be said that the power structure was involved even where we funded organizations other than the mayor's office, and that the mayor's offices were represented, and willingly, on the boards and governing bodies of community action agencies, which were nonprofit institutions. They very much participated, and in many cases the difference was insignificant. There were ultimately good programs and bad programs in both categories.

It has been the rare community action agency that has created situations of crisis in the community, because they had broad representation from every part of the community. In most cases, businessmen, clergymen, local governmental offices, welfare agencies—just about everybody, along with the poor—sat in these community action agencies. And it's because of that, one could argue, that they caused considerably less of a stir in the cities and rural areas than they might have. It happens that most of the instances of clash—of sit-ins in welfare commissioners' offices, organization of tenant groups [to] protest at housing authorities, things of that kind—were generated out of demonstration projects, which were very small in scope and which were very scientifically devised by the social scientists, with a complete set of hypotheses and so forth. It was the community action agencies, because they were consensus operations, that in many cases failed to make any kind of real impact. In other cases, in extreme cases, in some of the very largest cities, the poor had such a meaningless role in it that one can hardly think of them in this context that's being suggested here.

THE DEMONSTRATION PROGRAMS

TOLMACH: Some demonstration programs which were funded early on clashed with community action agencies. That's a whole different history. It's often that that gets confused with community action, [although] not so much these days, because the demonstration program has dwindled considerably in the last two years. There is now, for instance, a requirement that a demonstration program have the approbation of the local community action agency. It was one of the virtues in the very beginning that demonstration programs did not have to have the sign-off of the community action agency, or anybody else in the area, in order to receive funds. If they had, we never would have been able to make the kinds of experiments that we did make.

One such demonstration program that became a major headache for the agency took place in Syracuse, New York—where, incidentally, there was quite a fine community action agency. The demonstration program up there hypothesized that the needs of the poor would not be met until they were organized around issues. So community organizers fanned out into the community and got groups of poor people together around in some places housing issues, in other places welfare issues, with the ultimate aim of merging all of these groups into an organization of organizations. It was more of an Alinsky-ish approach, and it zeroed in on the community action agency as one of its enemies, causing no end of problems for us.

The R&D program was a vehicle for testing a lot of the concepts and assumptions in the legislation and probably went further, in areas such as resident participation and the employment of nonprofessionals from the low-income population, than the community action agencies themselves [did]. There had been a need to fund rather quickly communities around the country with comprehensive antipoverty programs, and to do that in a way that was more or less acceptable to everybody in town and everybody back here in Washington. Consequently, some of the key concepts of the legislation weren't really implemented as fully in the large-scale, communitywide programs as they were in the R&D program, especially in the first year. The idea was that innovative approaches, tried and evaluated in the R&D program, would, if successful, be adopted by the community action agencies which were operating the big programs.

I suppose the demonstration program largely reflected the kinds of people who were in it. It was administratively under the directorship of Richard Boone, who, as head of the program policy and planning division, had responsibility for the experimental programs. I mention that because Boone was one of the key people in the development of the concept of "maximum feasible participation of the poor," and accordingly, he staffed his R&D unit with people who in the task force days had, like Boone, been promoters of the idea.

So the demonstration program undertook experimental approaches, essentially, to just about every feature of the bill. There were housing demonstration programs; there were demonstration programs in the area of education, in health. These were all funded under section 207 of the [Economic Opportunity] Act. Quite a bit actually was learned from these demonstration projects, and many of them evolved as major thrusts which were adopted by the community action agencies. However, it was probably in the area of resident participation that the demonstration program left its deepest mark. Those demonstration programs in the areas of education, for instance, didn't ruffle as many feathers. But it was where we actually tried out new methods of bringing poor people into the operation of programs that we accomplished our most interesting work and probably caused the biggest stir.

There was a pattern to some of these; there was a design. We weren't haphazard by any means, and we proceeded systematically to explore the whole matter of how you involved poor people, or stimulated their involvement. Resident participation was, of course, an essential aspect of all of the endeavors, whether in housing, health, or any other area. But there were certain projects funded just to test that participation out in its pure sense, if it's possible to make that claim. There was one I had described in Syracuse, where one approach was tried; and then a slightly different approach [was] tried in Richmond, California—each of these making different assumptions about poverty communities. One making the assumption that there were no effective organizations and that it was necessary to go in and organize people around issues; another one attempting to utilize already-in-place associations of poor people and bolster those.

We got into trouble over so very many community-organizing projects and others that came out of the demonstration program. There were programs in Harlem—HARYOU—and there was the program in Syracuse. Each in its own way led us into confrontations as an agency in the kinds of things we were funding with political—capital "P"—powers in these communities. And it was from that that we gradually retreated in not funding these kinds of things. Along with this, we're developing more and more administrative rules and regulations and meeting demands from Congress and elsewhere that we have a greater degree of control over administrative procedures and personnel practices and what-have-you as we developed as a bureaucracy.

So we limited, gradually, the kinds of things that we started out. It was the feeling all along that Shriver never really had his heart behind the demonstration program; one sensed a kind of perverseness in him, though, that he in a way kind of liked it. It separated him from the average bureaucrat in town, and it gained him some credibility on the one hand with large groups of people who were for doing this kind of thing, and with the poor. He'd always say he was doing some of these things, and yet he was pulling back on them because he was eminently sensitive to political pressure.

COMMUNITY ACTION IN CHICAGO

Were you involved in the Lawndale project?

TOLMACH: Yes, I was involved in the Lawndale project.[8] I went to Chicago and was just about thrown out of [Deton] Brooks's office. As I walked in and was introduced, [he asked], "Are you the guy who has been working on this Lawndale project?" He wouldn't hear of it. And at that time it was not necessary, as it is today, that we have the clearance of the community action agency, which Brooks represented. I don't recall the exact date of this meeting that I had with Brooks, but we'd already begun trying to get the approbation of the higher-ups in town. Having been burned so badly in Syracuse and in so many other places, the process of getting sign-off, while not formal, was already under way. So we were trying to, in a sense, get his nod or at least [his] understanding of it. Well, very frankly, some of these demonstration programs depended on just the opposite.

What do you mean?

TOLMACH: If, as in Syracuse, you're going to allow poor people to question whether the poverty agency is the appropriate organization to represent the poor, you can't very well first get the poverty agency to agree to the organization of an effort which is going to question them—especially in the case where the poverty agency is headed by the mayor, as it was in Syracuse and, of course, in Chicago. As it happened in Syracuse, one of the first targets of the organizations that were formed in Syracuse was the community action agency, in spite of the fact that it was one of the better community action agencies.

CONWAY: Mayor Daley of Chicago got himself appointed the head of the Conference of Mayors Task Force on the War on Poverty, and he used Hubert Humphrey to put the blowtorch on us. Not successfully—we did what we were going to do anyway, and it was proper. But he was mad at us because we had funded The Woodlawn Organization [TWO].[9] He felt that all that stuff had to go through him and his agency, and we said no, it didn't have to, and we were going to do it this way. We had our confrontation, and I put a good guy in charge of the community action program in Chicago, a good solid Irish Catholic that knew the territory. He was able to keep things in reasonable balance. I knew Daley very well, and he knew me. He went through his ritual; I went through mine; and we just went on doing what we were doing.

Shriver was very good on these things. He stood up every time. I never had any serious policy disagreements with Sarge at all. We were very different in personality and style, but we had no differences. He never ducked out on any of these things.

HARDING: The Blackstone Rangers, or what's called the TWO Project, was a classic blunder on our part. Shriver thought that he had Mayor Daley's concurrence in putting the project on. There had been much discussion prior to its funding about its being operated by the Chicago community action organization, CCUO [Chicago Commission on Urban Opportunity]. It was decided not to do it that way, but apparently they never quite recovered from that decision. They wanted it. When it was funded directly, they objected very strenuously to it. The police never liked it. The mayor never liked it, although Shriver thought he had the mayor's concurrence. So they were at a standstill for a year. And the project did not bring any really substantive results. There was undoubtedly some fraud in connection with it. I don't think it was ever as bad as the *Chicago Tribune* and the police painted it, but it was certainly never as good as a viable project should have been.

Do you mean that the way the TWO Project was set up was a mistake, or are you suggesting that this kind of element in society can't be dealt with by OEO?

HARDING: No, I think we have to deal with this element in society. And I think this was an honest conceptual means of dealing with this element of society. But the political aspect with the mayor—the project design in terms of the amount of autonomy that it gave to these gang leaders in terms of conducting a manpower training program—was erroneous. You get back to this business of "maximum feasible participation." Here we leaned over too far in terms of putting uneducated, perhaps even dishonest, people in charge of a great deal of federal money and a very important program, without the proper supervision by the establishment. And I don't mean necessarily bureaucrats, but professionals. And we didn't have it in there; we tried midstream to get more of it in. By that time it was too far along to get it. So, no, I think it's a real part of the poverty program. If you're going to deal with the problem, you're going to have to deal with disaffected youth, and particularly ghetto youth. Somebody has got to do it. We stuck our necks out. We made a bad choice in the way we did it, but I think certainly our intentions were completely honorable. Our objective was completely desirable. And some way or another we have to find a modus operandi to deal with this problem in the future.

HARYOU-ACT

KELLY: HARYOU was a calculated risk in the summer of 1965. At that time, it was our judgment that in funding HARYOU, we were taking some risks in terms of the sophistication of HARYOU to operate its program. We were also taking some risks in terms of the capability of HARYOU to accumulate and distribute its money in an accounting system. But we proceeded on the basis that the city of New York was responsible for HARYOU. There was a sophisticated controller organization in the city of New York. The funds were being funneled through the city of New York; they were not coming directly from OEO. The city of New York, through its poverty board, was responsible for the operation, the accounting, the fiscal constraints, that were to be placed on HARYOU-ACT.[10]

HARYOU-ACT lost some money. To this day nobody has ever proven that anybody ever stole any money from HARYOU. They got a program off very rapidly. Harlem was cooled. The people in Harlem participated. There were no riots, no property burned. Nobody was hit in the head with rocks, and that was a very successful summer program. But the accounting procedures were very weak. As a result, I think there turned out to be ultimately about $100,000 that nobody can find. There is no evidence that it was ever stolen. There is evidence that it was paid for legitimate purposes; but vouchers weren't obtained, receipts weren't obtained—or, if they were obtained, they were lost. You write it off, in my judgment.

The thing that just kind of makes me angry in retrospect is that that was the first year of this program. It was the first of many long hot summers. Four years later, after the city of New York has had the opportunity to learn from their HARYOU experience, we find that there has been at least $1 million stolen in New York in the summer program last year, and God knows how much money stolen during the course of the regular year. Nobody makes much noise about that except the *New York Daily News* and the *New York Times*. I haven't heard a lot of speeches—or at least I've not read a lot of speeches—on the floor of Congress about that. I think the point I'm making is that there was hell to pay over HARYOU, and nobody has ever proven any money was stolen.

People's attitude is kind of benign now in a case where at least $1 million was stolen. So there tends to be a double standard, depending upon the spirit of the times. I think everybody in the country today is committed to the fact that you've got to have summer programs, and if people steal in them, well, what the hell. If they don't burn down the city, that's all right, that's the price you pay. Whereas in 1965, people weren't committed to summer programs, and because some money turned up not accounted for, then everybody says it is OEO's fault. It isn't OEO's fault. It's the city of New York's program. I would think that after having been there since they bought it from the Indians, in whatever year they bought it, they would have developed some sophistication in terms of handling their internal affairs, but they don't appear to have.

COMMUNITY ACTION AND THE GREEN AMENDMENT

Robert A. Levine was a senior economist in the logistics department of RAND Corporation from 1957 until 1965, when he joined OEO as chief of the Research and Plans Division of the Office of Research, Planning, and Evaluation. A year later, he became assistant director of the Office. Levine, a native of Brooklyn, had received his B.A. and masters degrees in economics from Harvard and his doctorate from Yale in 1957. Levine's military service extended from 1951 to 1954; he served in the Navy Supply Corps. He worked briefly as an economist for the Conference on Economic Progress in Washington in 1956.

LEVINE: [The relationship between the community action agencies and local governments] has been an evolutionary thing. The Green Amendment has made some difference at the margin in essentially the balance of bargaining power between the official and the community action agencies. But I think the trend was quite clear long before. This really began by early to mid-1966. In 1965 the mayors of the country descended on Vice President Humphrey, who was sort of the ambassador to the mayors, and said, "This kind of [conflict between the CAAs and local government] can't go on." This was communicated in no uncertain terms to Shriver. In fact, [the relationship] did begin to change then, so that 1966 politically was an ambiguous year. By 1967, when the new Congress came in, they were predicting that OEO would be thrown out. Shriver was able to use the mayors on his side to help preserve OEO, and that change took place that sharply.

I had an experience in one city, in which at the time of the Green Amendment determination, there was a big fight. There were hearings, and the mayor saying, "We're going to run it ourselves," and the community action agency was fighting. There was revolt. It was one of the more radical community action agencies that was in one of the more conservative cities. They were head to head and so forth and so on. During this period I happened to be in that city, and I talked to the mayor's special assistant. He said, "Hell, no, we don't want it. We've got to make the record look like they forced us not to take it, but we want to stay a little bit outside." I think that may be a typical pattern. This was a fairly smart politician—where if we have a dumb politician, he may try to really absorb it, and he may suffer for it because he's not really going to have the power that exists only in Chicago. I think that's the reason why the Green Amendment hasn't had more effect, and I think [this trend] is likely to continue.

PREVENTING RIOTS

PHILLIPS: The director's staff meetings were where the hot-spot problems were discussed. Shriver might lead off with: "Ed May, where do you anticipate next week's riots are going to be? Which cities?" And Ed would have a report. In the summer of 1966, these kinds of meetings were held each week. That was not the only thing that was ever brought up at these director's meetings, but that was one of the main things on the agenda every week from about May through September.

What could be done in this short span of time to prevent a riot?

PHILLIPS: There was certain discretionary money that Shriver had in our appropriation bill. He could, for example, expand a recreational component of a community action program in a city where we had a reliable report that there might be some trouble. He could announce such grants in a matter of hours by calling the city's newspaper that he was providing enough additional funds for a local CAP to keep the swimming pool open in the evenings or to light the tennis courts and the playground areas at night. I'm not talking about a lot of money, but an additional, supplemental grant that could be processed in a matter of hours. Perhaps a psychological boost that might [deter a riot].

Bertrand Harding found the Report of the National Advisory Commission on Civil Disorders (the Kerner Commission report) to be accurate in regard to OEO.

HARDING: Regarding OEO, I think they had a very good fix on the problem. I think our program did more to help than to hurt, certainly; there were very, very few people directly associated with the program that were involved in any of the rioting. But there were many, many instances where our community action people were working with the police and law enforcement groups to solve situations in the ghettos. Now, in the longer range, in terms of what does community action do to either repress or to bring forth violence within a community, that's probably something that the historians are going to have to answer. I don't know. But in terms of the direct action of people, I think it's true that people employed by the Community Action Program did not activate violence but in fact tried to calm it. And that's essentially what the Kerner Commission report said.[11]

EVALUATING COMMUNITY ACTION

LEVINE: I would argue that the Community Action Program has been very successful. I'm probably in a minority in that argument, but I would argue it. I think it has changed the institutional structure in city slums and ghettos drastically and favorably. I think this is necessary for a complete war on poverty.

There are three ways you evaluate it. One is that it's a bundle of services, and they can be evaluated as services: What is the health program doing today?

What is the legal program doing? This sort of thing. By and large, these evaluations were pretty good.

Second of all, it can be evaluated administratively. How does the machinery work? How is it coordinated? And other things. And by and large, these evaluations would look pretty poor.

The third thing, and I think the most important, the most different impact of Community Action is on the building of institutions in the community—particularly the black communities—and the changing of the institutional structure in which these communities are embedded to more favor the poor communities and the poor. How is this evaluated? Well, until now we've evaluated it largely anecdotally, but the evaluation staff at OEO now is getting quite deep into a project to quantify some of this institutional change. What sorts of things have been happening? How have they been happening? To make institutional change is inherently a qualitative aspect. That's to say: an apple is inherently not quantitative, but you can count apples. So you can count institutional changes in detail, kinds of changes, causes of changes, and so forth. They're doing this now, and that's the best way I think we've come across to try to really evaluate Community Action.

10

AN EARLY SUCCESS
Project Head Start

ALTHOUGH IT WAS NOT MENTIONED *in the Economic Opportunity Act, Project Head Start—the development program for preschool children—quickly emerged as the most popular feature of the Community Action Program. When Head Start was launched in the summer of 1965, it became an instant success. Half a million children attended the first summer's program, and a full-year version was introduced that fall.[1]*

Head Start was not merely a preschool educational program but a comprehensive child development program that offered health, nutrition, and social services as well. For seventy percent of the children enrolled, Head Start provided their first medical or dental examinations. The requirement that Head Start projects prepare a hot meal ensured that the children ate at least one nutritious meal each day.[2]

Several studies evaluating the Head Start experience focused on a decline in the performance of children who had completed the program and then attended inferior elementary schools. The researchers Max Wolff and Annie Stein observed this "fadeout" but did not consider significant differences between the Head Start children and those in the comparison group. Dr. Urie Bronfenbrenner and other advocates of the program used the data on "fadeout" to press for continuing Head Start through the first three years of elementary school. In 1967, Head Start Follow Through was launched as a pilot program, administered by the Office of Education. Another evaluation, by the Westinghouse Learning Corporation, reported only limited results in terms of the child's cognitive development.[3]

The two men whose support of Head Start mattered most, Sargent Shriver and Lyndon Johnson, understood the importance of an enrichment program for culturally deprived children. As director of the Kennedy Foundation, Shriver had become knowledgeable about environmental influences on the development of mentally retarded children. Johnson's experience as a teacher of impoverished Mexican American youths in south Texas had taught him that the intervention of a caring teacher can affect the lives of neglected children. Both Shriver and Johnson embraced Head Start and approved its expansion when additional funds were required. Lady Bird Johnson gave the program national visibility by visiting local projects and hosting Head Start events at the White House.[4]

THE CREATION OF HEAD START

SHRIVER: Somebody in the Budget Bureau prepared a pie chart of the poverty population of America, at our request. If you looked at the pie chart of who was poor in America, a certain percentage was rural poor; a certain percentage were mothers without husbands, running families. But the biggest chunk, about fifty percent of all the poor people in America, were *children*. I can see that chart as if I had just been shown it, and I said to myself, "My God, look at that. Fifty percent of all the poor people are children." What does that mean? It means that if we have a war against poverty and we don't have programs specifically aimed at children, nobody can say we're having a war to help the most numerous victims of poverty. It's just as if you had a war to conquer Germany and you didn't drop any bombs on the German soldiers—you wouldn't be conducting the war intelligently. So I said, we have to have programs for children. Well, then, what can you do for children, really?

It was the struggle to come up with programs for children, coupled with a second experience I had had, which produced Head Start. In the Kennedy Foundation, we were doing work for mentally retarded kids. A woman named Susan Gray at the Peabody School of Education in Nashville, Tennessee, had done some extraordinary research which showed that if you intervened early enough with children living in the slums—rural and city slums near Nashville— you could change their IQ.[5] Well, that shocked me. This was about 1957, 1958, 1959, 1961, when she did this research. I had always thought if you had an IQ of 90, that's what you had. That was what you were given by nature. That was your genetic endowment. The idea that you could take somebody with an IQ of 85 and make it 88 or 90, I had never heard of. But she proved you could do that with mentally retarded children. I knew about that research because I worked for the Kennedy Foundation with my wife.

So when I was looking at this pie chart with all these poor kids, I said, "Look, if we can intervene with mentally retarded children and raise their IQ, we surely ought to be able to intervene with children who are not mentally retarded and have a beneficial effect on their IQ and on their abilities in school." So I got in touch with a scientist named [Jerome] Bruner at Harvard. Like most good scientists, he was very skeptical about government programs. After [I talked] with him at some length, he wrote a paper for me and recommended that it would be feasible to try an experiment in early childhood intervention—which is what the experts call it—with a group as large as 2,500 children. We would get the baseline data, do the experimenting, and see whether we could have the effect on normal children that Susan Gray at the Peabody College had achieved with the retarded. I said, "Professor Bruner, that's wonderful, but that's no good. We've got to help 5 million children out there. What we can do with 2,500 is not large enough." He said, "Well, good luck to you, Mr. Shriver, but you can't succeed with a mass program in this field."

But I kept talking to people, and one day I had lunch with Joe Alsop, the famous newspaper columnist; and in the course of lunch I said, "Hey, Joe, what do you think about this?" and I trotted out this idea of early childhood intervention for the poor. He said, "My God! I think that's a great ideal." I nearly fell off my chair, because I had expected him to be very much opposed to it. I can remember going back to the office and saying, "My God, if Joe Alsop will support this idea, we can sell it, because he's such a hard-nosed conservative."

E. CAHN: Shriver had a sense of delightful disdain for professionalism per se. That came up in the context of Head Start and child development. Martin Deutsch and others were saying you've got to have Ph.D.'s, and it's a five-year process, and I remember he asked Dick Boone to get together what amounted to the equivalent of a developmental chart about what it would take to get a child development program off the ground. If you want to call it simplistic or realistic, I don't care, but he took the belief, if you could get the kids before they were destroyed, maybe you would have a handle on it. He flew into almost a rage, saying, "If I listen to the experts, this will take five years and a Ph.D. for every parent in the Head Start program. People have been raising children for a long time, and they've been doing a creditable job, and some of the children have worked out well and some of them haven't. But I'm not going to take this. We need high visibility. We need impact programs."

THE FORMATION OF THE HEAD START STEERING COMMITTEE

SHRIVER: Well, I just couldn't sit there and think about this myself. Obviously, I didn't have enough experience to do it single-handedly. So I talked to the head of the scientific advisory committee of the Kennedy Foundation, a great pediatrician named Dr. Robert Cooke. I said to him, "What about this?" And he said, "Well, I think it might work." And I said, "Would you get together a committee, and make an analysis of this thing, and come in with some recommendations to me?" So Bob Cooke and I—but I think principally Bob Cooke—went out and put together a committee. I think it had as many as somewhere around fourteen to eighteen people on it—men and women, medical doctors, sociologists, educators, and so on—and I just threw this problem, and this approach which I've just described, at them at that point [and] said we'll put $10 million behind it.

SUGARMAN: In the fall of 1964, there was a small group of people who were brought to Washington to look at the question of what might be done to develop programs for young children. It was in some senses a sort of an abortive effort. They prepared a piece of paper, which didn't get a great deal of attention in the agency. But I suppose it had enough of an impact that Mr. Shriver soon began to talk to a number of other people about the possibilities of a major effort in this area. And although I've never heard this directly from Sarge, I take it that he was greatly influenced by Mary Bunting, the former president of Radcliffe College; and by a number of people with whom he had been working in the mental retardation area.

So in early December or maybe November of '64, Mr. Shriver called Dick Boone and asked him to put into gear an effort to make a serious study of what we might do. He suggested that Dick talk to Dr. Robert Cooke, who was and still is the chief of pediatrics at the Johns Hopkins Medical School and Hospital and who had been very active in the mental retardation field. He also was the Shrivers' personal pediatrician, so there was a good deal of family and business and interest relationship there.

Dick, I recall, was sent out to Pittsburgh to catch Dr. Cooke between planes, and they had a very brief conversation around the idea of forming some sort of committee. Then Dick got involved in other efforts, and he asked me to take on this responsibility. So I met in Baltimore with Dr. Cooke and with Dr. Edward Davens, who is the deputy director of health in the state of Maryland. Simply sitting around the table, we put together a list of people who might be invited to participate in such a committee. We deliberately tried to make it an interdisciplinary effort, and I suppose that had a very profound effect on the kind of program Head Start eventually became. We—I don't know whether it was consciously or unconsciously—did not include a great number of educators. In fact, I guess there were only one or two people who could be called out-and-out educators. There was a heavy representation of psychologists and medical people. We put this list together, and as I recall, Mr. Shriver approved it pretty much as was.

This is what became originally the steering committee—and then renamed, later on, the planning committee—for Head Start. There were about twelve people on that committee. During the month of January and early February, we met two to three times a week, both in Washington and in New York, and hammered out a piece of paper which eventually became the Cooke report. That report said, in effect: There is a need for a program for preschool children; it can be mounted; the effort should begin with this summer, but that should be viewed only as the first step toward longer full-year programs and perhaps to[ward] longer-range programs in terms of entering into the school years as well. It said that that program ought to be comprehensive in its nature in involving educational services, medical services, social services, nutritional services; and that parents ought to be significantly involved in the program.

Well, we made this report to Mr. Shriver. We suggested to him that if we really worked at it, we could probably get maybe 300 programs going that summer, and we might involve as many as 100,000 children. He was pleased with it. Apparently, he immediately went to the president with the report, and the signals were given to go ahead.

As a little sidelight here, after we had written the report, Mr. Shriver said to me, "Now, what will this cost?" Of course, we hadn't figured the cost at all. I said, "Well, I'll look into it and let you know." He said, "Fine, you have an hour!" So another fellow and I sat down over lunch, and we figured out what Head Start was going to cost in the summer. We estimated it would average $180 per child. As it turned out, that first summer it averaged $186 per child, so we weren't too far off base. But we were very much off base in terms of the size of the program.

RECRUITING JULIUS RICHMOND

Julius Richmond was appointed the national director of Project Head Start and OEO's director of the Office of Health Affairs in 1965. Before he was recruited to help establish the War on Poverty's child development program, he had been professor and chairman of the Department of Pediatrics at the College of Medicine, State University of New York at Syracuse, from 1953 to 1965. Earlier, from 1946 to 1953, Richmond had been a faculty member at the University of Illinois Medical School in Chicago, his native city. He served as a flight surgeon during World War II.

RICHMOND: As Mr. Shriver proceeded then to think about where one could really get some help to do this, he began to look around. He had known of our work in Syracuse. At that point, I was chairman of the Department of Pediatrics at Syracuse. I had also just become dean of the medical school. With one of my colleagues, Dr. Bettye Caldwell, who's now down in Little Rock, Arkansas, I had been developing a program that had already demonstrated in a scientific way that you could interrupt the developmental decline. Let me explain what I mean by "developmental decline," or "developmental attrition." What we observed in very-low-income children that we were studying from the prenatal period on was that they developed by standard tests reasonably well up through the first year. But at about the first year, when language becomes more important to development and as children begin to explore their environments and interact more with others, these children underwent a rather steep decline in development—again, as measured by tests. Ultimately, of course, this gets reflected over the years in school performance, because all of the measures that we're talking about are basic to performing in the usual school environment.

Well, when we faced up to this naturalistic observation that these children were undergoing what we call developmental attrition, we then had to face up to the ethical question: since the parents didn't come to us for any intervention, should we try to intervene? We struggled over the ethical issues of whether we might be more intrusive than parents might desire, and we decided that it was worth trying to make a demonstration that one could, in fact, prevent this developmental decline. And we had demonstrated that. It was just prior to the time that the Economic Opportunity Act was passed.

But because of Mr. Shriver's involvement in mental retardation and my involvement in both mental retardation and this whole field of child development as a professor of pediatrics, he was quite knowledgeable about what we had been doing. So he invited me to come to Washington. In characteristic fashion, he wanted me to drop everything that day and get down there immediately. I had some appointments to see some patients, and some other commitments, so I suggested I would come down the following day.

We had a meeting, and he essentially laid out what he was interested in having me attempt to do. At that point I had not had any large-scale public health experience or large-scale managerial experience—although I'd certainly been involved in managing enterprises within the academic environment—but I had been deeply interested in public health and public health issues. So when I suggested to him that maybe he ought to try to find someone who had had more of a public health and managerial background than I had, Shriver, in his rather characteristic fashion, said, "Well, if I had wanted a bureaucrat, I would have looked for one." So I said, "But I've just taken on the deanship, and I have a lot of obligations, and I just really don't know whether I could drop everything and come and do this." He said, "Well, would you like to have me call the president of your university?" And I said, well, no, I didn't think that was quite necessary, that maybe we could settle this without that.

He had done his homework. He turned to me, and he said, "You know, you've been a very strong advocate of programs like this going way back to early in your career. In the late forties in Illinois, you were a very strong proponent of permissive legislation for what we then called nursery schools, preschools like Head Start." I said, "Yes, that's true. I was and still am." And he said, "Well, now put up or shut up."

So I found myself in Washington. The university was rather generous in making it possible for me to do this, and we then began to develop the program.

STARTING UP THE PROGRAM

RICHMOND: We were into early February of 1965, and I and the committee and my associate director for the program, Jule Sugarman, were struggling with when we could start the program. We started out thinking about a summer program, and the judgment we had to arrive at sometime during that month of February was whether we were going to run a program that summer of 1965 or whether we would wait until the year following. All of the experts that we talked to—well, when I say experts, I mean all of the people representing professional organizations—kept telling us, "Well, you can't do it this summer. It's already too late, and you'll never carry it off." [They said] we'd better wait a year or two, or three even. Some of them kept talking about "you don't have enough manpower, and you'll never be able to carry it off." With Jule Sugarman available to do the managerial side of this, which he had great expertise in—and he had a deep, personal commitment to this kind of program—I felt quite confident that we could carry it off, even though it would be pushing communities all over the country to get applications in and all.

Even getting the announcements of the program out, we couldn't do that until early March. By then our timing was such that all we could do was give the communities six weeks in which to write their applications. Again, I come back to the fact that these were comprehensive child development programs, not just preschool education. [They were] supposed to have health and nutrition and social services as well as the education components. We built in voluntary effort and participation of the various professions and all. Six weeks was really putting them under quite a gun. But that also meant that we had left ourselves only six weeks to review all these applications and process them and get these communities funded so that we could be off and running sometime in June. And yet we made the judgment that we probably could carry it off.

SUGARMAN: We had to decide, of course, how we were going to let people know this program existed. There was in OEO at that time a very dynamic public affairs director named Holmes Brown. Holmes said, "Well, I think Shriver ought to write a letter to every school superintendent and every health director and every welfare director in the country." At that time, I don't think he had any idea of how many people that was, and I suppose in total it was close to 50,000. The letter-writing firms collapsed under the strain, and while I think we probably wrote to every school superintendent, I don't think we reached all the health and welfare offices. One of Holmes's other brainstorms was the notion of putting a little three-by-five card in that people could send back for further information.

So we sent the letters out. In the meantime, Mrs. Johnson had decided that she would sponsor a tea at the White House to announce the program. We sort of got fouled up because that tea was scheduled, as I recall it, for the middle of the week, and earlier in the week Dr. Richmond, who by that time had been picked as the director of the program, and I had gone to a conference in Atlantic City where the Educational Writers Association was holding their annual conference. The idea was that we'd give them a background briefing so that when the tea was held they could write about it. However, they took the position that if we were talking for the record that was one thing; and if we weren't, they weren't interested in hearing from us. So after a hasty conference with the White House press office, it was decided that we would announce the program in Atlantic City. In that sense, we sort of scooped the White House.

But the tea went very well. It was attended by a very large representation of prominent women in America, a number of governors' wives, a number of leading ladies in business and the entertainment world, and it just went beautifully.

Sargent Shriver briefs educators, public officials, and members of the press on the
recommendations of the Head Start Planning Committee in the East Room of the
White House on February 23, 1965. *33918-12, 2/23/6.5 Presidential Collection,*
LBJ Library

We had sent out these cards, and the first few days, of course, there were just
a trickle of them coming back. Then all of a sudden we were hit with a deluge of
cards coming back saying, "Please send me further information."

RICHMOND: I'll never forget, there was a very interesting fellow who was on
Shriver's staff, and we came into his staff meeting—he used to hold a staff
meeting early in the morning, three mornings a week. This fellow flipped
through these cards, and he said, "Why, we haven't heard of places like
this since Kefauver ran for the presidency in 1952." People came out of the
woodwork manifesting their interest. Then what happened was that we had
to undergo kind of a role reversal—that is, people like me, who are accustomed to going through grant review processes for the National Institutes
of Health [NIH] or whatever, where your whole objective was to determine
what the very highest-quality were and then you discarded the rest. It was
a very ritualized process. And when I say "role reversal," in this process we
had to keep thinking of how we could get those communities that needed
the programs the most and had the least capacity to write an application
into the program. So it was exactly the opposite of what we had traditionally been accustomed to.

SUGARMAN: We convened a meeting of a group of young people here in Washington who were management interns in the various federal agencies. We said, "If you'll give up your weekends for the next six weeks, we'll pay your way to go out to the 300 poorest counties in the United States and help them write an application." We had, I guess, close to 125 kids who did that anywhere from two to six weeks. As a result, 225 of the 300 poorest counties were actually in the program that summer.

Now, this effort was greatly aided and abetted by a committee of congressional wives, who got together from both sides of the aisle, I might say, and who put together their resources of knowing people around the country and kept on the phone until they found somebody who was willing to talk about Head Start. Once they had that name, then we'd send one or two of these young people off to sit down with them. They literally wrote the applications for most of these communities and literally helped them to set up their centers, even though they knew very little about it themselves.

RICHMOND: Now, let me sort of get the final numbers. What we had come in were about 3,300 applications, and we ended up with 2,700 of them being funded for programs that summer. There were some that, if they just didn't indicate that they could carry it off, we couldn't in good conscience, no matter how great the need was, provide the funds. But by and large, the communities were in need and the populations had to be clearly defined.

How do you process 3,300 applications in six weeks? Here again, Jule Sugarman and I struggled over how to do this, and we decided to break the processing down into component parts so that it was manageable. But then we needed a staff that would be available on a short-term basis, because we couldn't hire several hundred people to do this processing and then keep them employed in Washington indefinitely. There'd be no need for them after we got the programs funded. We thought, where do you get people who could work on a short-term basis that intensively? I think it was Jules who got the idea, and it turned out to be a brilliant one, of tapping into the substitute teachers in the District who were generally not fully employed. The school district down there went along with the idea, so we brought all of the substitute teachers in to work on this processing line. Their educational level was such that they could be trained rather readily, and it turned out to be a very workable sort of thing. They appreciated the employment, and we needed their competence, and so it was a good match.

Just to show you how the thing ran, I was on a program one evening at the Mayflower Hotel—it was a conference on day care—and the head of the Child Welfare League of America, Joe Reid, and I were on that program. This was about ten o'clock in the evening when the meeting broke up. Joe said, "What are you going to do now? You want to have a drink or something?" I said, "No, I'm going back to the processing line." He said, "The processing line? What do you mean?" I said, "Well, we're processing the grant applications." He said, "Mind if I come with you?" And I said, "No."

So we went down, and the lights were blazing and people were working and things were really revved up by then. By this time, it was about eleven o'clock at night. His eyes popped. He was a marine in World War II. He said, "I haven't seen anything like this since World War II." And that's about the way it went, and that's how it took off.

SETTING UP PROGRAMS

SUGARMAN: In this period, a very crucial policy question arose. I say "crucial" because it involved the question of whether we should limit the program to communities with good resources, where we could be assured the kids would get a quality experience, or whether we should go as fast and as far as we could and go into places where there really was very great scarcity of resources. We opted to do the latter, but we opted to do it with the understanding that we'd go through with training and technical assistance and consultation and everything we could to bring the quality up. In this sense, we departed rather dramatically from the previous government grant programs, which, for the most part, are conceived of as quality experimentations, trying to develop new services in a quality fashion. As a result of that decision, we got a wide mix in the variety of programs, and we created an enormous range of backup services.

First of all, in the training area, around about March, somebody said to us, "Well, okay, you're going to have all these kids. We know there aren't enough teachers who've had experience in early childhood. How are you going to train them?" And so we had a staff meeting and we got the idea, "Well, we'll get the universities to train them." This was—understand you now—late March. We sent out a telegram that same day to some 200 universities, saying, "Please come talk to us about a training program." Strangely enough, they did! In the end, more than 200 colleges offered a six-day orientation program, and as I recall, something like 44,000 people actually went through a six-day training program before the end of June. So it was a pretty phenomenal operation.

Then somebody said, "Well, training's fine, but what you really need are people on the scene to help out in the technical assistance way." So we put two people on the telephone who knew the early childhood experts in the country, and we said, "Call them up and invite them to a meeting in Washington on Saturday." We had a lovely snowstorm that day, but nevertheless, about 150 of America's most dedicated women—the early childhood experts—came, accompanied by maybe five or ten men. We formed a technical assistance corps, and they just gave up everything else they were doing to work on this project. That corps now, I guess, in total exceeds over 2,000 people who work as part-time consultants to the program, and I think it's been a terribly valuable part of the effort.

TEACHER-CHILD RATIO AND AGE SPAN

RICHMOND: Just as one example of the things that might seem like small decisions that can have great significance: the third or fourth day I was in Washington, we'd been projecting the following number of children per teacher (on the basis of what elementary schools usually have)—one teacher per twenty or thirty children. And I said, "No, we can't have that." They said, "Well, what do you suggest?" I said, "I would suggest one trained teacher and two teaching assistants per fifteen children." They said, "You've just more than doubled the budget for teachers." I said, "Well, if it's necessary that we do a program for half as many children this first year, that's what we ought to do. I don't know whether we'll succeed if we have one teacher per fifteen children with two assistants, but I know we'll fail if it's one teacher with twenty to thirty children. One of the most important things about a new program is that it succeed and demonstrate successes. If that means reducing the scope and size of the program, then that's what we'd better do."

It turned out we didn't have to do that, because—again—of the response of the president and Mr. Shriver. Incidentally, each of these times I'd up the ante and go to Mr. Shriver, he'd say, "Well, let me talk to the president." The next day he'd say, "Fine." So you know, it kept going up and up. When we started announcing the grants, it was very interesting. We generally would go over to the White House, and the president would announce them in the Rose Garden before cameras and all. It was quite a festive occasion, so he personally played quite a role.

Another major decision that we had to make early on [was], are you going to cover all of the preschool years from birth on up, or will you focus? The advisory committee and I decided we would target the children who were the year prior to school entry. The reason I put it that way is that not all schools across the country entered children at the same age, because some had kindergartens and some didn't. Only about half the children of the country at that time had kindergartens. So in some instances, we were dealing with the four-year-olds where there were kindergartens, and other places we were dealing with the five-year-olds. The reason for that was, we felt that even though our resources were fairly good, that if we distributed them thinly over all of the preschool years we wouldn't have an impact on any one age period.

Did you think that the year before starting school was the most critical year of a preschooler's development?

RICHMOND: I don't think we could say critical, but I had the feeling that if we were going to impact on the children with a carryover to the school years, that it would be better if there were not a gap between the time they were in the program and the time in the school. There still isn't any good, absolute proof for that; but that, just more or less on a commonsense basis, was the way we decided to go.

PARENTAL INVOLVEMENT

RICHMOND: Bettye Caldwell and I had had enough experience with parents to know that things went better if the parents were involved. We also learned that parent involvement with low-income families was not necessarily what it would be with middle-class families, if you were going to have some impact—although I think we've learned subsequently, even for middle-income families, that they do better if they're involved. The point of difference that I'm getting at is that with middle-class families, there had been a history of parent education. That is, parents had some motivation. They wanted to learn about child development; they would be willing to sit in a classroom and have somebody talk to them about child development and the needs of children. We found that getting them involved in the actual program, letting them see what was happening, or letting them see how teachers worked with children was much more important.

Did you ever consider requiring a certain measure of parental participation in order to enter the kids in a program?

RICHMOND: Well, again, we didn't want to rule children out who were living in the worst circumstances. Our advisory committee was very alert to this. During that first summer and toward the end of the first summer, they kept saying, "Well, are we really getting the children who always fall between the cracks in those families that never get into programs?" We paid a lot of attention that first summer [to] how to contact such parents. For example, rather than relying exclusively on printed materials and the print media, we tried to do a lot over radio, where we had some reason to believe that these families were more in tune with radio than they were with the print media. So we did everything we knew how to do, but we still had not satisfied ourselves at the end of the first summer that we were really getting the most needy of the children.

OBJECTIVES OF HEAD START

Was part of the thinking in Head Start to provide some sort of day care? Did you consider what the parent might be able to do in terms of employment while the child was in the program?

RICHMOND: It had mixed goals and mixed objectives. Those [programs] that were child-centered, those that were oriented toward the parent, and particularly in relationship to social services—we proposed not to try to replicate what was available to families in the community. But we did specify that the Head Start program try to guide parents to the resources in the community: employment resources, welfare resources, social agencies that might be helpful beyond Head Start, the medical facilities in the community beyond Head Start. So all of these issues were initially part of the program, but I wouldn't say that we specifically designed Head Start so that mothers could be free to work. We felt [the program] was inherently good.

SUGARMAN: Broadly stated, [the goal of Head Start] was to try to intervene at a point in the life of the child in ways which would keep deficits from developing in that child and which would therefore make it possible for him to achieve his maximum potential in latter life. It was only in part a school readiness program, but really, I preferred the term "a life readiness program."

It wasn't simply a kindergarten program.

SUGARMAN: No, it wasn't. Quite explicitly, the effort was made to convince people that it was not a kindergarten program as such. Now, the other thing that should be very clear is that Head Start never developed—and to this day does not have—a single model of what you do with young children. There are all sorts of curriculum styles. There are all sorts of programs and approaches that have been approved in Head Start. I think that is essential to the future, because we simply still don't know exactly what the best methods and programs are.

NUTRITION AND HEALTH

RICHMOND: Since we wanted to ensure the best-quality nutrition, we thought a way of doing that would be to specify that there be one hot meal, because we felt if you didn't specify that, there wouldn't be all that much attention to the food that the children got. But if you were providing a hot meal, you had to pay some attention to setting up for it and getting people interested in what was going in that meal preparation rather than just putting out a little cereal and milk or whatever. So again, it was a nuance.

Was Head Start able to provide medical treatment and see that treatment was provided by a diagnostician?

RICHMOND: Well, we had an interesting internal debate going on about that, because a lot of the laypeople involved in Head Start thought that if we're going to get involved on the health side, then clearly, if you identify children [with medical needs], you just go ahead and take care of them. I was very concerned about that, because first, I recognized that if you started using the Head Start funds for medical care, you'd soon use them up at a rate that would have made it a medical program, essentially, for relatively few children. So that was one reason why I didn't. I just felt in terms of the resource situation that it was untenable, so for the first summer I said, "No treatment." That was an enunciated policy.

I don't think [that policy] was entirely observed, because if there were some communities where children couldn't get care in other ways, we tended to authorize it. But that didn't happen very often. The other reason why I took that stand was that for decades the American Medical Association [AMA] and other groups in the field of health were always saying [that] nobody needs to lack for medical care, that income is no factor, that everybody in the United States has access to care. Of course, they were referring to what essentially were charitable contributions that people might receive from the health professions. And I wanted to really highlight the issue that you really had to develop a design for more comprehensive health services. What began to develop in communities all around the country was that medical societies were saying, "We can't take care of all of these children; you're just giving us this terrible load." And my retort to that was always two things: one, you've always said that nobody needs to lack for medical care because they're poor; and secondly, remember, we didn't generate the need for medical care. All we're doing is generating the demand for medical care.

We didn't really have too much conflict about that that first year. But you have to remember, that was also the session of Congress that time when Medicaid was passed, and it was not yet in place as an operating program. I had this in mind too; that was the third reason for not just putting all of this money into medical care indiscriminately, because it would have set a precedent and it would get gobbled up. By the next year, Medicaid was coming in place, and then we began to relax and to say, "Well, look, if these children need medical care, you should be able to get the medical care supplied through Medicaid."

FROM SUMMER TO YEAR-ROUND PROGRAM

The program was originally designed as a three-month summer program. Wasn't there some question as to whether it would continue to be a year-round program?

RICHMOND: That's right. But while we got started, we began to lay the groundwork for a year-round program, because we were quite convinced from the onset that it would be better if these children had this kind of environment throughout the year rather than only during the summer. I don't think we could have mounted as large a program during the school year. That's another point that I didn't bring out in terms of our confidence that we could run a program in the summer. We knew that we could tap into a pool of teachers that were ordinarily underemployed in the summer and who would be interested in doing this. This involved giving them some short, intensive courses to bring them up to speed to working with younger children. But that worked out very successfully. But if we had had to start on that scale for a year-round program, I just don't think we could have carried that on.

HEAD START AND THE COMMUNITY ACTION PROGRAM

Do you think that having Head Start work through Title II and the Community Action Program was satisfactory? Or should Head Start have been another provision?

RICHMOND: Well, that's a very interesting question, and it relates to Mr. Shriver's managerial style, because even though we were part of the Community Action Program, managerially he never dealt with us as though we really were. He dealt with us quite directly, so we never felt as though we were being constrained by being in the Community Action Program. We tried to exercise the proprieties of going through the director of the Community Action Program. And on a formal basis, as budgets would go up and things of that sort, we dealt with those formalities. But in terms of major program decisions and all, it was really right out of Mr. Shriver's office, in effect. That occasionally made for some abrasions. Some of the Community Action people, particularly if they had come out of the old federal bureaucracies, thought that that violated all of the proprieties. Yet it was very functional. This is what always causes me to describe Mr. Shriver as the world's best antibureaucrat, since he really didn't pay all that much attention to the proprieties.

Did you have problems with community action agencies at the local level?

RICHMOND: We had something to learn, and we took this as a plus that we were in the community action agencies at the local level, because they had had experience in mobilizing people in the low-income communities; they had had experience in how you get people to work on boards, and that's what we were about. I would say by and large at the local level we found the arrangement to be rather helpful. At the local level, the proprieties were exercised much more than they were at the central headquarters level. It's an interesting point. I hadn't quite thought of it that way, but we talked a lot about the fact that we were in the Community Action Program out in the field, and by and large we always—I think Jule Sugarman and I at any rate—felt that that was more of a help than a hindrance.

Do you think that Head Start served to bring new elements into the Community Action Program on a local level?

RICHMOND: Oh, yes. No question. Yes. Because we were tapping into resources in the community from the educational establishment, the social services

Lady Bird Johnson participates in a press conference on Head Start at the Cleveland School in Newark, New Jersey, August 12, 1965. Participants (left to right) include Sargent Shriver; Governor Richard Hughes; Mrs. Hancock, a Head Start mother; Mrs. Jackson, a Head Start teacher; Lady Bird Johnson, Dr. Mildred Groder, administrator of the Newark Head Start program; Mrs. Venson, a Head Start teacher; Mr. Maurice Feld, director of Head Start at the Cleveland School; Mayor Hugh J. Addonizio; and Elizabeth (Mrs. Richard) Hughes. *34969-4, 8/12/65. Presidential Collection, LBJ Library*

programs, and certainly the field of health, which [meant] we had people coming in that never would have had anything to do with this program if it had been the broad-based community action agency. So the fact that these programs had to have boards of their own and had to have consultants of their own in the community made an enormous difference and brought in a lot of people that never would have known about community action.

What is the proportion of the sponsors of Head Start programs that are community action agencies?

SUGARMAN: In the full-year programs, about ninety percent of Head Start funds go through community action agencies. In terms of the actual program operators, just about one-third are public schools, about twenty-six percent are community action agencies, and the remainder are private nonprofits of one sort or another.

Now, there are quite a number of interpretations of what the purposes of Head Start were. There were a group of people within OEO who believed and still believe to this day that it was fundamentally contrary to the community action concept, because it offered what they termed a "package approach." In contrast to that, my own view was [that] this offered a neat balance between individual decision making and some assurance of a quality standard that would result in a good program. It is true that many—probably most—communities, particularly the smaller ones, began their community action effort with Head Start, and that it served as a vehicle on which they could build later on. The tragedy of it, of course, was, by the time they were ready to build, there wasn't any money. So many of them never went beyond that Head Start stage.

[There was] no new money for other parts of the Community Action Program. The initial legislation contained no mention of Head Start. It wasn't until the 1966 amendments that language was introduced in the bill which defined the Head Start program. It was later amended in 1967 to put in parent participation, which had always been a policy.

Again, I think there's a diversity of approach here. By and large, the official Community Action line was to deemphasize national emphasis programs; to encourage the growth of free money as opposed to earmarked money; and, at least in the case of substantial numbers of Community Action personnel, to sort of discourage communities from using Head Start. Although it was probably the most popular of the poverty programs among the public—and the Congress as well—it was, at least for a period of time, the least popular of the programs among the OEO staff. This was simply as a result of the fact that it had taken such a great proportion of the money, that it had been earmarked by the Congress, and that it simply seemed antithetical in nature to a community action program. That viewpoint moderated and shifted as time went along, but there was a very rough period of relationships for a while between Head Start and the rest of the Community Action staff. It is still the case today that as far as jobs within OEO go, Head Start is low man on the totem pole. An individual who comes in as a new employee will be assigned to Head Start as a break-in period, but he really isn't considered to have made it until he has advanced to a Community Action analyst.

Because Head Start was a popular program, there seems to have been pressure to fund it at higher levels than perhaps people in OEO would have liked. Is that correct?

RICHMOND: No, I don't think I ever got that perception; but, of course, whether something like that would have happened later on, I don't know. But I never felt that we were getting beyond the need and getting beyond communities' capacities to meet that need. As I indicated to you earlier, we were making a very determined effort to get the communities with greatest need in, and we didn't want to discriminate against the communities that had somewhat better resources and capacity to write grant proposals and to develop programs. And so if you were trying to get a lot of counties and school districts in that had never had these kinds of resources, then you were, of course, making demands for more funds than programs otherwise would. If we had just sat back and waited for these communities, it would have taken a long time.

But I never had the feeling that we were being pressed to spend money, and that's why I described the situation as going quite in the reverse. We would be apprehensive about whether there was enough money for these additional programs that we were coming up with, and we would go with considerable apprehension to Mr. Shriver, not knowing what the ceiling might be. But each time, after checking with the president that first year, he came back and said, "Well, we seem to be able to do that." Now, I think the way in part they were doing it, as it was explained then, was [that] some of the other programs were not taking off as fast, and there was a little tension within OEO. There were some of the people in the other programs that didn't have the visibility and the popularity, who I think felt, "Well, gee, if they weren't getting all that money, we'd be growing faster." But I never saw any good evidence for that, and I never saw any evidence that we were really taking it away from them.

HEAD START FOLLOW THROUGH

Do you remember how the Head Start Follow Through Program originated?

RICHMOND: The advisory committee was interested. That original document laid out that what goes before and what comes after [Head Start] are important. I was often inclined to say in that first summer that the Head Start program might do more for elementary education than almost anything that had ever happened—because what we were doing was demonstrating a model that was very functional: that is, a favorable teacher-to-child ratio, favorable curriculum development, favorable training programs, and all. What we were beginning to generate—and we anticipated that this would happen—was the demand on the part of teachers all over the country who were teaching kindergarten, first, second, and third grade, saying, "Well, we could do just as good a job as Head Start does if you just give us the same resources." I think we then began to generate some ferment. So we also, in order to make it more attractive to schools to do something with the Head Start children, began to wonder how we could institutionalize and bridge this and follow through [in] our effort to do that. So you'd give the school some funding for this. Since Title I of the Elementary and Secondary Education Act had come along at the same session of Congress, it also was to provide funds to do similar things. Many times it wasn't very clear as to which was to do which.

I think developing a follow-through program in many ways was much more difficult, because the schools were already there, and they had their patterns of activity. Do you give them money for after-school things, or, if you supplement the school curriculum, are you in a sense being intrusive in relationship to curriculum development? So we wanted to go slowly with this and explore it, and that's how the whole notion of alternatives in follow-through [developed]. Various options developed with the idea that no community knew precisely how to do this. It was called "planned variation," instead of just ad hoc variation in which you'd encourage communities to go different routes in terms of what they would add to the child's daily experience.

Did the Follow Through Program address the problem of children's relapsing, backsliding, after being out of the Head Start program for a while?

RICHMOND: Yes. Yes. This, of course, in the later concerns about Head Start, the attrition of the effects, became a fairly central kind of argument, and initially a lot of that focused around IQ test points and things of that sort. The interesting thing about that was that [with] virtually all of the programs, even with the very brief summer programs, by all conventional tests, while the children were in programs [they] would show a spurt in development, and then there was some decline over time. Of course, various people—and I think early on, when Moynihan was in the White House, he was one of them—tended to say, "Well, these children don't perform better forevermore; therefore it didn't work." That is what I tended to call the "immunization model." You know, you give them one shot, and they're all right for the rest of their lives. Of course, our interest in follow-through was precisely because we anticipated that there would be attrition if there weren't some enrichment program. So we were very interested in enrichment, and follow-through was just one way of accomplishing that. But we had hoped that the schools generally in low-income neighborhoods would do more of this, and I think to some extent they've been trying, with whatever resources are available.

But studies then began to emerge indicating that there was some "washout" effect, and that was a term that you might have been searching for, because that's what commonly was used. That turned out to be entirely true, because over time, as other studies developed, it's been clear that some children retain some gains indefinitely, and if there is reinforcement in the schools, it's understandable that they would do even better. So the long-term effects have been much more favorable now that we have rather long-term effects measured in a variety of studies. It's been a very encouraging facet. But I think [Dr.] Ed[ward] Zigler was inclined to feel very strongly that even if these children had gotten nothing more than the medical and the dental and the nutritional benefits, that one could have said that the program was well justified. But we think it has done considerably more than that.

The study that attracted most attention was the Westinghouse Study.[6] We felt even before they started the study—when I say we, Dr. Urie Bronfenbrenner at

Cornell and I made a trip to Washington to talk with the then acting director, Bert Harding, about the study, and it was stimulated to some extent by the fellow who was in... I've forgotten what they call the research unit in OEO. He was a social psychologist by the name of John Evans, who I think is still at the Office of Education now. We tried to point out that the design was such as to homogenize any differences. If you didn't look at subgroups of children, you'd get a leveling of differences. So that's just what happened with the Westinghouse study. It was a one-shot measure. They didn't know what had happened to the children in the program. They just took them a year later and compared them with controls. And there were so many criticisms of the design of that study that it spawned a whole cottage industry of studies, reanalyzing even those data showing that various children did indeed show significant gains. So the program just reflects the need for being thoughtful in relationship to designing a program of research and evaluation.

I wonder if you'd like to comment on the differences between the report by Max Wolff in 1966 and Bronfenbrenner's reply to it.

Sugarman: Actually, there were several themes [in Wolff's report]. One was a finding that between the time of entry into Head Start and the time of leaving Head Start, there was progression. The second was that for most children who left Head Start, they slipped back after they had left Head Start. Now, there is a third theme that has never been much noticed by the public, and that is that those children who left Head Start and went into a good teaching situation continued to grow.

Later reports essentially have been consistent with the Wolff thesis that there's something [that] goes wrong after you've been out of Head Start. But as yet, nobody knows whether that's because Head Start was poor or because something was wrong after you left Head Start.

In your relationship with the religious organizations and churches running Head Start programs, did you have a problem keeping religious activities or symbols out of the programs?

Richmond: Not significantly. There were some interesting developments. The *New York Times*, for example, would run an editorial emphasizing that there ought to be separation of church and state in this program as in all others. And on the other hand, they would run an editorial saying you must be sure that these programs are integrated. Well, in the South you couldn't have it both ways. That is, if we were going to have integrated programs, church buildings were about the only buildings that were available to us, and so a lot of the programs ran in church buildings. But we tried to emphasize that that was only a site for the program, and that these were not religious programs and that there was not to be any religious orientation.

JOHNSON AND HEAD START

Did Lyndon Johnson ever tell you what he thought about the Head Start program?

RICHMOND: I didn't have a great deal of conversation with him personally—more with Mrs. Johnson. But there were a couple of encounters that I had with him. At the time we made the first set of grants and I described our going over to the White House and his announcing them in the Rose Garden, Mr. Shriver and I went into the Oval Office together, and [the president] kind of shook his head and said, "You know, this whole thing is where I came in." I did a double take, and he said, "Well, you know, I'm a schoolteacher. I was teaching Mexican American children. This program is designed to do what we were trying to do way back then, and it just adds to what might be currently available." He, of course, was very intrigued and interested and very committed.

Then, a little more than a year later—it was March of 1967, [and] by this time we had developed in Head Start a film on a young Mexican American child: *Pancho.* They were to have the first showing in the White House, and Mrs. Johnson had arranged for the president to be there. They had arranged to give me an award. I had developed tuberculosis the previous fall. This is when I was sort of getting back into circulation, and they had decided to give me an award. It was on that occasion that they had the showing. I was sitting just

Johnson and Shriver present Head Start's poster child, Pancho Mansera, and his mother at the White House ceremony, March 13, 1967. C4713-8, 3/13/67. *Photo by Robert Knudsen, Presidential Collection, LBJ Library*

a little behind the president, and they had Pancho and his parents there. As the film began to be shown and he looked at it, he turned around toward me, and with tears in his eyes, [said], "This is all of what I used to see when I was teaching school down there in south Texas." So he clearly was very touched by it. Mrs. Johnson used to keep him posted on the program, so he knew a lot about it.[7]

[Head Start] was just so much a part of the president's overall commitment to the antipoverty effort that I think we just were supported almost to the limit of what we could do. I think our limitations during the period were only on what it was humanly possible to get going.

SHRIVER: By the time the program was finished, about the thirty-first of August, we had put in somewhere between $50 million and $70 million into that program. Now, that is an incredible story in recent government; I believe it's an incredible story. Just let me make these points: we never had to ask Congress for permission to start Head Start; we never had to ask the Bureau of the Budget for permission to start Head Start; we never had to ask anybody for any money to start Head Start, not even the president; we didn't have to go to any external cabinet officer to start Head Start. We were able, under the community action title of the War on Poverty legislation, to do that by ourselves. I don't know of many other instances in the recent history of the United States, especially in the civilian side, where anybody, anybody, anybody—I even include the president, almost—was ever able to start a program of national magnitude, involving, let's say, $70 million, without asking anybody for permission to do any of it.

11

ADVOCATES FOR THE POOR

VISTA and the Legal Services Program

SEVERAL OF OEO'S PROGRAMS *provided advocates for the poor to work in low-income areas. While the best-known of these initiatives, Volunteers in Service to America (VISTA) and the Legal Services Program, evolved differently, both became significant features of the War on Poverty.*

The initial efforts to establish youth training and community service programs in the late 1950s and early 1960s were inspired by the New Deal's Civilian Conservation Corps. President Kennedy's appeal to national service in his inaugural address and the creation of the Peace Corps in 1961 were further catalysts for a national volunteer program. Robert Kennedy and his lieutenants on the President's Committee on Juvenile Delinquency promoted the concept of a domestic Peace Corps in 1962. While chairing a cabinet-level study group that his brother established that year, Robert Kennedy sought to develop a formal way for Americans to serve their country. The resulting legislation called for the creation of the National Service Corps that would recruit volunteers for work in urban slums, depressed rural areas, Indian reservations, migrant workers' camps, and mental health institutions. After stalling in the House of Representatives, the proposal was repackaged the following year as one of the antipoverty components of the War on Poverty Task Force. Title VI of the Economic Opportunity Act provided for VISTA to recruit, train, and fund volunteers to spend a year working on behalf of the poor on antipoverty projects in both rural and urban areas. By June 1968, approximately 5,000 volunteers were assigned to 447 projects in every state except Mississippi, whose governor had vetoed the program.[1]

However, limited public awareness and a shortage of operating funds hampered the early efforts to recruit volunteers for VISTA. And because its volunteers, most of whom were in their twenties, were often assigned to community action agencies, Head Start projects, Job Corps camps, and other OEO programs, VISTA had to struggle to maintain a separate identity. The small program sought to maximize its impact by emphasizing community organization instead of casework. If these allies of the poor supplemented the other antipoverty initiatives through their labors, they also further sensitized the middle class to the problem of poverty in the United States. VISTA volunteers were even criticized for "overidentifying" with the poor.[2]

By contrast, the Legal Services Program was not stipulated in the original Economic Opportunity Act. Two young activist lawyers, Jean Camper Cahn and Edgar Cahn, had advocated legal aid to the poor as a basic tenet of the principle of equal justice under the law. Jean Cahn, as an employee of Community Progress, Inc.—a Ford Foundation Gray Areas Program in New Haven, Connecticut—had opened a "poverty neighborhood" law office in January 1963. Drawing on her experience, the Cahns had written an influential article in the Yale Law Journal, *advocating a legal services program. The article caught the attention of the War on Poverty Task Force, which drew the Cahns into the planning sessions.*[3]

As a lawyer, Shriver quickly grasped the significance of legal representation as an additional weapon in the antipoverty arsenal. The broad mandate of the Community Action Program allowed for the creation of the Legal Services Program, and support from the leadership of the American Bar Association (ABA) defused any serious local opposition. However, ABA did exact a price for its cooperation: it exerted strong influence on the program's board of directors. As a result, forty percent of Legal Services projects were administered by private legal aid societies. While the influence of the legal establishment may have minimized institutional changes and legal reforms, poverty lawyers made significant gains for their clients by filing class-action suits on behalf of migrant workers, tenants, and welfare recipients. In 1968, nearly 2,000 lawyers were working out of 800 neighborhood law offices to help the poor.[4]

VISTA: A NATIONAL SERVICE PROGRAM

Stephen J. Pollak was an assistant to the solicitor general in the Department of Justice when he worked on legislation to establish a domestic Peace Corps. In 1964 he was detailed to the War on Poverty Task Force to develop the VISTA program. After the passage of the Economic Opportunity Act, Pollak joined OEO as an assistant general counsel. He participated in the creation of the Legal Services Program before returning to the Department of Justice in 1965. Pollak was born in Chicago in 1928, was educated at Dartmouth and at Yale Law School, and was a navy veteran. He practiced law with the Washington firm of Covington and Burling from 1956 to 1961.

POLLAK: I did undertake some responsibility for Attorney General Kennedy in the summer or late spring of 1963 in connection with something called the President's Task Force on a National Service Program, which is the precursor of the domestic Peace Corps or VISTA. I was, for a period of from probably May or maybe even earlier in 1963 through the end of August and early September of 1963, the lawyer for this task force. That task force prepared the facts for and presented and supported legislation to create a domestic Peace Corps. The group that I became associated with that was working on the National Service [Corps] included a number of people who had worked with the President's Committee on Juvenile Delinquency [and Youth Crime], which was a Justice-HEW effort. A number of people who had worked in that juvenile delinquency effort then became involved with David Hackett, who was a special assistant to Attorney General Kennedy in this undertaking in support of a domestic Peace Corps. The going was sufficiently hard in securing approval from the Congress for creation of this National Service [Corps] that the thoughts of those working on it didn't move very much beyond achieving what we were trying to achieve. Had it been achieved, then the domestic Peace Corps would have, or could have, become a vehicle for a broader domestic antipoverty effort.

Was there any particular locus to the opposition in Congress?

POLLAK: That was summer of 1963. It was my first exposure to the legislative side of government, to the presentation of legislation. We presented the legislation first in the Senate, and there was a lot of support for it, and the bill passed the Senate. Passage, however, was by a smaller margin, 44–40, than we needed. President Kennedy lost the support of the southerners and of the Republicans, and the margin in the Senate was not enough to get the bill moving along in the House. It never came to a vote in the House. If I were to look at it coldly, there were many things the president was trying to achieve in the summer of 1963. While Attorney General Kennedy gave this effort as much of his support as he could, and while the service program effort was really sponsored by a task force which included all of the cabinet people, it just wasn't a big enough undertaking to command very much time of the White House, and we just couldn't swing it on our own. We were never without support from Attorney General Kennedy. It's just that when you're working on something like that, you really have to make it yourself—meaning [that] your team of people has to make it, or the project will not succeed. The White House can't really devote that much of its attention to that kind of undertaking.

The National Service [Corps] was not heavily identified with an antipoverty effort, as it was presented in the summer of 1963. It was impressed with the heavy poverty input in the spring of 1964 when it was added to the antipoverty bill. It was not added to the antipoverty bill until the antipoverty legislation was fully drafted. The original idea was associated with a cadre of young and not-young. The corps was going to spend its efforts in many different areas—poverty being one, mental retardation and the state mental hospitals being another. It was going to deal with the problem areas that exist in the United States. They weren't then, and they aren't today, only poverty problems. It had a broader focus.

Is it possible to pin down exactly who or what group of people originated the idea of a domestic Peace Corps?

POLLAK: Yes. The major sponsor was Robert Kennedy. I'm confident that the insertion of the VISTA program into the antipoverty bill, which came late, was at the urging and insistence of Robert Kennedy. It wouldn't have been in there if he hadn't pushed for it.

There was concern back in the summer of 1963 by the Peace Corps people—Sargent Shriver's people; and I could not be a witness to know whether this reflected the views of Mr. Shriver or not—but there was concern by the Peace Corps people at some levels that creation of a domestic Peace Corps would harm the overseas effort. Maybe they couldn't get enough volunteers; maybe it would tarnish the undertaking. In my work with the service program people—while I secured some very worthwhile suggestions and help from Bill Josephson, the general counsel of the Peace Corps; and while Sargent Shriver was on the task force, along with other cabinet people—the Peace Corps was not a big booster of the domestic Peace Corps. I never thought that it was created out of the overseas Peace Corps. Really the idea was developed and launched more from the Committee on Juvenile Delinquency; and Robert Kennedy, Dick Boone, Dave Hackett, [were] the ones that I associate with the idea.

VISTA IS BORN

POLLAK: Late in February, either Nick Katzenbach [Deputy Attorney General] or Norb Schlei came to me and asked me to draft a tide or section for the antipoverty bill, establishing a domestic Peace Corps.[5] I did that, drawing upon the bill that we had had before. The bill we had had the prior year was perhaps twenty, twenty-five pages long, and as a political matter, we determined that it should not be blown up so big in the draft legislation. In the end, VISTA, or the domestic Peace Corps, was one section in Title VI of the antipoverty law.

Was there any feeling that, because a domestic Peace Corps was an idea of Robert Kennedy's, it might not get into the antipoverty program?

POLLAK: The problems that Congressmen [Samuel L.] Devine [of Ohio] and [H. R.] Gross [of Iowa] had raised the previous year, the opposition that the domestic Peace Corps had had the previous year, had made Shriver—who, after all, was looking to the big picture and wanting to achieve a successful passage of the bill—desirous of not including this, not because he didn't like it or because it was a Kennedy item, but because it was thought possibly to be a liability. In the end, it needed a champion to overcome this understandable legislative tactical reluctance.

CANNON: I was in two meetings with [Kermit] Gordon and Shriver in which Kermit made a very strong plea to Sarge for VISTA, almost on a personal level. Kermit was a Quaker, and this kind of voluntary action was very dear [to him]. Sarge kept saying it wasn't very important; it wasn't good politics. It didn't have the title VISTA. It had the [name] National Service Corps or something. But Kermit asked him, "Really, as a favor to me, won't you do it?" I think that's why it got in the bill eventually.

POLLAK: I did provide an interim, part-time support for the Shriver task force in assembling facts and materials to back up the VISTA part of the legislation. Shriver asked a man named Dr. Glen Olds, who was then the president of Springfield University in Springfield, Massachusetts, to come down and take a position on the task force as the man for the VISTA program. And I educated, to the extent that I was able to do so, Glen Olds in the history and meaning of the VISTA part. So during March, April, and May of 1964, I provided this backup for Glen Olds and then another man named Glenn Ferguson, who subsequently became the director of VISTA and then ambassador to Kenya. Glenn Ferguson had been a director of training for Shriver at the Peace Corps, and Shriver put him into this part of the task force on the VISTA program.

While serving as the Peace Corps' associate director for Selection, Training, and Volunteer Support, Glenn Ferguson was assigned, in 1964, as a consultant to the War on Poverty Task Force to formulate the VISTA program. He became the first director of VISTA appointed by the president, and he served as director until he was appointed ambassador to Kenya in October 1966. Ferguson was born in Syracuse, New York, in 1929 and was a graduate of Cornell University and the University of Pittsburgh Law School. In 1961, while he was affiliated with the Washington, D.C., office of McKinsey & Company, management consultants, he was assigned to the Peace Corps to assist Sargent Shriver in staff recruitment. Subsequently, he established the Peace Corps program in Thailand before returning to Washington as associate director. Since leaving Kenya, Ferguson has served as president of four universities; as president of Radio Free Europe/ Radio Liberty; as president of Lincoln Center; and as founder of Equity for Africa.

FERGUSON: Because I was interested in the potential of creating a domestic counterpart of the Peace Corps, I volunteered to assist with the War on Poverty Task Force. Training, selection, and volunteer support were functions germane to a domestic volunteer program, and I had been responsible for those functions at the Peace Corps. On loan from the Peace Corps, I worked half time with each of the organizations for a period of three months, and then worked exclusively on the development of VISTA. Subsequently, I received a presidential appointment as the first director of VISTA.

What people on the task force were working with you on VISTA?

FERGUSON: Initially, the Job Corps and the Community Action programs received priority attention. The volunteer program was a mere appendage. The basic commitment of those of us associated with the volunteer program was to generate interest within the task force. As I remember, there were four of us concerned with VISTA development—Steve Pollak, a Washington lawyer; Doris Smith; and Hans Spiegel, who devoted time to the identification of volunteer assignments. During the first few weeks, Glen Olds also provided consulting assistance.

The VISTA component of the task force was located at the Old Court House at Pennsylvania Avenue and 17th Street. Our initial recommendation was that the volunteer program should be considered an integral part of OEO. We devised the acronym "VISTA," moved to an office at M Street and 15th Street; and became immediately operational. Under Sargent Shriver's guidance, we began the recruiting process to secure consulting assistance.

The continuity of VISTA was probably related to the fact that it was not a visible, politically oriented program (such as Job Corps or the Community Action Program) which enjoyed significant appropriations and external attention. As a result, it was possible to develop bipartisan support for the VISTA concept before the program became operational.

Did you attempt to use the Peace Corps structure?

FERGUSON: Because we were doing the same functions, many of the procedures that we used in the Peace Corps were appropriate in selection, training, and volunteer support; however, the organizational differences were profound. We used a few of the same organizational titles, but we employed consultants during the initial stages almost exclusively. Our training was only partially conducted at universities, because we felt—in contrast to the Peace Corps—that training could be done in the poverty environment in the United States. There were local organizations that could provide the kind of training that would be far better than the academic bill of fare at the universities. That didn't preclude the use of universities, but we found that there were groups like Hull House in Chicago, and other groups, that could provide training that was germane immediately to the needs of the volunteers. In addition, there were no field offices or regional offices. The Peace Corps was highly decentralized. Each Peace Corps unit in the field worked virtually alone, with minimal policy guidance from headquarters. VISTA had no field organization and no regional offices. The small staff worked almost by sufferance with the local officials. There was no direct chain of command. So, there were some profound differences.

What about the one-year commitment rather than the two-year enlistment, as you had in the Peace Corps?

FERGUSON: An intriguing question, because I don't think there was much discussion on the topic. We just assumed it would be a one-year assignment. In retrospect, I'm sure the rationale was that a shorter training period was required. We were dealing with English as the pertinent language. There was no in-country training required when they got to their local assignment. There was less travel, certainly no international travel; less expense. Most importantly, turnover became desirable. We were hopeful that an extensive number of volunteers every year would change—increase—the awareness of poverty. The one-year assignment, for the reasons that I've just cited, would be sufficient to make impact. We didn't see any objection to new volunteers succeeding the earlier groups.

Any recollections on the selection of the name "VISTA?"

FERGUSON: After my arrival, which was in April 1964, we realized that we would be branded as the "domestic Peace Corps." The leadership of the Peace Corps felt that the "domestic Peace Corps" terminology was inappropriate because it might make it difficult for them in their continuing recruitment. Also, there was almost a second-class citizenship implication related to being called the "domestic Peace Corps." We recognized that "domestic Peace Corps" would not suffice. We went to the drawing boards and tried to come up with something creative. My effort produced "VISA: Volunteers in Service to America." Then, I think that it was probably Steve Pollak who did a little research and found that there was an incipient VISA credit program. So we put the "T" in the acronym, and from the first days we were calling it "VISTA."

MANKIEWICZ: I named VISTA. We wanted to call it Volunteers for America, and I recalled that there was an organization called Volunteers of America, and I worried about it.[6] So I remember calling them up to find out what they did. And they were like the Goodwill Industry—you know, sheltered workshops, things like that. So then we began fiddling around with acronyms and VISTA—Volunteers in Service to America. We came up with that finally. And the White House liked that, even though it was clearly the domestic Peace Corps under another name.

Did you see any stigma at all connected with the National Service Corps, since it had not passed Congress in the previous session?

FERGUSON: Once the policy decision was made to couple VISTA with OEO—and that was the big issue: whether to keep the volunteer program separate or to have it an integral part of OEO—once that decision was made, then I think there was a desire to make VISTA, as a part of OEO, something fresh and different that would relate to the poverty syndrome. I'm not certain that there was anything negative about it with regard to the National Service Corps. It was just that the National Service Corps never got under way, and there was a feeling that freshness was essential at that moment.

Do you recall how the decision was made to couple the volunteer program with OEO?

FERGUSON: I think there was some natural reluctance on the part of the OEO to take on a program that was so different in character and in scope from the other programs, which related directly to poverty intrinsically, whereas VISTA program emphasized the use of volunteers. Volunteers are quite different from federal employees. There was a feeling that it might not be germane to have VISTA as a part of the OEO rubric. As I remember, it was Sargent Shriver who felt deeply that, if there were to be a domestic counterpart, that it should be an integral part of OEO and not off on its own trying to have impact in the field of poverty. The judgment was that poverty was the controlling element. The fact that it was so different from other elements of the War on Poverty was secondary to the major cause, which was to put volunteers into that environment.

VISTA VERSUS THE PEACE CORPS

Was there any sense among those working on the planning and implementation of VISTA that you were in competition with the Peace Corps?

FERGUSON: Every day there was an overt awareness that the Peace Corps was a competitor, but nothing direct, nothing that impinged on the ability to get VISTA launched. I never heard anyone on the Peace Corps staff suggest that we constituted a problem for them. I think it was more a feeling that Peace Corps represented a romantic mystique. Peace Corps was well known nationally and internationally. VISTA was perceived as a stepchild without that mystique.

Sargent Shriver was heading OEO and the Peace Corps, and his attention of necessity was on those programs. It would have been virtually impossible for him, given his priorities, to focus very much on VISTA. Initially, the competition related to being able to handle recruitment and other functions in a unique context.

In the beginning, there was some direct competition in recruitment, until we recognized that joint recruitment was the answer. Then, particularly on university campuses, we would have a VISTA recruiter—normally a local consultant—join the Peace Corps recruiters with a VISTA sign, because we recognized that we were complementary and not competitive.

We made a concerted effort to ensure that the Peace Corps and VISTA coordinated recruiting efforts and compared experiences. As a former deputy director of the Peace Corps, from his vantage point in the White House, Bill Moyers identified Peace Corps staff members in comparable functions who were available for consultation; but the basic objective of VISTA was to ensure that it was perceived as a separate entity distinct from OEO and from the Peace Corps.

PROMOTING VISTA

MAY: The most fragile program which I do know something about at that particular juncture was VISTA. VISTA really hung in there on a thread for a few months. We had serious discussions about closing it down. We couldn't get any volunteers. Shriver asked me to go over to VISTA as the deputy director. Glenn Ferguson, who is a very bright and talented person, was the director. And we literally didn't get enough volunteers. One of the first things I did over there is, I drafted people from all over OEO, my friends, to become recruiters. I sent management people out recruiting for VISTA, and we did a crash fourteen-day university tour and dredged up enough volunteers to keep the show on the road.

But we had a terrible identity problem, first. Half the places that you went to, they thought we were a Johnson Wax product, because they had a car wax named Vista. Nobody knew who the hell we were. And the Peace Corps had all this glamour about foreign countries and being a help to some poor African in some far-off, exotic place. Who the hell wanted to help some poor Africans, third-, fifth-generation residents of Harlem? But that changed. That's the interesting thing too. In later years, more people volunteered for VISTA than for the Peace Corps. The Indian reservations, migrant worker camps, the hollows of Appalachia, Harlem, and the South Side of Chicago, and Watts, all became exciting to American young people.

Ferguson: Name recognition, in my opinion, was the major problem of VISTA—certainly for the period with which I was affiliated, through October of 1966. We were preoccupied with that issue because we thought it might affect our recruiting efforts and that it would have a very specific negative impact on the evolution of VISTA.[7] In fact, it didn't, because recruitment could be done at the local level. Local publicity could induce people to come to discuss VISTA if we had a team visiting a given community. At the national level, name recognition was a major factor—very specifically in Washington, D.C. There was confusion on the Hill regarding Peace Corps and VISTA: What is the domestic Peace Corps? Is Shriver running both? These kinds of questions. We needed to clarify this issue, and it was very difficult at that particular time to command the attention of either President Johnson or the director of OEO and the Peace Corps, because they were inevitably preoccupied with very major policy questions.

Our first effort was to involve Mrs. Johnson, who was greatly interested in volunteers in the United States. We were able to convince her to give the first graduation address to volunteers in St. Petersburg, Florida, and she helped launch VISTA because the resulting publicity was very positive. Of equal importance, I think her involvement constituted a spur for President Johnson. Also, Bill Moyers was interested. So we created a constituency at very senior levels.

We were very naive. We assumed that the good works of our volunteers would constitute the best publicity. Rather than tooting our horn and saying, "Look, we're VISTA"—which wouldn't mean anything to anybody—we assumed that the media would recognize that the volunteers were unique, and were doing a good job, and that we wouldn't need extensive public relations. This approach worked later on, and we didn't have funds or personnel for publicity in the beginning. We did use press conferences, magazine interviews, and press releases. The Advertising Council helped us out, and we used public service announcements from celebrities.[8]

During that first year—to give you an example of the commitment of staff to public information—I visited fourteen states, thirty of the 100 projects, and six of the training sites to tell our story and to conduct local press conferences. All of the members of the staff were involved. It became a personalized public relations effort.

VISTA ASSIGNMENTS

Was VISTA initially conceived as more of a rural program—for Appalachia, for the Indian reservations—or was it seen as both a rural and an urban program?

WEEKS: There was a lot of ambivalence about whether it made any sense whatsoever to send VISTA volunteers into cities to deal with, I guess, what you call "urban development" projects of one sort or another. Because in part the rationale for many Peace Corps projects [is], "Here is a small village in the Altiplano of Bolivia which has no contact with the outside world and which has a lot of problems; let's send a few Peace Corps volunteers in and see whether they can help do something." That kind of concept doesn't have any relevance to Harlem, New York, where you obviously have an awful lot of people around there.

One of the things that was tried a great deal was to try to integrate VISTA volunteers with Head Start projects, with community action projects—the idea that the VISTA volunteers could be directly involved in many community action agencies and perform roles there. The success of the VISTA volunteers in major urban programs always got hung up on the fact that the people who lived in an urban ghetto, for example, were much, much less receptive to some college graduate from white suburbia coming into Harlem to run a nursery education program than a Bolivian farmer might be to the same kind of individual going to live in a village in Bolivia.

Was this dichotomy discussed in the task force?

WEEKS: It was kicked around in the task force, but it was perfectly obvious that VISTA volunteers were going to have to be assigned to cities as well as rural areas, and it couldn't be simply a rural program. And a lot of efforts were made simply to try to make an urban VISTA volunteer program work. I think it was probably one of the less successful areas.

One of the thoughts in VISTA, of course, was that there would be a benefit in taking college graduates and some technically qualified people and giving them assignments which would give them experience they otherwise probably would not have—working on an Indian reservation, or working in a poor Appalachian community, or working in an urban ghetto area—and that this kind of cross-fertilization between different areas of the country, different parts of the country, not only in terms of geography but in terms of rural-urban and the types of social areas of the country that we have, was a major benefit, and that understanding the patchwork-quilt nature of the country and what goes on inside of some of the other pieces of the quilt that we live in is important for all Americans in exactly the same way that it's important for all Americans to understand Bolivians and Ethiopians and Pakistanis better.

Will you discuss the range of VISTA assignments, particularly with regard to both the urban projects and the rural projects, which I guess were more comparable to the Peace Corps assignments?

FERGUSON: We didn't start with any specific bias, except we assumed that the preponderance of the volunteers would be assigned to urban projects. There were requests from almost 500 communities within the first six months. The majority of those came from urban areas. However, when we started negotiating with the local people who actually ran the projects—and keep in mind, they were not VISTA staff—we came to the conclusion that there was an extensive structure in urban America. There were people available who knew the environment well; and very few volunteers, as catalytic agents, were needed. In contrast, in rural America, there was no structure. There might be a person heading a poverty project in the Smoky Mountains who worked with the regional poverty program. That person could use more volunteers than an urban project, because there was literally no help. From the beginning, although we were involved eventually in fifty states, and the District of Columbia, and the United States territories, more than forty percent of our volunteers were assigned to rural projects.[9]

Was the assignment of VISTAs to Job Corps camps and Community Action projects seen as a major allocation of VISTA resources?

FERGUSON: I believe that Job Corps constituted one or two percent of the total number of volunteer assignments. It was not a major commitment. During the planning stage, we assumed that Job Corps assignments of volunteers would constitute one of the major areas of placement.[10] The Job Corps provided a very structured staff relationship. The skills required were quite different from a volunteer who had to create a job. The Job Corps found that they could hire local people as staff who had commitment and were able to work within the Job Corps context much easier in a structured, hierarchical kind of relationship. I don't think there was any bias against Job Corps placement.

About fifteen percent of our volunteers were involved with assignments on Indian reservations. That was a very large contingent. After the first year and a half, of the 3,000 volunteers on assignment, we had about 350 Indian reservation placements, because there was no structure and because each assignment had to be negotiated.

The volunteer's role was vital. It wasn't what the volunteers did, or where they did it, but the way they did it. The assignment in relative terms was easy. The volunteer lived and worked in the environment of poverty. Once he or she was there, it was possible to learn quickly the ambience, to associate, to develop areas where help was needed, even though initially it was not part of the job description. The critical issue was how the role was perceived. The debate right from the beginning was whether VISTA would be a politically action-oriented program with the volunteers committed to political action upon arrival, or whether it would be a program where the volunteer was politically neutral. If neutral, the volunteer went into the environment of poverty to learn and to work, but whether the application of skills became political or not was of no interest to the volunteer. The volunteer was assigned to improve the lot of the people without being committed to political action in any form. The latter point of view prevailed. The day I left, in 1966, we still were making that distinction—which we thought was profound.

VISTA VOLUNTEERS AS AGENTS OF CHANGE

Did you see the VISTA volunteers as agents of change and community organization as well as caseworkers?

MAY: Yes, I did. And again, that's what created the problem. They *were* agents of change. You know, I started out as a newspaperman writing about welfare, and I spent some time impersonating a caseworker in order to do that series of articles I told you about. I spent a year researching a book, so I didn't have a lifetime of experience. But you didn't need a degree from Harvard to figure who the bad guys are in these dramas. You really didn't.

It didn't take the VISTA volunteer a hell of a long time, whether he was in Harlem or in the South Side of Chicago or in Appalachia or in a Navajo reservation. In the latter, for example, it didn't take him long to figure out that if the white people have got a municipal water system, and the Indians have got to travel in the same county five miles to get enough water in a bunch of five-gallon cans, then there's something the matter with the public system here. Once you figured out there's something the matter with the public system, and if you're there to do something about poverty, you begin showing up at the water authority meetings, and you say things that they really don't want to hear. That's when the genie's out of the bottle. Yes, they're agents of change. We didn't need social workers; we didn't need a lot of people to teach little kids how to read.

Did their training include this element—community organization?

MAY: Yes. Again, it depended upon where they were trained, to what degree. I know the Appalachian volunteers certainly stressed community organization a great deal. And that's what got them into deep trouble.

Let me ask you to discuss the intention of those planning the VISTA program with regard to the extent to which the volunteers would engage in community action or community organizational efforts.

FERGUSON: The basic objective of the Office of Economic Opportunity was the eradication or reduction of poverty in the United States, which affected one-fifth of the citizenry. The volunteer program, VISTA, was affiliated with the poverty program—rather than being a separate entity or rather than being affiliated with some other government organization—because of the relationship directly to that mission: the eradication of poverty. The volunteer was a conduit. The volunteer was an instrument, bringing commitment and skills and maybe insight, but certainly time and concern, to help people make their own judgments with regard to the direction in which they wanted to go in every community, whether it was a migrant camp or an urban complex. In that context, the volunteer was not committed to any form of action. Action was certainly contemplated, but it was not political action, nor was it the antithesis of action—which became the fixation of later administrations, certainly the Nixon Administration. The commitment to action implied that the volunteer would help create his or her assignment in the process of understanding the community. If political action was the result, it would not be because the volunteer represented a particular credo or philosophy, but because the action-oriented effort of a catalyst had brought about a willingness of the group in that particular community, urban or rural, to bring about a specific kind of action.

In my opinion, that is not a subtle distinction. The volunteers discovered that if they became creatures of political action [and] were branded as a result, they were limited in their impact. I can remember several occasions where volunteers discussed this question with VISTA staff members. It's difficult to suggest that positive action can occur without political context. The volunteer had to be committed to a result that was not necessarily more specific than the generic quest to eliminate poverty.

How did local communities respond to the volunteers in their midst?

FERGUSON: Prior to assignment, there was some animosity, because we were perceived as a federal program superimposing people and ideas on the local environment. After the volunteers were assigned, I can't think of a single case where there wasn't a very positive reaction. Once they realized there was no federal structure, that volunteers were not supervised by federal employees, they were reassured. The volunteers were supervised by people who were known in the community. I think that we were successful in the early years in making certain that they were rated on their ability to do a job. Some volunteers obviously were better than others, and those who weren't able to adjust—as with any program—didn't make it. However, I think the perception of the volunteers, once they were in the community, was extremely positive. They were involved. They were enjoying it. It was working.

VISTA AND POLITICS

Was it a conscious decision on your part to protect VISTA from political whims?

FERGUSON: Within the broad policy guidelines and supervision of OEO leadership, it was our feeling that VISTA had to reflect bipartisan support. It was necessary to create a separate entity so that the "domestic Peace Corps" was not considered an appendage of the Peace Corps. Volunteer service in the United States was different. The nature of the volunteer assignments was different, and local political reality was important.

We were part of OEO, and we were proud of the association; however, we felt that it was a necessity to carve out a separate image. We recruited our own staff, and—in contrast to other OEO components—the staff was new to government and to the Washington scene. OEO recruited staff members who had been involved in significant public and private programs with strong public policy dimensions. In contrast, VISTA relied upon personnel who had lived and worked in the environment of poverty; from college campuses and from extremely varied backgrounds.

For the first two years, VISTA was different and energizing. After two years, major OEO problems of a political nature emerged which affected VISTA indirectly. We were able to maintain our bipartisan stance. It was reassuring to have the leading Republican members of the House of Representatives supporting VISTA objectives—Congressman Albert Quie of Minnesota, Congressman Gerald Ford of Michigan, and Congressman Charles Goodell of western New York state. In the Senate, Senators [John J.] Williams [Delaware] and [Charles] Percy [Illinois] were very supportive. There were many Democrats who were interested, but Vice President Humphrey was the most vocal and the most effective.

As the program evolved, the Community Action Program, in particular, triggered sustained local political opposition which had nothing to do with VISTA, but VISTA volunteers were assigned to many of the projects. I found it difficult to articulate a VISTA volunteer's presence in a local project which was becoming increasingly partisan. It was this evolving political reality, coupled with five consecutive years of service with Peace Corps and VISTA, which prompted me to accept readily the opportunity to serve in Kenya.[11]

THE POLITICAL ARM OF POVERTY

LBJ's conversation with Jack Vaughn, March 10, 1967[12]

JOHNSON: This VISTA thing is the political arm of poverty. I don't know whether you know it or not, but it's up to its knees in politics all over the country. All the governors tell us that when we go out. We've been to twenty governors now. That's what they tell us.

THE LEGAL SERVICES PROGRAM: EARLY ADVOCATES

Jean Camper Cahn was working in the Public Affairs Division of the Ford Foundation when she was hired as a consultant by OEO. Along with her husband, Edgar Cahn, Jean Cahn was the driving force in the creation of the Legal Services Program, which was patterned after a neighborhood legal aid project she had created in New Haven. She left OEO in March 1965, when Shriver decided, against her urging, to place Legal Services under the authority of the Community Action Program. After leaving OEO, Jean Cahn had a private law practice before she and Edgar Cahn directed the Urban Law Institute at George Washington University. The Cahns founded the progressive Antioch Law School, which ultimately became the District of Columbia School of Law. Jean Camper Cahn—the daughter of a prominent Baltimore physician who had been a civil rights leader and founder of NAACP's Baltimore branch—was educated at North-western, Swarthmore, and Yale Law School.

J. CAHN: Paul [Ylvisaker] put aside a small [Ford Foundation] fund for those of us who were involved in dreaming up the first steps of the Legal Services Program. So we had our own special fund—people like Adam Walinsky and Abe Chayes, Charlie Haar, Clyde Ferguson, maybe about one or two others. We would have weekly meetings and discuss how we were going to launch the next attack on the private sector in terms of starting legal services. But Paul had put up that money to give us some spending money for trips, for speech-writing, secretarial stuff. I was also his special assistant, by the way, during the final days before I came to Washington. In fact, right up until I went to the State Department, I was acting in that capacity.

Paul had planned to work the Ford Foundation out of this business after the government was fully involved in it. So he was not ego-involved in the government takeover of the program, because from his point of view that meant that it was a success. Ford's function, he felt, was seed money for things that should be taken over by government or by industry or by someone else. So as soon as in some sense the War on Poverty was off the ground, he turned to Leon Sullivan and the Opportunities Industrialization Center,[13] which I remember saying to him at the time I didn't think was a good bet, which he proved once again intuitively that I was wrong. He was right. It turned out to be a very good bet.

E. CAHN: I was told at a very early meeting—I think it was by Boone, but it was confirmed later, I think, by a couple of other people—that Justice [Arthur] Goldberg had gone to Lyndon Johnson and had asked him to include legal services in the War on Poverty. We had done some ghostwriting for Justice Goldberg, and we had talked about that. Lyndon Johnson simply turned him down flat, saying no, he didn't want that.

Did he say why?

E. CAHN: I had the feeling maybe that [he thought it] would clutter up what appeared to be the simplicity of a war effort to mobilize all resources to solve a problem.

POLLAK: One thing that history ought to record is that in the very beginning, when we were starting to develop these ideas about the Legal Services Program, Shriver, who is an attorney himself, and I were walking down the hall to his office, and he said to me that he thought the launching of the Legal Services Program would possibly be the single most important thing that he would do in the poverty program. He said he felt this way because making provision for attorneys to represent the poor and for the courts to recognize rights of the poor never before recognized would have such a far-reaching and continuing effect on the distribution of power in the society. I thought that was farsighted of him, and I shared his view.

NEGOTIATING WITH THE LEGAL ESTABLISHMENT

J. CAHN: Shriver told me that what he wanted was a legal service program that involved legal educators. That's what he foresaw as the new legal service program. I told him that if we had to work on legal education, we could all forget it and go home, that the best chance was the organized bar. Shriver said he didn't believe the organized bar could be gotten. I think he cited at that point the problems that were being had with the medical profession over the pending passage of Medicare. It hadn't passed yet. So he thought that I was stark raving mad when I said the only way to launch this program is going to be to get the organized bar itself and capture them. But what I'm remembering is the whole attempt to keep Legal Services tied to CAP and to be within CAP and be dominated by it, to run the money through it.

E. CAHN: Boone was an active aider, abettor—if you would, co-conspirator—in trying to make sure that Legal Services was enumerated as one of the list of possible services for which Community Action money could be spent. We understand that was step one. Based on getting that, he said to Jean, "All right, now that this is a service, we need to begin launching this. We need to get applications in. We need to begin seeing this develop." At that point Jean started both dealing with the organized bar, stimulating proposals, and dealing with all the old-line legal aid agencies, who all wanted to dominate it.

That's the stage where you begin to get the first national emphasis programs. Head Start gets a big ballyhoo, and I'm not sure what the date is. And then Legal Services is going to be the second one really to get off the ground with high visibility. There was a tug-of-war within both, but CAP could accommodate Head Start as sort of a special projects office. Legal Services immediately got more uppity. It got more uppity because in order to sell the notion of Legal Services, you had to get the organized bar in, or it was going to be viewed as socialized law. Once you had the organized bar in, which is what Jean pulled off over a series of negotiations....

The program that Jean had been associated with was still being attacked by the local bar. We understood that the local bar would attack, but maybe the national leadership would be more enlightened. Lowell Beck, who was then the Washington lobbyist for the ABA [American Bar Association], contacted Jules Pagano of Peace Corps, because he started finding out that all the speeches were coming from the same source. But the speech that particularly offended the bar was when Shriver in Chicago talked about setting up a supermarket of social services.[14] The idea of putting lawyers in shopping carts really turned [them] off. Chicago, of course, is the headquarters of the ABA, so that [speech] got high visibility.

It was at that point that they decided this thing had to be stopped, there was enough of this foolishness, and this was getting dangerous. So Lewis Powell, who was then president of the ABA, designated John Cummiskey [chairman of ABA's Standing Committee on Legal Aid and Indigent Defendants], Bill McCalpin [chairman of ABA's Select Committee on Availability of Legal Services], Don Chanel—who was simply [ABA's] Washington lobbyist, second-in-command—and Lowell Beck [an ABA lobbyist] to meet with Jean and me as the representatives of the big bad federal government at the Mayflower [Hotel] to find out what was going on, and to stop it and indicate that the bar would make sure that it was stopped, because this clearly constituted federal interference in the private practice of law, a threat to the integrity of the profession, and all things good, holy, and pure. I guess about six to eight hours . . .

J. Cahn: Oh, it was a good eight hours locked in one room.

E. CAHN: . . . of fairly heated negotiations about, "Either you can jump on and participate and help shape something that will make equal justice more closely a reality than it's ever been in this country, or you can stand aside and fight it and get a black eye and then have to spend all the money the AMA has [spent] in refurbishing its public image." That was basically the pitch that we had to take. And we were playing poker, because we weren't sure how many dollars or cards we had to play. We didn't even know who we were dealing with.

J. CAHN: [ABA's] legal aid [society] was very threatened by the advent of Legal Services, because the bar was spending at that time a total of $5 million a year nationally to deal with the problems of the poor.

What do you think turned the ABA people around?

J. CAHN: We reached an accommodation so that [by February 8, 1965] the historic meeting in New Orleans, the ABA unanimously voted to endorse the new Legal Services Program.

E. CAHN: But there were elaborate quid pro quos that were negotiated.

J. CAHN: They were very elaborate. One of them was that the organized bar would in fact oversee the Legal Services Program in order to see to it that Legal Services lawyers acted within the ethical dimensions of the code of professional responsibility, which was at that time just being rewritten by [Supreme Court Justice] Tom Clark.

E. CAHN: One of the commitments was that the code would be revised with this development in mind, because the fear was: If a lawyer's money comes from this source but he serves this client, does he listen to this source or is he accountable to the client? The tradition says he's accountable to the client. The intrusion of a third-party payer looked as if that lawyer might be influenced by monetary, political, or ideological agendas and use the client or manipulate the client for those agendas.

J. CAHN: So at this point in time, there are actually provisions within the code of professional responsibility that are meant primarily for Legal Services lawyers. Another of the agreements we had to have was that during the time between the February meeting and that meeting [i.e., the earlier meeting with ABA officials at the Mayflower Hotel], that if Lewis Powell and the staff at Chicago agreed to go ahead with their recommendation to go with this program, that I would have to agree that Lowell Beck would be able to read any application that I decided to fund, and that we would jointly agree on that.

So they would have a veto power over grant approval?

J. CAHN: Basically, it was an unofficial veto, and it wasn't a veto. Rather, let's put it in some terms that Zoya Mentschikoff [a law professor] once put it in: "We can agree that you have the power"—in other words, "The federal government has the power, and we're advisers, but we will now adjourn as the advisory committee and we will meet as the organized bar." So it was advice with a clear understanding that the program could run into very heavy waters if we didn't listen to advice.

E. CAHN: But there's a piece that you're leaving out, which is that you had the organized bar on the one hand, and then you had as a subdivision of the organized bar an organization of all of the legal aid and public defender agencies. Jean perceived that there was an interest in the leadership of the bar [in] new experimental, developmental programs that were different and that would countenance more experimentation, and that... the old workhorses working for the poor had a kind of myopia, [in] the same way that social workers looked at the new community organizers or looked at community action. "How dare you invade our turf? We've been tilling these fields unloved and unblessed, and all of a sudden it's fashionable and you're calling us duds and mediocrities, and all of a sudden here are these bright new warriors in the trenches, and we're left on the side."

Jean sensed that and understood that the power and the leadership of the bar would go with an innovative program and would deliberately reject what was demanded by the old-line agencies, which was an automatic monopoly—that they be the automatic designated grantee. So ABA involvement was then critically helpful, where you wanted to bypass the old-line agencies because they were ineffective. Where they were effective and you could build on them, that was fine, but some of them didn't want to set up neighborhood offices. Some of them wouldn't countenance any role for clients and poor people on the board, and yet the ABA leadership was willing to. So, in effect, by getting their involvement, it was not veto-negative; it was supportive of something that was really innovative.

J. CAHN: Subsequent to that meeting, I went to Chicago. Edgar was supposed to be with me, but he instead went to St. Louis with Shriver and left me to face about thirty-some very old white men—sitting around a very long table at the ABA center—who were all dead against legal services for the poor. It was my job to convince them that they were for it. The basic message that convinced them is that we're going to do it with or without you, so the question is: Are you going to be in there working in order to make it the best possible program and also a credit to the bar, or are you going to be on the outside? Now, if it were my money, as a taxpayer and as a member of the bar, I [would] prefer to be inside.

I suppose about two o'clock that afternoon there was general agreement that they would in fact support the Legal Services Program. These were the head staff members of all the various legal organizations that are represented in the ABA center. It was chaired by Bert Early, who was the director of the American Bar Association. Bert then went upstairs to his office, took me up to his office, and called Lewis Powell and said, "It looks like everybody is in line here and that we can go with it."

After that, it became a matter of people like John Cummiskey and Lewis Powell and, to a lesser degree, McCalpin—but Bert Early and Lowell Beck were very, very much in the forefront—working out the politics of how they were going to get the membership of the ABA to solidly endorse this program, knowing what the opposition was on the local level. They, in turn, did pledge their support to take care of the local bar associations, and therefore, for the first opening years of the Legal Services Program, every ABA president was on the road most of the time, trying to calm the local bars down, and state bars, and explain to them that Legal Services were all for the good.

D. BAKER: At that time, we also had an informal advisory group, and we worked on some preliminary guidelines for the administration of the program. And right up to the time and after the time of the Law of Poverty Conference [June 25, 1965], we were negotiating with people in the established bar—the people like Mr. Powell and people from the NLADA [National Legal Aid and Defenders Association]—and the various agencies about what would be in the guidelines in the way of the majority representation by lawyers of the committees, the governing boards, the Legal Services group in relationship to CAP, and all that sort of thing, and the degree to which there would be local control or federal control.

Was there any resistance to this on the part of NLADA?

D. BAKER: The national leadership of the bar association, Mr. Powell and the people, Orison Marden and Junius Allison and John Cummiskey of the NIADA, and others—they were very supportive of the idea. Jerry Shestack from Philadelphia and the former head of the Committee on Legal Aid—what's his name—[William] McCalpin from St. Louis. All of these guys were tremendously supportive. And the fact of the matter is, they were way ahead of their constituency in their liberal view on this subject. By and large, they just did everything they could to make it function.

Now, both they and we recognized that there were some problems with the state and local bar associations, and indeed, there happened to be some very difficult problems. In Florida, Tennessee, Mississippi, and various other places, lawsuits were started, with varying degrees of responsibility by the parties that were starting the lawsuits. But this almost became a cause célèbre at the Miami meeting of the bar association in 1965, when Mr. [Edward] Kuhn of Tennessee was the candidate for the ABA presidency. And the Tennessee bar had a resolution ready to offer, attacking the New Orleans resolution, attacking legal aid. I went down there and made a speech to the public relations section on the first day of the convention, and then Sarge came down later. I flew right back. I had not landed in Washington before Mr. Powell had called and asked Sarge to send me back again. I spent the entire ABA convention down there, living in a $40-a-day room in the Fontainebleu on my $16-a-day stipend, defending this Legal Services Program from various people who were ready to....

Wliat were the grounds of the suits?

D. BAKER: [That] this is group practice and is in violation of legal ethics, soliciting, and all manner of criticisms. There was a criticism made on the basis that the act did not mention legal aid, as in fact it did not. The original act didn't, although I'm reasonably assured of the legality of the grants that we made.

IMPACT OF LEGAL SERVICES

D. BAKER: I think in the long run that the impact of legal aid on the improvement of the lives of the poor—and in fact the improvement of the viability and the relevance, to use the terminology of the college kids today, of our whole political and economic structure—[that] legal aid may be the most important thing that we are doing. Legal aid will have more impact on [the] total structure of our social, economic, and political structures than anything else that OEO and perhaps even the federal government has done on the domestic scene in our lifetime. There's no question but that the decisions resulting from, for instance—to mention one which is one of the best—the California Rural Legal Assistance program out in California [have] probably done more to revolutionize within the legal structure of the society the operations of state, local, and federal government in the state of California than anything anybody has done in the last hundred years. They've challenged school systems in the way they have been treating kids. They have challenged the welfare system. They've challenged the Labor Department in the way that they use the migrants and permit migrants in.[15] They've challenged the governor. They've even undertaken a system of educating the justices of the peace out there.

There have been a great number of things that have not been discussed. For instance, in many public school systems, if a kid gets difficult or if the teacher simply doesn't like a kid, it's easy enough for the teacher or the principal to bounce him, just throw them out. It has now been fairly well established, I think, in a number of states, and probably for the nation as a whole, that kids are entitled to an education in this country, and that there has to be a sound and legally justifiable reason for removing them from the prospect of education, and I think that's all to the good.

Legal Services, I hope, is the most secure of any of our programs. Not only will it have impact and bring on needed change, but it's hard for anybody devoted to equal justice under the law to attack. And it's one program in which you can find the most vigorous conservatives lining up shoulder to shoulder with real liberals in the defense of what Legal Services is all about. And so I hope for that reason alone that it will be one of long life.

POLLAK: There are many Legal Services programs around the country. They have gotten into so many different areas where the poor never had lawyers. Throughout so much of the legal system, particularly on the civil side—and Legal Services is primarily on the civil side—persons of property and wealth had lawyers and used the legal system to preserve, protect, and improve their interests. The poor by and large did not have access to lawyers. Where they had good arguments, they weren't able to present them. Where they needed laws to protect them, our system requires lawyers to move the legislation along, and the poor didn't have lawyers. So this Legal Services Program changed the equation very greatly, and it still is.

12

DELEGATED
PROGRAMS

THE ECONOMIC OPPORTUNITY ACT *included programs that were to be operated by established departments. Since OEO made no serious effort to monitor these delegated programs, its influence was minimal. If this aspect of the War on Poverty illustrates how little the cabinet departments had focused on the poor, it also demonstrates their capacity to change direction to preserve their bureaucratic turf. Interagency rivalries notwithstanding, the War on Poverty did cause existing departments to address the problems of low-income Americans.[1]*

The two delegated programs discussed in this chapter—Title III and Title I of the Economic Opportunity Act—represent alternatives to primary thrust of the War on Poverty. Title III authorized thirty-year loans to local farm processing and marketing cooperatives when credit was otherwise unavailable. This was a contrast to OEO's urban orientation; and the Department of Agriculture's program of loans to cooperatives brought more than economic progress to rural communities. Aid to a black farmers' cooperative in southwest Alabama, for instance, challenged the closed economic order of the South.[2]

Although the Labor Department's grand design for a massive employment program was rejected and the Job Corps was awarded to the upstart OEO, Labor did receive a consolation prize. Title I authorized local work-training programs for high school teenagers. The purpose of the Neighborhood Youth Corps was as modest as its budget: to keep needy students in school by offering incentives: a stipend, work experience, and "aititudinal" training. The program offered both summer employment for high school juniors and an in-school version. Full-time training was offered to local young people who had left school permanently.[3]

"ON SOMEBODY'S DRAWING BOARD"

PERRIN: The Neighborhood Youth Corps was delegated to Labor, Adult Basic Education to HEW, the Work Experience Program to HEW, the Rural Loan Program to Agriculture, the Economic Loan Program to SBA [Small Business Administration]. We had five programs at that time. My office was responsible at that stage for relationships with the other departments on those programs. We were the conduit for information from OEO to them concerning the programs and vice versa. We held regular meetings with representatives from those offices.

I also was the point of contact in OEO for any information or any ideas that popped up in other departments that they wanted to express to us. Or if we had things that we wanted to get them to cooperate on, it would usually come through me from the program office within OEO.

Was delegating programs to other agencies a unique arrangement in government?

PERRIN: Yes. I think it's the first time that it has ever really been done on any scale at all.

What was the rationale behind it?

PERRIN: Part of it was political, and part of it was experimental. Politically, a number of programs that made up the OEO legislation were really on somebody's drawing board before OEO came into being. So they were all tossed into this particular pot. But part of the political understandings that went into the legislation—it was known that these were to be delegated to the other departments for actual operation. The leadership of the Labor Department didn't like OEO and didn't think we should have any manpower job. So as sort of the quid pro quo for our running Job Corps, they were, by God, going to head Neighborhood Youth Corps. And Adult Basic Education went to HEW. I think it should have. We shouldn't have been running a broad program like that—although the idea was that we would influence the direction, try to make sure that they involved poor people, and, to the extent we could, coordinate them with community action and the other activities in which we were engaging.

So the guidelines would be written at OEO, and the money would come through OEO appropriations. Is that right?

PERRIN: That's right.

Did this give OEO the kind of control that it needed to supervise these programs?

PERRIN: Well, it didn't then. It did and it didn't. It worked to a limited degree. An agency like ours was one that had the kind of influence it could bring to bear on an established department of the government. We probably were too busy taking care of community action and the programs that we were running to spend as much time as we should have spent on establishing a very sound basis of coordination and influence in terms of these other programs. It got out of hand. I think Shriver's view was: "Well, just let Labor and HEW run those things, and don't bother me with that; we've got enough problems of our own." And consequently, and given the political realities of Willard Wirtz and his desire to handle all manpower programs with a minimum of interference, we didn't exercise as great a control as I think we should have.

Of course, I wasn't in on that part of it. I came in after the relationship had pretty well been nailed down and in fact was starting to disintegrate or become quite altered. About that time legislation was starting to take various programs away and altering them, such as the NYC [Neighborhood Youth Corps], for example. It just became a part of a series of manpower programs which were being financed under our act and administered by Labor. And with the role of community action agencies being the sponsor of these programs, I finally got to the point where I turned over the relationship I had with NYC to [the] Community Action [Program] in OEO.

It got quite confusing and difficult to handle. Adult Basic Education was eventually transferred fully to HEW by legislation. The Work Experience Program was starting to be phased out, so it was diminishing. The SBA program was similarly being legislatively altered.[4] So that particular part of my responsibilities was starting to decrease.

What obstacles did OEO encounter in coordinating these programs with the old-line agencies?

PERRIN: There were several things involved: one was the very parochial attitude that a lot of departments had. They had been running their programs for all these years; they didn't want this upstart agency involved. There was the difficulty of Shriver dealing with members of the cabinet in terms of who influences whom. But programmatically, there was the tendency of many agencies and departments to run their programs on behalf of those who were not the poorest of the poor. And this was the way they had been operating for years. Our charter said very specifically that we deal with the very poor. To turn an agency around so that it was even thinking about these people was quite a feat.

The Labor Department was a good case in point where the programs were concerned. That's one of the areas we've had probably our greatest influence in, in how their programs are being operated. The Manpower Training and Development Act [MTDA], for example, in the years of its existence, had been directed mainly to helping people upgrade themselves—those who had jobs get better jobs [and] more training. Through our influence, MTDA began to take in the unskilled needs, the unemployed hard-core, jobless, and bring them into the circuit. The Employment Service traditionally waited for people to come into the office and look down the list of jobs that were available, or those who were on unemployment compensation, which meant they had been working and had some kind of a job record. They had never paid any attention to those who had no job record. Now it does, limited though it may be, but it meant quite a change in it. By using them as recruiters, say, for the Job Corps—for one thing, it has brought them into contact with a lot of people they wouldn't ordinarily see, forcing them to get out of their offices to go into the ghettos to set up an office in a neighborhood center, for example. These have had tremendous impact on a number of state employment services. Of course, they're all different. They're all creatures of their individual states, and this is a long battle that isn't restricted to OEO, by any means.

Another trouble that we had with the old-line departments was getting them to work with community action agencies. And it has been a continuing effort and struggle to see to it that the community action agency was the presumptive sponsor of many of these programs as they were implemented in the field. And we've been quite successful in that. But I think none of this was unexpected, and I think a great deal of progress has been made.

EDUCATIONAL PROGRAMS

SHRIVER: Francis Keppel, the commissioner of education, was a terrific fellow. He came to me when we were putting the so-called War on Poverty together administratively, and he said, "Listen, Sarge, I've been trying to get a program through Congress for the last"—whatever it was—"three years, and I haven't been able to get it through. If we could get it through, it would help poor kids a great deal. Would you put it into this War on Poverty legislation and see if you can get it through?" And I said, "What is it, Frank?" He said, "I call it 'work-study.' The idea is that we would give federal money to poor kids who would work and study so that they could work their way through college studying and working, and we would finance it into the schools." I said, "I'm all for it." I went through college myself that way at Yale. I worked and I studied, and they paid a large part of my tuition. So I said, "I'm all for it. What do you want me to do?" He said, "Here's our plan for it. Would you put that into your legislation?" That's the OEO legislation. And I said, "Sure, but when it goes through, you will run it, won't you?" And he said, "Fine."

So I took the plan that he had for work-study, put it into the OEO legislation, got the legislation passed, got the appropriation for it, and gave it to Frank Keppel to run.

D. BAKER: The work-study program that we originally had, Title I-C of our act, a work program subsidized in effect by our funds for college kids who were needy, was first delegated and then eventually transferred by legislation to the Office of Education. As a matter of fact, that transfer was initiated by us because of our feeling that these kids who had gotten to college were really a step above the type of kids that we really wanted to concentrate on, and also because we saw that the college work-study program really ought to be expanded upward in terms of income to get a larger number of kids. That program probably was helped by being transferred to the Office of Education.

THE DEPARTMENT OF AGRICULTURE'S ROLE

SUNDQUIST: The basic difficulty was that the OEO had a complete and thorough and unshakable distrust of the Department of Agriculture. They thought we were a department of racists and that the best thing we could do for the program was get out of it. Now when I say "they," this varied among individuals in the OEO, but our efforts were generally thwarted. One of our main thrusts was to try to get some money from them to put people on our payroll to get out and organize community action agencies, and we never succeeded in getting anything from them.

Boone was a very hard man to get anything much out of, because he moved so deliberately. But finally, when we went forward with our proposal for personnel, the Extension Service was to be our chosen instrument. This fell on deaf ears. Then we modified it. I guess Boone suggested that we should try in three states, and we picked out South Carolina, Minnesota, and Arkansas, because we were very confident that the extension services in those states would perform. We laid out with some care exactly how they'd be set up, and how they'd proceed. This got through Dick Boone and the Community Action shop and was vetoed by the general counsel, Don Baker.

On what grounds?

SUNDQUIST: On policy grounds, on the grounds the Department of Agriculture was essentially segregationist. I think he finally said it would be all right to let Minnesota go, "but we don't want to put any money on the Department of Agriculture in South Carolina and Arkansas." We did get some community action agencies started, but it was very tough going. Actually, while we worked hard at it, the job didn't get done until the state technical assistance agencies were set up and the money put into them. Then they tended to get complete coverage in particular states.

It may be that the department never could have done it, but at that time we were concerned that nobody else was doing it and that all the money was going into the cities. We did have a nationwide network of rural-areas development committees and technical action panels that we felt we ought to throw into the effort. We couldn't have avoided trying. It was very frustrating. Then we also wanted to get a piece of the research money, to do research on rural poverty problems. The only happy relationship with OEO was the Job Corps and the Forest Service. The Forest Service did its usual brilliant, methodical job of planning and preparation and building on the experience of the CCC. When they made their presentation to the Job Corps, which was at that time floundering, the Job Corps seized upon the staff work they'd done, and the conservation camps got moving rather well.

The Economic Opportunity Act and the Office of Economic Opportunity and the community action agencies all came into being because the old-line agencies had failed. It was quite explicit in the doctrine surrounding community action that the welfare bureaucracy and the other bureaucracies, the education bureaucracy, were not dealing effectively with poor people. This was certainly the attitude among the poor, and particularly the blacks. OEO then came into being with the assignment of challenging the established ways of doing things. The Agriculture Department and the Labor Department and HEW certainly represented established ways of doing things. As I said earlier, our proposal was to use the established Extension Service to go in and organize community action. It was very easy for OEO to say, "Those are the very people that we were set up to supplant." You got a new crowd in OEO that hadn't been in the government before, unsympathetic with the established ways of doing things.

I wouldn't want to say they were wrong. I don't think, as a matter of fact, the Extension Service would have done the job well. I certainly feel that way. But I was fighting their battle at the time. I was also very conscious that nobody had any better approach to the problem. So I argued, why didn't they put their money on us and let us see what we could do? Some of the people were extremely hostile. I remember Bill Haddad called the various departments to a series of meetings to talk about how the inspection function would work, and I had a real blowup with him, mainly on the point of whether or not their people would be able to relieve Department of Agriculture employees from their duties on the spot. I told him in no uncertain terms that Secretary [Orville] Freeman would never stand for somebody else firing his people. We didn't care how many reports they brought back and how much advice they gave us, but they weren't going to act on internal USDA disciplinary matters. I checked this point with two or three other departments to see if they were going to take the same stand, and obviously they were. So in this instance, the whole government ganged up against Haddad, who was obviously so far off base that he couldn't have held his position anyway.

SOUTHWEST ALABAMA FARMERS' COOPERATIVE ASSOCIATION (SWAFCA)

J. BAKER: I'll give you an example down the road a little ways that leads me to believe that we didn't get as much grants for Farmers Home Administration to use as we initially wanted. There was a loan and grant application from something called Southwest Alabama Farmers' Cooperative Association [SWAFCA].[5] By that time Sarge had taken so much beating from the conservatives on the Hill that he was scared of [SWAFCA]; and the Community Action Program assistant director—a guy from Cincinnati, Ted Berry—had gotten beaten over the head so much that they were skittish as hell with SWAFCA; and there were two relatively well-known communists on the SWAFCA board. Or maybe it was just their two New York lawyers that were suspect.

The Southwest Alabama Farmers' Cooperative Association was a black farmers' co-op, wasn't it?

J. BAKER: Yes, yes. In black-belt Alabama. And every member of the Alabama delegation, including both senators and all the members of the House, had already called on the White House and Sarge that they didn't want that [loan and grant] made.

I kept poking Freeman to talk to Shriver about it, and Shriver was so jumpy that Sundquist and [Kenneth] Birkhead [Assistant to the Secretary of Agriculture] told Freeman not to poke at Shriver about it. So I made a run at Ted [Berry]. I got Ted over in my office to talk to him about it. I said, "Look, Ted, if you'll make the damn grant, I'll make the loan. I won't look back. The Alabama delegations can't scare me a bit." Well, he mouthed around and went back home and two or three days later said it was a go. Me having the courage gave him the courage to go on and make the grant part of that particular loan. Now, that was the loans-to-cooperatives program.

We lost somewhere the grant component of the co-op loan program in the OEO package.[6] We later and almost simultaneously got authority under an entirely different piece of legislation for this land reform thing by not calling it land reform. We called them "grazing associations," in which a bunch of farmers would set up a cooperative and we'd make them a loan to buy 10,000 acres of grazing land in Montana, or maybe in Florida.

We were just absolutely in a system, because we were convinced that in a really tough social structure intertwined with economic structure, the only solution for poor folk was to get co-ops with competent management to be on their side. Partly we've been strengthened in that with the experience of the rural electric cooperatives. Part of the strength of the rural electric cooperatives were not the actual members of the cooperatives as such, but the fact that they had to have a lawyer and they had to have an accountant and they had to have this and that. And you started to get some upper-middle-class people who were being paid to represent these folks [who] didn't have any electric lights or washing machines.

We felt that we needed to do that with marketing and purchasing. We had had good experience in Arkansas, Louisiana, and Mississippi in purchasing and marketing cooperative associations in the old Farm Security days in the late thirties and early forties, as long as we kept it on purchasing and marketing. And there were a lot of very successful farmer cooperatives around all over the country, in addition to rural electric cooperatives. That's why we wanted the poverty program to have that component in it. When you start with people none of whom are functionally literate and not many of whom can even read or write at all, they're going to make a lot of mistakes starting the big sophisticated vegetable marketing business or something like that. And I guess we had been raised up in Resettlement and Farm Security that you don't make bad loans. You make good loans and then fill in the part that you need to with a grant, instead of making bad loans and then having delinquencies and foreclosure.

In that part of the South, as distinct from mine and your part of the South, part of the deeply believed folklore and beliefs was that "colored people," [as] they called them when they were polite, could grow crops like cotton and corn, but they couldn't handle livestock. Vegetable growing was too complicated for them, but they had to stick to things like cotton and corn, rice. And in the black belt, there was a problem of soil erosion and one-crop agriculture, partly because of that. Fay [Bennett, Executive Secretary, National Sharecroppers Fund] and Dr. [Frank P.] Graham [Chairman, National Sharecroppers Fund] thought the way to open up the society and also give them additional sources of income was growing vegetables, which they could sell in the northern cities, who were in favor of black people and so forth. Back at that time, the cities claimed they were pro-black.

That was the background. And I really think Fay Bennett rather than one of my people stirred up the business of them organizing the co-op down there right in the middle of the black belt. I think it was Fay Bennett and her crowd that did it. I don't know whether I would have done it if I had thought of it or not. But Fay is not short on guts; she's sometimes short on wisdom once in a while, but she wasn't short on guts.

Anyway, they organized and applied for a grant and a loan. In the process of organizing them, the organizers had to promise them the moon, I guess, to get them to engage in any kind of disciplined organization. And what they had heard over the radio and whatnot about the War on Poverty and all, they thought—in any event, I guess it first came to my attention in a purely routine way: Would I be willing to approve a loan if they gave a grant for this thing? So I guess I got Howard Bertsch [Administrator, Farmers Home Administration] to send some of his boys down there to look into it, and Howard and I decided we'd do it.

Then about that time, all hell broke loose on the Hill. Both senators and all members of the House from Alabama had old Sarge by the ear anytime the phone wasn't busy, or whoever was Sarge's replacement with them. They were giving Ted Berry fits. Alabama hadn't decided that black folks were as good as white folks yet, like they have since. They were still supported by their governor, their then governor [George Wallace], who has changed his mind some since, too. And it was a black-versus-white, white-versus-black, Democrat-versus-communist...oh, it was bloody. I couldn't see anything wrong with it. My experience had been, with some ski-jump loans in Illinois and Pennsylvania, that if you had guts enough to go on and do it, pretty soon the congressional delegation would be prouder than hell and they'd start claiming [it]. At any event, I kept urging them and goosing them to go on with it. About then, when it got so hot, I decided I had better keep Freeman informed. He said, "Well, have at it!" But he said, "Don't quote me." Finally, Sarge got Freeman on the phone.

Freeman backed me. Freeman and I between us just gave Sarge and Ted [Berry] enough guts to go on and do it.

The next thing I knew, the entire board—and their lawyer, who was alleged to be a French communist woman lawyer, was there; plus two of her assistants, both of whom were alleged to be communists; and some hangers-on—appeared in my outer office and said they weren't going to accept the loan with the terms and requirements of the Farmers Home.

By that time, I guess they were partly interested in giving us trouble as well as letting the other side give us trouble. They weren't going to accept the loan unless we met their terms, instead of them meeting our terms. I told them that all the members of the board and all of their employees of the board, representatives of the board, should come in. We'd close the door, and we wouldn't open the door until we came to an agreement, even if it was nothing more than to agree to disagree. I wouldn't even let them go to the bathroom. I kept them in there twenty-six hours, and [Calvin] Osborne, who was one of their needlers, had to go to the bathroom. I wouldn't let him back in. I didn't want a bunch of smart alecks sitting out there in my outer office or out in the hall double-timing me. We were just going to sit, by God, there until we came to an agreement. Thank God, I lasted.

How radical were the SWAFCA leaders?

D. BAKER: SWAFCA suffered primarily from the objections of some of those demagogues down there to having blacks have any control over their own destiny or their own economic freedom. Probably the biggest single factor in the opposition to SWAFCA was the fact that Shirley Meshner—a white civil rights worker who came to Selma as part of the march and stayed, who lives around in Negroes' homes and is a very militant lady—was in on the initial organizing of SWAFCA. That, and there were some economic reasons. It was not an accident that the local pickle manufacturer, who had been paying a very minimum for the cucumbers he bought, was the only businessman nonpolitico to make the trip up here. And after SWAFCA got going, the price per peck of small pickled cucumbers went up three or four cents. I think eventually they were selling their okra, making a couple or three cents more on a bushel of okra that was sold in Chicago than they had been selling to him.

THE NEIGHBORHOOD YOUTH CORPS

HOWARD: Within the whole Economic Opportunity Act [EOA] structure, there was constant pressure by the Labor people to enlarge the Title I-B, which is Neighborhood Youth Corps [NYC], to enlarge whatever programs we had, as well as not to diminish what we were doing under the Manpower Development Training

Act [MDTA]. The struggle was the allocation of funds, of course. We would get a budget cut, and then you had to split it up. We always felt we got hind tit—naturally, being in Labor—to the more expensive per capita things. Job Corps was $5,000, $6,000, $8,000 per capita, and we were held to sometimes $400 or $500 in Neighborhood Youth Corps. So we were constantly pushing on that. We made sure when we testified before Congress that they saw those figures, that they knew what we were up against. So that, in that sense, we were constantly pushing for jobs. Now, it's true it was youth jobs. It wasn't a public service job at that stage. I don't know at that time whether we were prepared, or whether the country was prepared, for public service employment. Later on in the second or third round of the EOA, we had the beginning of some jobs; we had New Careers and Green Thumb and began to have pieces for adult employment kind of snuck into the poverty program. But my best recollection is that we did not have a massive public employment program, although Wirtz pushed for it. But it didn't seem to fit into the poverty program at that stage.

OEO was responsible for oversight of the Neighborhood Youth Corps. Was this aspect successful?

HOWARD: From OEO's point of view, I'm sure it wasn't. Once the delegation was signed, from that point on, it was lip service to oversight. My position, which was bureaucratic, was that I was working under the direction of the secretary of Labor. The program was delegated to the secretary of Labor, and he delegated it to me, and therefore I looked to him. I did not take direction from Shriver. I did not take it from anybody else. And since the secretary of Labor didn't give me any direction, that left me in that particular situation.

We had a constant battle about the philosophy of the Neighborhood Youth Corps, whether it was a training program or whether it was a transfer-payment program. I refused to pretend that we were going to provide meaningful training and skilled training for kids working a couple of hours after school five days a week, or for the summer program. For one thing, I had seen the failures of the manpower training program, [in] which we trained for jobs that weren't there. They'd go through this training, and then where were they? I felt it was just completely bullshit for us to pretend that in this poverty program we were going to train them, and then not have jobs for them. So we severely limited the Neighborhood Youth Corps to a transfer-payment program. We refused to build in expensive training and expensive counseling, because I was convinced it was a grab by the administrators, especially by the school bureaucracy which administered our in-school programs. We refused to pay overhead. We set, as our minimum, eighty-five percent of every dollar had to go into payroll for kids, so we cut out their overhead. OEO wanted us to build in another ten percent for training, and we refused. We just said: We're not going to waste that money, because it will be wasted on the training bureaucracy, it will be wasted on the teaching bureaucracy, and we want it to get into the kids' hands. That was a constant running battle. I'm sure that OEO would say in that sense that oversight did not work.

Do you feel that there was sufficient training to make Neighborhood Youth Corps worthwhile?

HOWARD: We rationalized it on the basis of attitudinal training, on work habit, work attitude, and so forth. I think one would be hard-pushed to overstate the training component and the attitudinal component of the in-school program. There were certain things that were valuable there. There was work around the school. There was a time factor: they didn't show up, they didn't get paid. There was the factor that if they dropped out, we wouldn't let them go into the next program unless we'd try to get them to sign up to go back to school, etc. So there were some pressures there for staying in school, for showing up on the job, and for taking direction and doing what the people told them to do, and that's about all. I'm not going to call that skilled training, but it may be some attitudinal training.

The out-of-school program was a little different, because there they were working sometimes thirty, thirty-five hours a week. They had to show up on time. They had to perform functions, in the best programs. There were lousy programs too. But as theoretically designed, with adequate supervision, there should have been some attitudinal kinds of training.

Were there any jobs to be had after the training?

HOWARD: No, by and large. Certainly for the in-school program there were no jobs. The summer program—which we developed, and which became very popular, and which is about the only thing that now exists from the Neighborhood Youth Corps that isn't called that—the summer program was just that: it was a summer program principally for in-school people. The idea was, we did not want seniors going in. We wanted seniors to go into manpower training or something like that. It was aimed for sophomores and juniors, and the hook was to get back to school in the fall.

The out-of-school program, which was the more expensive program and hence was always limited in number—I don't know if we ever got over 100,000, because we were limited to a couple of thousand a year on that, compared to the Job Corps' $7,000, $8,000, $9,000, $10,000. We tried to link that program with MDTA, with manpower training. We tried to tell ourselves that our effort would be to pull the various programs together, either through the youth opportunity centers, where they existed, or through enhanced sensitivities of the local employment service, because the Employment Service was involved in the out-of-school program. So the theory was that if we could get these youngsters who had nothing some kind of job, some kind of beginning of an attitude toward work, an attitude toward showing up—then if we could, with some money from HEW or even out of the program, we'd build in some basic education, some kinds of remedial education.

The theory was, we would then at least perhaps get them to a point where they could move into Manpower Development and Training and get skilled training. In theory, MDTA slots were keyed to needs in the community. That was a job development aspect that the Employment Service was supposed to undertake that we didn't undertake. We were to get them up to a point where they could go into manpower training. In other words, some of the disadvantaged young people we were working with couldn't even get into manpower training because they were just so really, really not with it. So we did not have jobs. We tried to get training opportunities for them, and that's about it.

How cooperative were school systems in working with the Neighborhood Youth Corps?

HOWARD: By and large, very cooperative. By and large, they helped us turn on a politically sensitive program fast and big. They would help by accepting our assignment to get x numbers of people and find x numbers of jobs and administer this program for no overhead. They accepted the fundamental idea that it would be helpful for kids who needed money to earn a little bit in a school setting and with school people. See, we didn't reject out of hand the school system for the Neighborhood Youth Corps, even though we had a lot of reservations about schools that had not changed to reflect the community of the kids that were in the schools. For example, New York City, where the schools were largely black and brown and the hierarchy were largely white, middle-aged Jewish teachers. That's a big thing about the problem in New York. We didn't just reject that out of hand—maybe practically, because we couldn't.

We had to move fast. The bill was signed I guess in August. The appropriation was in August, and we had to get a program going by election day, which we did. So they helped us by running the program, by accepting the program, by accepting a lot of trouble. They accepted payroll problems. They used their systems for payroll. They accepted separate books. They accepted direct federal control, because we didn't sub out these things. The Neighborhood Youth Corps was run directly from Washington until we set up our regional offices. We could freeze bank accounts. We could review and hire and fire their staff. They accepted that, I would say, by and large. Of course, there were places that didn't.

We did not use the school system for the out-of-school program, and in that sense there was some struggle, because the school system wanted it and we didn't trust them. They wanted to give year-round employment or summer jobs and so forth. But I don't know, as a general characterization, it seems to me through the years of history that they were cooperative.

How about local government?

HOWARD: Local government was less cooperative, because they were less sure that they wanted to be involved fooling around with a bunch of disadvantaged kids. Also, some local governments saw it as a great rip-off opportunity and would use it for sons of chiefs of police and things of that sort. We still got some good cooperation. I guess, basically, the smell of money attracted most of them. We would make our allocations down, and we would tell our field people where we wanted to be: we wanted to be in these cities, and we wanted to be in these areas. We knew the poverty populations and so on. Especially in the South, some of the local governments gave us a lot of problems on our race situation. But on the other hand, there were some remarkable instances where—either under the guise that they couldn't control it or what—but southern cities and counties would have black kids in white offices. So it was mixed. I would say [local government] was somewhat more resistant, but still, the program rolled, and so we couldn't do it by ourselves. We had to have their cooperation.

How about private business?

HOWARD: Initially, there was a proposal that private business would run a lot of the manpower programs. That was a big deal over at OEO, and Job Corps especially. They were going to go to universities and private business [with] know-how and stuff like that. That didn't enter into any of our figurings at all. We used the community action agencies because we had to. Their theory was nice, but...we had a lot of trouble with community action agencies. We used cities; we used school systems.

Why did you have trouble with the Community Action Program?

HOWARD: [The community action agencies] were used to the way that the Community Action Program in Washington dealt with them, where they got a lot of money for overhead, they got a lot of money for staff, and they got a lot of stuff like that. And they weren't used to dealing with us, because we wouldn't pay for that bullshit. We wanted program, we wanted kids working, and we wanted all the money going to them. Also, some of them felt that we were too narrow, that we weren't philosophically attuned to the notion of more training and more counseling and all that kind of stuff. And quite frankly, in the in-school program, of course, it was difficult to work with Community Action, because often the school system didn't necessarily appreciate the Community Action Program, and so we couldn't get the jobs in the school. When the kid is working two days a week after school, it doesn't make much sense to move him across town to a park or some other place. The best job is going to be in the school, whether it's on the grounds or whether it's in the library or whether it's whatever, whether it's maybe helping the teachers with the younger kids on the playground or something. But we needed the cooperation of the school system, and Community Action couldn't provide that.

Was recruitment a major problem with the Neighborhood Youth Corps?

HOWARD: No, we always had more than we could get in the in-school program. No, we were always limited. We never could fund all the projects we had.

Was there a dilemma within the program, or within your own mind, with regard to what sort of corpsman you should get for the Neighborhood Youth Corps? Should it have been someone who just needed the money to stay in school, or someone with real cultural disadvantages who perhaps had a criminal record and was in fact somewhat of a risk?

HOWARD: My best recollection would be that we stated general principles, and the principles were that the enrollment should be limited to the people who were at or below the poverty line; that there must be an equitable performance on men and women, boys and girls; and that there could be absolutely no race discrimination. Now, in the in-school program, it was largely left to school counselors.

We would say [to the schools]: You know the kids that it would really help them stay in school, motivate them to stay in school, and so forth and so on; use it. Obviously, if [there] were good counselors and good people in the school, they would see it as an extra tool for motivating and working with difficult cases.

THE NEIGHBORHOOD YOUTH CORPS AND MINIMUM WAGE

HOWARD: The minimum rate in the Neighborhood Youth Corps I well remember— we had been rolling along on a dollar an hour. We figured that's a nice round figure. We'll get more bang for the buck on that and so forth. So we were going into a meeting one day. Wirtz and I were walking down the hall, and he said, "Jack, what are you doing on the minimum rate?" I think this was in the early planning stages. We'd just signed a few contracts. I said, "We're doing a buck an hour, because we're getting so forth." He said, "Well, guess what? It's now a dollar and a quarter; it's now the minimum rate." I said, "Okay." That was straight from [George] Meany and 16th Street [AFL-CIO]. Well, I had no problem with that at all; that's great. That gave us a whole series of moral arguments. I mean: minimum rate; we're not having a scab youth rate; we're teaching them work habits; etc., etc.

We had enormous problems in Texas, and not once did the White House intervene. The Texas school boards were paying their janitors sixty, seventy cents an hour until we came in. I was summoned to Austin to meet with Governor

Connally. I don't know whether he did it through the White House or whether the secretary of Labor would respond to the governor of the home state of the president, but I went down to Austin to meet with him and made it very clear we were not interested in screwing up his labor relations, but we did have a national program. We had national standards. I said, "We'll phase it in."

CONWAY: There was no explanation for it. I was just going through a straight reception at the White House for something else, and Lyndon saw me fifteen people down the line, and I could tell from the look on his face that he was going to scorch my ass when I got there for some reason. I could just tell. Sure enough, he just started talking *at* me, two or three people down the line, about the minimum wage. What the hell was I doing on this minimum wage question? Didn't I know that this was a difficult problem and so on? What I was doing was working out a formula with Jack Howard where we'd combined educational hours with work hours in such a way that we diluted the labor unions' [requirement that we pay] the minimum wage for the hours worked, but the hours required in the program included extra educational hours that diluted the value of the minimum wage. I think there was a little flak building up from John Connally in the state. He was blowing off some of that pressure on me.

THE COMPETITION FOR FUNDING

Did you ever get as much money from OEO as you wanted?

HOWARD: No. Did anybody?

We had internal meetings where we talked about budget. Then we'd have our budget hearings at the Bureau of the Budget. We would push for our amount, and the budget examiners would do some cuts. OEO had problems with BOB too. I'm not saying it's all OEO's fault. There were those kinds of struggles back and forth. Then, of course, the ultimate struggle was on the Hill, because after Sarge introduced the measure, then each of his program managers did our own thing. Inevitably, [Representative] John Fogarty would say, "Well, Mr. Howard, how much did you ask for from OEO and the Bureau of the Budget?" I'd tell him. "And how much could you use?" And I'd tell him. So there was that. That was always on the record, and Fogarty made it a flat rule. Anyone going up there knew that they were going to be asked that question.

Did the Bureau of the Budget think more highly of the Neighborhood Youth Corps than the Job Corps?

HOWARD: First of all, they were pretty down on the Labor Department anyway. In the Bureau of the Budget, they were desperately opposed to the Employment

Service, with fairly good reason. We had to live with them, and we had to try to make them work, but the Bureau of the Budget examiners could sit there and throw bombs at it. I don't know—frankly, I never got any encouragement from the Bureau of the Budget. I never got any indication they thought we were doing a goddamn for the program. In many senses, it was a fairly lonely job, because all the kudos went to Shriver, and all we did was churn out hundreds of thousands of kids. We spent our money well, and we had very few scandals. We had to get our reward in heaven or from an occasional congressional committee on testimony, but I never got any encouragement from Bureau of the Budget.

Were you ever able to get more money from the Congress for the Neighborhood Youth Corps than OEO wanted?

HOWARD: Yes, summer. We were always able to get more for [the] summer [program]. We always got more for summer because the program worked.

The cost comparisons between the Job Corps and the Neighborhood Youth Corps evidently were really a problem for OEO when programs would come up for appropriations.

HOWARD: We helped make sure it remained a problem. Now and then they'd get a complaint through [the] press or through a member of Congress or through the inspector general or something. After Haddad had gone, we'd worked that out, investigated, found out what it was. No, we were really fairly autonomous. Looking back on it, I am amazed, really, at, first of all, the authority that Wirtz gave me, and secondly, that maybe because of that we were a very tight-swinging operation that they really couldn't control.

Was there any preoccupation with quantity? Were you constantly faced with the statistical imperatives, the number of youths you could get enrolled, rather than the quality of the programs?

HOWARD: In all programs, I won't say just Job Corps, but all of us...all of us were. We were. It was a budget crunch, a bang for the buck. We've got so much money, and how many numbers can we get for it? We tried follow-up. We tried to say these kids stayed in school, and these kids went on to jobs and stuff; but because we didn't expect much from our program, we didn't expect our program to end up in job training. So we had rather slippery measures, and about the only firm measure we had were numbers, that we were helping this number of kids and eighty-five percent of the money is going into family incomes. We'd do dramatic things like tracking the checks that were cashed one week, and we showed they were cashed at the grocery stores and clothing stores and for bills. So that was our focus.

13

CHALLENGES TO
HEAD START

THE POPULAR HEAD START program frequently served as a political shield for the more controversial components, the Job Corps and the Community Action Program. An exception came in racially polarized Mississippi, where the intersection of Head Start and the civil rights movement touched off a two-year battle in which OEO came under attack from both the left and the right.[1]

The nation's largest Head Start program was launched in May 1965 in Mississippi, with a grant to establish eighty-five centers in forty-five counties to enroll some 6,000 children. The fact that the grantee was Mary Holmes Junior College, a private, historically black institution, enabled OEO to avoid the governor's veto. But the college then subcontracted the actual operation of the Head Start program to another entity, the Child Development Group of Mississippi (CDGM), which had been organized specifically for that purpose. The headquarters of CDGM were in Mount Beulah, a hotbed of civil rights activism and a center of the Mississippi Freedom Democratic Party (MFDP).[2]

It did not take long for the Head Start program to become entangled with the struggle for racial justice. CDGM was accused of diverting funds, rental cars, and employees for civil rights work. Financial irregularities and loose administrative practices plagued the CDGM operation, as did harassment from the white establishment. The Mississippi congressional delegation pressed for elimination of the program, while liberal groups accused Sargent Shriver of selling out. Within OEO, there were deep divisions regarding the project's merits. Even as popular a program as Head Start could not exist within a political vacuum.[3]

THE MISSISSIPPI CONTROVERSY

SUGARMAN: In the spring of '65, very shortly after Head Start was announced, a psychologist by the name of Dr. Tom Levin arrived on our doorstep to talk about Head Start. He identified himself as having worked in Mississippi the prior summer with the Emergency Medical Committee (that is not quite the correct title, but something like that). He wanted to hear what Head Start was all about, and he was very fascinated by it. He went away and came back a few days later and said, "Gee, there's a group of us that would really like to get this thing started in Mississippi, but we're pretty sure that school systems will do nothing about it. But we really don't have any resources with which to get started. I'd be willing to give up my practice and go to work on it for the summer, but I need money to survive on."

By that time, it was very clear that school systems in Mississippi in fact were not going to do very much about it. So we arranged to put Dr. Levin in touch with the AFL-CIO, and in some way they provided funds to get him off the ground. The next thing we knew, there was an application on our desk for a program for 3,000 children, which we funded.

RICHMOND: In the early days, we were very interested in getting a program going in Mississippi. We didn't have the notion of integrated programs and integrated schools in the South as an operational notion at that time. The governor was not particularly receptive, but he couldn't impede the development of the program because of a very creative, in my view, notion that we had generated. That is, that we would make the grant to an institution of higher education, which meant that the governor couldn't veto the program. And so that's how we got to Mary Holmes Junior College. And the question at one point—an amusing sidelight— came up: is it an institution of higher learning? Then I had to begin to try to define what is an institution of higher learning. I learned from the Office of Education that a loose definition they had was that if [a college's] credits had ever been accepted at an accredited institution, that it then would be regarded as an institution of higher learning. We couldn't find many students whose academic work had been accredited at traditionally accredited institutions, but we did find that there had been precedent, that there had been some, so it was an acceptable institution.

So we made the grant to the college, and it developed the Child Development Group of Mississippi. There was a great deal of imagination and energy and vigor in the program, and that first summer they were operating, I think, in eighty-six different communities across the state. We were highly enthusiastic about the program, but there were a number of problems that were developing down there.

I decided to make a visit in late July or early August of 1965. I went down there, and the program really was exciting. We traveled from community to community, often with cars loaded with rednecks following us; [and we] talked to some of the young people who had come from the North as volunteers in the program, who would be standing guard at night over their buildings with rifles and things of this sort. It was really a tense situation. One of the most beautiful programs we saw had been operating out of a wonderful little black church, I think it was in [Daleville], and it was burned down the day after we visited the place. The next day it opened under a tent. People in the community were willing to go ahead, and we provided the authorization for them to proceed.

SUGARMAN: Perhaps even before the program opened, it became apparent the registration was going to dramatically exceed 3,000. So they came back in for a supplemental grant, and I think that we probably funded somewhere between 5,000 and 6,000 children in that first summer. They organized from scratch programs for 5,000 or 6,000 kids that summer. They brought a lot of college students into the area from out of state. They got a lot of people who were interested in the problems of civil rights and the problems of Negro opportunities to come to Mississippi for the summer.

INVESTIGATIONS OF CDGM

SUGARMAN: It wasn't very long after the program was funded before we began to get some inquiries by the state's senators and congressmen. Soon the inquiries became much more pointed, and we began to get accusations by Senator [John] Stennis [of Mississippi, a Democrat] in particular that things were awry in the CDGM program and that money was being misused. It was being used for civil rights purposes rather than for the Head Start program. We sent investigators to CDGM, and at the same time the Senate Appropriations Committee sent one of its staff investigators to look into the program. He came back with a rather sensational report of things that were wrong. Our own investigators were not quite as sure about this, but they were sure that there were some rather serious problems, including some involving the director.

RICHMOND: We had been under considerable attack by Senator Stennis shortly after we got back to Washington. I incidentally invited to go with me Dr. George Gardner, who very fortuitously a number of years later I succeeded as director of the Judd Baker Guidance Center in Boston and chief of psychiatry in this hospital. He was with me on that trip, and when we got back to Washington, it was announced that Senator Stennis was going to hold hearings. So George Gardner came down. He and I and Mr. Shriver were in the hearings; the program was under very considerable attack by the senator. They had sent an audit team down, and I think out of the million and a half dollars that we were expending that summer, there were about $26,000 that they couldn't identify receipts for. And that became a very large cause célèbre for the senator.

Were you convinced that there had been some financial mismanagement or misuse?

RICHMOND: Oh, no. After all, $26,000 in a state where a black man couldn't ask a white vendor for a receipt and expect a response—so I was a little taken aback that it was that low. We had cautioned people about getting receipts and documenting everything, because we knew that sooner or later this kind of thing would come up. But to me, that was a ridiculously low figure not to have receipts for when you're expending a million and a half dollars, and particularly under those circumstances. So I viewed this as kind of a "Star Chamber" proceeding.

How about CDGM's participation in civil rights activities?

RICHMOND: Well, there was a lot of that kind of activity. For example, I was cautioned by some of our security staff people, people from our inspector general's office, about the problems of our riding in integrated cars. We were riding in integrated cars, but with the recognition that it was a very hazardous thing to do there at that time.

I mention that by way of indicating that the atmosphere was tense. The staff particularly that had come in from outside of the state was involved in civil rights activities. They viewed the integrated effort as an important step in civil rights.

The contrasts, of course, are so great. Nine years later, I was invited back to Mississippi to a governor's conference on education and youth. I decided it would be interesting to see how much change had taken place. Of course, I went back, and at the hotel in Jackson, Mississippi, there was the governor with blacks on the platform and a lot of interaction. The whole meeting was integrated, the hotel was integrated, and you had integrated professional staffs working in programs and all. So in nine years it was just a transformation.

Did the fact that the program was largely a black program—that it was in fact segregated—create problems for you?

RICHMOND: It did in that we had intended for it to be an integrated program and we couldn't get it integrated. I think there was a sincere effort to get the poor white community to participate, but the climate of the times was such that there was no way poor white people were going to participate in a program that was predominantly black down there. So we never could quite turn that around until school integration really started to take hold in the South.[4]

D. BAKER: In the year of its great crisis, CDGM came to be a tool of the black militants. I think it fair to say that our chief objection was that it ceased in many respects to be chiefly oriented toward providing Head Start to children and became an instrument of some of the black militant organizations. The fact of the matter is, a lot of our money went to pay for the automobiles and to feed the marchers on that Selma march. There were some of those centers that were feeding SNCC [Student Nonviolent Coordinating Committee] workers three meals a day out of food that was being purchased to feed Head Start kids.

Perhaps in some respects the worst thing about it was that in many areas it was converted from a child-oriented program to a public employment program for adult Negroes. They were hiring illiterate, untrained Negroes, and not infrequently requiring a certain amount of militancy from them, [to], in essence, what amounted to baby-sit the children—at least that was what our evaluators.... In order to spread the loot, so to speak, they would hire "Suzie Glotts" as the employee of record. Suzie might work two days a week; then she would be replaced in actuality, though never formally on the record, by somebody else who would work two days. And maybe a third person would work Friday and the following Monday, and they would be the third person on that payroll. And that is the way it was working. It got a little money into the hands of everybody. I'm sure the vast majority of those people who were being employed needed it very badly, but in point of fact it was not what we gave them the money for. There are legal and moral problems with federal funds being used for purposes, however good they are, other than what the money is granted for.

Another thing that was happening was, there were some cases where people would be on the payroll and spend the whole period up in New York recruiting for SNCC or [being] in school. There was a lot of that sort of thing going on. There just wasn't a hell of a lot of management.

Was that Senator Stennis's objection?

D. BAKER: Well, Stennis's main objection—he was reflecting accurately, I think, his white constituency, who basically, if the thing had been run 100 percent by Uncle Toms, if they'd been all black, they would have objected to it because that's not the way it's done down there. His more formal objections were that we were supporting the black militants down there; and there were people, in fairness to him, who were misusing some of this money for militant purposes. In fairness to us, however, some of the charges that he was making about the SNCC involvement, while they involved people who maybe had been part of SNCC or SCLC [Southern Christian Leadership Conference] or CORE [Congress of Racial Equality] or something, [they] really had severed all ties and, as far as we were ever able to determine, were doing the right thing.

Now, having said that they were doing a lot of things that were bad, the fact of the matter is, the situation under which people in CDGM were operating was also intolerable. And in some respects, the white community was making it impossible for them to do it 100 percent right. We require accounting of dollars. But Head Start in the state of Mississippi, because it did have something of a black militant cast—at least it was perceived so by the whites—there were many cases in which the white merchants selling food or milk or what-not wouldn't dare in the same county sell milk for the local program. So they would have to go into the next country. Well, that was very expensive. Other places, the merchants wouldn't take their checks; they had to pay in cash. And then they wouldn't give a receipt, because they didn't want anybody to ever have a record that they had ever dealt with these blacks. They wanted the business, but they didn't want the credit for having dealt with them. The police harassed CDGM in many, many ways, and it was a very difficult situation. It was a mixed bag.

SUGARMAN: We had enough problems raised from the two [investigative] reports that we felt some change in the operation was necessitated. One of the exacerbating issues here was the fact that they had chosen for their headquarters a small abandoned college which was also the focal point for civil rights activities in Mississippi—Mount Beulah. And accusation was made that we were in fact subsidizing Mount Beulah to Mary Holmes Junior College, which was almost 200 miles away.

Even though the program had only one or two weeks to run, it was decided that the headquarters would have to be moved. Our assistant general counsel, Jim Heller, was sent there to deliver this message. He delivered it and was met with terrific resistance. After what must have been almost a night-long discussion, he became convinced that it was ludicrous to insist that the program move. Accordingly, we reversed ourselves and left the program there. And they completed the summer program.

But in the meantime, the people in CDGM had begun to think about a full-year Head Start program and filed an application for approximately 6,000 children for the full-year program, which would have begun in the fall of '65, through '66. We were directed not to proceed with funding that application until the questions which arose out of the summer '65 program could be resolved. And we sent a number of auditors into the program. Those auditors found evidences of irregularities which in total never exceeded more than one percent of the total cost of the program.

Didn't CDGM have its own auditors?

SUGARMAN: Yes, they had their own auditors, an established international firm of CPAs; but despite this, there were problems.[5] There were also [other] problems that we were concerned about: what seemed to be a movement toward black separatism and toward discrimination [in] hiring, and the almost total lack of the involvement of white children in the program.

We went through a protracted period of negotiations. We sort of hammered away at it point by point. Eventually, I was sent to Mississippi to negotiate the final points, and we arrived at an agreement which involved them putting up, I think, approximately $30,000 as a bond against any eventual disallowances of money. I discussed the agreement with Mr. Shriver by phone from Mississippi and thought we had a complete understanding and said so. I returned to Washington and found we didn't have a complete understanding. So what seemed to have been an agreement to fund was not an agreement to fund, and we then went through another series.

Was this a misunderstanding between you and Shriver?

SUGARMAN: I suppose so, I suppose so. It really boiled down to the fact—at least [it was] my feeling—the fact that he added conditions after the agreement had been reached.

Had the funds been spent for purposes other than for Head Start?

SUGARMAN: In the end, I think less than $5,000, which was maybe one-hundredth of a percent of the total grant, was really disallowed.

At any rate, some five or six months after the program closed in the summer of '65, it was again funded, to run, I think, until September of '66. A number of conditions were imposed, including the importation of a good deal of management assistance from external sources. We literally worked days and nights, through the night, trying to recruit staff for them so that they would have greater management capability.

The minute we refunded CDGM, we were, of course, attacked by Senator Stennis. The [Senate] Appropriations Committee investigator returned to the scene, and our inspectors returned to the scene, and we went through a long series of battles.

Was it simply a political affair from the point of view of the Mississippi congressional delegation?

SUGARMAN: I think it had its origins in the fact that many of the people who were involved in setting up the program had been members of the Freedom Democratic Party, and that, in the senator's mind, this was simply an extension of the efforts of the Freedom Democratic Party. This he did not feel was appropriate. Specifically, he didn't feel the use of federal funds was appropriate to do this. This has been his public position, and I assume that that was his basic position [on] why he was so desperately opposed. At various times, he has also alleged that there were people who had even more serious problems. There were somewhat abortive attempts to identify people on the staff with the Communist Party, none of which ever really came to any serious charge. But he just believed in his heart, I think, that this was a bad thing for Mississippi, so he opposed it with all the vigor and prestige and strength that he had. Of course, by virtue of his membership on OEO's appropriation committee, he had a very good forum to do this.

What kind of pressure was put on Shriver about CDGM?

SUGARMAN: It was about this time there began to develop two sets of pressures, which were in contrary directions, because during this second grant we had a repetition of allegations of the same kinds of problems. Eventually, we shut the program down because of the extent of the allegations and the charges of mismanagement and misuse of funds.

MISSISSIPPI ACTION FOR PROGRESS

SUGARMAN: Around [the termination of CDGM's Head Start contract] developed what really became a debacle in terms of conflict between the people who would ordinarily be considered the friends of OEO but who in this instance were rather bitter about OEO.

Would that be the Citizens Crusade Against Poverty?

SUGARMAN: That was the core group, very heavily. A heavy number of church groups were involved, and other groups with liberal orientations, and some very responsible people who just believed that OEO had caved in to pressure in this situation. Part of the issue here was that, when we reached the decision that we could not continue with CDGM, we were reluctant to see a program disappear from Mississippi altogether, so we actively supported the formation of another group called Mississippi Action for Progress [MAP], which would develop programs to replace CDGM.

I believe there were charges at the time that the MAP group had been conceived in the White House.

SUGARMAN: Yes, there were charges to that effect. I never thought that was true, but I really frankly don't know exactly how MAP came into being. I do know that we had received word that there was a group of people—of whom Hodding Carter and Aaron Henry[6] were two—that would be willing to talk about sponsoring a large program in Mississippi. Of course, both Hodding Carter and Aaron Henry were people who had done progressive things in the state and who had a certain reputation. So when we made the decision, when we were almost sure that this was what was going to happen, Berry and I and some other people were sent to meet this group from Mississippi and to discuss with them the formation of a new organization. And we did. They submitted an application, an application which was written in considerable degree by members of our own staff. We announced that we were cutting off CDGM and we were going to fund [MAP].

That's when all hell broke loose. It was a very bitter battle, which probably reached its emotional climax in an ad which appeared in the *New York Times* headed, "Say It Isn't So, Sarge" ["Sargent Shriver"—the full name appeared in the heading], which deeply upset Mr. Shriver. I'd never really seen him as moved and as angry as he was. It was a terrible reflection on his personal integrity. It was one of those situations in which quite well-meaning people on both sides of the argument completely lost, in my judgment, perspective and were so engaged in fighting with one another that they couldn't stand together against what was really a common enemy.

In his reply to the New York Times *advertisement,[7] Shriver said that all the advice he had gotten—from the Office of Inspection, his general counsel, Community Action, Head Start, and so on—was to cut off CDGM.*

SUGARMAN: That is factually correct, but there were a vast number of OEO employees, who were not themselves involved, who took a very dim view of OEO's action and felt very bitter about what they believed was a cave-in to not only senatorial pressure but White House pressure. I have never seen or heard anything that really documented pressure from the White House. It is possible that it existed, but in the ultimate resolution of things, I do believe there was a call from the White House that was influential in leading us to re-fund CDGM.

People chose sides on this one, but meanwhile, a process of negotiation began. Again, I was sort of in the middle, between Mr. Shriver, on the one hand, and the CDGM board, on the other hand. A couple of visits to Mississippi, a couple of visits to Washington by the CDGM board; and shortly before Christmas [1966], we finally hammered out another agreement with another set of conditions— and an agreement which is still the subject of disagreement as to what I agreed to between myself and the CDGM board.

The night that these negotiations were held, I was supposed to be in Los Angeles for a Head Start party given by the Head Start center out there. I kept watching the clock with one eye and trying to negotiate with the other eye. Mr. Shriver had gone home and said, "Call me when you reach some degree of agreement." This time the agreements involved getting the National Board of Missions of the Presbyterian Church to guarantee against any disallowances [and] getting the Board of Missions to agree to pay the salary of what would really be a management overseer to try to strengthen the management of the program. But the nub of the problem, and the one that led to dissension between me and CDGM, was what was to happen with respect to MAP. We, after all, as a federal agency, had said to MAP, "Here you are; you can have a program in all these counties for this number of kids," which was roughly equivalent to what CDGM had had before. Now we were saying, "Well, we're going to put CDGM back in business, but not as large as it used to be, and only in certain counties." The question was, where do we take territory away from MAP and give it to

CDGM? The MAP board, I think quite properly, said, "Look, fellows, we got into this business because you said there was a need for a program, and now you are saying to us get out!" And we said, "Well, we're not really saying get out. We're saying you can keep the same size of program, but let's narrow the jurisdictions to those areas [where] you are actually engaged in program already." We hammered out a plan with MAP that was in agreement on all but five counties, and in those five counties there continued to be disagreement.

At this point, I said to the CDGM board—and this was that night in December—I would personally undertake to discuss with the MAP board whether an agreement could be reached on those five counties, and I would encourage them to accept the proposal, which was essentially to have them both operate in those counties but in different parts of the counties. I went to Mississippi, and I was unsuccessful in persuading the MAP board to do that, for reasons which I think were valid reasons from the perspective of the MAP organization. On that basis, and because of our prior commitments from MAP, we decided to honor their priority of right there and not to fund CDGM in those five counties.

I think to this day the people from CDGM believe that I did not honor a promise to give them those counties, a promise which I felt I hadn't made but they felt I did. So it was one of the misunderstandings that characterized the whole process.

At any rate, they did get funded. They went back into operation, and in those five counties a new group sprang up called the Friends of the Children of Mississippi [FCM], which was financially supported by the Field Foundation in small degree but which essentially operated the old CDGM centers on a voluntary basis. That group operated for well over a year on a voluntary basis, during which another series of negotiations took place between FCM and the Field Foundation, on one side, and the OEO regional office—which had now assumed jurisdiction of the program—and MAP, to see if some sort of agreement couldn't be reached between them. In the meantime, MAP had had a change in leadership on the part of its executive director, and eventually a series of agreements were hammered out, and FCM and MAP are now aligned together in a single program.

CDGM has now dissolved as an organization and been replaced by a series of county organizations which contract directly with Mary Holmes Junior College, which has become much more of a factor in the operation than it was in the past. So the net results of all of this—you have to add up the fact that Mississippi now has the largest Head Start program in the country. There are some 30,000 children in Head Start in Mississippi in the full-year programs, which is one-seventh of all the kids in the country in full-year Head Start, in Mississippi. And that's roughly fifty percent of all the children that are in the first grade in Mississippi. So it's a very big factor in the Mississippi programs for children, and it's a very big factor in the economy of Mississippi. The thing that made this possible was the authority that the director of OEO has to allot twenty percent of his funds on a discretionary basis. And whereas Mississippi would be entitled to something like $8 million in accordance with the allotment formula, in fact OEO is now putting closer to $35 million into Mississippi. This is something that we were never really successful in convincing people of, that they were getting not only their fair share but far more than their fair share. It was always believed that there was another million dollars somewhere.

THE SOCIAL AND POLITICAL IMPACT OF HEAD START

Do you think Head Start was effective as a tool for racial integration?

RICHMOND: Yes. In contrast to the public schools, which historically had patterns set, we could learn from what had developed by way of segregation and try to minimize that. So we started out with a very conscious determination from day one to try to develop integrated programs. As I indicated, in some places we weren't initially successful, but we highlighted the issue. We kept working toward this, and communities kept learning that we were serious about this. We had our Office of Civil Rights, with some people who were very ingenious. I began to learn the technology of civil rights enforcement, because they would tell me, "This application indicates they're going to run a segregated program," and I'd say, "Well, how do you know that?" They had built into our application form a map of how the bus routes would go, and they could tell from looking at a community whether that was going to be a segregated program or not. That's how we didn't squander our meager human resources. We didn't have very many people who could go around and look at communities, but they could pretty much smell them out.

Were you satisfied with the quality of Head Start teachers?

RICHMOND: Well, yes, by and large I think it worked out very well. When we started, there weren't very many really trained early childhood educators, because there hadn't been careers. Prior to Head Start, there were settlement house nursery schools, very small in number. There were co-op nursery schools, largely middle-class, where parents got together and pooled their resources. And there were university campus nursery schools. And that was it. So there weren't career opportunities, and relatively few people went into such careers. When Head Start opened up, people began to see careers. The universities then began to teach it, and so we had the burgeoning of career opportunities. It became very exciting for many people. Jule Sugarman and I tried to develop a career ladder so that people who didn't even have a high school certificate might come in as workers in Head Start centers and, while working, could work toward [career goals]. We had many anecdotal stories of people who had ultimately gone up through their collegiate experience and had emerged as trained teachers. So we had a design for increasing the numbers, and we've been in that sense largely successful. I think the quality on balance was really remarkably good.

What do you think of the participation of the nonpoor in the Head Start program? It evidently has appealed to a lot of people who don't fit into the poverty bracket.

RICHMOND: Well, the whole preschool educational movement always had great appeal to middle-class people. There just never was enough of it to satisfy their demand. Some of the most intense meetings I think I'd ever had were from middle-class groups who said, "Why should the poor be the only ones to benefit from programs like this?" That was a hard question to deal with. It was just more on the basis of need, because we knew that middle-class children would, in the overall, develop reasonably well, even if they did not go to [Head Start]. As a matter of fact, that was an interesting thing. Bettye Caldwell and I had reviewed the data on early childhood education for middle-class groups, and it was very difficult to see that it had really enhanced the development of the children. Their parents wanted it, and we didn't come out and say, "Well, you don't need preschool education for more affluent groups."

We did, however, feel that it would be desirable to have some mix. Because we didn't want to be criticized for making it a program for the more affluent, we limited that [to] ten percent. Then there was some criticism of that. We did that with the notion that you wanted children from those backgrounds to interact with low-income children and that that might be beneficial to both in social terms, but also—in learning terms—beneficial to the lower-income children. But the data for really establishing that firmly had not been very good. We did that on the basis of impressions and judgments.

It's been said that Head Start was one of the prime forces in giving impetus to Title I of the Elementary and Secondary Education Act. Do you have any knowledge of this?

SUGARMAN: Well, I don't think it can accurately be said that it gave birth to Title I, because Title I came along in '65—actually, [it] was enacted while Head Start was just forming. I do think it is correct to say, though, that it has significantly influenced the way in which Title I programs eventually came to operate. For example, the heavy involvement of aides in Head Start was an example that was picked up and used by many of the school systems. The increasing concentration of Title I funds on the elementary years, the primary years, and sometimes on preschool, is a reflection of experience that came out of Head Start. There has been some movement, although I think not enough in Title I, to make programs more comprehensive in introduction of more health and outreach services. And finally, the strong advice issued by Commissioner [of Education Harold] Howe last year, calling for the formation of advisory committees involving parents, I think, grew directly out of the Head Start experience. That also had a very significant impact in the social and rehabilitation service, the welfare programs. As you may know, we now have in statute a requirement for parent participation in our day-care programs, and also for the use of nonprofessionals and volunteers. Both of those, Wilbur Cohen has told me, came directly from his observation of the Head Start experience.

SPINNING OFF HEAD START

Was there an intention to ultimately spin off the Head Start program to HEW?

RICHMOND: We were always very conscious about the fact that OEO programs were not to stay in OEO forever, that it was an innovative agency. Oh, yes, this was a clearly expressed notion, at least as I understood it, from day one. Mr. Shriver always articulated that—that it was an innovative agency; it was to develop these new things, get them started; and then they'd be turned over, we assumed largely to HEW. It didn't necessarily have to go that way. Later on, all kinds of things began to develop in other agencies; [there were] the multiservice centers operating out of HUD and even some health programs out of HUD funds. You began to see Agriculture begin to develop some programs for the rural poor that they hadn't had up until then. So there was considerable impact. But we kept talking about the fact that these programs would end up largely in HEW.

Do you think that Head Start was kept longer in OEO simply because it was a good shield for the less popular programs?

RICHMOND: Gee, I don't know how to answer that. It just took quite some time to get it all gelled so that it could be moved over. It moved over—what, in about 1969? I would guess that the timing was about right. If one would not give it that kind of incubation period, it might have been premature, in terms of its survival, to move it. But I thought the timing was about right.

Do you think that Head Start, before it was turned over, had done a significant amount to get HEW to pay more attention to the poor?

RICHMOND: Well, I think OEO's presence generally did, because early on, in connection with Head Start, I would go over and talk to people in the Children's Bureau, and obviously they kind of wished that it had all been developing there, but under the circumstances it couldn't. I think they were very interested and concerned about what we were doing, anticipating that someday it would come over.

But it was also true of the health programs that we began to develop. I remember Mr. Shriver and Ms. Lee Shorr and I went over to brief Wilbur Cohen and his whole staff on what we were doing by way of developing neighborhood health centers. His staff went around the table, talking about how many programs for the poor they had. It turned out, it was very few. The assistant secretary for health, walking out of the room, said, "Damn it, 40,000 people in the Public Health Service, and nobody working for the poor." So it clearly began to focus their attention on doing more for the poor.

SUGARMAN: In the fall of 1965, when we were doing budget projections for a five-year period, I proposed that we operate Head Start for two years, that we delegate it for another two years, and that we spin it off completely in the fifth year to the Children's Bureau. But at the first level of review, it was decided that we would propose three years of direct operation and two years of delegation, and then we'd think about spin-off. To make a long story short, by the time the program went to the Budget Bureau, it made no provision for either delegation or spin-off, which was sort of an advanced warning of our arteriosclerosis in OEO's bureaucracy.

Are you implying that OEO simply was unable to let go of programs, despite the fact that they might have matured and could operate safely?

SUGARMAN: That's the way I read it, yes. I think that has been reflected in other programs as well. Actually, the issue arose again in the late fall of 1967, when I formally proposed to Mr. Shriver that we undertake to negotiate a delegation to HEW of the Head Start program. After considering the matter for two or three months, I was authorized by Mr. Shriver to proceed with negotiations for a delegation.

We had just barely begun negotiations when the roof fell in, in the form of the out-and-out assault on OEO in the Congress. At this point, Mr. Shriver, I think quite rightly, concluded that he couldn't afford to lose any weapon that might help him to maintain OEO. So discussions were dropped.

Why do you think OEO should have spun off Head Start?

SUGARMAN: For a series of reasons. First of all, I think that OEO should have tried to stay small, should have tried to encourage institutional change in HEW and other agencies by a careful spin-off and monitoring of programs. Actually, I probably have shifted my view a little bit, in the sense that I now favor a much more active role for OEO during delegation than I had originally conceived. For example, it is my view that a good delegation would involve things like having an OEO review of all policies, like having a portion of the funds reserved to OEO for monitoring and evaluation, and perhaps most importantly, having OEO act as an ombudsman for any organizations or individuals who feel aggrieved by the operation of the program by some other agency. Sitting over here in another agency now, I see the need and the desirability for some sort of outside influence which would counteract the inevitable pressures to conform to different considerations rather than some of those that are important to OEO.

THE DOMINICK AMENDMENT

The "Dominick amendment" of 1967 proposed transferring Head Start to the Office of Education, which would operate the program as grants to state agencies.[8]

SUGARMAN: It was in some ways a legislative fluke—a bill which I think was introduced without any serious belief that it would pass but which almost did pass. As far as the substance of the bill was concerned, it would have destroyed totally all that had been built up in Head Start. There's no question in my mind about that.

The Dominick amendment would have transferred Head Start out of OEO and given Head Start programs to the states, with supervision or some form of control by the Office of Education—is that right?

SUGARMAN: It really went beyond that. It really physically put an end to the Head Start program and instead provided a lump sum of money to the states which was to be used for early childhood purposes, with no standards, with no quality, with no legislative specification as to the nature of those programs.

With no regard for the prior experience?

SUGARMAN: That's correct, correct. However, when it did pass the Senate and became a serious threat, and when we got people to focus on the problem of the content of the bill, we found (a) that nobody really had bothered to analyze it and understand it, and (b) that when they did, even those who were still in favor of a transfer were quite willing and receptive to altering the contents of the bill to maintain the Head Start program as it is. It was not the Head Start program that they were seeking to destroy. It wasn't even necessarily, on the part of many sponsors, an attempt to put it in the education world, but rather it was a slap at OEO. Of course, motivations varied here, and I've never been sure exactly who stood where on that bill.

Are you saying then that Senator Dominick wasn't so much concerned with the fate of Head Start as he was with taking a stab at OEO?

SUGARMAN: I think he was concerned with the fate of Head Start. I think he was supportive of the Head Start program. I think that his prime motivation was to remove the program from OEO, where he had some doubts about how it would fare. Now, he was aware that there had been a whittling away of the funds for Head Start by the OEO officials, and he knew that there had been tremendous pressure, which eventually succeeded in producing a supplemental appropriation for Head Start, which he viewed as replacing the funds that had originally been appropriated for Head Start and converted to other purposes. Just giving OEO more money. So I believe that his prime motivation was protective or supportive at least of Head Start.

THE GOP'S OPPORTUNITY CRUSADE

SUGARMAN: In '67, the point of concern about Head Start was much more the "opportunity crusade" bill, which, you may recall, was Congressman Goodell's and Congressman Quie's attempt to recast the entire poverty program.[9] Interestingly enough, I found that the Quie bill was a pretty good bill. It introduced some rather novel concepts—at least novel for that time—which I thought had a lot of merit. First of all, it preserved all the essential features of Head Start as far as program content went. Secondly, while it involved state agencies, it specifically provided that those state agencies would not be the state department of education but a newly constituted state commission involving all the relevant public agencies and private agencies. Thirdly, while it required the state commissions to act on applications for assistance, it left the final decision on assistance in the hands of the federal government and provided a very adequate bypass in those cases where the state was acting out of conformity with the purposes of the act. So I was sort of encouraged by the bill in terms of the future of Head Start. Obviously, I preferred that it stay right where it was, in OEO. But if we were going to have a bill, then that wasn't too bad a bill.

To my recollection, the Dominick measure that year didn't get much attention. I don't recall that we took it very seriously. [But] 1968 was another matter, and we were all caught off base on that one, because none of us had any sense that it would go as far as it did. In fact, the White House congressional people had told OEO the day before the vote that it wouldn't get twenty votes. They were obviously very wrong.[10]

THE DIFFICULTY OF EVALUATING HEAD START CHILDREN

SUGARMAN: What we hope for, of course, is for kids who are living up to their maximum potential, who are able to fit into situations that they are going to run into in life and to do well and be happy and be healthy. But how to quantify those things and how to measure them is very difficult. We just don't know.

It seems to me such measurement might involve certain problems of social adaptability. What is socially acceptable, for example, to the black community may not be socially acceptable to the white community, and vice versa. Has this come up as a problem?

SUGARMAN: Yes; and of course, even the IQ tests are accused of having all sorts of cultural biases. The real answer is in the measurement of performance, but that's, again, a highly complicated thing that we don't have much experience in. I would just as soon dispense with all IQ scores if I had some other measures to work with—and maybe we will. There's a lot of investment going into the development of performance measures and the development or assessment of motivation and the assessment of social effectiveness and so forth.

Would you say that today's objectives are very similar to the objectives you had in mind back in 1964?

SUGARMAN: Yes, I think they are, except our concept of the family involvement and the value of the program for the family is much greater or deeper than it was in 1964. It's probably quite true that we were focused much more on the child, and now we're much more focused on child and family together.

RICHMOND: We were determined to have good accountability, so we tried to set up reporting systems that would assure accountability. We also wanted to try to collect data on whether the program seemed to be having an impact or not. My colleague Bettye Caldwell developed what was called a preschool "inventory" to see if we could get teachers to use this to rate the children and see whether they were making progress. Then we wanted to get health data, so we sent out a lot of health forms, and we just loaded that system with far more than they could manage. If you were taking care of the children, you couldn't spend a lot of time filling out forms. I think that was clearly our inexperience. But we kept being pressed, and to some extent this was important. We kept being pressed to come up with data to show that the program was effective, and we kept struggling with how are we going to do this. The answer was try to get them to report, and so we were killing the goose that laid the golden egg.

We hadn't yet developed a design for sampling. Mr. Shriver, for example, was very conscious of this, and he wanted a national sample. We did raise the question, "Well, you know, we could do just small samples." "No, we ought to sample the universe." But this was inexperience. Everybody had very good

Lady Bird Johnson reads to a Head Start class at the Kemper School in Washington, D.C., March 19, 1968. *C9080-17a, 3/19/68. Photo by Robert Knudson, Presidential Collection, LBJ Library*

intentions. Later on we learned that it was better to sample youngsters on what was going on in programs around the country rather than trying to draw on the universe. We did some innovative things that way. We funded some thirteen university-based centers to give consultation to programs regionally to develop training programs for teachers and things which did have a rather significant impact, and also to stimulate the collection of data.

THE NEED FOR INTEGRATION OF SERVICES

SUGARMAN: We have several elements in the Head Start program: the daily activities, the nutritional, the health, the social services, and the parent activities. My observation in visiting Head Start programs and reading evaluations is that, while all of those elements are present in most programs, there is very little interaction between them. For example, the doctor seldom gets into the classroom; the teacher does little in the way of health education in the classroom; the social worker or the neighborhood outreach worker, the nonprofessional aide, may never talk to the teacher about what they are finding in the home; and the teacher may never tell the worker what problems are going on in school. So I think there's a great deal of effort that needs to be made to make sure that it's not just a series or an aggregation of services but an integration of services.

SUMMARY

RICHMOND: There was a lot of national commitment, all the way from the top down to the grass roots, to the program that helped make it successful—from the president's commitment, Mr. Shriver's commitment, to the outpouring of volunteers. And in part, when I say the quality of the teaching was good, what you got essentially were teachers who were deeply committed, and, of course, a good part of teaching is the commitment that people bring to the task, as well as the skills. And then the ingenuity of people to improvise. You had programs operating in just all kinds of improvised facilities, not always at a standard we would have liked, but workable nonetheless.

People like Jule Sugarman were just remarkably imaginative and innovative in the way they went at the task and made it possible for something like this to happen so quickly. So I think it's a good demonstration of the fact that it is possible to change programs and change directions fairly quickly if a need is perceived and there's a design, and if there's imagination and commitment.

One other point that I would make is that it's a lot easier to start programs from scratch than it is to turn old ones around to do new things.

GAITHER: Some 2 million children have been helped now, and in their lives it makes a great deal of difference. The figures are really astonishing. Head Start isn't just an educational program. There's no doubt in our minds that the gains are lost in the school years if you don't follow through. What they don't lose is the first medical check they've ever had in their life, the first shots they've ever had. Ninety percent of the kids who go through there have never been to a dentist at age five or six; in some cases, never had a health checkup; they've never had shots; they've never gotten corrective treatment for their eyes. They may be totally unable to see [enough] at least to get along in a classroom, but they don't have glasses. They may have very serious bone deficiencies. And Head Start is providing complete health care for these children.

The difficulty is, over the last three and a half years we've gotten 2 million children, ages three to five, out of a universe of 9 million who needed that help. This year we have a little less than 800,000 children in Head Start, but only 250,000 of them are in full year; the rest are just in the summertime. Well, it's difficult to overcome the handicaps for four or five years just in the three-month summer period.

So in one sense, we've done a lot, but there's a lot more to do.

14

THE JOB CORPS UNDER SIEGE

BY THE END OF *1966, the Job Corps was in trouble. The program had been oversold and was having difficulty living up to expectations. For one thing, it could accommodate only a tenth of the young people who needed it. Also, its initial haste in opening and filling centers to produce quick results had made it vulnerable to criticism—to charges of poor planning and inadequate data. Some opponents doubted that the corpsmen were being trained for jobs they could actually fill; others challenged what they regarded as the program's excessive cost. Whenever a Job Corps youth committed a crime, it was invariably seen as a reflection on the program. When a riot occurred at a Job Corps camp, it was a scandal of major proportions.*[1]

Part of the Job Corps mythology had been that it needed a university president as director. In October 1965, Dr. Otis Singletary was replaced by Dr. Franklyn A. Johnson, the former president of California State College at Los Angeles. Franklyn Johnson lasted only a year; by the time he departed, it was apparent that the Job Corps needed a strong, experienced administrator, not an academic figurehead. William P. Kelly, a career civil servant, brought sound management systems and accountability to the program. Unfortunately, Kelly had to live with shrinking resources and congressional skepticism as he tried to polish the Job Corps' tarnished image.[2]

LYNDON JOHNSON'S VIEW OF THE JOB CORPS

Do you know what the White House attitude was toward the Job Corps in late 1966 and 1967, when you came in?

KELLY: Yes. I think that the president had always viewed Job Corps with a good deal of empathy. I think he understood Job Corps. Job Corps to him was kind of a combination of the CCC and the National Youth Administration, both of which he was very familiar with, having been an administrator in the National Youth Administration back in the thirties. His view in 1966 was that the Job Corps was not doing as much as it could have done. It wasn't getting enough kids into the program. When I talked to him in 1967, after Congress had reconvened and he was about to send my name up, his knowledge of Job Corps and what it ought to be doing was, I would say, complete. He understood what Job Corps ought to be doing. It ought to be getting tough kids—when I say tough, I mean kids that really needed assistance, tough cases. As he said, "We'd be doing them a really great service if we'd teach them how to brush their teeth, comb their hair, shine their shoes, sleep between sheets." So his knowledge and understanding of what the Job Corps ought to be about was excellent.

Did he seem disappointed by what had happened to it?

KELLY: If he was disappointed, he never expressed that disappointment to me. I don't think he thought that Job Corps was touching enough kids. I think that was an indication of some disappointment in terms of recruitment.

He never talked to me about the problems of disturbances or incidents that occurred in the Job Corps. Because there was a hiatus from the time that I became acting director of Job Corps until he decided for whatever reason to send my name and Bill Crook's name up to the Senate for confirmation. This was early March or late February. It had to be the 28th of February or the 1st of March. By that time, there was a notion afoot here in Washington, at least in the press, that the Job Corps was different. I think that that notion was present at the White House. At least Moyers, prior to his leaving—he left just about the time I was confirmed—was saying that there was a different understanding about what the Job Corps was, in even such a short period of time such as that. And there had been no incidents from December on. As a matter of fact, there had been no incidents in the fall of 1966. The last incidents had occurred in the summer of 1966.

What were your own feelings about the Job Corps at the time? How did you interpret the problems that it was undergoing?

KELLY: There were a number of things afoot in the Job Corps. The Job Corps had been largely leaderless during a whole year, a very important year—all of 1966. Its director had spent most of his time on the road. When he was here, he did not lead, because he was not that kind of a human being. He did not know how to do that. Other things he did very well. That he did not know how to do.

The Job Corps did not have any data. It had spent its life, up to that point in its life, doing a really enormous logistics job. It had built in excess of 120 centers, but there were other things that needed to be done. The recruitment was way off. The Job Corps had a capacity of about 35,000 youngsters on the first of December 1966 and only had 28,000 beds occupied.

The Job Corps was suffering some really terrible feelings of self-doubt. It had been beat about the head and shoulders by the Congress, by the public, by the press. It suffered an enormous inferiority complex. The one asset it had [was] some really good people, not all of them in the proper job. And it had some vacancies into which other people of good caliber could be moved to help any new director run it. He had an opportunity to pick some people, because there were some good jobs that were open.

So in viewing the Job Corps at that point in time, I viewed it as an enormous and interesting challenge, an opportunity to really do good things. At the same time, [it was] an opportunity to get your head beat in because of the fact that there were a lot of people in this town that did not think the Job Corps was salvageable.

You mentioned inadequate data as one of the Job Corps' problems. What kind of data are you talking about?

KELLY: We really didn't know what it cost to run the Job Corps center in Camp Kilmer, New Jersey. We didn't know whether youngsters made gains in reading, arithmetic, in any orderly manner. We didn't know whether kids were getting jobs as a result of Job Corps experience, or how many of them are going back to standing in front of the poolroom. We didn't know any of the details of financial management in the Job Corps. What were we spending for clothing? What were we spending for food? What were we spending for utilities? What were we spending for training? We really didn't have a very good property management system. We didn't know what we owned.

So that what we did in terms of that first two weeks in December was to lay on a list of priorities of things that we had to do. One of them was, we had to fill up the Job Corps. We just couldn't sit around with a capacity of 35,000 and only have 28,000 filled. At the same time, we were under the admonition of the Congress to go to 23 percent women, which meant we had to open still new centers. The budget for 1967 had called for having 39,000 youngsters in the Job Corps by the end of the fiscal year. I set the target at 41,000, because that was our capacity, and I said in December we would have 41,000 kids. We would first of all pick up the slack between the 28,000 and the 35,000, and we'd go to forty-one. Then I said we'd have a data system. I outlined the minimum things that we would have in the data system by the first of March, and the minimum things we'd have by July 1, and the minimum things we'd have by the following December, a year later. We achieved all of those. We got the 41,000; we got the data system.

Wasn't there some sort of data analysis of Job Corps from the very beginning?

KELLY: It wasn't systematic. The reporting of the raw data, the stuff that was coming out of the computer, was garbage. It was on a sampling basis, fundamentally; a lot of starts and stops had been made. People would start to put together a data system and then get pulled off into other areas—mostly logistics in 1965 and even into 1966. That became an excuse for not gathering data except on a kind of catch-as-catch-can [basis]. All of a sudden people would become very worried about data a month before a hearing. Then everything would stop, and they'd scurry around trying to put together enough data to get by. But there was no systematic method of doing it. When I arrived here and asked some very elemental questions, I couldn't get any elemental answers. So we laid on a data system, and we got it. It saved us in 1967, because by the summer of 1967 we had the most extensive data system of any manpower program in existence. We still do have the best data system in the federal government, in my judgment.

You really hadn't been faced with any major incidents or any incidents of the nature that the early Job Corps had to face.

KELLY: No. I think some of the things we did account for that. First of all, the first month I was here, we published a code of conduct. Job Corps had never had a code of conduct. We published a code of conduct not only for the Job Corps enrollees but for the staff, and I ran into some flak on that. People were telling me that I couldn't tell grownups what they could do. Well, I figured if they're going to work in Job Corps, and if they're going to set an example for disadvantaged youth, that there ought to be some standards. So we prescribed them. In the first six months, we fired twenty-eight center directors. That's always a horrendous thing to have to do, but we did. I think that put a little spine into the Job Corps.

On what basis do you fire and hire directors?

KELLY: We fire them on the basis that they're not running a good program, and we've got the yardsticks. Are the kids staying? Is it disciplined? One of the really terrible problems the Job Corps had at the outset was the whole notion that it should be a permissive Job Corps. My notion was that it should not be a permissive Job Corps. If we were going to have one thing, if we didn't have anything else, we were going to have a disciplined Job Corps. First of all, the taxpayers of this nation weren't anteing up their treasure to have a program in which there was no discipline. You just couldn't produce a kid that was going to be able to go to work, that was going to be able to adjust to an industrial society where there are all kinds of constraints upon you. You have to be at work on time. You have to deal with your boss in a certain way. You have to deal with your fellow workers in a certain way. Unless we could inculcate those kinds of notions into the kids, then we had a problem. And the only way you can do that is through a reasonably disciplined process. So the notion of the permissive Job Corps went down the drain.

A lot of people dug in their feet and said, "That's not the way to do it." But I was being paid to do it, and that's the judgment I made. We haven't had any incidents since then, and we're still taking the same tough kids. And the kids want that. The kids want to be told what to do. They want to know what their parameters are. They want to know what the boundaries are. They become very insecure in a world in which there's nothing proscribed for them. I don't care whether they're poor kids or middle-class kids. I've got six kids. They're always happier when they know what the name of the game is.

How do you recruit directors?

KELLY: In terms of the conservation centers, we depended pretty much upon the Agriculture and Interior Departments to do that. In terms of the contract operation, we assisted some of the contractors in the urban centers to find people, people that we knew, people who had been called to our attention. Those are pretty good jobs. They pay twenty grand a year. I insisted [that] either myself or my deputy see every potential recruit. In the case of some places where we had troubles when I first arrived, and where the first thing I did was to move to get rid of the center director—and a deputy in a couple of instances—I just called a corporation president and said, "I want somebody from top management. I want the best vice president you've got in there for thirty days, that is, if you want to keep the contract." So the industrial concerns that were dealing with us really came to the conclusion that we meant business and that we weren't going to take castoffs. We weren't going to take guys that were in their last two years before retirement. We wanted young, vital people out there that could run these centers.

We decentralized more and more of Job Corps activities to the field. That, I suppose, is organizational change, because when I came to the Job Corps, we had many more people in the headquarters than we had in the field, and now the reverse is true. We have got more people in the field than we have in the headquarters in the seven regional offices. In terms of great changes, of moving boxes all around, I haven't done much of that.

How would you describe the quality of people in headquarters who work for Job Corps?

KELLY: I think that we've had some really extraordinary people in OEO, and we've had some extraordinary people in the Job Corps, and continue to have. In any enterprise of this kind, you have people come and people go. I'd rather have a good guy for a year than a bunch of bums for five. So my feeling is that if I can get a commitment out of a really good guy to work a year, I'd rather have that than some gemouk that's going to make a home out of it. So I really think I've been blessed.

We used to call the Job Corps, back in 1967, the Tiger Team. We had buttons that we wore, kind of corny, but they had a tiger on them, and it just said,

"Job Corps Tiger Team" on it. Everybody wore them. We wore them to hearings. People appeared in the well of the House of Representatives with them on, members of the Congress.

CHANGES IN RECRUITMENT

What were some of the recruitment problems?

KELLY: The problem in recruitment was that the Labor Department, through the Employment Service, had been the chief recruiting arm for Job Corps. There had been starts and stops in 1965 while arguments occurred within this building as to whether or not they should have an exclusive monopoly on it. By 1966, although they did not have an exclusive monopoly, it was clear to everybody that they were the main instrument to do it and were being paid rather handsomely to do it. But the problem was that the performance on the part of the Employment Service was terribly spotty. It still is to this day. Some states are good; some states are terrible. Again, it's a classic kind of situation in the federal government that once the federal government merely becomes a check-writing instrumentality and gives something to the states and merely writes checks for its operation every year, it doesn't control it. That's the problem with the Employment Service.

We set some goals and did it in a very no-nonsense way. I talked to my people here in Job Corps who were in charge of recruiting and said, "If we don't make 41,000, there'll be some new guys here. It's as simple as that." And also I talked to the Employment Service. At that time, there was a new guy whose name was Frank Cassell. He'd been a vice president of Inland Steel. I just said, "Look, Frank, we can help you turn around the Employment Service, and we'd like to help you do that. I think by laying this very difficult task on them and just never letting them out from under the gun, you can serve my purpose and serve yours too." And somehow or other, we pulled it off. We did turn them into a fairly effective recruiting arm, and we did meet all of our quotas. We did have 42,000 kids in the Job Corps on the 30th of June 1967.

In early 1968 we had to close down sixteen Job Corps centers because of the Budget Bureau cutting us back. At that time, we had to turn off recruiting, and it took us a year to recover from it. I think it took us a year to recover from it for a number of reasons. One, I think it was fully expected within the Department of Labor that there would be further cuts in Job Corps, not by the Congress but by the administration, principally by the Budget Bureau. It's very hard to turn on something that you turn off. Because we turned it off for three months, and then it took us about nine months to turn it back on so that it could meet capacity. We didn't fill the Job Corps back up again until January of this year [1969], and we were down below capacity from June, so it was a period of about six months.

Did the Employment Service cooperate in focusing on your target population, the poor?

KELLY: No, they didn't cream on us. We set the standards; they didn't cream. Their figures, which we verified, showed that they screened seven kids before we'd get one. So we get the seventh kid. The other kids either go to Neighborhood Youth Corps, MDT [Manpower Development and Training], some other program. So that we've been getting really the toughest cut of kids. [The Employment Service hasn't] done well in rural America for us, because they don't have any outreach there. As a result, we've tried to utilize other institutions in rural America. Getting anything done in rural America is very difficult because of the lack of sophisticated human resources.

Now, our women have been recruited, I suppose, about fifty percent by WICS, Women in Community Service, an instrumentality the Job Corps created made up of the National Council of Catholic Women, Church Women United, National Council of Jewish Women, and the National Council of Negro Women. They do about fifty percent of the recruitment for women. But the other fifty percent is done by the Employment Service. And the Employment Service does a somewhat better job in recruiting women that it does men—which is really strange, because WICS was set up because nobody believed the Employment Service could recruit women and didn't until we went to the twenty-three percent in 1967. We had to meet that 30th of June target, which was a requirement of law, and WICS fell down on us. So I had to put the Employment [Service] into the breach during the months of March, April, May, and June, and they made up the deficit and have done it for us.

THE BUREAU OF THE BUDGET VERSUS THE JOB CORPS

GORDON: [The Job Corps] looked to us at the very beginning as though it was more romantic than practical. It didn't seem to be a very efficient way of providing intensive job training for delinquents and dropouts and low-potential kids from slum areas. And as you know, it has proved to be a very expensive operation. You can argue about what the cost is, but the Neighborhood Youth Corps, which is a work-study program right in the home community of the kids involved, I think has shown itself to be a more efficient way of producing the result than the Job Corps has.

KELLY: I think that the objective of the Budget Bureau has always been to get rid of Job Corps. Job Corps has always been harassed by the Budget Bureau, from the very moment it was created. Their notion is that you could do more to alleviate poverty if you took this money and did something else with it. They're never quite clear as to what the hell you would do with it.

And I made some very serious tactical errors with the Budget Bureau personally in 1966, when I took this thing over, by establishing an objective of 41,000 kids in the Job Corps. I wrote them and explained what I was going to do. It was kind of a slap in their face, because supposedly they'd milked the budget so that I could only have 39,000 kids. But we got 42,000 with the same money, and they never gave me permission to do it. Even though I requested it, they ignored my letter. They evened up the score, though, in January of 1968 by demonstrating that I couldn't be quite as autonomous as I thought I could be by whacking me $10 million, putting it in the concentrated employment program, and forcing me to close sixteen centers.

THE COST OF JOB CORPS TRAINING

KELLY: I can remember the first time that cost ever came up as an issue in Job Corps. It was in July of 1964, when we were putting together the first budget for OEO. The question was asked by John Forrer, who was the budget examiner: What was it going to cost to run Job Corps? And the estimate at that time was about $6,000 [per enrollee man-year].

When that [estimate] was sent over to the bureau, there was a great hue and cry, because they thought that the previous figure that had been talked about in the earlier spring or late winter was $4,500. That had been kind of a horseback guess. I don't even know where the $4,500 came from. I think Chris Weeks pulled it out from under his hat and gave it to Shriver, and Shriver used it. But when some analysis was done, it was obvious we couldn't run it for less than $6,000 if we were going to do the things that the Job Corps envisioned doing. And there was just a great hue and cry. There were conversations between Charlie Schultze and Yarmolinsky and myself that this would probably be unacceptable to the president. But finally, after a lot of discussion, we budgeted it on the basis of about $6,000 per enrollee man-year.

COST OF JOB CORPS TRAINING

Even before Johnson signed the Economic Opportunity Act, he expressed concern about the cost of training Job Corps youths.

LBJ's conversation with Bill Moyers, August 7, 1964[3]

JOHNSON: Can anybody explain to me why in the hell it costs $4,600 a year for a boy?

MOYERS: Shriver can better than I can, but it boils down to the basic fact— travel. You've got to have more instructors for this, because these boys are more undisciplined. So, per ten boys, you've got to have at least one instructor, until they test it and see whether or not it goes. That adds up to the cost. The other things are food and so forth. It's on a twelve-month basis, rather than on a nine-month basis, which a college education is figured at.

JOHNSON: Well, I know that anybody can board for a hundred dollars a month. That's twelve hundred. And I know you're going to pay them fifty. Isn't that right?

MOYERS: That's right. That's $600.

JOHNSON: So that's $1800. They say exclusive of your camp equipment, so you would have to, according to this, have about $2800 for teachers. That don't make sense.

MOYERS: I don't know enough about it...

JOHNSON: Well you find out enough about it, because you're not that dumb. And you're the head of this program, and you've been running it. And that's the big question I've been asked about every time I talk to somebody. You tell them I want to see why we can't cut that [cost per corpsman] down, because that's going to have to stand scrutiny. I'm going to put an auditor on that.

At the outset of the program, Shriver mentioned in a couple of speeches that the total potential capacity of Job Corps was 100,000. Is this beyond the actual capacity of Job Corps?

KELLY: Yes. I think what Shriver was talking about was the fact that at any given time there were probably 100,000 kids that could be recruited into the Job Corps. Nobody ever had enough money for 100,000. We built a plant that would accommodate about 41,000, 42,000 kids. The most money we ever had was for 39,000 kids. I took it to 42,000 by stretching the money. That was the high-water mark. After that, we went back to 36,000 kids in terms of the $10 million cut. That was what was in the 1969 budget. And for the 1970 budget, if the new administration hadn't cut us, we would have annualized the 36,000 at between 36,000 and 37,000.

Is it adequate, in your opinion, to enroll between 35,000 and 42,000?

KELLY: No, hardly. As we sit here, there are about 400,000 youngsters in the United States who need a Job Corps program. They need the total human renewal the Job Corps provides. They need to have their teeth fixed, and they need to have their psyche straightened out, and they need to get some weight on them, and they need to have a residential setting where they can get away from the pusher and the hooker and all of the other signs of failure that exist in their ghetto, whether it be rural or urban ghetto. Rural ghettos are bad too. These are the kids thirty percent of whom can't read or write; sixty percent of whom come from broken homes and suffer other debilitating factors. We would have managed, if we had been allowed to stay at the 41,000 level, to help about 60,000 or 70,000 kids a year.

Congress has limited the amount it can cost to train trainees. Has there been any decline in the cost?

KELLY: Oh, yes, the cost has rapidly declined. The cost in 1965 was about $10,000 per enrollee man-year. It came down to about $8,000 in the first half of calendar 1966. In the second half of calendar 1966, it came down to about $7,800. In the first half of calendar 1967, we got it down to about $7,300. In calendar 1968, it's running about $6,500. The Congress first in 1967 hung us with $7,500, as I recall; now it's $6,900. We're under the $6,900; we're running about $6,500.

Now, those are direct costs. Those do not include amortizations on capital. Those are direct operating costs and do not include the cost of my overhead here, the space we're sitting in, and the rent I pay for this portion of the building. Nor does it include the costs of the work supplies that are used to build picnic tables or roads out of the conservation centers.

The cost has come down dramatically. It has come down for a number of reasons. One, the Job Corps has become more efficient. We cut costs. We cut out a lot of frills that we discovered we really didn't need in this kind of a program. We've been running reasonably at strength over the last two years. With the exception of a period of about six months, we've been at strength.

But, yes, there were some political problems in the period 1965–1966. I think that most of the political problems had disappeared by the late fall, early winter of 1966. I inherited a situation in which community relations were starting to turn the corner. They hadn't turned it completely, but they were starting to turn the corner. The economic impact of Job Corps was starting to be more appreciated. People were working in Job Corps centers and getting Job Corps paychecks.

PRESENTING THE "NEW JOB CORPS" TO CONGRESS

KELLY: I knew that Mrs. Green [Representative Edith Green] was probably perhaps the most hostile member, at least in the Democratic Party, toward Job Corps. One of the first things I did when I became director of the Job Corps,

I went up to see her. She had a bill of particulars involving our women's center in Albuquerque, New Mexico. And I must say it knocked me right out of my chair, because she had stuff I didn't know about. I had only been acting Job Corps director about four or five days when I went to see her. So I put some people on an airplane that afternoon, sent them to Albuquerque, and we got it straightened out. I went back and reported to her in detail, and I don't think anybody had ever been that frank with her. [But] her mind was not changed about Job Corps; she doesn't think Job Corps is a program that ought to be supported. She never will.

For what reason, do you think?

KELLY: She's an educator in the traditional sense. She thinks that education ought to be one of those powers reserved to the states and the local communities. If you're going to provide any kind of assistance to the states or local communities, what you ought to do is write them checks, establish guidelines, let them submit plans. If the plan meets the guideline, then write them a check and let them carry it out. That's her hang-up. You're not going to disabuse her of that notion, because that's pretty well ingrained. She's an ex-schoolteacher, and she's of the establishment.

But I think that no one had ever been really quite frank with her in the Job Corps. As a matter of fact, she had gotten some snow jobs. And she found it refreshing that somebody said, "Yes, we've got a kid pregnant out at Albuquerque, and the guy that got her pregnant is a member of the staff. It's a violation of all the rules there are." She kind of fell out of her chair when I came back. So even though she didn't like the program, she did have some respect for me and has always been very gracious and courteous to me.

I think it was Representative Green who in 1966 came up with fairly accurate figures for Job Corps' training costs.

KELLY: Mrs. Green's figures, at least all the figures she has ever given me, are not accurate. They're biased. She takes a snapshot, a sampling, favorable to her point of view. I can remember during the markup in 1967, we were talking about the women's center in Tongue Point, Oregon, and we were talking about the costs of that center. She was trying to stick me with the construction costs of that center, which were costs that were incurred in 1943 by the Department of the Navy. We had a little colloquy, and I said, "Now, Mrs. Green, you know you can't stick me with those costs. Those were appropriated, paid for, and accounted for in an entirely different decade. They're not properly chargeable to Job Corps." But she would do that. She's a very clever woman, very politically clever.

There were a series of significant events leading up to Job Corps' appearance on the Hill in June of 1967, starting with the Perkins [Education and Labor]

Committee. First of all, we devoted an enormous amount of time to getting Job Corps ready, because it was very clear to me from my early reconnoitering on the Hill that Job Corps was in very bad shape with the politicians. The bad reputation of the Job Corps grew out of the fact that it had no data, or confusing data, or contradictory data. There was a persistent notion that Job Corps had, where it couldn't produce the answers, made them up. People kept using the word "snow job." As a result, it was very clear that if Job Corps was going to carry the day in Congress, there had to be a really very good presentation. There had to be a really excellent indication that the Job Corps knew what it was talking about, and that it had the data to support what it was talking about.

So we had worked very hard on putting together a data system that would provide us with facts. Not all that we wanted at first, but we arrayed the priority, and the priority was aimed at satisfying the Congress. By April we had the first materials coming out of the computer on the data system. We decided one of the things we would do would be to put together a congressional presentation separate from the standard OEO presentation. And we decided we would present it in really three ways. The first volume would be a volume in which we talked about the total program; highlighted the costs; made some comparisons between Job Corps and other institutions; and, going back over the previous year's testimony, creat[ed] an answer to every question that the Job Corps had been unable to answer or had answered in an unsatisfactory way in 1966. That we called volume 1.

Volume 2 was a complete cost analysis of what the Job Corps cost, center by center, down to such line items as what we were paying for gasoline at the Cispus Conservation Center, what we were paying for utilities at the Clam Lake Conservation Center.[4] The kind of detail that seldom exists in the federal government in any program, any that I've seen, and I've spent a few years in this business. That was volume 2.

At the same time in March, I had written a letter to some 1,000 addressees around the country in towns and villages, cities, adjacent to Job Corps centers. I wrote to the chiefs of police, the mayors, the presidents of the chamber of commerce, leading businessmen, clergymen. I asked them to evaluate for me what they thought of the Job Corps, what they thought of the youngsters. Had the Job Corps been a good neighbor? Had the Job Corps made a contribution to their town or city? Had the Job Corps participated in some meaningful ways in the affairs of their town and city? That was volume 3, and it was called "A Community Relations Résumé." So by May we had what in my judgment is the finest congressional presentation that was ever put together in this city to defend a program.

What kind of responses did you get, generally, to the letters you sent out?

KELLY: Extraordinary responses. They surprised me. As a matter of fact, there were so few negative responses that when we compiled the thing, we put all the negative responses in it because they were so few and they paled in contrast. I had the police chief of the city of Edison, New Jersey, which is right near Camp Kilmer, tell me that our youngsters were better than his "locals." This was the kind of thing that was reiterated time and time again—[as well as] the economic benefits that the Job Corps had brought to small towns, where in many instances it was the only federal presence, and in many instances it was the only substantial payroll.

We decided that we had to seize the initiative, that we just could not go before any committee—but particularly before the first committee—deliver ourselves a kind of a benign statement, and then be up for grabs in terms of questions. It was my judgment that what we had to do was to occupy the center of attention for at least an hour so that we could get our story told, so that we could anticipate the questions that might be asked. Frankly, I was trying to leave that committee sitting there with their questions answered; with the nasty little kinds of queries that only a congressional committee can level at you already snuffed out; and with the Job Corps in command of the situation, rather than a conservative congressman from Iowa.

We went before that committee, succeeded in getting the chairman to agree that he would block out a morning, or longer if necessary, for Job Corps and give us an hour to make a presentation. I must say that the finest moment I've ever had in eighteen years in the government business was finishing that presentation and having both sides of the aisle—Goodell (now Senator Goodell; he was congressman at the time); Congressman Quie; Mrs. Green; Congressman Gibbons; the chairman, Mr. Perkins—say that this was as good a presentation as they'd ever seen. I suppose that was Job Corps' finest hour, because it was very clear that here was a program that had come off the ropes, come off the canvas, knew what it was about, and had made a presentation that left no question that the Job Corps was in command of its data. The Job Corps was in command of its program, and the Job Corps could now take its place as a program that was respected.

Did you have any prior contact with people on the Hill before you went up there?

KELLY: Oh, yes, I spent a good deal of time [on that]. I spent maybe twenty-five percent of my time in the late winter, spring, and early summer of 1967 talking to congressmen and -women. I probably talked to 150 in their offices. On the Senate side, I talked to forty, maybe forty-five members of the Senate during that period. What I was saying all of the time to them was, "Reserve your judgment on the Job Corps until we come before the committees. Suspend the judgments that you have today until you see the new Job Corps." That was the theme that we harped on, that there was a new Job Corps. "Just hold your judgments in abeyance until we have an opportunity to appear. And if you're not there to see us, read what we have to say and talk to your colleagues about it." That was the thrust of what I was saying all during that period from January until June, when we made our first appearance.

Could you categorize congressmen and senators in terms of whether they would be friends or enemies of the Job Corps?

KELLY: Let me say this. In all the places I went at the Capitol—and I saw hostile people as well as people who wanted to be friendly—I was always treated with graciousness, with courtesy. Even those people who said to me in the opening moments of our dialogue, "I voted against the OEO; I don't believe in the program," still treated me deferentially. But there's certainly a way of categorizing people up there. There are people who are victims of their own mythology. They prefer to believe the myth rather than the fact, even after you lay out the fact. For a moment there may be enlightenment—the sun may break through—but they will invariably retreat back to the myth, because it's comfortable and it's something in which they take intellectual refuge.

There are people who have open minds, who want to hear the facts, who will question you carefully, closely, about the facts. Personal integrity is awfully important in dealing with the Congress. If they think that you're a trick-shot artist, you're dead. If you come across in terms of being sincere, reasonably bright, and if they can perceive that you are not trying to pull a trick shot on them, then the tendency of people with open minds is to believe you.

And then there are the people who are dedicated to this kind of a program. Some of the conservative publications call them the "flaming liberals," and they were committed. If we would have burned down the center of the Vatican, they would have been committed to the program, because it was poor kids who were burning it down. They're really kind of antiestablishment, although they can't be that overt in the way that they talk, at least publicly. They usually represent constituencies that are fairly liberal. And you find some Republicans like this. This is not restricted to the Democratic Party. Those are terribly broad categories, and they're terribly unfair.

Then you get way over on what's properly called the right, and you get guys who won't believe it regardless. They tend to be midwesterners. They're worse than the southerners in this regard, I must say. The southerners will believe you, but they have some very sticky political problems that won't allow them to support you. The people in the midwest won't believe you, and they don't have as many sticky political problems to prevent them from supporting you. But there are some people who are against everything, including social security.

Could you also comment briefly on how you and the Job Corps worked with the OEO congressional relations staff and the White House liaison people?

KELLY: My principal relationships were with the OEO congressional relations staff. George McCarthy, who headed that staff in 1967 and into 1968, is really one of the most extraordinary people I've ever met, particularly in terms of his knowledge of the Congress. He's a brilliant political tactician. He was just absolutely well schooled in how the Congress operates. He knows the mystique; he knows the mythology; he knows the system; he knows the people. But our principal relationship was with him and his staff, and we mounted a tremendous lobbying effort.

Would you call it a lobbying effort?

KELLY: That's what they call it outside. It's against the law, but this is taped for historical purposes.

Let's pursue this then, because Goodell did make that charge.

KELLY: Well, the fact of the matter is that I lobbied very, very hard for this program. I think that anytime you're charged with a program, you have to lobby for it. You can call it anything else you want. You can call it providing information to the Congress; you can call it being courteous to the Congress; but a rose by any other name—it's lobbying. What you're trying to do is get your program through. You're trying to get as many votes as you can get for it. You're trying to get it understood. You're trying to overcome the misunderstandings. You're trying to bury the mistakes. You're trying to do [these] kinds of things if you believe the program is worthy of passage.

We had congressional strategy meetings daily. We had congressional assignments daily. The thing we were trying to do was to get as much into the *Congressional Record* that was favorable to all of OEO programs as we could. I was in the process of making mass mailings, which continue right down to the present day. We were always trying to get favorable stories in publications, and we got an awful lot of them in the last couple of years. If something favorable turned up across the nation, I'd mail it with a nice letter to every member of the Congress. Then we'd have congressmen put it in the *Record*, and the same on the Senate side. Every time you opened the *Congressional Record*, if you could read something favorable about the Job Corps, that was to our benefit. If you could read something favorable about OEO, that was to our benefit.

There are a lot of people in this town that don't think that this is important. There are people in the old-line agencies who have become so used to the fact that they just merely have to troop up there for appropriations hearings. They don't have to go up there to get reauthorized. They're authorized forever, and they know that their budget is going to be plus or minus five percent, no matter what they do. They looked upon us over here in the OEO as being kind of theatrical, overdoing it. But the problem is, they've never been in the kind of a situation where they had such a controversial program, where they had to get authorized—never mind appropriated—every year, with the exception of this last year, when we got a two-year [authorization] in the 1967 cycle. The attitude was that the OEO made too much out of congressional relations, too much out of congressional lobbying. Well, that was not the case. It had to be done, or this institution wouldn't be here.

Did you have any dealings with the White House liaison people with congressional responsibility?

KELLY: I probably had some telephone conversations with [Mike] Manatos [White House Senate liaison]. I used to talk to [Joseph] Califano occasionally, not very often. I talked much more often to Moyers when he was there. When the Moyers crowd left—Moyers and Hal Pachios and Hayes Redmon and the people that represented that group over there—I really didn't have anyone inside the White House that I knew that well to talk to.

What happened to Job Corps? Did you have to close down any centers?

KELLY: What happened in 1968, of course, was really in some ways even more disappointing than what has happened in 1969, at least for me. I expected what happened in 1969 to happen; I didn't expect what happened in 1968 to happen. We won the legislative battle hands down in the Job Corps. Every debilitating amendment that Mrs. Green offered in committee, we'd beat. We had Republicans voting with us in that committee, at least two of them, sometimes three. The Democrats, with the exception of Mrs. Green, closed ranks. With all of her cajoling, trying to make deals with them, they held the line in the case of Job Corps. Let the record show, they did not do that in any other program in OEO. She had her Green Amendment in the Community Action Program. But they held the line completely in the case of Job Corps, which I think is a great tribute, first of all, to the lobbying job we did—to use that onerous word—and the presentation that we had delivered to the Congress.

One of the really extraordinary things that happened was in the House Appropriations Committee markup. At the end of that process, they had earmarked the entire $295 million for Job Corps to guarantee that it might not be shifted or used somewhere else. Now, when you get a committee that is fundamentally as conservative as the House Committee on Appropriations doing that, then you have won a magnificent battle, let me tell you!

Well, we won the legislative war, and we lost the war with the regular government. In January of 1968, the Budget Bureau decided it would divert $10 million of the Job Corps money to the concentrated employment program. That $10 million, coming at the start of the third quarter of the fiscal year, had the kind of impact on us as $40 million would have. It forced us into the position of closing sixteen centers in order to recoup the $10 million, else the Job Corps be in violation of the law and find itself in a deficit position come the 30th of June, or the end of the fiscal year.

We had been asked during the course of the 1967 congressional cycle what criteria we would use if we were forced to close Job Corps centers, and I had stated a criteria which we proceeded to use. It consisted of costs; [it] consisted of community relations; it consisted of placement; it consisted of thirty-day drop-out and length of stay. We weighed them equally, and we came up with the sixteen poorest centers, although there was at least one or two of those centers that couldn't be considered poor. We'd cut deep enough into the marrow of this program that we were forced to close at least a couple of centers that would have stayed open by anyone's measure, except we had to get $10 million.

Our objectivity was such that, if you looked at it from a political point of view, you would have thought we were insane, being a Democrat administration closing centers fundamentally in our friends' districts and our friends' states. We closed the only center that the late Senator Robert Kennedy had, and we closed the only urban center that Senator Edward Kennedy had, in New Bedford, Massachusetts. We closed centers in Gaylord Nelson's state [Wisconsin], [and Philip] Hart of Michigan. So that our objectivity on the criteria was good, but it hurt our friends.

It was a terrible time for all of us. We had to go and explain to these people what we had done. They thought that they'd earmarked $295 million for the Job Corps. They had not realized that that [earmarking] had been knocked out with our concurrence. We were consulted about it in the conference between the House and the Senate. We didn't see any reason why there had to be earmarking. We thought that the intent of the Congress was clear, and we didn't think that the establishment would gut us after the fine showing we'd made on the Hill. But they did.

Do you know why there was the $10 million cutback?

KELLY: My own judgment is that the $10 million cutback was the Budget Bureau flexing its muscle and indicating to us, "Don't do that again," because the previous year we had gone to 42,000 [enrollee capacity] when the budget had only called for 39,000.

I gather that there was great political pressure going on at this time, especially on this office, and probably on you. Could you go into that?

KELLY: There was a lot of pressure, particularly from [Senator Wayne] Morse, but there was pressure from other people—everyone that had a center closed. I can remember a conversation that I had with Congressman [John] Blatnik [of Minnesota], who's just a wonderful guy and had been so supportive of this program, who just said, "This is just killing me politically." You looked at those guys whom you knew were your friends, and it ate my gut not to be able to say, "Look, we won't close yours." But if you did that in one case, then your criteria would be demolished, and your credibility would be destroyed. We'd spent a whole year establishing the credibility of the Job Corps. When people called it political, I just said, "That's impossible. You can't call it political. Would I close the two Kennedy brothers' centers? Would I close Blatnik's center? Would I close Wayne Morse's center? There's nothing political about it."

Did Morse ever contact you personally?

KELLY: Yes. He said I was a dumb bureaucrat. He said, "I'll dismantle that program."

What did you say to him?

KELLY: I said, "I'm sorry, Senator. It's a lousy deal. I didn't want it to be cut. I think you ought to talk to the president. It's his Budget Bureau that cut it."

If it was recognized in OEO that closing those sixteen centers would incur the wrath of people like Morse—who could damage the whole program and not just the Job Corps—weren't attempts made to get out of the situation?

KELLY: Oh, yes. Mr. Shriver—who, of course, was in his waning days here—wrote a memo to the president, which I'm sure the president never got, in which he said, "Now, here are the implications of what we're doing here," and spelled out some of the same implications that I spelled out, the political implications, in a separate letter.

We tried to set up a nationwide clearinghouse. I put two people to work full time on it, where we sent telegrams to 600 school systems in the United States and said, "Look, here are the teachers we've got. Here's where they are. Here's how you can contact them." We got some teachers placed. We did the same thing with technicians, with the people that would not ordinarily be grabs for the public school system but who might teach in an on-the-job training program—people without certifications of one kind, but somebody that could repair your TV set or teach you how to repair your TV set. We did that. In the case of contract centers, the contractors placed as many people as they could back within the corporation. In the case of the conservation centers, Agriculture and Interior tried to absorb them.

WAYNE MORSE AND FORT VANNOY

D. BAKER: The closing of Fort Vannoy was one of the real problems. The community around Fort Vannoy had really opposed it quite a good deal. In Oregon, there's a great number of people, fugitives from the Civil War, the post–Civil War era from the South; and there's a fair amount of racism in that section of the state. They had opposed Fort Vannoy very vigorously, and Wayne Morse had defended it. He had gone back there and defended it and tried to sell it and worked in its behalf. He had always been very good to us.[5]

As part of [Kelly's] public relations gimmick and his presentation to the appropriations committee the previous year, [he] had laid out the criteria [for closing bases], which he was going to use if he didn't get his money. So he was committed to these criteria.[6]

As a factual matter, I think the criteria were faulty in a number of respects. One, they were based on at least one erroneous premise, and that is that all the Job Corps camps were getting kids of the same degree of difficulty. With respect to Vannoy, I later found out that was particularly untrue. It was sort of a repository of Latin American kids from southern California that were just regularly channeled up there. Their academic achievement was lower than elsewhere. Their language facility—that is, with English—was less in every respect. They were harder-case kids than were going elsewhere, even on the West Coast. Beyond that, several of the criteria measured the same thing, just over and over again. One of the criteria which was quite legitimate was also a bit subjective: that is, the community relations. The fact of the matter is, so far as Vannoy was concerned, I personally in my own investigation am satisfied that [in] the assessment and the placing of Vannoy on the scale that they use to measure community relations, they were reflecting the earlier response to Vannoy and not what was occurring within the last three to six months.[7]

And what was the community response then?

D. Baker: Pretty damned good. Wayne Morse had done a job of selling it, and the community had recognized that they had an economic interest. That was reflected in the fact that they fought like hell and got Wayne Morse to fight like hell to keep the camp.

And beyond that, there was the erroneous judgment that included, as part of this decision-making element, no consideration for the federal financial investment. Fort Vannoy happens to be bricks and mortar—some of the best facilities west of the Mississippi. It has got the finest machine shop in the whole four or five northwest states, just an elegant outfit in which we had about a million and a half bucks! Even in that same area, we had some of the early bases that we had put up in which we'd used portable housing—you know, trailer, mobile homes sort of things—which I'm willing to bet my bottom dollar by the time we close Fort Vannoy, or right now, are pretty much deteriorated and depreciated to almost nothing. In order to keep them going, it's going to require some very substantial investment.

Now, even if you assume that those criteria were good, it would have made more sense in some of those cases nearby to have moved the whole goddamned camp from one of these tempo outfits to a place like Vannoy—lock, stock, barrel, kids, equipment, kitchen pans, and the whole shebang. But they didn't do it.

Well, Wayne Morse, in his typical thorough, lawyer-like fashion, dug up all these facts, and he presented them, and he complained about them bitterly. And he made his judgment. This was a mistake insofar as he was concerned. The fact of the matter is, it was a goddamned mistake as far as Fort Vannoy is concerned. I think some of those other bases were a mistake. Hell, we've got a couple of those bases where we had a million, three-quarters bucks, where we never put a kid—there was never a kid in them! Just absolutely it was a disgraceful waste of money! And Morse knew it.

[Morse] called me up and asked if I would come up to the office. And he said to me, "You're someone that I admire very much and I'm very fond of. You're associated in that place in a responsible position, and because of our personal relationship, I want to be perfectly fair with you, and I'm going to tell you exactly what I'm going to do. If you people and Lyndon Johnson don't find some way of remedying that Fort Vannoy situation, I'm going to declare war. It's as simple as that, and you can count on me." And he did. But we were warned. He gave us a reasonable period of time to act, and we indicated that we were not going to do anything.

EVALUATIONS

HOWARD: The Job Corps had some heavy-duty problems coming into existence with a certain bag of predetermined philosophy with respect to movement, a certain difficulty with respect to not having real jobs there. They had many internal problems dealing with two different agencies and running the camps. With all [that], they promised a lot. They promised it was going to be the crown jewel. It was going to be their big operational program, and maybe they felt they had to do it because Neighborhood Youth Corps went to Labor. At any rate, they promised too much. It was a difficult program to begin with. It was not susceptible to starting big. It was a slow-startup program, and yet they pushed and pushed and pushed. All those things, I think, made it a disaster.

YARMOLINSKY: We optimistically figured that when [Job Corps graduates] went back [to their communities], if there were jobs, they would be motivated to get them. And once they got the jobs, they'd be all right; they'd have made it. Now, why wasn't that so? I suppose partly because there weren't jobs, and there weren't jobs above the poverty level. I don't know the answer to that question, and I haven't really looked at a systematic study of what happened to the people who graduated from the Job Corps. It may be that the problem was just [that] the Job Corps was so small, that in fact a sizable proportion of the graduates made it out of poverty and stayed out.

D. BAKER: The fact of the matter is, Job Corps is vulnerable. From a subjective and a personal point of view, Job Corps is the thing that really, I think, is probably my biggest disappointment. I expected many of the troubles we had with other programs, but Job Corps is a program that I am convinced is a sound idea. It works in a number of places and works not very well in others, but I'm reasonably convinced that where it works and where it doesn't work is the result of absolutely nothing that comes out of Washington. It works where it is, works because of the dedication and intelligence and sensitivity of the people who happen to be at a particular base.

I think it should be said in defense of Job Corps that the Employment Service has done an absolutely *miserable* job of recruiting. The state employment services have connived with the courts and the police and everybody in the sun to get kids into the Job Corps that had no business being there, who they had no hope of dealing with, who ran up their bills at a phenomenal rate, led to exorbitant dropout rates. They just did a lousy, lousy job, as they do in everything they put their hand to. But even so, some places are doing fantastically good jobs.

SINGLETARY: I knew personally some real success stories out of the Job Corps. I know, as every teacher knows, that while you may not have the solution of what to do about old folks or grown folks or anything else, it is still possible to affect the lives of young people. They are at that malleable age where things can happen to them that will alter their lives. I saw that happen many times. I saw many dropouts and failures as well, but I saw kid after kid after kid really avail himself.

One of the great pleasures that I remember is being down at Gary one time. Maybe this was even after I was out of the Job Corps and was back in Austin for a visit. I was there when a plane came in from Oklahoma from some corporation to pick up eight of the kids who had just finished the welding program there. I've forgotten the hourly wage that they were going to pay them, but it was unlike anything those kids had ever heard of before.

There was unmistakable evidence of a real problem and a real need that somebody had to fulfill. And if that program doesn't do it, they're still going to have to find some other way to do it. That body of youngsters out there is still there, and getting bigger.

SHRIVER: It's sometimes true that medicine hurts and people don't like to be cured even of what they've got because the medicine hurts. It's also true sometimes that if you're trying to build yourself up after you've allowed yourself to get into bad physical condition, there's an awful lot of what we call aches and pains attendant to an effort to get yourself into shape. Not only with respect to the Job Corps, therefore, do I say this, but with respect to the problem of poverty in general: I would say that most of us middle-class or upper-class white Americans were shocked to find out that there was poverty in the United States back there in the sixties.

Secondly, we weren't quite prepared for the bitterness and the antagonism and the violence—in some cases, the emotional outbursts—that accompanied an effort to alleviate poverty. There were an awful lot of people, both white and black, who had generations of pent-up feelings. I believe that when you take the cork out of a bottle like that, it's likely to burst forth because of a long period of compression. As a result, when we went into communities or when we took youngsters out of communities, like for the Job Corps, there was a lot of acrimony and wild activity, such that the placid life of most middle-class Americans was stunned, shocked, by all this social explosion. There was a lot of animosity revealed in the explosion, and then a lot of fear came into the hearts and minds of a lot of middle-class people—not only fear, but then real hostility.

KELLY: Why should you take a job at $80 a week that you can't get to because public transportation is so damned bad in the United States of America? Why should you take a job that you've got to get up at six o'clock in the morning to get there by eight and have to transfer three or four times? Particularly when your friends on the corner are saying, "You copped out, eh? Got a job! What's the matter? You losing your touch with the pool cue?" It's nonsense.

A job doesn't provide an exit to the suburb. A job doesn't allow you to buy a house in Prince Georges County or Montgomery County, where Negroes can't go. A job doesn't provide your child with a good school. It's no exit [from] a lousy school that your kid has still got to go to in Woodlawn or Harlem. A job doesn't teach you anything about nutrition. A job doesn't get your teeth fixed. A job doesn't teach you a darned thing about installment buying, or about how to avoid a usurer. The notion that a job is an answer to these people is crazy! It is naive! It's a view of the world that doesn't exist in the ghetto. Now we know about these things in the Job Corps, and lots of other people don't know.

So what do you try to do, then?

KELLY: What you try to do is effect some kind of a human rehabilitation. You try, first of all, to fix somebody's teeth. If they haven't got any teeth and they're fifteen pounds underweight, you give them some teeth so they can eat food.

What you try to do is change their attitudes about the world. You try to point out to them that work is dignified. You try to point out to them what is the relationship between the person who works and his colleagues who work, between him and his boss, and the institution that his boss represents. And what is a labor union, and what does it do, and how can you participate? Why is it important to be at work on time, and why is it important to take care of your employer's tools? Why is it important that your hair is cut and that your shoes are shined, and that you've got a clean shirt on, even if you're a blue-collar worker?

And why is it that we care? Why does the society care enough to be able to ante up out of its wealth $6,500 a year to teach you something? This is a society that hasn't abandoned you. This is a society that thinks that you deserve an opportunity and a chance, and it's willing to ante up all of its wealth to do this. We teach you how to read, and we teach you how to do arithmetic, and we teach you some skills that will put you on the first rung of the economic ladder, so that the only thing that you can see is not just a job as a busboy or a dishwasher. There's an opportunity for you maybe to own your own business someday. That's what we do.

15

"KEEPING THE TRASH IN ONE PILE"
Legislative Battles

IT DID NOT TAKE LONG *for OEO to encounter sharp criticism in Congress. In 1966 legislators added restrictions to the poverty program and earmarked funds for the favored Head Start program at the expense of Community Action and the Job Corps. The fight over the fiscal 1967 appropriation demonstrated how the support of a strong subcommittee chairman—Representative John Fogarty of Rhode Island—afforded protection to a controversial program.[1]*

OEO's 1967 authorization battle marked the emergence of Kentucky Congressman Carl Perkins, who succeeded the deposed Adam Clayton Powell as chairman of the House Education and Labor Committee.[2] OEO's dim prospects for authorization in the House led Perkins and the program's other supporters to adopt the crucial amendment by Representative Edith Green that placed CAAs under the control of local government. Republicans denounced this successful maneuver as a "bosses and boll weevil" strategy.[3]

OEO's aggressive lobbying in 1967 also influenced the outcome of the authorization battle. The agency mobilized its supporters around the country to pressure reluctant members of Congress. Shriver himself worked Capitol Hill as tirelessly as he had in 1964. In the end, OEO not only weathered the crisis but received its first two-year authorization.[4]

THE LEGISLATIVE PROCESS

PERRIN: Normally, they [OEO amendments] start here in OEO. We have developed a general pattern of circulating among the program areas and collecting from them ideas that they would have for amendments that would affect their programs, things that they believed were necessary or appropriate or for clarification, improvement, what have you. This exercise was run by the general counsel's office. Once these were pulled together and polished, the extraneous weeded out, or the politically impossible discarded, and other ideas cranked in, we would then begin the process of selling it to the admin-

"War-On-Poverty Is Hell Too"

"War-on-poverty is hell too." *A 1965 Herblock Cartoon, copyright by the Herb Block Foundation*

istration, which began with the Bureau of the Budget. And, of course, the White House got into that too. But this was the general procedure that was followed. The draft bill that was finally transmitted to Congress by the president reflected these kinds of looks and actions by the various people within the Executive Office.

What happens when the bill gets to the Coiigress? Does OEO have people on the Hill who provide information to congressmen about the bill and help to get it through?

PERRIN: We work very closely with the committees that handle the legislation. This contact is year-round; and then once the bill is transmitted, we work with the chairmen and their staffs to make sure, one, that we know what their time-table is, and that we know what they expect of us in terms of what kind of testimony they want and what shape they want it in.

The first order of business is the open hearing by the committee. We testify, sometimes at considerable length. Sarge used to open the testimony, and then on subsequent days, once they got finished with him, various program directors would take over and testify and answer questions. It was usually done on this kind of format.

Following the hearings, the committee, sometimes a subcommittee, would go into executive session. In the case of the House, Perkins was handling it last year [1968] as a full committee rather than a subcommittee. They go into executive session and start marking up the bill. And on those occasions, we also continue to work very closely with the committee staff by having certain key people right there on the Hill, and usually in another room, but they are available so that as matters are proposed in the executive session someone can check them out with knowledgeable OEO staff as to what the effect of this would be if it were accepted. And this continues really right on up until the House or the Senate passes the legislation.

Was Larry O'Brien involved?

PERRIN: Oh, yes. Larry was over usually when the going was the toughest and close. Moyers sometimes was there. But Larry and Mike Manatos, I think, were probably the two most directly involved. They'd pull all kinds of maneuvers to get a vote, to keep a vote, to get rid of a vote. I recall one time that some senator had a flight out of town. He had to go make a speech someplace. This was the kind of thing that always infuriated me about the Senate: how the Senate was run on the basis of what somebody's personal plans are, quite often. This particular senator had a flight out, so one of the White House representatives called the vice president of the airline, and he got him to hold this particular plane at the airport until the senator could get there. These are the kind of things that happen. Certainly you don't find them in the civics textbooks, but they're things that made the world go around as far as legislation is concerned.

Larry O'Brien was certainly one of those [White House staff members] who respected the integrity and the ability of members of Congress and was not one who threw his weight around, but he knew how to get things done too. And he was a very, very professional and capable spokesman for the White House in these sessions.

PLAYING GOLF WITH JOHN FOGARTY

PHILLIPS: On the appropriations issues, we pretty much put all our eggs, or a good many of our eggs, in John Fogarty's basket. John Fogarty was the chairman of the Labor-HEW subcommittee that handled our funds. He was an old friend of Sarge Shriver's for many years. They had a close personal relationship. John Fogarty and I had a close relationship too, from Democratic Study Group [DSG] days. Fogarty is not the kind of a member that most would think of as a gung-ho DSG guy, but he was an active member. There were some issues that we worked on together when I was at DSG. When I went down to OEO, Shriver called him, and the three of us had lunch and talked about how things were shaping up on the bill, the timetable on the appropriation hearings, the markup, and so forth. Shriver and Fogarty were great kidders; they just kidded the hell out of each other. Shriver got to know him through the Kennedy presidential campaign and in the Peace Corps operations.

Fogarty never hesitated to call me about antipoverty problems in his district or in Rhode Island. He sometimes became upset because of the role being played by the governor of his state. Governors had unique roles in the operation of the antipoverty program, because it was a federal-state-local program—even program veto power to some extent. The thing about congressional liaison at OEO was that you had vertical governmental liaison as well as a liaison between the executive and legislative branch of the federal government. Not many people have really thought about that aspect or analyzed the unique nature. It would not be unusual for me to have a call from a state legislator saying, "We've got a bill up in the legislature to provide local funds for this antipoverty program. Can you tell me something about how it functions in my district?" I once had a call from a county judge who was interested in a community action agency in his county. I've had calls from governors. I've worked with governors' staff. Of course, governors had initial veto power over individual programs in their state. The thing about OEO was that you never knew from day to day at what level of government you were going to be involved—vertical down to the local-community-city-town level, or horizontally at the congressional level. That was one of the things that was so fascinating about the antipoverty program.

The governor of Rhode Island then was John Chaffee, a Republican, now a senator from Rhode Island. He hated Fogarty; Fogarty hated his guts. They tried to outdo each other on grant announcements. A couple of times Chaffee got leaks from somewhere and announced OEO approval of such and such a grant. It was awfully difficult to prevent a governor—or his staff—from using his political muscle to get that kind of information from the regional level.

Fogarty would call me and say, "Hey, we got to figure a way to work this so I can get some credit out of this program. Hell, I'm doing all this work for you up here."

He loved to play golf and was pretty good. Representative Hugh Carey (who was on the authorizing committee), Chuck Roche (who was on the White House liaison staff then), John Fogarty, and I were having lunch at the Democratic Club one day. It was a day the House wasn't in session, a beautiful day. Fogarty said to Carey, "Let's go out to Burning Tree and play some golf. Roche here has got the White House limousine; he can take us out." Roche says, "The hell with that! If I'm going out, I'm going to play!" So they said to me, "Do you play?" I said, "Yes, jeez, but I don't have my gear; I don't have my clubs; I don't have my shoes; I don't have anything here." Fogarty said, "Well, that's all right. We can borrow some out there." So we all got into the White House limousine, and we went out to Burning Tree Country Club to play golf.

What makes the story so funny—it's a true story—is that a couple of days before, Shriver was telling me about an experience he had with Fogarty when he was director of the Peace Corps. Fogarty was appointed to the conference committee on the Peace Corps appropriation that year. He said, "[Fogarty] called me, and I tried to return his call, but there was no answer; it was in the evening. The next morning I had a speech to give somewhere, and I didn't get back to him. The next afternoon he called me and said, "Shriver, I tell you, not returning my phone call cost you $100 million in your appropriation, because I wanted to discuss an amendment that was being offered to cut it. You didn't feel that it was important enough to call me back, so the hell with you!" And he hung up on him. Sure enough, Fogarty cut $100 million out of the bill.

Carey and I were a twosome, and Chuck Roche and Fogarty were a twosome, and we had a few bucks' bet. The score was close; Carey and I were maybe one stroke up on them on the last hole, and we chipped up onto the green. We were all on in two; it was a par-four hole. I was about twenty feet away, and the others were a bit closer. I putted about two feet short and had that for my par. Roche hit by the hole. In other words, one short putt to go. If I sink this putt, we keep our one-stroke lead and we've won. Maybe we would have won fifteen bucks. We had a dollar bet a hole, or something like that. As I'm lining the putt up, Fogarty says, "Just a minute, Bill. I tell you what, let's make a side bet on this putt. If you guys win, I'll see to it that you get an extra $50 million in your OEO appropriation. If you miss it, it's going to cost you fifty." Hell! I know he means it because of the story Shriver had told me about the missed phone call and the Peace Corps appropriation. I said, "Come on, John, you're kidding." He said, "No, I'm not kidding." I missed the putt. It lipped the cup. Just thinking about it, I start to shake. John laughed. We went back to the clubhouse and had dinner and went home. It was a very pleasant afternoon.

The next morning I went into Shriver's office, and I said, "Sarge, I got some bad news." He said, "What's that?" I said, "I had a hell of a good day with

Fogarty yesterday. We played some golf. I think they're going to mark up the appropriations bill week after next. The bad news is he bet me $50 million on our appropriation on the last putt, and I missed it." It's one of the funniest things that ever happened to me. I told him the whole story. Sarge said, "Was he serious? Was he serious?" I said, "You know how serious he is. Of course, he was serious." He said, "Well, hell, how could you miss a damn putt that short?" He was mad as hell.

Fogarty and I spent a lot of time together in the next several weeks; this was coming toward the end of September and into October, when the Labor-HEW appropriation bill was coming up. One day he called me and said, "I've got a delegation of building trades people in town from my district. They're protesting one of the OEO grants at home—training young kids to be bricklayers—they feel is unfairly competing with the building trades apprenticeship program." It was very touchy, because Fogarty was a bricklayer. This was his union. These were his people. He said, "They're mad at me. You've got to bail me out." So he set up a meeting on a Saturday morning in his office.

There were about twenty in the delegation. He asked me to talk to them and explain this program and why it was necessary. I got briefed on it and found out who was involved and what was going to happen to these kids that were going to be trained. They weren't to be trained for bricklayer jobs in that area, but trained in such skills so that they could be hired by corporations who were doing that kind of work in other areas. I explained the program at the meeting and said some nice things about John's valuable role in the OEO program and what a great congressman he was. Everybody left happy, he smiled, and everything was great. Once in a while I had those kind of requests, not just from Fogarty but from other members. Just to come in, talk to constituents, and bail them out.

Did you get your $50 million back?

PHILLIPS: I'm getting to that. As I recall the figures, the House passed a [$] 1.5 [billion] authorization. There was a cutback from the original $1.75 billion requested because of escalating costs. The Senate had voted a $1.7 billion authorization. The conference committee was a very large committee—twenty-some members from the House and Senate. Out of those twenty-two—I think is the number— only five members of the conference committee had voted for the authorization bill in the House or Senate. Seventeen of the people voted against the authorization bill who were on the conference committee for our OEO money.

We were all very much concerned. Shriver and I had discussed the problem with Fogarty, and [George] McCarthy had some talks with Clark, Mansfield, and others on the Senate side. We did what we could. I remember waiting for Fogarty in the bar at the Democratic Club while the conference committee was meeting. He finally came in with a big smile on his face. I said, "How bad was it?" Just to split the difference between the two versions—$1.6 billion—would have been a miracle, because we didn't have the votes. But because of the controversial nature of the program, and the fact that seventeen out of twenty-two House and Senate conferees had voted against the authorization, we could have ended up with a lot less than that. We could have ended up with the $1.5 billion House figure, which would have been a disaster. It would have required a tremendous series of cutbacks in almost every program area. Fogarty said, "Well, you got your $50 million. I got you $1,625 billion."[5] It was a miracle to do better than a split with those kinds of odds against you. I said, "Gosh, John, how did you do it? How in the hell could you get these guys to vote $250 million more than half the difference when most voted against the authorization bill?" He just said, "I traded a few things." But that's Fogarty. So I bought him a drink, and that was it. He never told me what happened.

THE 1967 LEGISLATIVE BATTLE

PHILLIPS: Many of the programs were popular here on Capitol Hill. But there was an overall concerted attack on OEO by the Republican task force of the House Republican conference. Two Republican members were named in 1966 to cochair the antipoverty task force: Congressman Al Quie of Minnesota and Charles Goodell of New York. They were taking a hard-nose Republican policy line, which was to terminate most and to spin off some OEO programs like Head Start into established departments. Of course, our counterargument was that if you spin off the programs into the old bureaucracy, the innovative quality will be lost and they would be absorbed into the old bureaucracy, never to see the light of day and never to be effective. We argued that the reason OEO could be effective was that it could be creative, innovative, [that it] dared to do something differently than the old bureaucracy chose to do it.

H. Barefoot Sanders, as legislative counsel to the president during 1967–1969, worked with Congress during the last two years of the Johnson administration. Born in Dallas in 1925, Sanders earned undergraduate and law degrees from the University of Texas. He served as a United States attorney for the northern district of Texas in 1961–1965, and then joined the staff of the attorney general before moving to the White House.

SANDERS: The problem with the poverty bill initially was twofold: whether or not the Republicans were going to succeed in their effort to splinter off some parts of the poverty program from OEO—Head Start, the Job Corps, as I remember. In addition to that, there was the question of money for the poverty program. In 1967 and 1968, in everything we did, money was a big, big factor! Because the Republicans, with the southerners, could control the purse. We could always start out with 145–150 votes in the House by knowing the White House position, give or take twenty on a particular issue. But the rest of them you had to pick up from the moderates, and then you moved into the southerners or the liberal Republicans. You had to get it from one way or the other. So there was a lot of backing and filling on that. The president sort of gave me a free hand as to how to work this out, and I worked pretty closely with Carl Perkins; and with [Carl] Albert [Oklahoma], with the Speaker. Phil Landrum was involved in it. Mrs. Green was on the other side of the thing, so I couldn't do very much with her, although she's very key on the Education [and Labor] Committee in the House. The remarkable thing that we were able to work out was that the Republican effort began to splinter off. It did not pick up a single Democratic vote on tellers [the unrecorded votes] in the House. They lost it flat. This was partly because of their own blunders.

For instance, they needed the southerners to do this, but their appeals to the southerners were completely the wrong way to go about it. For instance, they talked about the boll weevil bloc. Well, you know how that would go with the southerners. And they could not show that this was going to do any good for the southerners. Why should the southerners take Head Start and give it to the Office of Education when the South had been having so much trouble with the Office of Education? This was one of my chief talking points. Why take the Job Corps and put it over to the Labor Department, where some areas were having trouble with segregation and the civil rights attitude of the Labor Department? So the only way they could come at them was on money. Well, without ever saying so, I always tried to let it be understood that we would take a reasonable cut on the authorization and not fight it, and I didn't fight it. And on the recommit motion ["recommit" is a device often used to kill legislation by returning it to committee], which was the final tie-up, they cut the bill $400 million; that's about a twenty percent cut. But I could stand that, because I knew we'd get some of it back in the Senate, as wc did—nearly $200 million, and the authorization is always above the appropriation anyway.

I've seen the Green Amendment interpreted in two different ways. One is that it saved OEO in 1967.

D. Baker: Well, I think in a sense it did. The fact of the matter is, OEO was probably in as much trouble in January of 1967 as it was in June or July—at least that was my perception. I remember writing a memorandum to Sarge to give to Larry O'Brien and Califano, arguing that the OEO legislation ought to be taken up as late in the year as possible. There had already begun some criticism of Lyndon Johnson on the part of the Democrats, who were getting very hysterical after the elections of '66 and not deciding whether they were going to be with Lyndon or not. And I argued—I guess erroneously, as it now turns out—that as 1967 came to an end there were going to be more of those guys coming to their senses and realizing that, whether they liked Lyndon Johnson or not, they were going to have to run with him, and they would be much more apt to be with his program. I had a whole series of political arguments that in my mind argued for a later rather than an earlier consideration.

I don't remember when it was in 1967, but another thing I did was give Sarge a memorandum in which I urged him that we really ought to have something like the Green Amendment. The legislation was not going to pass without something like that. The proposal I put to him involved a series of steps using the Council on Intergovernmental Relations to develop a model state law. One of the problems with community action in the public body has been the state law on constitutional division. I contemplated an amendment that would have let that agency work on it for a year or two and giv[en] us time for a transition. But my recommendation, which was all in oral form—it was never in draft form— was entirely consistent with what came out in the Green Amendment. To anybody who understood the House of Representatives, it was clear that between the absolute enemies of the program and some who were fairly favorably disposed to it but who were more public agency-minded, and some who were genuinely concerned about the establishment of this new political entity (as they saw it, who never stood for election and were responsible to nobody and yet had all this federal money to spend)—to many members of the House this was a very disturbing and stressful concept. A lot of these guys are lawyers, and they like neat and orderly things with responsibility and power going hand in hand. It was just quite evident that something was going to have to take place to put a new face on community action and to make it either actually or apparently more responsible, and "more responsible" meant tying it closer to state and local government than it had been, either really or apparently.

HARDING: The Green Amendment was a conscious effort on the part of this agency and friends of this agency to satisfy some very, very negative attitudes, particularly among southern members of the House, to the end that it was felt that unless some sort of compromise was put into the bill, it would never pass, and this agency would have come to a screeching halt on June 30, 1967, when our authorization expired. So this was done knowingly, albeit somewhat surreptitiously, to work out a basis and accommodation with those people that would allow them to vote for the continuation of the agency and the programs.

D. BAKER: Goodell's gripe was that we were winning, that we won—that's his big gripe. And he lost. He not only lost; he caught a lot of hell in doing so. He had an extremely critical editorial in the *New York Times*, which criticized in effect not only his judgment but his duplicity and the way he and Quie and those guys had tried to undermine the program.[6] And he was stung by the defeat. He thought he was going to win!

He could have been bought off. I sat down at a cocktail party or a dinner with him and Quie and Bert Harding early in 1967, at a very clandestine and quietly arranged dinner where we discussed what their price would be. And the fact of the matter is, their price was just about what we got in the House. "Spin off everything, and we'll let the programs go on."

And yet Goodell seems to be the big champion of community action—"Don't put it in the hands of the mayors!" Does he take that position because they're Democratic mayors and he's a Republican?

D. BAKER: No. He was "put it in the hands of the poor," but he divined that there was a great deal of antipathy to this participation of the poor and what he perceived as the revolutionary aspect and militant aspect of community action. And he played on this, thinking that there would be a backlash, particularly on the part of the southerners. Now, where he lost was with the South. He played to the South. He figured basically he would get his votes for his point of view from the majority of the Republicans—the middle and right wing of the Republican Party, all the Dixiecrats. He was trying all throughout to maximize the "maximum [feasible] participation" and to maximize those elements of the program that would have been most objectionable to the relatively conservative people and the big-city guys—the machine guys. It was a good strategy. I would have done it the same way.

But Goodell would have been held accountable for it, wouldn't he?

D. BAKER: Well, you've got to consider [that] in 1967 he didn't know Bobby Kennedy was going to get shot. He thought he would be a conservative congressman probably for the rest of his life. He made liberal noises, but if you go back and look at Goodell's record, he was anything but a liberal guy. He talked as a liberal, but he led some of the most conservative reactionary fights that were led in the House of Representatives, and he was tremendously effective.

Goodell has always been very difficult for me to understand. I have read that into his record, but you recall that at the time of the Green Amendment he used the phrase "the bosses and boll weevils."

D. BAKER: At that time he was so absolutely furious and hysterical that he made a very serious mistake in judgment. Just as he was playing to try to make this thing appear as ultraliberal so as to alienate the southerners, so Perkins and Green and the rest of us were trying to make it palatable to those guys. His strategy was to make the thing in its totality objectionable to as many of those people as he could. Then what he wanted to do—it was going to be very difficult for a lot of people to vote for killing Head Start, for killing the Job Corps, for killing Upward Bound. Some of these guys had interests in programs, so his idea was to spin them off. And he divined, at the time he made the "bosses and boll weevils" speech, that we were beating him at his own game. Essentially, we adopted the same strategy he did, only it was in reverse. We ended up getting the southerners on the tellers. William Jennings Bryan Dorn [of South Carolina] and Joe Waggonner down in Louisiana led their colleagues, along with two or three of the others, along with us on the tellers and most of the teller vote. Very few times did they vote against us. They were voting with Carl Perkins the chairman, and with Carl Perkins the southerner. Then came the record votes, and there were too many Republicans that couldn't stand the heat of voting against Head Start, so they turned around and voted for us while the boll weevils were voting against us. And that's exactly the way it was planned.

KELLY: Party loyalty is a very fuzzy thing. In the 1967 legislative cycle, it was awfully important for us to get some southerners to stay with us, particularly in the teller votes on the floor on amendments. We didn't expect that they were going to vote for us on final passage except in the exceptional instance. We had to come up with an extraordinary way to lobby them. You have to find out what they don't like. One of the things in 1967 that we were up against was the whole business of spin-off. They were going to take programs out of OEO and put them in HEW. I suppose the one that was in greatest danger, because it was the most popular and HEW wanted it, was Head Start. Now, it was very important for us, because it was obvious that a number of amendments would be introduced on the floor—even though we beat the ones that were introduced in committee— and we had to have the southerners go with us.

So what we really did was say to the southerners: "Do you want this program to go to the Office of Education?" Their feelings about the Office of Education and the whole business of desegregation and guidelines and all of the issues that remain even to this day—unfortunately, but they're there—they were so embittered about that that their reaction was, "No, we don't want it to go to the Office of Education, and we'll vote against that. Even though we won't vote for the program on final passage, we'll vote against its being put in the Office of Education."

I can remember the night that we sat around in this room, two or three of us, and wrote what is now the famous Congressman Joe Waggonner speech, Waggonner being from Louisiana. The speech will always be remembered by the line that said, "I don't want OEO broken up. I want to keep that trash in one pile."[7] That speech, of course, coalesced the South. It was a speech that was very beneficial to us, because the Republicans couldn't break up OEO because the southerners went with us because they wanted to "keep that trash all in one pile." I often walk through the Capitol building at the height of the tourist season and say, "My God, Americans, you don't know how your government is really run!"

MCCARTHY: In the Senate they were really working to spin off Head Start. I remember I went to Senator [James] Eastland of Mississippi. I got along with him pretty good. Poor old Doc [Harold] Howe then was head of the Office of Education. Doc Howe was a red flag to the southerners. So I went in to see old Eastland. He had some problems that I got on his phone and took care of them, down in Mississippi. He said, "Is there anything else you want to talk to me about, George?" I said, "Yes, Senator; there's going to be an amendment coming up." He said, "An amendment on OEO! You know I can't help you on that OEO business. I can't support that program." I said, "I know that, Senator. I'm not asking you to vote for OEO. What I'm doing is asking you to stop a part of the program from being administered by Doc Howe." He said, "By who?" I said, "Well, they want to transfer a good portion of the program over to Howe's administration." "George, I wouldn't vote to give a red turd to Doc Howe. When is that amendment coming up?" I said, "I don't know whether it's going to be today or tomorrow." He said, "Well, I tell you what you do, George. You watch, and when that amendment is coming up, you call me, because I want to be on the floor to vote against that amendment, and I'm going to get all my southern friends to vote with me."

THE EMERGENCE OF CARL PERKINS

Could you remark on the effectiveness or usefulness of Adam Clayton Powell as opposed to Carl Perkins?

D. BAKER: Well, I think there's no comparison, in a sense. Perkins was far more sensitive to the House of Representatives as an institution and had an instinctive feel for what was necessary to get bills enacted. Powell flouted the House. Whereas he, for reasons best known to himself, did things to infuriate his colleagues, Perkins always went out of his way to placate and ingratiate them. Needless to say, Perkins was absolutely essential to the strategy that was being used in the 1967 fight. His relationships with the "establishment" of the House—the big-city members and more particularly with the southerners—made it possible for him to get teller votes or to avoid negative tellers by encouraging members to be absent and not to vote against him. He was able to do this in a way Adam Powell never could have. Powell is, or at least was, a much more intelligent man than Perkins. I think Powell, as a matter of fact, in his best days probably was one of the most brilliant guys in the House, however much he may have wasted his talents.

When Perkins came in, it was an entirely different operation, and we were a little concerned. He's sort of a countrified gentleman who doesn't seem to have a hell of a lot of energy and doesn't seem to be too bright, talks a bit like a hick. The fact of the matter is, he's one of the most sagacious old gentlemen in the House of Representatives, who sometimes when he appears to be playing some childish games has really got something under way. And I've watched his staff grow in amazement over time as they've come to perceive that some peculiar thing that they've been laughing up their sleeve about him doing for the last two years is really part of a large tactical problem that he's interested in.

He was interested in the poverty program. His greatest concern in life is that of the poor people of eastern Kentucky; and next to them, the poor people of the state of Kentucky; and beyond that, the poor people of the rest of the country. He's really a very humane and decent sort of guy who wants to get things done. And he took great advantage of the fact that he was a chairman and that he was a southerner to really court—he really did—the southerners. On any pretext whatsoever that he could try to win them to his position, he did so. He involved them in a wide variety of ways in the process. He's a next-door neighbor to William Jennings Bryan Dorn. We had a number of meetings in William Jennings Bryan Dorn's office. Normally, Mr. Perkins used to call these meetings in Dorn's office because Mrs. Green was always going by his office and seeing him coming out of his office—or somebody like Shriver or me or O'Hara or Thompson or somebody coming out of his office—and she was very jealous that she hadn't been called to the meetings and all of this business. And she was trying to find out what was going on. He used to hold meetings in William Jennings Bryan Dorn's office, pleading with Dorn that he had to escape Mrs. Green. But I always had a sneaking suspicion that he was sort of enveloping William Jennings Bryan Dorn and getting him committed to Carl Perkins and this operation of trying to save the poverty program.

The fact of the matter is, nobody with any responsibility or knowledge, sophistication, in the House of Representatives expected the '67 bill to pass. Carl Albert told Sarge Shriver and me a week before the bill went to the floor that he just didn't see the votes; and when we showed him a list of our canvass, he just went down the list ticking off the ones that he doubted. I think it was the Friday before the bill was taken up in the House of Representatives, I was in the Speaker's office. The Speaker was talking about, "Isn't there some deal we can make with Goodell and Quie? We can't possibly pass that bill." And everybody was telling Perkins, "You can't do it." But he decided to fight it out on those grounds, and fight it out he did, and he came off. Well, you know he grew somewhat in his own estimation, as well as everybody else's estimation, with that singular victory. I think as far as legislative victories in '67, there were no more greater victories, at least based on people's expectations. He did a great job. He became a chairman in his own mind and in the minds of some of his committee people and others around the Hill.

THE HARDING NOMINATION

PERRIN: The president finally submitted [Bertrand] Harding's name to the Congress and nominated him for director. Bert had a lot to do with the fact that I was, shortly, then nominated for deputy director. Unfortunately, confirmation never came about, as I'm acutely aware of today. When we got our first paychecks under the new pay raise, [I discovered] that I'm earning now $192 a week less than I would be earning if I had been confirmed as deputy director, so it's a very real problem.

The nomination got snarled up basically with politics, the congressional situation. It's hard to tell precisely what motivates people in these situations. I guess you can point to certain things. One was the fact that at that moment Senator Dominick had chosen to introduce an amendment to the Vocational Education Bill, of all things, to transfer Head Start to the Office of Education.[8] And it passed the Senate through some freak maneuver, without hearings—it was a floor amendment. Senator Morse, who was floor-managing the bill in the Senate, went along with it, and we could only assume that he had a quid pro quo in there someplace. He was quite concerned about some kind of Japanese log bill that was affecting the state of Oregon, and he was trying to get votes for it in the Senate. In any event, after taking a look at this surprise amendment, our people quickly discovered many flaws in it that would have been very catastrophic to the Head Start program had it passed.

These matters are always taken very emotionally by our employees, and we found that one thing that we should do as soon as we can is reassure them on matters on where the leadership of the agency stands. In this case, we put out this memorandum, which Morse took violent exception to and got up on the floor of the Senate and castigated Harding personally and vowed that he would fight him to the death and all of these wild statements that only Wayne Morse can make.[9] I've heard them over the years, heard him stand up there and accuse the president of the United States of treason. These kinds of things begin to bother you after a while. But he took this on as a personal fight against Harding. Obviously, he was going to attack Harding in this fashion; and that meant that there wasn't any place for me to go, because Harding was occupying the deputy director's slot, and I could hardly be confirmed, despite the fact that I had a number of friends in the Senate and I was under no personal attack.

OEO'S LOBBYING EFFORT

HARDING: Certainly not to my knowledge have we engaged in any illegal lobbying activities. There has been developed within the general confines of this program a large number of civilian outside groups—the women, the churches, the labor unions, others who are interested in this program. They are related to us through advisory commissions generally. These people have a very deep and a very personal interest in the program. When anything happens that is adverse to the program, they mount the podium and start writing letters and attempt to influence the Congress. I don't think this is an illegal activity. The only illegal activity that I know of was: one young, ill-advised staff member at one point sent a wire to a mayor asking him to make some sort of intercession, and this was an improper action. But I think the reason for the allegations is that we do have a well-developed clientele that react rather rapidly in most situations.

As I recall, the Goodell objection was not illegal lobbying, but just the fact that Shriver undertook sort of a personal public relations effort—and a rather tremendous one, as a matter of fact—in connection with getting the authorization bill passed.

Over 100 witnesses testified.

HARDING: Yes. And Shriver was bombarding the Congress and everybody else with information—positive information—about the program. And Goodell resented this. I'm very fond of the senator from New York, but I think his problem was that he had been attacking this agency, and when Mr. Shriver, very properly in his administrative capacity, started a counterattack, Mr. Goodell and Mr. Quie didn't like it. There was nothing illegal about it, and in my view, [it] does not constitute lobbying. It constitutes normal PR activity of a federal agency. And Shriver was undoubtedly one of the best instruments in carrying on a program of that sort that I've ever known.

16

OEO'S STRUGGLE TO ENDURE

LYNDON JOHNSON OBVIOUSLY *had mixed and sometimes contradictory feelings about the War on Poverty. Since he intended the War on Poverty to be a "hand up" rather than a "handout," reports of graft and financial mismanagement deeply offended him. Although he envisioned a reenactment of his New Deal experience, he understood that the grinding poverty of America's ghettos and rural areas would be resistant to Depression-era employment programs. Breaking the cycle of poverty required a comprehensive approach that would address health, education, housing, employment, and behavior. Beyond the War on Poverty, the Great Society's broad emphasis on each of these elements reflected Johnson's commitment to improving the lives of the poor.[1]*

As with the 1965 Voting Rights Act, Johnson recognized that political empowerment was the path to broader participation in the nation's prosperity. Given his political sophistication and his parallel efforts to expand the circle of democracy, it seems naive to suggest that he did not intend for the poor to have a greater voice in the political system. Yet when the beneficiaries of his efforts actually denounced the system instead of joining it, Johnson angrily disavowed the excesses of community action. He undoubtedly felt that their radicalism and the backlash it would arouse made it more difficult for him to achieve his liberal agenda.[2] Given the political controversy that surrounded OEO, it is remarkable that the president continued to back the program to the extent he did.

There was also a less substantive reason for Johnson's frustration with the program. As his rivalry with Robert Kennedy became more intense, the premium that the president had always placed on loyalty became even greater. Although Shriver himself was the epitome of loyalty to the president, Kennedy partisans were numerous in OEO.[3]

Yet if any one factor was responsible for Johnson's estrangement from the poverty program, it was the great distraction of his presidency—the war in Vietnam. As the war expanded in 1965 and 1966, consuming more and more of Johnson's time and the nation's resources, his domestic agenda, including the War on Poverty, became yet another of its casualties.[4]

OEO AND THE STATES

PERRIN: In 1967, when the president directed that a specific effort be made to improve relationships with the states, I was tapped by Sarge to go on some of these trips. At the beginning, they were going to go to about five or six states, that was all. As it turned out, they went to forty within the next year. So the success of the early trips, and the fact that many of the other governors that were being bypassed were complaining, led to the expansion of the program. So I went on about thirty of the trips. Fascinating experience; I enjoyed it. I saw so many state capitals that I can't pin one capital down to a specific state anymore. They all tended to blend. Like taking a European tour and seeing thirty countries in five days.

I talked mainly with governors and state officials, and we did not meet with mayors and county officials. The governors—certainly not all of them, but a number of them—were concerned about money coming into their states over which they had no real controls. And they indicated interest in distributing the money. Some of them, I'm sure, were sincere in this. Others saw this as a political weapon of considerable magnitude if they could determine where the funds went after they came into the state. I facetiously told a number of governors that they didn't know how well off they were in not having to answer for some of these programs that were being funded with antipoverty dollars.

But there was a great concern among some of the state officials, or at least those who operated the state economic opportunity offices, that they didn't have enough power, really, over the programs in their states. And I couldn't really argue with this too much, because they didn't have that power, and they weren't intended to have that power.

A lot of governors seemed to be at the mercy of their state economic opportunity director, at least in terms of what their knowledge of the program was. A number of governors showed really quite a lack of specific knowledge as to how all of this worked, and consequently, their contact with the program quite often was when the state OEO director brought to them the papers or the applications for them to sign, either vetoing or approving. In a couple of instances, I think we helped clear this up with the governor and made him more aware of the problem.

Has the governors' veto power been exercised very much?

PERRIN: Not as much as one would have assumed from all the hullabaloo over it. I don't have the figures now at my fingertips, but I think there probably have been less than fifty vetoes out of 30,000 applications of one kind or another. And of those vetoes, probably less than half were overturned, overridden by the director of OEO. So in practice, it has not been a serious break in our ability to proceed; nor has it given the governors a feeling that we would simply ride roughshod over them, because in quite a few cases we have accepted their veto or have altered the program to the extent necessary so that they would withdraw the veto. At one point, Governor Reagan of California was bragging about the number of vetoes that he had issued on our program, and we never considered that quite a proper contest for a governor to engage in.

THE ECONOMIC OPPORTUNITY COUNCIL (EOC)

PERRIN: The Economic Opportunity Council [EOC] and the director of OEO were to assist the president in coordinating all antipoverty efforts of the federal government. It was something of a dream world to begin with, because the council never had the specific power that is necessary to instruct or to insist upon coordinative mechanisms. Furthermore, we ran into internal political problems. The director of OEO was named by the law to be the chairman of the EOC, so this put a noncabinet member supposedly chairing a cabinet committee. This just doesn't work very well in Washington's scheme of things. The Economic Opportunity Council had its first meeting in December 1964, at which time, according to the minutes, President Johnson held that meeting in the White House and gave it a very ornate mandate to coordinate this and study that and advise him on the other thing. He called it his "Domestic National Security Council"—a lot of rhetoric like that, which never came to pass.

Sargent Shriver did as well, I guess, as he could as chairman, but we had no full-time staff. The staff, such as it was, was operated out of my old office of Interagency Relations. Shriver is not one who likes to plan ahead very far either, and we were invariably coming to the day before the EOC meeting with an agenda that had been prepared out of blood and sweat over the preceding few weeks. And it would be submitted to Sarge, and he would arbitrarily knock out items and substitute others on which absolutely no staff work had been done. So it was not an easy kind of a committee either to run or to staff.

Also, as time wore on, we began having trouble with attendance by the cabinet members. We always had members present. All the agencies were represented at every meeting, but we began to notice that the representation was getting down into the third and fourth levels of the agency hierarchies, and therefore there came a reluctance on the part of many of these individuals to actively participate in the discussions. They came primarily as observers and listened to others talk and didn't really enter into the swing of it.

We also had difficulty in getting the other members to bring problems to the council—which, of course, they were supposed to do under the original thought. This was not an OEO forum, although it was accused of that, really. I'm sure this was one of the problems. Of course, with the other members failing to bring problems to the council, OEO was then more and more required to devise the agenda, and then this simply seemed to encourage the others in believing that it was an OEO forum. So it was a round-robin affair that was very difficult to break. Specific requests to the other agencies to come up with ideas and thoughts for the council's agenda simply produced very little, almost nothing. I think one of the things that held the council together was Vice President Humphrey, because he, in his usual enthusiastic and energetic way, created a considerable spark of interest at the council meetings which he attended, and he attended most of them. He took this quite seriously.

So the conclusion that I came to was that the council simply could not continue to function as it was functioning, and consequently we proposed in 1967 that there be a significant change in the law to give it a different kind of a complexion. We had our last meeting in December 1967, which was the same month that we got our new amendments. I took that opportunity to simply stop further meetings. I suppose we could have continued under the old system, even though we had this new legislative design for the EOC, but I felt that we weren't getting anyplace with it and might as well stop. So I proposed to Shriver that we simply not have any more meetings, and he agreed. Then, as you know, President Johnson never did pick up that particular ball and re-create the Economic Opportunity Council, as it was restructured by the amendments.

What was the National Advisory Council?

PERRIN: The National Advisory Council also was created by the act to bring together, at a high level, citizens simply to serve as an advisory group for the director of OEO. It subsequently, through congressional action, was divorced from OEO and made an independent advisory group. So today, while we cooperate with it in terms of supplying information and attending meetings and generally have good relationships, we have nothing to do with the direction the council takes. It has its own staff that is not only outside of OEO but it's outside of the building altogether.

THE COMMUNITY REPRESENTATIVES ADVISORY COMMITTEE

BOOKBINDER: When involving the poor became a standard aspect of our program, I had the general assignment to mobilize the private sector and institute a series of advisory committees, so that through the advisory committees we could get different sectors involved—labor, industry, women, religious, and others. I suggested at one point, "Hey, we were saying that every community has to have a committee of poor people. Why don't we have a national advisory committee made of poor people so that poor people from different districts would also come together occasionally and exchange experiences and insights?" We called that the Community Representatives Advisory Committee (CRAC). We had some twenty or twenty-five people who were selected by as many local poverty programs as individuals who were showing a particular skill in articulating the needs of the poor and who were already involved, either as volunteers in their own programs or maybe even as paraprofessionals in some of the funded programs. I must tell you that psychologically, emotionally, for me it was the most gratifying thing that I did in the whole period, even though at this moment I can't think of a single idea or policy recommendation that emanated from that group that was of any lasting consequence. But the very fact of their involvement was for me personally a very gratifying thing. I think [it was] a very useful thing, too, to help set a tone to demonstrate our sincere commitment to the poor.

At the very first meeting of this group, we got this selection of people, and they came to Washington. Shriver opened the meeting and had to rush to the Hill on appropriations or something, and I remember I chaired the meeting that day. We said we'd start the meeting by just going around the room and asking each person to take five or ten minutes to give us just a quick picture of the community they came from and the nature of the problem. And we had all kinds. We had rural communities; big-city, ghetto, inner-city type of programs; Indian reservations; textile mills.

About the fourth or fifth person that I called was a Reverend Bread—I think Scott Bread was his name—an Indian living off the reservation. He took about ten minutes and described poverty in the Indian community that he knew. It was such an eloquent and moving account that when he got through, there was a stunned silence. Then I went to the next one. The next one was a rather older man from a New England textile village [where] the textile plant was shut down, and I thought he was going to describe that. Instead he said, "Mr. Bookbinder, I can tell you about my problems here, but we just heard the Reverend Bread tell about Indian poverty. I don't even want to tell you my story. I think we ought to take the rest of the day just to ask ourselves, 'What can we do about his problem?' Let's at least try to solve his problems."

MULTISERVICE CENTERS

GAITHER: The more we got into the problems of the poor, particularly the urban poor, the more apparent it became how difficult it was for them to travel—also for the elderly—and that federal agencies were putting their offices all over: a lot in cities, most of them in downtown locations, not near where the people lived. The president was making a speech about urban America and wanted some ideas in terms of things that he ought to say and new directions he ought to propose, and that was one of them.

Do you recall the genesis of the idea for the multiservice centers?

GAITHER: We had been working on it, trying to get some established. I have a feeling the idea was coming out of the Budget Bureau. I'm not sure of that. They were pushing to concentrate and coordinate delivery of services. It was kind of a big thing in those days to figure out how the hell you did it. My guess is that it was Larry Levinson who put in the president's speech, "We're going to establish twelve centers." So the president announced it.

We convened a meeting in Califano's office with the secretaries of HUD [Housing and Urban Development], Labor, HEW, and the director of OEO—I think it was those four—and basically gave them a memorandum to work it out with Budget Bureau participation, maybe somebody from the CEA [Council of Economic Advisers], and to come back with recommendations on how to implement it.

I received word about three months later that the task, which had been assigned to the undersecretaries and the deputy director of OEO, was hopelessly stalled, and that what they had agreed that day was that they were each going to have their multiservice center. HUD was going to have so many, and Labor was going to have so many, and the whole purpose seemed to have been defeated. Joe [Califano] called them all and asked them to all come into the White House—at the cabinet level, I think, without the undersecretaries—to discuss it. I think we got it back on track. But I'm not sure whether those centers were even established before we left or not.

It was another example of how difficult it is to get the agencies to work together. I think there were differences as to who paid the bills, what was in them, where they were to be located, what they were to do; and they finally just threw their hands up and said, "Well, we'll each do ours." It was really a kind of pathetic display. But I think it tells you something about the nature of the government that we have. Those departments are very independent, and they don't do an awful lot to help one another.

SPINNING OFF OEO PROGRAMS TO THE AGENCIES

Wilbur J. Cohen, a longtime expert on medical aid to the elderly, had helped draft the Social Security Act in 1934. His association with John Kennedy had begun in the mid-1950s while he was a professor of public welfare administration at the University of Michigan. When the Kennedy administration began to study the question of poverty, Wilbur Cohen was assistant secretary of HEW for legislation. He stayed in Washington through Johnson's presidency, becoming undersecretary in 1965 and secretary in 1968.

COHEN: There's a great deal to the point that when you've got some completely new ideas, they will go farther and faster in a new agency than in an old agency. I don't think that's because people don't want to carry out what the president wants done. It's [that] what the president is trying to do is still uncharted, as the poverty program was. And what you're doing is, you're being experimental and innovative—which requires a somewhat different mentality and experience than an old-line fellow, who can take something and make it work in a methodical way. And that's why I favor, when OEO programs are once determined and something has been worked out, transferring them to the old-line agency and keep[ing] OEO as a creative, innovative-type agency.

PERRIN: The resistance [in OEO to spinning off programs] is based on several reasons. One of the most popular and most visible reasons is that, if we spin off all our popular programs, we're left with nothing but trouble. If you take Head Start away, which has given OEO considerable protection over the years, and take away Legal Services and health centers and these good programs that conceivably could stand on their own if they were under someone else's tent today, you'd just leave OEO with the almost impossible political problem of running community action agencies. And this agency just couldn't survive if that were its only task.

The other reason that is more important to me is the assurance that programs will continue to be operated for the poor. And had a spin-off taken place early in the game, I'm quite convinced that that emphasis, that focus, would have been lost. We've always had to fight this tendency of our programs' becoming middle-class programs in getting away from the poorest of the poor. Had these programs gone to other agencies early in the game, I'm sure that would have taken place very rapidly.

There was also the community action agency linkage that we were quite concerned about. We had tried to build into every program that the CAA is the presumptive sponsor of this program. And until you get that well established, you're just courting disaster if you spin programs off too early. So I think we're at the stage where this can be done now. But again, you have to look at it in terms of what's left and what the justification is then for a continuation of an OEO.

HARDING: Sarge was very ambivalent about the whole question of delegation and spin-off. One of the first jobs that I had when I got here—and I've forgotten exactly how I happened to inherit it—but we were involved in the Title I, the manpower activities, and there had just been a mandate from the White House that the Department of Labor was to operate to the fullest extent possible all federal manpower programs. So I became the chief architect of building a delegation order with the Department of Labor.

I used to have constant trouble with Sarge about how far we'd go on this thing. And when I say he was ambivalent, I mean that he would constantly reiterate the fact that this agency was set up to innovate, to develop, to mature, and then to hand programs over to the existing agencies of government. The only problem was that in Sarge's mind these programs never really reached that point—or at least I felt and still feel that. He'd kill me if he ever thought I had characterized him as a bureaucrat, but he really was. It tore his soul out to take one of these pieces and give it away to somebody else. And Head Start was a classic example, because this was his prime creation; and whereas it had by this point in time, in my view, been quite well developed—it was one of the better-developed programs that we had, guidelines all issued, most of the decisions made, the mechanism set up, the funding level established; all these things had been met—it was ready to be administered by somebody else. But Sarge, no matter what he said, couldn't stand the thought of that program being taken away from OEO.

And let me say, it was not just emotional; it was very political. He felt, and I think with a great deal of justification, that a program like Head Start constituted a shield for the agency against all of the other problems that we would get into with VISTA volunteers leading hunger strikes and Job Corps kids tearing up the dormitories and so forth—all the adverse things.

LBJ ON SPIN-OFF

Although Johnson understood that keeping the Office of Economic Opportunity intact was the best way to protect its more controversial components, he also considered spinning off the agency's programs to reduce the political heat they generated.

LBJ's conversation with Roy Wilkins, January 5, 1966[5]

JOHNSON: ...I have a task force report. It is rather an exceptional report. One thing it recommends is that we take Community Action and put it in HUD. I think that normally that would be reasonably good. The task force was all of them for doing that except two; Kermit Gordon wasn't and Whitney Young wasn't. But this fellow Robert Woods of Harvard [and] MIT, he headed it up.... He's exceptionally able. He has done an outstanding job.... [They recommend it] on the theory that the city is where the problem is and we have to have some muscle in the city cabinet agency and that is where the Community Action is and that's where it ought to be run.... I think it makes a very convincing argument, but I can't quite buy it now purely on the basis of politics. I think if we spread it out among the different cabinet offices where we don't have one salesman at the top of it that we (a) don't get the image and (b) we knock it off and (c) they can defeat it easier and can kill it easier. I think in due time we might do that, but I am a little afraid to do it now. I'm going to be a little bit different. Do you have any reaction on that?

WILKINS: My reaction has never been very strong on that, on the transfer of Community Action, that is, from the poverty program over to HUD.

JOHNSON: That is right. What they'd do is reorganize poverty out of existence. You would give Wirtz the Neighborhood Youth Corps and the Job Corps. You would give [John] Gardner the Head Start and educational angles.

WILKINS: That Head Start, Mr. President, is a ten-strike. I wonder if you thought about it or who thought of it.

JOHNSON: Oh, it's wonderful. It's the best thing we've got.

WILKINS: It's absolutely wonderful.

JOHNSON: No, I am not entitled to credit for it, although I have supported it, and Mrs. Johnson has supported it. We are very strong for it. We're crazy about it.

LBJ's conversation with Wilbur Mills, November 12, 1966[6]

JOHNSON: ... down in our country, the poverty thing didn't look as good as some things. I've been giving a good deal of thought to putting it in the old line agencies and cut it out of an independent outfit. Then I don't think there would be so much hell-raising. I get pretty good compliments from the manpower retraining and vocational education that Wirtz is doing with his program, but I get a lot of hell on poverty.

LBJ's conversation with Charles Schultze, December 30, 1966[7]

JOHNSON: [Shriver] says his big problem is delegating something to Labor or HEW, and his own people say, "You took that away from us." They want that gravy. And he doesn't want to hold both of those jobs, operate one and coordinate the other. I told him that what I thought we ought to do is to have the Budget director himself coordinate, and when we get the funds, allocate [them] from the Executive Office of the President, kind of along the lines that Heineman recommends and kind of along the lines that he recommends—allocate these funds that Congress appropriates; and that for him then to administer the War on Poverty, the stuff that's not allocated, if he doesn't want to coordinate it and allocate it too. I would do both for the balance of the year. Where the good programs—Head Start or others that are popular—could be absorbed, I'd have some other agency absorb them. I'd take on the new things. But he doesn't want to do that.

THE WHITE HOUSE AND OEO

GAITHER: What I saw in two and a half years of handling the White House side of the War on Poverty was that the president favored it largely because of his instincts for opportunity as contrasted with handouts. He was very strongly anti-welfare-type programs, and OEO kind of came at the problems of the poor in terms of opportunity. The president always seemed very supportive of that.

On the other hand, he was hit almost from inception with enormous problems, problems of really any program designed to help a small segment of our country. The fact is, this was not like an education program where seventy percent of the American people benefited. This was really designed to help those who couldn't very well help themselves, who had no political clout. And as a result, it and the nature of its programs caused a lot of problems. This is not unusual.

In terms of what he did, one, there were a lot of people in the Executive Office, even the president himself, who spent an awful lot of time fighting for the poverty program, keeping it alive. I think without his support it never would have survived during that period. Would he take on every one of the political problems? Clearly not. Did he like some of the trouble? Clearly not. And we worked very hard to bring more accountability to the program as it got off the ground. We worked very hard with Shriver and Harding and the others to make it a better program and to come to grips with some of the things that were causing political problems. Through the president and his staff, there was a great deal of support for the program, not in the sense of saying that fraud or political problems at the local level are excusable and understandable, but rather to take the strengths of the program and build on them and try to make something out of it.

[The president] absorbed political heat from start to finish to protect the poverty program. There's no doubt about it. He did for Title I [of ESEA]. Those two programs, without him being willing to take the heat and fight like hell for them, would have died the first year. There's no doubt about it. Those votes were very close. Shriver was on the Hill almost daily. At the outset, the other departments and agencies were trying to tear it apart and get hold of the money themselves. At one point we put together the administration's position with respect to OEO and asked all of the cabinet officers to come over and talk about it and accept that as their position and to quit having their people go up in the Congress trying to tear OEO apart. There was an enormous change. We used to have on any given day about five people working the Hill against OEO. There are still some cabinet officers who were very upset with me.

If all of the programs had been labeled by what they were doing, I don't think we would have had such a political problem as we had with the poverty program. Because we didn't have any problem with Head Start or Upward Bound or VISTA; where we had it was in something labeled "community action." The problem was that nobody ever knew what that meant. We didn't have a problem with Neighborhood Youth Corps or anything like that. But what was community action? And an awful lot of people, particularly the more conservative, felt that community action meant community disruption.

I'm sure some people had the sense of a takeover.

GAITHER: Oh, there's no question. That label was just dynamite. And if we hadn't had that problem, I don't think it would have been nearly that severe. But I'm quite confident that the president knew the importance of that program, particularly the flexibility that he had under the poverty program to do things that needed to be done, and the tremendous accomplishments. There's no question [the poverty program] had some impact on militancy and community disruption, but on the other hand, the changes that it was bringing about indirectly through its impact on other agencies of the government [were also indisputable]. Despite all of the pressure from the White House, the poverty program did more to turn the Labor Department around from an organization that served the high school graduate son of the union man to minorities who were disadvantaged; the same thing in student aid and HEW; the same thing in the Office of Education, and indeed in the country. In 1963 "preschool education" was a very dirty word in the educational community. After Head Start, the school systems wanted preschool education, and they wanted to take over Head Start. Now, the president wouldn't give up any of that; I'm sure he would have liked to have shed himself of some of the political problems, but some of them were problems that you have to tolerate.

E. Cahn: Johnson understood that when he started this thing off and didn't hand it over to any department and set it up in the Executive Office, he was raising hell. He really understood that. He was conscious of the fact that by giving it to nobody, he was in effect setting in motion a catalyst. In effect, he was telling his cabinet members, "Play ball," and he was giving Shriver cabinet rank. Nobody liked that, and he understood that.

I was at one of the legislative meetings at the White House where he talked about that. It may have been a signing ceremony for the act. I just know that it was early on in the program, and he was very explicit, just in a very magnetic way. He talked about himself as a rural teacher. He talked about how people were sort of dropping between the cracks, that they weren't being reached, and that he knew that as a rural teacher. And that somehow something had to be done, and it wasn't being done in any of the established systems that were set up. You get impressed when you go in the White House and you see the president. He was in an expansive mood, and he was magnetic. All I can say is, it made me feel that he knew enough about what he was getting into, that we were consistent with the spirit of that mission even though we were going to raise hell and he wasn't going to like it, and we were all going to catch hell. But that was what we were supposed to do. He didn't want to hear about it particularly anymore, because the more he heard about it, the more he would have to deal with it.

Shriver: Lyndon Johnson never, never, never uttered a word of criticism to me about OEO, never. And let me tell you, he took heat! He took a lot of stuff from John Connally. John Connally would come up here when he was governor of Texas and spend the night at the White House, and he would pump Lyndon Johnson full of stuff about all the junk we were doing that was wrong. And he took a lot of heat from other politicians. But I know I would remember if the president ever called me to complain; *he never did*. I was hesitating for a second to try to recall whether anybody on his staff ever called, and I can't remember anybody over there ever calling and complaining to me about what we did.

Could the White House staff have softened the blows that seemed about to come in?

KRAMER: I think that while Moyers was over there, Moyers was able to soften these blows to some extent. I think when Moyers left, there was nobody. Califano was ostensibly the person who was the champion of this program; and as a matter of fact, in our fourth or fifth press seminar, when there were vast and hard-line rumors that OEO was going to be cut apart by the president, Califano even went so far as to come over to this agency and speak to the press and answer questions and deny that this was being done, which was an unprecedented move. Jim Gaither, Califano's assistant, I worked with in the preparation of presidential messages and statements about poverty. But on the whole, I did not feel that there was anybody at the White House who really supported this program, who really understood it and was really trying to speak up for it in the highest councils.

This agency attracted people who were ardent enthusiasts and supporters of its social theories and who didn't feel loyalty to the president above their commitment to their social theories. When I came down here, this place was a sieve. Nothing could be kept a secret, even things which rightfully should have been kept secret. There was no such thing as an internal memorandum; there was no such thing as loyalty. Everybody had his own line to some reporter, and that's the way things were being done here. And the president would get furious when stories would be leaked around him of things that he knew nothing about. Now, this does not mean that the president was right in the kind of almost fanatic watchfulness he kept on the news ticker. I think Mr. Nixon has done a very wise thing in getting the ticker out of his office. The president would watch this thing like a hawk, and if something came over the ticker that he didn't like, bang! He'd be on the telephone to Shriver or to somebody else in the agency to get a story out, to get a story squashed, to get things corrected. I don't think that has to exist that way.

PERRIN: Certainly Vietnam was not a popular subject around OEO. On the other hand, most of us realized that we owed the existence of the agency to President Johnson, and there wasn't much point in attacking him—because, for all the faults, he nevertheless was the chief political backer of this program. Once he withdrew that backing, we were dead. After he withdrew from the campaign, we went into a certain state of limbo which we have never emerged from yet. We didn't look to him as our supporter particularly, although he certainly was in a position to influence matters. We still had to get our appropriations, and we had a new budget that he was submitting, so he had many opportunities to cause the program serious damage if that had been his desire. But that's a negative way of looking at it. Positively, we weren't looking to him for a great deal of support from then on.

I think his desire to help people was what got him into this. I think he was somewhat chagrined to find what he had done and was disturbed by some of the problems that arose in carrying out this program. Yet every time the chips were down, he was usually there. But he had a rather schizophrenic attitude toward us, I think. He loved us and he was repelled by us at the same time. I just don't know what went on in his mind. He was a very strange man. I was recalling his demand for loyalty—demand of his people for loyalty to the president. I was the recipient of this on two occasions. Once, when I first came to OEO, I was called over for the Marvin Watson treatment, at which time it was explained how important it was for members of the president's executive staff throughout the government to be loyal to what he holds dear, so I accepted that all right. But then the next time I was called over there was to be told of my nomination as deputy director, and I was questioned at some length as to the attitudes of people in the agency on Vietnam.

MAY: I knew that the president was talking to Sarge about various things and about various problems; and later on, when I had the job as deputy director to VISTA and then later in the inspector general's position, I was aware that the president was aware of our problems. What impressed me was the fact that he continued to support us when he knew our problems. Our problems were that we were a political liability. The older we got, the worse we were politically, because they began to understand what the hell we were really about, and what we were about was to make change. And the one thing that scares the living hell out of a politician, whether he's a state representative in little Vermont or in Texas or anyplace else, is a lot of unknowns...change. Then these crazy bastards were going to go around and register people to vote? Oh, my God! I think it was after the first year, second year out, [Congress] prohibited us from doing that.

They began to understand what the hell we were about. What came clear [was] that poverty isn't something that they measure in an emergency room and say, "Hey, brother, you got 104 degrees in poverty. Take two pills every hour and it'll go away." Poverty is caused by some of the very institutions that we were trading with. Education, school system. Once that "maximum feasible participation" phrase came into play, we uncovered a whole host of very bright poor people. They said exactly that. They said, "Hey, man, the school system doesn't work." That didn't get you any points with the local establishment, and all of that negativism piled up.

Lyndon Johnson had every opportunity to say, hey, I'm backing away, but he didn't. That's why I'm frankly an unabashed Lyndon Johnson fan. When the heat was on, when we were really no good politically—I don't think we were ever any real positive use for political purposes—but when it was clear that we were a political liability, Lyndon Johnson hung in there, because what we were doing was right.

SCHULTZE: [President Johnson] was all for doing a lot of things for the deserving poor. Of course, one of our major problems was: What do you do about the undeserving poor? That he was much less sympathetic about. So one of the characteristics of the Johnson administration—and [there are] all sorts of paradoxes—[is that] on the one hand you might say he is the last New Dealer, in the sense that he would do anything to feed kids: [that he is] for children, number one, and for old folks. They can't help themselves. So anybody that can't help themselves, really can't help themselves, "By God, we'll do for them." Food, education, social security. On civil rights, in terms of clearing away the legal obstacles, he was also sincere, clearly and deeply, although realistic.

At the same time, however, you get into the much more complex problem of a redistribution of political power, and the relationship of the Negro in the ghetto to the established political machine, and the fact—right or wrong—that the black community and Mexican American community felt that the established mechanism channels wouldn't do it. They wanted extra political channels through community action programs, community organizations, picketing. Forget the violence; I'm not talking about violence. But even within the limits of peaceful [protest]—this he found much more difficult to accept. He found much more difficult to accept a broadened welfare program, particularly where it was broadened to cover those who might be doing something for themselves.

A Mayor Daley would come in and complain about the Community Action Program; and he was intuitively and basically on Mayor Daley's side, on [the] grounds—trying to express it his way, I guess—[that] "Here's a good mayor who is trying to do something for his community. Why can't these people operate and gain power politically?" I think that explains part of his complex reaction: this combination of passionate conviction, on one hand, but a deep devotion to the existing political structure and order, on the other hand.

THE WAR WITHIN

KELLY: By the fall of 1965, there were people in the Budget Bureau who had . . . decided that this was a time in which they could wage a war inside the White House—because they are part of the Executive Office of the President—in order to bring some changes that they perceived were necessary in the War on Poverty.

So there were memos passing back and forth in the fall of 1965, and those memos were very critical of OEO's management, particularly very critical of Shriver. The Forrer Memoranda—named for its author, John Forrer, who had been one of the budget examiners on the OEO—said the only way that you could "salvage OEO is to get rid of Shriver."

The management survey was kind of an interesting exercise. It was clearly sponsored by two forces within the executive department, one of them the Budget Bureau, and the other the Civil Service Commission. Probably the chief architect of the management survey was John Macy [chairman of the Civil Service Commission]. Macy had been in the position of being in a head-to-head battle with Sargent Shriver over the grade levels, particularly in the field of OEO. It had been Mr. Shriver's notion that if you were going to conduct a War on Poverty, that in the regional offices which had been established as an integral part of the OEO—seven regional offices—he should get the very best people that he could possibly get to run those offices. Traditionally, within the government, the best government grades had been reserved for those bureaucrats who stayed in Washington and who had little to do with what went on at the grass roots, out where the people were.

Shriver's notion was that the War on Poverty ought to reverse that trend. So what he requested was seven grade 18s to be regional administrators, regional directors for the OEO. Because of the fact that the Labor Department and the Department of Health, Education, and Welfare had grade 15s or 16s at the best in the field, the Civil Service Commission, based on that precedent—in arguing as they traditionally do from precedent—turned them down. The first turndown came in the spring of 1965. Shriver entered a reclama [appeal], and the reclama resulted in a turndown.

So that by the summer of 1965—some seven months after the Job Corps, Community Action [Program], VISTA, all of the component parts of the War on Poverty had been created by the Congress—Shriver couldn't get a decision out of the Civil Service Commission on how to conduct at least the regional part of the war. They talk about management inefficiency! That's really probably one of the most monumental bits of management inefficiency that ever was called to my attention in some eighteen years in the federal service.

He finally took the issue directly to the president, which in the bureaucracy is always a violation. Bureaucrats don't like to have their decisions overturned, particularly at that level. In going to the president, he won his argument in that the president was willing to overturn the chairman of his Civil Service Commission and also his talent search director, because that was the role John Macy played. The commissioner and Macy and others chafed under this decision very badly.

It was just about this time when Sargent Shriver's first deputy, Jack Conway—who had come from the Auto Workers—left. It was really unfortunate that a relationship that had started out so very well....But the problem was that Jack was no sooner appointed as deputy director of OEO than he took what amounted to a rather lengthy leave of absence. He was gone January, February, and March of 1965, at a time when the program was just getting started. When he did return, he was only here for a short period of time at the end of March, when his father became ill; and for all intents and purposes, he was gone then until late May. So that he absented himself from a very important post at a very important time, and nobody was ever really able to restring the telegraph wires between the director's and deputy director's office.

Who functioned as acting head of the Community Action Program while Conway was gone?

KELLY: During the period of December 1964 until April 1965, there was really no one. Fred Hayes was handling the field operations side of the Community Action office. Dick Boone was handling the program planning and the resource side of the aisle. Ted Berry arrived as the second director of Community Action in April of 1965. So that there was a hiatus there also. This was really a period of time in which Jack Conway's presence was sorely missed.

In the fall after Conway had left—Conway left in August, as I recall, even though, really, when he came back he spent very little time here because he knew he was going to leave—Shriver, who had known Bernard Boutin very well during the Kennedy administration, convinced Boutin to leave the Home Builders Association, which was a lobbying organization that he had joined after he had left GSA [General Services Administration], and return to become his deputy. Boutin came in late September or early October of 1965 and took the job that had been vacated by Conway.

Shriver decided that the person who would serve as the OEO representative of the management survey was his special assistant Chris Weeks, who had been in the Budget Bureau. The rest of the task force, or management survey, was made up of people from the Budget Bureau, people who were representing the Civil Service Commission, although they were employed by NASA in the personnel area. The management survey's chief, or director, whatever you want to call him, was Bertrand Harding, who was then the deputy administrator in the Internal Revenue Service. I think it is reasonably clear that what the establishment—the Civil Service Commission and the Budget Bureau— wanted to come out of this report was something that would discredit Sargent Shriver as a manager, that would be of such a nature that it would even shock him, and that it would be the means whereby the establishment could reassert the control that it had never been able to exercise over OEO, and the kind of control that it exercised with ease over other government agencies.

The management survey, when it was finally published in June of 1966, did not shock Shriver. As a matter of fact, he paid it some small attention. Bernard Boutin by that time had resigned to accept a job of small-business administrator—and I might add, the telegraph wires between the director and deputy director's office were never really restrung even with Boutin's advent. Boutin never really understood what his role was supposed to be. Instead of carving a world out, he waited for one to be created. It wasn't created, because that's not the kind of an administrator Mr. Shriver was. Bernie Boutin was fundamentally a bureaucrat by nature, a man of orderliness, a man I think whom most everybody, including Mr. Shriver, liked.

The management survey was delivered. At the time there was a vacancy for deputy, and Mr. Shriver submitted a number of names, including Bertrand Harding's, to fill the vacancy of Boutin. Mr. Harding finally agreed to become the deputy, with his first task to implement the management survey. The management survey was implemented only partially and to this day lies fallow somewhere in a filing cabinet in this building with most of its recommendations incapable of implementation in the real world. I think that the purpose of the management survey to, one, discredit Mr. Shriver as a manager failed; and secondly, the purpose of seizing control of OEO was partially attained. Mr. Shriver told his third and newly appointed deputy that henceforth he would deal with the Budget Bureau, the Civil Service Commission, in whatever manner he wished to, and that Mr. Shriver would concern himself with the program operations and with dealing with the political problems of the agency.

HARDING IS HIRED AS DEPUTY DIRECTOR

HARDING: It started really in February of 1966, when I was the deputy commissioner of Internal Revenue. I received a call from the then director of the Bureau of the Budget, Mr. Charlie Schultze, who told me that there were some problems over at OEO, and that he and John Macy, the chairman of the Civil Service Commission, had decided that I was perhaps the best-qualified person around to do a management survey of OEO and to make recommendations for changes in the organization, management procedures, and so forth.

Toward the late spring or early summer, as the project was about at its conclusion, I discovered by a personal conversation with the then deputy director of OEO, Mr. Bernie Boutin, that Mr. Boutin was extremely unhappy in his job with OEO and was determined to leave. He had apparently discussed this with the president and others and had been given the assignment to find a successor. And depending upon finding that person, he would or would not be able to leave his present job. Mr. Boutin approached me at lunch one day about the possibility of taking over his job. I was extremely hesitant about that—being a career employee and moving into the political realm—and I thought about it for some period of time. I was called by John Macy to discuss it, and by Schultze, as I recall, and then ultimately by Shriver. Shriver in effect offered me the job and stated that he was aware of the fact that he had a reputation for gobbling up deputies, but that in fact he thought he was a pretty reasonable individual, and [he] asked me to go over and talk to Bill Moyers, who had served as his deputy in the Peace Corps.

So I went to talk to Moyers, and I'll never forget Moyers's view, and that was that Shriver was a reasonable person to work for but there was only one consideration, and that was [that] you could never become indebted to him or in any way dependent upon him; that if you were prepared each day as you went into the job to leave immediately, that you'd get along very well with Sarge, but if you ever got in his clutches, as it were, that you were in sad shape. So after much consideration and soul-searching that went over several weeks, I decided that I would take the plunge, and it was subsequent to that that I had my first really personal facc-to-face conversation with the president.

What happened in that June 1966 meeting with the president prior to the announcement of your appointment as deputy director?

HARDING: Well, I got a lecture from the president. My recollection of that meeting is that I said, "Hello, Mr. President," and "Good-bye, Mr. President." For the intervening twelve, fifteen minutes, the president talked. We met in a little side office just off of his main office, just the two of us. About halfway through the conversation, Bill Moyers joined us, obviously trying to push the president along; I guess he was running late in his schedule or something. And he came in more as an irritant than as a participant. As a matter of fact, he said nothing at all. The president talked to me about his problems with the OEO; he talked to me about the past, about his early days with NYA.

Shriver and I had sort of a beginning understanding that I was to be Mr. Inside and he was to be Mr. Outside. I took care of internal matters involving personnel, budget, and management systems, and so forth, and Sarge was the guy who worked the Hill. Of course, working the Hill primarily involved, at that time, the '67 legislation. That was really the key year. I was involved in staff meetings of a general sort of nature; I understood generally what they were doing. If I didn't agree with it, I expressed my disagreement. But I was not a key factor either in the design of the '67 bill or in its eventual enactment.

I think the relationship with Shriver was very good, very satisfying—at least from my viewpoint, and I think from his. It was never a close personal relationship. Shriver operated with a small group of inside people, people that he had been associated with for some period of time, largely; and people who were of his particular bent, very imaginative, very humorous, very light and gay. I didn't fit into that particular category, so on a personal basis it was very friendly; it was very sincere. He seemed to always be open and honest with me, and I, of course, always tried to be with him. And I was very satisfied with the relationship.

LBJ ON SHRIVER'S DEPARTURE

For more than a year, Shriver struggled with the dilemma of resigning or remaining in his increasingly frustrating assignment. He considered running for governor or senator in Illinois, but he ultimately accepted the president's offer to be ambassador to France. Although Johnson respected Shriver and wanted him to stay with OEO, he became increasingly suspicious of almost everyone with Kennedy ties. Shriver's arrival in Paris coincided with student protests and riots in a number of European capitals, prompting Johnson to imagine an amusing link to the domestic upheavals caused by the Community Action Program.

LBJ's conversation with Eunice Shriver, December 18, 1966[8]

SHRIVER: Mr. President, I'll only take a minute of your time. I'm calling without Sarge's knowledge or anybody else. But I wanted to tell you one thing, which is that when you're as busy you are, it's sometimes difficult to know. It's just that Sarge—and I wanted you to know that I don't think there's anybody who has worked for you in the last few years, who has more loyalty really to you than anybody else in your administration. And I think that there have been situations—and you can imagine that they are, of course, with Bobby and Teddy, in which there have been questions in the past which Sarge could have decided one way in which he would never have been accused of disloyalty to you, but he could have decided in one way in the poverty program, but at no time—and I've lived through this, so I know it. In every single solitary case, he's always said—even when it would cause difficulty with the family—he always said, "I'm part of the Johnson administration and this is the way it's going to be, and if your family doesn't like it, that doesn't matter to me. This is the way it's going to be." And that has been a hundred percent the whole time. Now, we don't have to go into the particular circumstances, but I think you can imagine yourself that there are situations when he could have gone the other way with appointments to the poverty program and funding of the poverty program to where—this is off the record—that could have caused some difficulty in the family, but at no time, and at all times, he has been almost painfully loyal in the sense that he has always chosen what was best for you and what would reflect to your glory. Now that the moment is coming at which—and I say I can't emphasize that enough—and I think now the moment comes quite frankly when he feels that his usefulness is over—I don't want to get into all that. Those are political decisions you have to make...but I think that in the end, if he does leave, and I think, quite honestly, I feel that he probably will leave. I expect that he will leave.... I want you to know that when he does go, I hope he will go with the greatest mutual admiration. I know he will go with admiration for you, and I hope you will for him....

JOHNSON: No, we don't want him to go. We just want to all try to do the best we can with what we have under the circumstances. I have no desire for him to go. I think he's the best person that we could possibly have in that or nearly any other situation. But all I do is just see the papers and see what is happening, and I'll go over it all with him. During this period, I always have a lot of problems with each department not getting enough, and tonight I've got a $143 billion budget and it looks like the biggest deficit [for] anybody in the history. I'm just doing my best to cushion it as best I can and see that every person gets what I think is a fair appraisal and allocation.

LBJ's conversation with Charles Schultze, December 30, 1966[9]

JOHNSON: [Shriver] wants to resign if he doesn't work it out like he wants to. If he does resign, he wants to at least tell us, after he divorces the wife, who she can sleep with, after he's gone. He's no longer the man in the house, but he wants to designate the man in the house. We spent all day and didn't get anywhere except I told him that I would have you and Bill Moyers and Joe Califano get with him and work out an agreement on how to propose it, and he could quit talking about resignations. He's going to hold that in abeyance, kind of gun's going to be above the door until he gets it worked out. My judgment is he won't get it worked out to satisfy him. But I would say that he's going to kill the poverty program. My judgment is it will never get off the ground if he resigns. That's exactly why I'm going to keep the ball. He's taking two positions. One, he's used up his IOUs; he has no strength; he has nothing. The ship is sinking, so he wants to quit it. I pointed that out to him yesterday. I said, "You can't hurt me, because I've been hurt with everybody quitting. When a man's got as much pain as I got, a needle doesn't hurt you. I get the big ones hit me. I would much prefer it wouldn't happen, but if it happens, I'd just go on and resign now."

LBJ's conversation with Dean Rusk, February 19, 1968[10]

JOHNSON: [Mayor Richard J.] Daley is not going to have anything to do with [Shriver]. He doesn't want to. He's just showing him the courtesy of letting him appear to let him down. Daley wants a fellow named [Samuel H.] Shapiro, who's lieutenant governor, to be the governor. If he wants anybody, he wants [Adlai] Stevenson, but he doesn't trust either one of them. He thinks they'll stick him. That's about the way it is. That's just for our information. He might change his mind, or he might take him. He says that Shriver's rather unpopular. The down-staters—they would murder Shriver and murder me. He said the gangsters he's got on the payroll out there have just ruined him with the good people of Chicago. They're in jail, and we send them checks every two weeks and stuff like that....

RUSK: Now, I actually think that he would be awfully good in Paris.

JOHNSON: He would except he might be a Stevenson on one of these [Mai van] Bo[11] deals. I'm afraid that he'll come up and say, "Well, I could have worked it out." Like Bobby did. "We've got a good deal here, but Rusk and Johnson wouldn't give an inch."

RUSK: This morning he said, by the way: "If I go to the UN, I wouldn't create any problems of the sort you've had with Adlai Stevenson."

JOHNSON: Well, he's sure got one here—the poverty. He does it every day to me. I think a man's got it in his blood—I think anybody that thinks more of himself than he does his job is a problem for you and me. I think that was true of Goldberg. I think it's true of Stevenson. I think it's true of Bobby. I think it's true of Shriver. Anybody that has personal advancement in mind is a problem.

LBJ's conversation with Everett Dirksen, June 4, 1968[12]

JOHNSON: Dick Daley said Shriver started all these riots out there in Chicago, you know, with the poverty program. I said, "By God, I didn't know he could get them going in Europe that quick." He got de Gaulle going the week after he got there. Now he got them going good in Oxford. And now he got them going in Italy.

DIRKSEN: Yes, he's got them going in Spain.

JOHNSON: I'm going to export my riots.

SHRIVER DEPARTS OEO

Why did Shriver leave OEO?

KELLY: My own judgment is that he came to OEO for a year. He came to OEO to get that very difficult piece of legislation in 1964 through the Congress. He did not leave the Peace Corps; he was working both programs in tandem. I think he

Shriver and LBJ discuss the OEO budget at the president's office in Austin, January 4, 1968. *A5362-14a, 1/4/68. Photo by Yoichi Okamoto, Presidential Collection, LBJ Library*

agreed to come for a year and ended up spending four. And I think at the end of four years, particularly with the magnificent victory in the 1967 congressional cycle, when everybody thought that the thing would be "partitioned" and "split up" and "spun off"—or what other popular terms they were using—he kept it together. He got his money. It was clear that after 1967 that this institution, if the Democrats were to remain in power, was going to be with this country a long time.

So it's kind of like reinventing the wheel. Was he going to do the same thing over again? 1968 was a very easy year. There were no authorization hearings, so that I think at that point in time he was ready to do something else.

HARDING: I think he was tired. He had been under great pressures almost on a continuing basis. I think he felt he had perhaps gotten a little sour in the job and that it would be good for him to leave. When he discussed it with the president, as I understand it the president told him that he would be happy to have him in almost any capacity in his administration [and] specifically talked to him about a couple of ambassadorships. The French one appealed to Sarge more than anything else, and he eventually took it.

PERRIN: At that time [March 1968], we were, of course, aware that Sargent Shriver was going to be leaving for somewhere; the exact destination wasn't known. But the rumor was becoming fairly strong that he was to become an ambassador, perhaps to France. I've forgotten the exact dates, but sometime after the first of the year, Bert Harding called me in and said that it was quite certain that Shriver would be leaving. The timing wasn't known; again, the destination wasn't known. But he asked me if, when this took place, I would be interested in serving with him as acting deputy director. While I was quite flattered and somewhat startled by this suggestion, I quite promptly agreed to do this if this was what he wanted and, of course, if the White House had no objections to this. He said that he had served previously as an acting commissioner of Internal Revenue, and that he found that this simply wasn't something that he could handle alone. He determined then that he didn't what to have to do that again, and he needed some assistance. So I agreed to serve. Neither of us thought that it would be a very long time.

Why did you think that?

PERRIN: It just didn't make sense that this would continue very long. It was in March, finally, when the announcement was made. Harding told me for sure that Shriver was leaving, and that we would be taking over right away, even though Shriver hadn't actually left town and wouldn't for several weeks. But we were proceeding as if he were out of it completely. This was at President Johnson's request. The election was in November, and at that time the president still hadn't withdrawn from the race. There was just no reason to believe that the nomination of a new director and deputy director could be very far down the line. So we were looking at it probably in terms of two or three months' duration.

All sorts of things began to happen then: the president's withdrawal; the Martin Luther King assassination. That was really my first feeling of the difficulties of running an organization like this. Mr. Harding was out of town at the time of the King assassination, and I was serving as "acting acting director," which I had taken to call myself when he was away. And I remember being in my office on Saturday watching the smoke rise up over Washington, D.C., and wondering how the events were going to be overtaking our building and our program.

There was also the Poor People's Campaign.

PERRIN: It had already been set in motion by King, but it was picked up as the holy cause then and subsequently came about during the summer. So it was a climactic summer in many ways, with these events, the politics, campaign, the poor people's arrival, our congressional problems; it just never really let up from then on.

Bert and I got along very well in handling the chores of the agency. He indicated he wasn't the kind that had to know everything, see every piece of paper, sign everything, everything that was going on all over the agency. He looked to me to handle as much of it as I could, keep as much of it off his desk as I could. I had an excellent working relationship with him, enjoyed it very much. As the year wore on and the president finally nominated Harding for director, Bert had a lot to do with the fact that I was, shortly, then nominated for deputy director. Unfortunately, confirmation never came about.

[Wayne Morse] prevailed upon Lister Hill, the chairman of the Senate Labor and Public Welfare Committee, not to hold hearings on our nominations—which wasn't difficult to do, Hill not being too interested in the subject anyway and not running for reelection. So there were three nominations being held here: Harding's, mine, and [Padraic] Kennedy as director of the VISTA program. So this was the situation, then, as Congress took off in August for its vacation. And when they came back, there was still no action and no promise of it. I made some efforts to crack it loose. I went up to see people in the Senate—senators and some of the staff people—in an effort to shake it loose. And there was simply no action. Finally—and I don't recall my dates here, but it was about the week before Congress adjourned—I finally got fed up with the situation, and I called Morse, who was then, I discovered, out in Oregon campaigning. He wasn't even coming back. So I talked to his assistant out in Oregon, and I asked him if he would ask the senator what he intended to do about this, that I wanted to know now whether he was going to continue to block it, or was [he] willing

President Johnson confers with Bertrand Harding in the Oval Office at the time of his appointment as acting director of OEO, March 21, 1968. A5868-17, 3/21/68. Photo by Yoichi R. Okamoto, Presidential Collection, LBJ Library

to try to let it go through. Within a couple of hours, I had word back that he certainly didn't intend to block it, and that, as a matter of fact, he had told Senator [Mike] Mansfield two weeks before that he was no longer blocking it.

So I got this cranked into the machinery over there, and my friends in the Senate Labor Committee and staff prevailed then upon—I know I called Senator Hill's office to make sure that they knew—to call a hearing. We knew the deck was stacked, really, at this hearing, because there was a problem of getting a quorum. There were just a few days before the end of the session, and there had to be nine senators present. I think we wound up with six that morning. Harding, Kennedy, and I sat around for about an hour while they attempted to get a quorum and could not, so that was the end of that.

We tried one last gasp of trying to get the committee to poll out the nominations, which they can do, although they have to have unanimous agreement to do it. Then Dominick refused to go along with that, so Congress then adjourned, and that was the end of our effort.

"BETTER AS A TEAM"

PERRIN: [Shriver's] enthusiasm, his intelligence, his persuasiveness, were such that I personally am convinced that OEO would not have lasted, probably would not have come into being—certainly in the way that it did—and I doubt whether it could have survived during those early years, without somebody like Sarge at the helm. There came a time, though, when for the good of the program it was probably proper that he left. Because we did need to settle down into a bureaucracy form that was really overdue, and I just don't think Sarge was capable of presiding over a bureaucracy. He certainly more than served his purpose as head of this agency, and I think did an excellent job. I think he could have done a better job, should have done a better job; but maybe that's asking for perfection that no one is capable of.

It is true that we have had difficulties, but it has never been as bad as is laid out. Now, Sarge had a peculiar way of operating. He did it more by personal assistant than he did by program mechanisms that had been established. This always creates problems in an organization. Or his assigning a problem to whomever he happened to run into in the men's room or thought of on the spur of the moment, no matter how many other administrative lines it crossed.

Bert Harding, of course, came in on the basis of having conducted the management survey, which isolated and surfaced a lot of the difficulties that had grown up in practice in a rush to get things done. He has had a considerable effect, bringing more stability to the administrative operation, not only here but in the regions. Bert has been quite responsible for the delegation of authority to the regions to minimize to the extent possible the red tape involved and confusion in bringing things here to Washington. In other words, settle as many things as you can on the spot [in] the region[s].

KELLY: Shriver is the most extraordinary man I've ever known in my life. He's extraordinary in so many ways it gets hard to categorize him. He's bright. He has the kind of sensitivity about issues—I've never met anyone that has that kind of sensitivity. In terms of his understanding of the political process, I don't know where he learned it, whether he learned it here in Washington, but he had the kind of political sensitivity and political savvy.... I was with him in the Peace Corps, but he seemed to have an awful lot of it when he first arrived in town. Maybe he learned it in the family. He understands politicians the best I've ever seen in any person.

He's so interesting to work for because his capability of generating ideas just keeps you flabbergasted all the time. The whole business of Head Start—the conceiving of it, naming it, coupling the idea with his obvious understanding of the poor and his obvious empathy toward poor kids. He always stretched you. He got the absolute best out of you. I don't care whether you were having a conversation about God or Elizabethan poetry or talking about how you might get a Job Corps center straightened out; he always got the best out of you.

His long suit is leadership. His long suit is attracting extraordinary people to work for him. He's tough, awfully tough to work for, because he demands of everybody else what he demands of himself, and that is the best. He is the most disciplined human being I've ever met. Anybody that can drive himself to the hours that he put into this program! And there's one word that's not in his lexicon—"failure."

What sort of changes in OEO did the succession from Shriver to Harding make?

GAITHER: I think there was an inevitable political impact. Shriver was unbelievably hardworking and dynamic and very effective with all kinds of people, particularly on the Hill. Bert just wasn't that kind of guy. I think that Bert concentrated more on running the programs as well as he could, but in fact they were in political trouble at that point. The budget was getting hit pretty hard. They were very difficult times. I'm not sure anybody could have turned it around. But they were very different kinds of people, much better as a team.

EPILOGUE AND ASSESSMENTS

THE OFFICE OF ECONOMIC OPPORTUNITY *lasted only a decade, as Johnson's successors espoused other explanations of the problem and alternative prescriptions for its solution. President Nixon initially offered the Family Assistance Plan, which proposed a guaranteed annual income for poor families. After that initiative failed to generate support, he took a different direction. In 1973, he appointed Howard Phillips OEO director with the mission of dismantling the agency. A flurry of lawsuits thwarted Phillips's efforts and resulted in his resignation before Nixon himself was forced from office. The Community Services Administration replaced OEO in 1975, but the new agency was abolished in 1981 as part of the Reagan administration's effort to "undo" the Great Society. Writing in his diary, Reagan expressed the belief that "it was LBJ's war on poverty that led to our present mess."[1] The "mess" to which he referred was an explosion in the number of single-parent families that had caused a spiraling increase in Aid for Families with Dependent Children. In 1996, the Republican-led Congress replaced AFDC with the Personal Responsibility and Work Opportunity Reconciliation Act. President Clinton signed the legislation, transforming the traditional welfare system with temporary assistance designed to push recipients into the job market.*

As a small agency with broad authority for innovation, OEO was better equipped to develop new programs than it was to administer existing ones as they grew. Even the officials involved in the creation of the War on Poverty seemed to accept the inevitability of spinning off OEO's components to the established cabinet departments. The bureaucracy not only exerted control; it also afforded protection. Even so, it is remarkable that all of OEO's major programs except the Neighborhood Youth Corps have survived for almost half a century. Their longevity reflects the continued relevance of their mission and the measure of acceptance they have won.

The Labor Department finally gained control of the Job Corps in 1969. The program, which has trained more than two million participants since it began, presently has 60,000 enrollees at 122 centers.[2] Although the Job Corps still faces criticism for the high cost of its training versus its economic benefit, evaluations cite its promise for improving the prospects of at-risk youth.[3]

The Department of Education administers Head Start, the Work-Study Program, Adult Education, and Upward Bound. Head Start, with an enrollment of 900,000 children and a budget of 7.1 billion dollars, continues to enjoy broad bipartisan support. Recognizing the importance of even earlier intervention, Congress created a companion program in 1995, Early Head Start, for children from birth to age three and for pregnant women. Upward Bound helps prepare 65,000 participants for college each year. The Federal Work-Study Program remains an avenue for students to obtain modest financial support for college education while gaining work experience; the program presently assists almost 800,000 students at 3,400 participating institutions. Each year, more than two million adults are schooled in workplace literacy and English literacy through grants to states from the Office of Adult Education and Literacy for some 3,200 local programs.

The Corporation for National and Community Service administers VISTA and Foster Grandparents, both of which have been expanded by the Edward M. Kennedy Serve America Act of 2009. VISTA, as part of AmeriCorps, has 6,500 volunteers in the field assigned to 1,200 projects. Foster Grandparents, once a favored project of First Lady Nancy Reagan, is now one of several Senior Corps programs.

The controversial Community Action Program and two of its offspring have evolved in different ways. The once-maligned community action agencies—there are now approximately 1,086 of them—survive with block grant funding, administered by the states, from the Office of Community Services of the Department of Health and Human Services (HHS). Although the influence of local government has muted the agencies' early defiance, citizen participation has gained widespread acceptance, and a former community organizer occupies the Oval Office. The Neighborhood Health Centers, launched as one of Community Action's national emphasis programs, has expanded into 1,200 Community Health Centers under HHS's Health Resources and Services Administration. These centers provide primary care to some 18 million low-income Americans. In 1974, Legal Services was recast as a private, nonprofit corporation, funded by Congress and governed by a bipartisan board of presidential appointees. More than its War on Poverty siblings, the Legal Services Corporation (LSC) has carried on the OEO tradition of controversy with its vigorous assaults on laws that adversely affect the poor. While its opponents have retaliated with budget cuts, hostile governing boards, and restrictions on its lobbying and class action lawsuits, the organization has strong support within the legal community and the Congress. LSC currently supports 137 independent nonprofit legal aid programs that staff more than nine hundred offices nationwide and process almost a million cases each year.

Since this book deals with the perceptions of the poverty warriors, their own evaluations of their efforts are offered in this concluding chapter. These reflections, recorded in the late 1960s through the early 1980s, reveal remarkable insights into the antipoverty programs, the planners themselves, and the times in which they lived.

"A FAR MORE INTRACTABLE PROBLEM THAN WE REALIZED"

YARMOLINSKY: I would not have been as sanguine about finding jobs for people who were prepared for the jobs. There are impersonal forces in our society that are making it harder and harder for people from low-income backgrounds with poor education and poor work orientation to find decent work—unlike the previous eras, when successive generations of immigrants were able to pull themselves out of that condition. I don't think it's the fact that these people have black skins. I think it's more the nature of the economy. You find pockets of that kind of thing among white populations, but only [in] Appalachia, I suppose. You find it in south Boston. There is a kind of circle, and it's harder and harder for them to break out of it. Now we've got the inflation-unemployment inverse relationship, which makes it harder still. I won't say I'm pessimistic, but I guess I am, because if I were in complete charge, I don't know what I'd do. I think there may be some sophisticated economic things that people like Jim Tobin have thought of that could get inflation in hand without having unemployment go up and therefore making this structural unemployment harder to break out of. But whether you could get the Congress to go along with that kind of thing?

If you can get the problem down to a reasonable number, then you can deal with it. But when it gets up above a certain percentage, the things that you can do with small numbers of people you can't do with these people. I certainly think that a welfare system that did not put a premium on not working, or that didn't put a fifty percent tax rate on working—but you do that, and you've got to stretch out the welfare system so far that you take in too large a proportion of the population. Then what is the effect of those consequent tax rates? I don't really buy most of this stuff about how high tax rates discourage incentive for the middle classes, but they sure do distort the economy. You see people doing all kinds of strange things and companies doing all kinds of strange things for tax reasons that are not good for productivity. I sometimes think that the best thing you could do for the poor would be to give corporate executives lifetime employment so they could plan beyond the next quarterly earnings report.

D. BAKER: There are some fairly basic problems. The racial problem is masking a much more pervasive problem that we're really not facing up to, and that is the fact that automation and technological changes, in spite of some of my economics professors, have made muscles obsolete. And today it happens to be the Negro that is at the bottom of the heap, with only muscle power to operate. If we had been back at this point fifty years ago, it would have been the Italians and the Poles, but it would have been the same problem. Fifty years before that, it probably would have been the Irish. But the fact of the matter is, as the years go by, my friends in the cybernetics and the automation and—what's that other word they use?—"computerization" tell me that within our lifetime we're going to be producing about ninety percent of the goods manufactured or produced in farming that we use with about five percent of the present working force. We are going to have problems, economic distribution problems; and we are going to have to find ways of occupying people and of deciding who's going to work and who's not going to work. I think we're sort of fooling ourselves that this business of inability to find uses in society, to find uses for Negro muscle power, is just a racial thing.

MERRICK: We were much more naive about [poverty]. We assumed that, given enough attention, we really could do something. It's a far more intractable problem than we realized. I had the excellent experience of going up to Boston and being the manpower coordinator for the city, which meant that in discussions between the mayor and the poverty program the connection was me. I understood these programs. Nobody else in the city of Boston had any exposure to them at all. I realized then for the first time the terrible gap between what was happening at the local level and reports on which the secretary of Labor thought he was getting the truth. Indeed, all he got were reports filtered through three or four layers of bureaucracy, and in the course of those filterings, [he got] the most misleading impression of what was going on at the local level. One could be convinced that one was doing a great job. You were able to say forthrightly to the Congress, "We've spent x million of dollars, but we've gotten numbers in thousands of people in employment who otherwise would not be employed." Well, boy, the capacity for statistical deformation was just unbelievable.

INADEQUATE FUNDING

HARDING: I think it is undoubtedly true that if there had not been a [war in] Vietnam, or that, conversely, if Vietnam were to come to a screeching halt right away, that there would be—I guess the present estimate is somewhere between $12 and $15 billion additional available for domestic purposes. I think OEO could have shared in such a peace dividend. But I don't think of it in terms of a criticism. We have commitments to do all sorts of things, including our national defense. So the fact that unfortunately this agency came into existence almost at the same time that we started making our heavy involvement in Vietnam is just an unfortunate historical fact.

KRAMER: In 1965 everybody in this agency had reason to believe that we would be able to carry out our expectations and our hopes for the War on Poverty, that we would get the appropriate budgetary amounts. It wasn't until the 1966 budget was returned by the Budget Bureau that the first shock of the impact of Vietnam seeped in. It didn't seep in; it hit with a hammer blow! And I well recall that Joe Kershaw, the director of research program planning and evaluation, indicated that he felt right then and there he wanted to resign because, instead of expenditures of the $3 billion magnitude, we were held to expenditures of $1.5 billion. Mr. Shriver did his best to put a good cloak on that and make it seem that these expenditures were adequate. He was at all times a loyal subject of Mr. Johnson, but there was no cloaking the fact that the program had to be drastically curtailed and cut back, and the expression "the War on Poverty" soon became rather a hollow mockery.

I don't think that anybody really knew how difficult it was going to be to eliminate poverty in this country. They spoke rather glibly of the $11 billion or $12 billion "poverty gap," but that simply was a gap that could be bridged if you gave everybody who was below the poverty line enough money to get over the poverty line. But that still wouldn't do anything for the interlocking causes of poverty which we found existed. It was a very, very tough, dirty, mean, unpopular kind of war to fight. And we fought it with every weapon at our disposal— not having the air force, let's say, to supply the air cover to carry the war to its successful conclusion—and that was the money that would be necessary really to do the kind of job that was required.

The OEO five-year plan was never calculated to be the only thrust against poverty. This agency in its second year was to be spending at approximately the $3.5 billion level; by the third year it might be $5 billion. But that was only supposed to be the point, the spearhead, of major efforts that were being made. By 1968 the nation was spending $25.7 billion in the so-called poverty budget, but much of that was in transfer payments—welfare, Medicare, and so forth.

YARMOLINSKY: One of the moves to kill the proposal, or at least to delay it, was the usual proposal, "Let's study it more." This was a Republican proposal, and one of the alternative bills they introduced would be for a study commission. I think we all felt that, politics completely to one side, we knew enough to mount a program which we could reasonably expect would have some useful effect, and in a year we wouldn't know that much more. The way to begin was to begin, and that was a typical Kennedy as well as Johnson approach. And I don't think it was hasty. We could have studied it for five years, and would we have come up with a better program? Well, I don't know. My own view is that the troubles of the program were very largely due not to misconception or internal conflicts or inconsistencies of conception—although there were some, of course—but much more so [due] to the fact that it suffered from level funding. So that every year you had the problem of: Do you cut off people who have just made it and [are] just getting their program started, or do you frustrate people who are just getting their program together and about to come in for new money? If you don't have enough money to keep expanding, particularly in community action, you're going to create more resentment and frustration than anything else. I'm afraid that's to a large degree what happened.

E. Cahn: During those days, initially particularly, it was permissible to raise people's hopes and expectations. Everybody was worrying about a tax surplus and how to deal with it through negative income tax distribution. The belief was that the rate of growth in the country would generate enough money to significantly impact on the standard of living of the poorest of the poor without taking anything from anybody else. And as a [consequence] of the Vietnam War, increasingly LBJ had to deal with the budgetary device of guaranteed loans for housing, so that that didn't show up in the budget. But he was caught paying for a war the Congress didn't pay for and trying to deal with the consequences of inflation and war, and a war that was in some sense sufficiently undeclared that it couldn't be dealt with or wasn't dealt with as a budgetary issue. That clearly fueled a lot of the problems.

J. Baker: On strictly OEO, the big problems were two, as I think back on it, and as I participated in it. One was, there was not enough money for a war left over from Vietnam. The other was a very strong urban bias in the high-level person-nel, both in and out of government, related to the OEO program, resulting from two things, as I analyzed it. One, that it was just there because they knew about cities instead of knowing about the country. In other words, they didn't grow up with it. The other was because [the cities were] where the demonstrations and the riots were taking place. It left the impression with an awful lot of relatively cynical, high-level bureaucrats that the War on Poverty was just simply a pacifi-cation program to prevent city riots more than a sincere effort, like the Resettle-ment and Farm Security had been. Therefore, it was fair game to get as much money out of the bastards as you could get to help people you loved instead of the people they were trying to keep from burning down the city.

STRUCTURAL PROBLEMS

Schultze: We didn't foresee all the problems involved. We didn't foresee, for example, that OEO, if it were to become an operating agency, could not exercise a coordinating role, because they couldn't speak for the president when they were in competition with other agencies. So OEO always had that problem of trying to do two things at once which were self-contradictory: operate programs and get bigger budgets and more power to itself, which is natural; and at the same time represent the president in coordinating. They were just another agency.

Harding: OEO has not been able to, for perhaps a multitude of reasons, serve as a coordinating role, which is really sort of a controlling role. At least two reasons occur to me. One is that in spite of the original concept of the direc-tor being a special assistant to the president, in addition to his job as director, that role never materialized. I don't know whether that was a function of just the dynamics of the situation or whether it was the chemistry between Lyndon

Johnson and Sargent Shriver. But it never occurred. Any coordination that was accomplished was really accomplished by the Bureau of the Budget or by White House staff, not by this agency.

The second reason, regardless of what that chemistry might have been, is that the way we set ourselves up and began to do business, we became a competitor with the Department of Labor, with HEW, with HUD, and others. And it's very difficult for one peer to coordinate the other. So perhaps it was conceptually wrong, and in terms of the individuals that were cast in the roles, [perhaps] it didn't and couldn't work.

I think the agency ought to be relieved of the role of coordination, that that ought to be consolidated into a bigger coordinating role, and that is a coordination in a structured fashion across the whole domestic front, with a very heavy emphasis and continued pressure on the poverty side of it forcing the old-line agency to do more and more and more in support of this particular segment of the population. But I think the coordination, the overall management of the domestic side, ought to be brought together in some mechanism—probably in the White House, almost necessarily in the White House—that would carry out that sort of role.

This would involve the delegation of OEO-operated programs, wouldn't it?

HARDING: Not necessarily. That could be part of such a package or not. OEO could continue operating everything it's operating, and its coordination role would go up above. Or it could delegate a lot of programs. It could maintain itself as an innovative operator. It could maintain itself as the spokesman for the poor within the federal council. There are lots of different configurations that might be undertaken, but I am convinced that without a rather substantial change in both the structure, the role, and the individuals involved, that the idea of OEO coordinating all of poverty is unrealistic. In addition to all of this, there's a basic conflict in the assignment of that role Mr. Weaver at HUD [Robert Weaver, secretary of HUD] is supposed to coordinate all activities relative to urban affairs. Wirtz [Willard Wirtz, secretary of Labor] is supposed to coordinate all labor [and] manpower activities throughout the government. Cohen [Wilbur Cohen, secretary of HEW] is supposed to do the same thing for health. All of these programs have very real impact on the poverty population. So unless you are a coordinator of the coordinators, it's a meaningless sort of assignment, because nearly everything you're going to talk about that you're trying to coordinate is going to be of an educational, health, housing, some other nature, and some other guy has been designated as the coordinator of all of those activities. So you're just chasing your tail around.

If OEO could not coordinate the other agencies that dealt with poverty—indeed, if it was receiving opposition from them—would it have been better to place the director of the War on Poverty in a position closer to the president so that he could coordinate better and direct the various departments involved in the program?

GAITHER: Well, there are a lot of questions involved in what you've just said. One is a kind of fundamental question of government reorganization. I think by and large the supercabinet idea on the domestic side makes a lot of sense that instead of splitting things up—which is happening again—they ought to be consolidated so that there can be more coordination, and the president can set direction and have a more clearly defined organizational structure to carry it out.

In terms of that enterprise, I doubt whether there was a way to have made it more effective than it was. The president did back Shriver and his people for a long, long time, and in fact they brought about enormous changes in the way the government conducts its programs. Maybe that was inevitable, but I doubt it. I think if they had not been outside with large amounts of free money available to do interesting and important things, they could not have caused the traditional agencies to change. I don't think you can administer large programs within the White House. Otherwise you're just building another bureaucracy there.

So I think with the White House and the White House staff, the Budget Bureau, the Council of Economic Advisers, and the president being behind the direction in which OEO was going, and the fact that they were out there completely independent—if you had stuck it into HEW, even with strong direction from the president, I don't think anything would have happened. Nothing very interesting. If you look objectively at the direction of benefits in the federal government as a whole, or redirection from the lower-middle and middle-income class to the poor and disadvantaged and minorities, one, it did happen, and an awful lot of it is a result of what OEO was doing. It might have lasted longer, but I'm not sure you could have been more effective in terms of meeting the needs of the poor, which was what their mission was.

Would it have worked to have a program that merely coordinated and did not operate at all?

YARMOLINSKY: No. Because it's like being a bench scientist: you've got to have some hands-on experience in order to be able to coordinate effectively. Coordination is a sometime thing anyway. The only person who can really coordinate is the president. If you had a special assistant to the president for poverty problems, he's got no constituency, really. If you're a special assistant on the White House staff, you cannot really dictate how the departments and the agencies spend their money, what they spend their money on. You're kind of snipping and snapping at the edges of the budgetary process and those programs. You've got to have a substantial thing that you're running, and then maybe you can do some coordinating along the way. You've got to have something to deal with. You've got to have some cards to deal with.

IMAGE VERSUS REALITY

D. BAKER: As time passed and our programs got older, there was a parallel development, and I don't think that they're causally related. The development of a change in the nature of the civil rights movement and the development of the concept of confrontation on college campuses nationally were concurrent developments that would have taken place whether or not OEO ever existed, and independently of it. I am convinced personally that what is going on on American college campuses today would have gone on, certainly, without regard to a poverty program and would probably have come about even had there never been a civil rights movement. Some of the developments within the civil rights movement would have occurred both without the poverty program and without what's going on on the campuses.

But we happened to catch a lot of hell for both the other two! The relatively simpleminded people—columnists, newspaper reporters, editors, congressmen, senators, mayors, and governors—perceive us as causing all that trouble out there. The fact of the matter is, there would have been riots if we'd never been thought of. The civil rights movement was moving in a tougher direction within this liberalized movement; the problem of a civil rights leader maintaining his leadership and staying ahead of the activists in his own organization was already becoming apparent much earlier than in '64, and the increasing militancy and stridency of the problem was apparent earlier.

The challenge by the blacks and the Latins within our economic and social structure, political structure, would have occurred without regard to whether OEO was in existence also. It was just bound to come. The development of the mass media of the TV brought home to everybody out there the fact that the gulf between the whites and blacks is growing broader and deeper and blacker with every passing year. It was just inevitable that that was going to cause resentment on their part.

GAITHER: I think, in terms of administrative difficulties, that this period is probably no different from any other history of government programs. The problem is that they're highlighted. Let me explain a basic difference. Every time some youngster who is given a job through the Neighborhood Youth Corps gets into trouble, it's a national issue. Now, all OEO does is make a grant to a city or a community action agency or other to hire kids in the summer, and they go ahead and he becomes a member of the Neighborhood Youth Corps. And it's blamed directly on Sargent Shriver and the president, when one of those kids comes from an impoverished family; he has faced all of his life discrimination, inadequate education, inadequate health care; and all of a sudden we assume because he's given a job that's supported by federal money, he's going to be a perfect child—and they're not, all of them. But by and large, and compared with any other effort, there are no more bad kids in OEO programs than [in] any other.

Now, you don't read anything in the paper about some Social Security beneficiary who goes out and commits a robbery. You don't read anything about some schoolchild who happens to be getting $300 a year from the federal government through an HEW education program and that kid goes out and tries to burn the school down. John Gardner doesn't get blamed for it, nor does the president. But that's what happens [to] OEO.

During the rioting in Detroit, in Watts, and elsewhere, there were always rather extravagant claims by some politicians that it was incited by OEO people. Every investigation proved that this was not true. I don't know how many thousands of people [were] involved in Detroit—I think only five kids who had been employed in the Neighborhood Youth Corps were involved. That's an incredibly small number. You had in the country some 350,000 kids employed by the Neighborhood Youth Corps in the summer, and Detroit, I assume, had maybe 15,000 of them, maybe higher. And five of them were involved out there. Now, the reports from the mayor went just the other way. He said the Neighborhood Youth Corps kids were extremely helpful. They worked not only to try to calm youth gangs down, but they worked in answering phones. They had one group of them working in police headquarters, taking some of the load off policemen so that they could get out on the streets.

I'm not saying there hasn't been a problem; there has been. It's a tough program to administer; we're giving grants to people who have not had any experience in trying to run something, or account[ing] or control[ling] the distribution of funds. And there are problems. But I think they've really been surprisingly few, and those that we have seen have always been exaggerated to a national scale.

The charge has repeatedly been made that the rhetoric of the antipoverty war has raised the expectations of the poor without providing the means to fulfill those expectations.

HARDING: I would say that that allegation is true on a factual basis: that there has been much rhetoric; that there have been words such as "unconditional war on poverty" and, "abolish poverty by 1976." And the whole concept of a war on poverty in and of itself is a bit of rhetoric. Mrs. [Robert] McNamara, who served on our National Advisory Council for several years, used to get almost apoplectic every time the expression was used, because she felt it was not only misleading but just bad psychology in talking about it in war terms. And we have this throughout the whole agency. Everything is a strategy of some sort or another, and we use that sort of jargon.

But in a larger and in a more philosophical sense, I don't think it has been an error to talk much and to continue to expose the total population to the problem. I think only out of an understanding that there is a very, very real problem are we ever going to have any movement at all toward its solution. So in a restricted sense, we've talked more than we have delivered; but in a broader sense, I think the talking and the publicity and the PR has awakened this nation to a very real problem that many, many did not even understand existed four or five years ago. So whereas I am by nature not a PR type and believe much more in the muted sentence, I think that a great service has been done by people—real salesmen like Shriver—who have gotten this idea across, awakened thousands and thousands of middle-class Americans to the need; and they've volunteered and they've given money and they've served on boards. The women have knocked themselves out, the churches. We have perhaps changed more institutions in the last four years than any other agency in the history of this country. The American Bar Association, the American Medical Association, labor unions—you can go through just a whole litany of very fundamental organizations and groups within the society that have awakened to this thing and have become absolutely consumed in their interest in it. So I think it has been a tremendous step in the [right] direction. It is unfortunate that the resources never came along to match the brave words, but I think they will come.

OEO'S ACHIEVEMENTS

PERRIN: The hardest impact to pinpoint is the actual emergence of people from poverty. Now, we can only assume that the accelerated rate at which this has been taking place must be due to the kinds of emphasis on the programs for the poor that OEO has been spearheading. The booming economy, while important, takes a long time to reach the people we are concerned with and just can't really explain the speed with which this has been happening. So therefore, we will justly take credit for that, particularly in the rate with which the nonwhites have been coming out of poverty.

The impact on other federal agencies is impressive and obvious to those who live with this business and can see the changes. The willingness of other departments to consider not only the needs of the poor but to consider the participation of the poor—this has become standard. The willingness of the existing programs to put more of their resources into reaching the poor rather than simply upgrading the not-so-poor. Certainly the impact on communities is without question. We've had mayors tell us that if they didn't have community action agencies, they'd have to invent them, because they have to have a means of expressing, of listening to the voice of the people, which they never had before.

GAITHER: The important contribution of OEO had already been made, and it had very little to do with the programs themselves. OEO played a major role in redirecting the government programs through example. When I got there, preschool education was in disfavor in HEW: the federal government should not be supporting that. Within a couple of years, preschool education was the darling. The Office of Education was supporting it, thought it was a good thing, thought that, indeed, the age level ought to be reduced. So the example of preschool education and the focus on poor kids had an enormous impact on what was happening in education, and this was true across the board. I don't know. I guess it might have been possible to do it differently and to have had less difficulty, but I doubt it. I think when you start focusing a lot of attention on the poor, who don't really have a very big voice, where there are likely to be some problems, that you're going to have a lot of difficulties. OEO is not the only example of this, but it is, I think, the most successful attempt in terms of redirecting the attention of government that we've seen in this century.

TOLMACH: There is much more going on—in the cities particularly, but in many communities of the country—in the area of social programming than there was before this all started. How deep some of these things have gone is certainly open to question; it's deeper in some places than in others. One would hardly speak today yet of a vastly improved public school system across the country. And welfare departments are as bad as they ever were, where they were bad. There has been little impact. Nevertheless, there has been a focusing of attention. This is important because it begins the process.

I suppose, really, of all our faults, the greatest one was in advertising the possibility of potential for change in a way that suggested that it would happen more quickly than it did. The process, of course, is extremely slow, even though one sometimes has to use what looked like quick starts; over time the process is slow. But just bringing the country to a point where poverty problems are considered to the extent that they are now is, I think, immeasurable gain.

It's interesting that even the communications media focus on this in a way, now that there are ghetto reporters. Papers cover the news of the ghetto, not just a robbery here and there or a major fire that occurs in a slum community; but the problems are covered and often in an unstructured way, as the Columbia Broadcasting System is doing now.

GAITHER: OEO was set up really without a program, a very ambitious goal, and a charter to go out and innovate and experiment and see if somehow we could provide opportunity and give people a chance to escape from poverty. None of these programs—Head Start, Upward Bound, Legal Services, Neighborhood Youth Corps—were in the original bill. They were all invented administratively by the administration. And we launched them nationwide. Now, it's rather phenomenal that as many of them have worked, and have worked extremely well. But we didn't know where we were going. We didn't have very precise goals other than eliminating poverty and providing opportunity. But somebody dreamed up Upward Bound, and through that program—I guess some 32,000 disadvantaged youngsters have been in the program. And whereas only eight percent of poor kids across the country go on to college, some ninety percent of the kids who've gone through Upward Bound have made it on to college, and they're starting to come out of the colleges now. That's rather phenomenal, but we couldn't set a goal when we started, because we didn't know where we'd end up.

I think the reason that you don't see as easily in the record of [Johnson's] presidency his extensive involvement in the War on Poverty is that the OEO program itself was a very small part of it. Most people tended then, and I think they do today, to look at performance within areas: education and health and manpower. And we did too. The question is: What impact did it have there? If you start looking closely there, you will find an enormous impact, pushed almost exclusively by the president. Manpower programs, when Johnson took office, were almost exclusively for white males: many programs for sons of union workers, people likely to break into the trades, and almost nothing at all available for minorities, who were the hard-core unemployed. Through the efforts of OEO and the president and, over time, the Department of Labor—but it really was over time—that all got turned around so that by the time Johnson left office, there was a very substantial program in the manpower area, a very significant amount of federal money being spent on programs for the disadvantaged, for the minorities, for the hard-core unemployed.

Now that was a fundamental part of the poverty program, but you wouldn't see it if you just looked at OEO. OEO really got it started, because it had money that it could concentrate on the disadvantaged. As a result, the Department of Labor, but more importantly, the state departments administering manpower programs, wanted to get those funds. Shriver wouldn't give them those funds unless they would redirect their own efforts toward the poor. The same thing happened in health, with neighborhood health centers and other programs. The big impact of OEO was not in its own neighborhood health center program, but the enormous impact it had in terms of redirecting what HEW was doing in the health field.

D. Baker: In the broad picture, I think I really don't apologize to anybody for what we've done. We've alerted the nation to the problem of poverty and set forth an awareness of something that people were not aware of before—in a way that they'd never been aware of it. We've developed some program ideas that have been good in and of themselves and that will go on and survive regardless of what happens to us or this agency.

Beyond that, I think there has been sort of an unmeasurable and imponderable impact that, I suspect, is of more long-lasting importance than what we've done directly, and that is the indirect impact on the operations of federal, state, and local agencies, public and private. They are never again going to do things in the area of helping the poor quite so badly as they were doing them beforehand.

It has been a really great experience. As Jim Heller once said to me, twenty years from now he expected that all of us would be looking back on this period of our life as our salad days, and very likely we'd be telling stories around the bar and around the office and at home and at cocktail parties, and boring the hell out of people, just like some of the old guys from the New Deal days are doing right now in this city. And I think he may be right.

Appendix: Oral History Interviews

NOTE: All interviews were conducted for the Lyndon Baines Johnson Library, Austin, Texas, unless otherwise noted.

Adler, James N. Los Angeles, California, 2/23/83, by Michael L. Gillette.

Alden, Vernon. Boston, Massachusetts, 10/7/81, by Michael L. Gillette.

Baker, Donald M. Washington, D.C., 2/24/69 and 3/5/69, by Stephen Goodell.

Baker, John A. Arlington, Virginia, 11/13/68, by Paige Mulhollan; 12/11/80, 4/21/81, and 6/12/81, by Michael L. Gillette.

Berry, Theodore M., Washington, D.C., 2/15/69, by Stephen Goodell.

Bookbinder, Hyman. Washington, D.C., 12/9/81, 5/19/82, and 6/30/82, by Michael L. Gillette.

Cahn, Edgar, and Cahn, Jean Camper. Washington, D.C., 12/10/80, by Michael L. Gillette.

Califano, Joseph A., Jr. Washington, D.C., XXXI, by Michael L. Gillette.

Cannon, William B. Chicago, Illinois, 5/21/82, by Michael L. Gillette.

Capron, William M. Boston, Massachusetts, 11/5/81, by Michael L. Gillette.

Cohen, Wilbur J. Silver Spring, Maryland, 12/8/68 and 5/10/69, by David G. McComb.

Conway, Jack T. Washington, D.C., 8/13/80, by Michael L. Gillette.

Ferguson, Glenn W. Storrs, Connecticut, 3/16/77, by Lyndon B. Johnson School of Public Affairs, University of Texas at Austin; 1/20/96, telephone interview by Michael L. Gillette.

Gaither, James C. Washington, D.C., 11/19/68, 1/15/69, and 1/17/69, by Dorothy Pierce; 3/24/70, by Joe B. Frantz; San Francisco, California, May 12, 1980, by Michael L. Gillette.

Goldfarb, Ronald. Washington, D.C., 10/24/80, by Michael L. Gillette.

Gordon, Kermit. Washington, D.C., 12/16/68, 1/9/69, 3/21/69, and 4/8/69, by David G. McComb.

Hamilton, Ann Oppenheimer. Washington, D.C., 10/22/80, by Michael L. Gillette.
Harding, Bertrand M. Washington, D.C., 11/20/68 and 11/25/68, by Stephen Goodell.

Hayes, Frederick O'R. Lexington, Massachusetts, 10/7/81, by Michael L. Gillette.

Heller, Walter. Minneapolis, Minnesota, 2/20/70 and 12/21/71, by David G. McComb.

Horowitz, Harold W. Los Angeles, California, 2/23/83, by Michael L. Gillette.

Howard, Jack. Washington, D.C., 10/20/80, by Michael L. Gillette.

Kelly, William P. Washington, D.C., 4/4/69, 4/11/69, and 4/16/69 by Stephen Goodell.

Kramer, Herbert J. Washington, D.C., 3/10/69, by Stephen Goodell.

Lampman, Robert J. Madison, Wisconsin, 5/24/83, by Michael L. Gillette.

Levine, Robert A. 2/26/69, by Stephen Goodell.

Mankiewicz, Frank. Washington, D.C., 4/18/69, 5/1/69, and 5/5/69, by Stephen Goodell.

May, Edgar. Springfield, Vermont, 10/6/81, by Michael L. Gillette.

McCarthy, George D. Washington, D.C., 4/22/81, by Michael L. Gillette.

Merrick, Samuel V. Washington, D.C., 9/28/81, by Michael L. Gillette.

O'Brien, Lawrence E., Jr. New York, New York, 4/8/86, by Michael L. Gillette.

Perkins, Carl D. Washington, D.C., 5/12/83, by Michael L. Gillette.

Perrin, C. Robert. Washington, D.C., 3/10/69 and 3/17/69, by Stephen Goodell.

Phillips, William G. Washington, D.C., 4/16/80 and 4/17/80, by Michael L. Gillette.

Pollak, Stephen J. Washington, D.C., 1/27/69, 1/29/69, 1/30/69, and 1/31/69, by Thomas Harrison Baker.

Richmond, Julius B. Boston, Massachusetts, 10/5/81, by Michael L. Gillette.

Sanders, Harold Barefoot. Washington, D.C., 3/24/69; and Dallas, Texas, 11/3/69, by Joe B. Frantz.

Schlei, Norbert A. Los Angeles, California, 5/15/80, by Michael L. Gillette.

Schultze, Charles L. Washington, D.C., 3/28/69 and 4/10/69, by David G. McComb.

Shriver, R. Sargent. Washington, D.C., 8/20/80, 10/23/80, 7/1/82, 2/7/86, and 11/29/90, by Michael L. Gillette.

Singletary, Otis A. Lexington, Kentucky, 11/12/70, by Joe B. Frantz.

Steadman, John M. Washington, D.C., 4/5/85, by Michael L. Gillette.

Sugarman, Jule M. Washington, D.C., 3/14/69, by Stephen Goodell.

Sundquist, James L. Washington, D.C., 4/7/69, by Stephen Goodell.

Sweeney, John L. Washington, D.C., 11/14/68, by David G. McComb.

Tolmach, Eric. Washington, D.C., 3/5/69, 3/19/69, and 4/16/69, by Stephen Goodell.

Weeks, Christopher. Washington, D.C., 12/10/80 and 9/28/81, by Michael L. Gillette.

Yarmolinsky, Adam. Cambridge, Massachusetts, 7/13/70, by Paige Mulhollan; and Washington, D.C., 10/21/80 and 10/22/80, by Michael L. Gillette.

Notes

Introduction

1. Daily Diary worksheet, 4/24/64, President's Daily Diary, April 1964, Lyndon Baines Johnson Library; *New York Times*, 4/25/64; President's News Conference of April 25, 1964, in Lyndon B. Johnson, *Public Papers of the Presidents of the United States: Lyndon B. Johnson, 1963–1964*, Vol. I (Washington, D.C.: U.S. Government Printing Office, 1965), 549; Lyndon Baines Johnson, *The Vantage Point: Perspectives of the Presidency, 1963–1969* (New York: Holt, Rinehart and Winston, 1971), 79–80; Lady Bird Johnson, *A White House Diary* (New York: Holt, Rinehart and Winston, 1970), 120–22.

2. Lady Bird Johnson, *A White House Diary*, 120; Douglass Cater, quoted in Barbara C. Jordan and Elspeth D. Rostow, eds., *The Great Society: A Twenty Year Critique* (Austin, Tex.: Lyndon Baines Johnson Library/Lyndon B. Johnson School of Public Affairs, 1986), 16.

3. For a scholarly study of Johnson's presidency, see Robert Dallek, *Flawed Giant: Lyndon Johnson and His Times, 1960–1973* (New York: Oxford University Press, 1998).

4. Annual Message to Congress on the State of the Union, January 8, 1964, in Lyndon B. Johnson, *Public Papers, 1963–1964*, 112–17.

5. Special Message to Congress Proposing a Nationwide War on the Sources of Poverty, March 16, 1964, in Johnson, *Public Papers, 1963–1964*, Vol. I, 375–80; 88th Cong. 2d, Economic Opportunity Act of 1964, Report #218, with Minority Report.

6. Robert K. Triest, "Has Poverty Gotten Worse?" *Journal of Economic Perspectives* 36 (1998): 97; Joseph A. Califano, Jr., "Seeing Is Believing: The Enduring Legacy of Lyndon Johnson," Keynote Address, May 19, 2008, LBJ Library.

7. Republication criticism of the Economic Opportunity Act is discussed in William C. Selover, "The View from Capitol Hill: Harassment and Survival," in James L. Sundquist, ed., *On Fighting Poverty: Perspectives from Experience* (New York: Basic Books), 166–67; *Congressional Record*, November 8, 1967, 31806–7.

8. See, for example, Robert Rector and William F. Lauber, *America's Failed $5.4 Trillion War on Poverty* (Washington, D.C.: Heritage Foundation, 1995), 44.

9. Johnson, *The Vantage Point*, 70–73; Bill Moyers in Jordan and Rostow, eds., *The Great Society*, 176; Transcript, R. Sargent Shriver Oral History Interview V, 11/29/90, by Michael L. Gillette, Lyndon Baines Johnson Library, 25.

10. Daniel Patrick Moynihan, *Maximum Feasible Misunderstanding* (New York: Free Press, 1969); Allen J. Matusow, *The Unraveling of America: A History of Liberalism in the 1960s* (New York: Harper and Row, 1984), 113.

11. Johnson, *The Vantage Point*, 69–71; Special Message to Congress Proposing a Nationwide War on the Sources of Poverty, March 16, 1964, Johnson, *Public Papers, 1964–1964*, Vol. I, 375–80.

12. Transcript, R. Sargent Shriver Oral History Interview V, 11/29/90, by Michael L. Gillette, Lyndon Baines Johnson Library, 24; Adam Yarmolinsky, quoted in "Poverty and Public Policy," Transcript of a Conference at Brandeis University, June 16–17, 1973, John Fitzgerald Kennedy Library, 302–3. For a discussion of the negotiations between Johnson and Byrd on the budget, see Irving Bernstein, *Guns or Butter: The Presidency of Lyndon Johnson* (New York: Oxford University Press, 1996).

13. "Policy and Public Policy"; Sar A. Levitan, *The Great Society's Poor Law: A New Approach* (Baltimore: Johns Hopkins University Press, 1969), 55–75.
14. Remarks upon Signing the Economic Opportunity Act, August 20, 1964, in Johnson, *Public Papers of the Presidents, 1963–1964,* Vol. II, 528.
15. "Poverty and Public Policy."
16. Levitan, *The Great Society's Poor Law;* OEO Administrative History, Lyndon Baines Johnson Library; Adam Clymer, *Edward M. Kennedy: A Biography* (New York: William Morrow and Company, Inc., 1999), 86–88.

Chapter 1

1. Arthur M. Schlesinger, Jr., *A Thousand Days* (Boston: Houghton Mifflin, 1965), 1009–13; Theodore H. White, *The Making of the President 1960* (New York: Atheneum, 1964), 106; Michael Harrington, *The Other America: Poverty in the United States* (New York: Holt, Rinehart and Winston, 1984); Dwight Macdonald, "Our Invisible Poor," *New Yorker,* January 19, 1963, 82; Homer Bigart, "Kentucky Miners: A Grim Winter," *New York Times,* October 20, 1963; Transcript, Robert J. Lampman Oral History Interview, 5/24/88, by Michael L. Gillette, 3, Lyndon Baines Johnson Library.
2. Nicholas Lemann, *The Promised Land* (New York: Knopf, 1991), 158–64; Daniel Patrick Moynihan, *Maximum Feasible Misunderstanding* (New York: Free Press, 1969), 62–65.
3. The anthropologist Oscar Lewis gave currency to the term "culture of poverty" in his book *Five Families: Mexican Case Studies in the Culture of Poverty* (New York: Basic Books, 1959).
4. Adam Yarmolinsky, in "Poverty and Urban Policy," 285. The President's Committee on Juvenile Delinquency and Youth Crime (PCJD) was established in 1961 by Robert F. Kennedy to combat the root causes of delinquency through comprehensive local planning and action. PCJD made grants to sixteen projects in sixteen cities. Transcript, David L. Hackett Oral History Interview, 10/21/70, by John Douglas, JFK Library, 69–76. Of the Gray Areas projects, which were sponsored principally by the Ford Foundation, four also received support from PJDC: Community Progress Incorporated in New Haven, Action for Boston Community Development in Boston, Philadelphia Council for Community Advancement, and Mobilization for Youth in New York. Other Gray Areas programs were Oakland Inter Agency Project, United Planning Organization in Washington, D.C., and North Carolina Fund. Peter Marris and Martin Rein, *Dilemmas of Social Reform: Poverty and Community Action in the United States* (Chicago: University of Chicago Press, 1982), 25–28.
5. Lyndon B. Johnson, *The Vantage Point: Perspectives on the Presidency, 1963–1969* (New York: Holt, Rinehart and Winston, 1971), 69–73; Annual Message to Congress on the State of the Union, January 8, 1964, in Lyndon B. Johnson, *Public Papers of the Presidents of the United States: Lyndon B. Johnson, 1963–1964,* Vol. I (Washington, D.C.: U. S. Government Printing Office, 1965), 112–17; Richard N. Goodwin, *Remembering America: A Voice from the Sixties* (Boston: Little, Brown, 1988), 286–87.

    During the 1960 presidential campaign, Kennedy had used the phrase "war against poverty." See Schlesinger, *A Thousand Days,* 1005.
6. Robert J. Lampman, *The Low Income Population and Economic Growth,* Joint Economic Committee, Study Paper No. 12, 86th Congress, 1st Session (Washington, D.C.: U. S. Government Printing Office, 1959).
7. Memo re: Letters in Response to Howard K. Smith Program on Poverty, Robert J. Lampman to Walter W Heller, 3/22/63, Box Ac 83–64, Papers of Robert J. Lampman, Lyndon Baines Johnson Library.
8. Memo re: Notes on Changes in the Distribution of Wealth and Income From 1953 through 1961–1962, Robert J. Lampman, 4/25/63; Memo re: Progress and Poverty, Walter W. Heller to the President, 5/1/63, Box Ac 83–64, Papers of Robert J. Lampman, Lyndon Baines Johnson Library.
9. Moynihan, as head of the Department of Labor's Office of Policy Planning and Research in 1963, became alarmed at a Selective Service estimate that about half of those called for physicals were either mentally or physically disqualified. He spearheaded the creation of

the President's Task Force on Manpower Conservation, which concluded that a third of draft-age men were unfit for induction into the armed services. President's Task Force on Manpower Conservation, *One Third of a Nation* (Washington, D.C.: U.S. Department of Labor, 1964); Douglas E. Schoen, *Pat: A Biography of Daniel Patrick Moynihan* (New York: Harper and Row, 1979), 82–83.

10. Economic Report of the President, together with the Annual Report of the Council of Economic Advisors, January 1964.

11. Arthur M. Schlesinger, Jr., *Robert Kennedy and His Times* (Boston: Houghton Mifflin, 1978), 409–16; Peter Marris and Martin Rein, *Dilemmas of Social Reform: Poverty and Community Action in the United States* (Chicago: University of Chicago Press, 1982), 132. As Marris and Rein have observed, "President's Committee on Juvenile Delinquency and Youth Crime" was a misnomer: it never met as a working committee; it derived its actual authority from Attorney General Robert Kennedy rather than from the president; and its primary concern was reform of local government and institutions, not delinquency and crime.

12. Daniel Patrick Moynihan, *Maximum Feasible Misunderstanding* (New York: Free Press, 1969), 76–77; Allen J. Matusow, *The Unraveling of America: A History of Liberalism in the 1960s* (New York: Harper and Row, 1984), 113.

13. Paul Ylvisaker, director of public affairs at the Ford Foundation, administered the Gray Areas program, a series of grants to community action projects in urban ghettos in the early 1960s. Mitchell Sviridoff, a former United Auto Workers official, directed Community Progresss, Inc., the Gray Areas project in New Haven, in cooperation with the city's mayor, Richard C. Lee. Howard Hallman, Sviridoff's deputy, also attended the task force discussions.

14. HARYOU (Harlem Youth Opportunities) was an indigenous community program which attempted to eradicate juvenile delinquency by empowering the poor and pressing for institutional change. It was combined with another Harlem project, ACT (Asssociated Community Teams), which was under the control of Rep. Adam Clayton Powell, Jr. Matusow, *The Unraveling of America*, 257–60; Charles V. Hamilton, *Adam Clayton Powell, Jr.: The Political Biography of an American Dilemma* (New York: Atheneum, 1991), 426–27; memo re: Background on HARYOU-ACT Project, Pat Anderson to Yarmolinsky and Weeks, 8/3/64, "Community Action Programs (Basic Information)," Box 2, Files of General Counsel, OEO Records, National Archives.

Under Governor Terry Sanford in 1963, the state of North Carolina obtained a grant from the Ford Foundation and the Babcock and Reynolds foundations, with local matching funds and grants from several federal agencies, to create a private nonprofit organization to combat poverty in the state. The mission of the North Carolina Fund was to improve the efforts of governmental agencies at all levels in assisting the poor through education, employment, health, and welfare services. Terry Sanford, *Storm over the States* (New York: McGraw Hill, 1967), 174–76.

15. Heller to Sorenson, 12/20/63, Box Ac 83-64, in WE 9, 11/22/63-2/28/64, Box 25, WHCF, Lyndon Baines Johnson Library.

16. Recording of Telephone Conversation between Lyndon B. Johnson and John Kenneth Galbraith, January 29, 1964, 11:55 AM, Citation #1620.

17. Galbraith's speech, "Wealth and Poverty," was presented to the National Policy Committee on Pockets of Poverty on December 13, 1963. See John Kenneth Galbraith, *A Life in Our Times: Memoirs* (Boston: Houghton Mifflin, 1981).

18. Recording of Telephone Conversation between Lyndon B. Johnson and Kermit Gordon, January 29, 1964, 12:20 PM, Citation #1625.

19. Recording of Telephone Conversation between Lyndon B. Johnson and Walter W. Heller, February 15, 1964, 6:50 PM, Citation #2091.

20. Recording of Telephone Conversation between Lyndon B. Johnson and Lawrence F. O'Brien, March 11, 1964, 1:31 PM, Citation #2477.

21. At the president's news conference on February 1, 1964, he announced that he had asked Shriver to serve as Special Assistant to the President in the organization and administration of the War on Poverty program. Johnson, *Public Papers, 1963–1964*, 254–60.

Chapter 2

1. R. Sargent Shriver, *Point of the Lance* (New York: Harper and Row, 1964); Gerard T. Rice, *The Bold Experiment: JFK's Peace Corps* (Notre Dame, Indiana: University of Notre Dame Press, 1985); Johnson, *The Vantage Point, 76–77*.

2. Shriver's recruitment style at the Peace Corps is described in Coates Redmon, *Come As You Are: The Peace Corps Story* (San Diego: Harcourt Brace Jovanovich, 1986). For discussions of the task force's operations, see especially: Transcript, Adam Yarmolinsky Oral History Interview, 7/13/70, by Paige E. Mulhollan, interview I, 7–8; Transcript, Harold W. Horowitz Oral History Interview, 2/23/83, by Michael L. Gillette, interview I, 4; Transcript, Christopher Weeks Oral History Interview, 12/10/80, by Michael L. Gillette, interview I, 16, Lyndon Baines Johnson Library.

3. Transcript, Robert J. Lampman Oral History Interview, 5/24/83, by Michael L. Gillette, 16–17. For an excellent published analysis of the task force's deliberations, see Adam Yarmolinsky, "The Beginnings of OEO," in James L. Sundquist, ed., *On Fighting Poverty: Perspectives from Experience* (New York: Basic Books, 1969), 34–50.

4. Sol Linowitz, an executive of the Xerox Corporation, was also an attorney in Rochester, New York. LeRoy Collins, former governor of Florida, was director of the Community Relations Service at the Department of Commerce.

5. Recording of Telephone Conversation between Lyndon B. Johnson and Sargent Shriver, February 1, 1964, 2:25 PM, Citation #1807.

6. Recording of Telephone Conversation between Lyndon B. Johnson and Sargent Shriver, February 1, 1964, 1:20 PM, Citation #1804.

7. Recording of Telephone Conversation between Lyndon B. Johnson and Sargent Shriver, February 1, 1964, circa 3:30 PM, Citation #1809.

8. Recording of Telephone Conversation between Lyndon B. Johnson and Sargent Shriver, February 1, 1964, 6:28 PM, Citation #1815.

9. Back of the Yards Neighborhood Council in Chicago was formed by the community organizer Saul Alinsky in 1939 to assert power in local affairs. Its name was derived from its location behind the Union Stock Yards.

10. Harrington, *The Other America*; Harry Caudill, *Night Comes to the Cumberlands: A Biography of a Depressed Region* (Boston: Little, Brown, 1963); Ben H. Bagdikian, *In the Midst of Plenty: The Poor in America* (Boston: Beacon, 1964); Herman P. Miller, *Rich Man, Poor Man* (New York: Crowell, 1964); President's Task Force on Manpower Conservation, *One Third of a Nation;* James Agee and Walker Evans, *Let Us Now Praise Famous Men* (Boston: Houghton Mifflin, 1941).

11. William T. Patrick, Jr., was assistant general attorney, Michigan Bell Telephone; Benjamin W. Heineman was chairman of Chicago and Northwestern Railroad, Co.; Howard J. Samuels was president of Kordite Corp.

12. HR 9876 extended the Juvenile Delinquency and Youth Offenses Control Act of 1961.

13. Special Message to Congress Proposing a Nationwide War on the Sources of Poverty, March 16, 1964, Johnson, *Public Papers, 1963–1964*, 375–80.

Chapter 3

1. Moynihan, *Maximum Feasible Misunderstanding*, 94–100; Moynihan, "What Is Community Action?" *The Public Interest* 5 (1966), 3–8.

2. The Ford Foundation, PCJD, and National Institute of Mental Health funded Mobilization for Youth (MFY), a nonprofit membership corporation of social service organizations and institutions on Manhattan's lower east side. MFY's goal was to eradicate juvenile delinquency by providing comprehensive neighborhood services, community organization, and opportunities for residents.

3. In a memo of November 1963, Hackett proposed only five demonstration projects. Memo re: 1964 Legislative Programs for "Wider Participation in Prosperity," Hackett to Heller, 11/6/63, reproduced in Poverty and Urban Policy, Summary Planning and Materials.

4. For a study of ABCD (Action for Boston Community Development), see Stephen Thernstrom, *Poverty Planning and Politics in the New Boston: Origins of ABCD* (New York: Basic Books, 1969).

5. Boone's views on community action are presented in "Reflections on Citizen Participation and the Economic Opportunity Act," May 7, 1970, in "Citizen Participation in Economic Opportunity Act Program—Richard Boone Comments—1970," Box 1, Subject Files of the Deputy Director, OEO Records.

6. Recording of Telephone Conversation between Lyndon B. Johnson and Bill Moyers, August 7, 1964, 8:35 PM, Citation #4817, Recordings and Transcripts of Conversations and Meetings, LBJ Library.

7. Frances Fox Piven and Richard Cloward, *Regulating the Poor: The Functions of Public Welfare* (New York: Pantheon, 1971), and Cloward and Piven, *The Politics of Turmoil: Essays on Poverty, Race, and the Urban Crisis* (New York: Pantheon, 1972).

8. "Chevrolet division" is an allusion to Shriver's use of corporate metaphors to characterize OEO's structure.

Chapter 4

1. James T. Patterson, *America's Struggle Against Poverty, 1900–1980* (Cambridge: Harvard University Press, 1981), 181; Adam Yarmolinsky, in "Poverty and Urban Policy," 287–88; Daniel Patrick Moynihan, ed., *On Understanding Poverty: Perspectives from the Social Sciences* (New York: Basic Books, 1969), 13.

2. Congressional Quarterly Service, *Congress and the Nation, 1945–1964: A Review of Government and Politics in the Postwar Years* (Washington: Congressional Quarterly Service, 1965), 1223–24. Office of Economic Opportunity, Administrative History of the Office of Economic Opportunity, 153–55, Lyndon Baines Johnson Library. The influence of the conservation lobby is explained in memo, Samuel V. Merrick to R. Sargent Shriver, 3/20/64, and memo, Vernon R. Alden to Adam Yarmolinsky, 4/30/64, "Youth Programs—Title I Legislation," Box 734, Subject Files of Otis A. Singletary, OEO Records, National Archives. For Weber's letter and proposal, see Letter, Robert E. Weber to Harrison Williams, Jr., 7/19/63 and "A Proposal for The Youth National Demonstration Training Project: A Dress Rehearsal for the World of Work, Citizenship, and Parenthood," in "President's Committee on Juvenile Delinquency," Box 735, Subject Files of Otis A. Singletary, OEO Records.

3. On March 25, 1964, Shriver announced the appointment of Vernon Alden to head the subgroup planning details for the Job Corps. OEO Administrative History, 166, 210. Christopher Weeks, *The Job Corps* (Boston: Little, Brown, 1967), 78–80; OEO Administrative History, 479.

4. For descriptions of the negotiations with the Bureau of the Budget and the Department of Labor, sec memo re: Job Corps Recruitment and Selection, John Carley to Adam Yarmolinsky and Sargent Shriver, 8/10/64, and James N. Adler to Shriver, 8/10/64, in "Miscellaneous," Box 734, Subject Files of Otis A. Singletary, OEO Records; Weeks, *The Job Corps,* 179.

5. It was Shriver who named the Job Corps. For some of the other names under consideration, see OEO Administrative History, 161.

Chapter 5

1. Transcript, James L. Sundquist Oral History Interview, 4/7/69, by Stephen Goodell, 10, Lyndon Baines Johnson Library.

2. For an extensive report on community action programs in rural settings, see National Demonstration Water Project, "Rural Community Action: Status and Recommendations," December 1977, in "Rural Community Action," Box 2, Office of Policy, Planning, and Evaluation, records relating to evaluation of programs, OEO Records. 88th Cong. 2d Economic Opportunity Act of 1964, Report #1218.

3. Under the broad authority of a 1935 statute. Section 32 of PL 74-320, the Department of Agriculture initiated a food stamp plan in the late 1930s. In 1961, the Kennedy administration used the same authority to launch a pilot food stamp program in eight areas. Legislation to extend the program and make it permanent was stalled in the House Agriculture Committee until a quid pro quo was arranged with southerners seeking a

cotton-wheat subsidy. The federal food stamp program, HR10222, was signed into law on August 31, 1964. Congressional Quarterly, *Congress and the Nation, 1945-1964*, 739-41.

4. In 1965, the Food Stamp program spent $36 million on 633,000 people. A decade later, 17.1 million recipients received $4.3 billion. Patterson, *America's Struggle Against Poverty, 1900-1980*, 164.

5. The Water Facilities Act of 1937 authorized the Farmers Home Administration to provide loans for water storage and utilization facilities in western states. Kennedy's first letter to Congress included a request for loans and grants for public facilities in Appalachia. Letter to the President of the Senate and the Speaker of the House Urging Enactment of a Distressed Area Redevelopment Bill, January 25, 1961, in *Public Papers of the President, 1961*, 7.

6. In 1965 Congress passed PL 89-240, authorizing $55 million in grants for water and sewer systems and increasing the FHA loan insurance limit to expand the number of utility loans that the agency could process. Congressional Quarterly, *Congress and the Nation, Vol. II, 1965-1968*, 501.

7. The "land reform" provision was Title III, Section 303(a), which authorized the creation of family farm development corporations.

Chapter 6

1. Transcript, Norbert Schlei Oral History Interview, 5/15/80, by Michael L. Gillette, 45; Johnson, *The Vantage Point*, 70-71. One indication of the auspicious timing of the antipoverty legislation was the fact that it was endorsed unanimously by the American Legion at its meeting in September 1964. *New York Times*, September 25, 1964.

2. Sar A. Levitan, *The Great Society's Poor Law: A New Approach* (Baltimore: Johns Hopkins University Press, 1969), 38-47; Transcript, Lawrence F. O'Brien, Jr., Oral History Interview, IX, 4/8/86, by Michael L. Gillette, Lyndon Baines Johnson Library.

3. The Senate select subcommittee amendment defined community action programs as being created "with maximum feasible participation of public agencies and private nonprofit organizations primarily concerned with the community's problems of poverty." See amendment #2, and changes effected by the select subcommittee and reported to the full committee, subcommittee print #3, July 6, 1964, in "Executive (Full Committee)," Box 13, Education Subcommittee, Senate Committee on Labor and Public Welfare–Sen 88A-E13. Records of the United States Senate, Center for legislative Archives.

    Rep. Hugh Carey of New York opposed the bill's prohibition of aid to private schools. In a compromise, the House report specified that "other programs could be carried on by nonpublic as well as public institutions." This formula was later used in the Elementary and Secondary Education Act of 1965. Levitan, *The Great Society's Poor Law*, 44-45.

4. The formula for allocating funds to states under Title II of the Economic Opportunity Act was based on three statistics: (1) total unemployment; (2) total number of welfare recipients; and (3) number of children in families with an annual income of less than $1,000. See "Allocation of Funds to States Under the Economic Opportunity Act," Box 1, General Counsel Files, OEO Records.

5. Senator Milton Young of North Dakota added amendment #120, providing for the indemnity payments to dairy farmers. 88th Cong. 2d. Economic Opportunity Act of 1964, Report #1218; Levitan, *The Great Society's Poor Law*, 45.

6. OEO Administrative History, "Job Corps," 179.

7. 88th Cong. 2d, Economic Opportunity Act of 1964, Report #1218, with Minority Report. The House Republicans introduced their own antipoverty legislation, H.R. 11050, on April 28. John F. Bibby and Roger H. Davidson, *On Capitol Hill: Studies in the Legislative Process*, 2d ed. (Hinsdale, Illinois: Dryden, 1972), 239. For Republican criticism of the Economic Opportunity bill, see also William C. Selover, "The View from Capitol Hill: Harassment and Survival," in Sundquist, ed., *On Fighting Poverty*, 166-67. Landrum's announcement on August 7, 1964, appears in *Congressional Record*, Vol 110, part 14, 18582.

8. Recording of Telephone Conversation between Lyndon B. Johnson and Lawrence F. O'Brien, February 10, 1964, 10:30 AM, Citation #1992.

9. Recording of Telephone Conversation between Lyndon B. Johnson and Lawrence F. O'Brien, March 11, 1964, 1:31 PM, Citations #2477 and #2478.
10. Recording of Telephone Conversation between Lyndon B. Johnson and Lawrence F. O'Brien, May 11, 1964, 2:54 PM, Citation #3395.
11. Recording of Telephone Conversation between Lyndon B. Johnson and Sargent Shriver, May 13, 1964, 2:45 PM, Citation #3422.
12. Recording of Telephone Conversation between Lyndon B. Johnson and Phil Landrum, May 14, 1964, 10:00 AM, Citation #3453.
13. Recording of Telephone Conversation between Lyndon B. Johnson and Bill Moyers, May 14, 1964, 8:30 PM, Citation #3456.
14. Recording of Telephone Conversation between Lyndon B. Johnson and Sargent Shriver, July 28, 1964, 5:11 PM, Citation #4365.
15. Recording of Telephone Conversation between Lyndon B. Johnson and Lawrence F. O'Brien, July 28, 1964, 5:29 PM, Citation #4369.
16. Recording of Telephone Conversation between Lyndon B. Johnson and George Smathers, August 1, 1964, 11:00 AM, Citation #4604.
17. Recording of Telephone Conversation between Lyndon B. Johnson and Carl Sanders, August 1, 1964, 3:53 PM, Citation #4618.
18. Recording of Telephone Conversation between Lyndon B. Johnson and George Mahon, August 1, 1964, 7:27 PM, Citations #4626 and #4627.
19. Recording of Telephone Conversation between Lyndon B. Johnson and John McCormack, August 4, 1964, 12:01 PM, Citation #4674.
20. Russell Tuten ultimately voted against the bill.
21. Recording of Telephone Conversation between Lyndon B. Johnson and Lawrence F. O'Brien, August 4, 1964, 9:02 PM, Citation #4703.
22. Recording of Telephone Conversation between Lyndon B. Johnson and Edwin L. Weisl, July 30, 1964, 9:02 PM, Citation #4454.
23. Recording of Telephone Conversation between Lyndon B. Johnson and Robert E. Jones, August 5, 1964, 2:45 PM, Citations #4724 and #4725.
24. Recording of Telephone Conversation between Lyndon B. Johnson and Olin E. Teague, August 5, 1964, 2:56 PM, Citation #4728.
25. Recording of Telephone Conversation between Lyndon B. Johnson and Lawrence F. O'Brien, August 5, 1964, 3:20 PM, Citation #4735.
26. Recording of Telephone Conversation between Lyndon B. Johnson and B. Everett Jordan, August 5, 1964, 3:34 PM, Citations #4745 and #4746.
27. Recording of Telephone Conversation between Lyndon B. Johnson and Sargent Shriver, August 9, 1964, 9:23 AM, Citation #4843.
28. Recording of Telephone Conversation between Lyndon B. Johnson and Phil Landrum, August 9, 1964, 8:25 AM, Citation #4833.
29. Recording of Telephone Conversation between Lyndon B. Johnson and Walter Reuther, August 9, 1964, 8:51 AM, Citation #4839.
30. Recording of Telephone Conversation between Lyndon B. Johnson and Sargent Shriver, March 26, 1964, 12:55 PM, Citation #2671.
31. Recording of Telephone Conversation between Lyndon B. Johnson and George Mahon, August 6, 1964, 9:30 AM, Citation #4770.
32. Recording of Telephone Conversation between Lyndon B. Johnson and John McCormack, August 6, 1964, 2:03 PM, Citation #4779.
33. Recording of Telephone Conversation between Lyndon B. Johnson and Bill Moyers, August 7, 1964, 8:35 PM, Citation #4817.
34. Recording of Telephone Conversation between Lyndon B. Johnson and Sargent Shriver, August 9, 1964, 9:23 AM, Citation #4843. Johnson summarizes the sequence of events relating to Yarmolinsky in Recording of Telephone Conversation between Lyndon B. Johnson and George Reedy, August 11, 1964, 10:55 AM, Citation #4880.
35. Although Yarmolinsky was never nominated for a position requiring Senate confirmation, he remained in the Department of Defense until March 1966, when he joined the faculty of Harvard Law School. *Washington Post*, March 21, 1966.

36. Cyrus R. Vance was deputy secretary of Defense. Alfred B. Fitt was the Department of the Army's general counsel and special assistant for Civil Functions.

37. The Economic Opportunity Act, Public Law 88–452, was signed into law by the President at a White House ceremony on August 20, 1964.

Chapter 7

1. Jack Conway served as deputy director from February to October 1965, when he returned to the AFL-CIO. He was succeeded by Bernard Boutin, a Democratic Party activist who had been administrator of the General Services Administration. Boutin lasted at OEO only until May, when Bertrand Harding replaced him. Richard L. Schott and Dagmar S. Hamilton, *People, Positions, and Power: The Political Appointments of Lyndon Johnson* (Chicago: University of Chicago Press, 1983), 117–21.

2. When other top government officials favored putting the Peace Corps inside the foreign aid program in 1961, Shriver and Johnson lobbied President Kennedy for an independent agency. *New York Times Magazine*, 3/15/64.

3. Levitan, *The Great Society's Poor Law*, 54–57.

4. According to one White House aide, Johnson's reaction to the proposed poverty budget was that it was impractical and politically motivated to benefit Robert Kennedy. Joseph A. Califano, Jr., *The Triumph and Tragedy of Lyndon Johnson: The White House Years* (New York: Simon & Schuster, 1991), 79. For discussions of OEO and the proposal for a negative income tax, see transcript, Robert J. Lampman Oral History Interview, 5/24/83, by Michael L. Gillette, 36–42; and transcript, Robert A. Levine Oral History Interview, 2/26/69, by Stephen Goodell, tape 1, 40–45, Lyndon Baines Johnson Library. Also, memo re: Preliminary Report on a Plan for Negative Income Taxation, Lampman to Kershaw; Lampman to Ackley, 7/22/65; Kershaw to Harold C. Marlowe, 12/20/65, in "Negative Income Taxation—1965," Box 4, Subject files of the Office of Planning, Research & Evaluation, OEO Records.

5. Mitchell Ginsberg was dean of the School of Social Work at Columbia University and a former commissioner of the New York City Department of Social Services.

6. Recording of Telephone Conversation between Lyndon B. Johnson and Sargent Shriver, January 22, 1966, 12:17 PM, Citation #11047.

7. Recording of Telephone Conversation between Lyndon B. Johnson and Willard Wirtz, October 1, 1966, 10:03 AM, Citation #10904.

8. For the House commitment, see Recording of Telephone Conversation between Lyndon B. Johnson and Adam Clayton Powell, September 29, 1966, 9:12 PM, Citation #10854.

9. Recording of Telephone Conversation between Lyndon B. Johnson and Richard J. Daley, December 14, 1966, 11:42 AM, Citation #11139.

10. Recording of Telephone Conversation between Lyndon B. Johnson and Bill Moyers, December 26, 1966, 10:17 AM, Citation #11206.

Chapter 8

1. OEO Administrative History, 181. Of the first 6,000 enrollees, 1,100 had dropped out, had been discharged, or had left for medical reasons. OEO Administrative History, 474. During the 1964 Congressional hearings, Vernon Alden had estimated that the first year's recruits would total 10,000, with a cost of $4,500 to $4,700 per corpsman. U. S. Congress, House Committee on Education and Labor, *Hearings on Poverty*, 88th Cong. 2d (Washington, D.C.: Government Printing Office, 1964), 1513–14. The annual cost per trainee proved to be almost $10,000 by mid-1966. OEO Administrative History, 521–22.

2. The Department of Agriculture operated forty-seven of the eighty-eight conservation centers. By 1968 the Job Corps had begun to meet the "overwhelming corpsmen demand for vocational training" at conservation centers by introducing new courses and facilities. Summary Report, Job Corps Conservation Centers Inspection Project, 3/28/68, in "OEO-Inspection," Box 6, Files of Job Corps Inspection Reports, OEO Records; Weeks, *The Job Corps*, 221.

3. Camp Gary in San Marcos, an air force base and later an army helicopter training station, had been deactivated in 1959. Of the 12,028 corpsmen who had entered Camp Gary by

July 1967, 3,175 had graduated and 450 had transferred to other Job Corps installations. More than 3,400 resigned; 483 received disciplinary discharges; 1,600 were terminated after being absent for an extended period. The most serious criticism of the center was the fact that 1,257 corpsmen were arrested by the police. A handwritten comment on the cover of the Camp Gary Inspection Report expressed the wish: "Would that all centers were as good!" Robert G. Emond to the Director, 10/6/67, in "JCCC/ Inspection—Gary," Box 1, Files of the Director of Job Corps: JCCC/Inspection, OEO Records.

4. Weeks, *The Job Corps*, 179.

5. Recording of Telephone Conversation between Lyndon B. Johnson and Dick West, August 31, 1964, 9:52 AM, Citation #5279.

6. *New York Times*, 6/9/66 and 7/29/66.

7. The episode of the NYA official who was sent to El Paso is recounted in Transcript, Albert Brisbin Oral History I, 2/6/79, 17-18, Lyndon Baines Johnson Library.

8. Of the first thirty corpsmen at Camp Catoctin, nineteen were from Kentucky and West Virginia and eleven were from inner-city Baltimore. David Gottlieb, "The First Thirty," in "14.09 Gottlieb's Papers," Box 787, Decimal File of Otis Singletary, OEO Records.

9. Dr. David Gottlieb, professor of sociology at Michigan State University, joined the Job Corps as a program analyst. His report attempted to explain why the dropout rate of whites was four times greater than that of blacks. Gottlieb cited the fact that white recruits were less traveled, less adaptable, and more prone to become homesick. OEO Administrative History, 200-201.

10. Governor John Connally actually established a nonprofit foundation, the Texas Education Foundation, to run the Camp Gary Job Corps Center. Robert G. Emond to the Director, 10/6/67, in "JCCC/Inspection—Gary," Box 1, Files of the Director of Job Corps: JCCC/ Inspection, OEO Records.

Chapter 9

1. Transcript, Donald Baker Oral History Interview by Stephen Goodell, 3/5/69, 2-5, Lyndon Baines Johnson Library; OEO Administrative History; 19.

2. National emphasis programs included Foster Grandparents, Operation Green Thumb, Legal Services, Library Services, Medicare Alert, Family Life Education, Head Start, Neighborhood Centers, Opportunities Industrialization Centers, Community Employment Program, Health Centers, Upward Bound, and Small Business Development Centers. "A Brief Description of Federal Anti-Poverty Programs" in "Management Summary of Anti-Poverty Programs, Oct. 1966," Box 1, Management Summaries of Antipoverty Program, 1965-1967, OEO Records; OEO Administrative History, 74-78.

3. Moynihan, *Maximum Feasible Misunderstanding*, 131; Matusow, *The Unraveling of America*, 246-69.

4. By February 1969, only fifty-two of 972 CAAs had been designated as public agencies. Final Report on Designation of Community Action Programs, Section 210, Economic Opportunity Amendments of 1967, prepared by CAP, OEO, March 3, 1969, in "Green Amendment: Miscellaneous," Box 1, Files of the Office of the Director relating to the Green Amendment, 1967-1972, OEO Records; *Washington Post*, 2/14/68.

5. Recording of Telephone Conversation between Lyndon B. Johnson and Bertrand Harding, December 6, 1968, 5:38 PM, Citation #13806.

6. In 1965, CAP awarded its first demonstration grant to Syracuse University's School of Social Work, where the Commuunity Action Training Center (CATC) tested Saul Alinsky's confrontational methods in organizing the poor. The organization's leftist rhetoric drew spirited opposition from the city, the newspapers, and the local community action board. Memo re: Syracuse, NY, Jack Williams to William Haddad, 4/27/65 in "CAP Syracuse Onondaga County Dec. '64-Aug. '65," Box 55, CAP Inspection Reports, 1964-1967, OEO Records.

7. After the race riot in Newark, Mayor Hugh J. Adonizzio accused the local CAA, the United Community Corporation, of stirring up dissent. Moynihan, *Maximum Feasible Misunderstanding*, 156.

8. Lawndale is a black ghetto neighbhood on Chicago's west side.

9. The Woodlawn Organization (TWO) was Saul Alinsky's political entity in that South Side Chicago neighborhood. In June 1967, OEO announced a $927,000 grant to TWO for a job-training program to be run by two rival black gangs, the Blackstone Rangers and the East Side Disciples. Nicholas Lemann, *The Promised Land*, 246–50.

10. HARYOU-ACT was the acronym for Harlem Youth Opportunities Unlimited, Inc., and Associated Community Teams. The Black Arts Theater of the playwright LeRoi Jones spent about $115,000 under the guise of operating "day camps." *New York Times*, 6/16/66. OEO's inspection reports document the program's financial irregularities, including paid consultants who performed no services and nonexistent individuals listed on the payroll. Edgar May to Donald M. Baker, 10/13/65, in "CAP HARYOU-ACT, Sept.-Nov. 1965 NY City," Box 83B, Inspection Division, OEO Records.

11. *Report of the National Advisory Commission on Civil Disorders*, New York Times Edition (New York: Dutton, 1968), 336.

Chapter 10

1. Edward Zigler and Jeanette Valentine, eds., *Project Head Start: A Legacy of the War on Poverty* (New York: Free Press, 1979), 38–39, 47.

2. OEO Administrative History, 83.

3. Max Wolff and Annie Stein, *Study I: Six Months Later—A Comparison of Children Who Had Head Start, Summer 1965, with Their Classmates in Kindergarten* (Washington, D.C.: Research and Evaluation Office, Project Head Start, OEO, 1966); Urie Bronfenbrenner, *A Report on Longitudinal Evaluations of Preschool Programs. Vol. 2: Is Early Intervention Effective?* (Washington, D.C.: Department of Health, Education and Welfare, 1974). Westinghouse Learning Corporation, *The Impact of Head Start: An Evaluation of the Effects of Head Start on Children's Cognitive and Affective Development: Executive Summary, Report to the Office of Economic Opportunity* (Washington, D.C.: Clearinghouse for Federal Scientific and Technical Information, June 1969).

4. Transcript, R. Sargent Shriver Oral History Interview, 8/20/80, by Michael L. Gillette, interview I, 83–85, Lyndon Baines Johnson Library. Shriver also described his involvement in education and preschool development in Zigler and Valentine, eds., *Project Head Start*, 49–59. Lyndon Johnson's experiences as a teacher in south Texas are recounted in transcript, Lyndon B. Johnson Oral History Interview, 5/21/65, by Robert McKay, Lyndon Baines Johnson Library.

5. Susan Ward Gray and R. A. Klaus, "An Experimental Preschool program for Culturally Deprived Children," *Child Development* 36 (1965), 887–98. Also see Zigler and Valentine, eds., *Project Head Start*, 143.

6. Westinghouse learning Corporation, *The Impact of Head Start*; Zigler and Valentine, *Project Head Start*, 187.

7. The White House screening of *Pancho*, featuring Frank "Pancho" Mansera, took place on March 13, 1967.

Chapter 11

1. Transcript, David L. Hackett Oral History Interview by John Douglas, 10/21/70, 79–80, John Fitzgeral Kennedy Library; Hackett, in "Poverty and Urban Policy," 223–26. For the legislative background and a comparison of the National Service Corps [S. 1321] and VISTA, see "Bill: Bill Notes, Memoranda, Correspondence, 1963," in Box 2, Files of OEO General Counsel: Records re: President's Task Force, OEO Records. One small-scale antecedent of VISTA was the Connecticut Service Corps, which had been inspired by President Kennedy's appeal for a National Service Corps. In this program thirty-three college students worked with mental patients during the summer of 1963. David K. Boynick and Wilfred Bloomberg to Richard Boone, 12/18/63, in "Program: Connecticut State Program," Box 6, Files of OEO General Counsel: Records re: President's Task Force, OEO Records. OEO Administrative History, 121–25; Schlesinger, *Robert Kennedy and His Times*, 413–14.

2. Levitan, *The Great Society's Poor Law*, 221–22.

3. Edgar S. Cahn and Jean C. Cahn, "The War on Poverty: A Civilian Perspective," *Yale Law Journal* (July 1964), 1316–41; Earl Johnson, Jr., *Justice and Reform: The Formative Years of the OEO Legal Services Program* (New York: Russell Sage Foundation, 1974), 21–23.

4. Johnson, *Justice and Reform*, pp. 45–70; Harry P. Stumpf, *Community Politics and Legal Services: The Other Side of Law* (Beverly Hills, California: Sage, 1975), 138.

5. The volunteer program was not included in a draft of the antipoverty bill in late February 1964. Pollak's efforts to enlist Robert Kennedy's aid in adding the provision are reflected in memo, Pollak to John Nolan, 12/23/63, and memo, Pollak to the attorney general, 2/27/64, in "General Correspondence, 2 of 2," Box 3, Files of OEO General Counsel re: records of President's Task Force, OEO Records.

6. The name "Volunteers for America" was used as late as April 1964, according to Pollak's memo, re: Volunteers for America—Planning and Action, 4/6/64, in "VISTA Planning 1964," Box 7, Files of OEO General Counsel re: records of President's Task Force.

7. The task force members realized early that VISTA recruitment would require more time than originally anticipated. Memo, re: Lead-Time for Volunteer Recruitment, Ferguson to Yarmolinsky, 5/8/64, in "VISTA Planning 1964," Box 7, Files of OEO General Counsel.

8. The staff's efforts to promote VISTA are described in memo, re: VISTA Status Report, Ferguson to Shriver, 9/9/64, in "Status Reports—CAP, Job Corps, VISTA—1964," Box 6, Files of OEO General Counsel re: President's Task Force.

9. In the first year, approximately sixty-five percent of the volunteers had been assigned to rural areas. Ferguson to Albert H. Quie, 12/31/65, copy provided by Glenn Ferguson.

10. The preliminary focus on the Job Corps for VISTA assignments is reflected in a draft paper projecting that the Job Corps could use 3,200 volunteers. S. J. Pollak, "V, VISTA—Job Corps," 5/6/64, in "VISTA Planning 1964," Box 7, Files of OEO General Counsel re: President's Task Force.

11. When Glenn Ferguson left VISTA in August 1966, he was succeeded by William Crook of Texas. Schott and Hamilton, *People, Positions, and Power*, 127–30.

12. Recording of Telephone Conversation between Lyndon B. Johnson and Jack Vaughn, March 10, 1967, 1:56 PM, Citation #11628.

13. Opportunities Industrialization Center, Rev. Leon Sullivan's job training project for Philadelphia's unemployed poor, was founded in 1964.

14. Shriver's speech in Chicago, November 17, 1964, was an address to the Eleanor Roosevelt Memorial Dinner. Johnson, *Justice and Reform*, 49.

15. California Rural Legal Assistance sued the U.S. Department of Labor because of its immigrant farm labor policies. Levitan, *The Great Society's Poor Law*, 187.

Chapter 12

1. Transcript, C. Robert Perrin Oral History Interview, 3/17/69, by Stephen Goodell, 42–43, Lyndon Baines Johnson Library; Levitan. *The Great Society's Poor Law*, 54–57.

2. Only about sixteen percent of the community action grants went to rural communities. Title III A, which was administered by the Department of Agriculture, authorized loans to very-low-income rural families for farm operations and nonagricultural income-producing enterprises, and loans to low-income family cooperatives. By June 1967, 37,873 families had received individual loans. OEO officials found the rural loan program to be well administered, "perhaps the best of the delegated programs." Memo re: Title III Land Program, Perrin to Levine, 10/25/67; memo re: Implication of Title III Loan Program, Donald D. Steward, in "Rural Loans," Box 30, Subject Files of Office of P, R. and E; memo, A Summary of the Economic Opportunity Act of 1964, in "Summary and Analysis of the Bill," Box 7, Files of the General Counsel re: President's Task Force in War against Poverty, OEO Records.

3. When Wirtz announced the inauguration of the Neighborhood Youth Corps on November 19, 1964, he estimated that about 150,000 men and women would enroll during that fiscal year. *New York Times*, 11/20/64. By the end of October 1935, the program had provided 37,769 jobs for youths in 1,000 local projects. *Baltimore Sun*, 10/29/65.

4. Full authority for the Work-Study program was transferred to the Office of Education in 1965 under the Higher Education Act; Adult Basic Education was spun off the

following year, when the small-business loan program was shifted to the Small Business Administration. Congressional Quarterly, *Congress and the Nation: Vol. II,* 763. Levitan, *The Great Society's Poor Law,* 56.

5. SWAFCA was formed in late 1966 in ten counties of the Alabama "black belt": Lowndes, Dallas, Perry, Hale, Green, Sumpter, Marengo, Choctaw, Wilcox, and Monroe. The average income of its 1,000 members, mostly African Americans, was less than $1,500 a year. SWAFCA farmers were able to increase their income significantly by growing vegetables on their idle land. OEO grants and loans enabled SWAFCA members to obtain trucks, tractors, supplies, marketing facilities, and credit. For a detailed report on SWAFCA, see "Monthly Evaluation Report on SWAFCA, OEO Contract B89-4285, Oct. 18, 1967," Box 1, Job Corps Office of Plans and Programs, Plans and Evaluation Division, Special Projects Branch, Contract Files, OEO Records.

6. The grant provision. Title III, Section 302 (b), was deleted through an amendment introduced by Hubert Humphrey. Levitan, *The Great Society's Poor Law,* 45.

Chapter 13

1. Harry McPherson, *A Political Education* (Boston: Little, Brown, 1972), 353–55. OEO Administrative History, chap. 3, 8–28. While OEO was sharply criticized by Mississippi's Congressional delegation, Shriver was denounced when he spoke at a Citizens Crusade Against Poverty meeting on April 13, 1966. Advocates of the poor faulted OEO for failing to involve the poor sufficiently in planning, for accommodating local politicians, and for delaying funds through the excessive paperwork requirements. *Washington Daily News,* 4/14/66; *Philadelphia Inquirer,* 4/15/66.

2. For published sources on the CDGM project, see Polly Greenberg, *The Devil Has Slippery Shoes: A Biased Biography of the Child Development Group of Mississippi* (Washington, D.C.: Youth Policy Institute, 1990); Larold K. Schulz, "The CDGM Story," in XXVI, 24, *Christianity and Crisis* (June 23, 1967), 317–20; James F. Findlay, Jr., *Church People in the Struggle: The National Council of Churches and the Black Freedom Movement, 1950–1970* (New York: Oxford University Press, 1993), 124–31; Kay Mills, *This Little Light of Mine: The Life of Fannie Lou Hamer* (New York: Dutton, 1993), 203–15. Shriver's view of the CDGM episode appears in Zigler and Valentine, eds., *Project Head Start,* 61–64.

3. OEO's Office of Inspection reports contain detailed information about the activities and problems of the CDGM programs. Memo re: Inspection Report on CDGM Application, Warren Silver to Jack Gonzales, 2/11/66; memo, Gonzales to Edgar May, 2/28/66; memo re: CDGM, Robert Martin to Edgar May, 5/11/66; memo re: Child Development Group of Mississippi—Potential Problems, Frank Sloan to Shriver, 7/18/66, in "HS MS CDGM, Jan.-Aug. 1966," Box 106, Files of Inspection Division, Inspection Reports, 1964–1967, OEO Records.

4. Out of fear of reprisals from local whites, no effort was made to recruit white children in seventy-seven of ninety-four centers. Memo re: CDGM Inspection Statistics, Jack Gonzales to Bob Emond, 8/25/66, in "HS MS CDGM, Jan.-Aug. 1966," Box 106, Files of Inspection Division, Inspection Reports, 1964–1967, OEO Records.

5. For audit information on CDGM projects, with the appeal of the program's auditors, see memo re: 1966 CDGM Audit Appeal, T. Berry to Harding, 3/15/68 (folder 1); and memo on behalf of the Board of National Missions and Mary Holmes Junior College, Ernest and Ernest, Jackson, Mississippi, 2/3/68 (folder 2), in "CDGM (Child Development Group of Mississippi)," Box 1, Deputy Director's Subject Files, OEO Records.

6. Hodding Carter, III, was editor of the *Greenville Delta Democrat;* Aaron Henry was president of the Mississippi State Conference of NAACP Branches.

7. The ad and Shriver's response appear in *New York Times,* 10/19/66.

8. Sponsored by Senator Peter Dominick [R. Col.], in 1967, the Dominick amendment to the Elementary and Secondary Education Act of 1965 called for transferring Head Start to the Office of Education in fiscal year 1969. The program would be under the control of state education officials, who would distribute the funds to local programs. The amendment was defeated by a vote of thirty-five to fifty-four. *Congressional Record,* September 27, 1967, 27067. The following year, the Dominick Amendment was

reintroduced as an amendment to the Vocational Education bill (HR18366). The measure passed the Senate by a vote of sixty to twenty-nine. *Congressional Record,* July 17, 1968, 21734; *Washington Post,* July 22,1968.

9. The Republican "opportunity crusade"proposed a larger, cheaper antipoverty program by offering incentives to private industry to develop job training initiatives. OEO would be dismantled, with community action components carried out by HEW, and the participation of the states would be increased. Head Start would be expanded. The Job Corps would be replaced by residential skill centers administered by vocational education officials. The Republican alternative, H.R.10682, was unveiled on April 10, 1967. Press Release, 4/10/67, and "RPP&E Critique of Republican Opportunity Crusade," in "Opportunity Crusade April 1967," Box 29, 1967, Subject Files of Office of Planning, Research, and Evaluation, OEO Records.

10. Head Start became part of HEW's Office of Child Development in 1969.

Chapter 14

1. OEO Administrative History, "Job Corps," 188-99.

2. Schott and Hamilton, *People, Positions, and Power,* 130-34.

3. Recording of Telephone Conversation between Lyndon B. Johnson and Bill Moyers, August 7, 1964, 8:35 PM, Citation #4817.

4. Cispus Job Corps Conservation Center in Randle, Washington, and Clam Lake Job Corps Conservation Center in Wisconsin were operated by the Department of Agriculture.

5. Fort Vannoy Conservation Center was located three miles north of Grants Pass, a town of 12,000 in the Rogue River recreation area of southern Oregon's Cascade Mountains. Some 2,000-3,000 citizens had petitioned to keep the Job Corps from opening the facility. While the area had no black population, thirty-seven percent of the corpsmen were blacks. The Inspection Report for Fort Vannoy in 1966 revealed that the few incidents that had occurred had been started by local young people, not corpsmen. Memo, Eric Biddle to Edgar May, 12/16/66, in "Vannoy Inspection Report," Box 1, Files of the Director of Job Corps, JCC Inspection, OEO Records.

6. The criteria established by the Job Corps for selecting the centers to be closed included operating costs, length of stay, thirty-day dropout rate, gains in reading and math, placement, and community relations. Fort Vannoy ranked ninety-seventh out of ninety-eight centers, with low ratings in academic gains, placement, community relations, and operating costs. Memo, re: Fort Vannoy Job Corps Center, Grant Pass, Oregon, with Job Corps Evaluation Chart, February 1, 1968, in "Job Corp Center Closures 1968," Box 1, File of Job Corps Office of Congressional Liaison Staff, Job Corps Center Closure File, 1969-1969, OEO Records.

7. In December 1966, the Fort Vannoy Inspection Report cited as deficiencies the fact that there were only 126 corpsmen in the center with a capacity of 224, the lack of qualified and dedicated resident workers, and a weak education program. Memo, Eric Biddle to Edgar May, 12/16/66, in "Vannoy Inspection Report," Box 1, Files of the Director of Job Corps, JCCC/Inspection, OEO Records.

Chapter 15

1. In HR 15111, legislators earmarked funds for Head Start. *Congressional Quarterly, Congress and the Nation: Vol. II,* p. 763.

Fogarty had ample incentive to support OEO, since the agency's grants to his congressional district were significant in comparison with other districts. In 1965, Community Action programs received $1,947,456; Neighborhood Youth Corps projects, $807,865; Head Start programs, $151,210. Charts prepared by the Office of Management, in "OEO-Anti Poverty Programs Management Summary, Sept. 1965," Box 1, Management Summaries of Anti-Poverty Programs 1965-1967, OEO Records.

2. In January 1967, the Democratic Caucus stripped Powell of the chairmanship for his misuse of committee funds for travel and staff. Hamilton, *Adam Clayton Powell, Jr.,* 445-52.

3. *New York Times,* 11/8/67 and 11/12/67; *Congressional Record,* November 15, 1967, 32648. Local politicians rarely exercised their newly legislated control. Only forty-eight of almost 900 Community Action programs were taken over by local governments.

4. Memo, George D. McCarthy to Barefoot Sanders, 12/15/67, Reports on Pending Legislation, 1967, Lyndon Baines Johnson Library.

5. The OEO figure for the total fiscal year 1967 appropriation was $1,688,000,000. *Congressional Quarterly, Congress and the Nation: Vol. II,* 746.

6. In a sharp criticism of Goodell's and Quie's "opportunity crusade," the editorial declared that the "opportunity" they sought was their own political advantage. "It takes a lot of gall," the editorial concluded, "to vote against the poor and then call it a 'crusade.'" *New York Times,* 11/7/67.

7. Waggonner argued that fragmenting the program would make it more difficult to monitor and track funding levels. *Congressional Record,* November 13 and 15, 1967, 32242 and 32676.

8. The Dominick Amendment to the Vocational Education Admendments of 1968 (HR 18366), passed on July 17, 1968, with the support of thirty Democrats and thirty Republicans. *Congressional Record,* July 17, 1968, p. 21734.

9. For Wayne Morse's denunciation of Harding's and OEO's lobbying tactics, see *Congressional Record,* July 30, 1968, 24189.

Chapter 16

1. Johnson, *The Vantage Point,* 75-82.

2. Goodwin, *Remembering America,* 286-87; Califano, *The Triumph and Tragedy of Lyndon Johnson,* 77-80. Califano notes that Johnson considered dismantling OEO and transferring its programs to existing government departments in late 1965.

3. For the rivalry between Johnson and Robert Kennedy, see Bernstein, *Guns and Butter,* 134-36; Califano, *The Triumph and Tragedy of Lyndon Johnson,* 79-80, 294-96; Matusow, *The Unraveling of America,* 142, 382-85.

4. Transcript, R. Sargent Shriver Oral History Interview V, by Michael L. Gillette, 11/29/90, p. 24, Lyndon Baines Johnson Library; Bernstein, *Guns and Butter,* 537-38.

5. Recording of Telephone Conversation between Lyndon B. Johnson and Roy Wilkins, January 5, 1966, 4:55 PM, Citation #9429.

6. Recording of Telephone Conversation between Lyndon B. Johnson and Wilbur Mills, November 16, 1966, Citation #11036.

7. Recording of Telephone Conversation between Lyndon B. Johnson and Charles Schultze, December 30, 1966, 12:15 PM, Citation #11230.

8. Recording of Telephone Conversation between Lyndon B. Johnson and Eunice Shriver, December 18, 1966, 6:55 PM, Citation #11155.

9. Recording of Telephone Conversation between Lyndon B. Johnson and Charles Schultze, December 30, 1966, 12:15 PM, Citation #11230.

10. Recording of Telephone Conversation between Lyndon B. Johnson and Dean Rusk, February19, 1968, 11:00 AM, Citation #12721.

11. Mai Van Bo was North Vietnam's representative in Paris.

12. Recording of Telephone Conversation between Lyndon B. Johnson and Everett Dirksen, June 4, 1968, 6:05 PM, Citation #13102.

Epilogue and Assessments

1. Ronald Reagan, *The Reagan Diaries* (New York: HarperCollins, 2007), 65.

2. The statistics from this section are found on the agencies' websites.

3. Peter Z. Schochet, John Burghardt, and Sheena McConnell, "Does Job Corps Work? Impact Findings from the National Job Corps Study," *American Economic Review,* IIC, 5 (2008): 1864-86.

Bibliography

Unpublished Sources

Johnson, Lyndon B. Presidential Papers, Lyndon Baines Johnson Library and Museum.

Lampman, Robert J. Correspondence and Reports. Lyndon Baines Johnson Library and Museum.

Munden, Kenneth W. "The Office of Economic Opportunity in the Nixon Administration." 1973. OEO Records, National Archives.

Office of Economic Opportunity. "Administrative History of the Office of Economic Opportunity." 1968. Lyndon Baines Johnson Library and Museum.

Office of Economic Opportunity. Records of the Office of Economic Opportunity and the Community Services Administration. Record Group 381, National Archives.

Oral History Project, Ford Foundation Archives.

Oral History Collection, John F. Kennedy Library.

Oral History Collection, Lyndon Baines Johnson Library and Museum.

"Poverty and Urban Policy." Transcript of Conference at Brandeis University, June 16–17, 1973. John F. Kennedy Library.

United States Senate. Records of the United States Senate. RG 46, Center for Legislative Archives, National Archives.

Books

Aaron, Henry J. *Politics and the Professors: The Great Society in Perspective.* Washington, D.C.: Brookings Institution, 1978.

Alden, Vernon R. *Speaking for Myself: The Personal Reflections of Vernon R. Alden.* Athens: Ohio University Press, 1997.

Asen, Robert. *Visions of Poverty: Welfare Policy and Political Imagination.* East Lansing: Michigan State University Press, 2002.

Auletta, Ken. *The Underclass.* New York: Random House, 1982.

Austin, David. "Influence of Community Setting on Neighborhood Action." In John B. Turner, ed., *Neighborhood Organization for Community Action.* New York: National Association of Social Workers, 1968.

Bagdikian, Ben H. *In the Midst of Plenty: The Poor in America.* Boston: Beacon, 1964.

Baldwin, Sidney. *Poverty and Politics: The Rise and Decline of the Farm Security Administration.* Chapel Hill: University of North Carolina Press, 1968.

Balzano, Michael P. *Reorganizing the Federal Bureaucracy: The Rhetoric and the Reality.* Washington, D.C.: American Enterprise Institute for Public Policy Research, 1977.

Bane, Mary Jo, and David T. Ellwood. *Welfare Realities: From Rhetoric to Reform.* Cambridge, Mass.: Harvard University Press, 1994.

Berkowitz, Edward D. *America's Welfare State: From Roosevelt to Reagan.* Baltimore: Johns Hopkins University Press, 1991.

———. *Mr. Social Security: The Life of Wilbur J. Cohen.* Lawrence: University Press of Kansas, 1995.

Berkowitz, Edward D., and Kim McQuaid. *Creating the Welfare State: The Political Economy of Twentieth Century Reform.* Lawrence: University Press of Kansas, 1992.

Bernstein, Irving. *Guns or Butter. The Presidency of Lyndon Johnson.* New York: Oxford University Press, 1996.

———. *Promises Kept: John F Kennedy's New Frontier.* New York: Oxford University Press, 1991.

Beschloss, Michael. *Reaching for Glory: Lyndon Johnson's Secret White House Tapes, 1964–1965.* New York: Simon and Schuster, 2001.

———. *Taking Charge: The Johnson White House Tapes, 1963–1964.* New York: Simon and Schuster, 1997.

Bibby, John E., and Roger H. Davidson. *On Capitol Hill: Studies in the Legislative Process.* 2nd ed. Hinsdale, Ill.: Dryden, 1972.

Blank, Rebecca M. *It Takes a Nation: A New Agenda for Fighting Poverty.* New York and Princeton, N.J.: Russell Sage Foundation and Princeton University Press, 1997.

Blaustein, Arthur I., ed. *The American Promise: Equal Justice and Economic Opportunity.* New Brunswick: Transaction Books, 1982.

Blecher, Earl M. *Advocacy Planning for Urban Development; with Analysis of Six Demonstration Programs:* New York: Praeger, 1971.

Block, Fred, Richard A. Cloward, Barbara Ehrenreich, and Frances Fox Piven. *The Mean Season: The Attack on the Welfare State.* New York: Pantheon Books, 1987.

Bookbinder, Hyman. *Off the Wall: Memoirs of a Public Affairs Junkie.* Washington, D.C.: Seven Locks Press, 1991.

Bowles, Samuel, Stephen N. Durlauf, and Karla Hoff, eds. *Poverty Traps.* Princeton, N.J.: Princeton University Press, 2006.

Boyte, Harry C. *The Backyard Revolution: Understanding the New Citizen Movement.* Philadelphia: Temple University Press, 1980.

Brager, George, and Francis Purcell, eds. *Community Action against Poverty.* New Haven, Conn.: College and University Press, 1967.

Branch, Taylor. *Parting the Waters: America in the King Years, 1954–1963.* New York: Simon and Schuster, 1988.

Braun, Mark Edward. *Social Change and Empowerment of the Poor: Poverty Representation in Milwaukee Community Action Programs, 1964–1972.* Lanham, Md.: Lexington Books, 2001.

Brecher, Charles. *The Impact of Federal Antipoverty Policies.* New York: Praeger, 1973.

Bronfenbrenner, Urie B. *A Report on Longitudinal Evaluations of Preschool Programs. Vol. 2: Is Early Intervention Effective?* Washington, D.C.: Department of Health, Education, and Welfare, 1974.

Burghardt, John A., et al. *Does the Job Corps Work? Summary of the National Job Corps Study.* Washington, D.C.: U.S. Department of Labor, Employment and Training Administration, Office of Policy and Research, 2001.

Burton, James W. *Black Violence: Political Impact of the 1960s Riots.* Princeton, N.J.: Princeton University Press, 1978.

Cahn, Edgar S., and Barry A. Passett, eds. *Citizen Participation: Effecting Community Change.* New York: Praeger, 1971.

Cain, Glen George. *Benefit/Cost Estimates for Job Corps.* Madison: Institute for Research on Poverty, University of Wisconsin, 1969.

Califano, Joseph A., Jr. *The Triumph and Tragedy of Lyndon Johnson: The White House Years.* New York: Simon and Schuster, 1991.

Caudill, Harry. *Night Comes to the Cumberlands: A Biography of a Depressed Region.* Boston: Little, Brown, 1963.

Cazenave, Noel A. *Impossible Democracy: The Unlikely Success of the War on Poverty Community Action Programs.* Albany: State University of New York Press, 2007.

City University of New York, City College, Social Dynamics Institute. *A Relevant War against Poverty: A Study of Community Action Programs and Observable Social Change.* New York: Metropolitan Applied Research Center, 1968.

Clark, Kenneth B., and Jeannette Hopkins. *A Relevant War against Poverty; a Study of Community Action Programs and Observable Social Change.* New York: Harper and Row, 1969.

Clark, Robert F. *Maximum Feasible Success: A History of the Community Action Program.* Washington, D.C.: National Association of Community Action Agencies, 2000.

———. *The War on Poverty: History, Selected Programs and Ongoing Impact.* Lanham, Md.: University Press of America, 2002.

Cleveland, Frederic N., et al. *Congress and Urban Problems: A Casebook on the Legislative Process.* Washington, D.C.: Brookings Institution, 1969.

Cloward, Richard, and Lloyd Olin. *Delinquency and Opportunity: A Theory of Delinquent Groups.* Glencoe, Ill.: Free Press, 1960.

Cloward, Richard, and Frances Fox Piven. *The Politics of Turmoil: Essays on Poverty, Race, and the Urban Crisis.* New York: Pantheon, 1972.

Clymer, Adam. *Edward M. Kennedy: A Biography.* New York: William Morrow, 1999.

Covello, Vincent T., ed. *Poverty and Public Policy: An Evaluation of Social Science Research.* Cambridge, Mass.: Schenkman, 1980.

Crook, William H., and Ross Thomas. *Warriors for the Poor: The Story of VISTA, Volunteers in Service to America.* New York: Morrow, 1969.

Cunningham, James V. *Urban Leadership in the Sixties.* Waltham, Mass.: Brandeis University, Lemberg Center for the Study of Violence, 1970.

Dallek, Robert. *Flawed Giant: Lyndon Johnson and His Times, 1960–1973.* New York: Oxford University Press, 1998.

Danzinger, Sheldon H., and Robert H. Haveman, eds. *Understanding Poverty.* Cambridge, Mass.: Harvard University Press, 2002.

Danziger, Sheldon H., and Daniel H. Weinberg. *Fighting Poverty: What Works and What Doesn't.* Cambridge, Mass.: Harvard University Press, 1986.

Danzinger, Sheldon H., Gary D. Sandefur, and Daniel H. Weinberg. *Confronting Poverty: Prescriptions for Change.* Cambridge, Mass.: Harvard University Press, 1994.

Darby, Michael R., ed. *Reducing Poverty in America: Views and Approaches.* Thousand Oaks, Calif.: Sage, 1996.

Davies, Gareth. *From Opportunity to Entitlement: The Transformation and Decline of Great Society Liberalism.* Lawrence: University Press of Kansas, 1996.

Davis, Karen, and Cathy Schoen. *Health and the War on Poverty: A Ten-Year Appraisal.* Washington, D.C.: Brookings Institution, 1978.

Davis, Martha F. *Brutal Need: Lawyers and the Welfare Rights Movement, 1960–1973.* New Haven, Conn.: Yale University Press, 1993.

Devine, Joel A., and James D. Wright. *The Greatest of Evils: Urban Poverty and the American Underclass.* New York: A.deGruyter, 1993.

Donovan, John C. *The Politics of Poverty.* New York: Pegasus, 1967.

Duncan, Cynthia M., ed. *Rural Poverty in America.* New York: Auburn House, 1992.

Edelman, Peter. *Searching for America's Heart: RFK and the Renewal of Hope.* Washington, D.C.: Georgetown University Press, 2003.

Eisinger, Peter. *The Community Action Program and the Development of Black Political Leadership.* Madison: Institute for Research on Poverty, University of Wisconsin, 1978.

Ellsworth, Jeanne, and Lynda J. Ames, eds. *Critical Perspectives on Project Head Start: Revisioning the Hope and Challenge.* Albany: State University of New York Press, 1998.

Fabricant, Michael B., and Robert Fisher. *Settlement Houses under Siege: The Struggle to Sustain Community Organization in New York City.* New York: Columbia University Press, 2002.

Ferman, Louis A., Joyce L. Kornbluh, and Alan Haber, eds. *Poverty in America.* Ann Arbor: University of Michigan Press, 1965.

Finks, David. *The Radical Vision of Saul Alinsky.* Ramsey, N.J.: Paulist Press, 1984.

Fish, John. *Black Power/White Control: The Struggle of the Woodlawn Organization in Chicago.* Princeton, N.J.: Princeton University Press, 1973.

Fisher, Robert. *Let the People Decide: Neighborhood Organizing in America.* Boston: Twayne, 1984.

Fishman, Leo, ed. *Poverty amid Affluence.* New Haven, Conn.: Yale University Press, 1966.

Frieden, Bernard J., and Marshall Kaplan. *The Politics of Neglect: Urban Aid from Model Cities to Revenue Sharing.* Cambridge, Mass.: MIT Press, 1975.

Frost, Jennifer. *"An Interracial Movement of the Poor": Community Organizing and the New Left in the 1960s.* New York: New York University Press, 2001.

Galbraith, John Kenneth. *A Life in Our Times: Memoirs.* Boston: Houghton Mifflin, 1981.

Gans, Herbert J. *The War against the Poor: The Underclass and Anti-Poverty Policy*. New York: Basic Books, 1995.

Gelfand, Mark I. "The War on Poverty." In Robert A. Divine, ed., *Exploring the Johnson Years*. Austin: University of Texas Press, 1981, 126–54.

Germany, Kent B. *New Orleans after the Promises: Poverty, Citizenship, and the Search for the Great Society*. Athens: University of Georgia Press, 2007.

Gilliom, John. *Overseers of the Poor: Surveillance, Resistance, and the Limits of Privacy*. Chicago: University of Chicago Press, 2001.

Ginzberg, Eli, and Robert M. Solow, eds. *The Great Society: Lessons for the Future*. New York: Basic Books, 1974.

Givel, Michael. *The War on Poverty Revisited: The Community Service Block Grant Program in the Reagan Years*. Lanham, Md.: University Press of America, 1991.

Gladwin, Thomas. *Poverty U.S.A.* Boston: Little, Brown, 1967.

Golden, Olivia A. *Assessing the New Federalism: Eight Years Later*. Washington, D.C.: Urban Institute, 2005.

Goodwin, Richard N. *Remembering America: A Voice from the Sixties*. Boston: Little, Brown, 1988.

Gordon, Margaret S., ed. *Poverty in America*. Proceedings of a National Conference held at the University of California, Berkeley, January 26–28, 1965. San Francisco: Chandler, 1965.

Gottlieb, David. *VISTA and Its Volunteers*. University Park: Pennsylvania State University Press, 1974.

Greenberg, Polly. *The Devil Has Slippery Shoes: A Biased Biography of the Child Development Group of Mississippi*. Washington, D.C.: Youth Policy Institute, 1990.

Greenstone, J. David, and Paul E. Peterson. *Race and Authority in Urban Politics: Community Participation and the War on Poverty*. New York: Russell Sage Foundation, 1973.

———. "Reformers, Machines, and the War on Poverty." In James Q. Wilson, ed., *City Politics and Public Policy*. New York: Wiley, 1969.

Hamilton, Charles V. *Adam Clayton Powell, Jr.: The Political Biography of an American Dilemma*. New York: Atheneum, 1991.

Handler, Joel F. *The Poverty of Welfare Reform*. New Haven: Yale University Press, 1995.

Handler, Joel F., Ellen Jane Hollingsworth, and Howard S. Erlanger. *Lawyers and the Pursuit of Legal Rights*. New York: Academic Press, 1978.

Harrington, Michael. *The New American Poverty*. New York: Holt, Rinehart and Winston, 1984.

———. *The Other America: Poverty in the United States*. New York: Macmillan, 1963.

Harris, David R., and Ann Chih Lin, eds. *The Color of Poverty: Why Racial and Ethnic Disparities Persist*. New York: Russell Sage Foundation, 2008.

Haveman, Robert H., ed. *A Decade of Federal Antipoverty Programs: Achievements, Failures, and Lessons*. New York: Academic Press, 1974.

Heath, Jim F. *Decade of Disillusionment: The Kennedy—Johnson Years*. Bloomington: Indiana Press, 1975.

Helfgot, Joseph H. *Professional Reforming: Mobilization for Youth and the Failure of Social Science*. Lexington, Mass.: Lexington Books, 1981.

Hollister, Robert M., Bernard M. Kramer, and Seymour S. Bellin, eds. *Neighborhood Health Centers*. Lexington, Mass.: D. C. Heath, 1974.

Hopkins, Kevin R. "Social Welfare Policy: A Failure of Vision." In David Boaz, ed., *Assessing the Reagan Years*. Washington, D.C.: Cato Institute, 1988, 211–21.

Horwitt, Sanford D. *Let Them Call Me Rebel: Saul Alinsky—His Life and Legacy*. New York: Knopf, 1989.

Iceland, John. *Poverty in America: A Handbook*. Berkeley: University of California Press, 2003.

Isserman, Maurice. *The Other American: The Life of Michael Harrington*. New York: Public Affairs, 2000.

Isserman, Maurice, and Michael Kazin. *America Divided: The Civil War of the 1960s*. New York: Oxford University Press, 2000.

Jacobs, Bruce. *The Political Economy of Organizational Change: Urban Institutional Response to the War on Poverty*. New York: Academic Press, 1981.

James, Dorothy Buckto, ed. *Analyzing Poverty Policy*. Lexington, Mass.: Lexington Books, 1975.

Jeffrey, Julie Roy. *Education for the Children of the Poor: A Study of the Origins and Implementation of the Elementary and Secondary Education Act of 1965*. Columbus: Ohio State University Press, 1978.

Jencks, Christopher. *Rethinking Social Policy: Race, Poverty, and the Underclass*. Cambridge, Mass.: Harvard University Press, 1992.

Jencks, Christopher, and Paul E. Peterson, eds. *The Urban Underclass*. Washington, D.C.: Brookings Institution, 1991.

Job Corps, *A Chance for Change: The Job Corps Story*. Washington, D.C.: U.S. Department of Labor, Office of Labor, Office of Job Corps, 1994.

Johnson, Earl, Jr. *Justice and Reform: The Formative Years of the OEO Legal Services Program*. New Brunswick, N.J.: Transaction Books, 1978.

Johnson, Lady Bird. *A White House Diary*. New York: Holt, Rinehart and Winston, 1970.

Johnson, Lyndon B. *Public Papers of the Presidents of the United States: Lyndon B. Johnson, 1963–1964*. Washington, D.C.: Government Printing Office, 1965.

———. *The Vantage Point: Perspectives on the Presidency, 1963–1969*. New York: Holt, Rinehart and Winston, 1971.

Jordan, Barbara C., and Elspeth D. Rostow, eds. *The Great Society: A Twenty Year Critique*. Austin, Tex.: Lyndon Baines Johnson Library/ Lyndon B. Johnson School of Public Affairs, 1986.

Kaplan, Marshall, and Peggy L. Cuciti, eds. *The Great Society and Its Legacy: Twenty Years of U. S. Social Policy*. Durham, N.C.: Duke University Press, 1986.

Katz, Jack. *Poor People's Lawyers in Transition*. New Brunswick, N.J.: Rutgers University Press, 1982.

Katz, Michael B. *Improving Poor People: The Welfare State, the "Underclass," and Urban Schools as History*. Princeton, N.J.: Princeton University Press, 1995.

———. *The Price of Citizenship: Redefining the American Welfare State*. New York: Metropolitan Books, 2001.

———, ed. *The "Underclass" Debate: Views from History*. Princeton, N.J.: Princeton, University Press, 1993.

———. *The Undeserving Poor: From the War on Poverty to the War on Welfare*. New York: Pantheon Books, 1990.

Kershaw, Joseph A. *Government against Poverty*. Washington, D.C.: Brookings Institution, 1970.

Knapp, Daniel, and Kenneth Polk. *Scouting the War on Poverty: Social Reform Politics in the Kennedy Administration*. Lexington, Mass.: Heath, 1971.

Kotz, Nick. *Let Them Eat Promises: The Politics of Hunger in America*. Garden City, N.Y.: Anchor Books/Doubleday, 1971.

Kramer, Ralph M. *Participation of the Poor: Comparative Community Case Studies in the War on Poverty*. Englewood Cliffs, N.J.: Prentice Hall, 1969.

Krosney, Herbert. *Beyond Welfare: Poverty in the Supercity*. New York: Holt, Rinehart and Winston, 1966.

Lampman, Robert J. *Ends and Means of Reducing Poverty*. New York: Academic, 1971.

———. *The Low Income Population and Economic Growth*. Joint Economic Committee, Study Paper No. 12, 86th Congress, 1st Session, Washington, D.C., 1959.

Lavelle, Robert, and the staff of Blackside, Inc., compiler and eds. *America's New War on Poverty: A Reader for Action*. San Francisco: KQED Books, 1995.

Lawrence, Susan E. *The Poor in Court: The Legal Services Program and Supreme Court Decision Making*. Princeton, N.J.: Princeton University Press, 1990.

Lemann, Nicholas. *The Promised Land*. New York: Knopf, 1991.

Lens, Sidney. *Poverty: America's Enduring Paradox: A History of the Richest Nation's Unwon War*. New York: Thomas Y. Crowell, 1971.

Levine, Robert A. *The Poor Ye Need Not Have with You: Lessons from the War on Poverty*. Cambridge, Mass.: MIT Press, 1970.

Levitan, Sar A. *The Great Society's Poor Law: A New Approach*. Baltimore, Md.: Johns Hopkins University Press, 1969.

Levitan, Sar A., and Clifford M. Johnson. *Beyond the Safety Net: Reviving the Promise of Opportunity in America*. Cambridge, Mass.: Ballinger, 1984.

Levitan, Sar A., and Benjamin H. Johnston. *The Job Corps: A Social Experiment that Works*. Baltimore, Md.: Johns Hopkins University Press, 1975.

Levitan, Sar A., and Garth L. Mangum. *Federal Training and Work Programs in the Sixties*. Ann Arbor: Institute of Labor and Industrial Relations, University of Michigan, Wayne State University, 1969.

Levitan, Sar A., and Robert Taggartt. *The Promise of Greatness: The Social Programs of the Last Decade and Their Major Achievements*. Cambridge, Mass.: Harvard University Press, 1976.

Levitan, Sar A., and Joyce K. Zickler. *Too Little but Not Too Late: Federal Aid to Lagging Areas*. Lexington, Mass.: Lexington, 1976.

Lieberman, Robert C. *Shifting the Color Line: Race and the American Welfare State*. Cambridge, Mass.: Harvard University Press, 1998.

Liston, Robert A. *Sargent Shriver: A Candid Portrait*. New York: Farrar, Straus, 1964.

Lynn, Laurence, and David Whitman. *The President as Policymaker: Jimmy Carter and Welfare Reform*. Philadelphia: Temple University Press, 1981.

Mackenzie, G.. Calvin, and Robert Weisbrot. *The Liberal Hour: Washington and the Politics of Change in the 1960s*. New York: Penguin Press, 2008.

Manski, C. F., and I. Garfinkel, eds. *Evaluating Welfare Training Programs*. Cambridge, Mass.: Harvard University Press, 1992.

Marcus, Isabel. *Dollars for Reform: The OEO Neighborhood Health Care Centers*. Lexington, Mass.: Lexington Books, 1981.

Margolis, Jon. *The Last Innocent Year: America in 1964, the Beginning of the "Sixties."* New York: William Morrow, 1999.

Markowitz, Gerald E., and David Rosner. *Children, Race and Power: Kenneth and Mamie Clark's Northside Center*. Charlottesville: University of Virginia Press, 1996.

Marmor, Theodore R., ed. *Poverty Policy: A Compendium of Cash Transfer Proposals*. Chicago: Aldine Atherton, 1971.

Marris, Peter, and Martin Rein. *Dilemmas of Social Reform: Poverty and Community Action in the United States*. Chicago, Ill.: University of Chicago Press, 1982.

Marshall, Dale Roger. *The Politics of Participation in Poverty: A Case Study of the Board of the Economic and Youth Opportunities Agency of Greater Los Angeles*. Berkeley: University of California Press, 1971.

Matusow. Allen J. *The Unraveling of America: A History of Liberalism in the 1960s*. New York: Harper and Row, 1984.

May, Edgar. *The Wasted American; Cost of Our Welfare Dilemma*. New York: Harper and Row, 1964.

McPherson, Harry. *A Political Education*. Boston: Little, Brown, 1972.

Mead, Lawrence M. *The New Politics of Poverty. The Nonworking Poor in America*. New York: Basic Books, 1992.

Miller, Herman P. *Rich Man, Poor Man*. New York: Crowell, 1964.

Moore, Joan, and Raquel Pinderhughts, eds. *In the Barrios: Latinos and the Underclass Debate*. New York: Russell Sage Foundation, 1993.

Morone, James. *The Democratic Wish: Popular Participation and the Limits of American Government*. New York: Basic Books, 1990.

Moynihan, Daniel Patrick. *Maximum Feasible Misunderstanding*. New York: Free Press, 1969.

———, ed. *On Understanding Poverty: Perspectives from the Social Sciences*. New York: Basic Books, 1969.

———. *The Politics of a Guaranteed Income: The Nixon Administration and the Family Assistance Plan*. New York: Random House, 1973.

Murray, Charles. *Losing Ground: American Social Policy, 1950–1980*. New York: Basic Books, 1984.

Myrdal, Gunnar. *Challenge to Affluence*. New York: Pantheon Books, 1964.

Naples, Nancy. *Grassroots Warriors: Activist Mothering, Community Work, and the War on Poverty*. New York: Routledge, 1998.

Nightingale, Demetra Smith, and Robert H. Haveman, eds. *The Work Alternative: Welfare Reform and the Realities of the Job Market*. Washington, D.C.: Urban Institute Press, 1995.

O'Connor, Alice. *Poverty Knowledge: Social Science, Social Policy and the Poor in Twentieth Century U.S. History*. Princeton, N.J.: Princeton University Press, 2001.

Office of Economic Opportunity. *Women in the War on Poverty*. Conference Proceedings, May 8, 1967. Washington, D.C.: Government Printing Office, 1967.

O'Neill, David M. *The Federal Government and Manpower: A Critical Look and the MDTA-Institutional and Job Corps Programs*. Washington, D.C.: American Enterprise Institute for Public Policy Research, 1973.

Ornati, Oscar, with J. S. Sweet. *Poverty amid Affluence*. New York: Twentieth Century Fund, 1966.

Papadimitriou, Dimitri B., and Edward N. Wolff, eds. *Poverty and Prosperity in the USA in the Late Twentieth Century*. New York: Macmillan, 1993.

Patterson, James T. *America's Struggle against Poverty, 1900–1980*. Cambridge, Mass.: Harvard University Press, 1981.

Phillips, Kevin. *The Politics of Rich and Poor: Wealth and the American Electorate in the Reagan Aftermath*. New York: Random House, 1990.

Piven, Frances Fox, and Richard Cloward. *The New Class War: Reagan's Attack on the Welfare State and Its Consequences*. New York: Pantheon, 1985.

———. *Regulating the Poor: The Functions of Public Welfare*. New York: Pantheon, 1971.

Plotnick, Robert D., and Felicity Skidmore. *Progress against Poverty: A Review of the 1964–1974 Decade*. New York: Academic, 1975.

President's Commission on Income Maintenance Programs. *Poverty amid Plenty: The American Paradox*. Washington, D.C.: Government Printing Office, 1969.

Quadagno, Jill. *The Color of Welfare: How Racism Undermined the War on Poverty*. New York: Oxford University Press, 1994.

Rank, Mark Robert. *Living on the Edge: The Realities of Welfare in America*. New York: Columbia University Press, 1994.

———. *One Nation, Underprivileged: Why American Poverty Affects Us All*. New York: Oxford University Press, 2004.

Redford, Emmette S., and Marlan Blissett. *Organizing the Executive Branch: The Johnson Presidency*. Chicago: University of Chicago Press, 1981.

Reeves, T. Zane. *The Politics of the Peace Corps and VISTA*. Tuscaloosa: University of Alabama Press, 1988.

Rice, Gerard T. *The Bold Experiment: JFK's Peace Corps*. Notre Dame, Ind.: University of Notre Dame Press, 1985.

Rich, Michael J. *Federal Policymaking and the Poor: National Goals, Local Choices, and Distributional Outcomes*. Princeton: Princeton University Press, 1993.

Rose, Stephen M. *The Betrayal of the Poor. The Transformation of Community Action*. Cambridge, Mass.: Schenkman, 1972.

Rothman, Jack, ed. *Reflections on Community Organization: Enduring Themes and Critical Issues*. Itasca, Ill.: F. E. Peacock, 1999.

Rubin, Herbert J., and Irene S. Rubin. *Community Organizing and Development*. Boston: Allyn and Bacon, 2001.

Schiller, Bradley R. *The Economics of Poverty and Discrimination*. Englewood Cliffs, N.J.: Prentice-Hall, 1973.

Schlesinger, Arthur M., Jr. *Robert Kennedy and His Times*. Boston: Houghton Mifflin, 1978.

Schochet, Peter Z., et al. *National Job Corps Study and Long-Term Follow-up Study*. Washington, D.C.: U.S. Department of Labor, 2006.

Schoen, Douglas E. *Pat: A Biography of Daniel Patrick Moynihan*. New York: Harper and Row, 1979.

Schorr, Alvin L. *Poor Kids: A Report on Children in Poverty*. New York: Basic Books, 1966.

Schott, Richard L., and Dagmar S. Hamilton. *People, Positions, and Power: The Political Appointments of Lyndon Johnson*. Chicago, Ill.: University of Chicago Press, 1983.

Schram, Sanford F. *Words of Welfare: The Poverty of Social Science and the Social Science of Poverty*. Minneapolis: University of Minnesota Press, 1995.

Schram, Sanford F., Joe Soss, and Richard C. Fording, eds. *Race and the Politics of Welfare Reform*. Ann Arbor: University of Michigan Press, 2003.

Schwartz, Marvin. *In Service to America: A History of VISTA in Arkansas, 1965–1985.* Fayetteville: University of Arkansas Press, 1988.

Schwarz, John E. *America's Hidden Success: A Reassessment of Public Policy from Kennedy to Reagan.* New York: W. W. Norton, 1988.

Seligman, Ben B. *Permanent Poverty: An American Syndrome.* Chicago: Quadrangle Books, 1968.

Shepard, Kris. *Rationing Justice: Poverty Lawyers and Poor People in the Deep South.* Baton Rouge: Louisiana State University Press, 2009.

Shesol, Jeff. *Mutual Contempt: Lyndon Johnson, Robert Kennedy, and the Feud That Defined a Decade.* New York: W. W. Norton, 1997.

Shriver, R. Sargent. *Point of the Lance.* New York: Harper and Row, 1964.

Silverman, Charles. *Crisis in Black and White.* New York: Random House, 1964.

Sirianni, Carmen, and Lewis Friedland. *Civic Innovation in America: Community Empowerment, Public Policy and the Movement for Civic Renewal.* Berkeley: University of California Press, 2001.

Smith, Allen N., and Sherrie S. Aitken. *An Annotated Bibliography of Head Start Research since 1965.* Washington, D.C.: U. S. Department of Health and Human Services, 1985.

Soss, Joe. *Unwanted Claims: The Politics of Participation in the U.S. Welfare System.* Ann Arbor: University of Michigan Press, 2000.

Spergel, Irving A., ed. *Community Organization: Studies in Constraint.* Beverly Hills, Calif.: Sage, 1972.

Stone, Clarence N., Robert K. Whelan, and William J. Murin. *Urban Policy and Politics in a Bureaucratic Age.* Englewood, N.J.: Prentice-Hall, 1986.

Stossel, Scott. *Sarge: The Life and Times of Sargent Shriver.* Washington, D.C.: Smithsonian Books, 2004.

Stumpf, Harry P. *Community Politics and Legal Services: The Other Side of Law.* Beverly Hills, Calif.: Sage, 1975.

Sundquist, James L., ed. *On Fighting Poverty: Perspectives from Experience.* New York: Basic Books, 1969.

———. *Politics and Policy.* Washington, D.C.: Brookings Institution, 1968.

Thernstrom, Stephen. *Poverty Planning and Politics in the New Boston: Origins of ABCD.* New York: Basic Books, 1969.

Thurlow, L. C. *Poverty and Discrimination.* Washington, D.C.: Brookings Institution, 1969.

Tompkins, Dorothy Campbell, compiler. *Poverty in the United States during the Sixties: A Bibliography.* Berkeley, Calif.: Institute of Governmental Studies, 1970.

Trolander, Judith Ann. *Professionalism and Social Change: From the Settlement House Movement to Neighborhood Centers, 1886 to the Present.* New York: Columbia University Press, 1987.

Tyson, Cyril Degrasse. *Power and Politics in Central Harlem 1962–1964: The HARYOU Experience.* New York: Jay Street Publishers, 2004.

Unger, Irwin. *The Best of Intentions: The Triumph and Failure of the Great Society under Kennedy, Johnson and Nixon.* New York: Brandywine Press, 1996.

U.S. Congress. House Committee on Education and Labor. *Hearings on Poverty.* 88th Cong., 2d sess. Washington, D.C.: Government Printing Office, 1964.

U.S. Congress. House Committee on Education and Labor. *Poverty in the United States.* 88th Cong., 2d sess. Washington, D.C.: Government Printing Office, 1964.

Valentine, Charles A. *Culture and Poverty.* Chicago: University of Chicago Press, 1968.

Vinovskis, Maris. *The Birth of Head Start: Preschool Education Policies in the Kennedy and Johnson Administrations.* Chicago: University of Chicago Press, 2005.

Warner, David C. *Toward New Human Rights: The Social Policies of the Kennedy and Johnson Administrations.* Austin: Lyndon B. Johnson School of Public Affairs, 1977.

Washington, Valora, and Ura Jean Oyemade Bailey. *Project Head Start: Models and Strategies for the Twenty-First Century.* New York: Garland, 1995.

Waxman, Chaim Isaac, ed. *Poverty: Power and Politics.* New York: Grosset and Dunlap, 1968.

Weeks, Christopher. *The Job Corps: Dollars and Dropouts.* Boston: Little, Brown, 1967.

Weissman, Harold, ed. *Community Development in the Mobilization for Youth.* New York: Association Press, 1969.

White, Richardson, Jr., and Beryl A. Radin. *Youth and Opportunity: The Federal Anti-Delinquency Program.* Washington, D.C.: University Research Corporation, 1969.

Wilson, William Julius. *The Truly Disadvantaged: The Inner City, the Underclass, and Public Policy.* Chicago: University of Chicago Press, 1987.

Wofford, Harris. *Of Kennedys and Kings: Making Sense of the Sixties.* New York: Farrar, Straus and Giroux, 1980.

Wolff, Max, and Annie Stein. *Study I: Six Months Later, A Comparison of Children Who Had Head Start, Summer 1965, with Their Classmates in Kindergarten (A Case Study of Kindergartens in Four Public Elementary Schools, New York City).* Washington, D.C.: Research and Evaluation Office, Project Head Start, OEO, 1966.

Woods, Randall B. *LBJ: Architect of American Ambition.* New York: Free Press, 2006.

Zarefsky, David. *President Johnson's War on Poverty: Rhetoric and History.* Tuscaloosa: University of Alabama Press, 1986.

Zigler, Edward, and Susan Muenchow. *Head Start: The Inside Story of America's Most Successful Educational Experiment.* New York: Basic Books, 1992.

Zigler, Edward, and Jeanette Valentine, eds. *Project Head Start: A Legacy of the War on Poverty.* New York: Free Press, 1979.

Zurcher, Louis A., Jr. *Poverty Warriors: The Human Experience of Planned Social Intervention.* Austin: University of Texas Press, 1970.

Periodicals

Aleshire, Robert A. "Power to the People: An Assessment of the Community Action and Model Cities Experience." *Public Administration Review* 32 (September 1972): 428–43.

Alexander, Ernest R. "Goal Setting and Growth in an Uncertain World: A Case Study of a Local Community Organization." *Public Administration Review* 36, no. 2 (March–April 1976): 182–91.

Alinsky, Saul D. "The War on Poverty—Political Pornography." *Journal of Social Issues* 21 (January 1966): 41–47.

Armour, Marilyn Peterson. "Alternative Routes to Professional Status: Social Work and the New Careers Program under the Office of Economic Opportunity." *Social Service Review* 60, no. 2 (June 2002).

Blank, Rebecca M. "Distinguished Lecture on Economics in Government: Fighting Poverty: Lessons from Recent U.S. History." *Journal of Economic Perspectives* 14, no. 2 (Spring 2000): 3–19.

Bonnen, James T. "Rural Poverty: Programs and Problems." *Journal of Farm Economics* 58, no. 2 (May 1966): 452–65.

Boone, Richard W. "Reflections on Citizen Participation and the Economic Opportunity Act." *Public Administration Review* 32 (September 1972): 444–56.

Borus, Michael E., John P. Brennan, and Sidney Rosen. "A Cost-Benefit Analysis of the Neighborhood Youth Corps: The Out-of-School Program in Indiana." *Journal of Human Resources* 5, no. 2 (Spring 1970): 139–59.

Bowles, Samuel. "Understanding Unequal Economic Opportunity." *American Economic Review* 63, no. 2 (May 1973): 346–56.

Brauer, Carl M. "Kennedy, Johnson, and the War on Poverty." *Journal of American History* 69, no. 1 (June 1982): 98–119.

Burchinal, Lee G.., and Hilda Siff. "Rural Poverty." *Journal of Marriage and the Family* 26, no. 4 (November 1964): 399–405.

Cahn, Edgar S., and Jean C. Cahn. "The War on Poverty: A Civilian Perspective." *Yale Law Journal* (July 1964): 1316–41.

Carroll, Stephen J., and Anthony H. Pascal. "Toward a National Youth Employment Policy: Mapping the Route from Problems to Programs." *Policy Sciences* 2, no. 2 (June 1971): 159–75.

Cazenave, Noel A. "Chicago Influences on the War on Poverty." *Journal of Policy History* 5, no. 1 (1993): 52–68.

Claffey, Barbara A., and Thomas A. Stucker. "The Food Stamp Program." *Proceedings of the Academy of Political Science* 34, no. 3 (1982): 40–53.

Cobb, James C. " 'Somebody Done Nailed Us on the Cross': Federal Farm and Welfare Policy and the Civil Rights Movement in the Mississippi Delta." *Journal of American History* 77, no. 3 (December 1990): 912–36.

Colby, David C. "Black Power, White Resistance, and Public Policy: Political Power and Poverty Program Grants in Mississippi." *Journal of Politics* 67, no. 2 (June 1985): 579–95.

Crenson, Matthew. "Organizational Factors in Citizen Participation." *Journal of Politics* 36, no. 2 (May 1974): 356–78.

Curren, Laura. "The Psychology of Poverty: Professional Social Work and Aid to Dependent Children in Postwar America, 1946–1963." *Social Service Review* 76, no. 3 (September 2002): 365–86.

Currie, Janet, and Duncan Thomas. "Does Head Start Make a Difference?" *American Economic Review* 85, no. 3 (June 1995): 341–64.

Cutler, David M., and Lawrence F. Katz. "Untouched by the Rising Tide: Why the 1980s Economic Expansion Left the Poor Behind." *Brookings Review* 10, no. 1 (Winter 1992): 40–45.

David, Stephen M. "Leadership of the Poor in Poverty Programs." *Proceedings of the Academy of Political Science* 29, no. 1 (1968).

Eggebeen, David J., and Daniel T. Lichter. "Race, Family Structure, and Changing Poverty among American Children." *American Sociological Review* 56, no. 6 (December 1991): 801–17.

English, Gary. "The Trouble with Community Action …" *Public Administration Review* 32, no. 3 (May–June 1972): 224–31.

Erlanger, Howard S. "Lawyers and Neighborhood Legal Services: Social Background and the Impetus for Reform." *Law & Society Review* 12, no. 2 (Winter 1978): 253–74.

Findlay, James F. "The Mainline Churches and Head Start in Mississippi: Religious Activism in the Sixties." *Church History* 64, no. 2 (June 1995): 237–50.

Freeman, Donald G. "Trickling Down the Rising Tide: New Estimates of the Link between Poverty and the Macroeconomy." *Southern Economic Journal* 70, no. 2 (October 2003): 359–73.

Freeman, Howard E., K. Jill Kiecolt, and Harris M. Allen II. "Community Health Centers: An Initiative of Enduring Utility." *Milbank Memorial Fund Quarterly, Health and Society* 60, no. 2 (Spring 1982): 245–67.

Gans, Walter I. "A Benefit–Cost Analysis of the Upward Bound Program." *Journal of Human Resources* 6, no. 2 (Spring 1971): 206–20.

Ginsberg, Mitchell I., and Bernard Shiffman. "Manpower and Training Problems in Combating Poverty." *Law and Contemporary Problems* 32, no. 1 (Winter 1966): 159–86.

Glennerster, Howard. "United States Poverty Studies and Poverty Management: The Past Twenty-Five Years." *Social Service Review* 76, no. 1 (March 2002): 83–107.

Goodman, John C. "Privatizing the Welfare State." *Proceedings of the Academy of Political Science* 36, no. 3 (1987): 36–48.

Gray, Susan W. "Enduring Effects of Early Intervention: Perspectives and Perplexities." *Peabody Journal of Education* 60, no. 3 (Spring 1983): 70–84.

Gray, Susan W., and R. A. Klaus. "An Experimental Preschool Program for Culturally Deprived Children." *Child Development* 36 (1965): 887–98.

Haddad, William F. "Mr. Shriver and the Savage Politics of Poverty." *Harper's* 231 (December 1965): 44.

Harpham, Edward J., and Richard K. Scotch. "Rethinking the War on Poverty: The Ideology of Social Welfare Reform." *Western Political Quarterly* 41 (1988): 193–207.

Hasenfeld, Yeheskel. "Organizational Dilemmas in Innovating Social Services: The Case of the Community Action Centers." *Journal of Health and Social Behavior* 12, no. 3 (September 1971): 208–16.

Haskins, Ron. "Congress Writes a Law: Research and Welfare Reform." *Journal of Policy Analysis and Management* 10, no. 4 (Autumn 1991): 616–32.

Hazard, Geoffrey C., Jr. "Law Reforming in the Anti-Poverty Effort." *University of Chicago Law Review* 37, no. 2 (Winter 1970): 242–55.

———. "Social Justice through Civil Justice." *University of Chicago Law Review* 36, no. 4 (Summer 1969): 699–712.

Johnson, Kimberley. "Community Development Corporations, Participation, and Accountability: The Harlem Urban Development Corporation and the Bedford—Stuyvesant Restoration Corporation." *Annals of the American Academy of Political and Social Science* (July 2004): 109–24.

Katz, Michael B., Mark J. Stern, and Jamie J. Fader. "The New African American Inequality." *Journal of American History* 92, no. 1 (June 2005): 75–108.

Kennedy, Mary M. "The Follow Through Program." *Curriculum Inquiry* 7, no. 3 (Autumn 1977): 183–208.

Kershaw, Joseph A., and Robert A. Levine. "Poverty, Aggregate Demand, and Economic Structure." *Journal of Human Resources* 1, no. 1 (Summer 1966): 67–70.

Kravitz, Sanford, and Feme K. Kolodner. "Community Action: Where Has It Been? Where Will It Go?" *Annals* 355 (September 1969).

LeCompte, Margaret D. "The Uneasy Alliance of Community Action and Research." *School Review* 79, no. 1 (November 1970): 125–32.

Lee, Valerie E., and Susanna Loeb. "Where Do Head Start Attendees End Up? One Reason Why Preschool Effects Fade Out." *Educational Evaluation and Policy Analysis* 17, no. 1 (Spring 1995): 62–82.

Lenkowsky, Leslie, and James L. Perry. "Reinventing Government: The Case of National Service." *Public Administration Review* 60, no. 4 (July–August 2000): 298–307.

Levitan, Sar A., and Robert Taggart. "The Great Society Did Succeed." *Political Science Quarterly* 91, (Winter 1976–1977): 601–18.

Macdonald, Dwight. "Our Invisible Poor." *New Yorker*, January 19, 1963, p. 82.

Mead, Lawrence M. "Poverty: How Little We Know." *Social Service Review* 68, no. 3 (September 1994): 322–50.

Miller, S. M., and Martin Rein. "Participation, Poverty, and Administration." *Public Administration Review* 29, no. 1 (January–February 1969): 15–25.

Miller, Zane, and Bruce Tucker. "The Revolt against Cultural Determinism and the Meaning of Community Action: A View from Cincinnati." *Prospects: An Annual of American Cultural Studies* 15 (2000).

Moynihan, Daniel Patrick. "What Is Community Action?" *Public Interest* 5 (Fall 1966): 3–8.

O'Connor, Alice. "Community Action, Urban Reform, and the Fight against Poverty: The Ford Foundation's Gray Areas Program." *Journal of Policy History* 22, no. 5 (1966): 586–625.

———. "Poverty Research and Policy for the Post-Welfare Era." *Annual Review of Sociology* 26 (2000): 547–62.

Orden, Susan R. "The Impact of Community Action on Private Social Service Agencies." *Social Problems* 20, no. 3 (Winter 1973): 364–81.

Owens, Emiel W. "Income Maintenance Programs in the 1960's: A Survey." *American Journal of Agricultural Economics* 54, no. 2 (May 1972): 342–55.

Oyemade, Ura Jean, Valora Washington, and Dominic F. Gullo. "The Relationship between Head Start Parental Involvement and the Economic and Social Self-Sufficiency of Head Start Families." *Journal of Negro Education* 57, no. 1 (Winter 1989): 5–15.

Perrotta, John A. "Machine Influence on a Community Action Program: The Case of Providence, Rhode Island." *Polity* 9, no. 4 (Summer 1977): 481–502.

Peterson, Paul E. "Forms of Representation: Participation of the Poor in the Community Action Program." *American Political Science Review* 64, no. 2 (June 1970): 491–501.

Pye, A. Kenneth. "The Role of Legal Services in the Antipoverty Program." *Law and Contemporary Problems* 31, no. 1 (Winter 1966): 211–49.

Quadagno, Jill. "Race, Class and Gender in the U.S. Welfare State: Nixon's Failed Family Assistance Plan." *American Sociological Review* 55, no. 1 (February 1990): 11–28.

Rawlins, V. Lane. "Job Corps: The Urban Center as a Training Facility." *Journal of Human Resource* 6, no. 2 (Spring 1971): 221–35.

Reitzes, Donald C., and Dietrich C. Reitzes. "Alinsky in the 1980s: Two Contemporary Chicago Community Organizations." *Sociological Quarterly* 28, no. 2 (Summer 1987): 265–83.

Reynolds, Roger A. "Improving Access to Health Care among the Poor: The Neighborhood Health Center Experience." *Milbank Memorial Fund Quarterly, Health and Society* 54, no. 1 (Winter 1976): 47–82.

Ritti, R. Richard, and Drew W. Hyman. "The Administration of Poverty: Lessons from the 'Welfare Explosion.'" *Social Problems* 25, no. 2 (December 1977): 157–75.

Rubin, Lillian B. "Maximum Feasible Participation: The Origins, Implications, and Present Status." *Annals of the American Academy of Political and Social Science* 385 (September 1969): 22–24.

Sarason, Seymour B. "An Unsuccessful War on Poverty." *American Psychologist* (September 1978): 831–39.

Sawhill, Isabel V. "Poverty in the U.S.: Why Is It So Persistent?" *Journal of Economic Literature* 26 (September 1988): 1073–119.

Schmandt, Henry J., George D. Wendel, and George Otte. "CDBG: Continuity or Change?" *Publius* 13, no. 3 (Summer 1983): 7–22.

Schochet, Peter Z., John Burghardt, and Shenna McConnell. "Does Job Corp Work? Impact Findings from the National Job Corps Study." *American Economic Review* 98, no. 5 (2008): 1864–86.

Schram, Sanford F., and Joe Soss. "Success Stories: Welfare Reform, Policy Discourse, and the Politics of Research." *Annals of the American Academy of Political and Social Science* 577 (September 2001): 49–65.

Schulz, Larold K. "The CDGM Story." *Christianity and Crisis* 26, no. 24 (January 23, 1967): 317–20.

Slesnick, Daniel T. "Gaining Ground: Poverty in Postwar United States." *Journal of Political Economy* (February 1993): 1–38.

Steinberg, Carl W. "Citizens and the Administrative State: From Participation to Power." *Public Administration Review* 32, no. 3 (May–June 1972): 190–98.

Sullivan, Lawrence A. "Law Reform and the Legal Services Crisis." *California Law Review* 69, 1 (January 1971): 1–28.

Torrens, Paul R. "Administrative Problems of Neighborhood Health Centers." *Medical Care* 9, no. 6 (December 1971): 487–97.

Triest, Robert K. "Has Poverty Gotten Worse?" *Journal of Economic Perspectives* 12, no. 1 (Winter 1998): 97–114.

Tsuchiya, Kazuyo, "Race, Class, and Gender in America's 'War on Poverty:' The Case of Opal C. Jones in Los Angeles, 1964–1968." *Japanese Journal of American Studies* 15 (2004): 213–36.

Vinovskis, Maris A. "Early Childhood Education: Then and Now." *Daedalus* 122, no. 1 (Winter 1993): 151–76.

Walsh, John. "Antipoverty R&D: Chicago Debacle Suggests Pitfalls Facing OEO." *Science* (New Series) (September 19, 1969): 1243–45.

Wise, Katherine J. "A Matter of Trust: The Elimination of Federally Funded Legal Services on the Navajo Nation." *American Indian Law Review* 21, no. 1 (1977): 157–81.

Wolfe, Deborah P. "What the Economic Opportunity Act Means to the Negro." *Journal of Negro Education* 34, no. 1 (Winter 1965): 88–92.

Wolman, Harold. "Organization Theory and Community Action Agencies." *Public Administration Review* 32, no. 1 (January–February 1972): 33–42.

Zwick, Daniel I. "Some Accomplishments and Findings of Neighborhood Health Centers." *Milbank Memorial Fund Quarterly* 50, no. 4 (October 1972): 387–420.

Dissertations

Ambrecht, Biliana Maria Cicin-Sain. "Politicization as a Legacy of the War on Poverty: A Study of Advisory Council Members in a Mexican-American Community." Ph.D. diss., University of California, Los Angeles, 1973.

Andrews, Theodore Howard. "John F. Kennedy, Lyndon Johnson, and the Politics of Poverty, 1960–1967." Ph.D. diss., Stanford University, 1998.

Applewhite, Bettie Lou. "A Decade Later: A Follow-up Study of Indigenous Paraprofessionals Employed in Community Action Programs of the 1960's." Ph.D. diss., Cornell University, 1980.

Ashmore, Susan Youngblood. "Carry It On: The War on Poverty and the Civil Rights Movement in Alabama, 1964–1970." Ph.D. diss., Auburn University, 1999.

Balbus, Isaac D. "The Evolution of the Community Action Program: A Case Study in American Policy Making." Ph.D. diss., The University of Chicago, 1966.

Ball, Ian Traquair. "Institution Building for Development: Office of Economic Opportunity (OEO) Community Action Programs on Two North Dakota Indian Reservations." Ph.D. diss., Indiana University, 1968.

Bauman, Robert Alan. "Race, Class and Political Power: The Implementation of the War on Poverty in Los Angeles." Ph.D. diss., University of California, Santa Barbara, 1998.

Beck, Harry Louis. "The History and Development of the Federal College Work–Study Program." Ed.D. diss., University of Kentucky, 1975.

Beck, Susan Abrams. "The Limits of Presidential Activism: Lyndon Johnson and the Implementation of the Community Action Program." Ph.D. diss., Columbia University, 1985.

Berglund, Donald Duane. "Job Corps and the Public–Private Debate." Ph.D. diss., Virginia Polytechnic Institute and State University, 1992.

Bers, Trudy Haffron. "Private Welfare Agencies and Their Role in Government-Sponsored Welfare Programs: The Case of the War on Poverty in Chicago." Ph.D. diss., University of Illinois at Urbana-Champaign, 1973.

Blackett, Joseph E. A. "A Legal History of the Job Corps." Ed.D. diss., Andrews University, 2002.

Blum, Stephen R. "An Unrequited War: The Office of Economic Opportunity's Upward Bound Program 1965–1969." Ph.D. diss., University of California, Berkeley, 1973.

Boland, Ronald Thomas. "The War on Poverty in Fort Wayne, 1965 to 1975—A Case Study." Ph.D. diss., University of Kansas, 1981.

Boo, Sung Lai. "A Description and Analysis of the Concept of the Participation of the Poor in a Southern Rural Community Action Program." Ph.D. diss., Florida State University, 1970.

Boyle, Kevin Gerard. "Politics and Principle: The United Automobile Workers and American Labor-Liberalism, 1948–1968." Ph.D. diss., University of Michigan, 1990.

Braun, Mark Edward. "Social Change and the Empowerment of the Poor: Poverty Representation in Milwaukee's Community Action Programs, 1964–1972." Ph.D. diss., University of Wisconsin, Milwaukee, 1999.

Camacho, Desmond Manuel. "Conflict within Community Action Programs: A Comparison of the Effects of Community Organization vs. Maximum Feasible Participation." Ph.D. diss., Brown University, 1980.

Carcasson, Martin. "Negotiating the Paradoxes of Poverty: Presidential Rhetoric on Welfare from Johnson to Clinton." Ph.D. diss., Texas A&M University, 2004.

Carter, Robert Lee. "Ghetto Lawyering: Law and Ideology in the Rise of Legal Services, 1963–1984." Ph.D. diss., Columbia University, 1986.

Chappell, Marisa Ann. "From Welfare Rights to Welfare Reform: The Politics of AFDC, 1964–1984." Ph.D. diss., Northwestern University, 2002.

Christensen, Terry Lynn. "Citizen Participation and the Participation of the Poor in the Community Action Program." Ph.D. diss., University of North Carolina at Chapel Hill, 1972.

Clayson, William Stephen. "Texas Poverty and Liberal Politics: The Office of Economic Opportunity and the War on Poverty in the Lone Star State." Ph.D. diss., Texas Tech University, 2001.

Cobb, Daniel M. "Community, Poverty, Power: The Politics of Tribal Self-Determination, 1960–1968." Ph.D. diss., University of Oklahoma, 2003.

Combs, Paul William. "Job Corps to 1973." Ed. D., diss., Virginia Polytechnic Institute and State University, 1985.

Crowley, John Charles. "The Federal College Work–Study Program, University Policy-Making and the Graduate Student." Ph. D. diss., Syracuse University, 1977.

de Abreu, Anabela Nobre Lopes Garcia. "Comparative Analysis of Health Centers in Allegheny County, Pittsburgh, Pennsylvania." D. P. H. diss., University of Pittsburgh, 1993.

Dubnoff, Caren. "The Lost War on Poverty: The Dynamics of a Federal Program in an Urban Political System." Ph.D. diss., Columbia University, 1974.

Dwore, Richard Barry. "An Exploratory-Descriptive Study of the Office of Economic Opportunity's Neighborhood Health Center Program." Ph.D. diss., University of Iowa, 1971.

Engleman, Stephen Robert. An Economic Analysis of the Job Corps. Ph.D. diss., University of California, Berkeley, 1972.

Entin, David Hudson. "Missions of Antipoverty Organizations: Change and Survival (Massachusetts)." Ph.D. diss., Boston University, 1987.

Evens, Wayne Carl. "The Effects of Idea Systems on Social Policy: The Case of the Economic Opportunity Act of 1964." Ph.D. diss., University of Iowa, 1996.

Fisher, Christopher T. "'The Hopes of Man': The Cold War, Modernization Theory, and the Issue of Race in the 1960s." Ph.D. diss., Rutgers, the State University of New Jersey, 2002.

Fisher, Linda Lou. "The Presidency and Implementation: A Case Study of the Johnson Administration." Ph.D. diss., George Washington University, 1982.

Fraser, Stephen Arnsdorff. "Citizen Participation in Decision-Making by Federal Agencies: Selective Service System, Bureau of Land Management, Office of Economic Opportunity, Department of Housing and Urban Development." Ph.D. diss., Johns Hopkins University, 1969.

Fukahori, Satoko. "The Long Term Effects of Project Head Start: A National-Scale Longitudinal Study." Ph.D. diss., Columbia University, 2000.

George, Michael Albert. "American Liberalism: The Welfare State and the War on Poverty." Ph.D. diss., Kent State University, 1992.

Gibson, Dennis Wayne. "An Evaluation of the Alabama Job Corps." Ph.D. diss., University of Alabama, 1990.

Gilbert, Neil. "Clients or Constituents? A Case Study of Pittsburgh's War on Poverty." Ph.D. diss., University of Pittsburgh, 1968.

Givel, Michael Steven. "Community Services—The Politics of a Block Grant." Ph.D. diss., University of California, Riverside, 1988.

Glass, John Franklin. "Organizational Dilemmas in the War on Poverty: Contrasts in the Neighborhood Youth Corps." Ph.D. diss., University of California, Los Angeles, 1968.

Grady, John Marshall. "Status Dynamics and Social Control in a Community Action Program." Ph.D. diss., Brandeis University, 1977.

Hamrin, Robert Douglas. "Performance Contracting in Education: An Economic Analysis of the 1970–1971 Office of Economic Opportunity Experiment." Ph.D. diss., University of Wisconsin–Madison, 1972.

Hicks, Thomas. "The Historical Development of the Educational Policy of the Edison Job Corps Center." Ed.D. diss., Rutgers the State University of New Jersey, 1983.

Hoffman, Richard Lee. "Community Action: Innovative and Coordinative Strategies in the War on Poverty." Ph.D. diss., University of North Carolina at Chapel Hill, 1969.

Houghton, Ruth Edna Meserve. "Adaptive Strategies in an American Indian Reservation Community: The War on Poverty, 1965–1971." Ph.D. diss., University of Oregon, 1973.

Humphrey, Daniel Craig. "Teach Them Not to Be Poor: Philanthropy and New Haven School Reform in the 1960s." Ed.D., diss., Columbia University Teachers College, 1992.

Hunt, David W. "Programs under Siege: Congressional Committee Oversight as a Defensive Strategy against Budgetary Retrenchment and Termination." Ph.D. diss., American University, 1986.

Illuzzi, Michael Joseph. "A Conceptual History of Equal Opportunity: Debating the Limits of Acceptable Inequality in U.S. History." Ph.D. diss., University of Minnesota, 2008.

Jackson, Mandi Isaacs. "Demonstration City: Urban Renewal and Organized Resistance in the 'New' New Haven." Ph.D. diss., Yale University.

Keegan, Rosemary Patricia. "History of Head Start in Denver, Colorado." Ed.D. diss., University of Northern Colorado, 1984.

Kiffmeyer, Thomas J. "From Self-Help to Sedition: The Appalachian Volunteers and the War on Poverty in Eastern Kentucky, 1964–1970." Ph.D. diss., University of Kentucky, 1998.

Knapp, Daniel Leo. "Scouting the War on Poverty: Social Reform Politics in the Kennedy Administration." Ph.D. diss., University of Oregon, 1970.

Knight, Muriel Bernice. "Community Action: Advocacy for the Poor." Ed.D. diss., Northeastern University, 1988.

Krasovic, Mark. "The Struggle for Newark: Plotting Urban Crisis in the Great Society." Ph.D. diss., Yale University, 2008.

Kurtz, Donald V. "Politics, Ethnicity, Integration: Mexican-Americans in the War on Poverty." Ph.D. diss., University of California, Davis, 1970.

Lawrence, Susan E. "The Poor in Court: The Legal Impact of Expanded Access." Ph.D. diss., Johns Hopkins University, 1986.

Lazar, Alan Edward. "The Failure of Reform: The War on Poverty in New Hampshire, 1965–1969." Ph.D. diss., Harvard University, 1972.

Lerman, Hilary. "Power to the People: Community Organizing in Southeastern Ohio, 1969–1973." Ph.D. diss., Miami University, 1997.

Lin, Chi-Wei. "Effective Work Competencies: Evaluation of Work-Related Attitude Change in a Job Corps Residential Center." Ph.D. diss., Kansas State University, 1999.

Ling, T-Tseng. "The War on Poverty and the Concept of Participatory Administration." Ph.D. diss., University of Tennessee, 1972.

Mantler, Gordon Keith. "Black, Brown, and Poor: Martin Luther King Jr., the Poor People's Campaign, and Its Legacies." Ph.D. diss., Duke University, 2008.

Miringoff, Marque Luisa. "External Integration and Social Policy: A Comparative Analysis of the Model Cities Program and the Community Action Program." Ph.D. diss., University of Chicago, 1977.

Moseley, Samuel Andrew. "Poverty Politics and Political Transformation in North Carolina: A Comparative Case Study of Three Cities." Ph.D. diss., Ohio State University, 1989.

Munk, Michael. "Policy Priorities in the War on Poverty: The Funding of 81 Big City Community Action Agencies, 1964–69." Ph.D. diss., New York University, 1974.

O'Connor, Alice Mary. "From Lower Class to Underclass: The Poor in American Social Science, 1930–1970." Ph.D. diss., Johns Hopkins University, 1991.

Pass, David Jacob. "The Politics of VISTA in the War on Poverty: A Study of Ideological Conflict." Ph.D. diss., Columbia University, 1976.

Perrotta, John. "Representation of the Poor in the Community Action Program in Providence, Rhode Island: 1965–1969." Ph.D. diss., New York University, 1971.

Peterson, Paul Elliott. "City Politics and Community Action: The Implementation of the Community Action Program in Three American Cities." Ph.D. diss., University of Chicago, 1967.

Pious, Richard Matthew. "Advocates for the Poor: Legal Services in the War on Poverty." Ph.D. diss., Columbia University, 1971.

Pollinger, Kenneth Joseph. "New York City's Community Action Program: Social Control or Influence Outputs? A Case Study of the Tremont Community Action Program." Ph.D. diss., Fordham University, 1972.

Pollitt, Frederick Anthony. "Participation of the Poor in the War on Poverty." Ph.D. diss., Pennsylvania State University, 1972.

Rice, Leila Meier. "In the Trenches of the War on Poverty: The Local Implementation of the Community Action Program, 1964–1969." Ph.D. diss., Vanderbilt University, 1997.

Rose, Stephen M. "Community Action Programs: The Relationship between Initial Conception of the Poverty Problem, Derived Intervention Strategy, and Program Implementation." Ph.D. diss., Brandeis University, 1970.

Rosenbaum, Karen J. "Curricular Innovations in Federal Youth Programs: A Comparison of New Deal and War on Poverty Education Efforts." Ph.D. diss., Johns Hopkins University, 1973.

Russell, Judith. "The Making of American Antipoverty Policy: The Other War on Poverty." Ph.D. diss., Columbia University, 1992.

Sachs, Andrea Jule. "The Politics of Poverty: Race, Class, Motherhood, and the National Welfare Rights Organization, 1965–1975." Ph.D. diss., University of Minnesota, 2001.

Sandler Brown, Patricia Evelyn. "Intergroup Relationships in the Development of Social Policy and the Management of Social Programs: A Case Study of the Job Corps Program." Ph.D. diss., Northwestern University, 1994.

Schmitt, Edward Robert. "A Humane Struggle: Robert Kennedy and the Problem of Poverty in America." Ph.D. diss., Marquette University, 2003.

Schwetz, John. "A Study of the Effectiveness of the Penobscot Job Corps Center Measured by the Success of Former Students in the Labor Market." Ph.D. diss., University of Michigan, 1984.

Selden, Paul B. "Foreclosing on the Poor." Ph.D. diss., University of Southern California, 1989.

Seliger, Michael. "Critical Elements in the 'Health' of Community Action Agencies in the Age of 'Reaganomics.'" Ph.D. diss., City University of New York, 1986.

Shepard, Kristoffer. "Poverty Lawyers and Poor People in the Deep South, 1965–1996." Ph.D. diss., Emory University, 2001.

Spitzer, Scott Jeremy. "The Liberal Dilemma: Welfare and Race, 1960–1975." Ph.D. diss., Columbia University, 2000.

Stern, E. Christa. "An Analysis of a Rural Community Health Service Project: Factors which Affected the Development and Decline of the Tufts–Delta Project in Mound Bayou, Mississippi. A Descriptive Case Study." Ph.D. diss., Tulane University, 1976.

Strickler, Gaynor Richards. "VISTA: A Study in Organizational Survival." Ph.D. diss., Bryn Mawr College, 1994.

Takagi, Dana Yasu. "Community Action in San Francisco: Class Structure and Ethnic Politics (Ideology, Marxism, Black, Asian, California)." Ph.D. diss., University of California, Berkeley, 1986.

Tolbert Denise E. "Characteristics of Job Corps Students: Their Relationship to Training Completion and Job Placement." Ph.D. diss., University of Northern Colorado, 2001.

Udom, Udoh Elijah. "The Politics of National Service Programs: A Comparative Study of the National Youth Service Corps in Nigeria and Volunteers in Service to America in the United States." Ph.D. diss., University of Texas at Austin, 1981.

Walker, Walter Lorenzo. "The War on Poverty and the Poor: A Study of Race, Poverty, and a Program." Ph.D. diss., Brandeis University, 1969.

Weber, Charlotte Marguerite. "Organizational Innovation and Precarious Values: Citizen Participation in the War on Poverty." Ph.D. diss., Johns Hopkins University, 1979.

Werner, Tammy Marvin. "From Hillbillies to Welfare Queens: Representation of the Poor in the Poverty Wars." Ph.D. diss., University of Kentucky, 2007.

Wilson, Beclee Newcomer. "The Role of Symbols in Forming the Public Policy of the War on Poverty." Ph.D. diss., University of Minnesota, 1979.

Websites

Americorps VISTA
www.americorps.gov/about/programs/vista.asp
Official VISTA site, providing a brief history of VISTA and a state-by-state summary of projects and statistics.

Census Bureau, U.S. Poverty
www.census.gov/hhes/www/poverty.html
A wealth of reports, tables, and analyses of the government's measurement of poverty in the United States.

Community Action Partnership
www.communityactionpartnership.com
National association of community action agencies with information on conferences and a directory of local programs.

Head Start, Office of Administration for Children and Families, U.S. Department of Health and Human Services
www.acf.hhs.gov/programs/ohs/
Official Head Start site, offering reports, statistics, and conference proceedings relating to the effectiveness of the program.

Institute for Research on Poverty, University of Wisconsin–Madison
www.irp.wisc.edu
One of three regional research centers funded by HHS Office of Assistant Secretary for Planning and Evaluation to study the causes and consequences of poverty; includes archives of publications and research papers.

Job Corps
www.jobcorps.gov/home.aspx
Official Job Corps site features annual reports, success stories, and a directory of Job Corps locations.

John F. Kennedy Presidential Library and Museum
www.jfklibrary.org/historical+resources/archives
Site includes searchable index of collections and online transcripts of selected oral history interviews.

Legal Services Corporation
www.lsc.gov
Official site provides a directory of LSC-funded programs and reports to and testimony before Congress.

Lyndon Baines Johnson Library and Museum

www.lbjlib.utexas.edu

Selected oral history transcripts are available online; a complete listing of released LBJ's recorded presidential conversations through January 1969, with a searchable database of topical summaries.

National Poverty Center, Gerald R. Ford School of Public Policy, University of Michigan

http://npc.umich.edu

Academic research center funded by the Department of Health and Human Services to conduct and disseminate research on the causes and consequences of poverty in the United States. Includes archives of policy briefs, working papers, and conference papers.

Presidential Recordings Program, Miller Center of Public Affairs, University of Virginia

http://tapes.millercenter.virginia.edu

Site offers LBJ's recorded presidential conversations for download in a variety of audio formats.

Rural Policy Research Institute

www.rupri.org/

A consortium of Iowa State University, University of Missouri, and University of Nebraska. Features an archive of research papers related to poverty.

Spotlight on Poverty and Opportunity

www.spotlightonpoverty.org/default.aspx

A clearinghouse of websites and online resources relating to poverty in the United States.

Urban Institute

www.urban.org

Features evaluations of antipoverty programs and related developments in U.S. cities; includes archives of policy briefs, speeches, reports, and congressional testimony.

Index